AF573849

# 800 PACES TO HELL

# *ANDERSONVILLE*

**A Compilation of Known Facts**

**and Persistent Rumors**

**Dr. John W. Lynn**

**Published & Distributed by**
**Sergeant Kirkland's Museum**
**and Historical Society, Inc.**
912 Lafayette Blvd., Fredericksburg, Virginia 22401-5617
Tel. (540) 899-5565; Fax: (540) 899-7643
E-mail: Civil-War@msn.com

Manufactured in the USA

The paper in this book meets the guidelines for permanence and durability of the Committee on Production Guidelines for Book Longevity of the Council on Library Resources, Inc.

Library of Congress Cataloging-in-Publication Data

**Lynn, John W. (John Worth), 1936-**
**800 Paces to Hell : Andersonville / by John W. Lynn.**
p. cm.
**ISBN** 1-887901-19-1 (alk. paper)
Notes: Includes bibliographical references and index.
1. Andersonville Prison. United States -- History -- Civil War, 1861-1865 -- Prisoners and prisons, Confederate. 2. Prisoners of war -- Confederate States of America. 3. Prisoners of war -- United States -- History -- 19th century. I. Title.
E612.A5L87 1999
973.7/71 - dc21 First Edition 97-040676
CIP

1 2 3 4 5 6 7 8 9 10

Cover drawing by Thomas O'Dea, late private Co. e, 16th Maine Inf., colored by Tish Hall, Oglethorpe, GA, 1984.
Jacket design and page layout by Ronald R. Seagrave
Text edited by Pia S. Seagrave, Ph.D.

# *Acknowledgments*

Work on this book was initiated after I had bought a Colt Pocket Model pistol that had *Major Richard Bayly Winder* engraved down the backstrap. This started my infatuation with Andersonville and my insatiable appetite to obtain books and items related to that prison.

I soon learned about a grandson of General John H. Winder, J. Winder Hughes of Wilmington, North Carolina. We corresponded and talked on the telephone. Later, I corresponded with one of the general's great-granddaughters, Mrs. John H. Winder, of Winston-Salem, North Carolina. Robert Stevens, of the Enoch Pratt Free Library in Baltimore, Maryland, put me in touch with Frank L. Byrne of the Department of History at Kent State University and sent me several other nice leads. Byrne told me of the existence of the thesis of Sarah Annette Duffy entitled *Military Administrator: The Controversial Life of Brigadier General John H. Winder, C.S.A.*

I found that Major Richard Bayly Winder's great-grandson, R. Bayly Winder, was a professor at Princeton, New Jersey. He and I corresponded dozens of times. He was the first to convey to me the idea that Major Winder had been a well-educated, erudite gentleman.

The Baltimore College of Dentistry forwarded the informative little booklet, *Hall of Fame of Great Maryland Dentists*, which contains a rather complete biographical sketch of Doctor Winder.

Another person with whom I corresponded was Frederick Louis McCoy, of Scotland, Maryland, who was the grandson of Louis Frederick Schade, Wirz' lawyer. After Frederick McCoy's death, I corresponded with his widow, who was most helpful in furnishing me with several photos and a wonderful biography of her husband's grandfather.

Many book dealers scoured their inventories for books, broadsides, or pamphlets related to Andersonville. Terry Murphy, of Mt. Sterling, Kentucky, was most helpful. Mike Miner, of Sevierville, Tennessee, furnished copies of several pertinent diaries.

Librarians and archivists at many colleges and universities led to the discovery of several small, but significant, pieces of the mosaic. Ms. Janet L. Kern, of the University Archives, Alderman Library of the University of Virginia, helped with the transcripts of Dick Winder's troubles at that university. Mrs. Cynthia McClelland, of the Seeley G. Mudd Manuscript Library at Princeton, related stories of the further undergraduate education pursued by Dick Winder at that university. The Howard-Tilton Memorial Library at Tulane University helped with the study of Doctor Joseph Jones. The Confederate Museum in Richmond, Virginia, had a nice photo of General John H. Winder.

I am particularly indebted to Dave Mark of Linthicum Heights, Maryland, who graciously gave me permission to reproduce his cartes-de-visites of Captain Henry Wirz and General John H. Winder.

The staff of several historical societies were helpful, especially those at the Georgia Historical Society in Savannah and the Virginia Historical Society in Richmond.

My thanks to Father Peter at the Delbarton School in Morristown, New Jersey, for sending me his wonderful booklet detailing the Catholic presence at Andersonville.

The staff of the Hall of Records at Annapolis, Maryland, was helpful in sending me an article from the *Maryland Historical Magazine* entitled "The College Green Barracks: St. John's During the Civil War."

Many museums provided information of benefit in writing this book. The Swiss National Museum in Zurich, Switzerland, examined a dubious photo of Wirz in a weird uniform. The staff and volunteers at the Andersonville National Historic Site, at the Andersonville Guild, and at the National Society of Andersonville have been of great assistance.

Rockwell N. Smith, Esq., of Mechanicsville, Virginia, forwarded a letter from Ross Graves, of Nova Scotia, chronicling the flight of Doctor R.R. Stevenson, who fled the country in order to avoid the possibility of prosecution for his activities at Andersonville.

Dozens of individuals provided tiny bits of information that helped put together the final pieces of the puzzle. Some of these were Chris Calkins of Petersburg, Virginia; Lee Joyner of Monroe, Georgia; Charles Hubbard, of Evansville, Indiana; Ronnie O'Connell of Richmond, Virginia; and Peggy Sheppard of Andersonville, Georgia.

Lastly, my greatest appreciation goes to Dr. Pia S. and Ronald R. Seagrave of Fredericksburg, Virginia, who patiently guided me through this first attempt at writing a book.

ANDERSONVILLE 1864
DEATH BEFORE DISHONOR

# Private James Jefferson Lynn

Company G, 2nd Battalion North Carolina Infantry
Enlisted August 13, 1864, in Raleigh, North Carolina.
Captured October 19, 1864, in Strasburg, Virginia.
Sent to Point Lookout, Maryland.
In prison hospital for "Diarrhea Chronica."
Exchanged and admitted to the General Hospital
at Camp Winder, Richmond, on February 14, 1865.
Furloughed for sixty days on March 2nd.
Paroled, Raleigh, May 25, 1865.

# Private Charles Lunsford

2nd Detachment, Martin's Battery B of the
12th Battalion Virginia Light Artillery.
Enlisted March 4, 1864, in Petersburg, Virginia.
Paroled by Lieutenant Colonel T. L. Barker,
Provost Marshal of the 36th Massachusetts Volunteers,
at Farmville, Virginia, on April 13, 1865.

# 2nd Lieutenant John Wesley Friend

He enlisted on May 27th, 1861, Greene county, as a
private in Company B, 11th Alabama Infantry
Regiment. Appointed 2nd Lieutenant and Assistant
Chief of Ordnance on January 7, 1864.
He was in Captain Eppes' Company of Johnston's
Artillery of the Virginia Heavy Artillery.
John Friend surrendered with General Robert E. Lee
at Appomattox Court House on April 9th, 1865.

"In the death struggles of the confederacy the feelings were very bitter, and it is but fair to believe that most of the officers in command of the prisoners did not trouble themselves much about the comfort of the prisoners, nor care particularly for an increase in the death rate."

James N. Miller
Company A
12th West Va. Inf.

# *Chapter Titles*

In order that the reader might comprehend the tremendous undertaking by the Confederates in establishing a prison for 35,000 prisoners in southwest Georgia, one must compare the population of the Post to some large cities of the period. The following was taken from the 1870 census:

| | |
|---|---|
| Cambridge, Mass. | 39,639 |
| Charleston, S. C. | 48,956 |
| Charlestown, Mass. | 28,323 |
| Columbus, Ohio | 31,274 |
| Dayton, Ohio | 30,473 |
| Fall River, Mass | 26,766 |
| Hartford, Conn. | 37,180 |
| Kansas City, Mo. | 32,260 |
| Lawrence, Mass. | 28,921 |
| Lynn, Mass. | 28,233 |
| Memphis, Tenn. | 40,266 |
| Mobile, Ala. | 32,034 |
| Paterson, N. J. | 33,579 |
| Portland, Me. | 31,413 |
| Reading, Pa. | 33,930 |
| Savannah, Ga. | 28,235 |
| Syracuse, N. Y. | 43,051 |
| Toledo, Ohio | 31,584 |
| Utica, N. Y. | 28,804 |
| Wilmington, Del. | 30,840 * |

---

* John McElroy, *Andersonville: A Story of Rebel Prisons* Volume 2, Washington, D.C. The National Tribune, 1899, p. 259.

# *Author's Preface*

Writings about Andersonville Prison often contain some simple fact with a single footnote from one source accepted as a true statement. In truth, the "fact" could vary widely from another source. This book will present the wide deviations apparent in numerous authors' works and allow the reader to choose the more logical view or at least the one that varies the least from the truth.

Over two hundred men wrote of their experiences while imprisoned at Andersonville and, as one would expect, their tales were different. Most first-hand accounts were written from personal recollections. A few prisoners kept crude diaries, which were heavily edited at the time of publication, sometimes fifty years after their imprisonment. The prison itself was so large that an incident might be witnessed by only those living in that particular area of the pen.

The communication of news within the pen was difficult; a story or rumor was spread by the telling and retelling which distorted it with each transmission. Sometimes the incident involved only two people and was not witnessed by a third party. For these reasons, the books varied widely in content and emphasis. Sometimes the authors exaggerated and distorted the truth. At other times they synthesized and fabricated details to substantiate their positions. There was just plain lying by both sides.

It was for this reason (i.e. the distortion of the truth) this book quotes so many passages verbatim. This will prevent putting meaning into the words the original author did not intend. It will allow the reader to interpret what an author meant and help explain why his description varied so significantly from other witnesses of the same event. At other times, quotes are used because, at this late date, it is difficult to interpret what was meant by the original words. It makes the original author responsible for his own interpretation or misrepresentation.

The date a prisoner arrived at or left Andersonville Prison determined his representations or descriptions of a situation or event. If he came in March, he saw only one palisade; if he arrived later, he would have sworn there were two or three. The hospital was moved from inside the pen to outside of the southeast corner and, still later, to a site parallel to the south wall. Even descriptions of something as fundamental as the height of the palisades or the width of the deadline varied by a distance of eight to ten feet.

There are probably a dozen books about Andersonville easily obtainable with little effort at most local bookstores. One can readily find copies of the books by Robert Kellogg, John McElroy, R. R. Stevenson, Ambrose Spencer, N. P. Chipman, or by any of a handful of others. Perhaps the historical novel by MacKinlay Kantor or the books by William B. Hesseltine or Ovid L. Futch can be found. Another dozen or so are seen once in a lifetime. Most of the other hundred or so sources are books or diaries found only after extensive searches. Some diaries found are the only known copies. Others are pamphlets used to raise money for a convalescent ex-prisoner.

Many authors will become very familiar to the reader as he reads this book. These authors' prejudices and idiosyncrasies will be apparent after reading several of their quotations. For instance, the Unionist, Ambrose Spencer, who lived in the vicinity of the prison, was very sympathetic to the prisoners' plight. He personally became involved in an attempt to punish the Confederate authorities who had served there. A couple of ex-prisoner authors, such as James M. Page, surprisingly defends the efforts of Wirz.

This book attempts to glean the small tidbits of "truth" or objective observations from some of these approximately two hundred sources written by ex-prisoners about their experiences at Andersonville. Some hundred-page books were so blatantly biased that but a couple of paragraphs qualify for inclusion in this book.

Sometimes a researcher wishes to know if there is any interesting incident that happened to a prisoner who is the focus of his research. It was for this reason that all interesting incidents as well as "interesting deaths" are included. If the prisoner died under abnormal circumstances, he was included in this work.

One must keep in mind that prisoners have always hated the men who take away their freedom and they have tended to heap the blame on the "warden" for all their hardships, real or imaginary. One must also remember that the sectional hatred which prevailed during this time may have distorted some truths. Finally, whenever the word "testified" is used to describe a quotation in this book, the reader will assume that the quotation was from the testimony disclosed at the Wirz trial at the end of the war.

This compilation of facts will rely heavily on quotes and, for this reason, the standard longer quote form (single-spaced with wider margins) will be modified so that the book will flow more easily and be more readable.

The quotes will be left in their original dialect to allow the reader to judge the competency of the original author and the educational level of the speaker.

Since the prison camp had only been in existence for about thirteen months, ten of those months occur in the year 1864. Since the events in this book are, more or less, in chronological order, the notation of the year 1864 will not be added to most month and day notations, which locate an event or occurrence.

At the end of the Civil War, only one man was tried and convicted of war crimes committed during the war. That man, Major Henry Wirz, was an officer at Andersonville Prison, which had been established in southwest Georgia. Wirz contended that he had been unjustly arrested since his case fell under the terms of surrender agreed upon between Sherman and Johnston. He felt, among other things, that he had been tried by a court without jurisdiction over him, especially since his trial occurred in a time of peace. One of the best sources of sworn statements about the conditions at Andersonville was the testimony of former prisoners during Wirz' trial.

The pen continued to fill until the 10,000-man capacity that Sid Winder originally designated was surpassed. With the horrible crowding came many problems. Foremost among the problems was simply the lack of space within which the men could sleep. Other problems were a lack of funds to properly run the prison, an inappropriate amount of nourishing rations, the inability to secure needed sanitary facilities, an insufficient and incompetent guard force, and the lack of cooperation and support from the upper levels of command. Providing for the captured prisoners did not rank very high on the Confederate list of priorities.

In reviewing books on Andersonville, the South's most notorious military prison, a common theme persists or appears in all the works by ex-inmates: the extreme suffering of the Federal prisoners caused by already harsh conditions made harsher by the Confederate garrison at the prison. Most Northern versions say the suffering was intentional; most Southern versions say the suffering was unavoidable. Somewhere between lies the truth.

## *Chapter One*

# The Post and Its Early Personnel

***Andersonville is "a disgrace to civilization."***

Colonel Daniel T. Chandler
Confederate Assistant Adjutant
and Inspector General

**Secretary of War James A. Seddon** - He issued the actual order in November, 1863, to General John Henry Winder to send someone to Georgia to search for a suitable site for the prison.

At the outbreak of the Civil War, Brigadier General John Henry Winder was asked by his close friend, President Jefferson Davis, to be the provost marshal of Richmond. His duties included the overall control of the military prisons in and around Richmond. Because of the crowded conditions of the prisons there, Davis requested the construction of another prison camp, which would not drain the supplies necessary for the Army of Northern Virginia. On October 28, 1863, General Robert E. Lee wrote to Secretary of War James A. Seddon, stating many reasons why the prisoners should be removed from Richmond. First, the Federals might launch a raid against Richmond to free the prisoners since it was the capitol of the Confederacy and of strategic military value. Lee also noted that, since supplies had to be brought into Richmond to support the prisoners, these military stores tied up the transportation system and, indirectly, inflated the prices of commodities for the citizens of Richmond. It was more expensive to bring the supplies for the prisoners to Richmond than to place the prisoners at some remote cantonment nearer the source of the food supply. Finally, Lee felt the prisoners in Richmond gathered military information and intelligence about troop movements and communicated these in some manner to the enemy.[1]

[1] United States War Department, *The War of the Rebellion: A Compilation of the Official Records of the Union and Confederate Armies* (Government Printing Office, 1899), Series II, Vol. VI, page 438. Hereafter cited as *O.R.*; all references will be Series II.

From time to time, the editors of the Richmond newspapers voiced opposition to the presence of so many prisoners in the city, whose presence endangered its citizens. On October 30, 1863, the *Richmond Examiner* recommended "... the Yankee prisoners be put where the cold weather and scant fare will thin them out in accordance with the laws of nature."[2] At other times, the papers expressed Richmonders' concern for their own health because of the stench or noxious vapors rising from the many prisons located there.[3] The northbound trains coming from southern, food-producing areas returned southward empty and were available to carry prisoners with little inconvenience or interruption of freight hauling capability.[4]

On November 24, 1863, Secretary of War Seddon ordered General Winder to send someone to establish a prison in the vicinity of Americus or Fort Valley, Georgia. By an order issued through the provost marshal's Department of Henrico. General Winder sent his son and adjutant, Captain William Sidney Winder, to select the site.

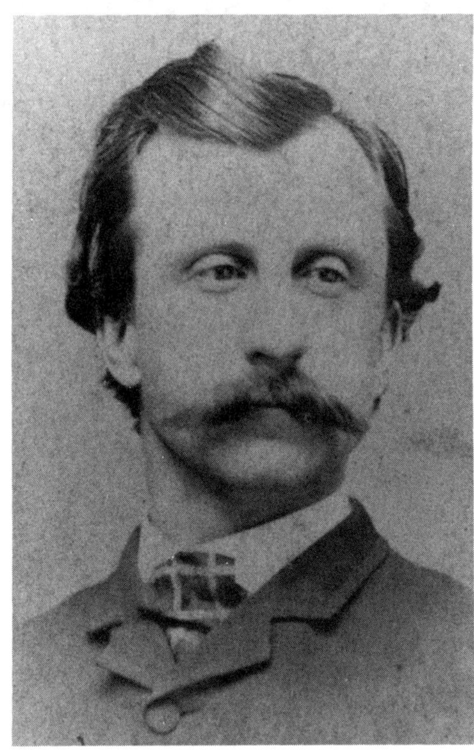

**Captain William Sidney Winder** - General Winder sent his son, his adjutant, to Georgia to search for a site for the prison and served as the first commandant of the post. (Courtesy of Mrs. John H. Winder, III)

*Headquarters Department of Henrico,*
*Richmond, November 24th, 1863*

*Captain-*

*The Secretary of War directs that a prison for Federal Prisoners shall be established in the State of Georgia. The General commanding the department directs that you proceed without delay to select a site for that purpose in the neighborhood of Americus or Fort Valley, a town between Macon and Andersonville.*

*You will go by way of Milledgeville to consult Gov. Brown; and also by way of Atlanta to consult Gen. Cobb.*

*You will hold yourself in readiness to return to these Headquarters as soon as ordered.*

*Very respectfully,*

*Your obedient servant,*
*J. M. Pegram,*
*A. A. Gen.*[5]

[2] Ambrose Spencer, *A Narrative of Andersonville* (New York: Harper & Brothers, Publishers, 1860), pp.120, 121
[3] S. S. Boggs, *Eighteen Months a Prisoner Under the Rebel Flag* (Lovington, Ill.: S. S. Boggs, Publisher, 1887), p. 13
[4] John L. Maile, *Prison Life in Andersonville* (Los Angeles: Grafton Publishing Company, 1912), p. 28
[5] *O. R.*, VI, p. 558.

"Capt. Winder did call upon Governor Joseph E. Brown, at Milledgeville, and, the legislature being in session, the Governor introduced him to many of the members from southwestern Georgia, with the request that they would assist him by any suggestions they might have to make.

From the governor and members of the legislature he received letters of introduction to many prominent men of Americus and Albany. After leaving Milledgeville, Capt. Winder went to Atlanta to consult Gen. Howell Cobb, then in command of that department, and received from him letters to several prominent citizens."[6]

"Winder considered locating the prison at Blue (now Radium) Springs, near Albany, but opposition by property owners there discouraged him. He then inspected the locality of Magnolia Springs, between Americus and Plains, and apparently would have established the prison at that place but for the objection of members of a Primitive Baptist church, who used the springs for baptismal ceremonies."[7] The site selected by Captain Sidney Winder was Andersonville or "Station #8" on the Southwestern Railroad. He immediately entered into an agreement to lease the land east of the railroad from Benjamin B. Dykes and Wesley W. Turner for a monthly rental of $50 and $30 respectively.[8] Benjamin Dykes, the railroad agent at Andersonville testified: "I own about a fourth of the ground where the prison was located. The other three-fourths were owned by W. W. Turner."[9]

Less than twenty people lived in the hamlet, which consisted of ten or twelve houses, a cotton warehouse, a frame church, and a dry-goods store. One author said, "There was but one house in Andersonville proper."[10] Another author, John B. Vawter, said of Andersonville, "There was one store, kept in part of the depot building."[11] Simon Helwig stated, "We found the place to consist of a dilapidated station, water tank and two houses."[12] The town originally had been called Anderson after John W. Anderson, who had been the Superintendent of the Southwestern Railroad. When it was extended from Oglethorpe to Americus in 1854, the U. S. Post Office Department changed the name to Andersonville in 1865, so it would not be confused with Anderson, South Carolina.[13]

General Winder sent his second cousin, Captain Richard Bayly Winder, to Andersonville on December 10, 1863, to be the prison's quartermaster.

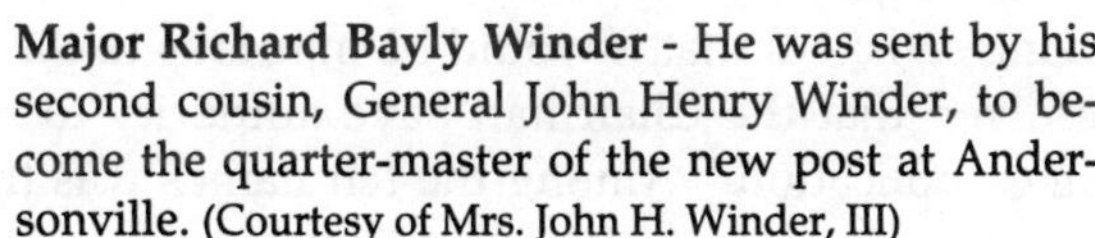

**Major Richard Bayly Winder** - He was sent by his second cousin, General John Henry Winder, to become the quarter-master of the new post at Andersonville. (Courtesy of Mrs. John H. Winder, III)

[6] Samuel B. Davis, *Escape of a Confederate Officer from Prison* (Norfolk, Va.: The Landmark Publishing Co., 1892), p. 23.
[7] Ovid L. Futch, *History of Andersonville Prison* (Florida: University of Florida Press, 1978), p. 3.
[8] *Blue and Gray* Magazine, "Andersonville," Dec.-Jan. 1985-1986, p. 7.
[9] *The Trial of Henry Wirz*, 40th Congress, 2nd Session, House Executive Document 23 (Washington, 1868), p. 372. Hereafter cited as *Wirz Trial.*
[10] P. A. Hanaford, *Field, Gunboat, Hospital, and Prison* (Boston: C. M. Dinsmoor and Company, 1866), p. 322.
[11] J. B. Vawter, *Prison Life in Dixie* (Chicago: Central Book Concern, 1881), p. 36.
[12] Simon Helwig, *The Capture and Prison Life in Rebeldom for Fourteen Months* (Canal Dover, Ohio: Bixley Printing Co., date unknown), p. 24.
[13] Futch, p. 3.

Richard Bayly Winder's father was Nathaniel James Winder, born December 16, 1794, a lawyer and Clerk of the Court of Northampton County, Virginia. The elder Winder was married to Sarah "Sally" Upshur Winder and he died on August 2, 1844. Richard Bayly Winder was born on July 17, 1828, at Eastville in Accomac County on the Eastern Shore of Virginia at Coventon, the old family home. Coventon, named for Coventon Simpkins, its first owner, was an eighteenth-century estate known to be in existence as early as 1790.[14]

Little is known about young Dick Winder, but it is clear he was instructed and tutored by a "... Mr. Mort, an Oxford graduate" in the classics and other subjects.[15] Many sons of aristocratic families throughout the South were sent to the Presbyterian-influenced College of New Jersey at Princeton. Dick was accepted by the College of New Jersey and was placed in the sophomore class by impressing the president of the college with his knowledge of Latin and Greek at his pre-admission interview. He entered the College of New Jersey, the forerunner of Princeton University, on August 18, 1845, thereby becoming a member of the class of 1848. He probably endured good-natured teasing by the other students over his Southern attire in fashion at that time, his "... broad-brimmed hat, bobtailed coat, baggy breeches, and high-heeled boots."[16] Records show he joined the Cliosophic Society, one of the two undergraduate, secret, debating societies. "The Cliosophic Society, or Clio Hall, as it was popularly called, was composed largely of northerners, while the Whig Society was considered to be a southern organization."[17] He was suspended on November 5th for, as the faculty minutes state, going "... out a gunning." The minutes of a faculty meeting held on November 17, read, "... resolved that Messrs. Silas Whitehead, Richard B. W. Winder and J. N. Richards, suspended by order, on the 5th inst., be permitted to return to college next Saturday." Winder was then absent from his first session exams on December 15. His grade average for the second session of his sophomore class was 31.9%. He apparently dropped out soon thereafter, for no further mention was made of him in the minutes.[18]

After his return from the College of New Jersey, Dick Winder was accepted at the University of Virginia for the 1846-1847 session into the School of Natural Philosophy composed of classes in the natural sciences.

At a faculty meeting on October 6, 1846, a Robert (sic) Bayly Winder, who was "...under age," applied to the faculty "... for leave to board at a Colonel Johnson's on account of delicate health." This request was granted.

Two weeks later, on October 21, 1846, he requested to leave the School of Natural Philosophy and sought admission to the School of Medicine. This request, too, was granted. At the faculty meeting on February 2, 1847, the Chairman called on the professors for the names of such students who were "... idle, inattentive and who are not making due progress in their respective schools." The professor of medicine reported that R. B. Winder had been absent seven times and the professor of anatomy and surgery reported R. B. Winder as being absent four times. Though most of the students were admonished by their professors for their several delinquencies, the faculty resolved the Chairman should admonish R. B. Winder for his frequent absences from lectures and for inattention. Such an admonition seemed slightly more forceful.

Two weeks later, on February 18, 1847, at the faculty meeting, Dick Winder made application through his Chairman for a leave of absence for two weeks. The faculty decided he could only have off until Thursday the 25th, when the intermediate examination in the School of Anatomy and Surgery would be held.[19]

At the faculty meeting on June 30, 1847, the faculty "... being satisfied, that it would be injurious to the University to readmit the following students of the past session, resolved that the Chairman have authority to refuse to grant them permission to matriculate, should any of them make application." Among the ten names was that of R. Bayly Winder.[20]

Following the completion of his abbreviated studies at the University of Virginia, he returned to Coventon where he managed a small mercantile business. While there, he met Miss Elizabeth S. Custis and married her on February 2, 1849. Dick and his wife moved onto a plantation with a lovely white clapboard home called The Folly, which she had inherited from her father. Dick and Elizabeth had no children, and their marriage was short-lived. Later, Dick Winder married Sarah M. Custis, the sister of his first wife. In 1854, the couple had a son, Richard Bayly Winder, Junior, and, in 1857, a daughter, Mary Custis Winder, followed. Dick Winder became a gentleman farmer, enjoyed raising horses, and maintained a racetrack on his property, where he kept several famous running horses.

A popular business man with a love for the South, Dick Winder went on to be instrumental in raising volunteers

[14] James E. Mears, *Virginia's Eastern Shore in the War of Secession* (Onancock, Va., 1946-1953) Photocopy made by Virginia State Library in 1956 of author's scrapbook of his weekly column "The Shoreline" in the *Eastern Shore News* 1949-1953. p.14.
[15] Burton Lee Thorpe, *Biographies of Pioneer American Dentists and Their Successors*, Charles R. E. Koch, ed., *History of Dental Surgery*, Vol. III (Chicago: National Art Publishing Company, 1909), p. 460.
[16] James O. Breeden, *Joseph Jones, M. D., Scientist of the Old South* (Lexington, Kentucky: The University Press of Kentucky, 1975), p. 20.
[17] Breeden, p.20.
[18] Personal correspondence, Mrs. Cynthia McClelland, Archives Assistant, Seeley G. Mudd Manuscript Library, Princeton University, 1980.
[19] Personal correspondence, Carolyn M. Beckham, Assistant Archivist. Archives, University of Virginia, Charlottesville, Va.
[20] *Ibid.*

for a regiment designated as the Thirty-ninth Virginia Volunteer Infantry. At Camp Huger, on a farm owned by Dr. George T. Yerby, Winder enlisted the men which composed Company A. William C. Wickings was elected captain.[21]

According to the "Proceedings of the Advisory Council of the State of Virginia," which met from April 21 to June 19, 1861, Governor John Fletcher nominated Richard B. Winder as Assistant Quartermaster and Assistant Commissary, with the rank of Captain of Volunteers for service on the Eastern Shore.

The field officers of the 39th Regiment were commissioned by Governor Fletcher on May 28, 1861. Richard B. Winder, as Captain and Assistant Quartermaster of the Thirty-ninth Virginia Regiment, wrote to Confederate President Jefferson Davis, "outlining the importance of the Eastern Shore peninsula and of defending its people who, by family heritage and geographic circumstances, were Southerners at heart."[22]

The 39th Regiment was composed of 800 men in eight companies of infantry, two companies of cavalry and one of light artillery, "... all poorly equipped."[23]

Dick Winder's participation in the 39th Virginia Regiment and this regiment's role in delaying the suppression of the Eastern Shore was a minor but interesting portion of Dick Winder's military career.

Once the opposition disappeared, the Federal expedition sent to the Eastern Shore embarked for home on December 2. By the middle of March, the Secretary of War was informed troops were no longer needed.

The men of the 39th were disbanded and mustered out of service on January 25, 1862, by order of the Secretary of War. Only twenty-nine officers, twelve non-commissioned officers and fifty-one privates succeeded in reaching the western shores of the Chesapeake Bay before the Eastern Shore was in complete control of the Federal troops. These men became part of the 46th Virginia Regiment, the 19th Virginia Heavy Artillery and the 24th Cavalry. Some men joined Maryland units. Later, fifty-eight more men escaped in small boats under cover of night and joined their comrades.[24]

A Confederate States Quartermaster Department document, dated November 26th stated, "We hereby certify that a number of privates of the 39th Reg't Va. Vol. by order of two of their officers, took the boat *Jenny Lind*, mentioned in the above account and fixtures, belonging to R. B. Winder, on the 18th inst., crossed Chesapeake Bay in her on the same evening, and said privates stated to us that said boat was crushed to pieces in the breakers at Cape Henry." A notation at the bottom of this document reads, "Received at Richmond, November 26, 1861 by Capt. R. B. Winder, A. Q. M., C. S. A., the sum of two hundred dollars in full on above account. Signed in duplicate, R. B. Winder."[25]

On several occasions during the war, Dick Winder was smuggled behind the Federal lines onto the Eastern Shore, which was blockaded by the Federal fleet. Louis J. Ross, a farmer who used his small sailboat to make the two-day trip from Folly Creek to the western shore, said, "He [Winder] would spend one night sailing to the area near the present town of Cape Charles, beach his boat, remove the mast, turn the boat upside down, cover it with marsh grass, and crawl underneath it to sleep during the day. The second night he would right and launch his boat and sail to the Western Shore."[26]

*The Baltimore Sun* of January 9, 1862, stated that R. B. Winder, Esq., of Accomack, had been appointed paymaster in the Confederate States Navy.[27] This appointment was substantiated by a second source as he was listed in the Roster of Officers of the Confederate Navy from Virginia as a "... Master not in line of promotion, Feb.1, 1862 (acceptance)."[28] The *Register of Officers of the Confederate States Navy 1861-1865*, said he "... served on Richmond station, 1862."[29]

By Special Order Number 233, Adjutant and Inspector General's Office, Winder was ordered to duty in Richmond from August 13, 1862, by command of the Secretary of War. He was placed on special duty in the Department of Henrico under the command of his cousin, General John H. Winder of the Maryland Line.

On December 10, by a special order from the Headquarters Department of Henrico, Dick Winder was told to proceed to Andersonville, located sixty-two miles south of Macon and nine miles north of Americus in southwestern Georgia to become the first quartermaster at the newly- conceived prison. As the new quartermaster, Winder immediately began his duties, the first of which was to prepare for the future arrival of the reluctant guests.

---

[21] Mears, p. 7.
[22] *O. R.*, Series I, Vol. LI, Part II, pp. 241, 242.
[23] Mears, p. 7.
[24] Mears, p. 17.
[25] *Ibid.*
[26] L. Floyd Nock, III, *Drummondtown, A One Horse Town* (Verona, Va.: McClure Press, 1976), p. 240.
[27] Mears, p. 34.
[28] Virginia State Library Compiled, *Confederate Service Rosters*, Vol. 19, p. 241.
[29] *Register of Officers of the Confederate States Navy 1861-1865* (Mattituck, N. Y.: J. M. Carroll & Company, 1983), p. 215. Compiled by the Office of Naval Records and Library.

General Winder said the site for the prison was selected "... about the 20th of December, 1863."[30] The size of the post was about one mile by a half-mile. When first ordered to build a prison stockade, the capacity specified was six thousand prisoners, but, at Dick Winder's suggestion, the inmate capacity was raised to ten thousand because "...the banks of the stream which was to supply the water were steep, and this would give me land more level and more available for the purpose at a very little more expense to the Government."[31] On February 3, Dick Winder said he expected 10,000 prisoners at the post.

When he was sent to Georgia, Winder was told he could get all the laborers he would need from the surrounding neighborhood. However, he met resentment and opposition from the local residents over the location of the military prison and the influx of Confederate support troops in their midst.

During a delay lasting well into January, Dick Winder wrote to Richmond and awaited permission to impress the necessary labor. He finally obtained permission from Major General Howell Cobb, commander of the military districts of Georgia and Florida, to impress 500 to 600 slaves from the neighborhood to begin construction. One out of every four slaves could be impressed from the planters in the vicinity. The construction of the prison began around January 10.[32] The builders used the Negroes, with implements gathered from surrounding farms, to begin clearing the land leased from Wesley W. Turner and Benjamin B. Dykes.

Most authors have said the immense, naturally straight pines were hewn into twelve-inch square, twenty-three foot logs. These logs were placed in five-foot deep trenches and the red Georgia clay tamped down tightly around them.[33] The trees, after being hewn, fit so closely the prisoners could not see daylight through the palisade.

**Prison Camp at Andersonville** – This fanciful print shows 4 thirty- or forty-foot-wide streets going north-south that never existed within the pen. Captain Wirz' headquarters, the bakery and a train are in the background. (Author's Collection)

[30] *O. R.*, VII, p. 541.
[31] *O. R.*, VIII, pp. 730, 731.
[32] *O. R.*, VII, p. 541.
[33] James N. Miller, *The Story of Andersonville and Florence* (DesMoines, Iowa: Welch, The Printer, 1900), p. 15.

In July, when the prison was enlarged, Captain Henry Wirz said the inmates were given the 1,000 posts, which made up the north wall to be used for firewood. He said these posts were twenty-three feet long.[34] When Captain W. M. Hammond inspected the prison on June 21 for General Braxton Bragg, he said the height of the pen was seventeen feet.[35] When allowing for five feet in the ground, these two officers independently corroborated the same length. Still, Colonel Daniel Chandler offered an incorrect opinion, after his inspection in August; the posts were fifteen feet high and hewn eight inches square.[36]

A prisoner, Morgan Dowling, said "... the upper ends were sharpened to increase the difficulty of getting over them."[37] Each log was spiked by a horizontal timber placed about three feet below the top of the wall on the outside.[38] Another author, Doctor Augustus Hamlin, said vertical logs were "... held in position at the top by long, slender pines, nailed on the outer side by large iron spikes" and positioned about three feet from the top."[39]

One can almost hear the syncopated axes swung in rhythm to old spirituals by blacks from the neighborhood. A work detail of fifty-four slaves and five free Negroes was stopped on its way to Savannah and put to work. They worked under the supervision of the "... experienced labor foreman, C. C. Sheppard, former plantation superintendent of Dougherty and Lee counties."[40] Captain William S. Winder felt some pressure to finish all construction quickly because all of the labor was impressed for only sixty days. Wagons and teams of mules and oxen proved difficult to obtain for the heavy hauling and stump removal. "All the transportation we ever had is what we were able to hire from a refugee, the Government furnishing none until June, 1864."[41] A Mr. S. Hays, "... a practical mechanic," was of great service in constructing the stockade.[42]

One of the great paradoxes at Andersonville was the apparent scarcity of building material at the prison, even though it was built within an abundant forest of tall Georgia pines. The Spanish moss that hung from many of these trees was more abundant in the lower-lying lands and was known as "death moss" because malaria was more prevalent where the moss hung.[43]

The prison held thousands of men willing and able to make cabins or shacks to protect themselves from the elements. These men were veteran soldiers and many were carpenters, who could take an ax and fashion comfortable quarters from a few pine trees in an afternoon.

Despite the ability of the prisoners to make shelter, one of the four or five main criticisms of the treatment of the Federal prisoners was the failure of the South to furnish shelter for them. Most Federal prison camps, such as those at Camp Douglas, Johnson's Island, Point Lookout, Elmira, and Fort Delaware, had some shelter, usually similar to barracks. These barracks were often poorly made, many with broken windowpanes, with only one stove to burn the very little fuel furnished to fend off the cold, blustery winds of the North. The vast majority of Confederate prisoners, however, did not completely lack shelter as the Federal prisoners at Andersonville did.

Captain William S. Winder had much difficulty getting nails. This was partly because only one factory produced cut nails in the entire Confederacy.[44] Right from the start, construction crept along slowly dependent on the supply of nails, lumber, and implements; manpower, however, was never a problem. By March 15, Winder said his commissary house would soon be finished; he had been using the local church for his commissary house, and was applying to the Secretary of War for permission to impress the sawmills.[45] On April 11, Dick Winder requested that a trainload of lumber, delayed at Gordon, Georgia, for twelve days, be forwarded immediately by Major J. G. Michaeloffsky, quartermaster at Macon.[46]

Plenty of sawmills operated nearby, varying in their sawing capacity, with some powered by steam and some powered by water; though the water-powered mills needed a good flow of water, there was never any diminishing of the streams powering the mills during the summer of 1864. The several large sawmills in the vicinity could have easily produced, in a few weeks, all the lumber required for the building of shelters.

By April 25, Dick Winder had received permission to impress lumber but lacked the means to transport it. He reported to General Marcus J. Wright:

"I have the honor to report the great difficulty I have had in procuring an adequate supply of lumber for the

---

34 *O. R.*, VII, p. 759.
35 *Ibid.*, p. 393.
36 *Ibid.*, p. 546.
37 Morgan E. Dowling, *Southern Prisons or, Josie, The Heroine of Florence* (Detroit: William Graham, 1870), p. 99.
38 Boggs, p. 21.
39 Augustis C. Hamlin, *Martyia or Andersonville Prison* (Boston: Lee and Shepard, 1866), p. 52.
40 Futch, pp. 4, 5.
41 *O. R.*, VII, p. 541.
42 *O. R.*, VI, p. 965.
43 John McElroy, *Andersonville: A Story of Rebel Prison* (Washington, D. C.: The National Tribune, 1899), Vol. I, p. 125.
44 J. William Jones, "Confederate View of the Treatment of Prisoners," *Southern Historical Papers* (Richmond: Southern Historical Society, 1876), p. 164.
45 *O. R.*, VII, pp. 1054, 1055.
46 *Ibid.*, p. 40.

construction of necessary hospital, commissary, and other buildings. Since authority to impress lumber has been given me, this trouble has been removed and now transportation for this lumber is the only obstacle. I have also had great difficulty in procuring necessary working implements and nails, and am still unsupplied. If I could succeed in getting the necessary lumber, nails and tools I could put these buildings up very rapidly, as I have no lack of mechanical force.

The troops here are suffering much for the want of tents. I used every effort in my power to obtain them, but without success."[47]

Dick Winder would complain after the war: "I could get no lumber scarcely at all, and after the power to impress mills was given me from Richmond, the railroads insisted that railroad transportation would give entirely out if I was allowed to impress the mills. I was then instructed to impress only those mills, which the railroads did not require. The result of this was that almost all the mills made contracts with the railroad for small quantities, did what they pleased with the balance, and I had to go without."[48]

Part of Dick Winder's problem of getting lumber was caused by his authority to buy planking at only $50 per 1,000 linear foot while the navy facility at Albany and hospital departments were authorized to buy the same lumber at $75 and $80 respectively.[49] Another obstacle Dick Winder had to overcome was his lack of funds to buy lumber from the private suppliers. He testified that for most of the summer of 1864, he was without funds, and that, although "... timely requisitions had been forwarded to Richmond, not one cent did I receive from them for the last four months that I was at Andersonville, and the few mills that were cutting for me refused to saw any longer."[50] Captain William S. Winder asked General John H. Winder to rescind his explicit order to construct all storehouses, hospitals, and quarters out of round logs but to allow him to use the planking obtained from trimming "stringers" for the railroads. The antiquated railroad lines in Georgia needed lumber cut into stringers, which were six by eight inches. These were placed, lengthwise, across the ties which had been laid in the usual fashion and into which the rails were spiked.

**View Looking North at the Depot c. 1868** – The depot was on the east side of the tracks of the Southwestern Railroad during the war. There was a Commissary Storehouse on the east side and the west side of the tracks. Notice the "stringers" that the iron rails were nailed into. The surplus boards from the trimming of these stringers were the chief building material at the post. (National Archives)

[47] *O. R.*, VII, p. 89.
[48] *O. R.*, VIII, p. 732.
[49] *Ibid.*, p. 732.
[50] *Ibid.*

Only a few of the officers of the guard lived in shanties, and these few were built of "... slabs and sheeting, which was the refuse of the mills."[51] "Nearly ever building in the encampment was built of rough logs and covered with clap-boards split from the trees and held to their places by poles."[52]

One of the Confederate physicians, Doctor John C. Bates said, "Immediately upon the west side of the stockade, and between there and the depot, there was timber scattered; on the north side, beyond the cook-house a little, there was plenty of timber; on the south side plenty had been cut in logs and lay there, and down by the hospital there was plenty. That is a woody country, and there was plenty of wood within a mile. It was fine timber, and could have been made into shingles or clapboards. I did not see any of it used to make shelter for the prisoners."[53]

Colonel Alexander W. Persons, of the Fifty-fifth Georgia Regiment was sent to Andersonville on February 26, "... by command of the Secretary of War," to become the second commandant of the post to succeed Sid Winder, who should be considered the first commandant of the post. Samuel Cooper, Adjutant and Inspector General, wrote to Major-General Howell Cobb on February 7, in Atlanta, and asked him to recommend a commander for this post. He said that, since the prison was located in the state of Georgia, he thought there should be a native Georgian in command. Cooper sought the name of an officer holding the rank of brigadier-general or colonel, who was unassigned because of wounds or disablement. Cooper said he also wished all the guards to be native Georgians as far as possible, but he knew this would be difficult because of the Yankee threat to that area.[54]

One of Colonel Persons' first acts was to place an order with a sawmill near Macon for one million linear feet of lumber. This was slowly brought in by rail and stacked at the prison "... for the purpose of building barracks."[55]

Dick Winder tried to provide shelter for the prisoners, scouring the state for tents. "I earnestly advised the use of tents, and gave as my reasons for it that they would be more healthy, less subject to danger from fire, and in case of a general exchange of prisoners, which we were all the time expecting, would be a great saving in expense to the Confederate States Government; but I was informed by the Quartermaster General that they could not be supplied for the simple reason they did not have them. There were some tents in Savannah, Ga., belonging to the State, which I tried in every way in the world to get, but could not succeed, as they said they needed them for their own troops."[56]

Spencer, the Unionist, said he was at Andersonville very frequently during June and July, and he noted that the guards' "... tents were all floored with good lumber, and a good many shelters of lumber were put up by the soldiers. I noticed a good many tents that were protected from the sun by boards. There seemed to be no want of lumber at that time among the Confederate soldiers."[57]

Colonel Persons cited lack of transportation. He faced the task of gathering materials to build barracks when General Winder arrived and, evidently, countermanded the orders:

"When I was there, the railroad upon which the prison was located was worked to its greatest possible capacity in feeding Lee's and Johnston's armies, and it was with the greatest difficulty that I could get transportation on that road. Perhaps in ten or twenty days they would give me one train. I held constant communication with the superintendent of the road, and every time I could get a train I would have that train loaded with lumber and brought through. During my stay, I had concentrated there, I suppose, about five or six trainloads of lumber. I suppose there were six, eight, or ten cars in a train. There were altogether about fifty carloads. I was in the act of erecting shelter, was just carrying the lumber, when I was relieved by General Winder. He arrived there about the same day I was relieved. I went into the stockade several times after I was relieved from duty, and saw no shelter there. I saw forty or fifty houses springing up outside of the grounds. The lumber disappeared in that way."[58] It is still unclear who used those forty or fifty houses.

Though the prison officials used the lack of transportation as an excuse for not sheltering the prisoners, the excuse was not substantiated by a witness at the Wirz trial. The court record relates that "W. A. Griffin lived in Nashville, Tennessee, and for the last eighteen months of the war was a conductor on the Southwestern Railroad on the run from Macon, Georgia, to Eufaula, Alabama, passing through Andersonville. He testified about the adequacy of the transportation to and from Andersonville. He was asked if he knew of any reason why lumber could not be carried to Andersonville? His answer was, 'I do not'."[59]

Besides shelter, Dick Winder had to obtain suitable sources of food for his soon-to-arrive guests. Evidently, Dick

[51] J. William Jones, p. 164.
[52] *Ibid.*
[53] Chipman, p. 131.
[54] *O. R.*, VI, p. 925.
[55] *O. R.*, VII, p. 136.
[56] *O. R.*, VIII, p. 732.
[57] Spencer, p. 151.
[58] N. P. Chipman, *The Tragedy of Andersonville* (San Francisco: The Flair-Murdock Company, 1911), p. 54.
[59] *Ibid.*, pp. 155, 156.

Winder was unable to secure any rations for these first prisoners because a local inhabitant and railroad agent at Andersonville, Benjamin Dykes, testified, "When the first batch of prisoners came, I loaned the quartermaster some meat and meal in consequence of not having any shipped."[60] Winder's correspondence, written in February, reveals many interesting shortages and problems which had to be circumvented. The Quartermaster-General instructed Winder to gather supplies from the nearby commissaries. On February 3, Winder wrote to Major A. M. Allen, Commissary of Subsistence, in Columbus, fifty miles away, that he needed "... beef, meat, flour, sugar, molasses, rice, soap, candles, &c." He did not wish the beef to be stripped of tallow, because he intended to make candles there at the camp. He did not need to be supplied with corn and meal, because he could draw it from the quartermaster's department.[61] On February 16, he wrote, asking his agent to proceed to Cartersville in northwestern Georgia, to purchase six, 100-gallon, iron kettles needed to boil meat for the prisoners.[62] On February 19, Captain Winder wrote he would be sending one of his agents to Albany in a day or two to arrange contracts with Drew's Mill at Adams' Station to furnish him meal made from corn obtainable in the region. As a part of his preparation for the prisoners, he told Major Locks, chief purchasing commissary for the state of Georgia, he would "... gladly feed any offal from the slaughter houses in Albany that could not readily be kept on hand or forwarded to the army to the prisoners at this post." For this offal, he had to pay $2 apiece for beef tongues, $1 for shanks, and 50 cents per pound for shank meat and pickled hearts.[63]

In his attempt to gather commitments for food, Winder made contacts to obtain beef cattle from Florida, which would have to be driven by "exempts," but he was unable to hire any because they found speculation much more profitable and the people willing to drive the cattle were physically unable to do so. Dick Winder said, "Arrangements are being made to feed prisoners on beef as far as can be obtained from Florida."[64] Because the Confederate Congress transferred the duty of feeding prisoners of war from the Quartermaster's Department to the Commissary Department in February, the Florida cattle drive was canceled. Soon after this law passed, a commissary officer journeyed to Andersonville and, after his arrival, the responsibility for feeding the prisoners fell on someone besides Dick Winder. Winder did have to furnish transportation for the rations from the commissary storehouse to the cookhouse and from the cookhouse to the prison.[65]

He wrote he did not need a second baker, nor did he need a commissary officer as everything was being handled by A. M. Allen, Major and Commissary of Subsistence. He still needed, however, a cook, nails, padlocks for doors, baking pans, window glass, and platform scales at once.[66]

In a letter written February 20, Dick Winder said he expected the prisoners to arrive on that date.[67] A Captain Walter Bowie of the Adjutant and Inspector General's Department said the prison was "... first established on the 23rd of February."[68] General Winder said the "date of organization" of the prison was February 24.[69] "Before the stockade was half completed the commanding officer, Captain W. S. Winder, was telegraphed from Richmond that it was impossible to feed the prisoners longer there and that they must come at once to Andersonville on account of provisions."[70]

---

[60] *Wirz Trial*, p.371.
[61] *O. R.*, VI, p. 914.
[62] *Ibid.*, p. 962.
[63] *Ibid.*, p. 985.
[64] *Ibid.*, p. 977.
[65] *O. R.*, VIII, p. 731.
[66] *O. R.*, VI, p. 1000.
[67] *Ibid.*, p. 977.
[68] *O. R.*, VII, p. 135.
[69] *Ibid.*, p. 524.
[70] *O. R.*, VIII, p. 731.

**Prisoners being escorted to Libby Prison by Confederate guards.** They were frequently subjected to the taunts of young Richmond kids directing them to "Hotel Libby." (Goss)

W. D. Hammock, of the 55th Georgia Regiment, testified he arrived at Andersonville on the 14th of February and the pen was about two-thirds completed at that time. He also said some prisoners arrived on the 20th of February.[71]

After being ordered on the 17th to be ready to leave Richmond the next day, at daybreak, the contingent of prisoners, considered by most historians the first, left Richmond's Libby Prison on the 18th, took nine days by rail, and arrived on the 27th between 10 and 11 a.m. Charles Smith took seven days and six nights in the cars with a rest of only one night at Charlotte.[72] James M. Page, a member of this first detachment, said the first group consisted of 1,000 prisoners. He also said there were about 2,000 prisoners already confined there upon his arrival at ten o'clock that morning of the 27th.[73]

The actual means of transmission of the prisoners was devised by General Winder, who said the prisoners would be sent by way of Raleigh and Columbia and they would be sent "... in detachments of 400, daily, which will require a guard of fifty privates, three officers, and four sergeants and four corporals."[74] He said the guards would be relieved by forming a relay of the guards. "I propose that the guard from here shall be relieved at Weldon, and return immediately; that guard from Weldon be relieved at Augusta, return immediately to Weldon; the guard from Augusta to go to Andersonville. I propose to place an officer at Charlotte, N.C., and one at Augusta, to procure, cook, and distribute the rations to the prisoners."[75] This grand design was never fully implemented, to say the least.

Some groups of prisoners had to depend upon the charity of people at the various railway stops along the way for food. George G. Russell told of the disposal of those who were too weak to make it to their final destination. "At every stopping place those of our number who died on the way were left along the route for burial."[76] The train on which Maile and his companions were conveyed, arrived in Augusta on Sunday at about church time. After learning of the plight of the prisoners, many ladies, instead of going to church, returned to their homes and emerged with baskets filled with sandwiches. They overcame the objections of the guards and gave the sandwiches to the men.[77]

When the first prisoners arrived at Andersonville, part of the south wall was not yet completed. "It being impossible to keep them in the cars, we had to put them in the completed end of the stockade and double the guards."[78]

---

[71] *Wirz Trial*, p. 497.
[72] Charles M. Smith, *From Andersonville to Freedom* (Providence: Soldiers and Sailors Historical Society of Rhode Island, 1894), p. 15.
[73] James M. Page, *The True Story of Andersonville Prison* (New York: The Neal Publishing Company, 1908), p. 61.
[74] *O. R.*, VI, p. 926.
[75] *Ibid.*
[76] George G. Russell, *Reminiscences of Andersonville Prison, A Paper Read by Comrade Geo. G. Russell before Post 34, G.A.R.* (Salem, Mass.: Observer Steam Book And Job Print, 1886), p. 5.
[77] Maile, p. 26.
[78] R. Randolph Stevenson, *The Southern Side: or Andersonville Prison* (Baltimore: Turnbull Brothers, 1876), p. 499.

"We were confined to the north side of the prison, the south side not being completed."[79] McElroy said the gap in the wall was several hundred feet wide when his group arrived on the 25th.[80] Edward Wellington Boate testified that, when he arrived on the 24th, he was placed in the second five hundred and "... one-quarter was not completed."[81] One man who arrived on February 29th testified: "When I arrived at Andersonville the prison was not completed. There was a portion between the north and South Gate on the east side that was not quite finished."[82] There were 200 men working on the pen when McElroy arrived.[83]

Charles Fosdick said, after the completion of the pen, "The first arrivals were assigned the south hillside, between the swamp and the stockade, which contained about six acres, leaving an alley running across the prison from the South Gate to the stockade at the east side. Each division fronted this alley and extended back to the stockade or down to the swamp, each hundred by itself, so as to form a line for roll call or drawing rations."[84] Sid Winder remained the commandant until approximately five or six lots of prisoners had arrived.[85]

There were several men who would have been happy to leave for Andersonville from Richmond, namely the six of Colonel Ulric Dahlgren's cavalry raiders who were captured while approaching Richmond to attempt the liberation of Union prisoners on Belle Isle. While in transit, these five hundred were ordered to destroy the mills, bridges, army stores, railroads, and to capture reserve artillery.

An uproar sounded throughout the South because some papers, taken from the body of the young leader of the raid, Ulric Dahlgren, revealed plans to destroy the city of Richmond and to kill Jeff Davis and his entire cabinet on the spot. This offensive document appeared later in all of Richmond's newspapers and in many others throughout the North and South, as well as in parts of Europe.[86]

The men on the Kilpatrick-Dahlgren Raid were, therefore, much despised by the Southerners. Among the raiders taken prisoner was S. M. Dufur, who heard, as he was marched into Richmond, small boys tauntingly shout: "Free carriage to the Libby Hotel: Right this way to the Libby."[87]

**Belle Isle Prison** – The skyline of Richmond with the State Capitol in the background. On this one-and-a-half-acre island prison in the James River were kept sometimes as many as 10,000 prisoners, mostly enlisted men. (Frank Leslie's Illustrated Newspaper)

[79] Chipman, p.172.
[80] McElroy, p. 134.
[81] *Wirz Trial*, p. 687.
[82] *Ibid.*, p. 373.
[83] McElroy, p. 134.
[84] Charles Fosdick, *Five Hundred Days in Rebel Prisons* (Bethany, Mo.: W. J. Wightman, Publisher, 1887), p. 30.
[85] *O. R.*, VIII, p. 731.
[86] The validity of these papers was discussed in an interesting article in the Civil War Times Liustrated Magazine of November 1983.
[87] S. M. Dufur, *Over the Dead Line or Tracked by Blood-Hounds* (Burlington, Vt.: Free Press Association, 1902), p. 35.

The captured raiders stayed at the Pemberton Building until dusk when they were moved to the nearby Libby Prison. There, the officials segregated them from the other prisoners. Dufur asked Dick Turner, the commandant of Libby, the reason for this. Turner said, "... the rest of the damned Yankee cutthroats were not going to be hanged just yet."[88]

They stayed at Libby Prison until the next day when, at about three o'clock, prison officials moved them to Belle Isle. At Belle Isle, prison officials told them to occupy one of the old ragged tents at one end of the prison and not to mix with the rest of the prisoners. They were also told that they would be severely punished if they were found in any other part of the camp.

Dufur found out that, the next day, six hundred men would be leaving and, since he feared for his life, he decided to "flank out" by pretending to be a man who had died a couple of days earlier or by "going out on a dead man's name." Dufur told how he and at least one other raider flanked out by disguising themselves to appear as old, emaciated inmates.

At a narrow gateway in the breastwork that surrounded the camp, Dick Turner was stationed, eagerly watching the men as they filed by him, and sorrow to him who was caught "flanking," where a man tried to pass out with a squad to which he did not belong.[89]

After the prisoners had been formed in two ranks, counted, and the roll called, Dick Turner stepped in front, and made the following remarks:

"Yanks, last night my dog was killed by some of you uns in this ere crowd. I want to know who killed him, and I'll be damned if I don't find out if it takes me a month. So now, you uns jest trot out the sneak that did it, and you're all right; and if you don't I'll chuck the whole of you back into that camp, and you'll go just seven days without rations. Do you hear?"

A young man standing near me stepped to the front, and taking off his hat, saluted the Lieutenant saying, "I am the man that killed your dog, sir."

A Confederate superior officer stopped him from being beaten by Dick Turner.

Walking up to the boy, he said:

"Was you the wretch that killed my dog last night?"

"I was, sir," came the prompt reply.

"And what did you kill him for?"

"For food," answered the young artilleryman.

"Then you eat dog meat, do you?"

"I do when I am hungry enough, and can get it" was the reply.

Turner then asked the fellow if he had any of the meat in his haversack; designating a small dirty cotton bag that hung from his shoulder.

The boy took a piece of the meat from the sack, and held it up before the heartless man, who should have blushed with shame, but instead he in a sneering tone said:

"You Yankee beauty, if you eat dog meat, eat a mouthful of that as it is," The poor fellow, not daring to refuse, took a piece of the raw meat in his mouth, whereupon the wretch struck him across the face with the side of his sword, saying

"It suits you too well, come with me, you damned Yankee dog-killer."

Near the gates there had been constructed an implement of torture called the "Jack." This consisted of two posts driven into the ground some six or eight feet apart; a plank was pinned or spiked to the side of these posts, about three feet from the ground. The prisoner was placed astride this plank, with his feet tied together underneath. His arms were pinioned and a stick of wood nearly the size of a railroad tie was placed between his legs, thus stretching the limbs and preventing the sufferer from falling from the edge of the plank. I think it was from five to ten minutes that the boy endured the suffering before the excruciating pain overcame him, and he fainted. In about fifteen minutes he revived.[90]

A higher-ranking Confederate officer came up at that time, ordered him removed, and let him be allowed to join the group of his comrades leaving the island.

The six hundred were taken, for some inexplicable reason, to Libby's second floor, where they stayed for thirty-

[88] *Ibid.*, p. 40.
[89] *Ibid.*, p. 49.
[90] *Ibid.*, pp. 52-55.

six hours. Dick Turner then aroused them with an oath, "... up and get into line! Fall into line, you damned Yankees nigger worshippers!"[91] The roll was then called and the men were counted. As the men passed out of the door of Libby, each was given a piece of cornbread weighing about two pounds. They knew because the "pone" was so large they were going to take a long trip. The six hundred were packed into ten cattle cars.

The prisoners left at about three o'clock in the morning of March 9, in the ten cattle cars with one passenger car attached to the end of the train for support of the forty officers and guards. They traveled by way of Danville. After nearly sixty hours, when the train had made it into South Carolina, the men were allowed out for the only time. The guards deployed themselves around the perimeter encircling about half an acre of ground with a few trees for shade. There, two or three men brought baskets filled with ears of raw corn and they emptied them on the floors of the cars and said, "Yanks, this is the best we can do for you now; you may eat it or throw it out. We can get nothing else here, it is impossible."[92] On the fourth day, they went through Atlanta, where they were given a little corn bread and a few pieces of hardtack. After passing through Macon and Americus, they arrived at Andersonville fifteen hours later, at about two o'clock in the afternoon on March 14th.

**Fresh Fish** – New prisoners arriving into the pen were a source of news of the war and of the prisoners exchange talks. Each new group of prisoners brought clothing, cooking utensils, and more currency to invigorate the prison economy. (John Urban)

The actual stockade, as first built, measured 1,010 feet long; its south wall measured 779 feet and its north wall measured 787 feet. Its long axis was configured more or less north-south.[93] The enclosed space was about eighteen acres, about three and one-quarter acres of which was swampy. One acre was within the deadline and one acre was set aside for streets and lanes, leaving "an inhabitable" space in the pen of twelve acres.[94] The actual area suitable for habitation was 740,520 square feet.[95]

A small, clear stream, a branch of the Sweet Water Creek, ran through the center of the stockade from west to east and soon became known as "Stockade Creek" to the prisoners. The stream divided the pen into two almost equal parts, which the inmates called "... North side and South side..."[96] The stream originated in two large springs about a half-mile to the west. Just before these two springs entered the pen, they merged into one, the rather swiftly flowing Stockade Creek. For this reason, some prisoners called it "Double Branch Creek." The branch, which ran through the prison, was described as being between three and five feet wide and between six and ten inches deep. Interestingly,

[91] *Ibid.*, p. 58.
[92] *Ibid.*, p. 65.
[93] Charles G. Davis, Commissioner, *Report of the Commission on Andersonville Monument* (Boston: Bright & Potter Printing Co., 1902), p. 21.
[94] *O. R.*, VII, p. 136.
[95] Chipman, p. 84.
[96] Vawter, p.37.

Confederate Captain Samuel B. Davis described Stockade Creek as being "... at least 20 to 25 feet wide."[97] Boggs, on the other hand, said the creek was four feet wide and five inches deep.

The creek usually had a thin layer of grease or scum on it, especially after the bakery and cookhouse began operation. James N. Miller described the stream as "... rather swift flowing, tinged with black and having a decaying vegetable taste."[98] Lyons stated, "The railroad station was so situated that all the drainage from that ran into it."[99]

The volume of the flow decreased during the summer heat and sun; it always acted as the primary source of water until the opening of Providence Spring, even though Stockade Creek, "... a great part of the time was completely covered with floating grease and offal from the cookhouse."[100] Despite its filth, Captain Samuel Boyer Davis said, "The guards who were stationed at the gate drank the same water."[101]

If the prison had been built across Sweet Water Creek proper, the prisoners would have had more than an ample amount of water for all of their needs. Major-General J. W. Wilson testified that the main part of Sweet Water Creek was fifteen feet wide and five feet deep, flowed at one mile per hour, and was only 250 feet from the corner of the hospital enclosure at the southeast corner of the pen.[102]

If the stream pollution was made up of grease and of by-products from the bakery, the Southern apologists have said that, since the bakers were Yankee prisoners detailed for that purpose, all criticism should be directed against their own comrades. After the war, Dick Winder admitted he had made a mistake in locating the cooking facilities upstream from the prison.[103] Also upstream from the prison were the camps of the guards. The Confederate guard was told to put latrines and stables for their cavalry horses and mules away from the stream. Still, the runoff from rain-washed stable and camp filth downstream. The guard who was encamped upstream could be seen, on a clear day, sitting along the banks of the stream, washing their dirty, lice-laden clothes.[104]

Located 450 feet from the southern wall of the stockade, and from thirty to fifty yards on each side of the branch, the stream was swampy. The swamp, on the north bank, stretched far wider than the swamp on the south bank. The north slope was also slightly higher than the south slope, and was about fifty feet above the branch level, or approximately 300 feet above sea level. Some authors described the swamp thus: "The place was very steep, rising up from the swamp; it could not be called a hill. It was a bank inclining at an angle of about 40 degrees."[105] "About one-fourth of the whole space enclosed by the stockade, which is wet and marshy and in its present condition, is altogether unfit for an encampment..."[106]

Vawter observed, "From the north side, by looking over the stockade where it crossed the hollow, we could see the Commandant of the Interior's headquarters above, and our hospital below. From the south side, in looking over the same way, we could see the quarters of a pack of bloodhounds, 'the old Redfield,' and a part of the town."[107]

McElroy noted, "When standing on the north slope or the south slope, one could see about forty acres to the east or the west at one time. Therefore the total acres that the men could see for the next year or so was 160 acres."[108]

When Sumter prison, as the locals called it, first opened, several trees stood within the pen.[109] Thomas Walsh, of the Seventy-fourth New York Regiment, arrived on the 29th of February and testified: "I think there were altogether about sixteen or seventeen trees in the stockade when I arrived there; a portion of them were old burned up pine trees; there were six or seven other trees on the south side which I believe were afterwards cut down and used, with the exception of one or two, in making a sink in the swamp for the accommodation of the men. But the other timber there, this blackened pine wood, was cut down by ourselves and used for firewood. I think the timber was all cleared out of the stockade in less than a fortnight after I got there. I think I was in the sixteenth hundred when I arrived."[110] One prisoner, Solon Hyde, said, "When we first came in here that swamp was covered thick with red-wood bushes as high as your head, or higher, and so thick that a rabbit could not get through them. Now it is as you see, - every inch has been worked over dozens of times, two feet below the surface, in search of bits of roots to cook with."[111]

Most of the stumps remained within the stockade when it first opened, but only the two, tall, Georgia pine trees

[97] Davis, p. 25.
[98] Miller, p. 16.
[99] Lyons, p. 42.
[100] Kellogg, p.168.
[101] Davis, p. 25.
[102] Chipman, p. 185.
[103] *O. R.*, VIII, p. 733.
[104] Urban, p. 313.
[105] Jean P. Ray, compiler, *The Diary of a Dead Man* (Acorn Press, 1979), p. 238.
[106] *O. R.*, VII, p. 136.
[107] Vawter, p. 38.
[108] McElroy, p. 129.
[109] Vawter, p. 36.
[110] *Wirz Trial*, p. 374.
[111] Solon Hyde, *A Captive of War* (New York: McClure, Phillips & Co., 1900), p. 210.

survived the inmates' need for fuel. "Two large pine trees were left standing in the southeast corner of the stockade, as before fuel became so necessary to our existence the prisoners collected in the immediate vicinity of these trees, and constructed their rude shelters or homes; therefore, we could not afterward fell them without endangering life."[112] Urban incorrectly located the two trees in the northeast corner. There were many pine stumps, limbs, and chips hewn from the logs scattered all around within the pen when Dufur arrived on the fourteenth of March. On that date, Dufur said there were six hundred prisoners in the pen. A couple of prisoners-turned-authors noted that oxen had been used to pull up all of the stumps. This probably indicates the authors had arrived later in the spring, when wood scraps and chips had been used up and the prisoners were attacking the stumps with penknives and any handy implement.

Confederate officer Samuel Boyer Davis attempted to explain the dearth of trees by saying: "If it be asked why there were no shade trees, I answer: all through the pine tree county and in the light sandy soil that produce the tall Georgia pine, you will find that whenever a house is to be built that the first move is to cut down all pine trees within reach of the house; that is all trees which by falling could fall on or in the immediate vicinity of the house. It is well known that the roots of tall pines have an insufficient hold on the light soil that produces them, and hence the necessity to remove the tree. The trees at Andersonville were cut down for this reason--all the trees that were in the enclosure were pines.[113]

Dufur, talking about the prisons at Andersonville and Florence, said, "Any able bodied man could stand on the inside of either of these prisons and with his arm cast a stone into the edge of a forest of mammoth pines miles in extent. The stockades were constructed from the bodies of these huge pine trees, and thousands of cords of wood were scattered over the ground in the immediate vicinity of those who were dying for the want of it."[114]

After the completion of the palisade, "... in a short time carpenters were put to work putting sentry boxes on the top of the stockade and then the deadline was made."[115] When first built, Andersonville had only eight sentry boxes.[116] As the number of prisoners increased, prison officials built more boxes. According to Captain Walter Bower, at approximately every 120 feet around the palisade, an elevated sentry box stood, with eight on each side of the pen or thirty-two total.[117] Most authors have noted that there were thirty yards between the sentinel boxes but Page asserts that one stood every thirty-five feet. At the same time, Fosdick counted forty-two guard towers around the pen.[118] Boggs, on the other hand, argued that there were forty-four, and Dufur said thirty-two. Smith said there were fifty-four. One author has even said sixty-four sentry boxes (eight at each end and twenty-four on each side) surrounded the pen.[119]

**Print *The Andersonville Stockade*** – Shows a guard in a Pigeon Roost shooting a pisoner for crossing the deadline. Note two trees in the pen, the bakery and a train in distance. (Author's Collection)

[112] Dufur, p. 83.
[113] Davis, p. 24.
[114] Dufur, p. 223.
[115] Typed transcript of Steven Payne's diary in private hands.
[116] *Blue and Gray* Magazine, Dec.-Jan., 1985-1986, p. 11.
[117] *O. R.*, VII, p. 136.
[118] Fosdick, p. 27.
[119] Earl Antrim, *Civil War Prisons and Their Covers* (New York: Collector's Club, 1961), p. 120.

These sentry boxes, or "pigeon-roosts" as the prisoners called them, were platforms about four feet by four feet. They allowed the sentry to stand protected by a slanting board sunroof. Each could be reached by a crude ladder. The top of the stockade reached up to about the sentry's waist. The pigeon-roosts were numbered serially with "Post Number One" at the South Gate. "Number one was on the right of the main gate, number two next and so on."[120]

After nine o'clock every night, and on every half-hour thereafter, the sentry would call out the number of the sentry post and the time: "Post Number 35. Three o'clock and all is well." The fall of Atlanta was learned about by the prisoners when the sentries yelled, "Post Number 35. Three o'clock and Atlanta's gone to Hell." Wild cheering erupted throughout the prison at the pronouncement. One prisoner described the dialogue, "At night the guards would call the hours, beginning with the one at the South Gate. If a guard wanted anything he would call out, 'Co' pal of the gua'd, post numbah foah.' It was very often hard to distinguish between the language of the negro slaves and that of some of the southern soldiers."[121]

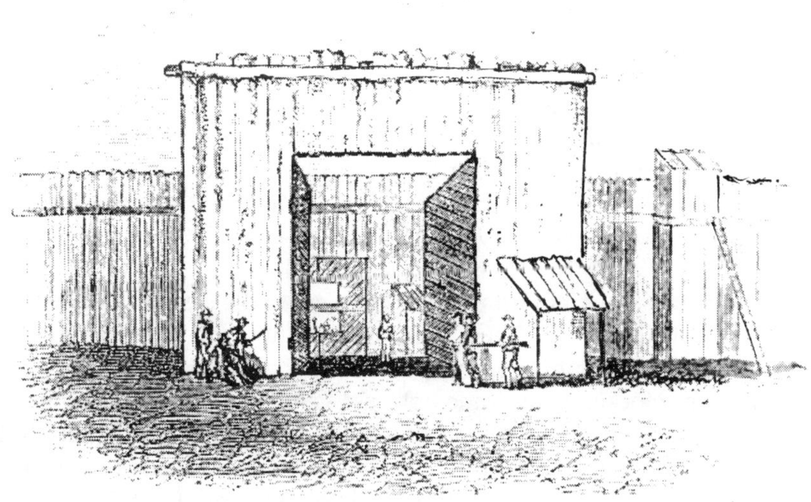

**North Gate** – Shows the small inner door or "wicket" within the large inner door of the porch and wooden support along the outside top of the palisade. The guard towers or "pigeon roosts" were not enclosed as depicted in this drawing. (From Sketch by R.K. Sneden)

**South Gate** – Shows the slant roofed tower the guard mounted by a ladder. The shack had guards who checked those who entered and left the pen. (From Sketch by R.K. Sneden)

[120] James Greacen, *Fourteen Months and Ten Days as a Prisoner of War During the Rebellion* (Kalkaska, Michigan: date unknown), Reprinted Royal Oak, Michigan, 1988, p. 7.
[121] Miller, p. 17.

It assured that the guards were keeping awake."[122]

Two gates marked the west wall, the Main Gate, or North Gate, on the north slope about 400 feet from Stockade Creek, and the South Gate, on the south slope, about 200 feet from the stream. As a rule, men entered by the North Gate and left by the South Gate. These heavy gates, which hung on massive iron hinges, were enclosed in a smaller, rectangular stockade or "porch" about 30 feet square and were arranged so a small holding pen was formed. The inner stockade gates were not opened by drawing a large iron bolt, until the outer pen's gates were closed on the same principle as that of canal locks. The prisoners noted the inner gate had a "... little wicket, that opens through the large gate."[123] *The Random House Dictionary of the English Language* defines a wicket as a small door forming part of a larger one, or as a window closed by a grating in a door. Depictions of the gates seemed to have had both kinds of wickets in them.

The gates were "... very large and as strong as the heaviest timber could make them, the tops being several feet higher than the timbers comprising the stockade; the hinges were of wrought iron and as long as your arm and I should say eight inches wide at the hinge center. In order to lessen the possibility of carrying the gate by storm, or charging it, as in the field you'd take a battery, General John H. Winder, had a small wicket made so that the main gate need not be opened only to admit the 'Ration Wagon.' Just outside of this little gate there was quite a large court or space about which was another stockade. This was occupied by the guards, 'Death Register Clerk,' and captain of the day.[124]

"A ten-feet wide street ran from each of these gates: South Street ran from the South Gate to the opposite wall. Broadway or Market Street, the main street of commerce, ran from the North or Main Gate. Enough space was left at the end of Broadway to allow the mule-drawn ration wagon to turn around. Later, when all the stumps had been removed for firewood, a pine stump remained in the middle of this turn-around. This stump served as a stage for various speakers and as a pulpit for religious services. Though no turn-around for South Street appears in the sources, presumably there was one.[125]

"North Main street was about ten feet wide. It ran from the North Gate to the opposite side of the stockade. That street went across the stockade parallel to the brook. There were two of those main avenues. There were quite a number of by-streets; I never counted them - about a dozen. They ran at right angles with the main street, and in some places across the whole length of the stockade and some not - not generally across the whole length; they were only two roads across the whole length; there were two main by-streets across the whole length; their width was about four feet. There were about two shorter ones; they ran from the main streets back toward the stockade; they would average about one hundred yards on the north side of the main street, and about 50 on the south side. That was the continuation of each one; I mean that half of them were fifty yards, and half of them a hundred yards. Those were the only avenues there I recollect. They were occupied at one time for sleeping purposes in the night. In the daytime they were occupied for walking purposes.[126]

The slant-roofed "Sutler's Shed" was located on the north side of Broadway, about midway between the east and west walls. Later, after the formation of the prisoners' police force, also called the Regulators, the "Police Headquarters" was located right beside it on Broadway. These were the only two structures within the pen until the sheds or barracks were built near the north wall. Still later, more sheds were built near the south wall.

The sutler was appointed by the commandant of the post, when General Winder was in charge.[127] On Wednesday, June 22, a Confederate quartermaster, by the name of Lieutenant James Selman, Jr., of Baltimore, set up the sulter shop on Broadway. Northrop said, in his diary, "We are told by rebel sergeants that he has a commission from Richmond." Selman used to come into the pen once each day to visit his shop. "The sutler had a partner; his name was Bush, a rebel sergeant; he was on duty. He came in and counted off the detachments. I cannot say what interest he had in the sutler's establishment. I do not know that all the goods came through Adjutant Selman. The goods were marked E.D. or E.B. Bush."[128] Since he sold many of the same things the prison issued, the prisoners thought their rations were cut to increase the sutler's sales. The quartermaster furnished the items to be sold there, and some thought he fixed the prices of them.[129]

Andrew J. Spring, of the 16th Connecticut Infantry, testified about the sutler: "I knew the sutler to the prison. The

[122] Maile, p. 34.
[123] Boggs, p. 47.
[124] Frank W. Smith, *Smith's "Knapsack" of Facts and Figures '61 to '65* (Toledo, O.: Spear, Johnson & Co., 1884), p. 23.
[125] Maile, p. 61.
[126] *Wirz Trial*, p. 573.
[127] *O. R.*, VII, p. 137.
[128] Northrop, p. 78.
[129] *Wirz Trial*, p. 581.

rebel sutler, when I first went inside the stockade, was a man named Selman; they called him Adjutant Selman. He remained there I suppose until he had got the biggest part of the prisoners 'greenbacks,' and there was not much use of his staying there. He was there in May, June and July, and I don't know but he was there a part of August. I never procured anything from him myself. One of our boys, after Selman went out, got permission to run the sutler stand himself. I saw him buy stock of this Selman. He kept a sort of sutlery over at the headquarters of General Winder. I say this man procured the articles from Selman; I have seen him carrying vegetables, such as watermelons and green corn, and also tobacco and such things as that."[130]

Wirz felt the appointment of the sutler ought to have been made by the officer in command of the prison (himself) and subject to the approval of the post commandant. Later, after leaving Andersonville, General Winder retained the ability to appoint the sutler there. Wirz' opinion was, "The appointment of the sutler ought to rest with the officer in command of the prison, subject, of course, to the approval of the post commandant of the prison. If the sutler is appointed by any one else he is not under the control of the commandant of the prison. Whatever he may do, be it ever so wrong, the commandant of the prison has no right to dismiss him. He must first make his complaint to the officer who appointed him, and if the sutler can lie well, he can get out of any scraps; and the officer of the prison becomes a puppet, who has no authority whatever. I, for my part, would pity any officer who had lost all self-respect and who would ever undertake to manage a prison and have a sutler in that prison who is not under his immediate control."[131] Spencer said Dick Winder selected and appointed the sutlers of the post. "It was notorious that he [Winder] shared a partnership with the sutler of the post and the sutler of the prison, and divided with them the proceeds of their gains."[132] Spencer even asserted Dick Winder set the prices of all the produce the neighboring farmers brought to the post to sell and that Winder allowed no one to buy any of the produce brought to the outside of the pen, until his sutlers had had their pick of that day's offering. The sutlers usually bought all the produce the poorer neighborhood farmers could offer. Sometimes the produce was bought from slaves or by the ladies left in charge of the farms, whose husbands had been killed in the war or were away, fighting. Winder did not set the price the sutlers charged their customers, but allowed them to set the price by the supply and demand in the marketplace. The amount of currency within the pen and the exchange rate of the Confederate money at that time was also taken into consideration. This situation allowed for someone to make large sums of money.

Butter could be bought from the farmers for twenty-five cents per pound in Confederate money and resold for a dollar-and-a-half in greenbacks. At that time, the exchange rate was about twenty bluebacks for one greenback.

Sutlers bought collards, a green vegetable common in the South, from farmers for ten cents per bunch of three stalks, and, later, sold them for fifty cents in Federal money or for a dollar-and-a-half in bluebacks. Spencer said, "R. B. Winder & Co." sold this money extracted from the prisoners "...to those who knew their value for what their market price demanded, and by these two operations cleared about one thousand per cent upon their labors."[133]

The men behind the counter of the Sutler's Shed, doing the selling, were two detailed prisoners, Charles Huckleby, of the Tennessee, and Ira Beverly of the 100th Ohio Infantry. Phillip Cashmeyer, a good friend of General Winder, came down from Richmond with him. Some authors felt he could have been the de facto sutler at Andersonville. His true role at the post was not well recorded. Phillip Cashmeyer told Colonel Norton P. Chipman, the Judge Advocate of the military commission which tried Wirz, that he was employed by General Winder as a "special agent" for him.

Northrop said, "Articles in stock consist of flour, molasses, small sticks of wood, plug tobacco, a vicious sort of whisky made from sorghum. We have to pay from 25¢ to $1 for an onion, 10¢ to 40¢ for miserable apples, 25¢ a pint for meal, 40¢ for wormy hog peas, 40¢ for 1/2 pint of flour, 10¢ for small piece of wood. With the advent of this installation rations grow less in quantity and quality. It is simply a scheme of this Rebel quartermaster to catch greenbacks, watches, rings, and things of value which men eagerly put up."[134]

One prisoner said that the sutler sold "... onions, beans, dried peas, potatoes, cornbread, eggs, flour soda, blackberries, meats, condiments, cakes and pies... " from the slant-roofed, clapboard shed.[135] Another author said that the sutler sold "... a little flour, soda, salt, cream of tartar, pepper, sweet potatoes, onions, etc. He charged one dollar per pint for salt, one dollar per quart for flour, ten cents each for very small potatoes, four to ten dollars per pound for tobacco, and everything else in proportion. A lemon did occasionally find its way within our prison, but I never saw one sold. I saw a few very small Irish potatoes that sold for five cents each, and were advertised to be ex-

---

[130] Northrop, pp. 77, 78.
[131] *Wirz Trial*, p. 111.
[132] *O. R.*, VII, p. 141.
[133] Spencer, p. 49.
[134] Northrop, p. 78.
[135] T. H. Mann, "A Yankee in Andersonville," *Century* Magazine, August 1890, p. 459.

cellent for scurvy."[136] These prices were relatively high and only those soldiers with a large wad of greenbacks could be steady customers and thus ward off starvation. Prisoners called the crude whiskey sold by the sutler, "pine top."

Though the men usually thought the sutler shop was just another method devised by the Confederate hierarchy to extract the last few greenbacks from the prisoners, the Confederates considered it a humanitarian effort to supplement the stark rations with some more nutritious varieties of foods.

Besides buying from the Confederate-run prison sutler, the prisoners could also buy from their fellow prisoners who had set themselves up in the business of selling various foods. These prisoner-sutlers bought their merchandise usually from four sources: the local farmers after the Confederate sutler had bought all that he needed, fellow prisoners returning into the pen after being detailed outside, Confederate officers who dabbled in speculation, and, possibly, Confederate officers who sold Confederate commissary supplies illegally. "A few things have been worked into camp by men who get out on duty or by Rebel sergeants. A fair sized onion goes for $1, apples 10¢ to 40¢, dry hog peas 40¢ per pint, plug tobacco $1.50."[137]

Some prisoners sold the foods in wholesale quantities and others sold individual-sized portions both cooked and uncooked (today's equivalent of a retail produce stand and a restaurant). These restaurants were usually just tents with crude signs advertising the specialty of the house.

"There were about thirty eating-houses there. There were a number of soup-jobbers there; I should think there were 300 soup-jobbers and meat peddlers together. At those eating-houses they sold ham and eggs, beefsteak, tea and coffee, biscuits and butter, honey, and sandwiches; some kept whiskey for $3. The price for a dish of ham and eggs and such things, was regulated by the price for the articles in the market... I could always get a good meal's victuals at one of these restaurants. A good meal's victuals there, as I understand it, was hot biscuits, coffee and tea, ham and eggs, fried potatoes, and fried onions; also steak and onions..."[138]

The prisoner Helwig wrote, "It was bean soup that I dealt in; of course I had nothing but a few beans and poor water to make the soup out of, with no salt or pepper, but I made soup all the same, boiling it in a half gallon tin pail. I had but one spoon, and borrowed a half canteen and then started out, and cried out, 'Here is your hot soup: only ten cents a dish!' I sold it all easily, but when I had two customers at the time, one had to wait until the other ate his; then I would dish out for the second man, not waiting to wash or wipe the spoon or dish."[139]

Others baked corn bread and wheat bread in tiny, dried-clay ovens, while others used sophisticated, large volume ovens. "There were five hundred bakers in the stockade; all of them had bake-houses; they were located in all parts of the camp except the swamp. There were five hundred bake-houses; some occupied a large space - some a small space. The largest one I knew of baked 22 dozen biscuits at a time; the smallest baked three platesful. The large ones occupied a space of ground about eight feet long and six fee wide; the smaller ones would occupy about two feet square. They were very few large ones there - only two that I recollect."[140]

An illicit enterprise also existed at a house five miles from the pen; commodities were sold there by members of the garrison: "... one sergeant would take out one man...sometimes we staid out there all the afternoon; some of the sergeants were with us; some were not; sometimes they left us; they did not all leave us, some remained with us; I have been out there when only two sergeants remained with six soldiers; that was almost an every-day occurrence; this house was about five miles off, at an angle from the southeast corner of the stockade; it was on a line with the hospital from the corner of the stockade nearest the hospital; we would go out past the hospital; we would pass through the woods to this house; always to that one house; we generally got cakes when we were there; sometimes we brought eggs and butter from there; sometimes none, but as a general thing we got cakes there; we got tobacco also, a different kind from what the sutler sold us. I do not recollect anything else except small articles of grapes, plums, and such things."[141]

Many other occupations were developed within the pen as time went on. A prisoner had to devise a source of income if he expected to buy extras to make his life more comfortable and healthy. Those who ate only the issued rations seldom survived. Supplementing the rations was necessary. Those prisoners who had a service or skill to sell or trade to their fellow prisoners ended up surviving the rigors of Andersonville.

Along Broadway, alongside the sutler's shed and Police Headquarters, hucksters with services for hire and items for sale set up fifty to seventy shops and stalls. There, the hucksters cut hair, repaired and sold watches, sold

[136] *Ibid.*, p. 460.
[137] Northrop, p. 65.
[138] *Wirz Trial*, p. 575.
[139] Helwig, p. 28.
[140] *Wirz Trial*, p. 574.
[141] *Ibid.*, p.578.

wood and jewelry, and ran pawnshops, games of chance, etc. Men stole sheets of tin from the tops of the boxcars they had arrived in, hiding the tin in their blouses, and making cups and pans from it. "Sweat boards or dice appear in camp, where men can stake 5¢ a throw, if he wishes to try his luck at gaming."[142] "Those who have razors shave for 5¢, cut hair for 10¢."[143] "A few razors found their way into the camp: consequently, several barber shops were running full blast most of the time. These shops consisted of army blankets supported by four small sticks or poles, one at each corner, from which was conspicuously displayed the good work done inside, together with the price-list, to the passing thousands. The price was usually ten chews of tobacco, five cents in greenbacks, or one dollar in Confederate money. Later, two or three dollars was the price."[144]

Other prisoners sold corn beer, which was a slightly alcoholic concoction known for its intoxicating effect as well as for its medicinal or antiscorbutic qualities. Dufur described the preparation and sale of corn beer; there was not only one, but more than fifty places in different parts of the camp where beer could be bought by the glass, pint, quart, or gallon. By adding a certain quantity of corn meal to a barrel of water, and exposing it to the hot sun for a certain length of time, it would ferment, and, with the addition of a little 'black-strap molasses, and one or two other trifling ingredients, quite a palatable mixture was formed. Barrels of it were sold to those who were fortunate enough to possess a little cash.[145]

"... it is meal beer made by letting corn meal sour in water. Molasses can be had for 5¢ a teaspoonful; a little is added to give it a twang and sassafras roots can be had by digging, the tea of which is often added to give it flavor. Those who have money, pay ten and fifteen cents for half a pint and drink it with a relish. Men crave something sour, and poor fellows with feverish lips and scabious tendency, without money beg and whine for it childishly. The vender cries, 'Here is your nice meal beer, right sour, well seasoned with sassafras'."[146]

Another of the flourishing occupations within the pen was tailoring. Tailors, by using only the most imaginative patches, were able to keep most men covered with some apparel. Most Civil War soldiers kept personal sewing kits called "house-wives" in their knapsacks, but most men lost their knapsacks before arriving at Andersonville. Within the prison, thread, cloth, and needles were quite scarce. Canvas from tent-flies made durable cloth. Tailors could obtain other cloth by flim-flaming the Confederates out of meal sacks and thread by unraveling them. They made needles from little slivers of bone ground down to points by rubbing them on bricks. By working meticulously, a fine wire could drill out the eye in the needle.

One prisoner testified, "If a man had money, he could buy sacks (made of strong, coarse cotton cloth) of the quartermaster who issued our rations. At the time of our capture, sacks two feet wide and three feet long cost two dollars each in greenbacks, or eight in confed. Thread to sew with was obtained by raveling out a piece of sack. Sometimes we drew rations in these sacks, and could keep them until ration time the next day. When this was the case, we were bound to return the sack or lose our next ration; but we could cut off the bottom of it two or three inches and not be detected, if we sewed it up as it has been. These strips furnished thread for the ninety."[147]

One prisoner described how the cotton potato sacks were acquired and sold: "... the sutler did not sell the sacks. The potato sacks had to be returned to the sutler. Sacks were an article of merchandise here. Towards the last period they brought one dollar a piece. They were sacks that would hold a bushel of corn meal. It would take two sacks for a pair of pantaloons. The tailor got from a dollar to $2 for making the pantaloons. They would be worth $4; I got two pair of pants made in that way myself and I paid from $3 to $4. The sacks were cotton - very rough cotton sheeting."[148]

Another prisoner told how prisoner–cobblers stayed busy repairing shoes: "...there were shoemakers there; they mended boots and shoes. I do not know what they charged for half-soling shoes... Labor was worth about a dollar a day there. There was no leather there, other than old boots and shoes. I do not know how long it took to make a pair of shoes. I have heard that men in Massachusetts make 24 pair a day... They are cut out by machinery and put together by hand. The shoemakers were paroled men who had been working for the confederate shop. Those that I saw there were constantly busy mending shoes."[149]

The men would go over to Broadway each morning to open their businesses. Each man quickly learned that he should always carry a cudgel or small billy club to use to ward off robbers.

---

[142] Northrop., p. 65.
[143] *Ibid.*, p. 66.
[144] Dufur, p. 123.
[145] *Ibid.*, p. 124.
[146] Northrop, p. 66.
[147] Vawter, pp. 47, 48.
[148] *Wirz Trial*, pp. 581, 582.
[149] *Ibid.*, p. 582.

A prisoner could enter prison completely destitute and, by saving and investing wisely in resaleable commodities, could amass a small fortune. One prisoner became "rich" by not eating his cornbread and living by eating only the peas and bacon of his rations. He sold his corn-bread ration for ten cents each day and invested in eggs for resale. He detailed his scheme like this: "I bought eggs and sold them, and then I bought soap and sold it. I commenced dealing in eggs about the 10th of June, I think. I bought thirteen dozen of eggs. I paid three dollars and sixty cents for them per dozen...When I left Andersonville, I had $520 in greenbacks, and I entered without anything. At one time there I had in my possession five thousand dollars, which I got by trafficking in that way. I was there from the 1st of June to the 24th of August. I purchased flour, beans, pies, potatoes, onions, tobacco, honey butter, grapes, apples, peaches, pears, and beer. I purchased sorghum at $324 a barrel in greenbacks or $1,300 in confederate money. I purchased two barrels of sorghum while I was there. I purchased them from the rebel sutler - the adjutant of the post... I bought flour. I paid seventy dollars a sack for it. I bought flour in sacks almost every day. Some days I sold as much as a thousand dollars' worth of flour. Almost every day I bought flour in the sack, Sundays and weekdays, from the adjutant of the post. I bought apples also; sometimes as much as a bushel at a time; not in the sack - merely piled up in a tent. I would go there and view them. They were piled up by the man owning them. Apples were brought in by the working parties. I paid sixty dollars a bushel for apples. I never bought apples from the adjutant. I did not buy them almost every day; they were a scarce article. I bought potatoes too; I bought them by the sack. I paid sixty dollars a sack for them. I bought the potatoes from the post adjutant. I bought onions by the sack. Potatoes and onions I bought daily. Of onions I bought but one sack a day on the average. Of potatoes I bought about three sacks a day on the average.[150]

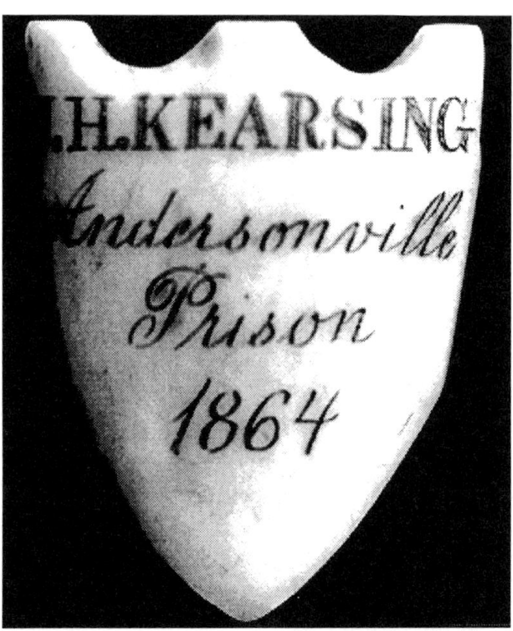


**Kerchief Slide** – This is an example of one of the ways that a prisoner could pass the time in prison. This kerchief slide was made from bone and was engraved with the following: "J.H. Kearsing, Andersonville Prison, 1864." He was in Company D, 43rd New York State Volunteers. (Author's Collection)

One of the most comprehensive descriptions of commerce within the pen was given by this same prisoner who ran a flourishing general merchandise store, which provided: "All kinds of trades that are calculated to make men comfortable were carried on there, such as shoemakers, tailors, watchmakers, &c. There were two watchmakers there, five or six shoemakers, and five or six tailors. The streets were full of soup jobbers; there were about thirty eating-houses there; they consisted of tables made out of rough boards and long benches; coffee, tea, ham and eggs, biscuits, butter, and honey could be got there; there were at least five hundred bakers in the stockade; they would bake biscuit, bread, pies, cakes. They would get the flour from the post adjutant and from the cookhouse and through

[150] *Ibid.*, p. 566.

the hospital; it would be smuggled in from the cook-house on wood wagons; it would be concealed below the wood and brought in. When the wood would be unloaded the flour would be taken out and delivered to the men it was sold to; it was always sold previously to being taken in; the bakers would manage to carry on their business very easily; there was always plenty of wood for sale and plenty of flour to be had and plenty of saleratus; I had a 50-pound keg of that; I had a store after I had been there a while, styled 'the novelty store.' I had a greater variety to sell than any other man in the camp; some of the articles I had for sale were potatoes, onions, peas, beans, apples, peaches, grapes, pears, plums, chickens, watermelons, saleratus, flour, red and black pepper, honey, butter, and beer; I had sorghum, about a barrel, I had to pay for a barrel of sorghum $1,300 of confederate money; that would be $325 in greenbacks. I had to pay $70 confederate money per pound for tea. We got the apples from the post adjutant; they cost us at the rate of $60 a bushel, potatoes the same, onions the same; flour cost us $70 a sack of 98 pounds; I had large quantities of tobacco; it was generally in 25-pound boxes, which would sell at $22.50; we got ale from the post adjutant; we bought it directly from him; he always came inside with loads of these goods; I had ginger and capsicum, and different kinds of roots and herbs in my store; I would buy them from the paroled men detailed in the hospital; I would get apples, grapes, and watermelons sometimes from the post adjutant; sometimes from the men who were on working squads; they would get them when out at work and would bring them in and sell them to the traders inside; we could get outside whenever we wanted to by giving the sergeant at the gate $5, generally to take us out to the country to a house where those articles were kept for sale; it was about five miles outside the limits; have very often helped sick prisoners, acquaintances of mine; I would give them medicine for scurvy and diarrhea; a dose of medicine there for diarrhea would cost about $1.25 in greenbacks; they would come around there to my tent every day when I told them to do so. There were clothing merchants there; there were only two that I particularly know of; but there were a great many on the streets selling clothing of different kind, shirts, pants, shoes, overcoats, caps and hats. Clothing was very cheap there; a good pair of army shoes could be got for 75 cents or a dollar; a very good overcoat for $4; pants for $2; shirts were about the dearest things there, they averaged about $3. There were quite a number of money brokers there; they would buy and sell State money, confederate money, gold and silver; there were about 50 of that class there; they would also deal in bounty certificates and watches, and would buy and sell bank checks. There were bank checks to buy and sell; they would be brought in by new prisoners; they would buy these bounty certificates at a great discount and run the risk of getting their pay on them; there was no place there for paying those bounty certificates; they would risk getting their pay when they returned north; it was not known there whether the certificates were genuine or not; most of them were on the State of Massachusetts; they gave about 50 per cent for bounty certificates. I should judge there was half a million of greenbacks circulating there when the Plymouth prisoners were brought in; confederate money was brought in any quantity. There were a number of barber shops there where men could get shaved, their hair cut and whiskers dyed, and some of them carried on the doctoring business. Only one carried on the doctoring business that I know of personally. They would buy their dyeing articles to work with, their soap and other things, from new arrivals. Those things were brought in large quantities... There were two watchmakers there that I know of. They repaired watches and jewelry. I have been at their shops. I saw upwards of 50 watches in one man's shop, and a number of articles, such as breastpins and rings, left to be repaired. This man kept a journeyman; the work was too heavy for himself. They had a full set of tools. They had a tent to work in. The tents were generally made of blankets stretched upon poles. Those poles were brought into camp by working parties. There were pole merchants there. I should say there were about 30 pole merchants... The working squads brought poles in - men who were taken out every morning to work and who were sent into camp in the evening; they would bring in such things as they could secure every day, fence rails, poles, and boards. The bakers could carry on their baking business very easily; everything that was needed to carry it on was to be had in the camp. Wood was for sale in large quantities. They constructed ovens of mud, some very large and others very small. They would buy the wood from wood merchants and also from the messes in camp. I cannot say how many wood merchants were there; they were passing around on the streets, all the time... The tailors had the business of making pants out of corn-sacks taken from the commissary wagons. There were a number of tailors - five or six I was acquainted with. They were always busy making pants for men who wanted a clean pair of pants to put on once in a while, to make themselves feel like being at home. They stole the sacks out of commissary wagons...

"There were gamblers there; quite a number of them. They would deal faro, honest john, euchre, seven up, and poker. There was an organized gang of gamblers there; also some detached gamblers who would make use of tents during the day-time to gamble in, and who would have runners hunting out men who wanted to gamble. There was a great deal of money won and lost every day; there were a good many 'chuckle-up' dealers, men who had a little board with numbers on, and boxes of dice. There was money there, so that that could be made profitable; I should judge there were a hundred 'chuckle-up' dealers on the main street, and they had a crowd around them at all hours of the day...There were about a thousand dealers, stores and such like, there I think."[151]

The prisoners knew there was a store over in town but they were not allowed to buy from nor to enter this store. One prisoner recounted: "I never saw any market stand or anything of that kind, no more than a store down at the railroad, a sort of country store, one that had been there apparently for years. It was there when I left. It was an ordinary store, not very large; about fifty feet by sixty, or something like that. I was never in that store. Yankees were not allowed to go in. I saw groceries upon the shelves, such as are generally found in any other grocery store. That was the only one there."[152] Doctor Bates testified, "There was no grocery store while I was there."[153]

As early as May 5th, work had begun on the reclamation of the wet, swampy land near the brook. Captain Walter Bowie, an inspector in the Adjutant and Inspector General's Department, inspected Andersonville on Monday 9th, and filed his report the next day. Bowie said, "Wirz is now endeavoring to reclaim this piece of wet land by draining, and expects to have it completed in a few days so as to make it a fit location for tents or barracks."[154] Solon Hyde recounted, "Room was so scarce that wheelbarrows were sent in and ground was made by wheeling sand from the north side and dumping it into the swamp."[155] Wirz indicated he would have started this work sooner, but was unable to do so because he was not able to obtain the necessary implements and tools.

Besides Broadway, this land became the main center of commerce and was called Market Square. "Market Square was a piece of made ground on the edge of the swamp in the center of the prison. Here men came together to barter trinkets they had made to while away the time, to exchange parts of rations, and to indulge generally, so far as they could, in the Yankee instinct for trade."[156]

Because of several attempted escapes by prisoners who tried to tunnel their way to freedom, surrounding the main stockade was first built an identical stockade to prevent this, supposedly by making the distance to be tunneled too great to be successfully completed. It was designed to be used as a back-up in case the inner stockade was stormed by the prisoners. "After the outer stockade was built, it greatly increased the difficulty of tunneling, as it would require a length of about two hundred and twenty-five feet to safely pass under both walls. Still there were men desperate enough to attempt it."[157] It, too, was about seventeen feet high made of unhewn logs, and was about 180 feet or 60 paces from the main palisade. Boggs said this second wall was built about one hundred and twenty feet from the inner wall. Redans were built in three corners of the second palisade and there was only one gate, that being in the west wall.[158] On August 4th, General Winder, even after the pen had been enlarged, said, "The present and constantly increasing crowded state of the stockade will, I fear, compel me to occupy the space between the present stockade and the stockade now being erected for defense for prisons. This will be a serious inconvenience, but I see no help for it."[159] General Winder seemed to have been making contingency plans in case a second enlargement of the pen was necessary.

Just as the second stockade had been designed to back up the main wall in case of an attack from within, a third palisade was begun in August, primarily to defend Sumter Prison from an attack from without by a Yankee cavalry raid intended to free the prisoners. This third palisade was planned to be a covered way to allow troops to march "... between the middle and outer walls." It was, however, never finished, and some of the surrounding forts also were never completed. Only the north and east walls were completed. They only reached a height of five feet and were positioned about twenty feet from the second palisade.[160]

In January, Wirz said the wood of the uncompleted third palisade could be used to make the stockade around the hospital as requested by General Winder. If it was ever thought necessary to complete the third palisade, they could easily get the wood from the near-by forests.[161] One author described the inner pen as being "... surrounded by successive and precisely similar palisades."[162] Doctor Mann described the third or the outer palisade as being 12 feet high.[163] In the summer of '65, a portion of the outer one was missing or "... seems never to have been completed."[164]

John McElroy told about the first attempt to escape before the deadline was .established: "Our first attempt was

---

[151] *Ibid.*, pp. 559-561.
[152] *Ibid.*, p. 211.
[153] *Ibid.*, p. 43.
[154] *O. R.*, VII, , p. 136.
[155] Hyde, p. 233.
[156] Maile, p. 50.
[157] Vawter, p. 80.
[158] *Blue and Gray* Magazine, Dec.-Jan., 1985-1986, p. 11.
[159] *O. R.*, VII, p. 541.
[160] *Blue and Gray* Magazine, Dec.-Jan., 1985-1986, p. 11.
[161] *O. R.*, VIII, p. 111.
[162] James D. Walker, *Pennsylvania at Andersonville, Georgia* (Penn., 1909), p. 65.
[163] Mann, p. 452.
[164] Walker, p. 67.

made about a week after our arrival. We found two logs on the east side that were a couple of feet shorter than the rest, and it seemed as if they could be successfully scaled. About fifty of us resolved to make the attempt. We made a rope twenty-five or thirty feet long, and strong enough to bear a man, out of strings and strips of cloth. A stout stick was fastened to the end, so that it would catch on the logs on either side of the gap. On a night dark enough to favor our scheme, we gathered together, drew cuts to determine each boy's place in the line, fell in single rank, according to this arrangement, and marched to the place. The line was thrown skillfully, the stick caught fairly in the notch, and the boy who had drawn number one climbed up... he slid over the top, and then heard the dull thump as he sprang to the ground on the other side...

"Thus it went on, until, just as we heard number fifteen drop, we also heard a Rebel voice say in a vicious undertone: 'Halt! halt, there, d---n you!' This was enough. The game was up; we were discovered, and the remaining thirty-five of us left that locality with all the speed in our heels, getting away just in time to escape a volley which a squad of guards, posted in the lookouts, poured upon the spot where we had been standing. The next morning the fifteen who had got over the stockade were brought in, each chained to a sixty-four pound ball...one of the N'Yaarkers betrayed us...The Rebels stationed a squad at the crossing place, and as each man dropped down from the Stockade he was caught by the shoulder, the muzzle of a revolver thrust into his face, and an order to surrender whispered into his ear. It was expected that the guards in the sentry-boxes would do such execution among those of us still inside as would prove a warning to other would-be escapes. They were defeated in this benevolent intention by the readiness with which we divined the meaning of that incautiously loud halt, and our alacrity in leaving the unhealthy locality. Another result of this abortive effort was the establishment of the notorious 'Dead Line'."[165]

When the prison first opened, no deadline existed. During that period, the prisoners could approach the wall, easily converse, and trade with the sentries. They could also sit and rest in the shade of the wall, which was no small benefit to the shelterless inmates. Another advantage to the prisoners was that the absence of a deadline made it possible to start tunnels very close to the wall with less digging needed to attempt to gain their freedom.

When Wirz arrived, one of his first orders was one issued to initiate the construction of the deadline. He sent in a gang of Negroes who drove in the wooden stakes at a distance of about twenty feet from the stockade. "Notification was given the prisoners by Wirz himself that no one should pass beyond this barrier under pain of instantaneous death to him who should transgress."[166]

Most authors felt the deadline was about fifteen feet away from the palisade and the small, frail fence was about waist-high, and had been made by nailing a small board across the top of two-and-a-half or three-feet high posts. Miller described the board as a "two-by-four,"[167] while Stevenson said it was a "three inch strip."[168] Clifton said the deadline, "... twelve feet inside of the main wall, was stakes driven in the ground with strips of plank or rope about two feet high."[169] That was the only time rope was mentioned as forming part of the deadline. "In some places the rail had been knocked off, and only the stakes marked the boundary between life and death."[170] The space between the dead line and the palisade was called the "deadrun." The width of the deadrun has been described by various authors as being 12, 17, 18, and 20 feet. Hamlin said it varied around the pen from 15 to 25 feet and averaged 19 feet in width.[171] Urban was probably the worst guesser, estimating its width at 35 feet.[172]

Anyone crossing the deadline would be shot immediately by the guard, with no warning given. The deadline was not a new or Southern concept; in fact, it was mentioned in the Federal regulations. There was a deadline at all Federal prisons with death being the result of anyone passing over this well-demarcated line. At Andersonville, several prisoners were shot for touching the deadline when they tried to reach the freshest water where the stream first entered the stockade. Some said there was no deadline put up adjacent to the creek just inside the pen where the water was the freshest. "No line is visible, which is the case for 60 yards at the point mentioned, parallel with the crossing from south to north. Old prisoners say there never has been a visible line at this creek crossing; that no man knows where it is except as he judges the distance from the stockade."[173] In the last stages of disease or because of insanity or suffering, many more prisoners ended their troubles by stepping across the deadline on purpose.

The width of the swamp around the stream varied from about fifty to a hundred feet, "...through which one

[165] McElroy, p 141.
[166] Spencer, p. 58.
[167] Miller, p. 15.
[168] Stevenson, p 541.
[169] Clifton, p. 7.
[170] Vawter, p. 45.
[171] Hamlin, p. 48.
[172] Urban, p. 314.
[173] Northrop, p. 66.

could not walk."[174] This area consisted of a "...lagoon of about two acres, which cannot be occupied except a few islands in the midst."[175] This lagoon was an iridescent green color because of the biliary excretions of the men trying to reach the sinks. As spring turned to summer, the heat caused the ground to actually move and bubble from the generation of swamp gases which in those days were called "noxious vapors" and were considered to be pathogenic. Robert Kellogg wrote, "Indeed, one or two could almost always be seen dying at the brookside."[176] Another prisoner related, "We called this ground 'death's acre,' for here could be seen more dead and dying than at any other place in the pen. There would be from fifty to a hundred men who were clinging to the last spark of life, wallowing in their own filth, many of them reduced to idiocy and some could not speak. The ground under them giving off the most suffocating stench to mingle with that of bodies decaying in the hot sun."[177] Boggs described the swampy area this way: "Along the swamp the human filth was from three to ten inches deep and from the frequent rains, had become liquid, and flowed out over the quagmire, where it fermented like yeast. Millions and millions of flies swarmed over it, and the mass of putrescent filth became a lake of rolling, squirming maggots. The largest would craw out on the hot sand, shed their tail-like appendage; wings would unfold, and an attempt made to fly; and thousands were clumsily dropping all over the camp. They tumbled into our mush, bedding-places and to the faces of the sick and dying.[178]

For some inexplicable reason, it took the men almost four months to build a small wooden bridge across the stream. The bridge was completed on July 3rd.[179] It spanned the stream about twelve feet from the deadline where the stream first entered the pen.[180] Few likenesses of the bridge exist.

**Little Wooden Bridge on Water Street** – It crossed the creek on the west side where the water first entered the pen and, therefore, was the freshest. Several prisoners were killed scooping water from the bridge area. The bridge finally was completed on July 3rd allowed prisoners to easily reach the sinks on the south side. (John Urban)

The most popular place to secure a drink of water before the stream became unpalatable was between the bridge and the deadline. The men would sometimes go down to the stream at midnight to fill their canteens or other containers so they would not have to drink from the stream when it was most contaminated during the day.[181] After six in the morning, it became undrinkable. "This little creek was our only water supply, and when we would go after water we would often sink to our hips in the mire, and men would often have to be dragged out by their comrades."[182]

[174] Miller, p. 16.
[175] Northrop, p.59.
[176] Kellogg, p. 137.
[177] Boggs, p. 53.
[178] *Ibid.*, p. 34.
[179] Miller, p. 46.
[180] Maile, p. 56.
[181] *Mass, Monument*, p. 31.
[182] Fosdick, p. 27.

Vawter described this area, "Just below the dead-line, where it entered, we had a place scraped out eight feet wide, by twenty long, and nearly two deep. We kept that pool as clean as we could, to drink from. Below this were a number of circular pools ten to twelve feet in diameter, and two feet deep in the center, to wash in."[183] These were called "wash pools." These seemed to have been the men's own doing and not part of Wirz' overall plan to improve the prison's sanitary facilities which was never completed. Northrop wrote, "Men with blotches, putrid sores, gnawed by lice and worms, squalid from weakness, scurvy and wasting diseases go there to drink, wash clothing and bathe. They are obliged to step into the stream the banks being two to three feet high, slippery, nasty."[184]

Some medical men thought that part of the high mortality at Andersonville resulted from the men's lack of bathing. Wirz proposed that a wooden washing facility be built in the western part of the creek. Doctor Isaiah H. White proposed in May each prisoner should be compelled to have a mandatory bath every so often.[185] Vawter said, "I believe half the men in the pen never washed at all."[186]

Northrop wrote in his diary of attempts to solve some of the sanitation problems on August 11th, "Recent improvement in camp are timbers laid across the swamp on the west side north of the stream for 20 rods, this will help escape the filth in passing from north to south. A flume and bridge has been made which improves washing facilities; also a road from the north to the stream in the east part."[187] "My tent was right there next to the creek on what we called Water Street. It was down next to the slough; it was the last tent before you got to the bridge near the stockade--the bridge made of stockade timber, which runs through from the north side of the slough to the south side."[188]

Alexander W. Persons was appointed lieutenant-colonel of the 55th Regiment Georgia Infantry on June 21, 1862, to take rank from May 17. After Person's command was captured at Cumberland Gap, Tennessee, he went back to Richmond and reported to the Secretary of War for duty assignment.[189] The part of the regiment which was not captured at Cumberland Gap on September 9, 1863, was consolidated into a detachment of three companies on February 24, 1864, by direction of the Secretary of War.[190]

Persons' selection as the second post commandant resulted from General Samuel Cooper's request, on February 7, of Howell Cobb, for the name of an officer from his state of Georgia. "It is due to Georgia that this commander should be a citizen of the State in which the cantonment is situated, in order, as far as possible, to allay any sectional prejudices which might be anticipated... I would have desired that the entire guard for the cantonment should be composed of Georgia troops, but this appears to be impossible on account of the threatening aspect of affairs in Georgia in the approaching campaign, which will require every able-bodied man from the State for the field."[191]

By Special Orders #49, dated February 26, Persons was assigned to duty as commandant of the post at Andersonville, which included the command of the prison guard and charge of the Federal prisoners.[192]

Persons testified, "I can simply state that General Winder's order to me was when I reported to him for duty under order of the secretary of war. He said to me that there were three separate and distinct spheres at Andersonville. He at the same time charged me, particularly, under no circumstances to let the commander of the troops take the command of the post; that when the post commander was necessarily absent, then the commander of the prison should go to his place."[193]

When Persons arrived, approximately half of one wall was not completed and 15 to 20 Negroes were working to finish it.[194] At that time, after five or six lots of prisoners had arrived, Sidney Winder was ordered back to Richmond. Colonel Persons said Sid Winder told him before he left for Richmond that he had "absolute discretion" in locating the prison.[195]

Colonel Persons was one of the few officers of the post at Andersonville whom everyone liked and admired. He was considered by all to be fair and just. He allowed individuals and whole squads to leave the stockade to bring in firewood and wood for building shebangs. Sometimes two or three hundred prisoners were outside of the pen at one time.

Northrop said Colonel Persons was "... quite familiar with a few of us and expressed a feeling that he would resign his command were it possible. He was sent for duty here because most of his command are prisoners. Earlier in

183 Vawter, pp. 55, 56.
184 Northrop, p. 64.
185 *O. R.*, VII, p. 171.
186 Vawter, p. 56.
187 Northrop, pp. 106, 107.
188 *Wirz Trial*, p. 139.
189 Chipman, p. 53.
190 Military Records from National Archives.
191 *O. R.*, VI, p. 925.
192 *O. R.*, VI, p. 1042.
193 *Wirz Trial*, p. 463.
194 Chipman, p. 53.
195 *Ibid.*

the war he was twice a prisoner, captured by Burnside's men, and was well-treated. He says men are sent here without any provision made for shelter, and he has no orders or means to furnish it; that it's not the fault of the local commissary that we are left to suffer."[196]

Colonel Persons wrote to General Samuel Cooper, Adjutant and Inspector General, on the 17th of April, explaining to him that the reason he had recently been absent from his post for three days was that he was away trying to secure some axes, hoes, spades, and shovels. These, he said, he needed to make improvements to the prison interior. "I had sent my quartermaster time and again but to no avail, as the things we so much needed could not then be had. I wrote through out the State and tried by proxy to supply the prison, all to no purpose. Up to my absence we did not have sufficient tools with which to bury the dead, and preceding the three days of my absence I learned authoritatively that I could be supplied with the things I so much needed in Augusta. I immediately went to my quartermaster, found him in bed sick with inflammatory rheumatism, where he had been a week previous, and had been since, scarcely able to turn himself over in his bed."[197] Persons testified, "I think the quartermaster did not have energy he might have had."[198]

The guard direly needed essentials. Colonel Persons scrounged throughout Georgia to obtain what most men in the Northern army took for granted. "The regimental quartermaster of the Fifty-fifth Georgia I had sent several days previous to Atlanta for tents for hospital purposes. The quartermaster of the twenty-sixth Alabama Regiment was off getting a supply of clothing for his regiment."[199]

On May 5th, Major-General Howell Cobb and his Chief Surgeon of the Georgia Reserves visited Andersonville and inspected the prison. Cobb observed: "The general management of the prison under Colonel Persons is good, and he manifests a laudable desire to discharge his duties in the most efficient manner."[200]

Colonel Persons must have had success in obtaining the tools he sought because, when the newly-arrived Captain Wirz wrote to Major Thomas P. Turner on May 8th, he described how he found the prison when he arrived and also told of receiving tools to distribute to the prisoners. "I found the prison in bad condition, owing to the want of tools, such as axes, spades, and lumber to erect proper buildings. The first commandant of the post, Captain W. S. Winder, and his successor, Colonel Alexander W. Persons, had left nothing untried to supply these so important articles. Only two weeks ago I received axes, spades, &c. I hope to have everything in the interior of the prison completed in two weeks."[201]

On May 23rd, Persons issued a General Order, "In future, no person whatever, whether citizen or soldier, officer, or private, shall have any communication with any of the paroled prisoners."[202] Again, on June 8th, he ordered that, "... no citizen or soldier will employ any of the paroled prisoners to do any kind of work without permission from post headquarters and the applicant must state what kind of labor he wishes the prisoner to perform."[203]

Colonel Persons left Andersonville near the middle of June before General Winder arrived on June 17th. Henry Wirz commanded the post for a short while when Colonel Persons had left. He signed a furlough for Colonel Fannin, "H. Wirz, Commanding Post." Extant is a letter written on June 20th from General Cobb recommending Persons for the position of commandant of the post at Macon left vacant by the resignation of Colonel Aiken. In July, he wrote Richmond asking for a 30-day leave of absence from August 1st because of a "... marriage recently contracted." He had plans to marry a college girl who had visited the prison during a school function. He tendered his resignation on the 24th of September, and his name appears on a document dated the 20th of November to the effect that his resignation was withdrawn. An official communication was addressed to him on December 11, 1864, as "Commanding, Fort Valley, Georgia."[204]

Nineteenth-century research yielded little information about the early life of Wirz. One biography, presented in the book *The True Story of Andersonville Prison, A Defense of Major Henry Wirz,* by James Madison Page, seemed very superficial and as though it had been enhanced as needed for continuity.

According to Page, "Major Henry Wirz, C.S.A., was born at Zurich, Switzerland, in 1822. He was the son of Abraham Wirz, an honest, respectable citizen of that city. After graduating from the University of Zurich, Henry Wirz took up the study of medicine, and, to fit himself for the profession, he attended the medical colleges of Paris and Berlin; in both schools he received the degree of M. D. He began the practice of medicine near his home, and

---

[196] Northrop, p. 72.
[197] O. R., VII, p. 63.
[198] *Wirz Trial*, p. 462.
[199] *O. R.*, VII, pp. 63. 64.
[200] *Ibid.*, p. 120.
[201] *O. R.*, VII, p. 169.
[202] *Ibid.*, p. 159.
[203] *Ibid.*, p. 215.
[204] Military Records from the National Archives.

soon after, while quite young, married. After giving birth to two children, his wife died, and Dr. Wirz decided to try his fortune across the sea.

"Leaving his children with his father and mother, he immigrated to the United States. His father was in good circumstances, financially, and the Doctor's children, Paul and Louisa Emily Wirz, had a good home. They remained in Switzerland, and both were living a few years ago [in 1908].

"Dr. Henry Wirz came to this country in 1849. He was a learned and skillful physician, and began the practice of his profession in Kentucky. Early in 1854, he married Mrs. Wolfe, a woman of good family, and a widow, the mother of two little girls, Susie and Cornelia Wolfe. The marriage took place at Cadiz, Kentucky, and was a happy one, as they were very much attached to each other. He was an affectionate husband and the kindest of fathers to his little step-children. On February 25, 1855, a little girl came to cement more closely the bonds of affection between this loving pair. They named her Cora...

"After his second marriage, Dr. Wirz removed to Milliken's Bend, Louisiana.

At the beginning of the Civil War, he had a large and lucrative practice as a physician in the locality in which he lived." [205]

Recently, Joseph P. Renald meticulously researched the early life of Wirz and said he was born November 25, 1823 (not 1822 as many have written), at 26 Froshaugasse, Zurich, Switzerland. He attended elementary school and the lower Gymnasium, began his commercial training at the Kaufhaus in Zurich, and completed it in Turin, Italy, in 1842. His interests lay in the direction of medical study, but his father objected and insisted on his entering the mercantile field. From 1843 to 1846, he worked with his father. In 1845, he married Emilie Oschwald who bore him two children, Emilie (1847) and Paul (1849). At some time between 1846 and 1849, he ran into trouble with the law. Just what his offense was "... is not clear but it had to do with money." Perhaps it was embezzlement; perhaps he lived beyond his means and incurred a debtor's sentence. At any rate, he served a brief prison term, his marriage ended in divorce, and, apparently, the Swiss government banished him. He sailed to America in 1849.

Wirz worked for a while as a weaver in a factory in Lawrence, Massachusetts, then wandered. In early 1854, he went to Hopkinsville, Kentucky, and became an assistant to a Doctor Weber. He left Weber after two months and went to work for a Dr. Edward Caspari, who practiced medicine in Louisville and Brownsboro, Kentucky. Shortly he moved to Cadiz, Kentucky, to set up a practice, and there, on May 28, 1854, he married a widow named Elizabeth Wolfe. If Wirz attempted to pose as a physician in Cadiz, he evidently failed to deceive the local doctors. He left Kentucky and drifted to the Marshall plantation at Milliken's Bend, Louisiana, where he was staying — possibly employed as the "doctor" for Mr. Marshall's slaves — when he decided to join the Confederate army.

Renald found no evidence that Wirz had earned a medical degree.[206]

Spencer said that, when Wirz came to America, he "... was unable to speak a word of our language, but, having some knowledge of woolen manufactures, he obtained employment in a shawl factory in Lawrence, Massachusetts. Here he remained for some years, when he emigrated to Louisville, Kentucky, and became a clerk or attendant to a homeopathic physician."[207]

In the highly-prejudiced work, titled *Demon of Andersonville*, written in 1865, some possible facts about Wirz' life surface. The book states that Wirz landed in New York and endeavored to become a physician and, after failing at that, went on to Lawrence. There, "... he became acquainted with the proprietor of a water cure establishment at Northampton in the same state. Here he picked up his first ideas of the healing art. From this institute of hydropathy, he went to Kentucky, and obtained a situation in a drug store at Louisville, where he finished his medical education...We next find him in Mississippi, practicing as a doctor on a plantation, and, in this vocation he continued till the outbreak of the rebellion.

"During the secession agitation which preceded the open acts of hostility on the part of the rebels, Wirz gained for himself a little local notoriety by his rabid denunciation of the United States Government, and the loyal people of the North."[208]

On May 25, 1861, he enlisted as a private "for the war" in Richmond, Louisiana, into Captain George C. Waddill's company "A" of the 4th Battalion Louisiana Volunteer Infantry. He was listed on company rolls in July, August, September and October as "present" and several of his pay vouchers for $11 per month are extant. On August 26, 1861, Private Henry Wirz, of the Madison Infantry, was requested to report to General John H. Winder in Richmond.

---

[205] Page, pp. 183-185.
[206] Futch, p.16.
[207] Author unknown, *The Demon of Andersonville; or the Trial of Wirz, For the Cruel Treatment and Brutal Murder of Helpless Union Prisoners in his Hands* (Philadelphia: Barclay & Co., Publishers, 1865), p. 117.
[208] William C. Harris, *Prison-life in the Tobacco Warehouse at Richmond* (Philadelphia: 1862), pp. 135, 136.

While Wirz was at Liggon's Tobacco Factory, also known as Rockett's Prison, No. 1, the officer in charge of Liggon was Lieutenant Todd, a brother of Abraham Lincoln's wife.

The following description of Wirz is interesting because it places him at Liggon Prison in 1861 in a book written in 1862. Thus, there were no pre- or post-trial biases influencing the author, because it was written before Wirz went to Andersonville.

"The Dutch Sergeant of the Post, - who, at the arrival of the Ball's Bluff prisoners, appeared to be the essence of authority at the prison. Commanding officer, officer of the day, and roll-sergeant, - all seemed blended in his German *factotum*.

"Was any thing wanted? Ask the Dutch sergeant. Would any thing happen soon? Ask the Dutch sergeant? Officers and men in the warehouse, and negro cooks in the yard, ignored the existence of all authority in the Confederacy, save what centered in our Dutch sergeant. He was a good fellow at times, and a very bad one at others. He would show his angular smile of half-stubborn good humor to-day, and curse us in his fragmentary English tomorrow. He was an infallible dog, - thought himself omnipresent and omniscient. Well do we remember, when Captain Bense and Lieutenant Merrill escaped, how our Dutch sergeant rushed into the warehouse, exclaiming, with his Teutonic accent, 'Gentlemen, two of you have got out. Must call de roll. I saw 'em but a minute ago.' (They had been gone thirty-six hours.) Completing the rollcall, and discovering the names of the absentees, he darted out of the door, exclaiming, 'I know where dey is! I can catch dem.' He aroused the town, and patrols were sent in all directions. But the Dutch sergeant was at fault for once, as they were rearrested at night, thirty miles from Richmond, by scouts searching for runaway negroes. He left us on the 22nd of November, 1861, for Tuscaloosa, in charge of Federal officers and men transferred thither as prisoners of war. By a letter thence we have been informed of his popularity, owing to his obliging nature. He fills the important post of commissary at Tuscaloosa, and is still noted for his infallibility and usefulness."[209]

In November and December, 1861, and also, in January and February, 1862, Wirz was listed as "... absent on detached service." For March, April, May, June, and July, he served under General Winder on "... detached service in Richmond, Virginia." During those first months of 1862, Wirz received $17 per month and held the rank of sergeant.

In his personal reminiscences, Major J. T. W. Hairston, who had command of the Richmond prisons in 1861 and 1862, said, "... my orderly Sergeant, Doctor Wirz, while he was with me seemed to be a very kind and efficient officer, but a very strict disciplinarian."[210]

At Seven Pines, Sergeant Wirz was severely wounded in his right shoulder and right arm above the wrist. The wound in his forearm was caused by a musket ball that shattered one of the bones. Others said the wound was caused by shrapnel. Small spicules of bone continued to work out for the rest of his life. He recuperated in the hospital for several weeks after being wounded, then rejoined his unit and earned a promotion to the rank of captain on June 12, 1862, "... for bravery on the field of battle."

The wound continued to ooze and fester, which made him unfit for duty at the front. He was detailed as acting adjutant-general to Brigadier General Winder. On June 19th, General Winder issued General Order 1 of the Department of Henrico that assigned Henry Wirtz (sic) Assistant Provost Marshal in command of the District of "... Manchester and vicinity including the whole of the bridges. He will have entire charge of all the bridges and will give the necessary orders to the guard."

Some more information about Wirz surfaces in William Marvel's biography published in the December, 1992, issue of the *Blue and Gray Magazine*. Marvel wrote:

"The bark *Sarah Boyd* dropped anchor in New York Harbor on the morning of April 23, 1849, after a three-week voyage from Le Havre, but not one passenger or crewman set foot on the wharf until the city health inspector saw everyone aboard. This sultry spring found Gotham authorities unusually vigilant for signs of pestilence: only four months before, another packet from Le Havre had brought an outbreak of cholera. The doctors examined about a hundred immigrants on the *Sarah* - mostly from Germany, Switzerland, and the Netherlands - and passed them all ashore by nightfall.

One of those who staggered down the gangplank under his heavy bundle of belongings was a slight, 25-year-old Swiss named Hartman Heinrich Wirz. A native of Zurich, Wirz had abandoned his very pregnant wife and a daughter nearly two years old. Some said he fled from the law, but Wirz denied it, blaming that rumor on the fraud conviction of his cousin, August Heinrich Wirz. Cousin August's business reputation does not seem to have suffered

---

209 William H. Jeffrey, *Richmond Prisons, 1861-1865* (St. Johnsbury, Vt.: The St. Johnsbury Republican Press, 1893), p. 86.
210 William Marvel, "Three Roads to Andersonville," *Blue and Gray* Magazine, December, 1992, p. 33.

any such blemish, however, and the banking-house job the immigrant said he held was actually August's occupation.

Sixteen years later, Wirz said he left New York for Connecticut and Massachusetts, where he worked in a woolen mill and a health spa for the next two years, but this part of his tale does not stand up to scrutiny, either. Within ten months of his arrival in America, Wirz was working as a bartender in New Orleans and lodging in a coffee house owned by some Germans by name of Webber.

The Webbers may have been related to Wirz, for one of his uncles was married to a woman of that family, and they could have been the vehicle for Henry's introduction to Augustine Webber, who practiced medicine up the Mississippi at Hopkinsville, Kentucky. Wirz wanted to become a doctor, and, in 1854, traveled upriver to study under the aging physician. After a few months, the apprentice concluded Dr. Webber was a quack who could teach him nothing, so he moved to a younger mentor in Louisville.

Wirz learned that his wife had divorced him for desertion. During his sojourn in western Kentucky, he met Elizabeth Wolfe, an illiterate grass widow who lived at her mother's home in Cadiz. By the time Wirz departed for Louisville he had married her. Eventually, Wirz achieved a diluted version of his professional goal. By the end of the decade, he hung out a shingle in homeopathy -- a health fad that did not long outlive Wirz himself.

According to Wirz' own account, he gave up his practice to oversee a plantation near Milliken's Bend, Louisiana, and that is where the census-taker found him in the summer of 1860. But Wirz did not represent himself to that functionary as the exalted boss of the entire spread; he gave the less-estimable occupation of a homeopathic physician. That career had not been very kind to him, either, for in five years he had accumulated no more property then he might have traded for a second-rate field hand.

By 1861, Elizabeth Wirz had borne two more children for her husband, but one of them died as a toddler. So poor were they that Henry saw better prospects in the army, and, with the outbreak of war, he enlisted in a local rifle company as a private. Early in August, he rolled into Richmond with the Madison Infantry, attached to the 4th Louisiana Battalion.

Within days of his arrival, Wirz turned down the road that would lead to his doom. Richmond was full of Federal prisoners from Manassas, and the Madison Infantry stood guard, for a few days, in one of the capital's makeshift dungeons. The chief prison keeper was John H. Winder, a crusty old man with the fresh stars of a brigadier general on his collar. On his daily rounds, Winder happened to take note of Wirz, whose nervous energy he coveted. The general asked for Wirz on a permanent assignment, and the Madison Infantry never saw him again.

Until the autumn of 1861, Private Wirz served as a clerk in the provost marshal's office. His superiors often remarked on his vigor and efficiency, and, in October, they ordered him to Tuscaloosa, Alabama, to assist the commandant of a new prison. He remained at Tuscaloosa through the winter and spring, occasionally commanding the prison, earning sergeant's stripes and the approbation of prisoners and citizens alike, until General Winder called him back to Richmond.

Once again, Wirz' story conflicts with the available evidence. His version brings him to Richmond in time to be appointed acting assistant adjutant general on the staff of General Joseph Johnston, only to be wounded in the wrist at the battle of Fair Oaks. Wirz was still in Tuscaloosa at least as late as May 15, however, and, while it would have been possible for him to return to Virginia in time for Fair Oaks, he is not mentioned as a staff officer in any official record of that fight. Besides, his commission, dated June 12, was rendered 11 days after the battle ended, and that document specifically assigned him to General Winder.[211]

One of Wirz' first orders from General Winder was to proceed to Alabama on a special assignment. James Page wrote, "On August 26, 1862, Captain Wirz was placed in charge of the military prison system in Richmond, where he remained on duty until September 26th, when he was ordered to Montgomery, Alabama, in search of missing records pertaining to prisoners captured in 1861 and the early part of 1862, and to report the result to Colonel Robert Ould, Agent for Exchange." After completing his assignment there, he was ordered by General Winder to go to Tuscaloosa, Alabama, to take charge of the military prison there.[212] The citizens of Tuscaloosa petitioned in April and recommended Henry Wirz, Assistant to Captain Elias Griswold be given the command of the prison when Captain Griswold was transferred. The petition states that, because of "... the large increase of prisoners here, present and prospective, [it] makes us anxious that his successor shall profess the prudence, discretion, firmness, decision and energy, which he has exhibited, during his continuance at this military post. We believe that Henry Wirtz (sic), efficient assistant, possesses all these qualities, in an eminent degree. We respectfully recommend him for that office."[213] This

---

[211] Page, p. 186.
[212] Military Records from the National Archives.
[213] *Ibid.*

petition was signed by forty-five or so of the more influential citizens of Tuscaloosa.

General Winder endorsed this petition by saying Wirz "... has been employed at this prison since its establishment and has been very faithful and efficient in the discharge of his duties and would, I think in every way, be a very suitable man for this place."[214]

Wirz' health was failing him; he applied for a furlough and was directed to proceed to Richmond. While there, he was appointed a special emissary by President Jefferson Davis on a mission to Paris and Berlin. He sailed for Europe on December 19, 1862. He carried secret messages to Mr. J. M. Mason in England and Mr. John Slidell in France and to other agents throughout Europe.

While there, Wirz decided to take advantage of the superior medical knowledge of the doctors in Europe. Page reported that, "While in Paris he had his wounded arm operated on to try to debride the chronic infection above his wrist. The physicians supposed that all the diseased bone was removed. As he began to regain his health, it was thought that the operation was a success. This was not the case, for after completing his mission in Berlin, the old trouble came back. When he returned from Europe in February, 1864, he was suffering as much as ever."[215]

Wirz was ordered to Andersonville when he returned. Of his arrival there, Wirz said: "I was assigned to the command of the prison by Col. A. W. Persons, the commandant of the post, on the 27th of March, 1864, having reported to him for duty by order of General J. H. Winder, commanding C. S. military prison."[216]

> *Orders No. 9*
> *Head-quarters, Confederate Military Prison*
> *Andersonville, April 12, 1864*
>
> *Captain Henry Wirz is assigned to the superintendence and management of the prisoners at this post, and will take charge of their custody.*
> *Supplies for their maintenance will be issued only upon his requisition and under his orders. Passes to visit the stockade will be granted by him alone, and all arrangements connected with its interior will be controlled by him.*
> *Captain Wirz will report directly to these head-quarters.*
>
> *By order of*
> *John H. Winder, Brigadier General.*
> *W. S. Winder, Assistant Adjutant General.*[217]

Colonel Persons testified at Wirz' trial: "I think he took command immediately. He was interrupted, however, by the arrival of Major Griswold, who had an order to take command of the prison. That order collided with the one that Wirz had. The matter was put in abeyance. I think Captain Wirz retired for some ten or fifteen days till the difficulty was cleared up. Subsequently Major Griswold was ordered away and Captain Wirz took command of the prison."[218]

Wirz' duties as Commandant of the Interior of the Prison included the command over the guards. He "... had control of the sentinels after they were put on duty -- after guard-mounting."[219] When he needed more sentinels, he had to requisition them from Colonel Persons.[220]

McElroy felt Wirz was qualified to be commandant by real or imaginary training. "Wirz had had some training as an accountant, and this was what gave him the place over us."[221]

Within days, Fosdick said, the following incident supposedly happened: "Nor was he long in making his new rank known and his authority felt. At the first provocation, whether real or imaginary, he ordered a squad out and then aboard a train, and sent them to New Orleans, where they were placed in buildings that had been emptied by the ravages of yellow fever. They were kept there until many died of the malady, when the Mayor of the city ordered that they be removed out of the infected district and placed in more healthy quarters, or removed from the city altogether. The latter order was obeyed, and thereby saved the lives of a small percent of this hapless little band."[222] It would be interesting to know if this incident actually happened.

---

214 Page, p. 186.
215 *O. R.*, VII, p. 169.
216 Spencer, p. 60.
217 *Wirz Trial*, p. 455.
218 Chipman, p. 53.
219 *Ibid.*
220 McElroy, p. 144.
221 Fosdick, p. 36.
222 *Wirz Trial*, p. 523.

When Wirz first arrived at his new assignment, he located his headquarters on the South Gate Road, a few hundred feet southwest of the gate on a slight prominence. "The headquarters were two large tents."[223]

**Wirz' Headquarters** – Looking north from his headquarters in the Star Fort with a view of the bakery, the garrison camps to the east, and pen. His first headquarters was a walled tent nearer to the South Gate. (From Sketch by R.C. Sneden)

Boston Corbett, who, the following year, would gain fame as the killer of John Wilkes Booth, the assassin of Lincoln, was captured near Centreville, Virginia, and taken to Andersonville. He testified that, when he arrived there on July 12th, Wirz was headquartered "... in some small tents."[224] Miller described what he witnessed while leaving the South Gate, as he headed over to the railroad station on approximately the 12th of September: "On the way to the station we passed the tent of Capt. Wirz, who was sitting there, looking very feeble from an attack of sickness."[225] The O'Dea print depicts Wirz' headquarters as being two, traditional, canvas-walled tents on the site, whereas other prints depict a crude, wooden cabin on the site. Wirz had a sign at his office which designated him as the "Commandant of the Interior of the Prison."[226]

A Mr. Martin, Wirz' chief clerk said, "All the clerks at headquarters slept in the tent with me... I took my meals in the second tent near to where we slept.[227] Another clerk was Benjamin F. Dilley, whose desk was right beside Wirz' desk.[228] Three clerks wrote at a table about two feet from Wirz' desk.

Some thought the second tent housed the headquarters of the medical director. Doctor G. G. Roy testified that, when he arrived at Andersonville on the 1st of September, "Captain Wirz' headquarters, when I first arrived at Andersonville, were in a tent adjoining Dr. White... it was there a week and a fortnight; I think, probably a month."[229] It seems to then have been moved to a wooden cabin over in the town proper.

Benjamin B. Dykes, the railroad agent, testified about where Wirz lived when he first arrived at Andersonville. "The house I lived in at Andersonville was about two hundred and fifty yards from the freight-house. I lived there from 1st January, 1861, to 24th January, 1865. I now live six and one-half miles from the place...Captain Wirz boarded with me about two months when he first came there."[230] Major Proctor testified, "I had occasion to go to the butcher, a Mr. Boss, who herded the stock; that was during the month of August. Captain Wirz was living at Boss' house, I think."[231] Doctor G. G. Roy testified: "Captain Wirz occupied half a house owned by a man named Boss, about two miles from Andersonville."[232]

One prisoner testified he had knowledge of possible illegal transactions transpiring at butcher Boss' house: "I have seen 800 pounds of flour go through that gate in one day. The flour came from the rebel butcher, I think. I do

[223] Chipman, p. 166.
[224] Miller, p. 34.
[225] Chipman, p. 122.
[226] *Wirz Trial*, p. 523.
[227] *Ibid.*, p. 673.
[228] *Ibid.*, p. 658.
[229] *Ibid.*, p. 372.
[230] *Ibid.*, p. 669.
[231] *Ibid.*, p. 558.
[232] *Ibid.*, p. 676.

not know what his name was. He was afterwards arrested for trading by Duncan, I understand. I know his shop was outside. I believe it was two miles away from the stockade. That was wheat flour, eight sacks., Molasses was taken in there by the barrel."[233]

Wirz' favorite horse was described by some prisoners as being a white mare and by others as being gray colored. The horses at Andersonville did not seem to be assigned to specific officers but were placed in a common pool to be requisitioned by any officer in need of transportation. "Captain Wirz trusted his horse to others; he gave it to Duncan, and to Mr. Bowers to get yeast to make white bread for the sick. I do not know how far they went with the horse. They were not on duty. They had flour for the sick men in the stockade, and wanted to get yeast, and Duncan came and asked him for his horse for that purpose. Duncan was acting as quartermaster. Bowers used to bring in rations to the camp."[234]

As spring turned to summer in 1864, Dick Winder and his cousin, Sid Winder, had fulfilled their respective jobs at Andersonville and began to take on further responsibilities. Though Dick Winder was taxed in his ability to feed the daily increasing numbers of prisoners, he would soon be asked to establish another prison at Millen, Georgia, and to establish a Confederate shoe factory. Sid Winder had completed his job of starting the largest prisoner-of-war camp the world would ever know, and of being its first Commandant. Sid Winder left Andersonville and returned to Richmond to rejoin the staff of his father, General Winder. He would soon select the site for the new prison at Millen. Colonel Persons would soon be replaced by an officer with rank equal to the responsibility of running a very large Confederate post. This officer was an infirm, sixty-year-old: Brigadier General John Henry Winder.

[233] *Ibid.*, p. 523.
[234] *Blue and Gray* Magazine, Dec.-Jan. 1985-1986, p. 9.

## *Chapter Two*

# Filling of the Pen and the Arrival of Brigadier General John Henry Winder and Captain Henry Wirz

*"The Duties of the inside command are admirably performed by Captain Wirz, whose place it would be difficult to fill."*

Major General Howell Cobb

For the entire spring of 1864, prisoners continued to arrive day and night at Andersonville. Most were brought down from the battlefields of Virginia but many arrived from the nearby battles around Atlanta. Several distinct groups made tremendous impact on the economy as well as the sanitary and living conditions within the pen.

Before the war, the train whistle signaled a train's arrival into Andersonville only about twice a day. "Normally two trains, one northbound and one southbound, passed daily. The train up from Albany stopped at 11 a.m., and the locomotive and cars down from Macon chugged in at 1:30 p.m. Besides taking on and letting off passengers and freight, the locomotives took on water and wood."[1] With the opening of the prison, the little hamlet became a stop for sometimes three, four, five, or six trains per day.

Most of the new prisoners arrived in cattle cars or common boxcars. William B. Clifton was one of the few who arrived on flat cars. Lewis Lake, Battery B, 1st Illinois Light Artillery, after his capture, was "... furnished a special train of flatcars, with a framework decorated with brush and pine boughs to protect us from the scorching rays of the sun."[2] They were usually packed sixty to seventy to a car. Some were placed in manure-strewn cattle cars immediately after the four-legged occupants had been removed. Kellogg was one of the few who had plenty of room, only having thirty-five to a car. One sentinel was stationed at each door and several guards rode on top. A special car sometimes brought up the rear of the train; the guards used this car. Maile rode "... fifty or sixty in a freight car, with twenty or thirty of our number on the top." The most desirable place within the box car was where one could avoid the heat and stifling odor by standing at a spot by the door or by having a place to sit at the door with one's feet dangling outside.

While traveling from Richmond, Dowling chipped though the rear wall of the rear car of the train with a pocket knife and dropped to the ground as the train ambled along at about ten miles per hour near Raleigh. He fled west and was captured by some Indians of the Creek nation employed by the Confederates to guard the passes of the mountains. The Creek guards received a reward of money and whiskey for their capture of Confederate deserters and escaped prisoners. While accompanied by these Indians, Dowling escaped again after getting them drunk on fire-water. He took off, again, temporarily, for East Tennessee, where he was recaptured and sent to Atlanta, and, finally, on to Andersonville. There, Wirz had the blacksmith rivet on a 32-pound ball and said, "I fix you God damned Yankees so you not get away again."[3] The prisoners sometimes called the ball and chain the wearing of a

[1] Author's collection.
[2] Typed transcript of Lewis Lake's diary in private hands.
[3] Dowling, pp. 85-97.

"watch and chain." Dowling was not stopped by his watch and chain, however. He obtained a file and lead bullet from a guard in exchange for money. He filed out the iron rivet and put a removable lead one in its place. Thus, he wore the ball only at roll call, and, in ten days' time, the Confederate authorities removed it.

The arrival of a trainload of prisoners (or fresh fish, as they were called) at first caused much celebration and excitement within the small town of Andersonville. The local inhabitants gathered because most had never seen a real live Yankee soldier before the opening of the prison. They would congregate around the station, a small group of curious men, women, and children, both black and white. These crowds were usually respectful and followed the prisoners to the entrance of the grounds.

Spencer described these curious crowds at the stockade: "Women went there day after day; forsaking more pressing demands upon their time at home and bearing their suckling babes upon their bosoms. They might be seen squatting upon the ground and gossiping in the interval, nursing their offspring, while they knitted socks and gloated over the novel sight of the prospect before them."[4]

Schools were let out so the students could see the spectacular events which would later be used as the subject of theme papers for school. "There was a high school - college it is called here in the South - for girls, that emptied its walls of its innocent but curious inmates, and in detachments, as the force of circumstances required, some loading the cars upon the railroad, others easily gliding in luxurious carriages, and many lumbering along in such conveyances as could be improvised, accompanied by the president and guardian professors, hurried in expectant curiosity to the center of attraction. When there, they chattered, flirted, stared, and ate their sandwiches, and took notes of what they saw as themes for their next weekly compositions.[5]

It was from one of these groups of college students Colonel Persons found his bride-to-be.

One prisoner described his reception at the prison thus: "Presently the commandant of the prison with a lieutenant and sergeant came down the line. I asked to go to the creek and fill some canteens, pleading our suffering condition. In a passion, pistol in hand, the officer turned with a ferocious oath, putting the pistol to my nose saying, 'I'll shot you if you say dot again.' Stepping back he yelled: 'If another man ask for water I shoot him.'

"To the left a poor fellow had squat in the ranks. This officer whom I found to be Captain Wirz, rushed upon him with an oath, kicking him severely and yelled savagely, 'Standt up in ter ranks!'

"The ground was covered with small bushes. While waiting some worked industriously pulling and packing in bundles to carry in for shelter. After two hours we started, but all were forced by bayonets to drop the bushes."[6]

Doctor T.H. Mann, in *Century Magazine,* described his arrival: "We had little time for thought before a round-shouldered, blustering little man upon a white horse rode the length of the train, and with many a curse and oath ordered us all out. During our exit from the close, cramped quarters we had occupied so long a fresh guard came, in the wildest confusion and unmilitary order, from the direction of the smoke (curling upward from a rectangular, substantial-looking pen), and after much blustering and more cursing we were formed into two lines, giving room for us to pass between, four deep. After some more swearing the officer on the white horse placed himself at the head of the column and ordered us to march. Upon reaching the enclosure we halted while a part of our number were formed into a detachment, and the remainder were ordered to be placed upon the rolls of the older detachments already in the pen.[7] John Urban described his actual transmission into the pen: "As we came near the gate we noticed that a regiment of rebel soldiers were drawn up in line to the right of us, and were kept in that position until we were inside of the prison. We were afterward informed by the prisoners that this was done every time a large number of new prisoners arrived, and that they were kept there for the purpose of guarding against an outbreak when the gates were open, and perhaps thinking that when the new arrivals discovered the hell-hole that was open to receive them, they would, in their despair and madness, make an attempt to overcome their fiendish jailers and escape: "As we entered the prison a mule-team that was coming from the gate got in position between us and the line of rebel troops. Captain Wirz, who was riding to and for, making as much fuss and putting on as much style as if he were in command of an army of fifty thousand men, discovered the team, and thinking his precious mules in danger should his captives make an attempt to escape, yelled out, 'Take them aisels away!'"[8]

The car Boggs was in had been used as a lime carrying car, and it had about a half-inch of lime dust on the floor when he was loaded into it in Petersburg. Because of the dust and heat, Boggs and his fellow captives grew very

---

[4] Spencer, p. 27.
[5] *Ibid.*, pp. 28, 29.
[6] Northrop, p. 57, 58.
[7] Mann, p. 453.
[8] John E. Urban, *Through the War and Thrice a Prisoner in Rebel Dungeons* (Philadelphia, 1892), pp. 307, 308.

thirsty by the time of their arrival. They begged to drink from the tiny brook near the station "... when a little grinny-faced Rebel captain, on a sway-backed gray horse, rode up and shook a revolver in my face and said; 'You Got tam Yankee! you youst vait, und you got so much vater vot you drown in booty quick!' As they marched to the pen between the double row of guards,"...the artillerymen stood with lanyard in hand at their canister-shotted guns." Once inside and because of their thirst, they rushed to the creek, "... as we were famishing from thirst. Two comrades, to get the clear water just above the 'dead line', and not knowing the danger, reached beyond it and both dropped dead in the water, shot by the guards on the water. We dared not move their bodies until ordered to do so by a rebel officer, who was some time in getting around. The water running red with our comrades' blood, stopped the drinking until the bodies were removed."[9]

"A large group of prisoners consisting of the garrison from Plymouth, North Carolina, were brought to Camp Sumter. They had surrendered Plymouth after four days of being hard pressed by the investing Confederate forces. Brigadier General Henry W. Wessells surrendered Plymouth to Brigadier General R. F. Hoke, C. S. A. on April 20th.

"As the Confederate commander approached Gen. Wessells, the latter reached him his sword, saying; 'Gen. Hoke, this is the saddest day of my life.' Gen. Hoke, as he received the sword, replied; 'General, this is the proudest day of my life.' And then, as if impressed by the wonderful and quiet bearing of the defeated commander, he handed back the sword, saying; 'Gen. Wessells, you are too brave a man to part with your sword; take it back! Have you any requests to make? 'I have but one request to make, General, and that is that my men are not robbed.' A quick and sympathetic response came from the victorious commander; 'Your request is granted.' And be it said to the credit of the Confederate soldiers, both officers and men, whose duty it was to guard the captives, this promise of Gen. Hoke's was faithfully kept. "[10]

This request worked out to the benefit of the prisoners because the paymaster had recently paid each newly enlisted man $100 bounty; each newly-reenlisted man had received the first installment of the bounty due. In addition, several months' pay had recently been issued. That was an especially sad day for many of the men because they had reenlisted a couple months prior and had due them a thirty-day furlough, a part of their contract for "veteranizing." About 2,300 men, including 99 officers, surrendered on April 20th.

On the first night after the capitulation, the men bivouacked about a mile in front of their works and received rations from their own stores. On the afternoon of the 21st, the men began their long march to Tarboro, arriving there on the 26th. There, they were placed in boxcars and told they were headed for the prisons of Richmond. After passing through Goldsboro, they realized that the train was headed south. They reached Wilmington on the 27th, Florence, passed through Columbia and Charleston, and arrived at Savannah on the 29th. On the outskirts of Savannah, they changed cars that passed through Milledgeville and Macon, and which arrived at Andersonville on April 30th.

Another distinctive group of new fish arriving during the end of April were all the "well" prisoners from Cahaba prison in Alabama. On April 20th, General Sam Cooper ordered General Leonidas Polk to send all the Yankee prisoners then at Cahaba to Andersonville. Probably because of the Federal Forces being in the near vicinity.

The guard at Cahaba were ordered to accompany the prisoners and to stay on at Andersonville.[11] By May 3rd, all Federal prisoners, except the very sick, had been sent on to Andersonville.

The prison population continued to grow rapidly, as a result, in part, of the following order:

*Adjut. Inspector Gen. Office,*
*Richmond, Va., May 2d, 1864*

*General Order No 45.*

*I. Prisoners captured south of Richmond will be sent direct to Andersonville, Sumpter (sic) county, Georgia.*

*(Signed)*
*Samuel Cooper*
*A. and In.-Gen.*[12]

The Cahaba prisoners were just one of several large contingents to arrive as a group. Some of them were very weak and debilitated. Most were very poor and poorly clad and did not effect the economy within Andersonville.

Many prisoners had asserted they had been robbed of all or most of their personal property by their captors in

---

[9] Boggs, pp. 18, 19.
[10] John A. Reed, *History of the 101st Regiment Pennsylvania Veteran Volunteer Infantry* (Chicago: L. S. Dickery & Co., 1910), p. 135.
[11] *Ibid.*,. 76.
[12] Samuel B. Davis, . 20.

the field, especially those prisoners captured by irregular troops or by secondary militia. "We were searched and robbed of everything valuable - watches, money, knives, extra blankets, and shelter tents, they telling us we should soon be exchanged, and could get more of the same kind. All that we were allowed to keep, except the clothing upon our backs, was our choice of an overcoat or a woolen blanket. Some of my comrades succeeded in secreting their money, and in some instances their watches. I saved my own watch by slipping it into my shoe under the sole and instep of my foot; and my money went into the lining of my jacket - both saved for a time."[13]

That Confederate commanders relatively high up were aware, if not responsible, for some of the thievery against Federal prisoners is illustrated by the following story. Lieutenant Colonel H. C. Hobart of the Twenty-first Wisconsin Volunteers wrote to his headquarters that, after the battle of Chickamauga, he accompanied the 1,800 men who had been taken prisoner. "At Tunnel Hill, Georgia, all the non-commissioned officers and privates of the above prisoners were ordered by the Confederate commander of the post to stand in line and give up their rubber blankets, which was done. At Atlanta, Georgia, the same prisoners were ... stripped by Confederate officers of [their] blankets and overcoats." Lieutenant Colonel Hobart protested to those officers it was "... inhuman and cruel and against the laws of civilized warfare." The Confederate officers said the order for taking their overcoats and blankets came from the commander of the department and must be followed.[14]

The prisoners often interpreted the confiscation of contraband items when entering Southern prisons as thievery on the part of the guard. Brigadier General W. M. Gardner said, in October of 1864: "When prisoners are captured their private property is taken from them at the first establishment in which they are confined and turned over to a quartermaster."[15]

Whether or not blatant robbery as described by some authors took place will never be proven. Because some of the incidents were generally corroborated by two or more witnesses, some larceny must have taken place.

At the end of the war, several of the men entrusted with the personal effects of these prisoners came forward with their very incomplete ledger books. Most of these books reveal the total number of a specific item taken, but did not list the names of each item's owner. If the prisoners were not robbed in the field when first captured, there was a good chance they would be robbed at their entrance into a prison. One prisoner wrote, "In Richmond, we were nearly stripped of everything; I however, had the luck to smuggle my woolen blanket through with me to Andersonville and it gave shelter for seven of us: and we were lucky too!"[16]

The defenders of Plymouth were some of the few prisoners who arrived with their kits intact. Most other prisoners arrived having already traded down to their last Eagle button for an extra bit of food or some other necessity. Larceny was ignored, by no means limited to those who wore gray. Many, many Southerners told of losing their personal property to Blue-bellies.

"Prisoner examiners" inspected all new arrivals at Andersonville ostensibly for weapons. Often the men ended up being relieved of money, hats, watches, shirts, and shoes. Augustus Hamlin asserts, "This system of robbery was open and audacious; it is positively stated that it was sanctioned by Wirz and Winder."[17]

Evidently, the Prisoner Examiners worked in shifts, because several men expressed gratitude that they had arrived when two men named Humes and Duncan were not working. They felt that if they had arrived when these two were working, they would have been admitted completely devoid of any personal property. Dufur wrote, "James W. Duncan, of New Orleans, and W. J. Humes, of Baltimore, were selected as the examiners of boxes, clothing, and pockets of the prisoners as they arrived, together with three police detectives, taken from the Richmond experts, to spy out and report to him the utterances and shortcomings of the people of the country. The services of these latter were in constant requisition, and they proved efficient aids."[18]

After General Winder arrived, he ordered that, since many of the prisoners captured in the summer of 1864 were soldiers of the raiding troops of General George Stoneman, all possessions should be taken from them on their arrival. J. B. Vawter was one of the 2,000 men with General Edward M. McCook's command of Kentucky cavalry with General William T. Sherman. Their mission was to cut rail lines, telegraph lines, destroy property and generally raise havoc behind the Confederate lines. Most of these prisoners were members of troops many had accused of pillaging and stealing from the plantations of Georgia. Sundry objects found in possession of the prisoners support this

---

[13]Author's library.
[14] *O. R.*, VII, p. 60.
[15] *Ibid.*, p. 987.
[16] Ray, p. 200.
[17] Hamlin, p. 54.
[18] Spencer, p. 48.

contention because those items would not normally be found on troops in the field. Silver flatware and beautiful, cased watches were taken and deposited with Captain Richard Winder, who later was ordered to return all identifiable objects to their rightful owners and the rest kept "subject to orders." Miller noted, "The Western troops were stripped worse than the Eastern, and cavalry worse than infantry. Their excuse for this was that the Western cavalry was always raiding and destroying their property."[19]

When Stoneman's raiders were brought in, an ex-prisoner testified General Winder supposedly had issued a special order: "The order was to take away from them everything we supposed they had taken away from citizens in passing through the country. We had no orders to take away anything that was their own or United States government property, with the exception of money. We had orders to take their money away from them; nothing else that belonged to the prisoners. We took the money and such things as we supposed they had taken from the citizens in passing through the country - knives and forks and spoons. They were generally silver forks and spoons. The things taken away from these men were put in a large box and put on a wagon, and, I suppose, carried to the quartermaster."[20]

Another prisoner told how his contingent was warned to hide any valuable items so that they might not be stolen or "confiscated" by the examiners: "When our train came to a stop at the Andersonville depot, we saw about twenty men, dressed in what had once passed for Confederate uniforms, but so raged and dirty as to be past recognition. They were loading wagons, and occasionally one of them passed close to the train. They never looked at us, but as they passed close by they were repeating over and over, as though they would forget it, this song: 'If you have any money, hide it. If you have any valuables, hide them.' We took it as a sign and acted on it. Some ripped a small hole and slipped money in the hems and collars of blouses, some in boots -- every safe place you could think of. I had one ten-dollar bill. I folded it small, peeled off the outside leaf of a plug of 'Ole Verginny,' wrapped it carefully around my bill, and laid it in my cheek. I didn't chew that quid very vigorously."[21]

Another prisoner further elaborated, besides telling how his group was robbed, gives a unique description of Wirz clad in a white duck suit and a Panama hat. The prisoner also describes the Germanic accent, though he was said to be able to speak English, German and French. "They marched us through the rebel camp, and about half way between it and the pen, on a sloping plain of bright yellow sand, they halted us and opened us into single ranks. After waiting awhile here, the sun roasting our heads and the sand stewing our feet, old Wirtz [sic] came out with a squad of men to search us. This was my first view of that notorious Switzer. He was dressed in a suit of white duck, with a Panama hat, and riding a white horse. He rode down our lines and cursed us for being raiders; then gave his commands so that all could hear: 'If any man stoops down, or sits down, or tries to hide any thing, shoot him!'

"'Strip 'im! Take eberyting he got! I make 'Im tink it is hell!"

"Two large boxes were brought to put the plunder in, and the search was begun. They made us take off all our clothes and lay them out in front of us, and stand there naked while they searched them. They turned all the pockets, then felt all the seams and hems, and if they felt a lump, they would throw that garment on their pile. They took and kept all watches, rings, knives, money, pipes, and even pictures of wives and sweethearts. One boy tried to make out that he could not get his ring off.

"'If te ring no come off, take te finger,' said Wirtz.

"After they were satisfied with their examination, they would throw back such garments as they allowed us to have."[22]

In stark contrast to the usual opinion was the statement of James Madison Page, who said in his book, "I have read much about our prisoners being robbed of money, watches, jewelry, and clothing upon entering Libby, Belle Isle, Andersonville, Salisbury, and other prisons in the South, but as far as I personally was concerned, I can truthfully testify that neither at Libby, Belle Isle, Andersonville, nor Millen, where I was confined, were any articles taken from me. I had $20 when I entered Libby and Belle Isle, and $30 or $40 of Confederate money when I entered Andersonville, and not one penny was taken from me. The Confederate officers and men at Libby and Belle Isle, also knew that I had a watch with me, for I made no secret of it. They did not demand it of me, though it was a valuable timepiece."[23]

For every soldier who said they were not robbed, there were hundreds who said they were relieved of all items

---

[19] Vawter, p. 44.
[20] *Wirz Trial*, p. 499.
[21] Vawter, p. 41.
[22] Vawter, pp. 42, 43.
[23] Page, pp. 39, 40.

of value.

For the first few weeks after the early prisoners arrived, they were grouped into "hundreds" and messes of "twenties." On Wirz' first day of command, April 12th, "The first day he went in the stockade he said he had to muster us all, to divide us into squads, detachments, and divisions, and if he did not get through by one or two o'clock in the afternoon we would get no rations that day; he did not get through, and consequently we had to go without anything to eat. ... It was impossible to get through all the work in the time specified."[24] John McElroy described the difficulty Wirz had in organizing the camp: "The next morning after his first appearance he came in when roll-call was sounded, and ordered all the squads and detachments to form, and remain standing in ranks until all were counted. ... It took Wirz between two and three hours to count the whole camp, and by that time we of the first detachments were almost all out of ranks. Thereupon Wirz announced that no rations would be issued to the camp that day." The same thing happened the next day and finally, on the third day, the count was completed and rations issued.[25]

Wirz ordered the prisoners grouped into "detachments" of 270 men commanded by a Confederate sergeant called a "chief sergeant." Later, Federal sergeants were made chief sergeants. A third of a detachment was called a "ninety" or "squad" consisting of ninety men commanded by a Federal sergeant. "A sergeant in charge of ninety men received a double ration for his trouble in calling he roll, reporting the sick, &c."[26] Other prisoners called the groups of 30 men, "thirties" or "messes" which were commanded by a sergeant or corporal. Lewis Lake said in his diary, "After the search we were divided into detachments of 270 men under the charge of a rebel sergeant, and each detachment sub-divided into companies of 90 men each and under charge of a sergeant or non-commissioned officer of our own men."[27] Dufur said the messes at Andersonville were of 15 men.[28] James C. Melvin wrote that, on June 19th, "... our men divided into squads of 10 -- a much better way."[29]

There seemed to be a definite disagreement or inconsistency in the nomenclature of the groups. To be assured of proper understanding, the best names for these groupings seemed to be "detachments," "nineties," and "thirties." Thus, a man would be identified as, say, "75th Detachment, 1st Squad" or simply, "75-1." The detachments were numbered sequentially, starting with those located in the north end of the stockade near the North Gate.[30] At one time, the 71st Detachment was located far from the north wall near the swamp. Every now and then they would fill in lower-numbered detachments that had been depleted by death, prisoners being detailed outside, and prisoners being transferred to other prisons. When Maile entered on May 23rd, his detachment was number fifty-five, he said, indicating the presence of fourteen thousand, eight hundred and fifty prisoners. This, of course, assumed the presence of "full" detachments.

The actual counting out of ninety men was done as follows: "After being searched, we were taken to the north gate; a door was opened in the gate-pen (a kind of ante-room, thirty feet square), and ninety men were crowded into it. The door was then closed, and another door was opened into the prison, and we were counted again as we passed through. ... Then a new ninety were let in and counted through, and so on to the end."[31] "... we were 'lock stepped' in by fifty and sixty at a time, or all the 'lock' would hold. . ."[32]

The reason the camp was reorganized by Wirz from 100's and 20's as first set up to 270's, 90's and 30's can not logically be explained. It definitely added to the inefficiency of the management of the post. Hours were added to various procedures such as all counting of prisoners and distribution of rations.

The actual description of Wirz, who also was known as the "Flying Dutchman," varied as much as the fifty to seventy-five authors who described him in the tales of the experiences they penned in their diaries, testimonials, and biographies. The more vindictive their stories, the more grotesque Wirz appears. In fact, he was probably the most despised man in America for fifty years. Any man who spoke at that time with a definite German accent, would be subjected to ridicule and made the butt of many jokes.

---

[24] Chipman, p. 175.
[25] McElroy, pp. 144, 145.
[26] Chipman, p. 168.
[27] Typed manuscript of Lewis Lake's diary in private hands.
[28] Dufur, p. 70.
[29] James C. Melvin, *The Melvin Memorial* (Cambridge: The Riverside Press, 1910), p. 110.
[30] McElroy, p. 20.
[31] Vawter, p. 44.
[32] William B. Styple and John J. Fitzpatrick, editors, *The Andersonville Diary and Memoirs of Charles Hopkins* (Kearny, New Jersey: Belle Grove Publishing Co., 1988), p. 73.

**Captain Wirz** – Drawing depicting him in McElroy's book. He seldom wore a regulation uniform and never his sword. He is sometimes depicted wearing a rectangular CSA sword belt plate. (McElroy)

**Captain Wirz** – Depicted as an almost Satanic figure in Chipman's book because of the sentiment prevalent at that time. (Chipman)

James Madison Page was, almost singularly, a defender of Henry Wirz and the treatment the prisoners received in southwest Georgia. He described Wirz thus: "… he was of good height, perhaps five feet eight inches slim in build, with a handsome face, equiline nose, even features and a high forehead. His eyes were gray in color. At this time he wore a short, partially full beard. There was a quiet, subdued expression of sadness in his countenance, particularly in his eyes. There was nothing of that 'short, thick-set Dutchman, repulsive in appearance, besotted, ignorant and cruel' we hear about, or of a countenance denoting ferocity and brutality."[33]

Wirz' superiors considered his abilities as a soldier and administrator at least satisfactory, if not exemplary. He had received a battlefield commission for bravery at Seven Pines and had climbed rapidly from infantry private to "Commandant of the Prison Interior" of the largest military prison in the South at that time. Officers from the Inspector General's Office inspected Andersonville at least four times and senior officers from Richmond visited it a like number of times; most gave Wirz high marks.

[33] Page, p. 80.

**Captain Heinrich Hartmann Wirz** - Wearing a Confederate uniform that he took with him when he went to Europe. He was very proud of his rank and accomplishments. This picture was probably taken while he was in Europe.

**Captain Wirz** - The uniform he is wearing in this photo could not be identified by modern Swiss authorities. It certainly is not a Confederate uniform. (Rutherford)

Major General Howell Cobb, accompanied by his Chief Surgeon of the Georgia Reserves, E. J. Eldridge, visited, on May 5th, to inspect the facility. He described Wirz' performance this way: "The duties of the inside command are admirably performed by Captain Wirz, whose place it would be difficult to fill."[34]

Walter Bowie, Captain and Inspector in the Adjutant and Inspector General's Department, came to Andersonville on Monday, May 9th, and, the following day, wrote this description in his report: "I take pleasure in this report in testifying to the ability and efficiency of Captain Wirz, the commander of the prison. His activity and zeal in the discharge of his arduous duties is highly commendable."[35] In this same report, he also described Wirz as being "... very firm and rigid in the discipline of the prisoners, and at the same time exercises toward them all proper acts of kindness."[36]

After Major Thomas P. Turner's inspection, which had been ordered by General Winder in the middle of May, Turner said Wirz "... deserves great credit for the good sense and energy he has displayed in the management of the prison at Andersonville. He is the only man who seems to fully comprehend his important duties. He does the work of commandant, adjutant, clerk, and warden, and without his presence at Camp Sumter at this time everything would be chaos and confusion; in my opinion, at least two commissioned officers should be assigned to duty to assist him."[37]

---

[34] *O. R.*, VII, p. 119.
[35] *Ibid.*, p. 139.
[36] *Ibid.*, p. 136.
[37] *Ibid.*, p. 168.

Lyons described Wirz' physical characteristics as, "Height about five feet ten inches; stoop shouldered; complection, dark; hair, black; mustache, black; goatee, black; eyes, black; and a heart as black as the fires of Hades could burn it."[38]

Miller described him by saying, "Wirz was old, sickly, peevish, small brained, incompetent, but at times kindly."[39] Spencer said he was five feet, eight inches tall, with stooped shoulders and that he walked with an "emasculated gait."[40]

The following was extracted from a statement written by the Hon. W. M. Hammond. On the 13th of June, Colonel W. M. Hammond was sent, by General Bragg, on a visit of inspection. He described the prison commandant this way: "Major Wirz was, when I saw him, apparently 40 years of age, born in Zurich, Switzerland and was a trained soldier, a little below medium height, slight of figure and lean almost to emaciation, with dark hair and brown eyes. His right arm had been mutilated near the wrist, caused by a fragment of a shell in an engagement near Baton Rouge, Louisiana, incapacitating him for field service. When I was on the point of leaving Andersonville he implored me, with tears streaming from his eyes, to urge upon the authorities at Richmond the absolute necessity for more and better food for the prisoners, for more medicines, tents and lumber and recommended that I should advise that they should send as many of the prisoners as could be furnished with transportation to Richmond or Savannah and there turn them over unconditionally to the Federal authorities."[41]

S. W. Ashe continued with Colonel Hammond's assessment of Wirz: "Colonel Hammond mentioned how Wirz passed, unarmed and unattended, with him through every part of the stockade, without receiving any unkind expression or threatening gesture; and, when questioned whether he had no fears for his personal safety, he replied; 'They know I am doing my utmost for them.' And Colonel Hammond added: 'It seems incredible to me that one guilty of the cruelties alleged against him by his executioners could have passed unharmed among thousands of his victims."[42]

McElroy said, when recaptured prisoners were brought before Wirz, "He would frequently give way to paroxysms of screaming rage, so violent as to verge closely on insanity. Brandishing the fearful and wonderful revolver of which I have spoken, in such a manner as to threaten the luckless captives with instant death, he would shriek out imprecations, curses and foul epithets in French, German and English until he fairly frothed at the mouth. One of the 'Old Switzer's' favorite ways of ending these seances was to inform the boys that he would have them shot in an hour or so and bid them prepare for death. After keeping them in fearful suspense for hours, he would order them to be punished with the stocks, the ball-and-chain, the chain gang or, if his fierce mood had burned itself out, as was quite likely with a man of his shallow brain and vacillating temper, simply to be returned to the Stockade."[43]

Kellogg tells of a rare act of charity by Wirz, "It again came my turn to go out with the squad after wood. We obtained our scanty supply, and were on our way back to prison, when we stopped for a few moments to rest. I improved the opportunity to dig all the Red root that I could, as it was a valuable remedy for diarrhea, which was distressingly prevalent in camp. The sergeant in charge of the guard was rather cross and surly, and allowed us but a little time to get breath, and then ordered us on again. In my haste I left my knife upon the ground, and did not discover my loss until I was nearly back to the stockade. The sergeant then refused to let me return for it. I was just giving it up for lost, when Captain Wirz came riding along, and as a last resort I appealed to him. For a wonder he told me to go with him, and walking his horse, he went with me to the spot where I had used the knife, and thus I recovered it. If I had failed to find it, he would have doubtless thought I was guilty of deception, and shot me through without any remorse whatever. As we went toward the prison-gate, we met other guards of prisoners going after the wood, under guard, and seeing me in company with the 'Old Dutchman,' they supposed I had been captured in an attempt to escape, and consequently had a great many jokes at my expense. The captain noticing this, remarked to me, 'They thinks you have pen up to some devilment.' The next day when the guard was called for again to go out after wood, no one wished to go, and I concluded to try it once more, though my feet were pretty sore."[44]

Phillip Cashmeyer, employed as a special agent by General Winder, submitted an affidavit dated September 22nd, 1865, to Colonel Chipman, Judge Advocate at the Wirz trial. In it, he described Wirz this way: "He was an extremely profane man and very strict in the discharge of his duties, oftentimes severe toward prisoners. While I was at

---

[38] Lyons, p. 29.
[39] Miller, p. 37.
[40] Spencer, p. 56.
[41] S. W. Ashe, *Trial and Death of Henry Wirz With Other Matters Pertaining Thereto* (Raleigh: E. M. Uzzell & Co., Printers, 1908), p. 31.
[42] *Ibid.*, pp. 30, 31.
[43] McElroy, pp. 374, 375.
[44] Kellogg, pp. 152, 153.

Andersonville attending to business with General Winder I there heard of his inhumanity toward Federal prisoners, but saw none of it myself at this place. I was inclined to the belief that he was spoken of in this connection more for the purpose of bolstering him as being a good officer than anything else."[45]

Other authors described their feeling towards Wirz. "This captain was the commandant of the interior of the prison, and was a wretch of the first or worst degree; insolent, overbearing, heartless, and of course a coward, for no man but a coward, would come into camp and draw a revolver upon helpless men as he had done. He was said to have been a deserter from our army, but I could not vouch for the truth of it."[46] "The 'Old Dutchman' was none other than Captain Wirz himself, who was best known in prison by that name. Indeed, a stranger would have thought it his only title."[47] "I believe he could sit and see his own father roasted over a slow fire, or his mother eaten alive by ants and never show the tremor of a muscle."[48]

General Winder described his perception of Wirz, "Captain Wirz has proved himself to be a diligent and efficient officer, whose superior in commanding prisoners and incident duties I know not.[49]

Berry quoted Wirz as having said, "I had rather shoot every one of you than see you exchanged."[50]

Ferguson quoted Wirz: "I am of more use to the Confederate Government than General Lee and his army, for I kill more damned Yankees."[51]

"Captain Wirz never wore an out-and-out rebel uniform; it was generally a mixture... In summer time, or during warm weather, he generally wore light clothes linen clothes. As the weather became colder, he wore woolen clothes. I don't remember; he may have had on gray clothing."[52]

Dowling felt that Wirz daily grew more bitter, morose and dangerous. He blamed this on Wirz' "... being continually retained at Andersonville in this capacity, the failure to promote him, as he thought his arduous and valuable services demanded, and incessant potations of fiery Southern corn whisky, all tended to make him sullen, liable to fierce bursts of passion and likely to explode into sudden atrocity when least expected."[53]

John McElroy recounted the last day Wirz ventured into the pen alone. "That afternoon Wirz ventured into camp alone. He was assailed with a storm of curses and execrations, and a shower of clubs. He pulled out his revolver, as if to fire upon his assailants. A yell was raised to take his pistol away from him and a crowd rushed forward to do this. Without waiting to fire a shot, he turned and ran to the gate for dear life. He did not come in again for a long while, and never afterward without a retinue of guards."[54]

Fosdick said, "He wore a long calico gown, and around his waist a leather belt with 'C.S.A.' in large letters, in which was placed a large dirk knife and a pair of pistols. He wore a loose fitting pair of gray pants, a heavy-soled pair of cowhide shoes, and a tight gray skull cap with a long bill or fore piece. Thin, shaggy beard, tinged with gray, hid his features, and gave him a very unsoldierlke appearance."[55]

Another prisoner testified at the trial, "Captain Wirz generally wore in the summer months a white pair of pants and a round coat; I suppose that it was a coat that he got in the regiment while he was a private or sergeant or something; it looked as if it had been a government coat; it had gold lace on the sleeves and strips on the collar; when he got to camp he would generally pull that off, or when he got to his headquarters. He would generally have on thin white pants, and I don't know the color of his vest. He would always pull off his coat; he would not be in his shirt sleeves; I think he always wore a vest."[56]

McElroy described Wirz as "... an undersized, fidgety man, with an insignificant face, and a mouth that protruded like a rabbit's. His bright little eyes, like those of a squirrel or a rat, assisted in giving his countenance a look of kinship to the family of rodent animals - a genus which lives by stealth and cunning, subsisting on that which it can steal away from stronger and braver creatures. He was dressed in a pair of gray trousers, with the other part of his body covered with a calico garment, like that which small boys used to wear, called 'waists.' This was fastened to

---

[45] *O. R.*, VIII, p. 754.
[46] Kellogg, p. 87.
[47] *Ibid.*, p. 115.
[48] Lyons, p. 30.
[49] *O. R.*, VII, p. 179.
[50] Chester D. Berry, *Loss of the Sultana and Reminiscences of Survivors* (Lansing, Mich.: Darius D. Thorp, 1892), p. 179.
[51] Joseph Ferguson, *Life-Struggles in Rebel Prisons: A Record of the Sufferings, Escapes, Adventures and Starvation of the Union Prisoners* (Philadelphia, Pa.: James M. Ferguson, Publisher, 1865), p. 79.
[52] *Wirz Trial*, p. 590.
[53] Dowling, p. 137.
[54] McElroy, pp. 144, 145.
[55] Fosdick, p. 36.
[56] *Wirz Trial*, p. 502.

the pantaloons by buttons, precisely as was the custom with the garments of boys struggling with the orthography of words in two syllables. Upon his head was perched a little gray cap. Sticking in his belt, and fastened to his wrist by a strap two or three feet long, was one of those formidable looking, but harmless English revolvers, that have ten barrels around the edge of the cylinder, and fire a musket bullet from the center. The wearer of this composite costume, and bearer of this amateur arsenal, stepped nervously about and sputtered volubly in very broken English."[57]

These descriptions of, possibly, the most despised man of the 19th century varied widely. Wirz' countenance, depicted by drawing or described by words, was grotesquely proportional to the amount of kindness or wrath he bestowed on the prisoners.

Wirz wrote, on May 8th, 1864, a self-assessment of his position at Andersonville in a report forwarded to Richmond. "I am here in a very unpleasant position, growing out of the rank which I now hold, and suggest the propriety of being promoted. Having the full control of the prison, and consequently of the daily prison guard, the orders which I have to give are very often not obeyed with the promptness the occasion requires, and I am of opinion that it emanates from the reluctance of obeying an officer who holds the same rank as they do My duties are manifold and require all my time in daytime and very often part of the night, and I would most respectfully ask that two commissioned officers (lieutenants) would be assigned to me for duty.[58]

Wirz felt, at that time, that he deserved a promotion to the rank of Major. He felt the position he held warranted a higher rank and that those under him would respond more promptly to a higher rank. He would obtain the rank of Major in the spring of 1865.

The following was taken from the very interesting monograph written by Fred Edmunds concerning the history of Jean Alexander Francois LeMat and the pistol he designed: "The sidearm used by (Wirz), and probably the most intriguing of all sidearms used in the Civil War, was the 'grapeshot revolver' devised by a Parisian-born medical doctor named Jean Alexander Francois LeMat. Born in Paris in 1824, LeMat went through school there, then came to New Orleans in the 1840s where he met the beautiful Sophie Leprete, the daughter of a wealthy planter. They were married, and LeMat became immediately enamored of the Southern way of life. Doctor LeMat practiced medicine in New Orleans, but was more interested in invention than medicine. His inventive genius produced a percussion revolver, which had more firepower than any of its contemporaries. It consisted of a nine-shot .42 caliber cylinder, rotating upon a central barrel of .63 caliber, which contained a cartridge loaded with buckshot or 'grapeshot' as it was then called. This grapeshot barrel was fired by an easy and fast manual adjustment to the face of the hammer. Truly an ingenious device...

"Receiving his U.S. patent on October 21st, 1856, LeMat shortly thereafter became acquainted with a major serving with the U.S. Corps of Engineers, and stationed in New Orleans, by the name of Pierre Gustave Toutant Beauregard, later to become a famous Confederate general. They struck up an immediate friendship which resulted in their becoming partners with Beauregard obtaining a ¼ share of the LeMat patent rights in exchange for promoting the pistol and some financial input. Through Beauregard's influence the LeMat revolver was tested by the U.S. Ordnance Bureau and was considered a great improvement over the Colt, showing 'a merit which is not known to be possessed by any other pistol now in use.' There was no follow-up by the U.S. Government, and the LeMat was not to see Federal service.

"Shortly after the U.S. tested the pistol, the political climate between North and South deteriorated to the extent that the bursting point was near, so Doctor LeMat proceeded with all haste to attempt to get his grapeshot revolver marketed for the defense of the South. He at first approached Cook & Brother in New Orleans, but they were too heavily engaged in manufacturing longarms and edged weapons to become involved in revolver manufacture.

"He traveled back to Paris and formed a business arrangement with Charles Girard, whereby the latter obtained ¾ths of the patent rights to the LeMat pistol, and took on the responsibility of its manufacturer and delivery to the South, filling the contract requirements agreed to by LeMat and the Confederate Government. Major Beauregard's ¼ interest was bought out by LeMat.

"July of 1861, saw an order of 400 LeMat revolvers by the Confederate navy, which were delivered approximately one year later to Richmond, and most of which (360 or so) were diverted to Confederate cavalry use, where they were badly needed.

[57] McElroy, pp. 142, 143.
[58] *O. R.*, VII, p. 170.

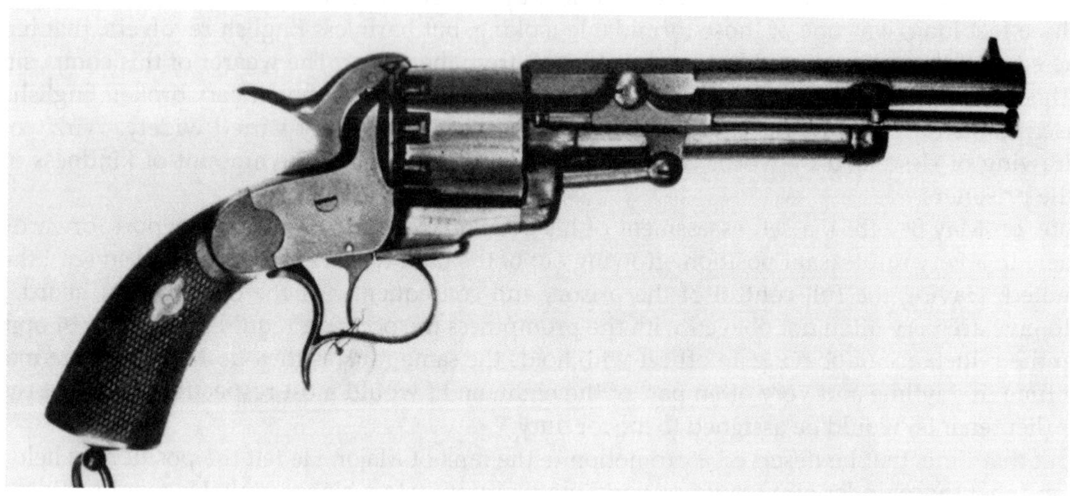

**Le Mat Two-Barrel Revolver (First Model)** - Type of pistol carried by Captain Wirz - Had 9-shot cylinder caliber .42 and a .63 smooth bore "shot gun." (Author's Collection)

"Many of these First Model LeMats found use by famous Confederates. J.E.B. Stuart's was #115; #163 had a silver inlay in the grip indicating use by 'Co. A 18th Ga.'; #189 by Henry Wirz, notorious commandant of Andersonville prison; #303 carried by a colonel in the Chesterfield Dragoons; #88 by General John Lewis, Louisiana State Militia.

By October, 1862, 1100 LeMat pistols had been shipped by the Confederacy, with subsequent production up to approximately #2500 having been shipped from 1863 to 1865."[59]

The prisoners always ridiculed Wirz for the large, bulky, ostentatious pistol he carried. Sometimes he carried the more customary Southern sidearm, a Colt pistol.

John Henry Winder was born in Somerset County, Maryland, on February 21, 1800, the son of General William Henry Winder and Gertrude Polk Winder. General William Henry Winder commanded the American forces in the War of 1812, whose defeat led to the burning and destruction of Washington by the British. John Henry Winder's birthplace was located on the Delmarva Peninsula just 50 miles or so from the birthplace of his cousin, Dick Winder, in the adjacent Accomac County in Virginia. He was a cadet at the U.S. Military Academy from August 5, 1814, until he graduated six years later on June 30, 1820, at the age of twenty, receiving his commission as second lieutenant on July 1st. At West Point, Winder "... was engaged in a meeting and joining in a combination against his superior officers." John C. Calhoun, then Secretary of War, saved him from punishment.[60]

He served in Florida for about a year and then resigned his commission in 1823. John Winder married Elizabeth Shepherd and had one son, William A. Winder. After the death of his wife and his father, he requested reappointment to the army and returned to West Point as an instructor of tactics and taught Jefferson Davis and Robert E. Lee when they were there as cadets. While still a young officer, stationed at Fort Johnson in Southport, North Carolina, near Wilmington, he again married. His bride was a young widow named Caroline Cox Eagles. They were married at the 250-year-old St. James Episcopal Church in Wilmington.[61] They had two sons, John Cox Winder,[62] born in October, 1831, at Southport, and William Sidney Winder, born in July, 1833.

Winder served from 1836 to 1840 in the Florida Territory, then served in Maine and, in 1845, went back to the Florida Territory.[63] He was brevetted major and lieutenant colonel for gallant and conspicuous conduct during the Mexican War of 1846. In 1849, Winder went to the garrison at Fort Columbus in New York. For the next decade he spent most of his time in Florida and at Fort Moultrie at Charleston, South Carolina.[64]

---

[59] Fred Edmunds, with permission of the author.

[60] Spencer, p. 45.

[61] Correspondence from Mr. J. Winder Hughes, the great grandson of John Henry Winder, in the author's possession.

[62] John Cox Winder lived in Portsmouth, Virginia, became a Major, C.S.A., vice-president of the Seabord Airline Railway, and died on March 22, 1896 at his residence in Raleigh, North Carolina.

[63] Sarah Annette Duffy, "Military Administrator: The Controversial Life of Brigadier General John Henry Winder, C.S.A." (Creighton University, Omaha: Master of Arts dissertation, 1961), pp. 27, 28.

[64] *Ibid.*, pp. 35-38.

**Brigadier General John Henry Winder** -wearing pre-war major's uniform. Note the "3" in the crossed cannon insignia on his Hardee hat. (Museum of the Confederacy)

Winder resigned his commission as major, Third Artillery, (the Maryland Flying Artillery), on April 27, 1861. Rather stout and too old to be an active line officer, he was assigned on July 16th by Robert E. Lee to command the Camp of Instruction at Hermitage Fair Ground (sometimes called the New Fair Grounds) in Richmond. Two days later, he was relieved of this command by Colonel Dimmock of the Virginia Volunteers and was made provost general of Richmond. This office not only gave him responsibility for the prison camps in the vicinity but also for the arrest of spies, the return of deserters, and the maintenance of order in a city swollen to more than twice its normal size by the war.[65]

General Winder mostly used soldiers to enforce his edicts but he also used many civilian Marylanders. These alien detectives were mostly from Baltimore, Philadelphia, and other Northern cities. They became known as "Plug Uglies" and were much dreaded and despised by many Richmonders who had been the subject of their quasi-legal searches and seizures. The term "Plug Ugly" was first used to describe the hooligans belonging to the Know Nothing elections of 1859.[66]

John B. Jones, in his diary concerning wartime Richmond said, "For some time past (but since the battle of Manassas) quite a number of Northern and Baltimore policemen have made their appearance in Richmond. Some of these, if not indeed all of them, have been employed by General Winder. They are illiterate men, of low instincts and desperate characters. But their low cunning will serve them here among unsuspecting men. They will, if necessary, give information to the enemy themselves, for the purpose of convincing the authorities that a detective police is indispensable; and it is probable a number of them will be, all the time, on the pay-rolls of Lincoln.[67]

Among these Plug Uglies were three detectives who would be seen later at Andersonville: James W. Duncan of New Orleans, W. J. Humes of Baltimore, and a man named Bowers.

Though hated by most of the citizens of Richmond, Winder, most critics agree, was an efficient and educated administrator who succeeded despite the complexity of his many duties and the emotional chaos of the times. General Winder commanded or controlled the camp of instruction, the detention of the POWs, the issuance of passports, the issuance of liquor licenses, mail between the lines by the Flag of Truce Boat, the arrest of subversives, the registration of soldiers visiting Richmond, the care of deserters, the care of the wounded, the burial of the dead and surveillance of enemy spies.[68]

For most of the first year of the war, the fixing of some commodity prices for the inhabitants of the Confederate capital fell upon Winder. In March, John B. Jones wrote, in his *Diary*, that General Winder's detectives were very busy. "They have been forging prescriptions to catch the poor Richmond apothecaries. When the brandy is thus obtained it is confiscated, and the money withheld for selling the banned alcohol. They drink the brandy, and imprison the apothecaries."[69] The apothecaries, arrested and imprisoned, were tried and acquitted by a court-martial. Jones said, "General Winder endorsed on the order for their discharge; 'Not approved, and you may congratulate your-

---

[65] *Ezra J. Warner, Generals in Gray* (Baton Rouge: L.S.U. Press, 1975), pp. 340, 341.
[66] Duffy, p. 65.
[67] John B. Jones, *A Rebel War Clerk's Diary*, Earl Schenck Miers, ed. (New York: A. S. Barnes & Co., Inc., 1961), p. 39.
[68] Duffy, pp. 44-47 and 87, 88.
[69] John B. Jones, p. 70.

selves upon escaping a merited punishment'."[70] In his eagerness to destroy all contraband whiskey, his Plug Uglies destroyed much of the Richmond apothecary Elijah Baker's celebrated patent medicine, "Baker's Bitters."

On March 5th, 1862, martial law was declared for the city of Richmond by the suspension of the Writ of Habeas Corpus within 10 miles of the city. This was later extended to include the city of Petersburg.[71] The *Richmond Enquirer* presented several editorials condemning the martial law and passport systems, both of which were quite stringent; the Richmond paper also condemned the new law's enforcement by military court martials rather than by civil courts.

On March 12th, according to Jones, "General Winder moved the passport office up to the corner of Ninth and Broad Streets. The office at the corner of Ninth and Broad Streets was a filthy one; it was inhabited - for they slept there - by his rowdy clerks. And when I stepped to the hydrant for a glass of water, the tumbler repulsed me by the smell of Whiskey."[72] The offices of the Provost Marshal were located in the new frame building at the southwest corner of Tenth and Broad Streets after having first been located on the southside of Main Street three doors above Ninth Street.[73] This building became known as the "Winder Building" and after the war it was occupied by the Freedmen's Bureau.

**The Winder Building in Richmond** - This was the building that housed General Winder's office. It was located on the southwest corner of Tenth and Broad Streets. (Harper's Weekly)

This office was almost constantly besieged by large crowds of people wishing to go to various points. "General Winder has established a guard with fixed bayonets at the door of the passport office. They let in only a few at a time, and these, when they get their passports, pass out by the rear door, it being impossible for them to return through the crowd."[74]

In April, Congress finally had to limit the punishment dispensed by Winder to thirty days hard labor and limit his arrests to persons who had committed offenses against the government.

The rumor circulated that, if the pockets of the Plug Uglies were lined, then a passport could be obtained.

The Baltimore papers constantly revealed information about the military situation in the capital of the Confederacy, and many times they would publish the passport allowing their source to pass through the lines. "I doubt not they are sold by the detectives, Winder being ignorant."[75] It became so universally thought people were using passports obtained from the alien policemen and to transmit military intelligence to the North, General Lee's pickets

[70] *Ibid.*, p. 71.
[71] *O. R.*, XI, Part 3, p. 403.
[72] John B. Jones, p. 69.
[73] The Confederate Museum and et., *Illustrated Guide to Richmond, the Confederate Capital* (Richmond: the William Byrd Press, 1960), p. 12.
[74] John B. Jones, p. 69.
[75] *Ibid.*, p. 91.

would not honor passports obtained from General Winder or from his Provost Marshal. Because of this military secrecy, many officers returning from furlough were unable to find the location of their regiment. They had to go to John B. Jones in the Secretary of War's office to get a recognized passport to Lee's headquarters.[76] Thus, passports could be obtained from the clerk, John B. Jones, but, on July 19th, 1862, "... the whole business of passports" was turned over to General Winder by the Secretary of War. This decision was later reversed to allow Jones to issue passports to persons going to the camps near Richmond, but Winder was responsible for passports to more distant points.[77]

General Winder wrote a letter from Richmond on April 30th, 1862, to the Secretary of War, G. W. Randolph, recommending that his son, Captain John C. Winder, be appointed a captain in the Engineer Corps of the Confederate States. Captain John Winder had served as an engineer with the North Carolina Troops at the mouth of the Cape Fear River at Wilmington. His commission "... expired by limitation," referring to a law stated that his commission expired at a given time if he did not raise a company. He was so busy in the performance of his duties that he was ordered not to take the time to raise a company.

A Confederate General Order No. 46 on April 20th, 1863, told the results of this or another General Court Martial trial of Major Elias Griswold for giving a written permit to another person "... to bring into Richmond ninety-one barrels of brandy, in violation of the lawful command of his superior officer, Brig. Gen. Jno. H. Winder." The Court was "...lenient in its sentence, because it is satisfied... [the offense] arose from inadvertence and was not accompanied with any evil intent or improper purpose... " and it sentenced the Major to be reprimanded "privately" by the Commander of the Department of Henrico (i.e., General Winder).

On Saturday, November the 21st, Major Griswold's head of the passport office, Lieutenant Kirk, was arrested on the charge of selling passports at $100 per man to a Mr. Wolf and a Mr. Head, who were in prison and made the charge.[78]

In December, another Winder appointee, Captain G. W. Alexander, of Castle Thunder, was arrested for malfeasance in office."[79]

Due to anti-Maryland sentiments in Richmond, a bill was introduced on January 15th, 1863, that subjected Marylanders to conscription, much to the delight of most Richmonders.

In April, 1863, the Honorable Herschel V. Johnson and Senator B. H. Hill wrote, without Winder's knowledge, asking the President and Secretary of War to promote Winder to major general. They cited Winder's efficiency, patience, industry, energy, and fidelity since assuming command in Richmond.

The Plug Uglies made lots of money in their speculating or, more correctly, smuggling operations. They went back and forth between the lines, carrying contraband or carrying items common in the North but scarce in the South. In December of 1863, "... a Baltimorean, last week seeing a steamer there loading with goods of various kinds for the Federal prisoners here, bought a box of merchandise for $300, and put it on board, marked as if it contained stores for the prisoners. He ran the blockade so as to meet the steamer here; and obtained the box, worth, perhaps, $15,000."[80]

In November of 1864, 100 passports were given by Winder's office to leave the Confederate States by the new Provost Marshal I.H. Carrington and the War Department. The illegal sale of passports continued throughout the war.[81]

One of the men who evidently made several trips through the lines was General Winder's son, William Sidney Winder. He was captured at least two times passing through the lines. It is not known for what purpose he was traveling between Baltimore and Richmond. Was he on assignment for the Government as a courier or spy? Or was he on some personal, greed-inspired, speculation business?

Port Royal, a small town about 35 miles south of Fredericksburg on the Rappahannock River, was thought, by the Federals, to be a regular stopping point for secret traffic traveling between Baltimore and Richmond. Because of his suspicion, Major General Ambrose E. Burnside, ordered the steamboat *Cooper's Point,* under the command of Captain O. Lachemeyer, to carry a small force of about thirty men with two brass howitzers to intercept any suspicious men commuting on this route. Contrabands told the Federals that "... recruits for the rebel Army were being

[76] *Ibid.*, p. 83.
[77] *Ibid.*, pp. 90, 91.
[78] *Ibid.*, p. 310.
[79] Emory M. Thomas, *The Confederate State of Richmond* (Austin: University of Texas Press, 1974), p. 154.
[80] John B. Jones, p. 318.
[81] *Ibid.*, p. 454.

ferried across the river to Port Royal, and passed thence to Richmond, and that arms, goods, and stores of various kinds were also safely sent by the same route." Nelson Provost, commander of the expedition reported to his commanding officer on August 16th, 1862, the particulars of the action. "About midnight a Negro named Richard Parker brought me word that a wagon load of goods had arrived and was waiting transportation across the river. Taking Captain Lachemeyer and ten men I ascended the bank and a short distance from the ferry found and arrested three young men, who acknowledged that they were on their way to Richmond to join the rebel Army. About half an hour later a party of ten more in a four-horse wagon came up and were met and held in talk by Captain Lachemeyer (who led them to suppose him to be a rebel soldier) until I arrived with a fresh detachment and took them prisoners.

Some of them were armed with pistols, but a careful search of their baggage revealed no papers except [a few] of little importance, which were sent to General Burnside, [along with a few] letters."[82] Among the prisoners was William Sidney Winder.

Another incident involving William Sidney Winder was described by Nelson Provost, when he told of the capture of the schooner *Exchange* on December 28th, 1862. The schooner was captured on the Rappahannock River for "... not having any permit or pass from the Department... There were two men on this vessel when captured, who stated that they came here on account of the weather for harbor, and also stated they were bound for Baltimore, where Mr. Trader, the owner, would meet them, he having the required papers. Their names are James Marchant and William Winder. They having no papers, I seized her as a prize to the United States."[83]

Another one of General Winder's two sons was captured, as is seen in the following anecdote of an incident that happened in the latter part of the summer of 1863. The incident, described by Frank E. Moran, probably involved Captain John C. Winder. "One day in the spring of 1863, two mounted men in the uniform and equipment of Federal captains appeared at a fortified Union camp in East Tennessee and presented an order from the War Department at Washington commanding them to make a careful survey of the post and an immediate report as to the number and condition of the troops present, the character of the earthworks, and the general facilities for defense in case of assault.

"In obedience to this order the colonel then in command of the post received the messengers courteously and afforded them every possible facility for the performance of their duty. Having made full and careful drafts of the breastworks, and sketched their surrounding exposures, they dined with their obliging host, who gave them all further verbal information they sought, thanked him for his courtesy, mounted their horses and departed. It chanced that at this very moment General James H. Wilson rode up to the tent, and casually glancing at the two officers leaving, and thinking vaguely that he recognized in one of them a former acquaintance whom he could not place, inquired carelessly of the colonel the names of his visitors. In answer the War Department's order was handed him, and this he proceeded to read with an interest that soon increased to suspicion, and, finally convinced that all was not right, he directed that the two men, who had now a good start on their return journey, should be overtaken and returned to his presence for further inquiry as to their mission and identity.

"A small but well-armed squadron was instantly mounted, and advancing rapidly by a parallel road, the two men were soon intercepted and informed that their immediate return to the camp was desired by General Wilson, who awaited them. Their protests were vigorous, but as they were informed that these orders were not debatable, and as a successful resistance was not possible, they sullenly accompanied their escort back to headquarters. The men were sharply interrogated by General Wilson; but they calmly reiterated their previous statements to the colonel, and pointed with cool dignity to the order of the War Department in confirmation of their authority and identity.

"General Wilson, confronting the man whom he first recognized, asked him directly if he was not so-and-so (calling him by name), whom he had known at a certain time prior to the war, at West Point, and if was not now an officer of the Confederate army, and his companion also. The officer with emphasis answered, 'No' whereupon General Wilson stepped quickly to his side, and, without ceremony drew the officers sword half-way out of the scabbard, and behold, upon the blade was the name by which the General had addressed him, and under the tell-tale initials, 'C.S.A.'...

"A court-martial was at once convened, composed of officers of the post. The evidence was clear and conclusive, a verdict of guilty was unanimously rendered, and in conformity with the stern military law and usages of war relating to spies, the bold but unlucky adventurers were hanged the next morning."[84]

The circumstances surrounding this hanging incident was again related by Moran: "A few days later the com-

[82] Author's library.
[83] *Naval O. R.*, V, p. 209.
[84] Frank E. Moran, *Bastiles of the Confederacy* (Baltimore, Md.: 1890), pp. 8-11.

mandant at Libby Prison summoned into one of the lower rooms of the prison all the Federal captives 'of the rank of captain.' Many of the prisoners, fondly hoping that this unusual summons betokened their exchange, fell into close ranks and were boisterously merry.

"But an ominous silence ensued as they looked into the colorless face of the Confederate officer as he opened with a nervous hand an official-looking document and proceeded to read it in a voice that revealed his strong agitation. It was an order from his superior, General John H. Winder, commanding that, 'by direction of the Confederate Secretary of War,' two Federal captains should be drawn by lot from among those now present for immediate execution, this measure having been decided upon in retaliation for the 'lawless execution' of two Confederate officers in Tennessee by the Federal commander of that department. The method of the drawing was with grim courtesy left in the lottery of death...

"The full name, rank and command of each man was plainly written on white ballots, cast into a hat, and shaken up... an aged Union chaplain then in Libby was induced to make the drawing.

"The venerable man, with his eyes bandaged and with a silent and fervent prayer on his lips, drew forth the first ballot; and the Confederate officer, amid the stillness of death, announced the name of Captain Henry W. Sawyer as the first victim, and the next slip bore the name of Captain John Flynn...

"The doomed men received the announcement of their fate with the composure that became brave soldiers. They were taken to a small, dark cell in the middle cellar, to their await their execution, which was to take place within a few days, and the rest of the officers were sent back to their former quarters...the execution of the two men was fixed to take place the next day at Camp Lee, near Richmond, the usual place for military executions. Both men wrote tender messages of farewell to their loved ones, and at an early hour next morning they left their cells, and mounting horses -- the death-sentence having been first read to them -- they proceeded, under a strong mounted guard, toward the place of execution...they were near the fatal ground when an officer, overtaking them on horseback, rode to the head of the escort and handed the officer in charge a paper...He saluted and dismissed the messenger with a few inaudible words, and giving the command 'right about!' the squadron,. . . began a brisk return in the direction of Richmond.

"The facts were reported to General Butler at Fortress Monroe, and were by him swiftly transmitted to Washington. The case was discussed in Cabinet meeting, and aroused deep indignation at the North. Mr. Stanton was authorized to place the matter in the hands of General Butler, 'with full power,' and Butler acted with characteristic promptness and vigor. He politely notified the Confederate authorities at Richmond, and without argument, that on the same day and hour that Captain Sawyer and Flynn should be executed, he would hang General William H. F. Lee and Captain Winder, both of whom were then his prisoners at Fortress Monroe. The former was a nephew of General Robert E. Lee, the latter a son of Jefferson Davis's particular friend John H. Winder, Commissary General of Federal prisoners.

"The checkmate was superb and complete."[85]

Harry E. Neal, in an article called "Rebels, Ropes, and Reprieves" published in the *Civil War Times Illustrated*, told about this incident. The two Confederate captains executed in Tennessee were William F. Corbin and T. G. McGraw.

The Libby prisoners were assembled at daylight on the 6th of July and Captain T. P. Turner read his orders:

> *Headquarters, Department Henrico*
> *Richmond, July fourth, 1863*
> *Special Orders No. 160*
>
> *Captain T. P. Turner, Commanding Confederate States Prison, is hereby directed to select by lot from among the Federal captains now in his custody, two of that number for execution.*
>
> *Signed,*
> *John H. Winder, Brigadier General*

The men themselves were given the option of determining how the two were to be selected. Captain Henry W. Sawyer of Company K, 1st New Jersey Cavalry, suggested that a number of black and white beans be mixed in a hat and held aloft by a Federal prisoner chaplain. The first two prisoners to draw black beans would be the two designated for execution. The first black bean was called the "First Death Prize" and the next was the "Second Death Prize."

---

[85] *Ibid.*, pp. 11-16.

Sawyer, who had been captured at Brandy Station, drew first and drew a black bean. Captain John M. Flynn, 51st Indiana, drew second and he, too, drew a black bean.

Captain Turner left immediately and reported to General Winder the names of the two prisoners. At ten o'clock, another officer came in and told them that they were to hang at noon that same day. They were given permission to write to their loved ones before being conveyed by an ox-drawn cart, with a cavalry guard commanded by an officer, to a hill overlooking the city. On the way there, they were overtaken by a Roman Catholic bishop who asked the Confederate officer to go slowly so that the bishop could plead before Jeff Davis for a delay. The Confederate officer promised not to hang them until the designated time of noon.

"The men's hands were tied behind their backs after arriving at a large oak tree on the hill selected for the execution site. After standing in the cart, Sawyer asked permission to sit down at 11:30. At about five minutes to noon, they were told to stand again. Off in the distance, a cloud of dust indicated the approach of a rider bringing a ten-day reprieve granted by President Davis.

After receiving a letter from her husband, Mrs. Sawyer went to see Lincoln on July 14th. The next day, Lincoln, "... after conferring with his advisers and Major General Henry W. Halleck," ordered Colonel W. H. Ludlow, his Agent for the Exchange of Prisoners, to notify Judge Robert Ould of his solution to the Confederate threat to execute two Federal Prisoners. Lincoln selected Brigadier General William H. F. Lee, who was recovering from wounds received at Brandy Station, as one of his two hostages. Ludlow selected Captain Robert H. Tyler, a captain in the Eighth Virginia Infantry, as the second hostage.[86]

Robert H. Tyler wrote to Colonel Robert Ould, Commissioner for Exchange of Prisoners and stated that he, a "... Captain Winder," and Brigadier General William H. F. Lee, were taken into close confinement at the Old Capitol prison in Washington on the 16th of July, 1863, to be held, supposedly, as hostages for the two Yankee prisoners. The letter was written on October 8th.[87] Prutsman said the two held were Captains Fitzhugh Lee and John S. Winder (sic).[88]

Sawyer and Flynn were kept in the dungeon for twenty days, then returned to the general prisoner population. In March of 1864, they were exchanged at City Point on the James River.

After his death, Stonewall Jackson's body was brought to Richmond where it lay in state in the Capitol. His body lay visible through a glass pane in the coffin until his funeral on May 12th. All the pallbearers were generals and among those generals was General Winder. The general's servant led his war-horse. The President Davis followed near the hearse in a carriage. The heads of the various departments followed the carriage, walking two by two, the first two being Secretary Benjamin and Secretary Seddon. All along the route were flags and people wearing black feathers.[89]

In August, John B. Jones, in his *Diary,* said the Adjutant-General, "by order" (he supposed of Jeff Davis), was annulling, one after another, all of General Winder's despotic orders.[90] "In both Houses of Congress they are thundering away at General Winder's Provost Marshal and his Plug Ugly alien policemen."[91] He was, near the 9th of October, ordered by the President not to issue any more passports to people desiring to head North.[92]

On October 29th, General Winder dismissed all of the Plug Ugly policemen attached to the provost marshal's office, for "... malfeasance, corruption, bribery, and incompetence." Their removal was probably ordered by President Davis, who had been prompted by the sentiments of the citizens of Richmond. Winder dismissed all his detectives except Cashmeyer, "... about the worst of them."[93]

Most descriptions of the Plug Uglies imply they were ignorant, stupid, graft-receiving, thugs. The writings of Phillip Cashmeyer demonstrate he was an erudite and articulate gentlemen. In one letter, Cashmeyer said he was there at Andersonville "... attending to business with General Winder."[94]

General Winder replaced the alien police of Marylanders with Virginians more acceptable to Richmonders.

By the fall of 1863, General Winder was looking for places to disperse the burdensome prisoners. He wrote, on November 3rd, to Major Sutherlin in Danville, asking what housing and provisions were available there for the 4,000

---

[86] Harry E. Neal, "Rebels, Ropes, and Reprieves," *Civil War Times Illustrated* (Gettysburg, Pa.: February 1976), pp. 30-35.
[87] *O. R.*, VI, p. 362.
[88] C. M. Prutsman, *A Soldier's Experience in Southern Prisons* (New York: Andrew H. Kellogg, 1901), p. 18.
[89] John B. Jones, p. 207.
[90] *Ibid.*, p. 93.
[91] *Ibid.* p. 95.
[92] *Ibid.*, p 106.
[93] *Ibid.*, p. 111.
[94] *O. R.*, VIII, p. 754.

prisoners he wished to forward from Richmond. The major replied that he had only been able to rent two houses to put up the prisoners, that there were no provisions available and that about thirty days' rations should be sent with the prisoners. He also said a very energetic officer should accompany them to provide supplies which would have to be scavenged from the surrounding district.[95]

General Winder lived in a house on Sixth Street, between Clay and Leigh Streets about five blocks from his headquarters in the wooden Winder Building at the corner of Tenth and Broad Streets. The home of General Winder, the person responsible for the protection and security of fife and property in Richmond, was burglarized on the night of November 18th.

Just as many Richmonders thought Winder too zealously enforced civilian regulations, most prisoners in the twenty-odd prisons in and around Richmond blamed Winder for their harsh treatment and for the lack of food.

Not all prisoners thought General Winder was brutal. Congressman Alfred Ely, of New York, who was captured at Manassas and held in Liggon prison, once described Winder by saying he "... has treated me with the utmost kindness and respect, and his demeanor and general courtesy of manner, when he visits the officers, indicate a strict disciplinarian, it is true; but a person at the same time of humane feelings, and not disposed to exercise his power beyond its proper limits."[96]

On January 14th, a letter was received by the Secretary of War from a Mr. Stephens, of Columbia, South Carolina, who, evidently, lived in Richmond. The letter meant to inform the President that Winder drank excessively, was brutish to all but Marylanders, and habitually received bribes. President Davis endorsed the letter; because of the absence of specifications, no action on his part was necessary.[97] During January, investigations in the courts continued to show that, during General Winder's "Reign of Terror," passports sold for as much as $2,000. each.[98]

Winder raised troops from the prisons in and around Richmond. "From the hodgepodge of deserters and reprobates lodged in Castle Thunder emerged four companies of infantry for Lee's army--'The Winders Legion'."[99]

A Mr. J. J. Sloan, from Greensborough, North Carolina, wrote, on February 2nd, 1864, to Secretary of War , and told of the loyal Carolinians' complaints about General Winder and his rule in Richmond. He wrote: "They call it an outrage on our rights to be governed by foreigners from Maryland; state that our people are insulted and cursed by General Winder, who is regarded here as a depraved, corrupt, and drunken man, who has received bribes on more than one occasion to allow men from this and the adjoining county of Alamance to carry liquor into Richmond, - a fact of which they declare themselves ready at any time to produce witnesses from among the parties who sold the liquor. These factionists complain that our people are hunted about the city by spies - low rowdies from Baltimore - under the control of General Winder and one Griswold; that it is not safe for them to walk the streets on legitimate business, for while doing so some of our people have been arrested by these detectives and carried before Winder and subjected to the most insulting treatment and profanely abused. Of these facts you will be made acquainted on the oath of some of our best citizens."

This letter carried the following endorsement by Seddon. "There is not a particle of justice in the allegations against General Winder. That officer may err in being sometimes over-zealous, but his honor, honesty, and loyalty are beyond all question. I wish his accusers had half his purity and devotion to our great cause."[100]

Even "Special Detective" Phillip Cashmeyer was imprisoned in Castle Thunder after being charged with "... giving information to the enemy by sending letters to the North." General Winder was able to get the charge against Cashmeyer "... reduced to simple indiscretion" and, after getting him released, Winder put Cashmeyer back on his staff in his original position.[101]

Two prisoners mistakenly placed General Winder at Andersonville in February of 1864. In fact, one of them, Ralph O. "Billy" Bates said he had arrived at Andersonville after dark on February 11, 1863 [sic], and that General Winder was there upon his arrival.[102]

On May 25th, General Braxton Bragg relieved General Winder from duty in Richmond and ordered him to report to General P. G. T. Beauregard, who gave him command of the Second District, Department of North Carolina and Southern Virginia, with headquarters in Goldsborough, North Carolina. Winder had jurisdiction over such cities

---

95 Letter in his military records, National Archives.
96 *Ibid.*, p. 61.
97 John B. Jones, p. 325.
98 *Ibid.*, p. 438.
99 Thomas, p. 171.
100 *O. R.*, LI, pp. 815, 816.
101 Duffy, p. 105.
102 McElroy, pp. 132, 133.

as Weldon, Goldsborough, Kinston, Plymouth and Washington.[103] When Winder left Richmond, he took some of the Plug Uglies with him, including his friend, "Special Confidential Detective" Cashmeyer.

So many Marylanders had been excused from service because they were refugees from an occupied territory; on June 15th, President Davis decided the Marylanders in Richmond were to be considered either "residents," or "alien enemies." If they were the former, they must fight -- if the latter, they were to be expelled.[104]

Winder's reputation in relation to the prisons in Richmond was so bad the *Richmond Examiner* said, when he was sent South, "Thank God that Richmond is at least Rid of old Winder! God have mercy upon those to whom he has been sent!" His love of alcohol beverages was implied by the following poem:

*At the head of Richmond post they've placed a Marylander,*
*And like the devil in regions lost there sits General Winder.*
*He snaps and snarls, he rips and swears, whether sober or tight.*
*The old villain's heart's as black as his head is white.*
*All through this vicinity they hate him as hard as they can,*
*Nor ever slander him with the epithet of decent man.*
*However mean, he's a patriot, that may be understood,*
*For when he left the Yankee land, 'twas for his country's good.*[105]

General Winder stayed in North Carolina only a few days before being ordered to Andersonville on June 3rd because General Howell Cobb stated that an officer of rank was required there.

Major Thomas P. Turner had been sent, on April 30th, to inspect Andersonville and, on May 8th, he wrote to General Samuel Cooper, Adjutant and Inspector General, the following recommendation: "I wish to say one word in regard to the command at Andersonville. Great confusion and serious difficulties have existed in regard to rank among the officers, quarrels and contentions as to who ranks and commands, all tending to disturb the good order, discipline, and proper conduct of the post and prison. I beg leave to suggest that if the commandant of the post is to command the prison he should be of such rank and experience as to silence all contentions; otherwise the commandant of the prison should be independent of the post commandant, and he himself should be of such rank as to control those who report to him from day to day for duty."[106]

General Winder left Goldsborough on June 10th, went by way of Charleston, South Carolina, and arrived at Andersonville on June 17th.[107] He brought with him Captain Sid Winder, Assistant Adjutant General and Lieutenant R. W. Brown, aide-de-camp. Spencer said Winder was made commander of the post at Andersonville, and the county of Sumter, in which it was located.

Mistakenly, Northrop stated that, on Saturday, June 4th, "Wirz, Gen. John H. Winder, commissary general of prisoners, Howell Cobb, and several minor personages came inside on horseback and rode partly through the prison and along the stockade over the dead line as far as possible."[108]

General Winder wrote to General Cooper explaining he had been told by the officer who established the post at Andersonville (i.e., his son, Sid Winder) there was but one house in the town. He, therefore, requested he be allowed to set up his headquarters and secure quarters for him and his family in Americus, a beautiful town about ten miles south of Andersonville, close enough by rail to allow him to "... exercise perfect supervision of the post." Secretary of War Seddon turned down the request, saying General Winder was needed at Andersonville proper because his presence alone "... would have a beneficial effect upon the guard and the prisoners. He can inspect frequently the prisons and see that subordinate officers discharge their duties fully, and in the event of any emeute (French: riot) to take prompt measures for quelling it."[109] General Winder was to report directly to the Secretary of War, since the prison was not considered a part of any military department in the State of Georgia.[110]

Warren Lee Goss described General Winder as, "... a man apparently about sixty years of age, dressed in homespun Secesh citizen clothes, butternut-coat and gray pants, tall, spare, and straight in figure, with an austere expression of face, a firm, set mouth, a large Roman nose, like a parrot's beak, and a cold, stony, stern eye."[111]

---

[103] O.R., XXVI, Part 3, pp. 832, 835, and 876.
[104] John B. Jones, p. 393.
[105] Author's library.
[106] *O. R.*, VII, p. 168.
[107] Duffy, p. 146.
[108] Northrop, p. 72.
[109] *O. R.*, VII, pp. 213, 214..
[110] *Ibid.*, p. 430.
[111] Warren Lee Goss, *The Soldier's Story of his Captivity at Andersonville, Belle Isle, and other Rebel Prisons* (Boston: I. N. Richardson & Co., 1873), p. 256.

**General Winder's Office** - in the Village of Andersonville. The second structure is thought to be Dykes' country store and the third one back is Captain Wirz' office.
(Peggy Sheppard, Weclome Center, Village of Andersonville, GA)

Prosecuting attorneys at the Wirz trial asked Ambrose Spencer to describe the "... general temper and spirit of General Winder with regard to those prisoners." He answered: "The opinion that I formed of him was anything but creditable to his feeling, his humanity, or his gentlemanly bearing. I am not aware that I ever had a conversation with General Winder in which he did not curse more or less, especially if the subject of Andersonville Prison was brought up. I can only reply to your question by saying that I considered him a brutal man. That I drew from his conversation and conduct as I observed them I looked upon him as a man utterly devoid of all kindly feeling and sentiment."[112]

Spencer described General Winder this way: "With an exterior and countenance repulsive by superannuation, and unsoftened by that suavity or courtesy of manner that marks the comity of a gentlemen: with a roughness of demeanor and a rudeness of speech that bespoke the bear instead of the officer, his presence shed around him an air of ungracious churlishness, that repelled the intimacy which his position ought to have invited. Unpolished and uncivil in his manners, his speech was, if possible, more ill bred. The vocabulary of invective might have been searched in vain for a novelty in imprecation which was not familiar to his lips; and, as the oaths rolled from his tongue in the most ordinary conversation, a listener could well be excused for the manifestation of astonishment at the fertility of the general's language, and the varied plenitude of his maledictions."[113]

On June 20th, there arrived a young lieutenant on General Winder's staff, Lieutenant Samuel Boyer Davis, Assistant Adjutant and Inspector-General.

Lieutenant Samuel Boyer Davis, C.S.A., was an aide to Major General Trimble, of Maryland, at the battle of Gettysburg. While with one of the divisions supporting Pickett's charge, he was shot "... through the lung" and was taken prisoner. Soon afterwards, he escaped and made his way back to Richmond. When he reported for duty in the later part of October of 1863, Davis was assigned to General Winder as his aide-de-camp and A.A.I.G. He remained in Richmond until the 27th of May, and stayed with the general during his brief stay in Goldsboro, North Carolina. He was then assigned to Andersonville and arrived there on the 20th of June, arriving three days after the general did.

After being at Andersonville only four days, General Winder sent Davis back to Richmond with letters to General Samuel Cooper, Adjutant General, to relay that no more prisoners be sent to Andersonville. The two main rea-

112 Chipman, p. 154.
113 Spencer, pp. 46, 47.

sons were: first, it was already overcrowded and food was difficult to obtain; second, the risk of concentrating so many prisoners at one place was extremely dangerous.

The documents conveyed to Richmond included the following letter addressed to General Samuel Cooper, Adjutant and Inspector-General:

*Camp Sumpter,*
*Andersonville, Georgia,*

*June 24th, 1864*

*General*

*The pressing necessity of the post and the great irregularity of the mails, have induced me to send Lieutenant Davis with this letter, though I can very illy spare his services as he is one of my most efficient assistants. The state of affairs at this post is in a critical condition.*

*We have here largely over 24,000 prisoners of war and 1,205 very raw troops - Georgia Reserves, with the measles prevailing, badly armed and worse disciplined to guard them. The prisoners rendered more desperate from the necessarily uncomfortable condition in which they are placed.*

*With the present force, a raid on the post would almost of necessity be successful, as the prisoners would occupy the attention of the troops. I do most conscientiously think the force should be largely reinforced, and I respectfully ask that it be done with the least possible delay.*

*There has been and I am satisfied that there is now going on, a correspondence in the prison, with disaffected persons outside and I have every reason to believe that just before my arrival an agent of Gen. Sherman had been here tampering with the prisoners. From the information I have been able to collect since I have been here, I am satisfied that there is a portion of the population around here who ought to be looked after, and who actively sympathize with the prisoners. In order to enable me to watch and counteract this influence, I respectfully ask that Capt. D. W. Vowles, with a detailed man by the name of Weatherford, on the police at Richmond, and two other well selected detectives, be ordered to Report to me immediately. It is difficult for those at a distance to realize the great responsibility of the command of this post, and the great danger of a successful outbreak among the prisoners; 25,000 men by the mere force of numbers can accomplish a great deal. If successful, the result would be much more disastrous than a defeat of the armies. It would result in the total ruin and devastation of this whole section of country; every house would be burned, violence to the women, destruction of crops, carrying off Negroes, horses, mules and wagons. It is almost impossible to estimate the extent of such a disaster; a little timely, prudent preparation will render it impossible.*

*The rawness of the troops, the almost impossibility of getting a court-martial from the 'Department of South Carolina and Georgia,' and other circumstances connected with the prisoners, renders it very necessary that I should have the power to order court-martials, and I respectfully request that such an arrangement be made.*

*Let me again press upon the attention of the Department the great danger hanging over this post, and to the necessary steps to avert it. Another prison should be immediately established as recommended in my former letter, and that no more prisoners be sent to this post. The force is becoming too ponderous, and, indeed, it is not possible with my present means to extend the post fast enough to meet the demands; within the last four days we have discovered two extensive tunnels reaching outside the stockade, showing great industry and determination on the part of the prisoners.*

*I am, very respectfully,*
*Your obedient servant,*
*John H. Winder,*
*Brig.-Gen.*[114]

Lieutenant Davis, the next morning after reaching Richmond, "... was sent to see President Jefferson Davis, that he might question me personally in regard to all matters connected with Andersonville." President Davis was then fully apprised of the horrible conditions at Andersonville. On the back of the letter written by General Cooper and carried back to General Winder by Davis, Cooper had written an endorsement that "... contained a very severe censure." General Winder wrote back to Cooper that he would not have censured Winder if he had fully known the circumstances and difficulties of running the post.[115]

Captain Davis arrived back at Andersonville on the 18th of July. There, he found that Captain Vowles and Captain Sid Winder had already left in search of a site for a new prison because instructions to do so had been tele-

---

114 *O. R.*, VII, pp. 410, 411.
115 *Ibid.*, p. 480.

graphed down from Richmond and had reached Andersonville before Captain Davis arrived back at the post.[116]

On the 21st of July, Lieutenant Davis received orders to take charge of the prison at Macon where 1,200 officers were confined. While at Macon, Davis allowed a couple of Federal prisoners to visit a friend of theirs, who was mortally wounded, for the purpose of conveying this officer's deathbed message to his wife and family. These two officers, who were on parole, were allowed to visit this Federal colonel in a hospital in Macon, accompanied not by a guard but by a Confederate adjutant who acted as a guide for a one-hour visit outside the prison. This excursion outside the pen elicited the wrath of the colonel, who commanded the post and removed Davis immediately from command and sent him back to Andersonville.

When Davis returned to Andersonville after a two-week absence, he asked that a court-martial be convened to clear his name of any wrong-doing. After hearing from the colonel commanding at Macon, General Winder refused to convene the trial and "... he said I had only done what any kind and humane man would have done under the circumstances."[117]

Davis was then assigned to assist Wirz and, when Wirz became sick a couple of days later, on either August 13th or 14th, Davis was made commandant of the interior of the prison. After Wirz recovered and returned, Davis was assigned to Richmond in October or November. After the first of the year, Davis volunteered for a secret mission to Canada.

Lieutenant Samuel Boyer Davis was sent, as a courier, to carry a manifesto from President Davis to help free a secret agent caught for espionage behind Union lines. The affidavit stated that John Beall, of Virginia, was a duly-commissioned officer of the Confederate States Navy. He had been ordered to capture Johnson's Island, in Lake Erie, and the gunboat *Michigan*. Lieutenant Davis also carried a copy of Lieutenant Beall's commission in the C.S.N. He arrived safely in Toronto and, after a week, started back, his coat sleeve's white, silk linings filled with military dispatches. On the second day of his return trip, Davis was recognized by ex-inmates of Andersonville, and was arrested near Sandusky, Ohio. He was tried and convicted, in Cincinnati, of being a spy. President Lincoln commuted his sentence just hours before Davis' appointment with the hangman.[118]

Captain Samuel T. Bayly was another of the four officers who were closely related at Andersonville. Captain Richard Bayly Winder's mother was Sarah Upshur Bayly.

Samuel Thomas Bayly, the son of Colonel Thomas M. Bayly and his second wife, was born in 1831, and he, too, lived on the Eastern Shore of Virginia. For three years, from 1847 to 1850, he took courses in Ancient and Modern Languages, Mathematics, Natural and Moral Philosophy, and Chemistry at the University of Virginia.[119]

Captain Samuel T. Bayly was adjutant of the 20th Regiment Virginia Infantry when its records, some arms and accoutrements, tents, and camp equipment were lost at the battle of Rich Mountain, Virginia, on July 11, 1861. On August 31, the regiment received orders to go to the Hermitage Camp of Instruction at Richmond where Captain Bayly, who had been sick, reported himself well.

On July 2, 1862, Captain Bayly wrote to the Honorable George W. Randolph, Secretary of War, and sought to apply for the position of Captain of Artillery. He stated that he was authorized by the Honorable J. P. Benjamin to enlist and muster into service a company of heavy artillery and sufficient companies of infantry to form a battalion or regiment. He said that he enlisted over 116 men and, on April 28th, was elected its captain. The company, called Bayly's Artillery, was ordered to quarters at Camp Lee until the 12th of May. Then, the company received orders to go to Drury's Bluff to serve as sharpshooters. Later, his company was sent to Battery #8 and then to Battery #9 where it was engaged in erecting fortifications along the James River until June 18th, at which time the company was disbanded. Samuel Bayly, evidently, wanted to continue to stay in the artillery service since he requested that he be made a captain of artillery.

On July 5th, 1862, General Winder wrote Captain Bayly and said, "If you are still commissioned, I would be glad to apply for your detail as Mustering Officer." He joined General Winder's staff after August 23rd, but, on that date, he still signed a pay allowance slip as "Captain Samuel T. Bayly, Bayly's Artillery. His office in the Bureau of Conscription was in the Winder Building in Richmond."

Bayly received his assignment to Andersonville on July 7, 1864, with General Winder, and followed him there where he served as Winder's Ordnance Officer, beginning the last of July.

William Sidney Winder, as detailed earlier, was the son of General Winder's second wife, Caroline. He attended

---

116 Davis, p. 20.

117 *Ibid.*, p. 21.

118 *Ibid.*, pp. 44-72.

119 Personal correspondence, Janet L. Kern, Assistant Archivist for University Archives, University of Virginia, Charlottesville, Virginia, June 15, 1982.

undergraduate school at Columbiad College near Washington, D.C., with his brother, John Cox. He then went on to law school and began the practice of law in Keokuk, Iowa, in 1858. In the late 1860s, he returned to Baltimore, then headed to Richmond, where he was commissioned a first lieutenant on October 29th 1861..[120] Ambrose Spencer said that "Sid Winder ... was about thirty-five years of age, rather below the ordinary size in stature, of no prepossessing appearance, and in many characteristics resembling his sire."[121]

Sid Winder was considered second in authority at Andersonville because he spoke for his father, "... legally as well as naturally." He was "... a humane man and gentlemanly officer ... and gave us plenty to eat (such as it was)."[122] The duties of Sid Winder as adjutant of the post were varied. He had charge of the detailed men outside of the prison, he wrote and issued all military orders for the troops on duty there as guards, he kept the records of the post, and had command over the provost marshal.

The only description of the provost marshal at Andersonville, Lieutenant W. Shelby Reed, described him as a "... youth of about twenty-two years of age, and a supple tool in the hands of his superiors."[123]

The pen continued to fill until the 10,000-man capacity that Sid Winder originally designated was surpassed. With the horrible crowding came many problems. Foremost was the simple lack of space for the men to sleep. Other problems were the lack of money to run the prison, the lack of nourishing rations, the lack of sufficient sanitary facilities, insufficient and incompetent guard force, and lack of cooperation and support from the upper levels of command. Providing for the captured prisoners did not rank very high on the Confederate list of priorities.

---

[120] Arch Fredric Blakey, *General John H. Winder, C. S. A.* (Gainesville: University of Florida Press, 1990), pp. 42-48.
[121] Spencer, p. 49.
[122] Thomas N. Way, *In the Jaws of Death, or Eighteen Months a Prisoner of War in Southern Prisons* (Salem, Ohio: Journal Stram Print, 1872), p.
[123] Spencer, pp. 48, 49.

## *Chapter Three*

# Shelters, Rations, Cooking Facilities and Sanitary Facilities

*"I saw men hunting around the sinks for food that had once passed through men's bodies."*

Chipman

Many of the first few thousand prisoners that were sent to Andersonville had been confined at Belle Isle, Pemberton, Libby, Liggon or Danville. Most were very sick and malnourished before heading south. They were so hungry that they were literally eating dogs to survive. These groups of several hundred sick continued to arrive at Andersonville almost daily all spring from the prisons and hospitals in Richmond. Later in the summer, prisoners captured just hours before were brought directly to the prison from battles and skirmishes in Georgia and Florida.

The prisoners' health, both mental and physical, began to deteriorate immediately upon entering the pen. As it seems that the largest fish out of water dies first, so it was at Andersonville. Usually the more heavy, robust youth died before the older, immuned, veterans. "Among the first to die was the one whom we expected to live longest. He was by much the largest man in prison, and was called, because of this, 'Big Joe.' He was a Sergeant in the Fifth Pennsylvania Cavalry, and seemed the picture of health ... I can recall few or no instances where a large, strong, 'hearty' man lived through a few months of imprisonment."[1]

In three months, one-third of Northrop 's company of 47 men who came in on May 24th, had died. These were all young and healthy and not alumni of Libby or Belle Isle. Many times, within a few days of arriving, some of the apparently healthy men were deathly ill. "I am witness to the fact, that many young men in good health, whose hair was black as the raven, did, in twenty-four hours, become raving maniacs, - whose hair became as white as the driven snow before the third day's imprisonment."[2] Samuel Melvin arrived on June 3rd in good health, had diarrhea in two days, and died September 25th from chronic diarrhea and scurvy.

After arriving at the pen, each prisoner had to find a bedding place or "spooning-ground" as a prisoner, S. S. Boggs called it, to build his shelter or "shebang" as they were called. A. E. Stearns called the hovels "cabooses."[3] At Andersonville, the word "tent" meant a prisoner's abode, whether actually a canvas tent, a cave in the earth or a wooden shebang. Thus, a "tent" was described "... as the place rigged up to sleep in was called, whether canvas, turf, or wood."[4] The prisoner would stay with his buddies with whom he was captured, seek out already-captured members of his regiment, or sometimes associate himself with members of another regiment from his home state. All the men of a detachment were not required to live with other members of that detachment, but, for convenience, most did.[5] "Each division or company was expected to remain together the best we could."[6] If they did not, when rations were distributed and at roll calls, they would have to trek to the place designated as "detachment headquarters" which, sometimes, was only a log or tree stump.

---

[1] McElroy, p. 154.

[2] James R. Compton, *Andersonville, The Story of Man's Inhumanity to Man* (DesMoines: Iowa Printing Company, 1887), p. 37.

[3] Amos E. Stearns, *The Civil War Diary of Amos E. Stearns*, Edited by Leon Basile (Fairleigh Dickinson University Press, 1981), p. 64.

[4] Dufur, p. 129.

[5] Miller, p. 19.

[6] Typed transcript of Lewis Lake's diary in private hands.

**"Mansions of Andersonville"** - This is probably a true representation of the quarters of the prisoners within the pen. (Moran)

The detachments were numbered and placed sequentially with Detachment Number One located near the north gate. "The old Dutchman, as he was called, Captain Wirz, riding a white horse, came along and escorted us to the prison gate. Here he left us with the guards and himself went inside to learn what part of the prison to assign us to."[7] Once a prisoner got his plot picked out, he had to choose a method of shelter. He could dig into the ground, which had certain advantages such as the retention of body heat which, what with the little amount of caloric intake, every effort had to be made to prevent its dissipation. One disadvantage of digging in was that rain water seeks its lowest level and, sometimes, only the greatest of engineering proficiency prevented a prisoner from floating away after a heavy downpour. Staying dry was a real problem because the average annual rainfall for the Andersonville area was nearly five feet. "Water comes from the upper part in swift brooklets, sweeping every pool of foulness below ... Men unable to go to the swamp sinks, have holes dug close by where they lay. The rains wash these away or overflow them, and the filthy contents are carried into our resting places."[8]

When the first prisoners arrived, the interior was littered with some stumps, branches, and limbs trimmed from the timbers used in constructing the stockade. Therefore, initially, when wood was less scarce, most shebangs were made from scrap wood and lumber. Sometimes the shebang was slightly elevated from the ground with sides of scrap lumber and a top of wood with the front entrance covered by a rubberized poncho or pup tent-half. Such accommodations were considered luxurious and were built by only those who were relatively wealthy or had a talent or trade whose services could be bartered. In May, Northrop bought three logs, four to six feet long, for fifty cents each, to make a frame for his blanket.

Urban described his shebang this way: "Some of the soil close to us was composed of brick clay, and we found that by mixing it up with water, and letting it dry, it would be almost as hard as stone. We gathered a lot of this clay, and built a wall about six inches high around out lot. After being in possession of our new quarters for a few days, we gathered more clay, and, at first only for amusement and pastime, commenced to build our wall higher and stronger. We then discovered that when exposed to the sun for several days, it would become very hard, and we commenced to think that we might secure some kind of a shelter by raising the wall higher and arching it part way in. We built the two sides and one gable end of our house about three and on-half feet high, and taking Gilbert's blanket for a roof, we had a pretty good protection against the heavy dews so prevalent after night in that part of the country."[9]

"The prisoner was counted lucky indeed who had what was known at Andersonville as a 'Brown Stone Front' or a 'Dug out.' ... A Brown Stone Front was made with sticks and mud something after the fashion of a southern chimney. Our blankets were used for roofs and siding or sometimes a blanket or piece of one would cover the top of a hole, umbrella like. This hole, many times, would be the opening into a larger one capable of containing ten or twelve men. A dug out was...like the home of a prairie dog... Both of these would do quite nicely until heavy rains came; then good-bye 'Brown Stone Fronts,' and 'Dug-outs'."[10] Some men would associate with three other men who had blankets and the four would make an "A" tent with two blankets, cover the ground with the third blanket and use the other to cover their bodies at night. They would sleep spoon-fashion and would reverse direction on the command of "spoon." "The nights being very cold and damp, we used to lie down close together, to keep each other warm, in rows of ten or twelve, lying spoon-fashion. Lying in this way one could not turn over unless all turned at once. When lying on our right sides, the cry of two or three voices: 'by the right flank!' would cause a turn, and bring

[7] Tyler, p. 41.
[8] Northrop, p. 71.
[9] Urban, p. 337.
[10] Frank W. Smith, p. 43.

us all on our left sides."[11]

"Some hundred or more would lie down in long lines opposite the 'Main Gates,' the streets being twenty feet wide and running clear across the ground from West to East, from 'Dead Line to Dead Line.' By eight o'clock a few boys would turn in; shortly after some fellow would come along, and touching one of the end men, would say: 'Look here, wake up.' Say, comrade, 'Can I spoon with you to-night:' and the one awakened would ask, 'Are you lousy?' 'No.' 'Well, all right: chuck up, spoon close, for it's cold.' By and by, the line containing sometimes three hundred men would be sound asleep...Suppose the middle man of the three hundred in line desired to rest the tired and sore hip, well the order would be passed both way left and right until the entire 300 were ready; then the command of attention! was given, prepare to spoon; soon after in sharp clear tones, 'Right Spoon.' turn."[12]

To be able to line the floor of the shebang with pine needles was a most sought-after luxury. "Some of the prisoners who had no shelter, and not wishing to die down in the mud, conceived the play of making what they called a sleeping-post. A number of them got close together, and after forming a centre-post, would get around it one against the other, and try to sleep. Fralich [a friend of Urban] informed us that he would try that play too. He had hardly got his position when the centre gave way, and the sleepy fellows fell, a confused mass, into the mud."[13] "Frequently we saw a group trying to sleep standing by having one man for a center piece, the rest huddling around and leaning towards the center."[14]

Just to sleep out at night on the damp ground could give a healthy man pneumonia and, to subject a person on a starvation diet to this abuse, would almost certainly cause some respiratory disease. Therefore, "inflammation of the lungs" was a major cause of death.

The average temperature in Georgia was very mild and pleasant, but it was known to have snowed in the prison compound on at least one occasion. It was so cold some nights during the winter and early spring, the prisoners had to walk at night so they would not freeze to death, and sleep in the daytime. Dufur described how he "went to roost" with his comrades to conserve body heat: "We would stand with our bodies pressed together in crowds of from twenty-five to two hundred men. This partially protected our bodies, but those who were barefoot suffered much from cold and the many bruises they received upon their unprotected feet during the long nights we remained in this uncomfortable position."[15]

It was reliably reported by Ambrose Spencer, the Unionist living nearby, that, when he glanced at a thermometer one night, it read $18^0$. Many prisoners with no blankets were very happy as the Georgia nights became warmer with the approach of summer. During the summer of 1864, it was said to have reached the 110 degree mark on at least one occasion and, on many days, the mercury stayed above the 100 degree mark. "The shade temperature of this place sometimes rose to the height of $105^0$, even $110^0$ and upwards, for the height of the walls prevented the free circulation of air."[16] Spencer read his thermometer and noted that the reading was 110 degrees in the shade. He put it out in the sun once on an exceptionally hot day in June and the reading was $127^0$ to $130^0$ that day.[17]

Because of the heat, the behavior of some of the soldiers was radically altered. "The weather was getting very warm, and to preclude the necessity of toiling and sweating in the hot sunshine, we adopted the plan of rising before sunrise, to cook our scanty breakfast, and we found it to add materially to our comfort."[18] So not only were the cold nights with little or no protection dangerous to their health, but exposure to the sun's rays caused much grief by burning the skin. "Under the influence of a scorching sun; the entire upper surface of the foot would become blistered; these would break, leaving the flesh exposed, and having nothing to dress it with, or protect it in any way, gangrene was inevitable, and this would be followed by the loss of the foot, if not a larger portion of the limb."[19] There was "... a tropical sun above us, sending its scorching rays down upon our uncovered heads, causing great, watery blisters to raise on our faces, arms and hands, and heating the sand until it would almost blister the soles of our bare feet."[20] Many, especially the blondes and red-heads, were known to have received blisters which became infested with maggots, thereby necessitating amputations. "Most of the old prisoners preferred rain to sunshine, as it

[11] Brownell, p. 11.
[12] Frank W. Smith, pp, 41, 42.
[13] Urban, pp. 319, 320.
[14] Greacen, p. 6.
[15] Dufur, p. 229.
[16] Hamlin, p. 32.
[17] Chipman, p. 151.
[18] Kellogg, p. 150.
[19] *Ibid.*, p. 268.
[20] Fosdick, p. 49.

was so hot when it did not rain for a few days that the men who had no shelter almost perished of the heat."[21]

The rapidity of the deterioration of their uniforms surprised most of the soldiers. The blue fatigues rapidly "dry-rotted" so that, by the end of the second month, usually the pants and shirt had become shredded. Miller did not wash his under clothing for four months because he felt that washing would cause them to deteriorate more rapidly. The boots, if one was lucky enough to not have had them appropriated by a guard, were beginning to wear out and the scrap leather was used to make other utensils and tools. Shoes and boots in the Civil War era were sometimes made by joining the upper leather to the soles by small wooden pegs. Some men became cobblers or shoe repairmen and used pocket knives to hand-carve the wooden pegs. Thus, after two months and, certainly, after four months, the prisoner who had entered with a new uniform, would be barefoot with possibly only a remnant of a shirt on his back and wearing, sometimes, only drawers to cover his posterior.

"My faithful old army shoes had become things of the past, my shirt dropped off a piece at a time until it disappeared, my hat was worn and had been added to the rubbish of the accumulating filth, my blouse sleeves were worn off to the shoulders and my pants worn off to the knees."[22]

One prisoner captured at Gettysburg related that, "... on the way from Richmond a woman gave him a petticoat which reaches just below his knees that whops about his legs as he strolls characteristically through the camp, the sailor's cap on his head, and not another rag on his person."[23] There were dozens who had only kepis; other dozens had nothing at all to wear. "Not two thousand had coats and pants, and those were late comers. More than one half were indecently exposed, and many were naked."[24] "One or two men were roaming around camp without a particle of clothing upon their bodies."[25]

Every day, at about 7 o'clock, a roll call was taken, requiring the prisoners to stand for long hours in the streets under the threat from Wirz: "May God Almighty damn me forever and ever if I don't shoot the first man who attempts to leave the ranks."[26] "On these occasions there were two sentries in each sentry-box, and directions were given that we should not leave the ranks until the second sentry went down."[27]

"At ten o'clock every forenoon a drum call was beaten from the platform at the South Gate. At this signal the prisoners fell into line by detachments, forming as best they could in the narrow paths.

"At the same moment a company of Confederate sergeants entered the two gates for the purpose of counting and recording the number of prisoners. To each of these officers a certain number of detachments were assigned. The men had to remain standing during the entire count. If a number less than that of yesterday was in evidence, the Federal sergeant had to account for the deficit. Sometimes a number of men were too ill to stand up, so the line was held the longer while the Confederate official viewed the sick where they lay."[28] Boggs said everyone was counted every morning at eight o'clock.[29] Captain Walter Bowie, an inspector in the Adjutant and Inspector General Department, on May 5th, said the roll call was at 7 o'clock.

Each Confederate sergeant would count several detachments. W. D. Hammack of the 55th Georgia said; "I called the rolls of six divisions, and there were three nineties in each division - eighteen nineties altogether ... Our instructions from Captain Wirz were to call the roll, but I could not pronounce the names of so many. I merely counted the men."[30]

"I remember one morning at roll-call, out of ninety men, there were thirty-two who were not able to stand up when the rebel sergeant came to call the roll. They were unable to stand up principally from scurvy and diarrhoea. This was on Aug. 21st."[31]

"To insure correctness in the roll-call, the guards of the stockade were instructed to fire upon any men who should attempt to cross the brook from one side of the prison to the other. Thinking it would be no violation of orders to step to the side of the brook, to wash my hands, I did so, when snap went the cap of the gun of the guard near

---

[21] Urban, p. 321.
[22] Fosdick, p. 49.
[23] Northrop, p. 70.
[24] Sanitary Commission, p. 77.
[25] Sidney S. Williams, "From Spottsylvania to Wilmington, N. C. by Way of Andersonville and Florence," *Personal Narratives of Events in the War of the Rebellion, Being Papers Read Before the Rhode Island Soldiers and Sailors Historical Society, Fifth Series - No.10* (Providence: Snow & Farnham, Printers, 1899), p. 13.
[26] *Wirz Trial*, p. 376.
[27] *Ibid.*
[28] Maile, p. 36.
[29] Boggs, p. 27.
[30] *Wirz Trial*, p. 498.
[31] Chipman, p. 64.

me. On looking up I found he had intended to shoot me, but his gun had missed fire - thanks to a good providence."[32]

"While awaiting the completion of the new stockade, the roll-call was omitted a few mornings and lest some have a wrong idea of this, I will here say, that names were never called, but every morning a rebel Sergeant would make his appearance, at which time we would fall in, four ranks deep, when he would count us, and make sure that everything was right before he left us."[33]

If someone was missing at roll call, he had to be accounted for by his sergeant as either escaped, sick elsewhere in the pen, dead, detailed outside the pen, or in the hospital outside. Absent prisoners were punished by not receiving their rations that afternoon.

The prisoners soon learned they could sneak from the back rank or row of a ninety that had been counted to another that had not been counted. In this way, if a man had died from that ninety, the ration would still be issued until the deception was discovered by the authorities.

The purpose of the roll call was mainly to determine how many rations should be issued later that day. Another important reason for the roll call was so that an escaped prisoner would have less than twenty-four hours' head start in leaving for parts unknown. Therefore, the dogs would have a relatively fresh scent to track. After roll call, the men would gather at the South Gate for sick call. The Confederate Medical Director thought the close association between the sergeants and the prisoners could be used to an advantage in improving and monitoring their health. Doctor Isaiah White recommended, on August 5th, in a report to General Winder on the sanitary condition of the pen: "It should be the duty of Confederate sergeants attending roll-calls, or others, to see that all men of their command bathe at stated intervals and that their clothes are washed at least once a week. For this purpose soap should be issued to the prisoners."[34]

One of the Confederate sergeants who took roll of McElroy's detachment was called "Wry-necked Smith" because his head was permanently twisted to the right. The men accounted for the abnormality by saying that his colonel had once commanded "eyes right" and then forgot to give the order "front."[35]

"Smith was sergeant at the hospital after the hospital was established outside... Smith rode Captain Wirz' horse a good deal, about as much as Captain Wirz did. Smith was a tolerably tall man, not over tall. He wore his head on one side."[36]

If the detachments became very depleted by death, hospitalizations and so on, the prisoners would be ordered to fill the lower numbered detachments back to their 270-man capacity. This was the process of "reorganizing" the camp. On many days, less than half of those in the detachment could stand in the streets and be counted. Northrop said that, on one day of his detachment of 270 men, only 123 were able to "appear in line."[37]

W. D. Hammack of the 55th Georgia testified: "As soon as the number was ascertained to be correct I would dismiss them, except when the camp was going to be organized. They reorganized the camp twice, I think, before they moved the prisoners to Millen, and then the order was for the men to stand in the ranks at the place where they answered the roll-call until the whole stockade was called over. That was reorganizing."[38]

"Another time he came in, counted us off, and told us the orders were to remain in line till all the prisoners were counted. In the daytime they used to have a sentinel on every other post, but that day there were two sentinels on each post. He pointed to them and said, 'you see that they have orders to fire into any squad that breaks out or attempts to break out.' The rebel sergeant said that. 'But,' said he, 'it is not by my orders I assure you.' Some of the boys asked by whose order it was, and he said by Captain Wirz' order."[39]

Without the aid of paroled prisoners, the prison could not have functioned. Because of the small number of garrison troops, few could be spared for duties other than actual guard duty. Hundreds of prisoners were allowed outside the pen to work at various jobs around the post. "At Andersonville there were more than 1,500 prisoners out on parole in the Quartermaster's, Commissary and Medical Departments."[40] General Winder didn't like having so many outside and one of his first orders upon his arrival was to get all he could back inside.

---

32 Kellogg, p. 65.
33 *Ibid.*, p. 145.
34 *O.R.*, VII, pp. 559, 560.
35 McElroy, p. 131.
36 *Wirz Trial*, p. 511.
37 Northrop, p. 113.
38 *Wirz Trial*, p. 498.
39 *Ibid.*, p 304.
40 Davis, p. 35.

All prisoners paroled were given double rations; these were probably of a slightly better quality than those received by the men in the pen. They slept outside. One author said they camped in the "porch" or space between the outer and inner gates of the two gates. "About two hundred prisoners were detailed outside, on parole, to help handle rations, to cook, and to dig trenches to bury in, etc. They slept in the gate, or ante-room, at night - at least part of them did."[41]

Those out on parole could be of service to those friends left on the inside. For instance, they had access to wood for constructing shebangs. "When the inside door would be opened, on a morning, they would pitch them in beyond the dead-line to their friends. If you had no friend out on parole, the set, two stakes four feet long, and a pole six feet long, would cost you fifty cents."[42]

The parolees were given better clothes and some boxes of clothes, forwarded through the lines, were distributed only to those outside. "These men were well clothed and presented a stout and healthy appearance, and as a general rule they presented a much more robust and healthy appearance than the Confederate troops guarding the prisoners."[43] Because of the personal interplay, the men got better treatment and became friends with their keepers.

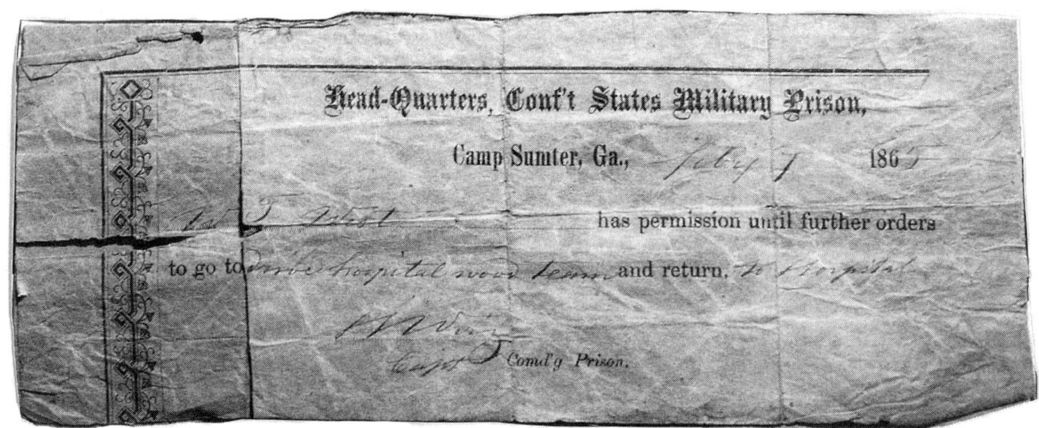

Head-Quarters, Conf't States Military Prison,

Camp Sumter, Ga., 186

has permission until further orders

to go to and return.

Comd'g Prison.

**Parole Issued at Andersonville** - Allowed W. T. West "to drive hospital wood team, and return to hospital." It was dated February 7, 1865. This was initialed by Wirz on the front and signed by him on the back in a purple oval stamp. (Author's Collection)

Once outside, parolees were not allowed back inside, nor to communicate with those inside to prevent a conspiracy precipitating a general insurrection. "There was an order issued so that we could not get into the stockade; the men who were paroled outside did not have permission to go in to see those inside the stockade; one day I was bound to go in, and I applied to the lieutenant of the guard at the gate and gave him twelve dollars in greenbacks to let me go in and stay an hour, to see our boys; I went in and spent an hour inside the stockade."[44]

On July 2nd the Governor of Georgia wrote to Secretary of War Seddon, complaining that it had been brought to his attention that there were hundreds of paroled prisoners wandering rather freely around the post at Andersonville. The Governor's un-named informant said, "I can state, on information from prisoners as well as our soldiers, that there are about 300 or a little over. They pass about as freely as our own soldiers do, go into the country, buy vegetables, &c., talk to and trade with our soldiers, though trading with prisoners is strictly forbidden. They have a camp of their own without guard; only one Confederate officer in it, whose duty it is to call the roll at stated times. These prisoners do not work under guard, and are never confined in the stockade. Some are chopping logs for the new stockade; some are employed in the bakery, cooking provisions outside for the prisoners in the stockade; some are employed as carpenters, some to bury the dead, some as teamsters, some as litter-bearers, &c. These prisoners have it in their power to do us and the country an immense amount of mischief. I am not able to state anything of

[41] Vawter, p. 48.
[42] *Ibid.*
[43] *O.R.*, VIII, p. 603.
[44] Chipman, p. 173.

consequence they have done, but they get all the information relative to the war supplies, troops, the position of armies, &c., that our own soldiers get. I hear them sometimes quote the telegrams exactly. By acting in concert with the prisoners on the inside, the whole could probably escape. If they should be exchanged or escape to the enemy, they could give much valuable information that would be encouraging to the enemy.

The negro prisoners are worked under guard in daytime and put back in the stockade at night. So are a few of the other prisoners."[45]

In response to a letter from the Secretary of War concerning the large number of paroled prisoners allowed outside of the prison, General Winder asked Lieutenant-Colonel T. M. Furlow, commander of a battalion of Georgia militia serving as guard, to write and comment on this situation. Lt. Col. Furlow said his quarters were on the other side of the railroad from "... a camp and workshops occupied by quite a number of paroled prisoners." He said, "I... never noticed anything in their conduct calculated to create a suspicion that any danger or evil would result from their parole. Their condition is so much improved and the penalty for any impropriety (a return to the stockade) so feared by them, they have every inducement to strictly obey orders and avoid every impropriety. Several cases have come to my knowledge of conversations with the negroes at work around the post, but invariably on the subject of a purchase of watermelons or peaches..." Furlow also said that, if the Confederates had to bury the Yankee dead or attend their sick, it would tax the guard force and cause universal complaining.[46]

General Winder said that the practice of keeping so many parolees outside the pen was disliked by him and "... on my arrival [I] set to work to try and get rid of it, but I found it impossible, and I was obliged to adopt such a system as was forced upon me."[47]

Most of the men arriving at Andersonville left their mess equipment in Richmond because, when they left, they had been told that they were being exchanged. These men, thinking they would not need the mess equipment, left it with those men left behind at Richmond. If they did suspect that they were only being transferred to another prison, then they still had to smuggle the mess equipment past the guards who, sometimes having none of their own, confiscated it. Pots and pans were very scarce among the first prisoners to arrive at Andersonville. However, canteen halves usually sufficed. Others cooked in discarded "... fruit cans, such as we could beg or buy from the guards."[48]

Those being transferred recognized the value of possessing raw materials for trade or manufacture. For instance, when Boggs' train wrecked, he had the presence of mind to roll up some of the tin which made up the railroad car roof and hid it within his blouse. Others stole railroad spikes and broken bolts. With these, Boggs made a cooking pan which he rented to his comrades. With the return of this pan, he would be given a spoonful of mush as rent.

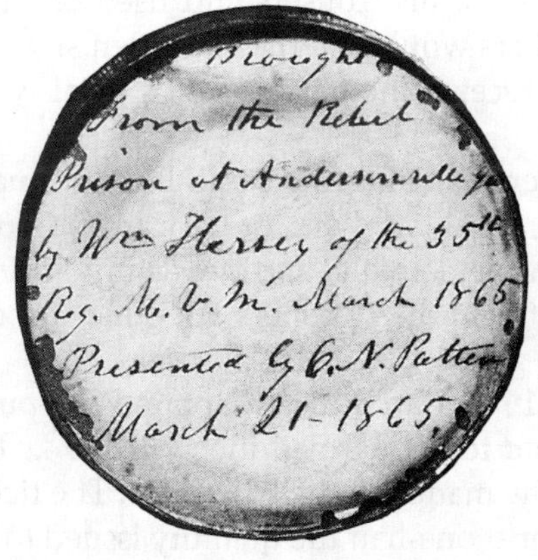


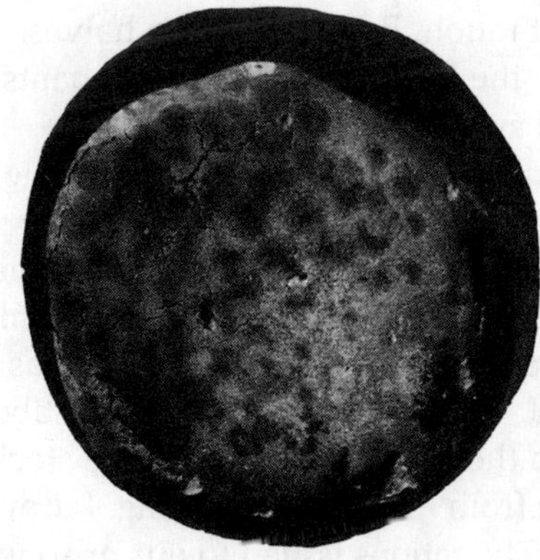

**Biscuit Issued at Andersonville Preserved in Tole Tin** - Note states: "Brought from the Rebel Prison at Andersonville, Ga., by Wm. Hersey of the 35th Reg. Mass Vol. Militia. March 1865. Presented by G. N. Patten March 21, 1865." (Author's Collection)

45 *O.R.*, VII, p. 437.
46 *Ibid.*, pp. 601, 602.
47 *Ibid.*, p. 624.
48 Author's library.

Few men ever mentioned that they were issued any cooking paraphernalia. When the prison first opened, "... the first two thousand prisoners were issued skillets, one to fifty men, but these were soon taken away."[49] As noted previously, Captain Dick Winder had tremendous difficulties getting vessels in which to cook. At first, the provisions were issued uncooked and the prisoners had to cook their own. This was during the period when wood for fuel was relatively plentiful.

Rations varied from day to day in quantity as well as content. The most common item issued almost daily, was corn meal. This was prepared by a group of five or six prisoners who would pool their rations and eat the prepared meal together. One man's job would be to gather fire-wood, which was no easy task. The most common method was to be detailed outside the prison to perform a duty, and, when returning, the prisoner would usually be allowed to bring in an armful of wood. Another man's job might be to start the fire and keep it burning. This, too, was no easy task because, many times, the wood was wet or very few matches were available. Another prisoner, perhaps, sifted the corn meal and another did the actual cooking.

If one had no way to cook rations, a prisoner would walk the prison and yell, "Who wants to trade some cooked for some raw?" By offering, say, a large penny as an inducement, the trade would be consummated.

"If a man was sick and unable to eat his meat, a comrade would take it, stick it on a sliver, and walk up and down the street crying, 'Who's got bread to trade for meat?' Presently some one would call out 'Here!' and then they would banter. One would say, 'Your bread is too small;' the other would say, 'Your meat isn't good!' After a wordy discussion, there would either be a trade or a fight. It is surprising to see how much hungry men think of their honor and how quickly they resort to blows to defend it. Fights were the order of the day. Look in any direction at almost any time of day and you might witness from one to a dozen fistic arguments in full swing. It was a good place for a young man to learn to mind his own business."[50]

One of the duties of a dedicated sergeant of a ninety was to cook for his comrades who were too sick to cook for themselves. Kellogg said, "... it would keep me busy nearly the whole day drawing rations and cooking for the poor sick boys who were unable to cook for themselves."[51] The rations were kept by the individual soldier in his haversack if he was lucky enough to possess one. Common objects were utilized as containers. The destitute prisoners, some with no earthly possessions, had no containers in which to receive their paltry rations. "We were put to our wit's end to know how to receive our rations. We had no vessels except our little coffee cans, and many did not have even these. Some would draw in their hats, mixing meal, peas and beef altogether; others would tear out a shirt sleeve, tie a string around one end, and draw it in, and others still would draw theirs in a corner of their blouse."[52]

Cow horns were found around the site of the slaughter of the beeves. These were hollowed out and, with a leather thong, made a very serviceable container for solids or liquids. They were used as ladles and scoops for beans and the very soft soap occasionally issued. The Confederates, also, utilized the horns for many of their utensils and accoutrements, (i.e., powder horns). Lyons cut the pockets out of his trousers and used one for his bread and the other to hold his meat ration. Besides canteen halves, the soldiers would interlace wooden slivers to form crude mats or plates. Sometimes, the man who loaned the pants leg to receive the detachment's meal would receive an extra spoonful of corn meal as rent.

Southerners usually defended the rations of the prisoners as being the same in both quality and quantity as those eaten by the Confederate garrison troops. After the war, Mr. L. M. Park, of LaGrange, Georgia, testified, "I was for three months a clerk in the Commissary Department at Andersonville, and it was my business to weigh out rations for the guards and prisoners alike; and I solemnly assert, that the prisoners got ounce for ounce and pound for pound of just the same quality and quantity of food as did the guards."[53]

However, John H. Goldsmith testified: "On or about the 1st of March 1865, Captain Wirz put me in charge of the rations to be issued to the prisoners inside of the stockade, and to the paroled men outside ... He used to make out tickets for me to draw from Captain Armstrong. I drew what he made out the tickets for. The ticket specified the articles and the quantity. The rations issued to our prisoners was just one-half the quantity issued to the rebel troops."[54]

Accounting for some of the big difference in mortality must have been the fact that the guards could supplement their diet with vegetables and fruits bought with their own money from vendors from the neighboring farms. The

[49] Sanitary Commission, p. 77.
[50] Lyons, pp. 44, 45.
[51] Author's library.
[52] Fosdick, pp. 31, 32.
[53] Stevenson, p. 450.
[54] *Wirz Trial*, pp. 298, 299.

food issued must be viewed in the light of the food that was usually eaten by the poorer Southern families at that time. Their main staples were pork and corn bread, and it was only natural that these would be so in the prison.

Just for comparison, Vawter was fed the following rations after being recaptured and held in the Columbus jail, "... we had two good meals per day, consisting of good corn bread (not the Andersonville kind), bacon, cabbage, rice, etc., all well cooked and enough of it." Fellow inmates in the jail received from friends on the outside peanuts, oranges, and other delicacies to supplement their rations.[55] It would be interesting to see the difference in the mortality rates if the diet of the prisoners had been supplemented by an occasional sweet potato, cabbage, tomato, or fruit.

"The quantity of corn meal allowed to the rebel soldiers by the rebel government was about one and one-third pounds daily; this would give about 28 ounces of bread, allowing 30% of water, which is the rule among bakers."[56] "The United States allowed to the rebel prisoners held by them thirty-eight ounces of solid food at first; but afterwards, in June, 1864, they reduced the ration to thirty-four and a half ounces per day. The range of articles composing the ration was the same as with our own troops, the exception being in the weight of the bread."[57]

The corn meal fed the prisoners was ground very coarsely and, in it, were large chunks of husk and cob. This should have been sifted to remove the foreign matter. It was stated by Dick Winder that he was unable to obtain any iron wire necessary to make a sifter.[58] Some soldiers attempted to sift it by taking half of a canteen and punching holes in it with a 6-penny nail. This was done by many soldiers at first but, later, in their debilitated condition, they were too weak perform this task. The list of foreign matter in the corn meal was a lengthy one and included such things as gravel, sand, feathers, mouse excretion, and a wide assortment of bugs and worms.

It was often stated there were no vegetables or fruits in the neighborhood to supplement the diet of the prisoners. Yet, that part of southwestern Georgia was termed "... the garden of the Confederacy" because there were grown many of the provisions of the Southern army. "The average of this land would be one bale of cotton to the acre; the wheat would average about six bushels to the acre; the average of corn would be about eight bushels to the acre. This is for the total number of acres in the counties contiguous to Sumter county. There are some lands that produce 35 bushels of corn to the acre."[59]

Some Southern apologists have said that, even though they raised plenty of corn, they did not have enough mills to mill the corn. Ambrose Spencer said that there were five gristmills within a ten-mile radius of the prison and two more gristmills near Americus that were about twelve miles from Andersonville. At Drew's Mill, at Adams' Station, was located a gristmill as well as a sawmill and it was contracted by Dick Winder to furnish meal for the post. Those near Americus were also contracted by Captain Craft to furnish meal to Andersonville.[60] Some of these mills were water mills, which could not function during a drought, but these were able to grind all during the occupancy of the prison.[61]

James Van Valkenburg lived near Macon for nineteen years and was familiar with the crops raised in southwestern Georgia. He testified the provision crop was larger in 1864 - 1865 than before the war. There was a regulation in the South that required farmers to give the government one-tenth of the crops that they grew. This regulation was applicable to corn, wheat, potatoes, and a certain proportion of their meat. When he visited Americus, James Van Valkenburg said there seemed to be very large quantities of stores in various warehouses there.

Mr. Van Valkenburg had a son-in-law who lived in Americus, and he told Mr. Van Valkenburg that he raised more wheat in that year than ever in his life. Some of the flourmills were what were called merchants' mills. Some mills, especially those doing a smaller business, merely ground for the tolls. He knew there was a large flour mill in Macon. He said, though Georgia was considered a corn growing state, it was generally considered a good country for wheat also and he thought that some of the best wheat was raised in southwestern Georgia.[62]

Augustus Moesner, of Company G, 16th Connecticut Volunteers, was captured April 20, 1864, sent to Andersonville, and arrived there on the evening of May 3rd. The prisoners were kept outside the pen overnight, and, the following morning, Wirz, with some Southern sergeants, counted off the men into detachments and sent them into the pen. On May 24th, he was paroled as a clerk to work in Wirz' office. Interestingly, Moesner testified: "I was not well acquainted yet with the English language." He said that, "... among other duties I had to carry orders down to

[55] Vawter, p. 127, 128.
[56] Hamlin, p. 86.
[57] *Ibid.*, p. 81.
[58] *O.R.*,
[59] Chipman, p. 151.
[60] *O.R.*, VI, p. 972.
[61] Chipman, p. 150.
[62] *Ibid.*, pp. 156, 157.

the stockade, and to carry returns and morning reports to General Winder's headquarters, and I also had to go to the commissary with returns."

Every morning, after roll call, a list was made out with the detachments listed and with each detachment's three squads listed adjacent to them. Beside each squad was placed the number of rations that squad was to receive as determined by that morning's roll call. This number was obtained by subtracting those men who were detailed outside of the pen or in the hospital from ninety. There was not one squad which had ninety "men in line." Augustus Moesner would carry this list down to James W. Duncan at the cook-house, leave it there, and return to his quarters. As soon as Mr. Duncan learned how many rations were to be issued, the Federal prisoners, paroled as cooks, began to cook that number of rations. The rations were then carried by Mr. Duncan to the stockade.

The hospital staff would send down to Mr. Duncan the number of rations needed at that facility. This hospital requisition was made out by Dr. Isaiah H. White; in fact, Moesner said that no requisitions for anything for the hospital were made out in Wirz' office or signed by Wirz.[63]

Moesner said that he did not remember rations being withheld from the entire prison population. However, the rations were sometimes withheld from a squad whenever a man was "missing" from roll call. The other members of the squad were then dismissed to search the pen for that man. When it was determined where the missing man was, the list was altered accordingly. If he had escaped, the ration list was decreased by one and sent down to the cook-house to Mr. Duncan, who would give the squad their rations by order of Captain Wirz. If Wirz was not there in his office, Moesner said that the clerks themselves had the power to order the rations issued.[64]

"It was shown that on one occasion Duncan came into the stockade with bread as usual. The witness who testified was detailed to go and bring the bread for his squad, with a man from a Tennessee regiment to assist him. After they had received their quota of bread, and Duncan was dealing out to another squad, a piece of crust broke off and fell under the wagon. The Tennessee man stooped to pick it up, when Duncan leaped to the ground, and kicked and beat the man so severely that soon after he died. Some time from that Duncan was again issuing bread, and a poor half-witted fellow was standing near, looking on, but saying nothing. Duncan asked him, with an oath, what he wanted there? He replied, 'Nothing.' 'Well, there's something for you,' said the ruffian, when he knocked him down and stamped upon him, then threw him over the dead line, when a sentinel shot and killed him.

On another occasion Duncan and Bowers seized upon James Armstrong, and put him in the spread-eagle stocks for saying that he did not get his full rations of bread. They robbed him of his money and a picture of his sister, which Armstrong begged might be returned to him. In six hours, they returned and released him, when he again asked for his sister's likeness, but was told by Duncan, with an oath - all swore there, from Winder down to the negro who blacked his boots - 'that he might consider himself damned lucky to get off with his life;' and threatened to put a ball and chain on him if he said anything more to him about it. The amount of money that Duncan stole was nine dollars in greenbacks."[65]

This incident was corroborated by W. W. Crandall, who testified about Duncan, "He had charge of the cook-house there. During the first time, I was there, he used to come into the stockade with rations. During the latter part of the time, they said he was acting as detective. In the first days of October, 1864, I was in the ball-and-chain-gang. I saw him and another man named Barr bring a man to put in the stocks. His name was James Armstrong. He belonged to an Ohio regiment; the number of the regiment I cannot tell. They put him in what they called the 'spread-eagle stocks,' and after putting him in they took from him his money and a picture. I heard Armstrong plead with Duncan for the picture, saying either that it was the picture of his sister or of his mother. He did not get it. He was left there three or four hours, when Duncan came back alone and took him out, saying that he was going to send him away on the cars. I heard Armstrong at that time ask Duncan if he could not give him back that picture. The answer was, 'You may consider yourself damned fortunate to get away at all, and that you are not put in the ball-and-chain-gang with those other boys.' I did not notice how much money. The man told me the amount while he was still in stocks. I think he stated the sum was about eight or nine dollars in greenbacks."[66]

"But perhaps the most pitiable meanness, where meanesses were so common, was a trick which this man Duncan played off upon a poor, scurvy-stricken prisoner, James Hamilton. It has been observed that orders were issued prohibiting the purchase of any vegetables by the prisoners, and if any were obtained in contravention of these orders, if the transgressor could be pointed out, not only were his hard-earned vegetables confiscated, but he

---

[63] Chipman, p. 159, 160.
[64] *Ibid.*, p. 161.
[65] Spencer, pp. 116-119.
[66] *Wirz Trial*, pp. 367, 368.

was severely punished for an infraction of the rule. Hamilton was one day lying upon the ground, calling, in his weariness and distress, for his mother, and begging for some vegetables to eat, for his instinct told him they would be better for him than any medicine. Just then Duncan drove into the stockade with the daily rations of bread, and passed near where Hamilton lay, having upon him an overcoat of somewhat better appearance than was usual there. Duncan inquired of him what he wanted there? He replied that he wanted some onions, and would give any thing for them. Duncan told him if he would give him his overcoat he would bring him some, and the poor fellow eagerly accepted the offer, and took off his coat and gave it him.

Duncan told Wirz of it, and on the following day, when he went in with the bread, Wirz accompanied him. He threw two bunches of shallots to Hamilton, exclaiming, 'There are your onions; I've done my part.' Wirz stepped up and seized the vegetables, and bore them off with him. But he did not stop here; he had Hamilton taken out, and, weak, exhausted as he was, placed him in the foot-stocks, and kept him there for twelve hours in the broiling sun. He went stark, staring mad; and, with horrid imprecations upon the robber of his coat, mingled with piteous appeals to his mother in her far-off home - these two thoughts alone rioting in his mind, which insanity had not driven from their strong-hole - thus he lingered and died."[67]

By far, the most common food issued at Andersonville was raw corn meal, corn meal mush or corn bread. On many days, one of these was all that was issued.

If the meal was issued raw, then it was many times eaten raw. This was not as repugnant as it seems because many soldiers in the field would eat it raw, when necessary. The men thought they were luckier if they received the raw rations unless they were sick or destitute. If they were healthy and had the means to cook their rations, they would much rather cook their own meals. "A portion of the camp drew raw rations, and fared somewhat better than those whose food was prepared before issued to them."[68] "The decision depended upon the state of the stomach. If very hungry, we made mush; if less famished, dumplings; if disposed to weigh matters, bread."[69]

The easiest method of cooking the meal was simply to make corn meal cakes or "Johnny cakes." These were patties made by mixing water with meal and frying them in a pan or canteen-half greased with some pork fat. When brown, it was flipped over and the other side browned. They could be baked by being placed on a board or canteen-half, and by tilting the board up near the fire at 45 degrees. They were sometimes called "hoe cakes" because slaves cooked the meal on their hoes in the field. This bread would become totally unfit to eat by the next day.[70]

The most popular and the most elegant method of preparation of corn meal was to cook little square chunks of pork or bacon in water, making a watery sauce, and then plopping in little balls made of corn meal and water. These dumplings then rose to the surface and, when brown, would be served, cut open and the pork sauce poured over them. This was the top gourmet meal served by the prisoners at Andersonville.

"We could not cook what raw rations we got; I very often mixed up the meal and ate it raw for want of wood and cooking utensils. We got a little more than a pint of meal; that was before Captain Wirz took command; we got a little better than that after he took command. The rations consisted of about a pint of meal and a half a pound of very coarse beef; we took it to be mule flesh; it looked more like horse or mule flesh than beef; we got about a teaspoonful of salt; that was our rations for twenty-four hours; I very often ate my beef or mule flesh raw."[71][76] "Some of the time they would give us beef, about once a week. They called it beef but it resembled mule or horse meat more than beef. The boys would eat it raw without salt, as they got it. It was generally full of fly blows, but we did not care for that."[72]

When meat was difficult to obtain, the Confederates issued sorghum molasses sometimes as a substitute. This was sometimes of very poor quality and was called "lasses" by some rebels.

"The food allowed to the prisoners at Andersonville, according to the statements of the prisoners and other witnesses, was from two to four ounces of bacon, and from four to twelve ounces of corn bread daily; sometimes a half pint to a pint of bean, pea, or sweet potato soup, of doubtful value. Vegetables were unknown. Thus giving a total weight of solid food, per diem, of six to sixteen ounces of solid food. The amount was not constant; some days the prisoners were entirely without food, as was the case at Belle Isle and Salisbury. Neither was the deficiency afterwards made good. The amount given was oftener less than ten ounces than more."[73]

[67] Spencer, p. 119.
[68] Abbott, p. 199.
[69] McElroy, p. 199.
[70] Abbbott, p. 197.
[71] Ray, p. 238.
[72] Clifton, p. 9.
[73] Hamlin, p. 80.

Besides issuing the corn meal raw and as corn bread, many times it was served a third way -- as a soft corn meal mush. This was the way many soldiers prepared their corn meal when they were in the field without access to a fire. Under what conditions the Confederates decided to prepare the meal as mush is unknown. They probably made mush when they were rushed and/or when the number of prisoners became too great for the cooking facilities. The prisoners called the meal mixed with water into a mush "chicken feed." "I remember of them hauling in large boxes full of mush which had fermented, and the box would be running over like a yeast crock."[74]

"As there were continual additions to our numbers our cooks could not bake bread for all, and large kettles were placed in the cook house and mush made for and issued to a part of the prisoners. They would fill these kettles about three-fourths full of water, and while one would stir with a great paddle another would dump in a fifty-pound sack of meal at a time, which would form in lumps as big as a quart cup, the inside of which would be dry, uncooked meal. This was hauled in a wagon-bed and measured in a large box to the respective divisions, giving each man something over a pint of mush. This would be scooped out on blankets made of old coats, shirts, and pieces of canvas sewed together, and while thus spread on these would become polluted by the multitudes of lice that filled the sand and the myriads of maggot-lies that swarmed overhead."[75]

Miller said the mush was dumped into "pine boxes" and then brought into the pen in wagons. "The Johnnies brought in our mush in barrels. After it was distributed the prisoners would tip the barrels over and go in head first trying to get what was not scraped out. They fought like cats and dogs about who would get in first."[76] At "nearly night," a mule team came in after the "mush-boxes."[77]

Another gastronomic delight was to place in a tin plate one of the big, round biscuits or crackers occasionally issued. Water was heated in a skillet and poured over the biscuit, then another tin plate was turned over it. After a few minutes, on removing the upper tin plate, the biscuit would have swelled so that it filled the plate. A piece of fat pork or bacon was then put in the skillet, and, when the fat was well-fried, the biscuit was put in the hot fat and placed over the fire.

"Sometimes I drew more rations than I could eat, the stomach revolting. In this case the surplus corn meal would be made into a beer or vinegar, used for the scurvy, or it would be traded with other prisoners for vegetables."[78]

Very rarely, but occasionally, the prisoners were issued wheat instead of corn meal. Captain Samuel B. Davis said, "Wheat was a rarity, not only at Andersonville, but everywhere else in the Confederacy. I was sent with official papers on one occasion from the War Department at Richmond to Gen. Lee's headquarters at Orange Courthouse. I arrived at night, about 1 o'clock. The next morning I was asked to breakfast with Gen. Lee and his military family. On the table in front of the General was a little piece of wheat bread, possibly 4 inches long, 2 inches wide and 3 inches thick. The good old gentleman asked each one at the table to have a piece, but all of us knew the scarcity of such food, and each one refused and ate corn bread. If the officers at the Commanding General's table ate corn bread, why not the prisoners at Andersonville?"[79]

Salt was always sought after at Andersonville. It was issued about every other day for the first couple of months but then it was issued only occasionally. The men continually complained about how bland the menu was at Andersonville.

"We traded buttons to the guards for red peppers and made our mush, or bread, or dumplings, hot with the fiery pods, in hopes that this would make up for the lack of salt, but it was a failure One pinch of salt was worth all the pepper pods in the Southern Confederacy."[80]

"Salt was a luxury in the stockade. I speak of my own positive knowledge when I say that salt was sold by the bakers at the bake-house to the traders inside the stockade in quantities to suit purchasers, and it was tied up in bags, and thrown over the stockade at night. The scarcity of salt affected our rations to this extent, that we had no salt at all in our bread for a long time; that is, no quantity which was appreciable; we could not taste it...One day about the middle of October I wrote to Captain Wirz that owing to the way in which our salt was disposed of, it was impossible to obtain any through the medium of our cooks, and I therefore requested him either to issue the salt to us personally, as the other provisions were distributed, from the wagons, or else to stop the supply altogether, so as to break

[74] Helwig, p. 29.
[75] Fosdick, p. 51.
[76] Tyler, p. 29.
[77] Dufur, pp. 128-130.
[78] Miller, p. 18.
[79] Davis, pp. 26, 27.
[80] McElroy, p. 199.

up this trading. He immediately issued an order which was posted on the sutler's shop, prohibiting the sale of salt inside the stockade, and authorizing the police to seize upon it wherever exposed for sale, and to confiscate it. I do not know for whose benefit it was confiscated. Immediately after that, for a few days, the taste of salt was perceptible in our bread, but matters relapsed into their former state in a short time."[81]

Sweet potatoes were issued the first few weeks the prison was open, but they, like the issues of salt, soon disappeared. Sometimes the rations consisted of a pint or a pint-and-a-half of what are called today, "black-eyed" peas. In the pen, they were known as "stock peas" because they were fed to livestock, "nigger beans" or, most commonly, "cow peas." The cow peas were usually issued raw and were welcomed because they were thought to be more nutritious than corn meal. They usually were of very poor quality with worms or grubs. They were said to have "occupants" by the prisoners. Because they were dry, they were easily carried and bartered. When being cooked, some prisoners skimmed off the bugs while others favored eating the additional protein. "The bugs in the peas bothered me by trying to crawl out of the cup when the boiling process commenced, but by careful watching, and pushing them into the soup, it made the food more nutritious and palatable."[82]

Lyons described the beans issued to him. "These beans were of a peculiar variety - small, speckled red ones, I think it is not exaggerating to say that one in every three beans contained a small, black bug. When we put these beans in water, some of the bugs came to the surface and we skimmed them off. Those that did not float we cooked and ate."[83]

Besides cow peas, another vegetable sometimes issued by the Confederates was rice, both raw and cooked. "A little weak vinegar unfit for use," was sometimes issued. It was thought this had some beneficial effect as an anti-scorbutic. "Corn meal coffee" was made by burning or charring bits of bread and boiling them in a tin cup.

Whole beef heads were issued intact several times. "When they would slaughter beef for their own men, they would give the head, and shanks from the knee down, to the prisoners. Just imagine ten men getting a cow's leg below the joint for a day's rations, and it not skinned or cut up. The head would be given to a mess of twenty men. Two or three would take the skin, singe the hair off of it and boil it, and thus have pretty fair soup, when two or three spoonsful of meal were added." It was then divided into twenty pieces and distributed. "Those getting the horns generally had a tough time. They would place them on a stick and hold them in the fire until they were broiled almost to a cinder. Then the owner would eat as far as burned, then put it into the fire again, and so on until he would get away with a whole cow's horn. The brains, eyes and nose would be eaten -- not one ounce would be wasted that could be used."[84] This was continued for only a short time and then the old fare was distributed.

Clifton told of a very lucky find in the sands of Georgia. "I was passing around close to the rebel's cook house one day and I saw a black greasy object lying in the sand. I picked it up. It was a piece of bacon skin. I scraped the sand off it. We were craving salt or something like bacon, and I can say for a truth, I don't think I ever did in all my life taste anything that I so relished or tasted so good though I have eaten of many finely prepared meals, but nothing compared to the old black skin."[85]

"I have seen the rebels bring in beef lung and throw it into a crowd of us prisoners to see us grab and scratch after it. I never could tell where it went. All I could see of it was bloody fingers. The one that could eat the fastest got the most of it."[86]

Ambrose Spencer related that the ration wagons drivers dared not enter the prison when the it became terribly crowded, for they feared an attack by the starving prisoners. This was highly unlikely, and never was corroborated by another writer. "When the number of prisoners increased to over thirty-seven thousand ... the custom of carrying the prisoners' food into the stockade was abolished. They drove up to the gates, which were slightly opened, and the scanty food, foul and unhealthy as it was, was thrown inside by the guard, to be scrambled for by the wretched prisoners, the strongest and those nearest the gate getting the largest share, the weak and sickly getting none."[87]

---

[81] *Wirz Trial*, p. 590.
[82] Miller, p. 18.
[83] Lyons, p. 44.
[84] Fosdick, p. 66.
[85] Clifton, p. 9.
[86] *Ibid.*
[87] A. C. Roach, *The Prisoner of War and How Treated* (Indianapolis, Ind.: The Railroad City Publishing House, 1865), p. 224.

**Bakery** - The one story, two-room bakery housed two ovens. Each oven was 14 feet in length by 7 feet in width. It was located on Stockade Creek before it enterered the pen. (Gross)

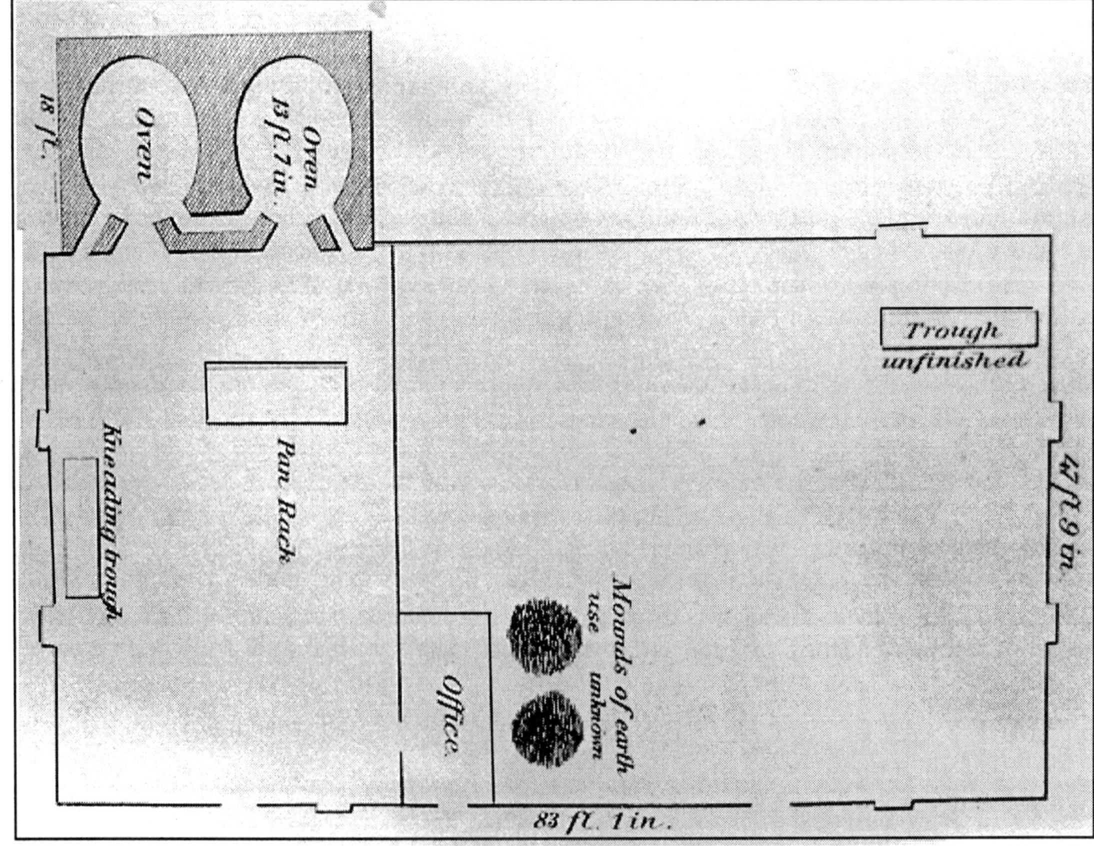


**Floor plan of the Bakery** - showing the two ovens. The bakery measured about 83 feet by 47 feet, 9 inches. (Goss)

The inmates complained and thought that Dick Winder was not interested in setting up a cooking facility when, in truth, he was unable to do so. The date that the bakery was started is unknown, but, on the direct orders of Captain Dick Winder, the bakery was located to the west of the palisade wall, which was a point that would, later, be between the two palisades on the edge of Stockade Creek. The bakery, or "bake-house," was constructed by prisoners who had been detailed for that purpose. They were taken out in the morning and returned to the pen before nightfall.[88] On the 8th of May, Captain Wirz wrote to Major Turner, "... the bakery, which could not be completed for want of lumber, is now in operation."[89]

There was a small spring behind the bakery, which was the source of the water utilized in making the bread. Dr. Bates said that only bread was cooked at "Cook House No. 1. "The bread furnished to the prisoners was simply mixed with salt and the dirty water from the brook, or the foul spring in the rear of the bakery, and then dried in the heat of the oven."[90] It must be remembered that, even as it was, the bakery was located downstream from the camps of the guards with their horses' stables. There was some run-off from these, even though it was said the soldiers did use slit trenches for latrines and the stables were relatively far from the water's edge. The garrison had been ordered not to foul the stream. "So little care was observed for the comfort or the health of the prisoners, that all the washings of the bakery, all the filth of the out-houses of the workmen, were allowed to pass down and mingle with the current of the stream only thirty feet above the point of entrance into the stockade. Besides this, the drains of the camp and town above emptied themselves into this stream which supplied the prison with water."[91]

"I have seen it completely covered, almost with floating greases, and dirt, and offal. I have gone in barefoot, when it was so dirty that I had to go out, as I was getting all over with grease and filth. It was not always so, but very frequently so."[92]

Dick Winder, after the war, admitted that he did make a rather bad mistake in locating the bakery where he did.

The bakery was a two-room, one-story shed made of rough boards. It measured 47 feet, 9 inches by 83 feet, 1 inch.[93] In one of the rooms, were two large ovens of common brick, in which was baked all the corn bread obtained by the prisoners. These ovens in the bakery were brought from Richmond,[94] and were about 14 feet long and 7 feet wide.[95] If they had been kept red hot day and night, they had the "extreme" capacity of baking nine thousand, six hundred rations of corn bread. The "ordinary" capacity was probably between four and five thousand rations per day.[96]

The interior of the bakery was described this way. "Here was a large, long box, in which was soured corn-dough sticking to its sides and bottom, over which swarmed millions of flies, a wagon-load of meal was scooped into this box, burying flies and gnats; water was dipped from the filthy branch to wet this meal, then stirred with poles and shoveled into large pans, marked off in half-brick sizes, and, when baked, sent into the pen, and a half-brick-shaped piece given to each man on the north side of the creek. The next day, the north side got dry meal while the south side got the baked bread, and so on, alternately."[97]

"Sometimes they would cook it. They had a big vat something like we make lime mortar in. It was swimming with fleas; they could empty a half wagon load of meal into it and mix it up with dirty water from the run that came down through there."[98]

Some prisoners implied they thought the authorities added fecal material to some of the rations. Dufur said that filth "... of the vilest and most outrageous kind that the human mind can conceive" was purposefully added to the mush fed the prisoners.[99]

There were 200 prisoners detailed as cooks, two shifts of 100 men each. They were housed outside the pen. "There were only four of our detailed men at both the cooking and baking houses and the balance of the force, some 100 and odd men, were paroled prisoners."[100] By having men detailed from their number, arguments about the in-

[88] Boggs, p. 30.
[89] *O.R.*, VII, p. 169.
[90] Hamlin, p. 86.
[91] *Ibid.*, p. 60.
[92] Chipman, p. 166.
[93] Hamlin, p. 60.
[94] Davis, p. 26.
[95] Hamlin, p. 60.
[96] *Ibid.*
[97] Boggs, pp. 40, 41.
[98] Clifton, p. 8.
[99] Dufur, p. 115.
[100] *O.R.*, VIII, p. 733.

ability of the cooks or possible shortages would be negated. Some southern apologists say that, since Yankees were detailed to do the cooking, these men would not knowingly foul the water that was to be drunk by their fellow prisoners.

James K. Davidson, who worked as a teamster hauling rations and the dead, testified: "While outside, we got our rations at the bake-house -- the first one. We had a sergeant of the wood squad, who drew the rations and brought them to us. That sergeant was a Union prisoner. The rations were generally brought to us in pails and boxes. The bread consisted of corn, ground cob and all, and beans that were not fit for any human. We had plenty of it such as it was. It was not fit to eat. I do not know who furnished us the wagons to carry out the dead. A man named Duncan had charge of them. He was a quartermaster. He had also charge of the bake-house. I saw Duncan in the stockade while I was there. He used to come in there. I believe he divided the rations to the prisoners inside the stockade awhile; also a man named Humes, and Captain Bowers. I cannot tell what portion of the time, while I was in the stockade, Duncan provided the rations. I do not know who did provide the rations while I was in the stockade. I know that part of the time they were not provided at all. Duncan provided them while I was outside of the stockade, and a man named Bowers, and a man named Humes. I believe Duncan issued rations to us all the time we were outside of the stockade. I believe the other two men went inside the stockade with rations. I do not know where Duncan's headquarters were. I do not know whether he had any headquarters or not. I believe he was generally recognized there as quartermaster. He was at the cook-house nearly all the time. He was a confederate. He did not belong to any regiment that I know of. I do not know where he ate his rations. I have no means of knowing whether he ate the same as he furnished to me. I do not know who furnished the wagons; Duncan had charge of them. I drove six mules all the time. I did not take care of the mules. I drove them to the depot at night and turned them into the corral. I had to go there every morning to get my mules. I do not know that I saw Duncan there at the depot. I never saw any other man at that place acting as or being called quartermaster. I had no orders in reference to these mules, only, after we were done our day's work, we were to return them to the corral. I do not know how many mules and horses were kept at that corral. There was a corral there with about two acres of ground, and was pretty well crowded with mules and horses. I could not go and select for myself my horses and mules. I had one team all the time. The man who had charge of the corral gave them to me. When I went to the corral for my team, I would ask for it, and tell the man what team it was, and he would get it... I was ordered to take the same team to draw rations in that I used to haul out the dead. Mr. Duncan, the quartermaster, ordered me. He had ordered me, when driving past the cook-house with the dead, to fetch a load of rations as I was coming back; and I obeyed him, of course. Captain Wirz never ordered me to do that. I looked up to Duncan as my boss or employer there. I did not consider that Captain Wirz had anything to do with me -- nothing more than hearsay. He never interfered with me while I was at work with Duncan. Captain Wirz never assaulted or bruised me while I was at work there."[101]

The authorities found it difficult to cook rations for more than half of the prisoners. One side of the prison would get cooked rations and the other would get raw rations; the next week, each would receive the opposite type rations. "When the number of prisoners exceeded 15,000, the facilities of the cook-house were inadequate. Therefore, raw rations were issued alternately every two weeks to each side of the prison."[102] Maile and Lyons said they alternated every two weeks, but most said the rations were alternated weekly. Boggs said they were alternated daily.

Jasper Culver of the 1st Wisconsin Infantry "... was at work in the bakery from the 27th of June, 1864, to the 12th of September, 1864. There were two reliefs, and in each relief thirteen men, working at the bakery, and four or five extra hands, making about thirty-two hands in the bakery. Those were all Union prisoners. There were no rebel soldiers or officers over them but this Duncan. Each of those reliefs had one of our men as boss-baker. All the boss-bakers did was to see that the bread was baked. We baked night and day - one relief for the night, and the other for the day. Duncan and a man named Humes took it to the stockade after it was baked. Humes went into the stockade and issued it. There was a clerk there who received the orders, who told me how much to issue to each detachment. He received those orders from Captain Wirz. The clerk was one of our own men. He had his station at the bakery; he staid at the bakery all the time. I saw Captain Wirz at the bake-house quite often; he would generally come down and go through it, and then go out again. I never heard him give any orders. I never saw him interfere with the management of the bake-house. This Duncan seemed to have the care of the surroundings of the bakery - the keeping of it clear. Some of us men were detailed as a police around the bakery. They seemed to attend to their duties properly. It was not made clean, and properly kept around the bakery. Immediately round, near the door, and in the bakery, it

[101] *Wirz Trial*, p. 144.
[102] Maile, p. 39.

seemed to be kept clean, but the filth of the cook-house and bakery was thrown off some distance from the bakery into a swamp, and that was very filthy. That swamp ran down to the brook. The offal was thrown in there by Duncan's order; at least I heard him order the men to throw their trash out in the swamp. It was five or six nods from the creek where they threw most of the stuff. I heard the men ask Duncan where they should throw some grease and stuff that came from the cook-house. This was before the cooking was removed. The stuff was liquid, and in a barrel; Duncan told him to throw it out there, pointing to a place in the swamp. There was very little to be thrown into that swamp after the cook-house was removed; nothing more than the sweepings of the bake-house. This did not make the water in the creek greasy. We used to take water from that creek to mix the bread with. It could not help to be otherwise than unclean, because the rebel camps were above, and they always used the creek to wash their clothes, and for every other purpose. The water in the well above the bakery was not good. I do not know what caused the water in the well to be bad; it seemed to be clear, but it was very bad-tasted. There was a small spring above, where they used to get drinking-water from. We often used to speak about the uncleanness of that brook."[103]

A prisoner named Goldsmith testified: "Captain Wirz made out provision returns day by day. I saw these returns. They stated the number of men and the number of rations. They calculated the rations. The number of pounds of meal was calculated. They were made out and brought to me every morning, showing the number of pounds I was to have issued. We used to draw five days' rations at a time from the commissary, and have them put in another room. They were issued in bulk to Mr. Bowers, who had charge of the bake-house. He used to come with the teams and take it to the cook-house. After that I had nothing to do with them."[104]

Again Goldsmith testified: "... the requisitions made out by Captain Wirz were made by the number of men. Captain Wirz would make out the number of rations to be issued to that number of men. He would put it down in pounds. Captain Wirz would give me tickets to issue next morning a certain number of pounds. I kept those tickets and returned them next morning to Captain Wirz' office. When this requisition was made out I would take it to Captain Armstrong and draw the rations. He would make out these tickets from his morning reports. They were yellow paper tickets. There would be on those tickets just the number of rations - peas, so many pounds; meal, so many pounds; molasses, so many gallons; salt, so many pounds - and the number of men in the stockade. When the requisition was made out it went from me to the commissary. The requisition remained in Captain Armstrong's office after he filled it for me."[105]

Jasper Culver of the 1st Wisconsin infantry was detailed to unload the meal that came to the bakery by the stream and to load the bread into the wagons for the stockade. "The bread was baked in cakes about eighteen inches long, ten inches wide and two inches thick. Ten of those loaves or 'cards' were sent out to a detachment of two hundred and seventy men for one day. They were four or four and a half of them sent to each 270 men. They were generally very poorly baked. The center of them was almost always raw. They never could be baked properly. Those large 'cards' that were baked in the night and sent in the afternoon frequently became sour and stringy; it became stringy from the sour dough and the heat of the bread, and it was impossible to eat it."[106]

It is assumed that most of the meat that was fed to the prisoners was obtained from cattle slaughtered on post because later, when a shoe factory was contemplated, it was stated that there were many cow hides present on the post. After the slaughter, the meat was butchered into portions to feed the thirties. The meat would then be carried to the "kitchen" to be boiled. The original kitchen, or second cooking facility, was located on Stockade Creek just west of the bakery because Dick Winder thought, "... they would require much water in the use of them."

By June 10th, Dick Winder said that he had built two large bakeries, and, at that time was in the process of constructing a third one.[107] Near the 1st of August, this second facility was torn down and re-established north of its old site. In one 19th-century print it was identified as the "cookhouse."[108]

They were in the process of moving it when Colonel Chandler made his inspection tour on August 1st. General Winder said, "When the number reached 12,000, immediate steps were taken to increase the baking, cooking, and other arrangements, but the impossibility of procuring the necessary material has prevented the completion. In a few days, the cooking arrangements will be completed; the baking is, and I fear will be, delayed for want of the necessary material."[109]

---

103 *Wirz Trial*, p. 305.
104 *Ibid.*, p. 301.
105 *Ibid.*
106 *Ibid.*, p. 302.
107 *O.R.*, VII, p. 222.
108 Mann, p. 542.
109 *O.R.*, VII, p. 541.

**Cookhouse Number 2 or "Kitchen"** - It measured about 100 feet in length and about 50 feet in width. It contained two medium-sized ranges and four boilers of fifty gallons capacity each. This was where most of the meat was prepared. (Gross)

Captain Richard Winder had great difficulty getting paraphernalia for his cooking facilities.

*"Andersonville, Ga.,*
*"June 10, 1864.*
*"General A. R. Lawton, Quartermaster-General, Richmond, Ga.:*

*"Sir: I would respectfully state that I am in great need of some sheet iron to make some baking-pans to cook bread for prisoners of war and cannot get along at all without it. I can have the pans made at the post, if I could only get the iron and wire, much cheaper than they could be purchased. Tin is entirely too expensive, as it burns out in a few weeks. I have tried everywhere in Georgia to get this iron, but cannot succeed in finding any. Please give this matter your immediate attention, as the prisoners are really suffering for the want of these pans. I have built two large bakeries and am now constructing a third. We have 22,000 prisoners here and are now extending the stockade, enclosing two more acres of ground. Please find below memoranda of necessary iron and wire.*

*"Ten bunches, twenty-four sheets in bunch, sheet iron, thirty inches by ten, sixteenth inch, or as near this width and thickness as possible. Two coils No. 8 wire.*

*"Please answer me by telegraph in regard to this matter, and should you order these things shipped from Richmond please have them sent through by express.*

*"Very respectfully, your obedient servant,*
*"R. B. Winder*
*"Captain and Assistant Quartermaster.*[110]

The wire being requisitioned was to make sieves to sift the corn meal. This explains the very poor quality of the meal the prisoners received.

Probably in response to the prisoner complaints of there being grease and contamination in the brook, Dick

[110] *Ibid.*, p. 222.

Winder began the third cooking facility about two hundred paces from the outer palisades of the prison towards the north-west. The exact date that construction was begun is unknown. This structure was sometimes called the "kitchen," the "soup house" or "cook house No. 2." After the original cooking facility No. 2 was torn down, this new kitchen became known as cooking facility No. 2.

It was a rectangular-shaped, one story shed of rough boards about 100 feet long and less than 50 feet wide. This was set up by Captain Dick Winder far enough away from the Stockade Creek that the waste products would not find their way into the prisoners' water supply. "The kitchen contained inside 2 medium sized ranges, and 4 boilers of 50 gallons' capacity each.[111]

"When the kitchen began cooking is unknown. It seems that corn bread was baked in that facility as well as at the bakery. "There were two cook-houses outside, and they generally cooked and baked in them; I have seen bread come from both."[112] "With constant cooking by industrious men, this kitchen would have been able to cook rations for about 5,000 men in any 24 hour period."[113]

During the first part of the war, prisoners were turned over to the Quartermaster-General to be kept and fed by his subordinates, under the direction of the Secretary of War. After February 17th, 1864, the feeding of the prisoners devolved upon the Commissary-General's subordinates. Dick Winder said: "In February, 1864, the C.S. Congress passed a law relieving the Quartermaster's Department of feeding the prisoners of war and placed it in the hands of the Commissary Department. Soon after this a commissary officer was sent to Andersonville, and after his arrival, owing to a misunderstanding about the orders, I for a time receipted to him for the prisoners' rations, which the commandant of the prison ought to have done, and which he, as I suppose, did so as soon as the orders were properly understood. After this I had nothing on earth to do with the prisoners' rations, except to furnish transportation for them from the commissary store-house to the cook-house and from thence to the prison."[114]

On July 25th, General Winder wrote to General Samuel Cooper, stating: "There are 29,400 prisoners, 2,650 troops, 500 negroes and other laborers and not a ration at the post. There is great danger in this state of things. I have ordered that at least ten days' rations should be kept on hand, but it has never been done."[115]

The supplies for the prisoners at Andersonville were furnished by the district commissary, Second District of Georgia. The vast majority of the supplies in this district were forwarded to the army in Virginia where they were urgently needed. In fact, L. B. Northrop, Commissary-General of Subsistence, endorsed on the back of General Winder's letter to Cooper, "Had General Winder's orders for ten days' rations for over 32,000 men to be kept ahead been complied with, I should have countermanded it to the district commissary. The reasons against such accumulation are greater now than before." Because of a severed West Point Railroad line from Alabama at this time, Georgia must supply food to both the Army of Tennessee as well as the Army of Northern Virginia. "Meanwhile we have no money either to buy or impress provisions...the army may be restricted in a day's ration."[116]

Even if the supplies were available, some Southerners rationalized that, since the Yankees burned the Shenandoah Valley of Virginia, where much wheat and corn was grown, the Yankees should be the prime beneficiaries of these actions. Dick Winder, too, did not have the support of the men further up the chain of command. In fact, Colonel Northrop, who was rather anti-Yankee in his sentiments, once stated: "The state of the commissariat will not allow the issue of a full ration to our own troops in the field, much less to prisoners of war. It is just that the men who cause the scarcity shall be the first to suffer from it ... Present appearance indicate the prospective necessity of a still greater reduction of the ration."[117]

Spencer commented on the sentiment of the citizens living in the neighborhood of Andersonville: "It was not uncommon to hear suggestions that the provisions which the prisoners consumed ought to be saved for the use of the rebel armies; that shooting every one who attempted his escape and was caught; poisoning those who were prostrated by disease, to rid the Confederacy of their sustenance by food or medicine; hanging those who were mutinous, and clear the country of their presence. Such were the feelings of a large, very large proportion of the inhabitants living in the county and country adjoining the Andersonville stockade."[118]

Almost every afternoon at or near four o'clock, both gates would swing open and two uncovered army wagons

[111] Hamlin, p. 62.
[112] Chipman, p. 171
[113] Hamlin, p. 63.
[114] *O.R.*, VIII, p. 731.
[115] *O.R.*, VII, p. 499.
[116] *Ibid.*
[117] *O.R.*, VIII, p. 161.
[118] Spencer, p. 35.

drawn by four-mule teams ("two span of mules") would be driven in simultaneously.[119] On the wagon would be a Confederate officer and a Confederate sergeant. Usually Captain Humes would be in one wagon and Captain Bowers in the other. At times, Captain Duncan drove one wagon and Captain Humes the other one. The food wagon was guarded by eight men with bayonet-tipped muskets.[120] The Negro driver sat on the left mule closest to the wagon ("near mule behind").[121] The Confederate sergeant would call for the sergeant of the detachment to receive the rations and he would draw the rations based on the morning count which had been taken earlier.

**Prisoners Receiving Rations** - The common army wagon was usually drawn by two spans of mules with a rider on the "near mule behind." The sergeant of the squad would receive the rations and return to the Thirty's headquarters where it would be divided out to the men. (Kellogg)

When Frank W. Smith was asked how he could tell when the ration wagon was coming into the stockade, he stated, "Millions of flies would follow the wagon in and out of the stockade, the buzz of the fly would warn us if the cheer of the comrades outside did not."[122]

"In the afternoon our drummer would put in an appearance and play 'grub call,' which unlike the morning summons, would elicit a cheer from nearly every throat of the six thousand inmates, making the old prison resound, and the same six-mule team and wagon that had hauled away the dead would come in with our rations, which would often be contaminated by the excrement from the dead, and was extremely offensive even to famishing man."[123] "The carts which were used to draw our rations into the prison, were during the forenoon made use of to convey the dead from the dead house to the trenches in which they were buried, and no pretense was made of cleansing them. Our rations of rice, beans, etc., were put into these carts in bulk, and those who got their rations from the sides or bottom of the cart, got more than they cared for."[124] Leonard also said that, after delivering the dead to the cemetery, "... on the return trip the same 'dead wagon' brought our food from the cook house to the Stockade

[119] Maile, p. 38.
[120] Lyons, p. 43.
[121] Kellogg, p. 110.
[122] Frank W. Smith, p. 36.
[123] Fosdick, p. 42.
[124] Russell, p. 8.

and hospital."[125] "To show the utter want of decency which ruled all things connected with the prison, it is stated, by positive eyewitnesses, that the same carts that transported the dead, went forth (without being cleansed of their reeking and disgusting filth), to the shambles and the depots for the meat and corn for the living prisoners."[126]

Therefore, if one were to receive cooked rations, the wagon would be loaded with "cards" of corn bread measuring about fifteen inches by twenty inches and three inches thick. The sergeant of the detachment would spread a blanket on the ground on which to place the cornbread. These would be separated into three equal stacks for each of the sergeants of the nineties to take back to their men and to sub-divide further to the thirties. The sergeant of a thirty would cut the morsel into pieces equal to the number counted that morning; the size of the morsel was about the size of half of a normal brick.

"A man was struck with a club and nearly killed, by one who helps unload rations... The man who was struck yesterday is dead. The murderer is sentenced by the chief of the regulators, to wear a ball and chain here and to our lines."[127]

On June 6th, Wirz wrote to Colonel Persons, calling to his attention the fact that the bread issued to the prisoners was fully one-sixth husk, that it was almost unfit for consumption, and was, almost certainly, increasing the dysentery and other bowel problems. He wished the colonel would order the meal bolted and sifted before being issued. He felt that if it were sifted, the corn bread rations would be smaller by fully a quarter of a pound.

Wirz also wished that some container or receptacle be issued to the men so that rice, beans, vinegar, and molasses could be received by the prisoners. "If my information is correct, any number of buckets can be got from Columbus, Ga., if the quartermaster of the post would make the requisition for the same."[128]

Brownell, having arrived before Wirz, remembered that the men were divided into twenties instead of thirties. "We finally adopted the plan of shipwrecked sailors - the meat was first cut into twenty pieces, as fairly as possible, then one man turned his back to the meat, while the Master of Ceremonies put his knife on a piece of meat and asked: 'who shall have this?' - he with his back turned called out some name, and this went on until every man got his piece."[129] When the rations were "touched off," there must not be the variation of a word, or any change in tone or emphasis.[130]

**"Allotting Squard Rations by Number"** - Note the "cards" of corn bread with the small pieces of meat (probably pork) on top. A man with his back turned would call out a number from 1 to 30 as another man passed his hand over a stack of rations. (Chipman)

"Each wagon was accompanied by a guard while being driven within the stockade and distributing its load at the headquarters of each detachment. The detachment sergeants issued it in equal lots to the three squad sergeants

[125] A. C. Leonard, *The Boys in Blue of 1861-1865* (Lancaster, Pa.: A. C. Leonard, Publisher, 1904), p. 59.
[126] Hamlin, p. 57.
[127] Northrop, p. 119.
[128] *O.R.*, VII, p. 207.
[129] Brownell, p. 11.
[130] Smith, pp. 11, 12.

and they again, dividing it as equally as possible, gave the portions to the individual men. After the bread and meat had been divided into the requisite number of pieces they were placed upon a log, which I was informed was the property of the squad. One piece of bread, about half the size of a brick, and a piece of meat, as large as two of my fingers, was the ration for each man for a whole day.

It would be impossible for any man, however nice his judgment, to divide the bread and meat into exactly even pieces; some would have a mouthful or a mouthful and a half more than others, and some pieces would be better in quality than others; in either case an item not to be overlooked by starving men."

Did the prisoners receive all the rations that they were authorized to receive by the appropriations of the Confederate Government? The prisoners were to have received the same rations in quality and quantity as did the Confederate soldiers in the field. If they did not, was it due simply to poor communication, poor transportation, and poor distribution? Some subordinates in the department were so prejudiced or anti-Yankee that the subsistence of prisoners was considered only slightly more important than feeding livestock.

Was there corruption or graft in connection with the securing and distribution of food? There was speculation, even during the war, that all was not right at Andersonville. Rumors circulated throughout the South and North concerning the deprivations carried on at Andersonville. "In some cases, newspapers in the vicinity heralded, some with boastful pride, others with reprehension, the enormous mortality which was daily occurring there."[131]

Inspectors were sent several times from Richmond to examine and report back their findings about the conditions there. General Howell Cobb, with his personal staff surgeon, inspected the prison to ascertain what was taking place 60 miles from his headquarters in Macon.

Doctor Joseph Jones, a Confederate officer sent to inspect the medical aspects there, rationalized: "If the Federal prisoners did not receive the rations to which they were entitled by the act of the Confederate Government, the deficiencies and irregularities were due either to the impossibility of securing regular supplies of provisions in the impoverished condition of the Confederacy, with the imperfect lines of communication, dilapidated but crowded railroad transportation, and with a currency depreciated to an almost nominal value, or to frauds committed by the officers in immediate charge of the subsistence department of the prisoners, and by the Federal prisoners themselves detailed to distribute rations within the stockade and hospital. ... The stealing of rations by those detailed to distribute them in the prison and hospital is a subject of continual complaint on the part of the prisoners themselves."[132]

The competency of the assistant commissary officer was called into question by Colonel Daniel T. Chandler after his inspection on August 1st. "Capt. J. W. Armstrong, assistant commissary of subsistence, left the post shortly after my arrival on sick-leave, locking up nearly all his books and papers. I was consequently unable to make a satisfactory examination into his affairs. Enough information, however, was elicited to show that he is a very inefficient officer and entirely incompetent for the discharge of his duties of his position, and should at once be removed."[133] One wonders if he was truly sick or whether there was some cover-up as in the medical department.

One of the witnesses who testified at Wirz' trial was Benjamin B. Dykes, the railroad agent at Andersonville. He became the railroad agent at Andersonville in 1861 and continued to hold that position through 1864. When he came to testify, he brought his railroad books with him that "... contained the original entries from the freight lists of goods and stores unloaded at his depot.

In the month of July, there were sixty-four barrels of whisky left at his agency, of which forty-three were for the medical director. In August there were ninety-six barrels, sixty of which went to Dr. White for hospital use. In September there were thirty-six barrels, all for the hospital. Here, then, in three months only, were one hundred and thirty-nine barrels of this so-much-called-for stimulant deposited in the hands of the medical director for the necessities of the hospital."[134] These were forty gallon barrels, so over fire thousand gallons of whiskey most of which went, according to Spencer, "... down the throats of Dr. White and his friends."

Uriah B. Harrold, a commissary of the Confederate Government stationed at Americus, was also a witness at the trial. He appeared with his abstracts of shipments of provisions to Andersonville, sent there after being requisitioned by the authorities there.

---

131 Spencer, p. 99.
132 *O.R.*, VIII, p. 617.
133 *O.R.*, VII, p. 551.
134 Spencer, p. 104.

"In the month of July he shipped to that place as follows:

| | | | |
|---|---|---|---|
| Bacon | 102,000 lbs. | Rice | 14,000 lbs. |
| Meal | 63,000 bush. | Sirup | 94 bbls. |
| Flour | 1,000 sacks | Whisky | 15 bbls. |

In August:

| | | | |
|---|---|---|---|
| Bacon | 113,000 lbs. | Rice | 10,000 lbs. |
| Meal | 90,000 bush. | Sirup | 131 bbls. |
| Flour | 1,000 sacks | Whisky | 20 bbls. |

In September:

| | | | |
|---|---|---|---|
| Bacon | 124,000 lbs. | Rice | 6,000 lbs. |
| Meal | 70,000 bush. | Sirup | 150 bbls. |
| Flour | 1,500 sacks | Whisky | 30 bbls."[135] |

"These shipments were made by but one commissary, it will be remembered, while there were fifty others to answer any requisitions upon them from the officials at Andersonville for the supply of that poet and prison. The commissary stores at Albany, fifty miles from Andersonville, it was shown, were much larger than at Americus, and the warehouses there were literally breaking down from the weight and quantity of stores assembled there. The commissaries at other points, near and easily accessible to Andersonville, were continually sending supplies to that point, as the requisitions were made upon them."[136]

"The article of rice amounted to thirty thousand pounds in ninety days, or more than three hundred pounds for each day; the flour, estimating the three thousand seven hundred sacks at fifty pounds each, would make over two thousand pounds for each day for the same period; the sirup, rating the three hundred and seventy-five barrels at forty gallons each, would have afforded more than twenty pints per day; and the whisky would give more than three hundred pints per day for the use of the patients in the hospital."[137]

To the question, what was done with all these supplies; the testimony of Dykes might clear up some points. Dykes testified that "... he knew James W. Duncan, who was in charge of the bakery and cook-house, and who was also a detective under Winder. He offered to sell me some sirup, ten barrels at one time, and said that Bowers another detective, would show it or bring it to me. He told me that he had a large lot of flour which he wanted me to sell for him."[138]

The following is a list of supplies and provisions that were received at Andersonville for consumption by the garrison and Union prisoners by March 31, 1864:

| | |
|---|---|
| Beef & Bacon | 13,269 lbs. |
| Wheat | 2,024 lbs. |
| Meal | 11,880 lbs. |
| Potatoes | 15,103 lbs. |
| Beans & Peas | 13,460 lbs. |
| Hardbread | 160 lbs. |
| Syrup | 489 gal. |
| Salt | 18,037 lbs. |
| Candles | 25 lbs. |
| Sacks | 351 |
| Barrels | 13 |
| Buckets | 5 [139] |

The toilet facilities within the pen at Andersonville were of two types. One type was the latrine, which was simply a hole in the ground outside of an individual's shebang. Perhaps a slit trench would serve a mess or thirty. These were horrible obstacles for those who wandered through the pen at night. Others, from laziness or sickness, simply "... filled the knapsack of Nature" outside their shebang.

[135] *Ibid.*, p. 105.
[136] *Ibid.*, pp. 105, 106.
[137] *Ibid.*, p. 106.
[138] *Ibid.*
[139] *O.R.*,VII, p.137.

On May 10th, Captain Walter Bowie, after his inspection for the Adjutant and Inspector General's Department, reported back to Brigadier General R. H. Chilton in Richmond that fifty men were detailed each day to police the interior of the pen. They were divided into two groups of twenty-five. "Every morning the fatigue squad used to go out and bring in lots of spades, picks, and other things to clean the camp with."[140] Each squad was supplied with shovels by the Confederates to rid the encampment of noxious material, which was then burned and the ashes thrown into the creek. One member of each squad was appointed superintendent and it was his duty to report daily to the camp commander any detailed men shirking their duty or any detachment chronically violating police rules.[141]

Doctor White recommended to General Winder on August 5th, "... if necessary sentinels should be instructed to fire on any one committing a nuisance in any other place than the sinks. ... Some stringent rules of police should be established, and scavenger wagons should be sent in every day to remove the collection of filth, a large quantity of moldy bread and other decomposing matter scattered through the camp and beyond the dead-line, which should be removed at once."[142]

The other, more elaborate, facility was a wooden, fence-type structure built along the stream near its exit, or the eastern wall, of the stockade. The facility was designed and partially completed by order of Wirz. It was to have consisted of two dams. The first dam was to have retained water just after it entered the stockade and was to have been used by the prisoners for drinking and cooking purposes only. The second dam was to have been further downstream and was to retain water for bathing and washing. The overflow from this second dam was suppose to have been lowered to wash away the excrement. This series of dams was begun with the urging of Captain Wirz, but was never finished. Only the "sinks" or latrine portion seemed to have been completed. The artificial banks of the sinks increased the velocity of the cleansing stream.[143] They were built on the south edge of the stream and were fully accessible only to those on the south side. Those on the north side had to wade through the marsh or cross the small bridge, which was, finally, completed on July 3rd. Most prisoners simply used the north edge of the stream for relieving themselves. "Sinks are dug on the bank near the swamp on the east side, but not sufficient to accommodate a tenth part of the persons on the south side to which it alone is accessible; so the north edge of the swamp, parallel with the stream, is used for the same purpose."[144]

Kellogg said the construction of the sinks was begun in the middle of May when, "... a number of men were set to work in widening the brook, with the idea of having it planked upon the bottom and sides, in order to give the men a clean place in which to wash. We watched their progress with the deepest interest, all the while hoping that summer would not pass away without its completion."[145]

Northrop said that, on Tuesday, May 31st, work began to be done to bury the filth near the stream. A squad of prisoners was furnished with carpenters' tools with which to make spades and handbarrows. The men were given these implements after they pleaded for them from Wirz and other officers of the post. The plan was to cover the filthy part of the swamp on each side of the stream with "dirt from the banks." The improvement was to extend along the stream for about 155 feet (10 rods) and into the bank for about 77.5 feet (5 rods). Northrop said that Wirz was persuaded to begin this by the argument that a prison uprising or riot would be more likely to occur under the unsanitary conditions that prevailed. Also, there was a greater chance of an epidemic of disease that would attack both the prisoners and the guard.[146]

Doctor Isaiah H. White, Surgeon-in-Charge of the Post, said, on August 2nd, that the swamp had recently been drained.[147] When Doctor White reported to General Winder on the sanitary condition of the pen on August 6th, he said: "The bottom land should be covered over with sand, the stream be made deeper and wider; the walls and bottom covered with plank, the same arrangements to continue outside, conducting the drainage freely to the creek beyond, and if necessary build a line to prevent the overflow of the banks. The stream from the stockade to the railroad should also be improved, and prohibit the use by troops or others outside. Sinks should be at once arranged over the stream of such a nature as to render them inviting. At present those who have an inclination to use them have to wade through mud and faeces to use them. At the upper part of the stream proper bathing arrangements should be

[140] *Wirz Trial*, p. 521.
[141] *O.R.*, VII, p. 137.
[142] *Ibid.*, p. 559.
[143] Ashe, p. 8.
[144] Northrop, p. 60.
[145] Kellogg, p. 85.
[146] Northrop, p. 69.
[147] *O.R.*, VII, p. 525.

constructed."[148]

Northrop said on, August 11th, that there had been other new improvements down in the swamp: "Timbers laid across the swamp on the west side north of the stream for 20 rods, this will help escape the filth in passing from north to south. A flume and bridge has been made which improves washing facilities; also a road from the north to the stream in the east part."[149]

To reach the sinks was sometimes out of the question for those with a real problem and so there were many miscalculations in the swampy mire around the sinks. This swampy area became iridescent green from bile and was covered by crawling maggots. One of the faults of the design of the sinks was that, at the point of exit of the stream through the walls of the stockade, it was "... not sufficiently bold" to allow a free passage of the fecal matter. "Gradually the filth clogged up the opening in the stockade, making a dam. As filth accumulated it rose and spread out over the banks, until it became three or four feet deep - spread forty feet wide, and backing up the stream seventy-five yards - making in our midst a lake."[150] It was said that the sinks could be smelled for several miles when the wind was "right."

[148] *Ibid.*, p. 559.
[149] Northrop, pp. 105, 106.
[150] Vawter, p. 57.

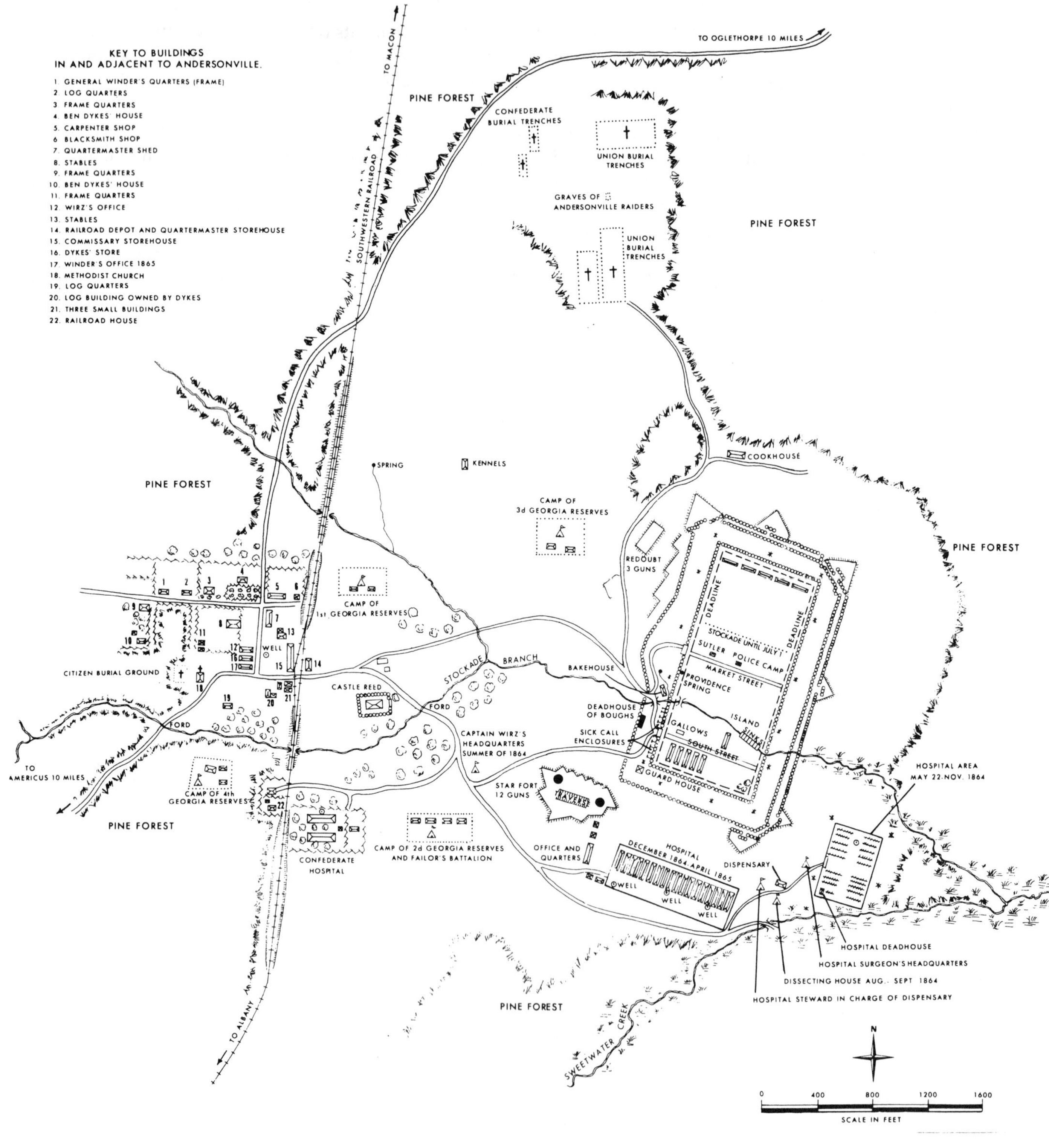
KEY TO BUILDINGS
IN AND ADJACENT TO ANDERSONVILLE.
1. GENERAL WINDER'S QUARTERS (FRAME)
2. LOG QUARTERS
3. FRAME QUARTERS
4. BEN DYKES' HOUSE
5. CARPENTER SHOP
6. BLACKSMITH SHOP
7. QUARTERMASTER SHED
8. STABLES
9. FRAME QUARTERS
10. BEN DYKES' HOUSE
11. FRAME QUARTERS
12. WIRZ'S OFFICE
13. STABLES
14. RAILROAD DEPOT AND QUARTERMASTER STOREHOUSE
15. COMMISSARY STOREHOUSE
16. DYKES' STORE
17. WINDER'S OFFICE 1865
18. METHODIST CHURCH
19. LOG QUARTERS
20. LOG BUILDING OWNED BY DYKES
21. THREE SMALL BUILDINGS
22. RAILROAD HOUSE
TO MACON
SOUTHWESTERN RAILROAD
TO OGLETHORPE 10 MILES
PINE FOREST
CONFEDERATE BURIAL TRENCHES
UNION BURIAL TRENCHES
GRAVES OF ANDERSONVILLE RAIDERS
UNION BURIAL TRENCHES
PINE FOREST
SPRING
KENNELS
COOKHOUSE
PINE FOREST
CAMP OF 3d GEORGIA RESERVES
REDOUBT 3 GUNS
PINE FOREST
CAMP OF 1st GEORGIA RESERVES
WELL
DEADLINE
STOCKADE UNTIL JULY 1
SUTLER
POLICE CAMP
DEADLINE
MARKET STREET
PROVIDENCE SPRING
ISLAND
SINKS
GALLOWS
SOUTH STREET
GUARD HOUSE
CITIZEN BURIAL GROUND
STOCKADE BRANCH
BAKEHOUSE
CASTLE REED
FORD
FORD
DEADHOUSE OF BOUGHS
SICK CALL ENCLOSURES
CAPTAIN WIRZ'S HEADQUARTERS SUMMER OF 1864
TO AMERICUS 10 MILES
CAMP OF 4th GEORGIA RESERVES
PINE FOREST
STAR FORT 12 GUNS
HOSPITAL AREA MAY 22-NOV. 1864
CONFEDERATE HOSPITAL
CAMP OF 2d GEORGIA RESERVES AND FAILOR'S BATTALION
OFFICE AND QUARTERS
HOSPITAL DECEMBER 1864-APRIL 1865
DISPENSARY
WELL
WELL
WELL
HOSPITAL DEADHOUSE
HOSPITAL SURGEON'S HEADQUARTERS
DISSECTING HOUSE AUG.- SEPT 1864
HOSPITAL STEWARD IN CHARGE OF DISPENSARY
PINE FOREST
SWEETWATER CREEK
TO ALBANY
N
0
400
800
1200
1600
SCALE IN FEET

## *Chapter Four*

# The Medicine and Hospitals of Andersonville

*The average duration of life at Andersonville was 95 days.*

(A.C. Leonard, p. 53)

Perhaps a quick survey of the state of the art and science of Civil War medicine should be attempted. Though crude by today's standards, the most modern medical techniques and practices of the early 1860s were the culmination of the trial and error of prior centuries. It must be remembered that there was, as there is today, a time lag of several years or even decades between the time that a discovery was made in medicine and the time that it became part of the practitioner's armamentarium. Surgeons still probed open wounds with bloody hands covered with "laudable pus."

In America, only a very few surgeons were beginning to wash their hands before operating. It was not uncommon to see the surgeon take the scalpel from between his teeth, strop it on his leather-soled shoes to sharpen it and ask for the next patient. Some Civil War surgeons kept spare suture thread dangling from their mouths for quick accessibility.

Since Crawford W. Long, a rural Georgia physician, began performing surgery in the 1840s with the patient unconscious, the terrifying days of wide-awake surgery had ceased. Chloroform and ether were the most commonly used anesthetics, but chloroform was preferred because it was not flammable. The chloroform was dripped on a wad of gauze over the nose and mouth until the patient went limp which was a fairly good indication that the patient was at a plane deep enough to begin the surgery. "This was a time when the doctor rarely handled a clinical thermometer and the Harvard Medical School reportedly did not own a single stethoscope!"[1] "... stethoscopes, thermometers, syringes, ophthalmoscopes, laryngoscopes, and the like were used widely in Europe, many doctors here at home had never seen them let alone used them."[2] "They washed their hands only when smelly or sticky and wiped off their knives and saws only when the day was done."[3] Even the youngest doctors had not heard that diseases could be caused by microscopic animals but still were taught the soon-to-be archaic concepts that the causative agents were miasmas and noxious effluvia. "There are two kinds of miasma laid down by medical writers: the kino and the ideo; one consists of exhalations from the human body in a state of disease, and the other of exhalations from vegetable decompositions and saturations generally. There were both kinds there. The miasmatic effluvia emanating from the hospital was very potent and offensive indeed."[4]

This concept stated disease was caused by breathing smelly "bad" air or by drinking smelly "bad" water from a low, swampy source where putrescent organic matter was present. At that time it was thought one could contract lung disease by breathing air that had become "bad" by its having passed over fulminating gum disease. The concept

[1] Stewart Brooks, *Civil War Medicine* (Springfield, Illinois: Charles C. Thomas, Publisher, 1966), p. 9.
[2] *Ibid.*, p. 22.
[3] *Ibid.*, p. 92.
[4] Chipman p. 130.

was perfectly logical for the state of the art of medicine at that time. It explained a logical genesis of disease but did so, in fact, for the wrong reason.

Lister was doing his experiments in Europe and the gospel of germ theory was slowly being disseminated to the people in practice in Europe. Soon this theory would be introduced to America. In the decades immediately after the war, surgeons would begin using meticulous antiseptic regimens.

The training and preparation of a young person to be awarded the Doctor of Medicine degree varied little from state to state and from region to region. The noted surgeon John A. Wyeth described the entrance requirement at his medical school this way: "... there was no preliminary or entrance examination. Any white male who could read or write and who had mastered the rudiments of English was eligible. Neither Latin nor Greek was essential."[5] "Like most of the approximately thirty-five medical schools in the United States in the middle of the nineteenth century, the University of Pennsylvania's medical department had a seven-man faculty... Expenses included a three to five dollar matriculation fee, tuition amounting to fifteen dollars a course paid directly to the professors, and a fifteen to twenty dollar graduation fee. The term ran from the middle of October to the beginning of March. Two terms, the second covering the same material as the first, were required for graduation... Schools also required three years of private study under a respectable practitioner for graduation. But like the admission standards this requirement was generally modified and sometimes waived entirely."[6]

Some army surgeons had not manipulated live tissues nor had some handled tissues of the dead because many states prohibited any kind of dissection of cadavers. Simon Baruch, a class-mate of Andersonville Surgeon Isaiah White at the Medical College of Virginia, Class of 1862, used to say that he was appointed assistant surgeon in the Confederate army "... without ever having lanced a boil."[7] Other medical schools thought anatomy and other kindred subjects could be mastered by lectures with no "hands- on" instruction. "A few far-seeing, perhaps opportunistic, physicians moved to remedy this evil by establishing private schools of dissection."[8] "Working with cadavers was thought to be potentially dangerous, and various precautionary steps were taken. Dissection rooms were heated only enough to prevent the corpse from freezing, necessitating that students dress warmly. Street clothes were forbidden in the anatomy rooms and aprons and sleeves tightly secured with rubber wristbands were prescribed. Each part of the body was disposed of as soon as it had been dissected."[9]

"Doctor Oliver Wendell Holmes, in an address to the Massachusetts Medical Society in May, 1860, asserted, '... if the whole materia medica, as now used, could sink to the bottom of the sea, it would be all the better for mankind, - and all the worse for the fishes.'"[10]

At the start of the war, there were twenty-one medical schools in the South.[11] Each year, a larger percentage of physicians were receiving formal educations at legitimate medical colleges. The newly-formed American Medical Association fought for standardizing and up-grading the requirements for the M.D. degree. Unfortunately, one could obtain an M.D. degree from one of several hundred "diploma mills" which required only a few weeks' study and a very large "tuition." These were not "uncommon" in the early 1800s, but the number increased dramatically in the 1850s. "Everyone was allowed to practice medicine by 1850, and it was only mild exaggeration to say that everyone did! Planters, house-wives, overseers, pharmacists, secretaries, quacks - all had a hand in the game."[12] These would soon be stopped by public outcry. The profession was still "young" and growing in knowledge and esteem. It would mature greatly in the following four years.

When the war broke out, there were, in the Federal Army, one Surgeon General, thirty surgeons, and eighty-three assistant surgeons. Of these, three surgeons and twenty-one assistant surgeons resigned to enter the Confederate service. Of the one hundred and forty-eight medical officers in the Federal navy, twenty-eight joined the Southern navy.[13]

At Andersonville, some of the physicians attended the guard whereas other physicians treated only the prisoners. Those who treated the prisoners were further broken down to those assigned to hospital duty and those who sat in the small pavilion outside the South Gate and examined the prisoners at the sick call held each morning. Doctors

---

[5] Breeden, p. 23.
[6] *Ibid.*
[7] Simon Baruch Papers, Archives Department, Tomkins-McCaw Library, Medical College of Virginia, Virginia Commonwealth University, Richmond, Virginia.
[8] Breeden, p. 26.
[9] *Ibid.*
[10] H. H. Cunningham, *Doctors in Gray* (Gloucester, Mass.: 1970), p. 17.
[11] *Ibid.*, p. 11.
[12] *Ibid.*, p 16.
[13] *Ibid.*, p. 31.

were classified into two categories. Some were civilian "contract doctors" who received a monthly stipend as long as their services were needed. These tended to be less competent and were avoided by the prisoners. The other physicians were the "regular army" doctors who had passed Medical Boards which seemed to have been more stringent in the South than in the North.

The number of doctors at Andersonville varied from month to month. On June 20th, when there were about 26,000 prisoners in the pen, Doctor Isaiah H. White, Chief Surgeon of the prison, said there were twelve doctors at the prison. Seven attended sick call at the South Gate and five were on duty at the hospital where there were 1,134 patients.[14] Doctor White thought an additional ten officers were needed to bring the medical staff up to strength at that time.[15]

The number of physicians was gradually increased as the summer wore on. When Inspector-General Colonel Daniel T. Chandler visited Andersonville on August 1st for his tour, he described the medical staff this way. "Of the medical officers but eleven hold commissions; nearly all of the others are detailed from the militia, and have accepted the position to avoid serving in the ranks, and will relinquish their contracts as soon as the present emergency is passed and the militia is disbanded. But little injury would result from this, however, as they are generally very inefficient. Not residing at the post, only visiting it once a day at sick call, they bestow but little attention to those under their care."[16]

A prisoner said, "Some of the physicians were educated men, from whose hearts the law of human kindness was not wholly effaced, but some were unfitted in every possible way for the work assigned them."[17]

By the time Doctor Joseph Jones, a pathologist, arrived in the middle of September, many physicians had left, accompanying the men when most of the prisoners at Andersonville were dispersed to Millen, Charleston, and other places of confinement. On September 15th, 3 surgeons, 11 assistant surgeons, and 8 acting assistant surgeons remained, for a total of 22 surgeons in attendance at the prison.

Dozens of Federal prisoners were detailed as nurses and drug dispensers because of the paucity of doctors. Since there were barely enough Confederates to guard the prison, there were no Confederate nurses. At least one worker in the hospital was a captured Federal physician: "Dr. A. V. Barrows, hospital steward of the 27th Massachusetts regiment, and acting assistant post surgeon at Plymouth, North Carolina, arrived at Andersonville on the 28th of May, and remained there six months. Owing to his knowledge of medicine and efficiency, he was paroled as a prisoner, and assigned duty in the hospital."[18] Many nurses were men who had been cured or were convalescent and, a few days earlier, had been patients themselves. "Yankee hospital attendants held passes from Captain Wirz, which allowed them to go out and come in between the hours of six in the morning and six in the evening."[19]

A few Yankee nurses were accused of causing increased suffering and the deaths of their comrades by their lack of training, sloppiness, and inattention. Some prisoners complained that their comrades, detailed as nurses, caused increased sickness and death in order to fall heir to the clothes and or the belongings of their charges. A few were accused of cross-contaminating sores by smearing pus from one gangrenous sore to another while the unsuspecting victim slept. Some nurses were very kind and did all in their power to alleviate the pain and suffering of their sick and wounded comrades. "About the middle of July, I was fortunate enough to make the acquaintance of a most excellent young man from Philadelphia, a member of the 7th Pennsylvania R. C. Volunteers, Joseph Egalf by name, who was actively engaged in caring for our neglected wounded men. From morning 'til night he went about dressing their wounds and ministering to their wants, and was unremitting in his efforts to benefit and comfort them. All in suffering had his sympathy and compassion, and his aid, so far as it was in his power to render assistance."[20] One man, detailed as a steward, said he dispensed what had been prescribed to the men in his ward. Seven of the patients died from these medicines the doctors had prescribed. He quit the detail after this first day.[21]

At least some of the nurses hoped to gain the double ration issued to all detailed men. Certainly many nurses and doctors were truly kindhearted and shed tears of compassion in response to the plight of their patients.

Doctor White said that the reasons he had great difficulty in filling the medical positions at the prison were:

(1) "the duty was so arduous."

---

[14] *O.R.*, VII, p. 427.
[15] *Ibid.*, p. 287.
[16] *Ibid.*, p. 548.
[17] Kellogg, p. 259.
[18] Dowling, p. 210.
[19] Charles M. Smith, pp. 30, 31.
[20] Abbott, p. 201.
[21] Berry, p. 309.

(2) "the exhalations from the sick and filth of the prison was so deleterious, that it was impossible for the medical officers to stand the service for any length of time."

(3) "the absence of many of the facilities for the treatment of the sick."

(4) "the great and numerous depressing agencies and the consequent unsatisfactory results of practice."

(5) "the more energetic Confederate surgeons and assistant surgeons endeavored to get transfers to other fields of labor, preferring the hardships and exposure of service at the front."

(6) "there [is] a scarcity of physicians in the Confederacy, [and] it is especially difficult to command the services of competent physicians in this sparsely settled country."

(7) "the serious wounding of thousands of Confederate troops have absorbed the attention and commanded the abilities of almost every available physician in the State."

(8) "the very conditions and results of the contest also, without doubt, tend to excite such prejudices as would disincline medical officers from seeking service amongst their captive enemies."[22]

"Each morning, at 9 o'clock, a lone drummer appeared at the South Gate and beat 'sick call,' when the worst cases of sick would be carried up and examined by two attending physicians, a few of which would be admitted to the hospital and the rest returned to their respective divisions."[23]

**Prisoners Waiting For Sick Call** - This depiction by McElroy shows some of the several hundred sick and infirm prisoners who waited at the South Gate each morning. They hoped to be either taken out to the hospital or to be taken out to the prescribing doctors in the stalls just outside to be examined. (McElroy)

Every morning the sick in the stockade would crawl and gather around the inside of the South Gate. Most would be brought on blankets and "... would be laid on the ground beside the path leading up from the bridge across the stream to the South Gate."[24] The sergeants of each squad would be responsible for getting the sick of his ninety to the appointed place. Each sergeant would call his men together and then the men would be taken out in single file through the wicket in the gate. About a third of the sick would be brought in blankets by their comrades to see the doctors. "It was my duty at seven o'clock each morning to call the sick, and immediately after roll-call to have them all fall in and march up to sick-call at the South Gate. Sometimes three or four thousand prisoners would collect around this gate to gain admission outside. There was a very small space to pass through the gate. Two sentinels were ordered to prevent the crowd from getting close to the gate near the dead-line."[25]

At about eight o'clock, the gate would be opened and the men would be allowed out in groups of about fifty. The sergeant would sometimes detail men to carry the very sick and would carry them to the doctors' shed. They had to return inside the gate until they received orders to go back outside to help return their comrades inside.

"Not having a sufficient number of stretchers, they were carried out on blankets, or on sticks of wood, and the bearers thus found admission to the hospital, where they were likely to find some untasted portion of food that had been given to the sick, and this they would obtain to appease their hunger. They could also get wood in this way, by which they could cook their small allowance, so that it was esteemed a double gain among these half-starved men

[22] *O.R.*, VIII, pp. 600, 601.
[23] Fosdick, p. 41.
[24] Lyons, p. 117.
[25] Chipman, p. 182.

which they realized for their dreadful work."[26]

Some were carried out on wagons; "They had two ambulances and an army wagon, in which they always carried the patients. An ambulance would hold four, and from this number I have often seen two taken out dead, having breathed out their lives on the way, and many died while waiting outside the stockade for some one to come to their relief."[27] The sick had to be brought out because the doctors were not allowed to prescribe for a patient unless they actually saw the patient. The number of doctors in the sheds varied from two to about twelve or fifteen. Each doctor in the stalls would be assigned a certain number of detachments depending on the number of doctors on call at the stalls and the population of the pen at that time. At one time each doctor had assigned to him six detachments or 1,620 potential patients. When the population became so great, only a few detachments' sick were seen each day. Northrop said, on Friday, the 7th of August, because there were so many crowding the South Gate at sick-call, the doctors decided only the sick from eleven detachments would be seen that day. Starting the next day, only the sick from selected detachments were to be brought to there.[28] Most prints of the period show the doctors' shed being approximately two hundred feet long against the outside of the inside stockade wall. One print showed it on the interior wall of the middle stockade. Another showed that both sheds had been built facing each other. Each shed was about "3 rods wide" bounded by a rail fence and had a slanted roof of wood or pine boughs to protect the doctors from the Georgia sun.[29]

The number admitted to the hospital each day was equal approximately to the number that had died in the hospital the previous day. On Saturday, the 20th of August, Northrop said that, of "The sick again admitted to the gate for prescription; but three [were] taken to the hospital out of several hundred applicants."[30]

"I have taken men out to the stall of a doctor named Williams, I think, and I have seen men crawl up there on their hands and knees with just life enough to get to the stall and plead to be either taken out to the hospital or to have proper medicine given them. He would say, 'Take him back into the stockade; he will live until tomorrow.'"[31]

In one of the letters of Edmund Riedel to Ira Pettit's sister, he said, "Ira never got any medicine, although he often went to the hospital at sick call."[32]

On several days, there was no sick call. Sometimes there would be several days in a row when no call would be sounded. On July 9th there occurred the first sick call in over a week. The sick were still at the South Gate late that night after being ordered not to leave until ordered back. Six patients died that day at the gate.[33]

Colonel Daniel T. Chandler and Major W. Carvel Hall were sent, on July 25th, by Colonel R. H. Chilton, Inspector General in Richmond, to Andersonville for an official inspection visit of the prison and post. They arrived on or about the first day of August. They wrote a "report of inspection" on the 5th of August and a copy was sent to General Winder. In the report Chandler described the sick call by saying, "The crowd at times is so great that only the strongest can get access to the doctors, the weaker ones being unable to force their way through the press; and the hospital accommodations are so limited that, though the beds (so called) have all or nearly all two occupants each, large numbers who would otherwise be received are necessarily sent back to the stockade. Many - twenty yesterday - are carted out daily, who have died from unknown causes and whom the medical officers have never seen."[34] On August 10th, 300 died or about 1 1/4% of the total number of men in the prison.[35]

General Winder sent a copy of Colonel Chandler's inspection report to Wirz, telling of the horrors seen by Chandler. Wirz wrote, on September 24th, to General Winder, defending himself against the inspection report of Colonel Chandler. "It becomes my duty to add a few words in regard to the sick-call, as this is under my direct control. Colonel Chandler states that the room was too small; that only a few could get to see the doctors; that the stronger ones pushed the weaker ones aside, &c. If Colonel Chandler had remained at the sick-call (which commences at 8 a.m. and very often continues until after 2 p.m.) longer than fifteen minutes or half an hour, he would have again, reported differently. I take the pleasure to explain in a few words the modus operandi of the sick-call. At 8 a.m. all the doctors are at their stand. Each doctor has a clerk (who is a prisoner) to take down the name and the

---

[26] Kellogg, p. 277.
[27] *Ibid.*, pp. 276.
[28] Northrop, p. 98.
[29] Kellogg, p. 258.
[30] Northrop, p. 107.
[31] Chipman, p. 182.
[32] Ray, p. 203.
[33] Author's library.
[34] *O.R.*, VII, p. 547.
[35] Miller, p. 28.

disease of the patient. The first that are attended to are those who are merely to be prescribed for without being admitted to the hospital. The number of this class is very large. The sergeant (Yankee) of each detachment must come with his sick to the stand of the doctor. When this class of patients are all prescribed for and returned to their quarters in the stockade then come all those to be admitted to the hospitals. As many as can be accommodated in the hospital are sent there, whilst the balance, if any, are returned to the stockade for the day, to be brought out the following morning, or when the hospital accommodations are such as to receive them.

"At 4 p.m. the clerks of the doctors receive the medicines, which in the meantime have been prepared for those prescribed for but not admitted to the hospital in the morning, carrying the same to the place where the sick-call is made, where the sergeant (Yankee) of each detachment receives the medicine for his men."[36]

Steven Payne of Company I 16th Illinois Cavalry went out for sick call, "On the 3rd of August, I was taken out to the hospital with the scurvy. There was near 1,000 taken out that day. We were taken out & there examined by the Drs. & those that were near enough dead they would mark for the hospital. As I was pretty bad, I had no difficulty to get put down for the hospital.

"We had to lay just outside of the stockade nearly all day waiting to be hauled out but about 4 o'clock the officer told us all that could walk had better walk out or we would have to stay out all night, & we did not like that much so there was a great many of us walked out to the hospital & were let inside & told to make our beds down on the ground in the streets as there were no tents empty."[37]

Because of the blockade, all drugs were scarce within the Confederacy and many of the most commonly used drugs of the day were unobtainable. The physicians at Andersonville had to resort to herbs, berries, roots, and barks from the surrounding forests. Those few drugs dispensed were requisitioned but due to the irregularity of the postal system, the approval was not received by return mail for eight to ten days. These approvals then had to be sent to the medical purveyor at the laboratory at Macon, where they were promptly filled. By that time, half of the month had passed and the previous month's supply had been exhausted.[38] When this occurred, there was no alternative but to resort to barks and roots. At other times, the requisitions seemed to be made twice per month for a two-week supply.

On a requisition form for Medical and Hospital Supplies for the two-week period from May 16th to the 31st, the number of Federal prisoners was listed at 15,000. Doctor White, as Chief Surgeon of the prison, requested small quantities of about 20 common medicines under the heading of "Medicines." Under the heading of "Hospital Stores," he requested "10 pounds of Ginger, ground, Jamaica; 12 oz. Nutmegs; 40 gallons Whiskey and 20 gallons of wine."[39] Whiskey, wine, and other stimulants were more frequently prescribed by Civil War physicians than they are today, but there were persistent rumors that whiskey was offered for sale by the barrel to neighboring residents by those in the medical department. It was alleged that several doctors were inebriated on the job. They rationalized their drinking of the stimulants was necessary to protect them because of their close contact with sickness and the unhealthy environment in which they worked.

Under other headings on the requisition form, Doctor White requested 12 stretchers, a pint of red ink, and 20 yards of muslin to add to the 10 yards he had on hand.

On July 31st, Dr. White wrote to the Surgeon General, Samuel P. Moore, in Richmond, asking permission to requisition directly from Macon without having to first write for approval from Surgeon Stout, Medical Director of Hospitals in Atlanta.[40] He was immediately given permission to draw supplies from the Medical Purveyor with the terse note, "... not having supplies is his own fault."[41]

On July 31st, he requested and received from Dick Winder 109 tent flies, 9 hospital tents, 10 mess pans, and 10 camp kettles by order of General Winder. On September 1st, he needed 45 walled tents for the "... use of the sick under his charge."[42]

The requisition for the month of November for the hospital was a long and extensive one. The hospital capacity was listed as 4,000. Besides the twenty-five or so medicines needed, there was a request for 2 barrels of whiskey, 100 yards of muslin, 5 pounds of lint, 10 papers of assorted pins, tape, 5 pounds of sponges, 1,000 pillow cases, 1,000 pillow ticks, 1,000 sheets, 400 towels, 10 bed pans, and 100 chamber pots. This requisition was signed by the new sur-

---

[36] *O.R.*, VII, p. 760.
[37] Steven Payne diary, in private hands.
[38] *O.R.*, VII, p. 427.
[39] Military Records of Dr. Isaiah White from National Archives.
[40] *O.R.*, VII, p. 430.
[41] *Ibid.*, p. 526.
[42] Military Records of Dr. Isaiah White from National Archives.

geon-in-charge, Richard Randolph Stevenson.[43]

Doctor A. V. Barrows, acting assistant post surgeon at Plymouth, described, in his testimony, some of the remedies available to him at Andersonville: "When we made requisitions, we got sometimes tonics and sometimes opiates, but in very small quantities (three-fourths of the time we were without opiates,) and products of an indigenous nature, such as white-oak bark, and such things as we could get there. Sometimes we got small quantities of drugs. We never got a solution of corrosive sublimate. Once or twice we got a little lime-water, for a cooling wash. I treated those cases of vaccine sores with lime-water, partly. We never got any brandy. I did not get any blue ointment. I think I have seen a small quantity of borax issued. I got aqua fortis, but in very small quantities. I have made requisitions for it in the treatment of gangrene. I have seen aromatic sulphuric acid there. I do not remember that I got any calomel. I think I have got blue pills in small quantities, but not very often. Blue pills are considered as mercurial. I did not have much occasion for their use; the patients were depleted enough without adopting mercurial treatment. More tonics were what we needed. I do not remember ever seeing any yellow dock or anything of that kind. I have seen very small quantities of carbonate of ammonia - a very excellent remedy. We did not get any oranges or lemons, nor pine-apples. We got iodine and iodide of potash, in very small quantities. Sometimes I got it in very quantities. I got very few escharotic medicines or things coming under that head. I think I have seen some white vitriol there - I could not state as to the quantity. Books recognize mercurial preparations as a specific for syphilis.[44]

There were few, if any, physicians within the pen among the general prisoner population. The few physicians who were placed in the pen were routinely removed to the hospital and detailed as stewards. However, in the pen were many barbers who did prescribe and diagnose. "There were quite a number of doctors inside the stockade among the prisoners; some of the barbers were acting as doctors. There were not any doctors there exclusive of the barbers."[45]

One prisoner testified that, along with his many money making schemes, he sold drugs and remedies. "I was selling medicine… by charging them $1.25 per dose… I sold blood-root and also a root that was called red-root; I had different kinds of herbs for sale there… I was the only man who could be called a druggist; I sold medicines to the barbers; there were others who sold medicines; some of the barbers sold medicines; they bought of me and sold again; they bought of me and also of men who had access to the hospital. For diarrhoea I sold a dose composed of capsicum, ginger, flour, and an egg, mixed with water or beer as the case might be; I would mix it, and I charged $1.25 to $1.50 for a drink... It contained one egg, about two tablespoonfuls of flour, half a tea-spoonful of capsicum, and a tea-spoonful of ginger; the balance water or beer."[46]

There was at least one prisoner who was practicing dentistry. Charles Hopkins said, in his diary, on July 23rd, that he "… had a root of a tooth pulled by a good dentist this morning. A rare cure in a Bullpen." The next day his face was very swollen from "neuralgia." On the following day, he again visited this prisoner-dentist and had him lance his gum.[47]

When they arrived in the spring of 1864, some of the new prisoners were sick and infirm from their stays in prisons in Richmond. The Richmond winter had been colder than usual. In fact, the men of Belle Isle said the swift-flowing James River had frozen three times, sometimes thick enough to support the weight of the prisoners walking over it.[48] Most of the men had been prisoners for less than a year when they were brought from Richmond; the older prisoners usually had been exchanged in some manner. The rations of most of the prisons in Richmond were basically the same: scanty corn bread and bacon issued at Andersonville, sometimes, with very infrequent substitutions of rice, stock peas, or potatoes. When some of these men arrived at Andersonville they were, in truth, dying.

These sick were put within one area of the pen and, for want of a better word, it was called a hospital. At first, the hospital consisted of one tent with five patients. Then it was simply an area that straddled the stream with half on the north slope and half on the south slope. "A small portion of ground was divided from the rest of the prison by a railing, and a few tent flies were stretched. And in those they used pine boughs for beds… The ground required for it compelled a general reduction of the space we all occupied, for some who had shanties built with pine boughs were now compelled to tear them down and we were so crowded that we could scarcely all lie down at the same time."[49]

---

[43] Military Records of Dr. R. R. Stevenson from National Archives.
[44] *Wirz Trial*, pp. 55, 56.
[45] *Ibid.*, p. 575.
[46] *Ibid.*, pp. 578, 579.
[47] Styple, p. 103.
[48] Boggs, p. 24.
[49] Compton, pp. 52, 53.

In May, Dr. White said that the drainage from the sinks of the prison passed through the hospital grounds.[50] "The first hospital was erected inside of poles and brush… The poles or logs were left several inches apart, and as sickly men were put in them the place became as odious and no more commodious than a backwoods hog-pen. A portion has a loose floor, no beds, no bunks, no blankets, no straw."[51]

The hospital within the pen was described by various authors as "straddling the creek" and it seemed to have been relocated "… in the northeastern corner of the stockade." "A makeshift of a hospital was established in the northeastern corner of the Stockade. A portion of the ground was divided from the rest of the prison by a railing, a few tent flies were stretched, and in these the long leaves of the pine were made into apologies for beds of about the goodness of the straw on which a Northern farmer beds his stock… Save a few decoctions of roots, there were no medicines, the sick were fed the same coarse corn meal that brought about the malignant dysentery from which they all suffered… the official records show that seventy-six per cent. of those taken to the hospitals died there."[52]

The hospital within the pen was divided into two divisions, with a full surgeon in charge of each. One of these divisions was subdivided into three wards and the other was divided into two wards, each ward being under the care of an assistant surgeon, usually a contract surgeon. Nurses and hospital stewards to attend to the sick were detailed from well prisoners or sick patients who were convalescent. A surgeon was appointed each day as professional officer of the day, whose duty it was to see that the hospital was well-policed and that the nurses and stewards discharged their duties promptly and efficiently. This officer of the day was required to make a daily morning report to Chief Surgeon White.[53]

By April 25th, Doctor White said, as of that date, there had been 2,697 patients treated with 718 deaths.[54] In early May, there were less than two hundred patients within the hospital and nearly all of these were from Belle Isle. By the tenth of May, 35 tent flies, that were very badly worn and full of holes, were sheltering 582 patients. These "pieces of canvas" were the only shelter for the first few patients. There were about 500 other patients undergoing treatment living in the non-hospital portion of the pen. From the time of the prison's establishment to this time, the number of cases treated was 4,588 with 1,036 deaths.[55] The prisoners avoided a stay in this hospital, if at all possible. After a short time, its reputation was that anyone who was admitted would not leave alive. Most of the men would rather stay with their friends, who could attend to them in their final hours. All doctors feared the closeness of the campfires and other foul exhalations of the pen would be a source of disease. "The sink was dug within a single rod of these men."[56]

The doctors almost immediately recommended that the hospital be moved outside of the pen for several reasons. First, the hospital was too near the noxious vapors arising from the sinks and low swampy areas. Secondly, the doctors noticed that some of the patients living in the hospital found that their personal property, such as blankets, clothing, and shelter. had been stolen by the forays of desperate men living in the rest of the prison. They sometimes sneaked into the hospital at night and stole from their weakened comrades and, more importantly, they stole the skimpy rations from their sick friends. Sometimes friends of patients would mistakenly feed them food that was incompatible with the wishes of the doctors. Doctor White said diseases in the hospital would be transmitted to the well prisoners living adjacent to the hospital.

General Samuel Cooper, Adjutant General in Richmond, ordered Major General Howell Cobb to learn about the conditions at Andersonville in order that Cobb might more correctly know the types and numbers of troops needed for guard duty there. Cobb ordered Doctor E. J. Eldridge, the Chief Surgeon of the Georgia Reserves, to accompany him on a tour of inspection of that post on about May 5th. At that time, there were 12,000 men in the pen and the hospital was still straddling Stockade Creek. Eldridge considered "… the establishment of a hospital outside of the present enclosure as essential to the proper treatment of the sick, and most urgently recommended its immediate construction."[57]

Colonel Persons testified: "Captain Wirz came to me and urged me to take the hospital out. I told him I had no authority to do anything of that sort. I addressed a communication, however, to General Winder, asking for permission to remove the hospital outside. My impression is, though I will not state positively, that it was declined by Gen-

[50] *O.R.*, VII, p. 125.
[51] Northrop, p. 111.
[52] McElroy, pp. 166, 167.
[53] *O.R.*, VII, p. 139.
[54] *Ibid.*, p. 89.
[55] *O.R.*, VII, p. 138.
[56] Kellogg, p. 251.
[57] *O.R.*, VII, p. 121.

eral Winder. Captain Wirz remonstrated, and I told him to remove the hospital - that I would take the responsibility. Shortly after it was moved out, General Winder sent an order from Richmond giving us permission to do it."[58]

The site Doctor Eldridge recommended for the new hospital enclosure was the wide, deep, swiftly-flowing Sweet Water Creek proper, located a few hundred yards from the existing palisade. For some unknown reason, this site was not chosen. A grove of shade trees adjacent to the southeastern corner of the pen was selected.

On about the 22nd of May, the prisoners began to make the long, painful, thousand-yard, trip out of the South Gate, around the south wall and through the gate of the new hospital. They went as rapidly as they could, because they looked forward to their new quarters in the shade outside of the stockade. They staggered past the sentinel stationed on each side of the fifteen-foot-wide main entrance of the hospital.[59]

The new hospital consisted of about two acres of tattered tents located within a thin board fence about six feet high. It was adjoining the pen at its southeast corner on a tongue of land sloping to the southeast between "... two small creeks on each side of which are swamps forty or fifty yards in width. All the excrement from the pen flowed along the north brook within yards of the patients' tents."[60]

The dimensions of the original hospital were 260 feet by 340 feet or 2.03 acres in the shape of a parallelogram.[61] It was one of Dick Winder's tasks to try to get shelter for the patients in the hospital. There were three main reasons that he "... advised the use of tents, [I] gave as my reason that they would be more healthy, less subject to danger from fire, and in case of a general exchange of prisoners, which we were expecting any time, would be a great saving in cost."[62] He tried, in Savannah, to get some tents that belonged to the state, but they said they needed them for their own troops. Though he could not get these, he was able to procure 209 tents of all descriptions which would hold 800 patients comfortably. In the "A" tents, four patients were placed; in the larger, walled tents, the doctors placed eight patients; and, under the common fly, they would place six or eight of the sick.[6463] "Now and then a tent was to be seen, but most of them were nothing but square pieces of canvas spread over a pole, which formed a roof, but left it all open below, so that the patients were exposed constantly to the rain, sun, and night dews."[64] Doctor White said, on August 2nd, the number of tents needed were 200 hospital tents or 500 walled tents to properly house the sick.[65]

About one third of the inmates were lying on some sort of bunk or scaffolding. The other two-thirds were lying on the bare ground with no straw or anything else to protect them from respiratory aliments.[66] "Along one side of it was a long shed, under that shed bunks built up out of plank to lie on, but nothing to lie on but the plank."[67] On August 2nd, Doctor White said there was a smaller wheat crop than usual that year, that local transportation was a problem and that farmers were unwilling to hire out their teams to haul the straw. Doctor White would try to get more at the post as soon as the present crop was thrashed.[68] "It would require five wagons, constantly employed, to furnish an adequate supply. The chief surgeon has instructed the agent for the purchase of supplies after subsistence or comfort of sick to purchase wheat straw and ship by railroad, the quartermaster having failed to supply us."[69] The chief surgeon said pine tags were used as a substitute for the straw until recently but it must be changed every two weeks because of vermin.

Work continued on the hospital for a couple weeks after the sick were taken out of the pen. About the 1st of June it was completed.[70] In keeping with the medical concepts of the times, Doctor Hamlin felt the fence "... only served to obstruct the circulation of free air, which was of vital importance; and besides, the fence was of no service whatever as protection against the escape of the inmates, as they were before admission generally far too feeble to make even an effort."[71]

By the time this first hospital outside was designed and built, the inmate population had doubled from twelve thousand to twenty-five thousand. In the hospital, a Confederate sergeant named "Stafford called the roll of the

---

58 *Wirz Trial*, p. 455.
59 Frank W. Smith, p. 26.
60 *O.R.*, VIII, p. 629.
61 *Ibid.*, p. 386.
62 *O.R.*, VII, p. 732.
63 *O.R.*, VIII, p. 629.
64 Kellogg, p. 253.
65 *O.R.*, VII, p. 524.
66 *O.R.*, VIII, p. 629.
67 William B. Clifton, *Libby and Andersonville Prison, My Actual Experience* (Indianapolis: 1910), p. 5.
68 *O.R.*, VII, p. 524.
69 *O.R.*, VI, p. 558.
70 Kellogg, p. 252.
71 Hamlin, p. 101.

sick... Stafford was a young man of 22 or 23 years of age, a very nice-looking young fellow."[72] By June 20th, they had crowded 1,022 men into the tents designed to hold 800 comfortably. Conditions soon became little better than those in the pen. A Confederate sergeant described it: "... they might as well go to hell as to the hospital. It is a right hard place; the doctors can do nothing."[73]

**Hospital at Southeast Corner of the Prison** - This print, entitled "Bird's-eye View of Andersonville Prison" from the South east shows four sheds perpendicular to the south wall and five parallel to the north wall of the pen. (Author's Collection)

General Winder telegraphed Richmond to see if the old tents that had been used on Belle Isle could be obtained. Doctor White wrote, "For humanities sake, please assist me in obtaining 200 tents at once."[74] Whether they were shipped or not is not known, but, since Belle Isle never completely closed down, it is assumed they stayed in Richmond.

With the hospital full, Doctor White said, on June 26th, there were 3,000 more sick within the stockade, "in quarters." He said, "It is impossible to get tents from the quartermaster in this military department. They seem to have nothing, or all act upon the principle that prisoners can do without them."[75] Soon there were 1,035 prisoners in the hospital with only five medical officers in attendance. With the five in attendance, Dr. White had eight more assistant surgeons who attended sick call each morning. He had squeezed 1,200 into tents suitable for 800 sick.

Near the end of June, the surgeons in attendance of the Federal sick were suddenly ordered off, probably to the battlefields around Atlanta.[76]

Doctor Thornburg said that, for the entire summer, the cooking facilities within the hospital consisted of "... two large salt kettles placed on a furnace in the open air."[77] To this hospital, the corn bread was brought cooked but all other foods were brought in raw to be cooked inside the hospital grounds.[78] Doctor Jones said there were four, large, iron pots similar to those used for boiling sugar cane, used to cook for the 2,000 patients.[79]

Doctor White was able to give the patients about the same rations that the men received in the stockade, plus perhaps, "...a little flour porridge, arrow-root, whiskey and wild or hog tomatoes."[80] Doctor Thornburg said he sometimes had some peas, potatoes, and collards to distribute. When McElroy went to the hospital, he received some rice and okra soup. One ex-prisoner said he saw no medicines dispensed but "... camphor, whiskey, and a decoction of some kind of bark - white oak."[81] This same man said that Doctor White often expressed regret that he did not

---

[72] *Wirz Trial*, p. 511.
[73] Northrop, p. 104.
[74] *O.R.*, VII, p. 417.
[75] *Ibid.*
[76] Kellogg, p. 157.
[77] *O.R.*, VIII, p. 630.
[78] Chipman, p. 171.
[79] *O.R.*, VIII, p. 605.
[80] Sanitary Commission, p. 79.
[81] *Ibid.*

have some medicines for his patients.

Doctor A. V. Barrows, the acting assistant post surgeon at Plymouth, testified about the diet issued in the gangrene wards. "Sometimes there was a little rice soup; perhaps a gallon of rice to thirty gallons of water... In July we got a very few vegetables; collards, which is a species of cabbage, but not sufficient to give the patients a spoonful of vegetable matter per day. Later I had more vegetables, though not every day... I drew sweet potatoes for them; perhaps they would get one a piece each day with their other ration of corn-bread. There has been a few times a little tea was issued; perhaps a quarter of a pound to a ward of a hundred persons for a week. That was not all over the hospital, merely in gangrene and surgical wards."[82]

In a report of Doctor White to Colonel Chandler on August 2nd, he said that supplies for the sick were purchased with hospital funds. "Heretofore we have been able to supply the sick with vegetables; but during the entire month of July the commissary has been without funds."[83] Doctor Bates testified: "Instances of misappropriation of bread and other articles of food by the hospital attendants occurred on a small scale several times... I therefore, myself, organized in the hospital a secret police of 23 members.. Charles Williams, of New Jersey, being at the head of it, to protect sick men against the ravages of some who were in the hospital, who would cut tents, run their hands through, and appropriate clothing and eatables... I wish the court to understand that Dr. Clayton and Dr. Roy were two men who did their duty. When they came in charge, the hospital then reached such a condition that I was able to report for one day not a death in the hospital. The condition of things began to improve on the very first day of January, 1865... I do not remember that I ever made a suggestion in my morning report that Dr. Clayton and Dr. Roy did not take notice of. Prior to that time I could not say that my reports were ever read."[84] "Sometimes there were foragers there whose duty I understood it to be to forage for the hospitals."[85]

Augustus Moesner, a prisoner detailed in the office of Captain Wirz, said that the requisitions for the hospital did not go through Wirz' office but through Doctor White's.[86]

The doctors attempted to keep the sanitary conditions of the hospital in better shape than the deplorable conditions in the pen. They had a police squad formed that patrolled the grounds twice a day to see that better hygienic conditions were maintained. Wooden boxes or "night boxes" were located at convenient intervals within the hospital and were supposed to be emptied daily. Being made from wood prevented their being emptied and cleaned properly. Metal or ceramic jars would have been more serviceable.[87] There were men detailed to empty the boxes and utensils were issued to police the hospital interior. Sometimes the sick simply could not make it to the boxes and there were accidental miscalculations all over the grounds. Colonel Chandler said, in August, that: "The management and police of the general hospital grounds seem to be as good as the limited means will allow, but there is pressing necessity for at least three times the number of tents and amount of bedding now on hand. The supply of medicines is wholly inadequate, and frequently there is none, owing to the great delays experienced in filling the requisitions."[88]

"About a month after the removal from the stockade, they enlarged the grounds so that they could accommodate twenty-five hundred; and at its completion, Doctor White, Surgeon in charge, admitted seven hundred men in one day. Nearly half of these could walk, but the remainder of them went in just as they could, some of them on their hands and heels, their legs being drawn with scurvy that they could not keep in an erect position."[89]

Near the middle of July, Kellogg said, "One morning the rebel authorities issued an order to the effect that all who were too sick to walk should be carried outside the prison-gate by their comrades. Such a great number went up that they were not all allowed to go out, and those who did were left nearly all day in the burning hot sun, before they were conveyed to the hospital, without a drop of water. We were told upon good authority, that about thirty of them died while lying there in that wretched condition."[90] "I remember that on the 27th of July an order was given, I think, for 500 - five from each detachment; there were over a hundred detachments in the prison at that time. The orders were generally read from the gate, but whether they came from the surgeons or from Captain Wirz, I do not

[82] *Wirz Trial*, p. 45.
[83] *O.R.*, VII, p. 525.
[84] *Wirz Trial*, p. 666.
[85] *Ibid.*, p. 43.
[86] Chipman, p. 160.
[87] *O.R.*, VIII, p. 605.
[88] *O.R.*, VII, p. 548.
[89] Kellogg, pp. 253, 254.
[90] *Ibid.*, p. 169.

know."[91]

The enclosed area was described, by several authors, as being four or five acres in area. Doctor Jones said the hospital was "... five acres of ground covered with oaks and pines."[92]

On August 2nd, Doctor White wrote to Colonel Chandler that the number sick on morning report was 1,305 in the hospital and 5,010 were sick in their quarters (i.e., the pen).

Many of the patients were harsh in their criticism of their doctors, "... many of whom had no feeling for them." "All were conscripts, and chose the profession in which they were engaged, rather than shoulder the musket and go to the front. They were allowed eleven dollars a month, which was about equal to one in greenbacks and the government ration of meat and bacon. They availed themselves of the opportunity to acquaint themselves with surgery, and were therefore not slow in performing amputations if they saw fit. They had also a dissecting house not very far distant, where they continued their experiments. They commenced their duties about eight in the morning, and finished about one in the afternoon They would stand in the middle of the street, and with folded arms ask the patient how he felt, and then very indifferently tell the clerk to renew the prescriptions of a previous time. In justice to some, however, we can say, they were kind to the sick and did what they could for them, but they were reluctant to go into the tents on account of the lice which were there in such quantities."[93] It is assumed this "dissecting house" was the temporary structure set up by Doctor Jones. There was no permanent structure where autopsies were performed.

Dr. Joseph Jones described this hospital when he was there in the middle of September this way: "The patients and attendants, near two thousand in number are crowded into this confined space and are but poorly supplied with old and ragged tents. Large numbers of them were without any bunks in the tents, and lay upon the ground, often times without even a blanket. No beds or straw appeared to have been furnished. The tents extend to within a few yards of the small stream, the eastern portion of which is used as a privy and is loaded with excrements; and I observed a large pile of corn bread, bones, and filth of all kinds, thirty feet in diameter and several feet in height, swarming with myriads of flies, in a vacant space near the pots used for cooking. Millions of flies swarmed over everything and covered the faces of the sleeping patients, and crawled down their open mouths, and deposited their maggots in the gangrenous wounds of the living, and the mouths of the dead. Mosquitoes in great numbers also infested the tents, and many of the patients were so stung by these pestiferous insects, that they resembled those suffering with a slight attack of the measles.

"The police and hygiene of the hospital was defective in the extreme. Many of the sick were literally encrusted with dirt and filth and covered with vermin. When a gangrenous wound needed washing, the limb was thrust out a little from the blanket, or board, or rags upon which the patient was lying, and water poured over it, and all the putrescent matter allowed to soak into the ground floor of the tent. I saw the most filthy rags which had been applied several times, and imperfectly washed, used in dressing recent wounds. Where hospital gangrene was prevailing, it was impossible for any wound to escape contagion under these circumstances."[94]

**The Interior of the Hospital at the Southeast** - This drawing shows the doctors standing in the center of the tent, not being attentive to the patients. (Kellogg)

[91] Chipman, p. 179.
[92] *O.R.*, VIII, p. 599.
[93] Kellogg, p. 256.
[94] *Wirz Trial*, pp. 626, 627.

"General Winder visited the hospital after I was sent there; I know something about his ordering men to be shot about the 20th of July: I was standing at the gate; there had been no dead-line established inside the hospital, never; in fact there was no dead-line except right in front of the gate; in order to keep the gate clear he ordered the guard to shoot any damned Yankee who would trespass on the dead-line; it was only a mark sometimes made in the dust with a bayonet; he said, further, 'Any Yankee son-of-a-bitch you catch bathing in that creek down there shoot him.' The nurses and attendants had a parole at that time; the pass was taken away from us, and we were refused the privilege of bathing in the creek; we bathed below the hospital; we had a ditch dug through one end of the hospital for washing-water, and a sink at the lower end; it was a tributary of Sweet Water branch; I did not see any reason why I should not be allowed to bathe there; it was all swamp waste land beyond that."[95]

This new ditch was dug to detour one of the streams to flow within the confines of the hospital. "A sluggish stream of water flows through the southern portion of the hospital grounds from west to east. The upper portion of this stream is used by the patients for washing whilst along the borders of the lower-portion logs have been ranged upon which the patients may sit and evacuate their bowels. This part of the stream was a semi-fluid mass of human excrements and offal and filth of all kinds. This immense cesspool fermenting beneath the hot sun emitted an overpowering stench. The banks of this stream south of the hospital enclosure are bordered by a swamp, which spreads out toward the southeast. North of the hospital grounds the stream which flows through the stockade pursues its sluggish and filthy course. The exhalations from this swamp, which is loaded with the excrements of the prisoners confined in the stockade, exert their deleterious influences upon the inmates of the hospital."[96]

Escape from the hospital was possible. "The boards of the fence came down to the surface of the water, where the Creek passed out, but we found, by careful prodding with a stick, that the hole between the boards and the bottom of the Creek was sufficiently large to allow the passage of our bodies, and there had been no stakes driven or other precautions used to prevent egress by this channel. A guard was posted there, and probably ordered to stand at the edge of the stream, but it smelled so vilely in those scorching days that he had consulted his feelings and probably his health, by retiring to the top of the bank, a rod or more distant. We watched night after night, and at last were gratified to find that none went nearer the Creek than the top of this bank."[97]

During the trial, Doctor Bates was shown the print of Felix La Baume and made the following comments: "I have seen that before; it was given to me in the Andersonville Prison by Felix De La Baume. The tents, chimneys, fence, trees, cart and mule, etc., are correct. One sketch here of 'Dr. Bates' is pretty good, but rather spindle-shanked. The great point in which it is not facsimile is that too few men are represented. If there were forty delineated where there is one it would be more correct. These men walking on their hands and knees and on crutches, some carrying their tin cups in their mouths, represent men who could not go there otherwise. They were afflicted with scurvy as a general thing. One man represented here I recognize as a man named Ison, who was a subject of dementia; he only crept along on his haunches and feet. I recognize several others whose names I never learned, but whom I frequently saw. That man with the bucket in his mouth, I frequently saw crawling up for his rations. I see one man here representing 'Dr. Bates examining the character and quantity of the beef,' together with the Confederate surgeon and Ed. Young, boss of that cook-house. I also see one figure representing 'Dr. Bates giving beef-bones to the cripples.' It was my prerogative as officer of the day to supervise the cooking and administration of the rations, and to attend to anything that generally belonged to the hospital. When rations were being issued I would frequently go there. Those detailed to cut up the meat would put the bones in one pile and count the rations and put them carefully in another. When I would go there from twenty to one hundred or more would ask me, some of them very imploringly, for a bone I would say, 'Yes, you can have all the bones.' I see that I am represented here as handing bones to those cripples. I would hand them out as here represented. The general representation in this diagram is about correct, save that there were twenty or forty men to one represented here. They were very thick about the cook-house."[98]

"The rations, for twenty-four hours, for those poor sick ones, was a piece of corn bread about two inches square, and two ounces of meat. In case of very severe sickness, they might have two gills of flour, enough for a biscuit, and this would be baked by the nurse of the ward, and sometimes they had a little rice, but so miserably cooked as to be almost loathsome. It would be boiled in two large kettles, and then filled up with cold water to make it hold out, for the supply of those who needed it. The meal of which the bread was made, was a mixture of the cob and corn, for it

[95] Ray, pp. 241, 242.
[96] *O.R.*, VIII, p. 604.
[97] McElroy, pp. 364, 365.
[98] Chipman, pp. 131, 132.

was all ground together."[99]

For water, the men dug wells, hitting cool, clear water of sufficient quantity at the depth of forty feet. "Wells are being rapidly sunk in the prison hospital. A good and sufficient supply of water is obtained about forty feet from the surface of the ground."[100]

Just as at the pen, there was much trading between the guards and patients facilitated by the low permeable fence. Clifton traded with a guard at night and for his pocketknife, he received "... about a gallon of goober peas and a dozen big sweet potatoes."[101] Some guards were not as cooperative, as illustrated by the following incident that happened at the hospital. "One night I was startled by the sound of a musket, and immediately after, I recognized a human voice, uttering the exclamation, in plaintive, 'Oh, I am shot.' I instantly arose and hastened to the spot from whence the sound proceeded, and there found that one of the poor fellows in my ward had gone to the fire that was kept by the guard who were stationed inside the fence, for the purpose of warming himself. Some one from the outside passing by, called out gruffly to him 'Get away from there,' and without giving him time to obey the heartless order, fired upon him, breaking his leg just above the knee. The following morning he was subjected to amputation, but he never rallied from it. He lingered about three weeks and died."[102]

Chief Surgeon Stevenson complained almost daily about the "... prisoners stealing hospital property and selling it to members of the guard stationed at the hospital, and because of the frequent escapes by patients within the hospital."[103] In the fall of '64, General Winder ordered Wirz to replace the short, six-foot fence around the hospital with a higher more substantial palisade but, because of more pressing improvements to the post and the lack of teams to haul the logs, the construction was put off. Wirz recommended using the logs lying around on the ground that had been cut to use to make the third stockade. It seems that the fence was never replaced; instead, they decided to build a new hospital parallel to the south wall that was surrounded by a palisade.

When someone died in the hospital, he was simply laid in the street in front of the tent in which he had resided. From that place he was removed by the black Federal soldiers detailed for that purpose. If he died during the night, he would lie there until the next day. Even if he died in the daytime, he would sometimes lie in state for several hours.[104] Kellogg said that the Dead House was within the hospital ground, "So that it was a wonder to ourselves that we had no contagious diseases from having so many decaying bodies in our midst."[105] Reverend Clavreul gave the dimensions of the Dead House as 50 feet by 30 feet and said the dead were lined up in four rows.[106]

Doctor Bates testified, "... the dead-house of the hospital was in the southwest corner. When I first went there, what was called a dead-house consisted of some boards put up into a kind of shed. These boards were used by the inmates of the hospital or somehow else; at any rate, they disappeared. For some time the dead were laid there without any shelter. Every time I came on duty as officer of the day, which was every six days, I reported that there was no dead-house, and called the attention of the authorities to the erection of a dead-house or some place to deposit the dead, not to let them lie without shelter and exposed to the sun... They did not allow the corpse to lie long enough to cause any exhalations from putrefaction.

"We needed a dead-house, so as to have some place to lay the corpses decently. At one time we got a tent erected for a dead-house, but that did not last very long. Every morning when I would go in I would find a blanket or a quilt sliced off. The men would appropriate them to wrap themselves up. At first the top commenced going, and in a few days all was gone I remarked that it was no use to erect such dead-houses as that, except to supply the men with blankets, though I had no objection to their being erected every night, if the men could thereby get blankets. If my memory serves me right, no more dead-houses were erected. I think that tent I managed to get erected was the last."[107]

With the dispersal of the prisoners from Andersonville starting the first week in September, the entire post was turned into a Confederate military prison hospital facility. "In September or October," a large number of "rude, black artisans"[108] were detailed to help with the construction of a new, larger hospital on the high ground a couple hun-

[99] Kellogg, p. 262.
[100] *O.R.*, VII, p. 1076.
[101] Clifton, p. 6.
[102] Kellogg, pp. 260, 261.
[103] *O.R.*, VIII, p. 111.
[104] *Ibid.*, p. 605.
[105] Kellogg, pp. 277, 278.
[106] Clavreul, p. 7.
[107] Chipman, pp. 132, 133.
[108] Hamlin, p. 103.

dred yards away from, but parallel to the south wall.[109] "... Dr. Stevenson developed a very fine place for an extensive hospital. He laid off the grounds and had several wells dug. His plan was to erect a number of long, narrow buildings to extend north and south on each side of a wide street running east and west. At the west end of this street and immediately in front of it, was to be a large two-story building about twenty-five by eighty feet, to be used as dispensary, laundry, storeroom, office, etc., the upper story to be devoted to the use of Confederate attachés. But the work progressed so slowly that up to the time of my departure the main building only had been completed, and we made a second move of the dispensary."[110]

For the next few months, under Surgeon-in-charge H. H. Clayton, the detailed workers erected a series of twenty-two, open sheds [111] within a "high" palisade measuring 925 feet long and 400 feet wide.[112] "Early in December they got the main building of Stevenson's plan completed, and we made another move with the drug department; one which gave us very good quarters, though we had to make a log heat outside to warm by."[113]

By the time of the abandonment of the Post in April, the hospital had not been completed nor had any patients been admitted to its grounds, according to Doctor Bates.[114] Doctor Thornburg said, "It was not entirely completed... but... it was used."

A few days after the first groups of prisoners arrived from Richmond, the first prisoner was diagnosed as having smallpox. He was put in the hospital, which consisted of a single tent within the pen. There were four other patients in this tent. This first patient stayed there until he died.[115] Doctor White established a smallpox hospital and placed Doctor E. Sheppard, P.A.C.S. in charge of it. More than half of the cases admitted to it ended in death.[116]

Frank W. Smith said, "I was getting very much reduced when, April 28th, it was discovered that I had the smallpox, and I was sent to the smallpox hospital. This was in a pleasant wood some distance east of south from the prison, where we had room and air, and an opportunity to wash if we survived the disease. The wash for both clothing and person I prized, for I had worn every article of clothing eight months without change or washing. And when I had bathed in the nice clear waters of the creek which ran near the smallpox hospital, and had washed my clothing with soap and water, and boiled it, when I put it on clean, and sweet, and fresh, I was in no mood to dispute the old saying, 'Cleanliness is next to Godliness.'

"The smallpox is a much dreaded disease, but it, no doubt, saved my life. We were not guarded at the smallpox hospital, nor did the citizens come near. But the swine ran at large, and the young porkers came into the camp. A tall Tennessean, looking down one day, saw a glistening stone, and he said to me, 'Charley, I believe I could rub your knife down to a point on that stone so we could stick some of these pigs with it.' Finally pigs were missed. The Confederate steward told our Yankee steward, 'The boys must stop killing pigs.' The Yankee steward said to us, 'Steward says, 'you must not kill any more pigs,' and I say so; but if you find any dead ones cook and eat them.' The smallpox is a cold weather disease. It died out in the summer. In July the smallpox hospital was abandoned, and on the 19th of that month I was sent to the general hospital as attendant."[117]

Near the first of June, Doctor Isaiah White established a hospital for the garrison troops at Andersonville to accommodate 100 sick and placed Assistant Surgeon W. B. Harrison in charge of it.[118] It was called, "Sumter Hospital."

Doctor Augustus Hamlin, a physician, said, "... the garrison hospital at Andersonville offers a terrible contrast to the open space, the wretched agglomeration, which the rebel authorities called a hospital for the prisoners... The hospital system of the rebels was quite complete, and most of their hospitals throughout the country were well constructed and equipped; and some of them were models of neatness, comfort, and scientific arrangement."[119]

"Farther to the west, along the same airy and commanding ridge, and close to the track of the railway, appear the large two-story wooden buildings which were built and arranged, carefully and comfortably, for the sick of the Confederate guards."[120] "Their invalids were well cared for also in the large hospital which was erected expressly for the garrison, and which consisted of two large two-story wooden buildings, admirably arranged, with the conven-

[109] Chipman, p. 168.
[110] Hyde, p. 265.
[111] Hamlin, p. 103.
[112] *Ibid.*, Figure opposite p. 21.
[113] Hyde, p. 293.
[114] Chipman, p. 131.
[115] *Ibid.*, p. 172.
[116] *O.R.*, VII, p. 548.
[117] Frank W. Smith, pp. 24, 25.
[118] *O.R.*, VII, p. 417.
[119] Hamlin, p. 103.
[120] Charles G. Davis, p. 22.

iences proper to the service. The kitchen, the dispensary, the ventilation, and the general arrangement, showed that scientific care and forethought had been observed there."[121]

Doctor Stevenson reported to Doctor White, on October 31st, "I am having the Sumter Hospital completely renovated. The unfinished building will be completed in a few days. The normal capacity of it will then be 120.[122]

**Garrison Hospital** - In the foreground is the officers' stockade known as Castle Reed. This drawing is looking south from the prominence northwest of the prison. One of the two-story buildings in the distance was the hospital for the Confederate garrison of the post. (Hamlin)

Solon Hyde, one of the four druggists detailed outside the pen at Andersonville, describes the dispensary this way: "The dispensary was a sixteen-foot square log house without any window, a style peculiar to that section of the country, and had formerly been the negro quarters to the double log house. It stood on the north side of the earth-work, two pieces of artillery being planted just on the east side, bearing on the pen. There were two other druggists besides myself and Schroeder, a Norwegian named Oyen, and a New Yorker named Reed."[123] Hyde also said, "We had a man helping us at the dispensary, named W. A. White, a tailor."[124]

Hyde gave some insight into the inventory of the dispensary. "The stock of drugs was meagre, consisting, in the main, of 'roots and yarbs' packed by the Confederate Medical Dispensary at Macon, Georgia... We had only a limited quantity of quinine, opium, mercurial preparations, etc., though what we had were generally good and bore the stamp of English manufacture. But the way we sent out those 'yarbs' was a caution, - sumac berries, white-oak bark, prickly ash, prickly alder, willow bark, dogwood bark, sassafras bark, sweet-gum bark, black cohash, blackberry roots, boneset, burdock, yellow dock, bayberries, snakeroot, golden seal, juniper berries, etc., being the ones in most general use. From these the attendants in the hospital made decoctions which they issued to the sick 'in quantities to

[121] Hamlin, p. 103.
[122] *O.R.*, VII, p. 1076.
[123] Hyde, p. 245.
[124] *Ibid.*, p. 272.

suit.' We had no vessels in which to prepare them at the dispensary, nor bottles to put them in, and I am at a loss to know how they prepared them inside the hospital to make them effective."[125]

"Our dispensary was the only place where medicines could be procured within a number of miles of Andersonville, and citizens sometimes came, with orders from headquarters, to draw from us for family use. One afternoon three ladies, having such an order, came up on horseback. As they had not sufficient bottles of their own, and we had none to spare, in order to supply them, it was necessary, when they all wanted the same thing, to put it all into one bottle. They were laughing about it and wondering what they could do in order to get all they wanted. I suggested that they would have to let the one who lived most convenient to the other two take all the medicine to her house. Then she could get up a quilting-bee some afternoon and invite the other two, who in the mean time could hunt up spare bottles and have them in readiness to divide the medicine and make a social visit too. They thought that a happy solution to the problem."[126]

"The manner in which the surgeons performed their duty was to visit their wards every morning, visiting each patient and writing their prescriptions in a book which was then turned over to a wardmaster. This officer made a computation of the number of doses, if of roots, barks, or herbs, and we in the dispensary issued them in bulk. It was rather a unique way, but we could do no better, as we had no paper in which we could divide the doses. Every other day we made pills of various kinds, generally about seven thousand in number. This work generally kept us busy until the middle of the afternoon."[127]

Druggist Solon Hyde gave an interesting insight into the chronic infection in Wirz' arm: "He had some very bad ulcers on his limbs, of a character that required mercurial treatment, and he usually came to the dispensary after an ointment that we prepared from simple cerate and calomel rubbed together. As I was one day mixing him a portion he said, -

"'Make him strong mit the calomel.'

"Being told it was already of more than official strength, he said, -

"'Py Gott! I cares not for dat; I takes de law into my own handts. Make him two-three times as stong.'

"I then mixed it as stiff with as I could, which seemed to please him, as he exclaimed:

"'Hi-yi, dat is goot! Dat is right.'

"The next time he came, he said:

"'Make him shust like dot last; it was shust right.'"[128]

The doctors at Andersonville were probably as good as any in the rural South. The prisoners' opinion that the contract doctors were less competent than the regular Confederate Army medical officers was probably correct. The contention that the inmates were vaccinated with material made from syphilis chancre scabs was utterly ridiculous. The quality of medicine that was practiced was encumbered by the clumsy drug-dispensing system under which the doctors were forced to endure. However, little of the suffering at the prison can be directly attributed to the medical department.

---

[125] *Ibid.*, pp. 245, 246.
[126] *Ibid.*, p.273.
[127] *Ibid.*, p. 259.
[128] *Ibid.*, pp. 294, 295.

LET US FORGIVE, BUT NOT FORGET.
SPECIAL CASES
12TH WARD
COOK HOUSE
15TH WARD PATIENS TENT
50 CTS PER COPY

## *Chapter Five*

# The Doctors of Andersonville

*"Take him back to the pen again for he shall live another day."*

Doctor's instruction to
his clerk at sick call

The following is a compilation of the material readily available about some of the physicians who served at Andersonville mentioned in works by those associated with this prison. Of course, as expected, it is very sketchy and incomplete. The prisoners tended to blame the doctors for conditions beyond their control. The prisoners called the doctors "incompetent" and "butchers" when, in fact, they did the best they could under the limited conditions under which they were forced to practice.

John C. Bates was one of several very compassionate doctors at Andersonville. Doctor Bates practiced medicine for about fifteen years after his graduation in 1835, and resided in Georgia for most of the war. After 1857, his home was in Louisville, Jefferson County, Georgia. When the war broke out, he was a practicing physician who also operated a drug store. Doctor Bates was reluctantly inducted into Confederate service. Bates attempted to aid the starving prisoners by ameliorating the harsh orders given him by his superiors in the medical department. He was very sympathetic to the prisoners' plight.

"Up to June 1864, I remained at home practicing medicine. I was exempted by the confederate congress, being a physician over thirty years old, and having been in practice for seven years prior to the 17th of December, 1864…

I was arrested and taken to Augusta, and was given thirty days for the purpose of showing my exemption on the plea of being a physician. I got up the testimony, and the plea was refused. I bothered no more about it, but reported to Colonel Brown, and told him where I stood. I told him that Surgeon Green, of the confederate hospital at Macon had sent word to me to go up there and help him. Colonel Brown said, 'If Doctor Green wants your services, your contract will be as good an exemption as you want.' I therefore entered into the contract, and it was endorsed by the surgeon general, and I was put on duty in the City Hall hospital. One day a lieutenant came up and asked me if my name was Bates. I told him it was. He said, 'You are under arrest.' I asked, 'For what?' He said, 'I do not know; but bring your blankets and duds.' I said I had none. He walked me out to Camp Cooper, adjacent to Macon, and there I was confined. Next morning I was taken out to be enrolled and to have my personal description taken. A testament was shoved up to me. I asked what it was for. The answer was, 'To take the oath.' Said I, 'Hold.' I was not allowed to speak or say anything to anybody. I then asked for Major Roland, commandant of the post, and said I wished to see him. He was in an adjoining room. He sent word to me that I was under orders and that he wished no conference with me. They stuck up a book to me. I asked them what the oath or obligation was. They said it was that I should support the constitution. I was surrounded by bayonets, and the book stuck at me. I took the oath under duress. All the acts I did in the southern confederacy were in consequence of my being compelled."

Doctor Bates, having signed as a contract surgeon, was assigned to Andersonville on the 19th of September and reported for duty on the 22nd of September as an Acting Assistant Surgeon. He was ordered by Medical Director S. H. Stout to report to Doctor White, surgeon-in-charge. Doctor White had been hurt in a railroad accident while transferring prisoners, so he reported, instead, to Doctor Stevenson. Bates was assigned to the fifteenth ward of the third division of the military prison hospital, under the direction of Doctor Sheppard.

Later, Doctor Bates was ordered to report inside the stockade. "I was some time on duty in the fifth division of the stockade. That was the best division at Andersonville. It was under the immediate charge and care of Dr. Mudd, a very efficient officer. I strove heartily to get with him, believing him to be a man with whom I could work. He had the best hospital there and made the best provision for his men." At that time, the disbursement of the prisoners to Millen and Florence had begun. All the remaining prisoners were located on the south side. The north side was vacant except for the construction of the barracks or sheds that fit "...pretty well across the north end of the stockade..." "One of two were not completed in the northeast corner" These were used as a hospital and designated the fifth division. Bates served as "... visiting physician to the stockade only two days... not beyond three."

When a patient of Doctor Bates was felt to be in extreme need of extra nourishment, Bates would write a note to the head cook of the hospital, Bob Allen, from the state of Illinois. Bates would send a cryptic note that he had prearranged with the cook. Only three-word messages were valid requests, for example "Bob-meal-Bates" was a valid request. Bates realized that when a patient received an extra portion of food, he was decreasing the general supply available for the rest.

Bates said that there were several cases of chilblains or frost-bitten feet. These would usually become gangrenous, necessitating amputation. If the gangrene reappeared by attacking the stump, reamputation would be necessary. "For a while amputations were practiced in the hospital almost daily... and some few successful amputations were made. I recollect two or three which were successful."

Whenever Bates went into the hospital with any abrasion on his person, he would cover it with an adhesive plaster to try to prevent any open wound from becoming infected with gangrene. Bates did not think that Chief Surgeon White "... did all in his power to relieve the condition of those men, and I made my report accordingly." He also said that Doctor Stevenson did not manifest much interest "... on his part to relieve the necessities of the prisoners."

In addition to corn meal, beef, and bacon, he saw, occasionally, rice, peas, port, and potatoes issued in his hospital, but he never saw any turnips, carrots, tomatoes, or cabbage. He would order potatoes sent in for a week or two but then saw them disappear from the menu. He stated that, though western Georgia was famous as a corn growing country, he only occasionally saw green corn issued. It was considered a good, anti-scorbutic remedy. Bates felt that man needed a varied diet and, if fed a monotonous diet consisting of only "... four or five articles of diet for one year... he could not live." When Doctor Clayton took over as chief surgeon after the first of the year, Bates felt that the food improved in quantity and quality.

After the first of the year, Bates was ordered, by Doctor Clayton to make a "... special report of every article that was issued." He went to the commissary, and saw the provisions brought in and weighed. He figured 16 oz. of meal would make 28 oz. of bread, and 16 oz. of flour made 22 oz. of bread. Doctor Bates figured each prisoner got 32 and "some tenths" ounces of food per day. Six days later, he was asked to check again and that time it worked out that each patient got 28 ounces of this monotonous food. He said, "When I pointed out my deficiency [Dr. Clayton] would ask me to interest myself personally and remedy it, and he would do anything that could be done."

When he came to work at the hospital one morning, Bates saw his chief clerk tied up or bucked in front of the gate. Doctor Bates, Doctor James, and Doctor G. G. Roy called him their chief clerk. It was Doctor James who wrote a letter to someone high in authority, possibly the commandant of the post, or the chief surgeon, concerning this treatment of their clerk. The altercation originated because someone neglected to report that a man was missing. Wirz thought the clerk was negligent. Doctor James thought the Confederate Sergeant, a man named Stafford who called the roll of the sick, was the one responsible.

Bates said, "It was my prerogative as officer of the day to supervise the cooking and administration of the rations, and to attend to anything that generally belonged to the hospital. When rations were being issued I would frequently go there. Those detailed to cut up the meat would put the bones in one pile and count the rations and put them carefully in another. When I would go there from twenty to one hundred or more would ask me, some of them very imploringly, for a bone. I would say, 'Yes, you can have all the bones.'"

On the witness stand, Doctor Bates was asked, "From your observation of the condition and surroundings of our prisoners - their food, their drink, their exposure by day and by night, and all the circumstances you have described - state your professional opinion as to what proportion of deaths occurring there were the result of the circumstances and surroundings which you have narrated."

He answered, "I feel myself safe in saying that seventy-five per cent of those who died might have been saved, had those unfortunate men been properly cared for as to food, clothing, bedding, etc."

Doctor Bates remained at Andersonville until the latter part of March, 1865. The above summary of Doctor John C. Bates was gleaned from his testimony at the Wirz trial.[1]

Doctor F. G. Castlen was the regimental surgeon of the Third Georgia Reserves. During the last two years of the war, he was in the Confederate army and, from May until September, 1864, he was stationed at Andersonville. He described the stench as only intolerable when an east wind was blowing, though his camp was located a half-mile from the pen.

He testified that the farms nearby raised cucumbers, squash, cabbages, potatoes, collards, and melons. He didn't think that members of his regiment procured their vegetables from these farms but that they were brought from their own homes. Once, in June, his regiment was very unhealthy but this was only for a short while.

Doctor Castlen witnessed the wrath of Wirz only twice. When the prisoners were being dispersed, "... one prisoner was out of the ranks; Captain Wirz jerked and struck him, I think, once or twice...

"I saw one man who had been bitten by the dogs. I saw the dogs bite him. I saw the dogs running down the swamp below my camp. I went down, and when I reached the brow of the hill, I heard the dogs baying; going down, I saw this man up the tree. I heard someone order him down. I don't know who it was. He came down, and I saw the dogs seize him. Captain Wirz was there with the hounds."[2]

Doctor Bedford J. Head was a surgeon who had practiced for many years in Americus and had come to Andersonville to work as a contract surgeon with the rank of Acting Assistant Surgeon. When he arrived the first day, he was so sick that several days passed before he was able to report to Doctor White for his assignment. His duty was to manage one of the wards in the hospital. He was very conscientious and did the best he could under the circumstances. Dr. Head began a habit which endeared him to those he tried to aid. He carried to his scurvy patients foods which were beneficial such as biscuits and light bread, tea, rice and vegetables, especially tomatoes. Doctor Eiland allowed him to bring in the food by turning his head the other way if not actually aiding him in his endeavor. "Dr. Head was not only threatened with death by the brutal Wirz, but was actually imprisoned for a short time for giving to the dying some vegetables which he had gathered from his little garden."[3]

Doctor Head's negro servant accompanied him some days when he carried these favors for the prisoners. This was how the servant described what he saw on one visit; "'My God!' said he, and the tears stood in his eyes as he said it, 'I never thought to see a white man so low down as those there. Why, sir, there was one whose bones were through his skin, and he was lying right on the bare ground! Yes, sir, he'd made a hole where he'd turned and rolled... There were two holes, sir, just so he could roll on to one and off into the other... He didn't have more than a rag on him; and as for the lice... When I give 'em what I had in the basket, and after they'd ate it all, one got down on the ground and picked up what was scattered, like a dog!'"[4]

When Doctor Head first arrived at the hospital, he prescribed for his patients in the usual and customary fashion. After a couple of days, he found that his patients had not received the medicine he had ordered. He was told by his detailed Yankee clerk that, to get a remedy dispensed, he would have to order by the number system that was in use there. Doctors were allowed only to prescribe the thirty-odd drugs which were numbered sequentially, beginning with number one upwards. If a patient was troubled with diarrhea, he would be prescribed perhaps "No. 1;" perhaps "No. 2" for dysentery; perhaps "No. 3" for scurvy; "No. 4" for another ailment, and so on for thirty-odd ailments or symptoms. This system was despised by the doctors who felt it was "utter quackery" because this method did not allow the doctor control over what was prescribed, the strength of the drug dispensed, nor the dosage. This was determined by the Medical Director. Doctor Head said that many times he had nothing to give his patients but "... a little red-oak bark as an astringent and other barks" indigenous to the forests nearby. This method of dispensing was soon abandoned because of the legitimate complaints of the physicians.[5]

Doctor Head only stayed at Andersonville a couple of weeks in July. "The names of Thornberg (sic) and Head will always be preserved as among the only few redeeming acts in the story of the great wrong. The sympathy of these men was undisguised, and when protest failed to produce kindly impressions, or to bring alleviation to misery, they secretly sought to succor the dying men from their own scanty store at the peril of their lives."[6]

T. S. Hopkins was a physician who had received his M.D. degree in March, 1845. He lived in Thomasville,

---

[1] *Wirz Trial*, pp. 27-43 and pp. 662-668.

[2] Chipman, p. 119.

[3] Hamlin, p. 111.

[4] Spencer, pp. 91-82.

[5] *Wirz Trial*, p. 363.

[6] Hamlin, p. 111.

Georgia, about one hundred and ten miles from Andersonville. In July, 1864, an order was issued by Governor Joseph E. Brown of the State of Georgia, putting physicians into militia service. Governor Brown claimed that they were liable to serve in the state militia, although they were exempt by Confederate law. Thus, Doctor Hopkins had a choice of either going into the medical department or serving as a private in the militia. Hopkins did not feel that he was able to stand the rigors of the field. Hopkins was ordered to report for duty to Chief Surgeon White on the 22nd of July. He was assigned as surgeon in the engineer department of the post. None of his charges died except one man, who died while away at home. He was at Andersonville until the 8th of September, when he was ordered to accompany some of his patients to Camp Lawton, the newly-formed prison at Millen.

While at Andersonville, Hopkins received orders, on July 28, from General Winder, to make a thorough inspection of the prison, report the causes of diseases at the post, and to make recommendations to decrease the diseases prevalent there. General Winder also assigned Chief Surgeon White and Acting Assistant Surgeon H. E. Watkins to serve on this committee.

On the following day, the three surgeons made their inspection. Two of the surgeons wrote a letter stating their recommendations, which they submitted to Doctor White, who was then to have forwarded the document to General Winder. White did not forward the first inspection report and, after much prodding, sent a report that was not that of the two surgeons.

This inspection occurred only a week before Colonel Daniel Chandler's inspection. Doctor Hopkins testified that he "... could not see any great difficulty in carrying out those suggestions I made. I think I could have had it done without much trouble." When asked if Wirz was the cause of the situation at the pen, Hopkins thought "... it was the implicit confidence which General Winder had in Captain Wirz."[7]

When the three surgeons were touring the pen, they were observed by at least one man who recorded it for posterity. "One day some men came in who I was told were doctors, and as they crossed the swamp they put their hands over their mouths and noses to keep out the stench. I went up to one of them and asked him for medicine for a sick comrade. His answer was, 'The medicine is all locked up and we can't get it.'"[8]

The following is Doctors Hopkins' and Watkins' report:

**THE CAUSES OF DISEASE AND MORTALITY**

1. The large number of prisoners crowded together.
2. The entire absence of all vegetables as diet, so necessary as preventive of scurvy.
3. The want of barracks to shelter the prisoners from sun and rain.
4. The inadequate supply of wood and good water.
5. Badly cooked food.
6. The filthy condition of prisoners and prison generally.
7. The morbific emanations from the branch or ravine passing through the prison, the condition of which cannot be better explained than by naming it a morass of human excrement and mud.

**PREVENTIVE MEASURES**

1. The removal immediately from the prison of not less than 15,000 prisoners.
2. Detail on parole a sufficient number of prisoners to cultivate the necessary supply of vegetables, and until this can be carried into practical operation, the appointment of agents along the different lines of railroad to purchase and forward a supply.
3. The immediate erection of barracks to shelter the prisoners.
4. To furnish the necessary quantity of wood, and have wells dug to supply the deficiency of water.
5. Divide the prisoners into squads, place each squad under the charge of a sergeant, furnish the necessary quantity of soap, and hold these sergeants responsible for the personal cleanliness of his squad; furnish the prisoners with clothing at the expense of the Confederate government, and if the government be unable to do so, candidly admit our inability and call upon the Federal government to furnish them.
6. By a daily inspection of bake-house and baking.
7. Cover over with sand from the hillsides the entire "morass" not less than six inches deep, board the stream or water-course and confine the men to the use of the sinks, and make the penalty for disobedience of such orders severe.

---

[7] *Wirz Trial*, pp. 376-379.
[8] Lyons, p. 101.

**FOR THE HOSPITAL**

We recommend -

1st. The tents be floored with planks; if planks cannot be had, with puncheons; and if this be impossible, then with fine straw, to be frequently changed.

2nd. We find an inadequate supply of stool-boxes, and recommend that the number be increased, and that the nurses be required to remove them as soon as used, and before returning them see that they are well washed and limed.

3rd. The diet for the sick is not such as they should have, and we recommend that they be supplied with the necessary quantity of beef soup with vegetables.

4th. We also recommend that the surgeons be required to visit the hospitals not less than twice a day.

"We cannot too strongly recommend the necessity for the appointment of an efficient medical officer to the exclusive duty of inspecting daily the prison hospital and bakery, requiring of him daily reports of their condition to headquarters."[9]

As expected, there was a wide range of abilities and prejudices exhibited by the doctors at Andersonville. One doctor was described, by Solon Hyde, the apothecary, as having shown deep, anti-Yankee feelings and as having a habit of drinking medicinal whiskey.

"Dr. Johnson was an individual from upper Georgia, whose medical ability, if he had any, was known only to himself. His latent hatred of the Yankees was extremely bitter, and when his better judgment was warped by intoxication his maudlin abuse was irritating in the extreme and knew no bounds. On one occasion, when in this condition, he came into the dispensary and attempted to help himself to more whiskey from our supply. On being refused, he broke out into an abusive tirade against us for daring to offer any objection. He became so loud in his talk as to attract the attention of Mr. Dance and Mr. Robertson, Confederate attaches, who came in and dragged him out on his back, heels foremost, into the rain. He was always fastidiously dressed, silk plug hat and all, but dragging out gave his a very unpresentable appearance... The doctor left Andersonville a few days later for a visit home, and he never returned. After my return from prison I became acquainted with Dr. Boyd, the surgeon of an Ohio regiment. He asked me if I ever knew a Dr. Johnson at Andersonville. He said that he had come across a man of that name after the fall of Atlanta, - near Jonesboro, I think, - who said he was at one time in attendance at Andersonville. He told Boyd how inhumanly the men had been treated; how he had lain awake and wept nights thinking of their condition and trying to devise ways to render them even passably comfortable; and how he had spent a fortune of his own in trying to do something for them. He made himself out to be an immaculate saint, and for his great benevolence our officers had put a guard around his property and furnished him a great many supplies from our commissary. I described our Dr. Johnson to him, and the picture fitted his Dr. Johnson so well that we concluded the two were identical."[10]

**Dr. W. J. W. Kerr** (CV)

Doctor W. J. W. Kerr, was ordered to Andersonville in July, "... to take charge of the dispensary and to superintend the building of a hospital and other government buildings connected with the prison."[11] "Dr. Karr [sic]... seemed to be a kind of roustabout whose duty was to superintend the hospital attendants and enforce orders (I do not think he held any commission) was addicted to inhaling ether and chloroform and getting into a kind of drunken state, when he was full of 'Old Nick.' Taking him all in all, he was... 'any how a funny fellow.' He took special delight in watching close to the hospital gate after night, trying to catch the guards and men trading. He was acting as hospital steward."[12] He was superintendent of the stewards and medical attendants at Andersonville.

[9] *Wirz Trail*, pp. 377-379.
[10] Hyde, pp. 253-255.
[11] W. J. W. Kerr, "Sad Ending of a Wedding Trip," *Confederate Veteran*, (July, 1915), p. 318.
[12] Hyde, pp. 250, 251.

While Doctor Stevenson was chief surgeon, "Dr. Kerr was the rebel hospital steward; he would come into the hospital enclosure disguised as one of our men; he would wear different disguises; one night he would wear a ragged uniform, and the next night a very good uniform. I have seen him come into the hospital enclosure and strike a man across the face with his pistol for merely standing and talking to a guard. He carried a heavy pistol. He would strike a man right across the forehead. This he did frequently, although I never saw him do it but once, but I saw men whom he had struck. Once he robbed a man. He went and took some staff buttons from a sick man in my ward; he had them in his pocket and Dr. Kerr could not get them in any other way - so he confiscated them. Buttons were used as money to purchase goods; they were worth five dollars apiece..."[13]

Spencer stated, "... some of the Andersonville historians have published an account of Dr. Kerr 'brutally striking a sick prisoner.' Permit one who is familiar with the circumstances to give the correct version."

"One day in August Dr. Kerr caught a hospital attendant, a paroled prisoner, selling a blanket to a guard. Dr. Kerr investigated the matter and ascertained the fact that the Federal prisoner had stolen it from a patient. He as good as caught him in the act, and when he remonstrated with the thief the latter, being a desperate man, attacked the Doctor, and but for the surgeon's agility he would have been injured. As it was, his sleeve was cut through with a knife, grazing the skin, whereupon the Doctor promptly and very properly struck the thief over the head with the butt of his revolver, knocking him down and disarming him. Simply that and nothing more, except that the thief lost his detail and the sick prisoner found his blanket."[14]

Solon Hyde, at the dispensary, told about a nice humanitarian act done by Dr. Kerr, "... Dr. Kerr, in one of his predatory raids at the hospital, confiscated a part of a caddy of tobacco in the act of being transmitted through the lines. This he brought into our department and told us to take charge of it. Now, anything that came into our hands we felt at liberty to dispense for the needs of the sick; consequently, when we found a patient who we thought would be benefited by tobacco, we prescribed it for him, or allowed him to prescribe for himself, until it was all gone."[15]

"Dr. Mudd was a bitter, red-hot rebel from Kentucky, who suffered his prejudices to bias his judgement. In his eyes a Yankee was no better than a dog. He was a surgeon of no mean ability, of phlegmatic temperament and well-defined muscle. If there was a soft phase to his nature he left it at his quarters, and to the prisoners he was always distant and haughty. He took some pride in his profession and boasted of his relationship to President Lincoln's wife, who he thought was 'no great shakes' after all."[16]

Benjamin F. Dilley, a paroled clerk, testified, "I have seen Dr. Mudd come into the hospital when they would be amputating a limb; he would hold his thumb over the artery just at the thigh, and when the operator would be tying up the arteries, he would take his finger off the artery and sent the blood up into the man's face; he would laugh at the time as if he thought it was something funny; I have seen him do that on two different occasions; I never saw him do anything but that; he did not appear to care about taking care of our men."[17]

Doctor Bates assured the court that it was proper procedure to release the artery to allow it to "display itself." The following morning report was placed in evidence by the prosecution at Wirz' trial.

*First Division C. S. Military Prison Hospital*
*Surg. E. D. Eiland,* *September 5,1864*
*In Charge First Division C. S. Military Prison Hospital*

*Sir: As officer of the day for the past twenty four hours I have inspected the hospital and found it in as good a condition as the nature of the circumstances will allow. A majority of the bunks are still unsupplied with bedding, while in a portion of the division the tents are entirely destitute of either bunks, bedding, or straw, the patients being compelled to lie upon the bare ground. I would earnestly call your attention to the article of diet. The corn bread received from the bakery, being made up without sifting, is wholly unfit for the use of the sick, and often, as in the last twenty-four hours, upon examination the inner portion is found to be perfectly raw. The meat (beef) received by the patients does not amount to over two ounces per day, and for the past three or four days no flour has been issued. The corn bread cannot be eaten by many, for to do so would be to increase the diseases of the bowels, from which a large majority are suffering, and it is therefore thrown away. All then that is received by way of subsistence is two ounces of boiled beef and a half pint of rice soup per day, and under these circumstances all the skill that can be brought to bear upon their cases by the medical officers will avail nothing. Another point to which I feel it my duty to call your attention is the*

[13] *Wirz Trial*, p. 682.
[14] Spencer, pp. 83, 84.
[15] Hyde, pp. 272, 273.
[16] *Ibid.*, pp. 252, 253.
[17] *Wirz Trial*, pp. 681, 682.

*deficiency of medicines. We have but little more than indigenous barks and roots with which to treat the numerous forms of disease to which our attention is daily called for the treatment of wounds, ulcers, &c., we have literally nothing except water. The wards, some of them, are filled with gangrene, and we are compelled to fold our arms and look quietly upon its ravages, not even having stimulants to support the system under its depressing influences, this article being so limited in supply that it can only be issued for cases under the knife. I would respectfully call your earnest attention to the above facts, in the hope that something may be done to alleviate the sufferings of the sick.*

*Very respectively, your obedient servant,*
*J. Crews Pelot Assistant Surgeon,*
*Provisional Army, C. S., Officer of the Day*[18]

"Dr. McVeigh,, a Virginian, was a tall, easy specimen of 'don't-care' activity, whose attenuated form required the support of a cane. He was easy in his manners and cordial in his intercourse with the boys. He was well posted... in medicine."[19]

Doctor G. L. B. Rice served at Andersonville from about August 1, 1864, to March 10, 1865. He was ordered to report to Doctor White, who assigned him to duty outside the stockade where he prescribed for three or four weeks and then was sent to the hospital. Because of the prescribing by numbers, he complained to his colleagues and asked them if there was any chance of getting rid of this clumsy system. They said that there was not. Some of them had gone to the chief surgeon and complained, but they were not able to initiate any change.

Doctor Rice mentioned to Doctor Stevenson one day that he had a great excess of vegetables at his home and that they would be rotting soon if not eaten. He asked Dr. Stevenson if he would allow him to go home for a few days and bring those vegetables down for the prisoners without any charge. If he were not allowed to go, then could Doctor Stevenson send some men to get them as they were all going to waste and would do no one any good. Stevenson observed that he would have liked to have had them but said no more about them ever again. They were never sent for.

Doctor Rice said he did not know whether or not Captain Wirz had had anything to do with the quantity or quality of the rations in the hospital. He did think the rations were approved by the chief surgeon.[20]

Doctor G. G. Roy was ordered, on September 1st, 1864 to Andersonville by Doctor Stout, the medical director of the Army of Tennessee. "Dr. Roy was a dapper young man who carried with dignity and honor the medical lore of two continents without its seeming to hurt him in the least. He was a true gentleman, who bowed as slow to the prisoner in his rags as he did to the officer in his tinsel. He lived about two miles north from Andersonville on a farm. Whether that was his home or not, I cannot say. His knowledge of medicine was theoretically good. I noticed that his opinion was sought after and respected by all the surgeons there. Practically he was a novice, having only taken his diploma some nine months before in Paris, and then run the blockade. He was justly proud of his profession and his professional attainments, and he sought every chance to investigate disease."[21]

Concerning the hierarchy of the medical staff, Roy said that there were two chief surgeons at that time at Andersonville. Surgeon White acted as Chief Surgeon of the Post and concerned himself mainly with the general administrative duties of the post. Doctor Stevenson was acting chief surgeon in charge of the hospital, and of the medical department prescribing at the stockade.

Doctor Roy was dismayed by the deplorable condition of the hospital. He said that the tents and the dry-rotted pieces of tents were not laid out "... with any particular regularity." Doctor Roy was sent there under orders that he was to be placed in charge of a division. There was a six-day delay while they re-organized the three divisions there to form another division, the fourth division, for him. He said that, by that time in September, there were only a few new cases of gangrene because "... most of the surgery had been done."

Concerning the control which Wirz had over the hospital, Roy said the power was absolute but Wirz did not exercise control but once. At one time, the chief clerk of Assistant Surgeon James, one of Roy's assistant surgeons, was "bucked" and placed outside the gate of the hospital. Roy and his staff called Wirz' bluff and demanded to see the orders which gave him the power over the hospital personnel, the guard, and interior. Wirz showed him the order giving him this power signed by General Winder which, in effect, said the medical men had no rights and a guard could do anything in the hospital without consulting a staff member. There was always a sergeant at the gate who

[18] *O.R.*, VII, pp. 773, 334.
[19] Hyde, p. 255.
[20] *Wirz Trial*, pp. 381-383.
[21] Hyde, p. 257.

was under the control of Captain Wirz.

After the first of the year, when Doctor Clayton took charge of the hospital, Roy said they had fewer patients and "... were pretty well supplied with food and medicine."

He was still at the post until the last of April of 1865.[22]

Solon Hyde described an elderly man and his son, both of whom were physicians. "Dr. Shepherd, Sr., was an old man in his dotage, who claimed to have been a surgeon in the United States Army or Navy, which I think likely, as it is a notorious fact that all the old wards of the government who found their way into the rebel army showed the meanest, most vindictive spirits we had to contend with... The doctor was an imperious, arbitrary old fellow, who, for all I know, may have forgotten more medical lore than an ordinary faculty possesses, but the fact was patent that he had not so retained it as to make it available at Andersonville. He was one of the bitterest men I ever met, yet without any clear reason for being so, and he was the only surgeon in the 'outfit' who dressed in out-and-out Confederate uniform.

"Wherever you met the old veteran, you would always find him shadowed by his son, Dr. Shepherd, Jr., a man perhaps fifty years of age. A peculiarly marked trait of the younger doctor was his veneration for his father, whom he called 'Pap-pay.' Wheresoever you met them walking, the son's position was always about a rod in the rear of the old man, which peculiarity might have been accounted for by the fact that he was very deaf, and, lest he should lose the old fellow, as he could not keep his ear on him, it became necessary for him to drop behind, so that he might the more readily keep an eye on him. The old gentleman's solicitude for his son was equally great. My opinion of the younger fellow was that he was daft; but I might have been prejudiced; at any rate, he was an inoffensive person affably inclined, his deafness possibly rendering him a little diffident. He was a hobbyist as a doctor, his constant medical theme being the fine therapeutical effects he had seen in the use of 'camphor water,' from which we are led to believe that if he did the sick in his ward no particular good he did them no particular harm. One day, when in a particularly good talking mood, he said to me, tapping a demijohn of camphor water with his cane, 'There is one of the finest remedial agents in the world, "Aqua Camphorata".' After that we all knew the couple as Dr. Camphor Water and 'Pap-pay.' They disappeared from Andersonville before I left."[23]

Richard Randolph Stevenson was born in Mercer County, Kentucky, the grandson of a Professor Stevenson, a native of Londonderry, Ireland. He was the son of Captain James Mayes Stevenson who served in the War of 1812. On his mother's side, he was descended from the Randolphs of Virginia. He studied in Louisville, Kentucky, and, at the outbreak of the Civil War, he enlisted as a private but was, later, commissioned as an army surgeon.[24]

Doctor Stevenson told about his career in the early part of the war in a petition to Major General J. C. Breckinridge seeking to explain how his rank should be considered retroactive back to 1861.

"In April 1861, I was forced to leave my home in Greencastle, Indiana on account of my political precedents. I went to Louisville, Kentucky with the intention of joining Blanton Duncan's Regiment and going to Virginia. When I arrived there I was advised by some of my old friends (Dr. H. M. Bullite, among others, who had previously befriended me in my early days) not to join Duncan's Regiment as there would be other regiments formed in the state with better men and more competent leaders, I was referred to Governor Magoffin by Mr. W. N. Haldeman and had an interview with him. He advised me to go to some point where I was best acquainted and known, and get up a company or as many men as I could and put them in the Confederate Army, I done so. I went to Anderson County, where I was well acquainted, and partly raised and I, in conjunction with Captain McBrayer and G. W. Dedman succeeded in raising a large company of good men. We started on foot from Lawrenceburg and made the march to Camp Boon, Tenn. We all took the oath as privates and risked the chances afterwards for office. That company now is "Co. I" 2nd Regiment Kentucky Volunteers, Captain Dedman commanding. I was soon afterwards appointed by Lt. Col. Johnson acting Assistant Surgeon of the regiment. Shortly afterwards I was notified by the Secretary of War, to appear before the Army Medical Board for examination. I appeared before the Board at Bowling Green and passed as Ass't. Surgeon, D. W. Yandell, President. I was shortly afterwards, selected and appointed by I. H. Lewis Colonel 6th Reg't, Kentucky Vols. as surgeon of his regiment. I was ordered as Surgeon by the Secretary of War to report to General Beauregard, commanding at Corinth for duty with the 6th Reg't. Kentucky . Vols. on the 22nd day of May 1862. This order was suppressed as I suppose by Dr. Yandell. I received a copy of it a short time since under Gen'l Orders from the War Department. I appeared before the Army Medical Board in November last and passed as Surgeon, D.

---

[22] *Wirz Trial*, pp. 81-85.

[23] Hyde, pp. 255-257.

[24] Military Records obtained from the National Archives.

W. Yandell, President."[25]

On August 11, 1864, he was ordered to proceed to Fort Valley, Georgia, in charge of the hospital and stores of the Newman Hospital.

Doctor Stevenson soon was assigned to Andersonville where he became a suspect in another scheme which possibly increased the suffering of the men.

Surgeon Stevenson was assigned by Chief Surgeon Isaiah White to duty at the prison hospital sometime near the first of September as Surgeon-in-Charge. Finding no building of any kind there and no accommodations for the sick and wounded but tents, Stevenson proposed building a series of sheds built in a space of ground covering 450 by 900 feet. He was firmly against using tents for the hospital since he felt it was impossible to keep tents properly policed.

He said that the sheds could be built rather quickly using wood found nearby. He felt that "... a hospital of this description can be easily erected at this post, or any other where lumber and material are so easily procured." He thought this pavilion hospital would cost much less to the government than any other configuration. The sheds would be 100 feet long, 22 feet wide, and 8 feet high at the eaves. He proposed to cantilever off a streamer running the entire length of the shed, an awning made from old tents, "... of which any quantity can be procured." This awning could be raised and lowered as desired. These sheds could house fifty patients and he proposed to build 40 of them. There would be ten sheds to a division with a capacity of 500 patients to the division for a total of 2,000 patients in the hospital. Each division was going to have a cooking facility, baking facility, and a convalescent dining room. There would be one special diet kitchen, a laundry, and a depot building for the reception of commissary stores and medicines for the entire hospital and the entire affair would be enclosed in a stockade.[26]

Doctor Stevenson was accused of embezzling a large sum of money from the hospital fund. Dr. G. G. Roy testified, "There was provision for a hospital fund, which was in the hands of the chief surgeon; all of the confederate hospitals drew on the hospital fund, which amounted latterly to about $3.13 per day for each patient; this hospital fund was for the purpose of procuring such articles as the sick needed and as the commissary did not supply, or as the medical purveyor could not furnish, and which could be purchased outside; when I first went there the hospital fund amounted, I think, to about $190,000 a month, between that and $200,000; I do not know that it was drawn; this was in confederate money; it ought to have been drawn from the commissary of the post; when I first went there Major Proctor was the commissary; I do not know whom he succeeded; I never had control of any of that fund; the chief surgeon, Dr. Clayton, and after him Dr. Stevenson, drew the funds and supplied me; I made requisitions for articles in kind, not for the funds to buy them; latterly, within three or four weeks of our abandoning the place, I got all I wanted; then we had very few patients, and our facilities for getting what we wanted were much greater."[27]

This was the way Doctor Thornburg described what he knew about the incident, "I only knew that there were orders from the war department, the assistant inspector-general's office, that the prison hospital should be on an equal footing with the Confederate hospitals, and that the surgeon in charge should be allowed to draw the same fund. A portion of the time the fund was a dollar a day for each patient, and after a while it got to be two dollars and two and a half dollars a day... I know of no reason why it could not have been drawn at Andersonville. It was generally drawn at other hospitals. The fund was sufficient to buy vegetables for the Confederate hospitals, and sometimes large amounts of the fund were turned over to other and more needy hospitals... There was an order issued from Richmond directing that the surplus fund be turned over to the quartermaster at the end of each month... I saw the weekly account current one time in the hands of the hospital steward, Mr. Kerr. I had made complaints to him about the condition of the patients and the condition and the amount of the rations that came in and the amount of vegetables and other nourishing diet that was to be bought with the hospital fund. Mr. Kerr, to convince me that these things were sent in, showed me the weekly statement for that week. In looking at it, I remarked that those things never came into the hospital at least, that no considerable part of them had come in and I made some little complaint about it to the other surgeons, and we began to talk about having an investigation of the matter. We called on Mr. Kerr after that for the book, but he remarked that Dr. Stevenson had it in his charge, and we were not allowed to see it. I never saw it after that until Dr. Stevenson left and Dr. Clayton took charge. At that time, myself and three or four other surgeons went up and asked Dr. Clayton to let us see the account current. He showed it to us, and on examination we found that large quantities of things which appeared by the book to have been bought had never come into the hospital. We made a statement of the facts to the surgeon-general and forwarded it by mail. A few days af-

[25] *Ibid.*

[26] *O.R.*, VII, p. 711.

[27] *Wirz Trial*, p. 83.

terwards Dr. Eiland was ordered to Montgomery. He had taken an active part in this investigation, and we requested him as he went through to Montgomery to stop at Columbus, Georgia, and make a statement to the medical director. He did so. At the time he made that statement, Dr. Gilliard, one of the surgeon-general's assistants, happened to be at Columbus, in the office of the medical director. He and Dr. Flewellen came down immediately and investigated the case, and found that there had been some errors in regard to the hospital fund. Dr. Stevenson went to Columbia, South Carolina, and was there the last news I had from him."[28]

R. R. Stevenson, Surgeon-in-charge of Post, sent a report for the month ending October 31st through Doctor White, who, by that time, was "Chief surgeon and inspector of hospitals, Georgia and Alabama," to General Winder. In his report, Doctor Stevenson said, of the hospital fund, "Great difficulty has been experienced in drawing from the general hospital fund; this, with the difficulty of drawing necessary bedding from the medical purveyor, has partially prevented me from making the sick and wounded as comfortable as I would wish."[29]

In this same report, he said, "There has been a marked improvement in the health of the prisoners and the guard forces during the past month; the cause of this is too obvious for comment."[3029] Using biased statistics that did not take into consideration the dramatic decrease in the prison population, Stevenson said, "By the use of vegetables in such quantities as could be procured, and an acid beer made from corn-meal and sorghum molasses, the death rate fell from about 3,000 in August to 160 for the month of December."[31]

Doctor G. L. B. Rice was also familiar with the alleged embezzlement by Doctor Stevenson. "He was tried for making away with the money that was sent there for the use of the hospital ... I think he was found guilty. I was called into the room where they were carrying on the investigation, and was asked a few questions by the committee. I do not know the amount of money Dr. Stevenson embezzled. I heard it was from $100,000 to $150,000."[32]

Doctor Stevenson was transferred on or about January 1st to Camp Maxey Gregg in Columbia. His place was filled by Doctor H. H. Clayton.

On February 13th, 1865, Stevenson was ordered, by Doctor White, Chief Surgeon, from his Headquarters of the Military Prisons East of the Mississippi River, in Columbia, to proceed from the Prison Hospital at Camp Maxey Gregg with his hospital property and ten attendants to Charlotte. There, he was to organize a hospital in connection with the prison at that place and assume command of it. Thirteen days later, he was ordered to High Point, North Carolina, to form a depot and to await further orders. Doctor Stevenson wrote, in moving from Columbia, that Captain Sharp, the Transportation Quartermaster, refused to furnish him with any transportation whatever. "After his refusal, I succeeded by great personal exertion in getting off all my stores and supplies I had in Columbia and Camp Maxey Gregg, safely to his place. I had several paroled Yankee prisoners and a number of buckets on the train with my stores and by bailing water for the engines at the several stations (the water tanks being given out). I fortunately assisted in not only saving my own stores, but several engines and trains."[33]

He was found at the General Hospital No. 3, in High Point, North Carolina, at the end of the war.

Another doctor described by Solon Hyde was Doctor Thompson, a Unionist, who anxiously awaited the return of the South to the Union. "Dr. Thompson was a South Carolinian, whom to use his own language, '... fought the false idea of secession like a devil, stumping his State in favor of the Union, but drifted with the tide.' He was a voluble talker, always ready to laugh at a good yarn, and to go one better, but never suffering himself to be outspun. He was attentive to his patients and kind withal, but too reckless to be trustworthy, - a true type of Southern abandon. He declared that rum, women, and tobacco had been his ruin, and that his love for them was his only fault. He did not have much confidence in the stability of the Confederacy, and often said that he was 'only waiting until he could get back home.' - meaning under the old flag and government."[34]

Another very compassionate physician at Andersonville was Doctor Amos Thornburg, Assistant Surgeon. He received his commission on October 29, 1862, and served in the field for a little over two years except for the short time he had been held prisoner. Because of poor health, he was relieved from duty in the field and sent back to a hospital in Oxford, Georgia. He stayed there two or three weeks, and was then ordered to Andersonville. He reported for duty to the commandant of the prison, Colonel Persons, on the 14th of April. Persons sent him to Doctor White, who assigned him to sick call at the stockade. He "prescribed in quarters" there for two or three months while

[28] *Ibid.*, pp. 334, 335.
[29] *O.R.*, VII, p. 1076.
[30] *Ibid.*
[31] Stevenson, p. 25.
[32] *Wirz Trial*, p. 382.
[33] Military Records obtained from the National Archives.
[34] Hyde, p. 253.

the hospital was inside the stockade, and then at the gate until the latter part of June. He was then sent to the hospital at the outside of the southeast corner. Doctor White left to follow General Winder when the prisoners were removed to Camp Lawton at Millen. Surgeon R. R. Stevenson succeeded Doctor White as Chief Surgeon on about the 25th of September. Surgeon H. H. Clayton succeeded Dr. Stevenson about January 1st and continued to be in charge until the pen was captured by General Wilson.

When Doctor Stevenson was in charge, Doctor Thornburg was in charge of the surgical ward in the second division, which was generally known as the gangrene ward.

"I had for that ward some scaffoldings fixed up for bunks, and I frequently made application for bed sacks, sheets, &c. I got a few bed sacks, but they would soon become dirty and I would send them off to be washed, and perhaps not see them any more. The next thing I would see would be some prisoner with a pair of pantaloons on made out of bed sack, and I would make application for more. I made no complaints about their taking them. I very seldom got anything that I made requisition for...

"The food that was issued was such as the other prisoners and the soldiers outside could get from the commissary, mostly bacon, beef, or pickled pork. The bacon was generally very good; the beef sometimes was rather poor. The pickled pork that came in was very frequently partly spoilt; it smelt badly, was hardly fit for use, and we had at times condemned it and sent it back. The meal that was issued was very coarse, and at first was not sifted even for the hospital. Sometimes we would get a few collards, and tomatoes, and sweet potatoes, &c., but in very small quantities. That was under Dr. White. It was a little better under Dr. Stevenson...

"The supply of medicines was generally insufficient. The surgeon in charge would generally make a requisition for medicine to have it on the first of the month, but it was usually the 10th before we got the supply, and when we did get it, such articles as opium, quinine, and other valuable medicines, which were very scarce in the Confederacy, would be exhausted in the course of ten or twelve days, and we would have to rely on such indigenous remedies as were furnished by the medical purveyor. They were generally put up in decoctions or infusions by the hospital steward...

"I would sometimes prescribe while at the stockade gate for five hundred patients in a day. In order to do that we had to prescribe by formulas; to make out formulas for different diseases and number them, and then just examine a man and set down the number of the prescription that he was to take opposite his name, with directions. Frequently there would be no vacancies in the hospital at all. Some days we could not send any to the hospital. At other times perhaps fifty, sixty, or a hundred men would have died during the day previous and there would be that many vacancies, and we would be allowed to send in a pro rata number to fill those vacancies. There were generally some ten or twelve surgeons and assistant surgeons prescribing at the stockade gate; and each one would be allowed to send in a certain number to fill the vacancies. Some days we would send in one, two, three apiece, sometimes ten apiece, and some days, when the hospital would be enlarged, as high as thirty or forty apiece. One day we sent three or four hundred among us out of the stockade to the hospital ... Sometimes the sergeants who drew the rations and had charge of the squads would represent to the surgeons the cases of men who were not able to come out, and had requested them to get certain medicines; and if the diseases were such as we could prescribe for, we would very frequently set the name of such a man down and the number of the prescription that he should have, and that medicine was then issued to the sergeant, and he delivered it to the man...

Sometimes there would be a very sick man brought from the stockade, and he would be marked in the surgeon's book for admittance to the hospital; he would have to remain at the gate until all the surgeons got through prescribing, so that the men who carried them to the hospital could be discriminate and take the proper ones. It generally took us from eight o'clock in the morning till twelve o'clock noon before we would get through prescribing, and sometimes very bad cases would die while waiting there to be carried to the hospital. I had charge of so many divisions in the stockade, and frequently when a man from one of my divisions would die in that way, the clerk who kept the death register would ask me the man's rank and regiment and name, and the squad to which he belonged. Several men might have died at my post when I was prescribing and I could not recollect anything about any particular one. There would be two or three dead, and we could not identify them. After that I adopted the plan of writing the name, rank, regiment, and disease of each man on a piece of paper and pinning it to the breast of his coat or some part of his clothing. It worked very well, and I recommended Dr. White to issue an order requesting all the surgeons who prescribed at the stockade gate to adopt the same plan. He did issue such an order, and the system was adopted June, 1864...

"So far as the names of the men and the diseases that they had, the hospital register was kept with great accuracy. If a man came to me I would diagnose his case, and send him to the hospital with a statement of the disease which I considered that he had. That was generally entered upon the register, but, perhaps, he would have half a dozen supervening diseases after he went into the hospital. The supervening diseases were hardly ever entered on the register, but generally only the disease with which he went from the stockade. I do not know what entry was made on the register when a man was shot in the stockade. I suppose the cause of death would be called 'vulnus sclopeticum'; that is the technical name for gunshot wound."[35]

Many patients listed in the hospital register had, beside their names, the phrase,"died in quarters." This notation meant that the patient had died in the stockade. It is interesting to note that the cause of the deaths of the six Raiders who were hung by their comrades was listed as "asphyxia," which means there was a lack of oxygen to the brain, in this case caused by the sudden tightening of a noose.

Doctor Amos Thornburg thought "... that one half might have been saved if we had had proper nourishing diet and the proper kind of hospital accommodations."[36]

In about the middle of August, Doctor Thornburg reported that his patients were in a "deplorable condition." "In the first, second and third wards, we have no bunks, the patients being compelled to lie on the ground, many of them without blankets, or any covering whatsoever. If there are any beds in 'Dixie,' it is to be hoped that they will be procured. We need straw very badly, especially for the fifth ward. We have men in this ward who are a living, moving mass of putrefaction, and can not possibly be cured of their wounds unless we can make them more comfortable."[37]

A new system of patient identification devised by Doctor Thornburg, was described by Kellogg this way: "These would have a piece of paper, with their number and name, put upon their clothes, or in their pockets, and it was not a strange thing that they were left in the hot sun all day, without anything to eat, or water to drink, and with a burning fever in their veins."[38]

"Before the plan of marking and numbering was observed, those who died while waiting to be carried to the hospital were buried with the single word upon them, 'Unknown.''[39]

Hyde though that "Dr. Thornburg was a man of fine feeling and medical ability, with a high sense of justice, that saw in the sick prisoner before him a human being who required medical attention and medical sympathy. His heart was with his patients, and he took pleasure in doing all he could to render them comfortable, carefully diagnosing his cases and noting every change in order to meet the necessities of the case promptly. I frequently heard him lament the absence of requisites to render the men comfortable. More than that, he read me a paper he had prepared for transmission to the Surgeon-General at Richmond, in which he fairly portrayed the condition of the men and asked that means might be put at the disposal of the medical staff to ameliorate the condition of the prisoners, or that some arrangement might be made to have them sent North. He also reported the fearful mortality."[40]

Colonel D. T. Chandler, A. A. & I. G., after his inspection near the first of August, said that he was told by the chief surgeon that Surgeon E. Sheppard, Assistant Surgeon R. E. Alexander and Assistant Surgeon A. Thornburgh [sic)] were "incompetent and inefficient."[41]

Isaiah H. White, the son of Samuel C. White, was born on July 24, 1838, at Onancock, in Accomac County on the Eastern Shore of Virginia. He was educated at the College of William and Mary in Williamsburg, Virginia, and then at the Medical College of Virginia in Richmond. He matriculated there on November 4, 1859, for the First Term of Medical School and on September 26, 1860, for the Second Term. He listed his home at that time as being at Yorktown, York County, Virginia. He said that a Doctor Thomas P. Bagwell of Onancock was the physician under whom he had spent his required preceptorship. After completing his two terms of study at the Medical College of Virginia, Doctor White, on October 21, 1861, returned to his alma mater from which he had just graduated to serve as a Demonstrator of Anatomy for the 1861-1862 session.[42]

Isaiah H. White was appointed assistant surgeon in the Confederate Army on April 8, 1862, and, four days later, was told to report to Surgeon J. B. McCaw, in charge of Chimborazo Hospital in Richmond.

On May 24, 1862, he was relieved from duty at Chimborazo Hospital and told to report to General Joseph E. Johnston for duty with the 14th Louisiana Volunteer Regiment. He was still in Richmond until the end of December,

---

[35] *Wirz Trial*, pp. 332-336.
[36] *Ibid.*, p. 338.
[37] Kellogg, pp. 271-273.
[38] *Ibid.*, p. 259.
[39] *Ibid.*, p. 278.
[40] Hyde, p. 252.
[41] *O.R.*, VII, p. 551.
[42] Original documents, Archives Department, Tomkins-McCaw Library, Medical College of Virginia, Virginia Commonwealth University, Richmond, Virginia.

but then he went to the Louisiana troops because, on April 17, 1863, he signed a Certificate of Disability attached to the resignation of 2nd Lieutenant A. C. Dickinson, Company D, Wheats Louisiana Battalion, as Assistant Surgeon, P. A. C. S. He had a regimental appointment with the 1st Texas Cavalry and was "in the field" in October, 1863.

Doctor White must have been one of the first officers sent to southwest Georgia because, on February 5, 1864, he was found at Camp Sumter as a surgeon. On that same day, he asked for a steward for the post. On May 25th, he was named surgeon-in-charge of the guard and prison.

On February 29th, he drew his pay from R. B. Winder for $162 for the month. He received no other pay until June 30th, when he received four months' back pay, totaling $648, from Dick Winder.

Doctor E. J. Eldridge, Chief Surgeon of the Georgia Reserves, after his inspection on July 5th, described the surgeon-in-charge. "I will add that as far as I have been able to judge from my short visit, the management of the medical department of the prison, under the direction of Chief Surg. I. H. White, reflects credit upon that officer, who seems well qualified for the position he occupied."[43] One prisoner described Doctor White in this manner, "I saw very little of Dr. White in his official capacity; he seemed to pay but little attention to the hospital. He was very seldom there that I saw. Sometimes he would ride there in his buggy."[44]

Doctor White was a very controversial figure at the prison. One of the complaints of several of the doctors was they had no stimulants to give to their weakened patients. During the Civil War, whiskey or brandy was given as a tonic to patients suffering from dozens of debilitating diseases such as most of the fevers and infections. Medicinal whiskey was prescribed very often for many of the most frequently-seen diseases at Andersonville, such as malaria, typhoid fever, gangrene, and pneumonia. In fact, there were few diseases for which alcohol was not an acceptable remedy. On September 5th, Doctor J. Crews Pelot said that whiskey was so "... limited in supply that it can only be issued for cases under the knife."[45] A Doctor W. A. Barnes said, "In regard to 'stimulants to support the system,' there were in September forty-three barrels of whisky under the order of the medical director and intended for hospital uses, but it was reported that visitors to Drs. White and Stevenson had all that they did not drink for themselves."[46] Yet the doctors at roll call felt that they did not have any whiskey to prescribe. Doctor Thornburg, who was a surgeon assigned to the hospital, said "... the whisky was drank by the medical director and his friends."[47]

Spencer said there "... were five distilleries in the county of Sumter alone, working under special contract with the government, a portion of whose produce must go to its agents, to be dealt out, on requisition, for hospital purposes."[48]

Benjamin B. Dykes was the railroad agent for the years 1861 through 1864 at Andersonville and he testified, while referring to his original railroad books, about the quantity and types of goods and stores that were unloaded at the Andersonville depot. Doctor White was made "... chief surgeon and inspector of hospitals, Georgia and Alabama," which was the title he had on October 31st.[49] On November 28th, Doctor White was assigned to Camp Lawton, in Millen, as Chief Surgeon of hospitals attached to Military Prisons East of the Mississippi River by command of the Secretary of War. Brigadier-General Winder, to consolidate his command, sent him as chief medical officer to Columbia to the headquarters of C. S. Military Prisons, East of the Mississippi River, on January 2, 1865. He continued to report to Samuel Moore, Surgeon General, in Richmond. On March 25th, he was at the headquarters at Augusta by order of General Daniel Ruggles.

On June 4th, he was ordered to be arrested by order of W. L. Burger, A A.G., United States Army. He was indicted for conspiring with Wirz, Dick Winder, et al. Only Wirz was ever brought to trial.

Below appear a few brief descriptions of doctors about whom no further information or identification is readily available.

A surgeon named Reeves reported in August, "I find the tents in bad condition, a great many leaking, and a great many of the patients lying on the ground and getting very wet when it rains. I would most respectfully recommend that straw of some kind be secured for bedding; also some arrangement to raise them from the ground. Without a change in this respect, it will be impossible for me to practice with success."[50]

---

[43] *O.R.*, VII, p. 121.
[44] Chipman, p. 171.
[45] *O.R.*, VII, p. 774.
[46] Spencer, pp. 102, 103.
[47] *Ibid.*, p. 104.
[48] *Ibid.*, p. 107.
[49] *O.R.*, VIII, p. 1075.
[50] Kellogg, p. 271.

The Confederate surgeons, Doctor Bemis and Doctor Flewellen, "... inspected the condition of the prison, and protested against the cruel management."[51]

"One of the chief medical officers of the rebel army of the South informed the author (Hamlin) that the medical men at this prison were without any influence whatever; and although the prison was within his department for a time, he had no more voice or influence in its management than the man in the moon; and that everything relating to the prison was controlled and devised by the authorities at Richmond."[52]

"A Kentuckian, and a Surgeon in the Confederate army, said to me one day, 'I believe that slavery is a divine institution. The negroes are placed in our hands, and we will be held accountable at the last day, for the manner in which we have treated them.'" The surgeon said that he "... brushed his slaves up a little when they needed it."[53]

**Doctor Joseph Jones** - He was a pathologist sent to Andersonville by Richmond to study the effects disease had upon men subjected to prison life. He spent the last two weeks of September with the help of his secretary, Louis Manigault, and man-servant, Titus, dissecting cadavers and collecting valuable statistics. (Joseph Jones Collection, Tulane University)

Doctor Joseph Jones, a pathologist, was not assigned to Andersonville, but was sent there in mid-September for investigative research by the authorities in Richmond

Joseph Jones was born on September 6, 1833, in Liberty County, Georgia, to a prominent family. He matriculated at South Carolina College, the forerunner of the University of South Carolina, in January of 1849. After staying there two years, he transferred to the College of New Jersey at Princeton, where he was asked to join the Cliosophic Society. Dick Winder had been a member of this same debating club. After finishing his undergraduate studies at Princeton in 1853, he continued his studies at the medical school at the University of Pennsylvania, from which he received his Doctor of Medicine degree in 1856.

It was during his studies that he decided to pursue his interest in research rather than engaging in full-time private practice. He went back south and taught chemistry at the Savannah Medical College. Jones accepted an opening on the staff as a professor of natural science at the University of Georgia in Athens. He left almost immediately for the Medical College of Georgia in Augusta, where he became a professor of medical chemistry. During the following few years, he studied infectious diseases and especially the fevers that were endemic to the South. He became nationally-known as a researcher, author, and scientist.

With the outbreak of the Civil War, Jones served as a private from October, 1861, to March, 1862, in the local militia, the Liberty Independent Troop, as its surgeon. With the expiration of this six-month enlistment, and after a short time at home, he accepted a commission as a full surgeon with the rank of major.

Because of his interest in medical research, Jones received permission from Surgeon-General Samuel P. Moore to tour the various hospitals, camps, and prisons throughout the South for the purpose of investigating the etiology of some diseases such as typhoid fever, tetanus, malaria, smallpox, pneumonia, scurvy, diarrhea, dysentery, and typhus that were filling the hospitals. He visited hospitals in Savannah, Charleston, Columbia, Charlottesville, Gordonsville, Lynchburg, and Richmond. He inspected some of the twenty-odd prisons in Richmond, including Castle Thunder, Libby, and Belle Isle. There have always been great advances in medical knowledge made during times of war and Jones would play a large role in this advancement.

It was while Doctor Jones was in Richmond the second time, in August of 1864, that he asked permission from the Surgeon-General to visit the prison at Andersonville. The Surgeon-General, on August 6th, ordered Surgeon Jones to Andersonville to begin an "... extended investigation upon the causes, pathology, and treatment of fevers and the

[51] Hamlin, p. 160.
[52] *Ibid.*
[53] Kellogg, p. 194.

relations of climate and soil to disease." He was to have the cooperation of all medical officers and facilities and would write up his findings in "substantial volumes."[54]

Doctor Moore gave Doctor Jones a letter of introduction, telling Doctor White and all his staff to cooperate fully with Doctor Jones. Doctor Moore hoped that this research would benefit the "... medical department of the Confederate Army." Doctor Jones accompanied by his private secretary, Louis Manigault and black manservant, Titus, went to Andersonville where he was welcomed. He arrived the day after the horrible train wreck that killed and injured so many prisoners. He saw and followed their cases for the time he was there. He was given permission to visit and have free access to the prison hospital and the dead house. He was however, denied access to the prison interior by Captain Wirz. Doctor Jones, as a result of this, wrote to General Winder to get him to reaffirm the order of Doctor Moore that gave him access to all the facilities there. General Winder, on September 17th, wrote to Wirz, "... you will permit Surg. Joseph Jones ... to visit the sick within the stockade..."[55] Wirz backed down. At the time of Jones' visit, the four sheds inside the north wall held 2,000 of the 15,000 prisoners still within the pen with only one doctor in attendance. Jones thought twenty physicians should have been.

Jones, at first, had selected a site to place his tent on the high ground just west of the South Gate, but had been advised by one of the surgeons that that very site had been where some guard troops had been camped when they suffered heavily with a "... fatal form of continued fever" and they had moved to a safer camp ground. Several black prisoners were detailed to set up Jones' camp near General Winder's headquarters "... across the railroad on a shady hill."[56] Around the camp, which consisted of two tents and cooking and mess facilities, Jones found it necessary to post a permanent guard, "... not against Yankees, but thieves, cows, hogs and dogs."[57]

**Louis Marigault's Sketch of Joseph Jones' Camp at Andersonville** - Jones, with the help of several paroled Federal prisoners, set up a pathology laboratory on the post where he did his dissecting, investigating the causes and sequelae of various conditions at the post. (Joseph Jones Collection, Tulane University)

Jones then "... instituted careful investigations into the condition of the sick and well and performed numerous post-mortem examinations. The medical topography of Andersonville and the surrounding country was examined, and the waters of the streams, springs, and wells around and within the stockade and hospital carefully analyzed."[58] Jones entered nearly all the tents in the hospital and examined all the interesting cases. Jones' dissection room was a "... small structure surrounded at the sides with old tent cloth, and covered with boards." That was where he carried on his scientific analyses and autopsies; it had been put up courtesy of Surgeon White. It had been "... erected extemporaneously for the occasion in an open space just outside the hospital grounds."[59] Though the staff was supposed to help Jones with his work including the autopsies, Jones did not demand it because he was "... fearful for their health." He did, however, invite their cooperation, but they were unwilling to help.

[54] *O.R.*, VII, p. 557.
[55] *O.R.*, VIII, p. 589.
[56] *Ibid.*, p. 616.
[57] Breeden, p. 158.
[58] *O.R.*, VII, p. 1012.
[59] *Ibid.*

Doctor Jones bravely went about, handling the rapidly decomposing flesh of the cadavers. He was in a fair amount of danger for he worked in a "... confined, unventilated room, exposed to the burning autumnal sun." It was interesting how Doctor Jones protected his hands from contamination in a time when there were no rubber gloves. "To safeguard his own health Jones adopted the policy of immersing his hands in a strong solution of alum, which he allowed to dry thoroughly, before undertaking any postmortem examination or handling any diseased structure.

At the completion of each autopsy he washed his hands in successive strong solutions of alum, chlorinated soda, and tincture of camphor, allowing these to dry completely. Every cut or abrasion was painted with tincture of iodine." In response to criticism that he used the Union prisoners as guinea pigs, it should be noted that Doctor Jones refrained from taking blood to analyze because he was so fearful that their puncture sites, where the blood was taken, might become infected by the exhalations of the pen. One prisoner, Martin Hogan, of the First Indiana Cavalry, testified that he saw Doctor Jones there. "I saw one doctor who came down there searching after medical science. He erected a dissecting room there, and went at dissecting. ... The dissecting room was just outside of the hospital, within about fifty feet of the walls. It was composed of boards nailed up roughly and a sort of canvas thrown over it. I was in there in attendance on some of the doctors while they were dissecting. I saw them dissecting several bodies there. They were the bodies of Federal prisoners. I saw them saw the skulls of men in two; I saw them saw the skulls off and open the bodies in that dissecting room. It continued four or five days, to the best of my knowledge."[60]

Jones went from Andersonville to Macon and Columbia to study gangrene for six weeks at the Confederate hospitals at those prisons. He worked, during the spring of 1865, on his research paper concerned with gangrene and was working on the paper researched at Andersonville when the war ended. The paper on Andersonville was supposed to have been submitted to the Surgeon-General, but was never delivered to him because the war ended. With the cessation of hostilities, Jones went home and hoped that he could just get some "peace and rest." This was not to be, for he would soon become a star witness in the trial of Henry Wirz.[61]

"After the war, Jones returned to the Medical College of Georgia. He was appointed by the faculty to edit the *Southern Medical and Surgical Journal*. However, his stay in Augusta was short-lived.

"In 1866, Jones accepted a professorship at the University of Nashville where he also held the chair of pathology. He also served as co-editor of the *Nashville Journal of Medicine and Surgery* and as chief health officer of the city of Nashville.

"At that time, Doctor Jones began his important archeological investigation of Indian civilizations in Middle Tennessee.

"Jones had been at the University of Nashville for less than two years when he was appointed to the chair of chemistry and clinical medicine in the Medical Department of the University of Louisiana (later the Tulane University School of Medicine) and visiting physician to the New Orleans Charity Hospital.

Joseph Jones and his family arrived in New Orleans in late 1868. After the death of his wife, who died soon after coming to Louisiana. Jones, in June, 1870, married Susan Rayner Polk, the daughter of the renowned Confederate general and Louisiana clergyman, Bishop Leonidas Polk. On a trip to England and France with his new wife, Jones learned of the revolutionary and epochal developments in bacteriology and Immunology emerging from the discoveries of Pasteur and Lister. Well ahead of most of his American contemporaries, Jones readily embraced "germ theory."

In 1880, Jones was appointed president of the Board of Health of Louisiana.In 1889, he was appointed Surgeon-General of the United Confederate Veterans. In 1892, he received an honorary degree of doctor of laws from the University of Georgia. His advice was sought for the establishment of the Johns Hopkins Hospital in Baltimore.

Joseph Jones' health began to fail in 1890. He suffered a stroke three years later, which caused partial paralysis in his left arm and leg, forcing him to resign from Tulane. Death came in 1896 from cerebral thrombosis.

With Jones' death, the South and the nation lost one of its leading scientific investigators.

At the time of his death in 1896, the *Journal of the American Medical Association* stated, "America has never produced a more earnest student, and a more painstaking and diligent scholar.'"[62]

From the organization of the prison on February 24th until September 21st, about 40,611 prisoners passed through its gates. Of these, 9,479 died or 23.3 percent. One out of every 4.2 prisoners died.[63] The number that had

[60] Chipman, pp. 171, 172.
[61] Most of the sketch was taken from the book on Jones by James O. Breeden.
[62] Harris D. Riley, Jr., "Joseph Jones: A Remarkable Deke Physician," *The Deke Quarterly*, c. 1985, pp. 14-17.
[63] *O.R.*, VIII, p. 615.

died in the stockade was 3,254 and, in the hospital, 6,225.[64]

Jones found no record of the sick within the stockade prior to September 14th. No record was kept by the authorities of the number of the various types of diseases that caused sickness and death within the pen. From Jones' report, it appears that, at the time of his visit, the maximum number of patients in the hospital was 1,730 sick prisoners. The sick were admitted roughly at the same rate that there were vacancies caused by deaths, so that the population of the hospital remained relatively constant. For the week of September 14th, there were 37 to 58 deaths each day. After a large admission from the pen, on the following day there would be a very small number admitted. On the 15th they admitted 114, the next day 16, on the 17th they admitted 109, and, on the next day, only 3.

The Morning Reports of Acting Assistant Surgeon F. J. Wells, who was in charge of the Federal sick and wounded in the stockade, showed, for that same week of September 14th, that the number of the sick each day was between 1,000 and 2,008.[65] The exhalations of the pen affected the disease rate for the Confederate guard. For the first "two or three months," the guard was camped very close to the palisades and, as a result, their morbidity was nearly equal to that of the prisoners. They were later ordered to move to the adjoining hills about a half- to three-quarters of a mile away. By July and August, this move resulted in a much healthier garrison.

**Consolidated Report of Sick Prisoners at Andersonville, March-August 1864** [66]

| | March | April | May | June | July | August |
|---|---|---|---|---|---|---|
| **Remaining last report** | - | 636 | 1,022 | 2,621 | 4,078 | 6,412 |
| **Cases during month** | 1,530 | 2,425 | 8,583 | 7,969 | 10,624 | 10,915 |
| **Supervening diseases** | - | - | - | - | 210 | 431 |
| **Aggregate** | 1,530 | 3,061 | 9,605 | 10,590 | 14,912 | 17,758 |
| **Returned to duty** | 353 | 1,463 | 6,276 | 5,311 | 6,548 | 9,443 |
| **Died** | 283 | 576 | 708 | 1,201 | 1,952 | 2,992 |
| **Remaining** | 894 | 1,022 | 2,621 | 4,078 | 6,412 | 5,323 |
| **Mean Strength** | 7,500 | 10,000 | 15,000 | 22,291 | 29,030 | 32,899 |
| **Percentage of mean strength taken sick during month** | 20.4 | 24.3 | 57.2 | 35.5 | 36.6 | 33.2 |
| **Ratio of sick to mean strength. One sick in every:** | 4.9 | 4.1 | 1.7 | 2.8 | 2.7 | 3.0 |
| **Percentage of sick that died during month** | 18.5 | 23.8 | 8.2 | 15.1 | 18.4 | 27.4 |
| **Percentage of mean strength that died during month** | 3.8 | 5.8 | 4.7 | 5.4 | 6.7 | 9.1 |
| **Ratio of deaths in mean strength. One dead in every:** | 26.3 | 17.2 | 21.3 | 18.5 | 14.9 | 11.0 |

There were no records kept of the sickness of the garrison troops until the months of July and August. During these two months, 2,494 cases of disease, affecting 66.4 percent of the force, were recorded. The death rate was 2.3 percent for those months but, if this had continued for the entire year, it would have worked out to an annual death rate of 13.2 percent.[67] General Winder said that measles and whooping cough were prevailing in his command on June 20th.[68]

[64] *Ibid.*, p. 601.
[65] *Ibid.*
[66] Breeden, p.186
[67] *O.R.*, VIII, p. 616.
[68] *O.R.*, VII, p. 386.

**Consolidated Report of Sickness among the Confederate Guards at Andersonville, July-August 1864** [69]

| | Cases | Deaths | Mean Strength |
|---|---|---|---|
| **July** | 1,258 | 29 | 1,881 |
| **August** | 1,236 | 33 | 3,629 |
| **Totals** | 2,494 | 62 | |

At least one of the guards who had never even entered the pen was a casualty of gangrene. Thomas J. Cole was a boy of sixteen when he left home to go to Andersonville to be a private in the Third Georgia Reserves. This poor young man had not been accustomed to wearing shoes and one of his shoes irritated a small abrasion on the side of his left foot below the ankle. He arrived on July 20th and, by September 12th, he had a lesion so bad he had to be admitted to the hospital. For the next two weeks his condition rapidly deteriorated while Jones was there. The final outcome is unknown.[70]

Besides Wirz, many officers stationed at Andersonville were stricken with sickness and disease. Even General Winder had gangrene of the face and was told by Doctor White not to go within the stockade. In the monumental fictitious work, *Andersonville*, by MacKinlay Kantor, he stated that Winder's sickness was caused by his having been scratched by a Negro slave. Doctor G. G. Roy examined General Winder at his headquarters in September because he "... had a rising, as he called it, in his ear."[71] Colonel George C. Gibbs, one-time Commandant of the Post, also had gangrene of the face and was given a medical furlough by the authorization of a medical certificate signed by Surgeons Wible and Gore, of Americus. Doctor R. R. Stevenson had gangrene together with scurvy that he contracted while on duty there.[72] Doctor Jones said he saw a full surgeon in charge of a ward with the classic signs of scurvy.

In correspondence dated August 13th to Samuel S. Cooper, Adjutant and Inspector General in Richmond, General Winder reported, "Colonel Henry Forno is quite sick and has been for some time. Captain Wirz is very sick, produced entirely by overwork for want of assistance. He ought to have gone to bed two weeks ago, but kept up because he had none to whom the command could be turned over. Lieutenant R. W. Brown, my aide-de-camp, is partially paralyzed, and I fear it will be long before he will be able to do anything ... I am, during Colonel Forno's illness, obliged to be the immediate commander of the troops ... I would beg to leave to remark that disabled officers, if much disabled, cannot stand the labors at this post."[73]

James Selman, Jr., the sutler, had to leave for a thirty-day sick leave in October.

Upon reviewing the credentials of the physicians at Andersonville, it can be assumed that the doctors were a fairly representative cross-section of the medical doctors in other areas of the rural south. It was a time of learning and maturation of the surgeons. Doctor Simon Baruch said that he had not even lanced a boil before he was made a Confederate surgeon. There were some who were sympathetic to the pain and plight of the prisoners, while others let sectional hatred take precedent over kindness.

---

[69] Breeden, p. 187
[70] Military Records obtained from the National Archives.
[71] *Wirz Trial*, p. 658.
[72] Stevenson, p. 29.
[73] *O.R.*, VII, p. 589.

## *Chapter Six*

# Diseases and Medical Problems

*"The condition of the prison at Andersonville is a reproach to us as a nation."*

Col. R. H. Chilton, C.S.A.
Ass't. Adjt. and Insp. Gen'l.
August 18, 1864

Doctor Jones listed about 135 distinct diseases or conditions that caused sickness and death at Andersonville during the six-month period from the first of March to the 31st of August, 1864. That period of time was when the prison "flourished." After the first of September, with the dispersal of all the ambulatory prisoners, Andersonville, for all practical purposes, became a hospital prison camp.

Many of what Doctor Jones called diseases are no longer recognized as distinct disease entities but are now known to have only been symptoms or sequelae of other conditions. There were 42,686 cases of disease reported during that six-month period. This figure is lower then the correct figure because many died without medical attention, and some prisoners wished to die, in their shebangs among their friends. No record of the sick within the pen was kept after the hospital was moved outside except for the couple of weeks during Jones' visit.

During the Civil War era, broken long bones were not "set." If a minie ball smashed into a bone of an extremity and shattered it, the treatment of choice was amputation above or proximal to the wound. There were two types of amputation operations. One was the guillotine type, which entailed a straight incision through the soft tissue and the bone would be sawed flush to that same plane. Blood vessels were tied off and suture material was left dangling from the stub, to be removed at a later date. Hopefully, when it was yanked out, the patient would not bleed to death. The other type of amputation operation involved laying a flap and cutting the bone a couple of inches proximal to the plane of the incision. By taking the flaps and by intricate manipulations, the stump would be covered with soft tissue. Most surgeons had better success with the guillotine type and, since it required less surgical skill, it was the most frequently-performed type of operation. Another reason to amputate was the appearance of gangrene. Some patients required re-amputation if gangrene appeared in the stump.

Many amputations were done at Andersonville with very infrequent success. Some patients died on the table before the chloroform wore off, especially if the patient was very debilitated. Some writers said there were no survivors. "The amputations would average as many as half a dozen every day, and I knew not a single instance of recovery from them."[1] D. H. Stearns, a steward at the hospital, testified, "I do not remember a single case of recovery after an amputation."[2] Doctor Jones also noted the extremely low survival rate of the amputees. "Almost every amputation was followed finally by death, either from the effects of gangrene, or from the prevailing diarrhoea and dysentery ... so far as my observation extended, very few of the cases of amputation for gangrene recovered."[3]

"The Rebel doctors at the Hospital resorted to wholesale amputations to check the progress of the gangrene. They had a two hours session of limb-lopping every morning, each of which resulted in quite a pile of severed members. I presume more bungling operations are rarely seen outside of Russian or Turkish hospitals. Their unskillfulness was apparent even to non-scientific observers like myself. The standard of medical education in the South - as

[1] Kellogg, p. 269.
[2] Chipman, p. 176.
[3] Dowling, p. 219.

indeed of every other form of education - was quite low. The Chief Surgeon of the prison, Dr. Isaiah White, and perhaps two or three others, seemed to be gentlemen of fair abilities and attainments. The remainder were of that class of illiterate and unlearning quacks who physic and blister the poor whites and negros [sic] in the country districts of the South; who believe they can stop bleeding of the nose by repeating a verse from the Bible; who think that if in gathering their favorite remedy of boneset they cut the stem upwards it will purge their patients, and if downwards it will vomit them, and who hold that there is nothing so good for 'fits' as a black cat, killed in the dark of the moon, cut open, and bound while yet warm, upon the naked chest of the victim of the convulsions.

"They had a case of instruments captured from some of our field hospitals, which were dull and fearfully out of order. With poor instruments and unskilled hands the operations became mangling."[4]

One of the few times cancer was mentioned in the hundreds of books by prisoners was the following in McElroy's book. "One form that was quite prevalent was cancer of the lower lip. It seemed to start at one corner of the mouth, and it finally ate the whole side of the face out. Of course, the sufferer had the greatest trouble in eating and drinking. For the latter it was customary to whittle out a little wooden tube, and fasten it in a tin cup, through which he could suck up the water. As this mouth cancer seemed contagious, none of us would allow any one afflicted with it to use any of our cooking utensils."[5]

The diet of abrasive, irritating corn meal and rancid, raw, greasy pork was devastating. Two medically-accepted methods of causing a bowel movement are by ingesting a lubricant such as mineral oil, and another is by irritating the bowels, by using phenolphthalein, for example, which is the main ingredient of one of America's best laxatives today. The lubricating pork grease and irritating corn husks were perfect purgatives; unfortunately, over a long period of time, the dehydration took its toll with steady, continual weight loss. The physicians at Andersonville did recognize that the pork and corn husks were causative factors, but, not being knowledgeable of germ theory, they did not realize that another irritant could be bacteria. Thus, they did not think of something that, today, would be so elementary as reminding the men to wash after using the sink. Doctor Jones thought that "... the foul exhalations from the innumerable small sinks and deposits of excrement ... must have caused derangement of the intestinal canal."[6]

Diarrhea, caused by the rapid passage of the food through the digestive system, did not allow the absorption of the nutrients nor the reabsorption of water. Thus, it is, theoretically, possible to starve to death even with the ingestion of an adequate diet, if the diarrhea is severe. It was, by far, the most prevalent disease at Andersonville. It existed in both the acute and the chronic forms.

Jones said the best treatment for someone suffering from this devastating disease was "... good fresh milk (combined when necessary with lime water), beef and chicken tea, boiled milk and rice, and alcoholic stimulants. Opium was used in immense quantities in the hospital practice, but with only temporary benefit."[7] Paregoric, a camphorated tincture of opium, was sometimes prescribed as a treatment for diarrhea. Miller said the taking of blackberry root, white oak bark, and charcoal were good treatments for diarrhea. Kellogg said sweet fern was a good remedy, also.

Dr. Jones thought a number of cows should be procured as a source of milk for the use of the sick. Jones, as well as most of the medical staff, realized treatment was useless without a change in diet and improvement in the sanitary conditions within the pen.

Kellogg said, "I have known many of them to eat nothing for a week at a time, except a little flour paste, while all the while their evacuations would be nothing but blood, and attended with the most excruciating pain. We always expected death as the inevitable result of such cases, for none were ever cured."[8]

During the six-month period of March through August, there were 12,000 cases of diarrhea resulting in the deaths of 3,530 prisoners.[9] Doctor Jones's post-mortem examination of the gastrointestinal tract showed "... congestion of the mucous membrane was intense, and was often accompanied with ulceration and mortification."[10]

In contrast, there were two-hundred-and-fifteen thousand cases of diarrhea treated in the United States Army in 1862. Of this number, only one thousand, one hundred died, showing what better care, using contemporary medical knowledge, could accomplish.[11]

---

[4] McElroy, pp. 360, 361.
[5] *Ibid.*, p. 360.
[6] *O.R.*, VIII, p. 617.
[7] *Ibid.*
[8] Kellogg, p. 264.
[9] *O.R.*, VIII, p. 614.
[10] *Ibid.*, p. 622.
[11] Hamlin, p. 135.

How severe was a typical case of diarrhea? Melvin, a prisoner who suffered from the most prevalent disease of the Civil War said he "... was called up 30 times in 24 hours."[12]

| | Diarrhea | | Dysentery | |
|---|---|---|---|---|
| | **Cases** | **Deaths** | **Cases** | **Deaths** |
| **March** | 481 | 77 | 185 | 41 |
| **April** | 1,149 | 335 | 184 | 76 |
| **May** | 2,337 | 422 | 1,277 | 101 |
| **June** | 2,476 | 777 | 811 | 103 |
| **July** | 3,145 | 847 | 1,179 | 242 |
| **August** | 2,502 | 1,072 | 1,046 | 436 |
| **TOTALS** | 12,090 | 3,530 | 4,682 | 999 |

Effect of Diarrhea and Dysentery on the Prisoners at Andersonville March-August 1864

Dropsy was another clinical sign that was thought to be a disease entity. Dropsy was simply the retention of body fluids in various parts of the body, (i.e., in the head, the chest, the abdomen or in the extremities). Today, this is considered edema and results from a malfunction in the cardiovascular system. Faulty valves, an enlarged heart, kidney disease, liver disease, respiratory disease and lymphatic disease were some of its many causes. It has only been in the recent past that the hydrodynamics of body fluids have been understood.

The patient's skin swells to about twice its normal size until it, sometimes, bursts. If pressure were to be placed on the tissue with one's fingers, the fingers would leave depressions where the edematous tissue was pitted.

"In dropsy... I have seen the limbs of some patients so badly swollen, they would burst, and for the want of proper treatment become filled with living things. Sometimes it would settle in the face, and in such cases they would not see at all."[13]

Dropsy today is considered a rather archaic term; the modern, preferred, term is edema. Its main cause at Andersonville was malnutrition and its treatment was to restore the balance of electrolytes by the consumption of a proper diet.

Unsanitary conditions in the stockade also caused the perpetuation of another type of "looseness of the bowels," i.e., dysentery. In the vernacular of the times, the "bloody fluxes" or "alvine fluxes," which was dysentery, was really one of two forms of the same disease, bacillary (Shigella) and amebic (Entameba histolytica) dysenteries. Both forms were transmitted from person to person by contaminated food, fingers, and flies. The main signs of the disease were frequent, bloody stools with tenesmus or straining, whereas diarrhea's signs were frequent stools with no straining. If left unchecked, perforation of the bowels, peritonitis, and death were the possible courses that this disease usually ran.

It is interesting to note that, at that same time, with the same medical technology, the Federal Army was able to save, proportionately, more men than did the Confederate Army. Of thirty-seven thousand cases of dysentery treated in the United States in 1862, only three-hundred-and-forty-seven died.[14]

Gangrene "... was classified as a surgical fever, along with erysipelas and pyemia, and was thought to be miasmatic in origin."[15] Jones, with his crude microscope, had seen the bacillus that caused gangrene, while he was examining fluids from sores. He saw "Animalcules of simple origin, and endowed with active rotary action abound in hospital gangrene."[16] With the state of the art of medicine at that time, medical researchers could not connect the bacillus in the pus to the disease. "In the present state of our knowledge we are unable to demonstrate that these animalcules are in any way connected with the origin and spread of hospital gangrene."[17] "When nurses infected with

[12] Melvin, p. 125.
[13] Kellogg, p. 267.
[14] Hamlin, p. 135.
[15] Breeden, p. 205.
[16] *Ibid.*
[17] *Ibid.*

the foul odor of the worst gangrene cases went directly to a healthy, granulating wound, and with the same fingers which but a moment before were employed in cleaning and pulling away gangrenous sloughs, the recurrence of the disease was almost inevitable."[18] With the noxious vapor theories in vogue, Jones said the "foul odor" was carried via nurses to other patients.

Doctor Thornburg said that he, "... having never tried the experiment of inoculation with gangrenous matter," could not be sure that he could cause the disease in another patient. The physicians at Andersonville felt that it was probably contagious and that they should have had more than one sponge and one wash basin per tent or ward.

"Gangrene first made its appearance in the stockade in the latter part of April or first of May last. The first that came under our observation was the result of frostbite. These cases (three or four in number) occurred among the [men] who had been imprisoned on Belle Island last winter, where they received the injury. The parts attacked from this cause were usually the toes. The treatment was cold water dressing, and the whole affected member enveloped in cloths spread with simple cerate, with tonics to support the system. This treatment usually succeeded, with the loss, perhaps, of one or more of the affected toes."[19]

Sometimes at Andersonville, a prisoner would scratch a mosquito bite and, in a few days, the area would fester, swell, ulcerate, turn a bright pea-green or blackish color and, without heroic medical intervention such as amputation, cause death within a few days. Any insignificant break in the skin, such as from a blister, sunburn, or a tiny splinter, could precipitate a life-threatening crisis.

Steven Payne told of his experience in the hospital. "I could hear the cries of men in distress over in one part of the hospital particularly. I asked my nurse what was the matter with them men & he told me that they were dressing the sores in the gangrene ward. I had heard of gangrene but never knew what it was so as soon as I got so as I could walk with crutches, I borrowed another man's & went down to see them dress the wounds & Oh what a sickening sight I did see. There were men that told me the first beginning of his sore was first a little hide knocked off of his hand or arm & then perhaps there was a sore as big as the palm of a man's hand & still getting larger & not unfrequently they lost a leg or an arm."[20]

Doctor Jones thought that the rapid break-down of the tissue was due to the exhalations and noxious effluvia emanating from the pen and because of the "... depraved and depressed condition of the systems" of the prisoners due to their poor diet, home-sickness, and depression. Doctor Jones thought that the prisoners' longing for home and their resentment and bitterness towards the Federal government because of their not being exchanged, played a large part in the depression of the bodies' response to infection.

Because of slovenly-kept records and the "imperfect organization" of the hospital, Jones was unable to accurately determine the number of amputations that were necessitated by gangrene supervening upon these slight injuries. In fact, the Confederate sick reports at Andersonville did not recognize gangrene as a distinct disease entity until the first of July. Also, prior to August, if gangrene was what killed a patient in the hospital, who had been admitted for scurvy, his cause of death would be listed as the disease for which he had been admitted. That is, no supervening disease would be listed as the cause of death, only the condition admitting the prisoner to the hospital. Using a very inaccurate hospital report, Jones thought that there had been 266 cases of gangrene, with 67 amputations and 25 deaths. Because of the inherent inaccuracies of the reporting system, those figures could be safely doubled.[21] Most of the prisoners felt that there had been no cases of gangrene followed by amputation that survived. Northrop said that "... in no case as I can hear, has gangrene been cured by amputation. Slight wounds are not healable owing to weak blood."[22] About 120 of the cases of gangrene had supervened upon gunshot wounds and the rest arose "... from scorbutic or deranged condition of the general system."[23] Twelve cases of gangrene ulcers had supervened at vaccination sites.

The treatment for gangrene in all its forms was the use of tonics, such as quinine, and of tincture of iron and other indigenous remedies that the stewards obtained from the forests of Georgia. The local treatment was to apply pure nitric acid, silver nitrate, or tincture of iodine, followed by poultices of cotton. Sometimes thickening a strong decoction of red oak with corn meal made a common mush poultice.

"The most conspicuous suffering was in the gangrene wards. Horrible sores spreading almost visibly from hour

[18] *Ibid.*
[19] *O.R.*, VIII, p. 627.
[20] Steven Payne diary, in private hands.
[21] *O.R.*, VIII, p. 619.
[22] Northrop, p. 112.
[23] *O.R.*, VIII, p. 619.

to hour, devoured men's limbs and bodies. I remember one ward in which the ulcerations appeared to be altogether in the back, where they ate out the tissue between the skin and the ribs. The attendants seemed trying to arrest the progress of the sloughing by drenching the sores with a solution of blue vitriol. This was exquisitely painful, and in the morning, when the drenching was going on, the whole Hospital rang with the most agonizing screams.

"But the gangrene mostly attacked the legs and arms, and the legs more than the arms. Sometimes it killed men inside of a week; sometimes they lingered on indefinitely. I remember one man in the stockade who cut his hand with the sharp corner of a card of corn bread he was lifting from the ration wagon; gangrene set in immediately, and he died four days after."[24]

As the men lost hope, and with the pain of their ill health, many began to behave rather weirdly. They began to wander aimlessly and to babble unintelligibly. Throughout the prison could be seen men who had lost touch with reality. Many became despondent simply because they were being kept from their homes and loved ones. Thus, "home-sickness" was given a rightful place in the list of causes of death at Andersonville. "Homesickness and the disappointment of daily longings for release appeared to be as potent agencies in the destruction of the Federal prisoners as the physical causes of actual disease."[25] Compton observed, "We did everything we could to keep the boys roused up as we well knew that when despondency set in upon them that death was the inevitable result."[26]

One of the Plymouth Pilgrims, a middle-aged member of the 101st Pennsylvania Regiment, surveyed his new surroundings and became very despondent. He only reluctantly built a shelter and learned the ways of prison life. A few days later, he became so depressed, he refused to eat and became psychotic. He imagined that he was sitting down to supper with his family and continually offered food to his imaginary family members. He died within a month after he had arrived.[2727]

Charles Hopkins, in his diary, said, "The cases of insanity were numerous. Men, strong in mentality, heart and hope were in a few short months, yes, often in a few weeks, reduced to imbeciles and maniacs. Today they know you and look upon you as friends and comrades; tomorrow they are peevish, whining, childish creatures, or raving maniacs. Some would beg for something to eat; others asked for wife, mother, children or other relatives; some, in their delirium were home talking to their friends, enjoying the good eating that Mother set before them - they seemed happy, many forever talking of hunger and a goodly number were furiously wild, and had they been strong they would have been dangerous - not knowing their closest friend, trusting no one, raving and cursing in fearful language. Happily, may I say it, all such died soon, worn out and exhausted by their emotion."[28]

Dowling described the deranged he saw. "The pitiful cries of the starving prisoners for bread were fearful, and the unearthly and inhuman sound of the dying man's voice was mournful and sickening to hear - sometimes crying for help, at other times, while in a sort of a delirium, talking to a loving wife at home, or a mother or father, asking of them their last blessing; others would mention the name of their sweetheart or a dear friend, but to them, alas, no help came until death relieved them of their suffering."[29]

"Some of the men were giving up all hope of ever being released, and some became so despondent that they became insane. The ravings, prayers, and curses of these men added much to the horrors of the prison. Some of them wandered around the prison in the most helpless manner, and begged piteously for something to eat. Some of the poor wretches imaged themselves animals, and moved around on their hands and knees, hunting for something to eat. Some of them gathered the undigested beans lying around on the ground and ate them. The number of these poor unfortunates who were becoming idiotic was fearfully on the increase, and this had now become the worse feature of our prison-life. On one occasion I was going through the prison when my attention was attracted by the cries of some one, and going in the direction from which it proceeded, I found one of these poor unfortunate ones, who although in a dying condition was trying to make a speech to a few men who had gathered around him. He was entirely out of his mind, and I am sorry to say that some of the men around him were making a jest of it."[30]

The gathering of undigested food by the insane was described by several authors. "One man [was] considered insane by us. He would go around among the debris of the swamp and pick up undigested food, beans and meat, that had passed through men."[31] Willis Van Buren, of the Second New York Cavalry, said, "I frequently saw the men

[24] McElroy, p. 360.
[25] *O.R.*, VII, p. 615.
[26] Compton, p. 54.
[27] McElroy, pp. 170, 171.
[28] Styple, p. 95.
[29] Dowling, pp. 267, 268.
[30] Author's library.
[31] Author's library.

hunting around the sinks for food that had once passed through men's bodies, undigested food to eat."[32]

Kellogg observed, "One young man, of excellent education, and evidently of good birth, while in this sad condition, would go down to the little brook nearly every day, at noon, when the heat of the sun was most intense, and taking off his clothes, or more appropriately rags, would wade backward and forward, but rarely, if ever, washing himself. Seeing him one day, while performing his accustomed round, I said to him, 'Why don't you wash and come out, and not stay there in the sun?' His hopeless reply was, 'I am waiting for the water to become clear.'"[33] Kellogg described another pathetic figure. "Another man would constantly imagine that he was some sort of an animal, and he would strip himself of all clothing, and persist in wallowing through the swamp on his hands and knees. Still another occupied his time in making curious sketches, in which rebels and devils would figure in intimate companionship."[34]

"One man in particular had a great penchant for bathing. He never missed a forenoon without taking his regular bath. The queer thing about it was the place he chose for cleaning himself. Instead of going above the sinks, he chose to go below."[35]

Northrop told of one pathetic prisoner who was insane and seen on Sunday, July 3rd. "I noticed one today without any clothing, having been naked for two weeks. He lay within four rods of the South Gate, arms extended, exposed to the sun, in full view of everybody. His whole body was blistered, his countenance frightfully distorted, giving utterance to unintelligible sounds, frothy matter oozing from his mouth and nostrils, his eyes appearing blind."[36] On July 21st, Northrop noted, "... a man near the stream cut his own throat today."[37]

This was how other pitiful victims were described. "They seemed to lose all power of speech and memory; they could not tell their own names and did not know whether they had been in prison a day or six years. If spoken to, their only answer would be a far-away look as if they were trying to recall something beyond the reach of their memory. They wandered aimlessly about and kept their comrades constantly watching to keep them from the deadline."[38]

George W. Murray described how, after one of his brothers had sunk into a state of idiocy and had begun raving incoherently, he began "... gnawing the flesh from both of his arms as far as he could reach." After suffering this way for a few days, he found relief in death.[39]

The guards almost constantly told the prisoners that a prisoner exchange was just around the corner or that an agreement would be consummated in the near future. The guards always built the inmates' hopes up, and dashed them when the anticipated date was passed. Some of this ruse, probably, was to placate the prisoners when the number of guards per thousand prisoners was very low. It was certainly pulled on the prisoners when they were being transferred by train when there were very few guards to ride shotgun.

The prisoners always thought that the leaving of bodies out in the Georgia sun, sometimes for a couple of days, the slinging of the bodies into filthy wagons, the bodies being buried naked, being buried with no coffins, being buried in slit trenches, etc., was used as a means to depress the prisoners' spirits. In reality, it was the only means, under the circumstances, that the job could get done. "The manner of disposing of the dead was also calculated to depress the already desponding spirits of these men."[40]

After a few weeks in the pen, most of the men were covered with soot from tending to their small fires. They had to get on their hands and knees to blow on the kindling to start their fires or to keep wet fuel burning. This pine soot from the smoke was greasy which caused dirt to adhere to the skin. Most of the men had some degree of diarrhea, which added to their discomfort and body odor.

One of a man's most prized possessions at Andersonville was a piece of soap. It could be bartered a bath at a time or could be sold by the bar. When Lieutenant Colonel D. T. Chandler officially inspected the pen near August 1st, he incorrectly reported that "...no soap or clothing has ever been issued."[41] Kellogg said that there were but two issues of soap made to the prison from May to September, "... and then we only received about a table spoonful of

[32] Chipman, p. 177.
[33] Kellogg, p. 197.
[34] Kellogg, p. 197.
[35] Sidney S. Williams, pp. 13, 14.
[36] Northrop, p. 83.
[37] *Ibid.*, p. 92.
[38] Boggs, p. 64.
[39] .George W. Murray, *A History of George W. Murray, and his Long Confinement at Andersonville, Ga.* (Northampton, Mass.: Trumbull & Gere. Steam Printers), p. 27.
[40] *O.R.*, VIII, p. 605.
[41] *O.R.*, VII, p. 548.

soft stuff, of the poorest kind, for each man."[42] The soap was usually very soft and probably the crude, yellow soap made from the tallow of animals butchered on the post.

Most soldiers considered it absolutely necessary to cleanse themselves of lice two or three times a day. "Immediately after roll call they 'have a louse,' or a 'skirmish' or a 'peeling off' as they expressed it from head to heels to give the 'gray backs' a cleaning out. These pestering varmints infest clothing, sticking along the seams. Where the torments come from, how they grow in a day, or an hour, is a mystery. Drawing our minds down to hunting lice is humiliating; but the man who don't isn't respectable, we feel disgraced in his company. Once a day is tolerable, twice better, three times makes a man of the first order. Neglect this, and he is soon over run, pitied, loathed, hated, sneered and snarled at. Lice pollute and sap his blood, he loathes himself and dies. They crawl in droves over the sick, herd in his ears, gnaw him, shade in his hair deep as the hair is long."[43] "... whenever a man stopped picking greybacks off his clothes we counted him gone, and he was about to die."[44]

**Prisoners searching for body lice or "skirmishing"** - This ritual was practiced daily. Comrades who did not practice personal body hygiene were not welcomed as tent-mates. Races between lice on a warm canteen half, with wagering by their owners, helped pass the time at Andersonville. (Abbott)

Each mess would pressure the members of that mess to perform this inspection of themselves and if a member was found to neglect this duty, he would be kicked out of that mess. Some said this had to be done two or three times a day. Some called this "skirmishing up" the lice.

Charles Smith told that, just by running the lice comb through his hair one time, he would find thirty or forty of the enemy.[45] "It was three hours' work every day, in my comparatively healthful condition, to keep my own body tolerably free from the lice. I have had men's hair cut, when, if these had been measured, there would have been in bulk a half pint of lice, and in size about a quarter of an inch."[46]

One of the main inducements for a prisoner to seek a parole, was that he would be allowed to bathe and get new clothing. To a soot-covered man wearing clothes full of lice made from a meal sack who was sun-burned and starving, it is surprising anyone stayed within the pen.

Because of the filthy flies and lack of screening, the wounds of the prisoners became infested almost immediately at Andersonville. Not all physicians thought their presence was a bad omen. Maggots ate only dead flesh and,

---

[42] Kellogg, p. 217.
[43] Northrop, p. 106.
[44] Helwig, p. 43.
[45] Charles M. Smith, p. 13.
[46] Kellogg, p. 270.

therefore, debrided wounds by selectively eating only dead, useless tissue. Doctor Joseph Jones, while at the prison, said, "I saw several gangrenous wounds filled with maggots. I have frequently seen neglected wounds amongst the Confederate soldiers similarly affected, and, as far as my experience extends, these worms destroy only the dead tissues and do not injure specially the well parts. I have even heard surgeons affirm that a gangrenous wound which had been thoroughly cleansed by maggots healed more rapidly than if it had been left to itself."[47]

From the vantage-point of the victim of the attack of the maggots, things were entirely different. One of McElroy's friends had ulcers on his abdomen infested with squirming maggots, causing extreme pain. The doctors gave this poor patient some turpentine to apply locally and he was carried out to die. D. H. Stearns, of the First Regiment United States Sharpshooters, was detailed as a steward in the hospital. He described very vividly the pain and agony that one man experienced who was covered with maggots. He said they attached the victim's eyes, nose, ears, and rectum, causing excruciating pain. Blessedly, the man died quickly.[48]

The scientists of the 1860s did not understand that maggots were the larval stage of the blow-flies that pervaded the prison. To look down and see maggots eating away one's flesh, knowing the main treatment, if available, was to pour fuming nitric acid on it, must have been one of the most terrifying experiences at Andersonville.

During the six-month period from the first of March through the end of August, there were 2,966 cases of malaria which caused 119 deaths

In the 1860s, fevers were usually characterized by describing the duration of the fever. Malaria was described as an intermittent fever, remittent fever, autumnal fever, marsh fever, or periodic fever. This parasitic disease is transmitted by the female Anopheles mosquito to the bloodstream of the human who acts as the intermediate host. The one-celled parasite, the plasmodium, causes fever, chills, nausea, vomiting, and sweating followed by a period of normalcy. This fever seldom caused death but, sometimes, was so debilitating that the person became susceptible to some fatal disease.

It was known that malaria was more prevalent in low, swampy areas, but the actual mode of transmission was unknown at the time of the Civil War. It was thought by Doctor White to have been caused by "... vegetable mold or other cryptogamous growth." Cryptogamous was the archaic division used in botany containing non-flowering fungi, molds and mosses, versus flowering plants with seeds.

Mosquitoes were pests and some prisoners would get up at 4 a.m. and smoke their tents to rid them of mosquitoes.[49] "... Mosquitoes swarm in untold myriads and render life at night all but intolerable by their everlasting buzzing and their troublesome bites. It was almost impossible to sleep, except under nets. During the first night that I slept at this place my face and hands were thoroughly peppered with the bites of these insects, and throughout my stay at Andersonville my face appeared as if covered with an eruptive disease. I observed that many of the prisoners and the Confederate soldiers had been similarly treated by the mosquitoes. It is probable that the immense amount of filth generated by the prisoners may have had much to do with the development and multiplication of these insects."[50]

| | Cases | Deaths |
|---|---|---|
| **March** | 72 | 7 |
| **April** | 49 | 5 |
| **May** | 1,162 | 19 |
| **June** | 662 | 22 |
| **July** | 506 | 24 |
| **August** | 515 | 42 |

Effect of Malaria on the Prisoners at Andersonville March - August 1864 [51]

An interesting observation was noted by Jones concerning the incidence of malaria at Andersonville. The number of cases "... did not conform to the almost universal law of the progressive increase of these diseases during the months of May, June, July, August, and September in the Southern States." It can be seen that, after a high of 1,162 cases of malaria in May, the number decreased rather sharply, considering the increase in the prison population.[52]

47 *O.R.*, VIII, p. 605.
48 Chipman, p. 176.
49 Stephen, p. 23.
50 *O.R.*, VIII, p. 594.
51 Breeden, p. 188.
52 Breeden, p. 188.

This may be attributed to the drying up of the ponds and puddles which are the breeding places for mosquitoes.

The Confederate guard sustained 581 cases of malaria during the months of July and August. That is 15.4 percent of the mean strength of the Confederate troops. For the six-month period, the Federal prisoners saw malaria affect 7.2 percent of the mean strength. That was just the opposite of what one would expect. The native, Southern boys should have developed some natural immunity, thought Jones, but he found that malaria prevailed to a greater extent among all the soldiers in all sections of the South than was seen among the inmates at Andersonville. Before the true vector of transmission was known, Jones incorrectly deduced: "We can only account for the comparative immunity of the Federal prisoners on the supposition that the artificial atmosphere created by the immense accumulations of filth and human excrements within and around the stockade and hospital counteracted or destroyed in some unknown manner the malarial poison."[53]

The treatment and preventive course for malaria were, as they are in some parts of the world today, derivatives of the bark of the cinchona tree or quinine, usually taken with a couple of shots of whiskey. This drug was most sought-after by those in the blockaded South. Exotic tales were often told about smuggling this much-needed pharmaceutical through the lines in dolls held in little girls' arms, in the petticoats of ladies' hoop skirts and via funeral corteges with no bodies in the coffins. "In addition, quinine was considered one of the best medicinals available for syphilis, rheumatism, neuralgia, diarrhea, and fevers, to name a few; and if there happened to be a little extra on hand, it was put to use as an antiseptic, dentifrice, gargle, or hair tonic."[54]

In July, out of 10,621 cases of sickness that were treated at sick-call, only 505 were of a "malarious character." The garrison troops were not immune from malaria with 145 cases of malaria out of the 1,603 cases of sickness involving the guards.[55]

Another big killer of Southern soldiers in the field was pneumonia. Jones felt that about twenty-five percent of all soldier deaths due to disease was "inflammation of the lung."

Into this class of diseases fell such diseases as bronchitis, pneumonia, tonsillitis, laryngitis, tuberculosis, catarrh, pleurisy, diphtheria, and asthma. These were usually treated by bleeding, blistering or purging. Jones began to recognize that perhaps these "cures" were too drastic, so he advocated a good, nutritious diet as the most advantageous treatment. He did, occasionally, use the lancet for bleeding, however.

Of the 42,686 cases of sickness among the prisoners during this six-month period, about 4,000 were of a respiratory nature; of the 7,612 deaths during this period, about 400 were from respiratory causes.[56]

Besides "diarrhea chronica," the other most devastating disease was scurvy. This was caused by a vitamin C or ascorbic acid deficiency. At the time of the Civil War, scurvy was thought to have been the result of "... impure air, bad water and improper food."[57] Vitamins were unknown, but physicians did recognize that the disease did respond to fresh vegetables. Every school child knows the story of the English sailors who were called "limeys" due to their rations of fruit on long voyages. Almost any fresh vegetable has enough vitamin C to reverse the horrible effects of scurvy. McElroy said, "It usually manifested itself first in the mouth. The breath became unbearably fetid; the gums swelled until they protruded, livid and disgusting, beyond the lips. The teeth became so loose that they frequently fell out, and the sufferer would pick them up and set them up and set them back in their sockets. In attempting to bite the hard corn bread furnished by the bakery the teeth often stuck fast and were pulled out. The gums had a fashion of breaking away in large chunks, which would be swallowed or spit out. All the time one was eating his mouth would be filled with blood, fragments of gums and loosened teeth."[58]

For the six months of March through August, Doctor Jones found there were several categories of disease that should probably have been added to the category "Scorbutus" to give the correct number of prisoners suffering from scurvy. He felt that at least some of the deaths listed under, "ascites," "anasarca," "morbi varii," and "marasmus" were due to scurvy. "Ascites" was an accumulation of fluid in the belly. "Anasarca" was a generalized dropsy or edema. Those listed under "morbi varii" were men who "... died without having received sufficient medical attention for the determination of even the name of the disease causing death." "Marasmus" means a "slow wasting," until death could intervene.

[53] *O.R.*, VIII, p. 616.
[54] Brooks, p. 65.
[55] *O.R.*,VII, p. 541.
[56] *O.R.*,VIII, pp. 609, 610.
[57] Urban, p. 391.
[58] McElroy, p. 205.

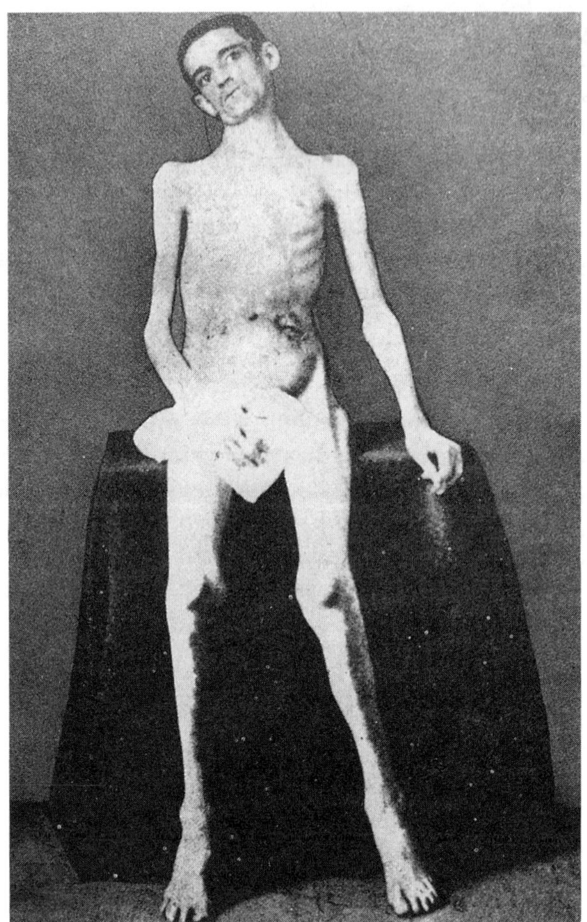

**An example of the extreme cases of malnutrition exhibited by ex-prisoners from Andersonville** - They show the edema of their lower extremities. Many survivors were photographed at Annapolis, Maryland, to document the extreme state of starvation of some prisoners. (National Archives)

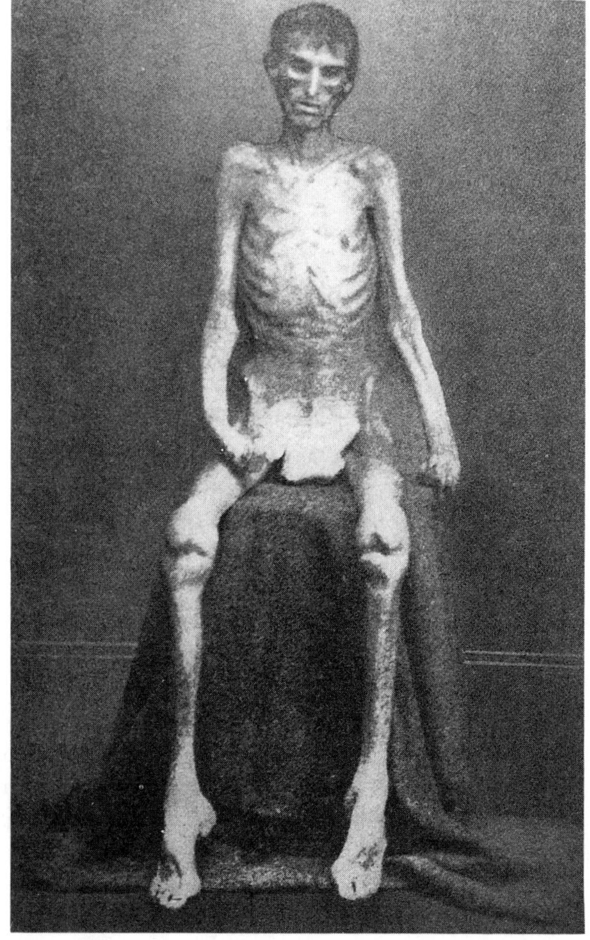

**Another ex-prisoner showing extreme malnurishment** - He did have stomach cancer which could explain some if not all, of his debilitated appearance. (National Archives)

| | Cases | Deaths |
|---|---|---|
| **Scorbutus** | 9,501 | 999 |
| **Anasarca** | 1,510 | 315 |
| **Ascites** | 46 | 4 |
| **Morbi varii** | 474 | 565 |
| **Marasmus** | 53 | 53 |

This table shows that over one-fourth of the prisoners were diagnosed as suffering from some scurvy or scurvy-like syndrome. In fact, Doctor Jones said, "... it appeared that almost every one of the older prisoners was more or less scorbutic."[59]

| | Cases | Deaths |
|---|---|---|
| **March** | 15 | 0 |
| **April** | 50 | 0 |
| **May** | 1,221 | 14 |
| **June** | 2,097 | 68 |
| **July** | 3,092 | 195 |
| **August** | 3,026 | 722 |
| **TOTALS** | 9,501 | 999 |

Effect of Scurvy on the Prisoners at Andersonville March - August 1864 [60]

With the loss of chewing efficiency, even the food available was difficult to eat. After a couple of days of sweet potatoes, these oral manifestations would become abated. When these or other vegetables were not available, sometimes a handful of sumac berries would accomplish wonders. On August 23rd, Kellogg felt he had developed the symptoms of scurvy within his mouth; he went to the sick call that day and was prescribed "...to receive at night about a table spoonful of sumach berries, the usual remedy for the disease, the tea made of it being very sour and astringent."[61]

Urban noticed the miraculous benefit of vegetables. "Terrible as this disease was, it could be easily checked when it first made its appearance, if the afflicted one could get potatoes, onions, or any kind of fruit or vegetables. Raw potatoes and onions were especially beneficial. When in its first stages, I have known it to be checked by the use of one raw potato."[62]

The underlying cause of the teeth loosening was the destruction of collagen fibers which make up the connective tissue of the body. This is the protein that binds the different parts of tissues together. When absent, tissues separate and, when vital organs cease to function, eventually, death is inevitable. After death, the prisoners' bodies were lifted by the arms, and sometimes all the skin would separate like peeling off a sweater, leaving the underlying muscle bundles exposed. If fresh vegetables were given soon enough before the vital organs became involved, then the whole process was reversible. This was the tragedy of Andersonville; if vegetables were available, they were not fed to the prisoners. One escapee stated that, within a few miles of the pen, were seen luscious vegetable gardens with an

[59] *O.R.*, VIII, p. 618.
[60] Jones, p. 192.
[61] Kellogg, p. 231.
[62] Urban, p. 392.

overabundance of vegetables which, if they had been fed to the prisoners, would have cured them of any scorbutic disease. "The neighboring plantations produced the potatoes in great quantities. In the everglades of Florida the lime tree, which furnishes a positive antidote, grows in wild luxuriance; and the woods everywhere, the corn and potatoes of their fields, furnish vinegar by distillation."[63]

Colonel Chandler said that he was "... confident that, by slight exertions, green corn and other anti-scorbutics could readily be obtained."[64] One prisoner escaped from the pen and said he "... came across very fine corn-fields within fifteen miles of the prison. I saw melons and apples, beans, tomatoes, &c.; I do not remember seeing any peaches."[65]

One might argue that, if these antidotal vegetables could not be bought or obtained by the quartermaster, why were the prisoners not allowed to have small gardens in which to raise their own food? Why did not General Winder let more prisoners outside to farm? There were a couple of indications of insignificant plots within the pen. "Our mess had a stalk of green corn, about knee high, growing by our sleeping ground, and guarded it as though it were gold. A crazy fellow came along one day, snatched the stalk, and ran away into the crowd, eating it as fast as he could, destroying our summer's crop."[66] Another prisoner said, "... in the immediate vicinity of our camp there was nothing green. It would soon be trodden down by the tramp of so many feet. In this way a few stalks of Indian corn were permitted to grow."[67]

Scurvy was thought to appear as three or four distinct clinical entities. Sometimes it would appear in the limbs, and the tendons or "cords" would be so drawn up that the victim could not walk. "It is strange to see so many young men moping about with canes... Some entirely loss [sic] their voices, can only whisper."[68] The flesh would become discolored due to the rupture of millions of tiny capillaries because their walls were weak from a lack of collagen. It would cause pitting of the skin or edema because of the pooling of intercellular fluids. Sometimes the men felt that the scurvy would be confined to the bones, and not show itself clinically. They considered this the more painful type of scurvy. The other was the intra-oral type, previously discussed, which left the patient toothless.

This was the way one man described scurvy: "Its first symptoms are eruptions on different parts of the body. Soon it locates - generally in the ankles. Here large sores begin to form similar to the first appearance of boils. These deepen and spread. The limbs become swollen. If not checked, it soon covers the whole body, and the flesh actually rots away and falls off the bones. It generally proves fatal by attacking the glands of the throat. These swell enormously, and the patient is often strangled. Sometimes it locates in the mouth; in this case the gums become softened and the teeth drop out."[69] Another said, "In some cases the body became covered with scaly, yellowish spots, and these soon developed into running ulcers, and the entire body of the poor victim was soon in the most horrible condition. In some cases the limbs swelled and face puffed up until the skin burst. A most painful diarrhea or discharge from the bowel, largely composed of blood, almost always accompanied it. Often the lower limbs became full of holes, and in some cases almost rotted off. Streams of offensive blood poured from the nose, mouth, and different parts of the body. Gangrene also often got into these sores, and finally mortification took place and ended the terrible sufferings of the poor victims.[70]

Jones "... strongly urged the preparation of large quantities of soup made from the cow and calves heads, with the brains and tongues, to which a liberal supply of sweet potatoes and vegetables might have been advantageously added. The materials existed in abundance for the preparation of such soup in large quantities, with but little addition expense."[71]

One disgruntled prisoner thought the vinegar or sour beer made in the pen was better-tasting than that dispensed by the Confederate doctors for its medical value. "The only thing he ever gave us in the way of medicine was some sour meal-water. Twice they gave me that as belonging to the scurvy patients. They called it vinegar. It was merely water laid upon sour meal. Our own men made a better article inside the stockade, which they call sour beer."[72]

---

[63] Author's library.
[64] *O.R.*, VII, p. 548.
[65] Chipman, p. 171.
[66] Boggs, p. 47.
[67] Kellogg, pp. 131, 132.
[68] Northrop, p. 122.
[69] Williard W. Glazier, *The Capture, the Prison Pen, and Escape* (New York: United States Pub. Co., 1868), p. 52.
[70] Urban, p. 391.
[71] *O.R.*, VIII, p. 603.
[72] Chipman, p. 168.

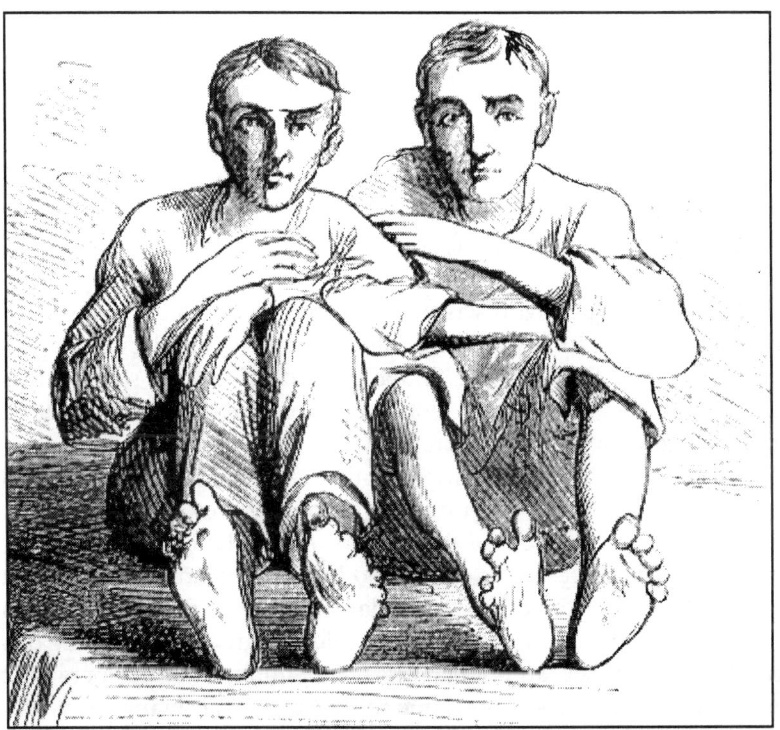

**Smith and Churchill, Two Boy Prisoners** - lost their toes from frostbite and were so crppled by scurvy that they could not stand up or walk. These boys were known to the rest of the prisoners by the nickname 'Siamese Twins.' (LaBaume)

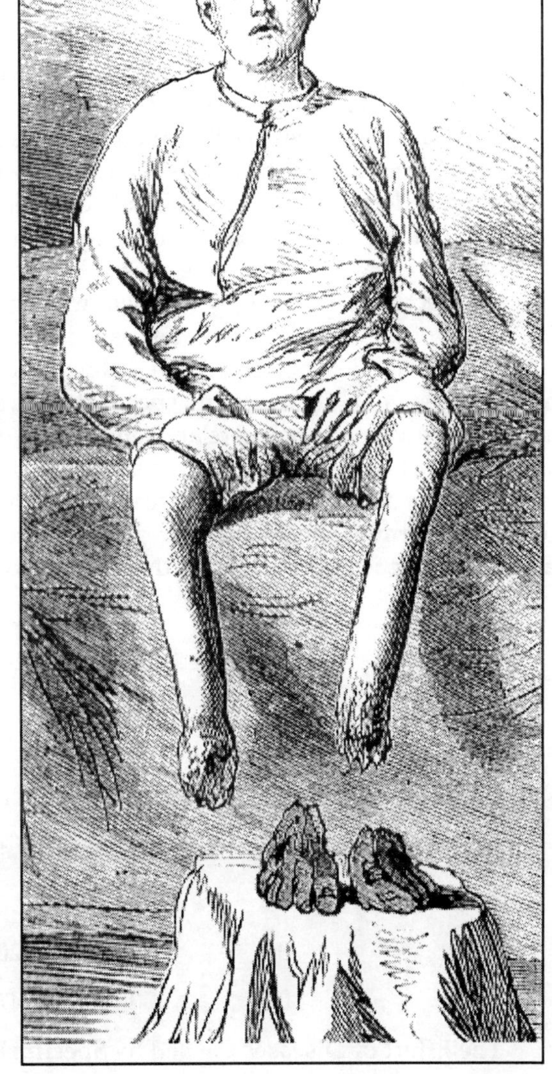

**Calvin Bates, Corporal Co. E., 20th Maine Infantry** - This shows him with his recently dropped off feet due to gangrene having set in after his bout with scurvy. Most of the time, this dropping of the feet did not hurt nor did the patient bleed excessively. He testified at the Wirz trial. (Abbott)

Helwig, who could not walk, "... made a trade with one of the guards, exchanging my gilt-edged testament that was in the knapsack I picked up when I was captured, for three or four large yams. I ate them raw, and made them last as long as I could. By the time I had them eaten I was able to hobble."[73]

The prisoners, eventually, were able to recognize when a comrade's case of scurvy became terminal. "The last change was ushered in by the lower parts of the legs swelling. When this appeared, we considered the man doomed. We all had scurvy, more or less, but as long as it kept out of our legs we were hopeful. First, the ankle joints swelled, then the foot became useless. The swelling increased until the knees became stiff, and the skin from these down was distended until it looked pale, colorless and transparent as a tightly blown bladder. The leg was much larger at the bottom than at the thigh, that the sufferer used to make grim jokes about being modeled like a churn, 'with the big-

[73] Helwig, p. 43.

gest end down.' The man then became utterly helpless and usually died in a short time."[74]

Northrop, on Monday, June 6th, "... noticed a man with the whole lower part of his body buried in dirt as a remedy for scurvy."[75] "I have seen hundreds of poor men sitting about the prison, with their legs buried in the sand, to keep them from bursting, they were so swollen with the scurvy."[76] "First, Isaac and David Loudenbeck, Co. B, 5th Iowa. They were now in the last stages of rotting scurvy. Their flesh had entirely wasted away, leaving the skin shriveled and calloused on the bone, except on the feet and legs, and this was puffed full of watery matter, which oozed out through fractures in the skin, and was very offensive to the smell. Their bony faces, sunken eyes and thin lips, closing over toothless mouths, gave them a sickening appearance. The following is the number of their graves; Isaac Loudenbeck, No. 9,438; David Loudenbeck, No. 10,224."[77]

"Next to me lay Daniel Bixler, Co. B, 5th Iowa, who was afflicted with scurvy and gangrene sores on his feet and legs. Where the sun had blistered them they had become running sores and were filled with wriggling larvas, deposited there by the hideous maggot fly. No. of his grave, 9,846."[78] Fosdick said, "I, too, was afflicted with scurvy until my feet, ankles and knees swelled almost to bursting, and turned to a purple color. I could place a thumb or finger on my foot or leg and press in an inch, which dent would remain twenty-four hours."[79]

In the Federal army, there was only one death from scurvy for every thirty-five thousand men. During the first two years of the war, there had been eighty-six hundred cases of scurvy and only one percent of these victims died.[80]

Smallpox was a viral disease caused by contact with a person who had the disease or who had come in contact with an object contaminated by a patient with the disease. The disease was contracted by the inhalation of the virus. The course of the disease varied, but usually it began with a fever of about 7 to 21 days' duration. Then, a couple of days later, small blisters formed that scabbed and fell off after about a month or so. Besides the ugly scarring, the disease could be fatal. There was no specific treatment. Edward Jenner, an English physician, noticed that farmers who milked cows with cowpox, a related and mildly eruptive disease, became immune to smallpox. Vaccination was recommended as early as 1800 and most of the prisoners had been vaccinated when they arrived at Andersonville. Smallpox was considered a "cold weather" disease. I became clear that the incidence of smallpox decreased with the coming of warm weather. The four diseases listed in the chart below were the four that Doctor Jones thought to be caused by specific poisons (versus those caused by exhalations and derangements of the victims' systems).

| | Typhus | | Typhoid Fever | | Smallpox | | Measles | |
|---|---|---|---|---|---|---|---|---|
| | Cases | Deaths | Cases | Deaths | Cases | Deaths | Cases | Deaths |
| March | 0 | 0 | 67 | 28 | 28 | 5 | 10 | 0 |
| April | 0 | 0 | 56 | 18 | 73 | 34 | 6 | 1 |
| May | 0 | 0 | 92 | 17 | 13 | 10 | 40 | 3 |
| June | 0 | 0 | 18 | 32 | 1 | 10 | 8 | 2 |
| July | 0 | 0 | 39 | 58 | 4 | 8 | 3 | 0 |
| August | 0 | 0 | 200 | 32 | 0 | 1 | 1 | 1 |
| Totals | 0 | 0 | 472 | 185 | 119 | 68 | 68 | 7 |

**The Effect of Diseases Caused by Specific Poisons on the Prisoners at Andersonville March – August 1864.** [81]

Within a month of the arrival of the first prisoners, smallpox was first noticed among those sent down from Richmond. As a result, the physicians were ordered to vaccinate "... all who could not show a healthy scar." Within a week or ten days, between 2,000 and 3,000 men were vaccinated. Out of this group, nearly every man who had scurvy "... was attacked with ulceration of the pustule." "These small ulcers soon began to slough and extend over a large extent of surface. These sloughs would become detached, the parts beneath suppurate, as in the case of other

[74] McElroy, p. 205.
[75] Northrop, p. 72.
[76] Compton, p. 55.
[77] Fosdick, p. 65.
[78] *Ibid.*, p. 57.
[79] *Ibid.*
[80] Hamlin, p. 135.
[81] Breeden, p. 189.

ulcers in a sloughy condition, until, at last, the ulcer could become phagedenic and destroy every structure in its track for a considerable extent. In this condition, gangrene would set in, and, if the disease be not speedily arrested by powerful escharotics, emollient poultices, and the proper vegetable diet, amputation became necessary, or the poor wretch would sink under the irritation; diarrhea or dysentery would supervene and speedily destroy the patient."[82] Isaiah White said, on the 25th of April, that smallpox was on the decline.

Of course, once the prisoners noticed the sequela that resulted from their vaccinations, most tried to keep from getting vaccinated or, if they could not avoid this, they would rush back to their tents or to the creek and wash the area of the vaccination. They thought the Confederate doctors had used contaminated vaccine and they raised this accusation at that time. After the war, it was brought up. At least twelve amputations were necessitated as a direct result of the patients having been vaccinated.

This supervening of gangrene or other secondary infections at the site of the inoculation was rather common during the war. Jones thought that the situation at Andersonville was caused by the scorbutic state of the prisoners' blood and that any puncture would have become infected even if made by a sterile instrument. Therefore, Jones never took any blood samples, fearing he might cause harm or death. Even the extremely biased Doctor Augustus Hamlin said that the stories about the spurious vaccinations were "doubtless untrue." He said that similar results had been seen "... in civil communities" and the Federal armies and hospitals.

One man, detailed as a ward master in the hospital, testified: "It was sure death for a man to be vaccinated there if it took. His arm would have to be amputated, and I know of only one successful case of amputation; there was a bet of $150 on that. It was the case of a young doctor who had charge of a man. I think he bet $100 that the man would live, and $50 that he would save the man's arm. He won the money. He supplied the man with a new sponge and a wash-basin, and attended him himself, for three or four weeks. That was the only case I saw of a cure, and I saw many a case there.[83]

Doctor Isaiah White said, on September 15th, that no case of small pox had occurred since July. "One hundred and fifteen cases have been treated, with sixty-seven deaths, an apparently large ratio of mortality. However the debilitated condition of these men before the attack should not be lost sight of, which rendered them unable to resist the sequelae, a large number of them dying after the subsidence of the primary disease."[84]

The Confederate physicians knew the possibly lethal consequences of vaccinating a patient. A very lucky clerk of Wirz, from Pennsylvania, testified for the defense. "I asked Dr. White to vaccinate me. I think it was during May. Dr. White did not say that the vaccine matter which he had was bad; but he gave me to understand so. He shook his head; as much as to say 'Don't be vaccinated.' He told me he would get a scab from a child in the country and vaccine me with that.[85]

A disease that one would have seen at Andersonville was tetanus or "lock-jaw." In fact, there were only 505 cases recorded for the entire Union army during the Civil War. This is remarkable, since there had been hundreds of thousands of dirty, deep wounds. There was probably a similar number of lock-jaw victims for the Southern army. This infection is caused by the bacteria, Clostridium tetani, which inhabits soil contaminated with manure. Luckily, most battles of the war were fought on unplowed, un-manured fields. Unluckily, many barns and stables were used as temporary hospitals where wounds were sometimes infected with the germ. The bacteria multiplied and flourished when introduced into a deep, penetrating wound where no oxygen could get to it. It would release a toxin, which attacked the central nervous system, causing a specific syndrome characterized by spastic flexing of the back, and clenching of the teeth, which usually relaxed only in death.

Jones described a patient with the classical symptoms of tetanus who had been wounded three weeks earlier. When seen, he would let out "... a shrill, piercing, cry, the head and neck are drawn back and downwards towards the heels, whilst the lower extremities are drawn in like manner backwards towards the head with great violence... The patient, cannot lie down, even in the intermission of the spasms, and is compelled to sit upon the edge of the bed, his lower extremities being forcibly bent backwards over the bed."

In that time of the miasmas, Jones thought tetanus was caused by "animal effluvia" and he "... treated the case's most pronounced outward manifestations - pain, restlessness, and constipation. His primary treatment was a concoction of chloroform, sulphuric ether, and tincture of opium and a diet of chicken and beef soup, corn gruel, and milk punch. He supplemented this course of treatment when the situation seemed to demand it with large doses of

---

[82] *O.R.*, VIII, p. 627.
[83] *Wirz Trial*, p. 675.
[84] *O.R.*, VII, p. 758.
[85] *Wirz Trial*, p. 680.

calomel, quinine, and laudanum and enemas of molasses and common salt and water."[86]

In that era of misdiagnoses, one wonders if this was a true case of tetanus because miraculously, the patient fully recovered in spite of this treatment. Typhoid fever or "camp fever" was caused by what we now know as the Salmonella bacteria, from fecal material, and was transmitted by flies, dirty fingers, and contaminated food. Jones felt fully one-fourth of all Southern casualties from disease was caused by typhoid fever. It was a warm weather disease, whereas the respiratory diseases peaked in the colder months. This same bacteria caused abdominal pain and acute diarrhea. It was often called "continued fever" because one of its characteristics was that the body temperature stayed elevated for two or three weeks.

During the six-months from March 1st to September 1st, there were 472 cases of typhoid fever recorded; 185 deaths resulted from it, for a 39.1 percentage of deaths or one death in 2.55 cases reported.[87] Among the Confederate guard, which had a mean strength of 3,755 for the months of July and August, there were 102 cases of typhoid fever with 38 deaths. The ratio of deaths to cases of typhoid fever for the guard was similar to the ratio for the prisoners: one death in 2.68 cases or 37.2 percent of the cases died. The ratio of cases of typhoid fever to the mean strength for the Confederates was nearly three times as great as it was among the Federal prisoners. For the Confederates, there was one case of typhoid fever for every 36.8 men, or 2.71 percent of the entire command; for the Federal prisoners, there was one case for every 86 prisoners or 1.16 percent of the mean strength.[88]

Jones mentioned that, at one time, the guard camped very close to the stockade at which time they died at a much faster rate that approached that of the prisoners. Since the records were not kept for those first few months, he was unable to substantiate this assertion.[89] Concerning typhoid, Jones "... attributed it to a combination of foul camp air, night exposure to the atmosphere of the swamps and marshes, bad water, and poor diet." Its symptoms were a "... low muttering delirium, loss of muscular & nervous power, & total derangement of the bowels & alteration & contamination of the blood."[90] This seeming susceptibility of the guard is probably due to the fact that the guard was composed of young boys and old men who had not endured the rigors and the naturally-immunizing effect of camp life.

Another "highly fatal" fever, characterized by a steady, "continued fever," was typhus. Jones found that there had been no substantiated cases of typhus or "ship fever" at Andersonville. This was very surprising, considering that this rickets-like disease was usually found in crowded, filthy places. Body lice transmitted the epidemic form of typhus from one person to another. Fleas transmitted the endemic form from rats to humans. An early description of this disease described the symptoms as "... sudden chills, severe headaches, pains in the back and limbs, and a steady fever which remitted slightly each morning. Some patients developed respiratory symptoms, especially coughs while others vomited often."[91] At that time, when bacteriology was in its infant stages of development, it is, of course, reasonable to assume that the various gastrointestinal disturbances were misdiagnosed. Complicating the diagnosis of the dying soldiers was the problem of parasitic worms. There were, basically, three types of worms: roundworms, threadworms, and flat worms. All are transmitted by the patient eating infected food, by not washing the hands after a trip to the sinks, or by larvae burrowing through the skin.

After the war, there was an interesting article about an ex-prisoner at Andersonville, Josiah G. Brownell, in *The Glen Cove Gazette* on December 16, 1865. It stated that he had recently been cured of a tapeworm - reportedly sixty-six feet long, "...four or five feet of the neck and head being no larger than a cotton thread." He attributed the parasite to the "... unwholesome and raw bacon which he was forced to eat while a prisoner."[92]

The above discussion of the possibility of the prisoners having been infected by worms may be only theoretical but there was an extreme likelihood that many, if not most, of the prisoners were infected with parasitic worms. Since there seems to have been no diagnosis of parasitic worm infection made by the physicians at Andersonville, the discussion is moot. At Andersonville, the Confederate authorities made a bold attempt to establish a community of about fifty thousand people in rural Georgia. Besides the complexities of supporting the prisoners, there were the logistics of supporting and providing for a garrison at the post whose population numbered from five to ten thousand men who suffered from the same problems of disease, sanitation, and nutrition.

---

[86] Breeden, pp.

[87] *O.R.*, VIII, p. 615.

[88] *Ibid.*

[89] *Ibid.*, pp. 615, 616.

[90] Breeden, p. 127.

[91] Todd L. Savitt, *Medicine and Slavery* (Chicago: University of Illinois Press, 1978), p. 72.

[92] Josiah C. Brownell, *At Andersonville* (New York: Published as a joint project of the Glen Cove Public Library and the Friends of the Glen Cove Library, 1981), Introduction by Daniel E. Russell, p. iv.

## *Chapter Seven*

# The Garrison and Interesting Prisoners

*"My treatment here is killing me, mother,*
*but I die cheerfully for my country."*

Sanitary Commission

During the spring of 1864, there was much activity at Andersonville. The prison population was ever growing, its capacity exceeded by each arrival of a prisoner-laden train. By the time one batch of four to six hundred prisoners had settled in, another train-load would arrive. All facilities and services were over-utilized. There was physical overcrowding in the pen and in the hospitals. The number of doctors, the amount of food, mortuary services, storage, transportation, and sanitary facilities all were inadequate. General Winder always had felt that post security was insufficient due to the paucity of well-trained guards and to an imagined insurrection on the part of Union sympathizers in the region. The changeover of guard troops was continuous. By the time one problem would be solved, three new ones would arise. There was never an established routine that could be maintained for any length of time. There were always difficulties, obstacles, and fears. Dick Winder, as Post Quartermaster, was particularly overworked.

Within a few weeks after Dick Winder arrived at Andersonville, he had the further burden of a request from the Quartermaster-General's office to establish a shop to manufacture army shoes at Americus. Because of this request, Confederate officers went into the pen and announced they sought prisoners with any prior experience in working with leather. Shoe manufacturers were asked to establish an army shoe-making factory in the nearby town. The prisoners were offered the inducement of double rations. Besides getting out of the pen, detailed prisoners were given better clothes and were permitted to bathe. Those who went out were usually frowned upon by their fellow inmates and considered by them to be weak in resolve. They were not considered turncoats as were those who took the Confederate oath of allegiance, the so-called "galvanized" Yankees. "Rebels came in nearly every day, trying to get mechanics to take the non-combatant's oath and work in their shops; the oath was to never bear arms, or to assist directly or indirectly, in any military operations against the Confederate States of America, or obligated us to work in such places as that government might direct...A few raiders went out."[1]

*Capt. R. B. Winder*
*Richmond,*
*Assistant Quartermaster* *April 15, 1864*
*Americus, Ga.*

*Sir:*

*I hope you are making some progress in establishing a shoe shop at Americus, Ga. Major Dillard has reported that he will supply you with leather; Major Cunningham, at Atlanta, that he will send to you an experienced man to aid in the organization of the shop, and Major Hillyer, at Selma, that he has forwarded a lot of shoemakers' tools, &c. The steamer Denbigh has fortunately just arrived at Mobile with a large lot of shoemakers' tools and findings, and Major Barnewall, the depot officer at that point, has been instructed to send you all you may require.*

---

[1] Boggs, p. 40.

*These arrangements, it is hoped, will make quite a productive establishment at Americus. It is of the greatest importance that the production of army shoes should be increased, so you must spare no effort to attain success. Do not be discouraged by rumors of exchange. Nothing is ever certain on that point, and it may be that inducements can be held out that will content the competent shoemakers to remain. Should ever a general exchange be resumed you can compensate them fairly for their services and in such a form as may prove most acceptable, and I have been assured that the unclaimed packages forwarded from the other side will in time be devoted to such as may elect to remain for a while and continue their labor. Report progress.*

*By order of Quartermaster-General:*
*W. B. B. Cross*
*Major and Quartermaster*[2]

A month-and-a-half later, on May 30, Dick Winder wrote Major William B. B. Cross, detailing the problems he was having setting up the shoe factory. First, Mr. Smoot, the man Major Cunningham had assigned as superintendent of the factory, had to be released from service. Winder had great difficulty obtaining the scarce "upper leather." He said there was no reason to begin production since he could obtain enough leather to last only three days, assuming he could find 50 workers. Winder said the two government tanneries at Americus could supply almost all the leather needed by his shoe factory and, by using this leather, he could save transportation costs.

In the South, shoes were put together with quarter-inch, hard wooden pegs and Winder had great difficulty obtaining these "shoe pegs."[3]

Over a month later, on June 23rd, he wrote to a bonded agent in the Quartermaster Department, Henry De Veuve, and told him to select suitable buildings without delay in which to establish the shoe factory. De Veuve was to procure any tools and machinery he thought would be useful "... to carry this shop into successful operation."[4]

In the latter part of July, Confederate officers again tried to entice prisoners to go outside to work in the shoe factory. Northrop told about a Yankee who had previously taken the oath and had come into the pen on Thursday, June 16th, hoping to obtain the 200 names of the men willing to take the oath and accompany him outside to work in the shoe factory being established. This man, however, was only able to get the names of about 50 potential shoemakers. The men inside became so riled, they took his papers and forced him to swear not to assist the Confederates any more. To reinforce their threat, they shaved half of his head. After Wirz heard about the incident, he sent in a small guard force to escort him outside and to arrest those who had assaulted the turncoat. Wirz ordered rations withheld until the man who did the shaving gave himself up. Rather than deprive the entire pen of its rations, the shaver reported to the gate. He was taken out and locked up, but refused to name his helpers. Wirz rescinded his order and issued the rations.[5] "A Yankee traitor who works in Americus, making shoes for the Jeff Davis government, said to be first and foremost in the shop, came into camp and was caught trying to entice out others to work with him. It excited the indignation of many, and as a fit punishment for what was esteemed his villainy, he was taken and half of his head shaved, and then left to make his way out, hooted and jeered at by the whole crowd."[6]

McElroy said a shoemaker from Macon came into the pen, was seized, thrown into a well and confined there for a whole day. He was only released when rations were cut off that day and it was announced none would be forthcoming until his safe return to the gate. "At one time a Yankee deserter, who was an overseer in a shoe shop which furnished shoes for the Southern army, came into Andersonville and undertook to persuade some of the prisoners to go and work in his shop. As soon as it was generally known what he was doing, he was treated to a prison haircut and shave. Several men took him and shaved off one-half of his hair and beard and kicked him outside."[7]

Dick Winder started another shoe shop near the 1st of August, at Oglethorpe and placed Henry De Veuve in charge of it. On August 3rd, Winder requested $50,000 to be turned over to Henry De Veuve to be used in its establishment. On August 19th, Dick Winder said, "I am about establishing a large Government shoe-shop. I can furnish from 500-1,000 shoemakers at once..."[8] As of September 3rd, he had not received the funds requested.[9] It is not known if both of these shoe factories actually stared production.

---

[2] *O. R.*, VII, p. 56.
[3] *Ibid.*, pp. 181, 182.
[4] *Ibid.*, p. 402.
[5] Northrop, p. 76.
[6] Kellogg, pp. 140, 141.
[7] Lyons, p. 100.
[8] *O. R.*, VII, p. 624.
[9] *Ibid.*, p. 762.

One of the leather workers at one of the shops became an admirer of Dick Winder and made him a beautiful pair of boots. He also reworked one of his leather saddles and presented it to him as a gift. This shower of good will was an indication the men were on good terms with their keepers, according to Dick Winder at the time of his indictment after the war.[10]

McElroy was approached over a dozen times to go out and work as a printer. One Confederate officer, from Columbia, offered him a job paying "... two dollars and a half a 'thousand' for composition." Before the war, McElroy's usual wage had been thirty cents a thousand. Since a man could set 35 to 50 "thousand" a week, this was very enticing, even if paid in Confederate money worth ten to twenty cents on the dollar.[11]

In June, a number of Confederate artillerists came into the pen in an attempt to persuade some of the prisoners to go out to join them, "... probably to drill their ignorant conscripts at the guns."[12] The poor response indicated the Yankees considered this aiding and abetting the enemy.

Walter Bowie, captain and inspector of the Adjutant and Inspector General's Department, was ordered, on April 29th, to proceed to Andersonville for an inspection tour. He arrived on Monday, the 9th of May.[13]

Major Thomas P. Turner was sent to Andersonville by General Winder on April 30th for the purpose of making an inspection of that facility. He reported, "Judging from the energy which has marked Captain Wirz' conduct in respect to the management of the prisoners at Andersonville, there is every reason to believe that there will be a continued improvement."[14]

Major Turner on May 28th recommended to General Winder in Richmond that a new prison be built on Sweet Water Creek proper. This site was selected because the creek had a "... volume and velocity at least ten times greater than the one which runs through the grounds now occupied."[15]

When the first contingents of prisoners arrived on February 27th, part of the south wall had not yet been completed. Two pieces of artillery loaded with canister guarded the breach day and night until the pen was completed. Due to the scarcity of guards during the first few weeks, those accompanying the first few loads of prisoners were retained temporarily. Some Confederate soldiers arrived at the post for guard duty with no guns. As a result of newly-enacted legislation to conscript all men from 17 to 50 years of age, most guards were either very young or very old. "Some of the guards that is a guarding us hear in the stockade aren't over ten years. They are all boys and old men, old grey headed men."[16] The guard force was described, on May 25th, by Major Thomas P. Turner, in this way: "There is scarcely one man out of a hundred who knows the manual of arms or who is capable of marching a company."[17]

When the pen was first built, the guard was camped near the base of the palisade but, because they suffered a "... fatal form of continued fever" and other diseases at the same rate as the prisoners, the guard moved to the high ground a few hundred yards to the west of the west wall. The guard had the option of putting its camps either upstream or downstream from the pen. Their choice, of course, was the high ground to the west. They made small sheds of unhewn, round logs with wooden shingles held down by small round poles. Dick Winder wrote, on April 25, "The troops here are suffering much for the want of tents. I have used every effort in my power to obtain them, but without success."[18]

The rabid Unionist, Hamlin, said the guards had comfortable quarters. "The guards furnished themselves with comfortable huts, arranged with the common conveniences, and their bunks were suspended above the contact of the treacherous ground."[19] "To the south, on the high land which overlooked the prison and appendages, was erected the two-story building which served as quarters and offices for the officers and clerks. Along the same elevated ridge were located the well-build huts of the guards..."[20]

Dick Winder said: "In fact, I used no materials for any purpose that could be done without, and positively refused to put up either officers; or soldiers' barracks until a sufficient hospital arrangement should be completed both for the prisoners and our own sick. For this I was much abused and complained of, but I held to my text and never

[10] Author's library.
[11] McElroy, pp. 348, 349.
[12] Kellogg, p. 194.
[13] *O. R.*, VII, p. 135.
[14] *Ibid.*, p. 167.
[15] *Ibid.*
[16] Blessing diary.
[17] *O. R.*, VII, p. 168.
[18] *Ibid.*, p. 89.
[19] Hamlin, p. 103.
[20] *O. R.*, VIII, pp. 732, 733.

did put up but one house, and that was under peremptory orders, and even that was not quite completed when I was ordered away in September."[21] Chandler testified: "The banks of that stream are hilly, and there were troops, the Georgia reserves, camped on it, and the washings from the camps came down into the stream and flowed through the stockade. I pointed that out to General Winder as wrong, and before I left there he had moved one regiment and the other was under orders to move."[22]

Colonel Fannin of the 1st Regiment Georgia Reserves testified: "My regiment was ordered to take the quarters of the 26th Alabama. We remained there from about the 11th of May till somewhere in June, when we moved above. We had sinks in the rear of the regiment, and the orders were for the men to use them. We were then removed from that place to a hill, a quarter or a half a mile - nearly a half a mile from the stockade. We used well-water. I recollect Captain Wirz objecting to Colonel Harris of the third regiment carrying his troops as far away from the stockade as he wanted to, saying that he was afraid he would be too far away; that he needed him very much, as he was scarce of troops. Colonel Harris located a little nearer the stockade on that account. One regiment, in June, July or August, of last year, was encamped near the depot - the 4th regiment; and the latter part of the year the 55th regiment was moved over there, near the same place, near the depot, about a half a mile above the stockade. I do not know whether they were ever removed, for the purpose of relieving that brook, or anything of that kind. I never heard any fuss made about it at that time. I never heard complaint from any one in relation to the troops polluting the water of that brook. Whenever we were camped near the stockade, I desired to get my regiment further from it. There had been some cases of small pox at the stockade which had been brought out, and I desired to carry my regiment further from the stockade. I did so on that account, together with others."[23] Though the camps of the guard were on the banks of the streams, their sinks were far off in the rear. There were issued orders not to "muddy" the water, much less defile it by using it as a latrine.

By Special Orders dated February 26th, Lieutenant Colonel Alexander W. Persons, with his 55th Regiment Georgia Infantry, was assigned to Andersonville as the second Commandant of the Post. Fannin had command of the prison guard as well as command of the Federal prisoners. On the following day, February 27th, he sought to remedy the scarcity of weapons by contacting the Macon Arsenal; from there he received "... 75 British muskets and bayonets and 2000 Buck and Ball cartridges." On the same day, the guard received, "... 50 Tower muskets and bayonets along with 125 cap pouches, cartridge boxes, cartridge box belts, bayonet scabbards and waist belts."[24] Boggs said that the guns of the guards were "... Queen Anne muskets loaded with ball and buck-shot."[25]

"There were two regiments guarding us; the 26th Alabama and the 55th Georgia. The Alabamians were intelligent and kindhearted, and would not shoot a prisoner unless he was trying to escape or disobeying orders. The Georgians were ignorant and brutal and seemed to delight in shooting and torturing the prisoners. It was a 26th Alabamian who shot the one-legged Hubbard, for which he was not to blame. Hubbard violated orders in crossing the deadline and refused to go back when ordered. Had it been a 55th Georgian, he would not have been warned, but shot down without a word.

"The Alabamians would talk to us from their posts, while the Georgians were liable to shoot if we spoke to them. There were some other Rebel troops garrisoned there, but I do not know what regiments."[26]

The guards were not held in very high esteem by the men in the pen. For instance, the men in Kellogg's 16th Connecticut regiment, after hearing some good news, "... showed their enthusiasm by singing *America, [The] Star Spangled Banner, Red, White and Blue,* at the top of their voices, probably much to the disgust of our guards on the stockade, though possibly not, for many of them were so ignorant it was doubtful if they knew one song from another."[27]

On March 15, the guard received "... seven saddles, bridles, saddlebags, and blankets" from the Macon Arsenal. "Our guards, generally, were an ignorant and superstitious class of men, and spoke the Southern dialect in all its native purity. They would sometimes ask us, 'What makes you 'uns come down here to fight we 'uns?' They seemed to think that we had come South merely to dispossess them of their property. Many of these were poor whites, and although they do not own slaves themselves, they stand up as firmly for it as the more wealthy and intelligent."[28]

[21] Hamlin, p. 20.
[22] *Wirz Trial*, p. 242.
[23] *Ibid.*, p. 438.
[24] Military records of Lt. Col. Persons from National Archives.
[25] Boggs, pp. 18, 19.
[26] *Ibid.*, p. 33.
[27] Kellogg, p. 79.
[28] *Ibid.*, p. 194.

Edward A. O'Neill, colonel commanding the 26th Alabama Regiment was described this way: "The Colonel of this regiment protested against the unnecessary cruelties that were daily practiced against us, and urged that we be better fed and cared for, but his protests were unheeded by the cravens in charge of the prison, over which the Colonel could exercise no authority. In the early spring he rode in among us almost daily and seemed to feel sorry for us in our wretchedness. He told us if he had the privilege he would allow us more room, shelter us from the burning sun, and provide us some comforts in the way of wood, cooking utensils and blankets. But as our condition grew rapidly worse his visits became less frequent, and when he came in he would say that he did not feel like fighting for a government that treated men as we were served, and would resign, or asked to be relieved from duty as commander of prison guards where such scenes met his vision. He was probably relieved at his own request, and sent to Atlanta, where he surrendered his regiment as prisoners of war without firing a shot. They were either paroled or sent North. Intelligence of their surrender was conveyed to us by new prisoners from Sherman's army and the 17th Corps, to whom they had surrendered."[29]

Sidney B. Smith was captain of a company in the 26th Alabama stationed at Andersonville from the latter part of February until the 14th of May, 1864. Captain Smith was present and an active participant in a conspiracy by the officers of the 26th Alabama to make known to General Samuel Cooper, the Inspector General in Richmond, the horrible conditions in Andersonville. The officers defended their colonel, who had been relieved from duty at the post.

During the first week of May, General Samuel Cooper sent Major General Howell Cobb, commander of the Georgia State Militia, from Macon to Andersonville to make a visit of inspection. He was accompanied by E. J. Eldridge, the Chief Surgeon of the Georgia Reserves. He reported his findings in a letter sent to Richmond on May 5th. He said, "I have arranged to send two regiments of infantry there within the next week which with the detached companies of Colonel Persons's regiment will be an ample infantry force. Captain Gamble's battery is there, but I would recommend that it be returned to Florida and Captain Tiller's battery sent in its place. My reason mainly for this recommendation is that Captain Gamble's battery is very ill supplied with horses and they are not needed at Andersonville, whereas Captain Tiller's horses have been so reduced that he is unable to move his battery in the field. I recommend a cavalry company because its presence would have a salutary effect in restraining the prisoners from any attempt to escape. I would recommend that the entire prison grounds should be surrounded by fortifications which could be put up by the troops, whose health would be promoted by the employment."

The visit of this local Georgia hero was the cause of a great celebration. "The ladies in the vicinity gave a picnic to the rebel soldiers in honor of the occasion."[30] "Cobb came down in person from Macon; the Confederates formed a square around him; he stood under a shady tree on some high ground not far from the prison, and made a fiery speech of a half hour's duration, appealing to them, as the future hope of Georgia, asked if they would turn this horde of Lincoln's brutes and hirelings loose upon the sacred soil in Georgia?--this band of assassins, who had cost the lives of so many of your fathers and brothers; to put them where you can hold them, and thus help your bleeding country's cause? Turn them loose, and how long would your property, and your mothers and sisters be safe? He implored them to do their duty, obey their officers, and the prison commander."[31]

In the early spring, the strength of the whole guard was:

| | |
|---|---|
| 57th Regiment Georgia Volunteers, rank and file | 625 |
| A detachment of the 55th Regiment Georgia Volunteers | 153 |
| A detachment of the 26th Regiment Alabama Volunteers | 288 |
| Captain Gamble's Florida battery of light artillery | 127 |
| Total | 1,193 [32] |

"The battery consists of four guns, two 10-pounder, rifled, and two Napolean guns. The artillery is posted -- a section of two guns on the summit of a hill within close range and commanding the gates and one slope of the interior of the enclosure; the other section of two guns is planted in a like manner on another hill commanding the gates and the other slope of the prison enclosure -- the two sections thus supporting each other and commanding perfectly the gates and the whole interior of the prison."[33]

Northrop said the Confederates had a fine rifle battery, captured at the battle of Olustee, Florida, planted on the

---

29 Fosdick, pp. 62, 63.

30 Kellogg, p. 62.

31 Boggs, p.38.

32 *O. R.*, VII, p. 137.

33 *O. R.*, VII, p. 138.

ridge overlooking the prison.[34]

A funny incident happened one warm night in March. "Nosey" Payne, a boy with a superb tenor voice, was singing patriotic songs with a large group of men around the campfire, with the entire camp joining in on some choruses. They were singing, *Brave Boys Are They* and other well-known songs of the times. All of a sudden, a shot rang out from a 55th Georgia sentinel who had just come on duty. He could be heard reloading, ramming home another ball. Then another shot rang out. The whole camp of Confederates came to life, thinking there was a riot. Finally, some prisoner yelled up to him and inquired as to his target. With curses, the sentinel said that a big Yankee near the deadline was his target. By that time, the Reserves had come up at the double-quick. The sentinel had been shooting a big piece of wood brought in and stood up near the deadline.[35]

McElroy told about another incident illustrating the alleged cruelty of the Georgia troops: "I was standing one day in the line at the gate, waiting for a chance to go out after wood. A Fifty-fifth Georgian was the gate guard, and he drew a line in the sand with his bayonet which we should not cross. The crowd behind pushed one man till he put his foot a few inches over the line, to save himself from falling; the guard sank a bayonet through the foot as quick as a flash."[36]

In mid-May, Captain Charles E. Dyke's company of light artillery arrived at Andersonville, which was "... an efficient body of men, well drilled, disciplined, and officered."[37] The seventy-five horses of Captain Dyke's Battery were turned in, on May 23rd, to Captain B. J. Dallas, bonded agent, to be re-assigned for duty by Major Norman W. Smith, Chief Quartermaster Transportation.[38] The horses would not be needed while the artillery was in place around the prison.

Kellogg had the following conversation with one of the guard. "I had a boy who was a prisoner with our people at the North. 'Indeed,' said I, 'how was he treated?' 'Very kindly, sir, very kindly' he replied. 'Did you receive letters from him while he was in prison?' I continued. 'Yes, sir, he wrote to us and we wrote to him.' 'He probably fared much better than we do in this prison; said I, 'did he not?' With great frankness he answered, 'Oh! Yes, sir, I reckon you fare pretty hard in there, but we ain't to blame for it. The 'Old Captain' is as hard on us as he is with you. A heap of us were taken right off our farms, and we left the crops standing, with nobody to ten 'em but the women folks.'"[39]

In the middle of May, while General Judson Kilpatrick and General George Stoneman were having success over Johnston, "... the rebels were particularly watchful over us, evidently fearing something would escape their notice, and they would in some way lose their hold upon us."[40]

In May, "... the guard held a 'sham fight', which drew admiring crowds of people from all the surrounding country to see how the thing was done. After their sport was over in that line, many of the women came down to our prison, crowding around the gate, amusing themselves by throwing in bread, and witnessing the eagerness with which our half starved men would scramble to get it, for at this time life was sustained only by a miserable pittance of poor corn bread, and a small bit of boiled bacon."[41]

Near the end of May, "... the rebels showed unmistakable signs of alarm about something. The working parties were all ordered inside the stockade, while their soldiers were posted around the outside of the prison, as if in expectation of an immediate attack. They finally returned to their camps, and everything went on as usual. We afterwards learned the whole thing was occasioned by a report that a body of our cavalry had crossed over the Flint River, at a point only twelve miles from us."[42]

"When General Johnston was being badly pressed by Sherman's army, it became necessary for the rebels to send every available man to the front, the soldiers who had been our guard were ordered to Dalton to aid in repelling him and their places were filled by some of the Georgia militia. The former looked upon these latter with supreme contempt, and applied to them the name of 'new issues'."[43] "The 26th Alabama and the 55th Georgia had been sent to fight Sherman and some eight or ten thousand Georgia reserves took their places. These were nearly all ignorant boys, who had never been away from home, and knew but little about the war, except what they had heard in

---

[34] Northrop, p. 63.
[35] McElroy, p. 158.
[36] *Ibid.*, p. 159.
[37] *O. R.*, VII, p. 548.
[38] *Ibid.*, p. 159.
[39] Kellogg, pp. 192, 193.
[40] *Ibid.*, p. 98.
[41] *Ibid.*, pp. 71, 72.
[42] *Ibid.*, p. 114.
[43] *Ibid.*, p. 84.

the fiery speeches of the Rebel leaders."[44] The number of the guard force was rather inflated.

These men were the men of the First Regiment Georgia Reserves and, within a few days, they were joined by the Second, Third, and Fourth Regiments Georgia Reserves. Colonel Fannin, of the First Regiment Georgia Reserves, testified: "When my regiment first went there it occupied the quarters of the twenty-sixth Alabama, I think. There were forks placed in the ground and boards from the pine timber were placed on them and covered. My regiment went into those quarters. Some of the houses which the fifty-fifth regiment had were sold and removed, and I had to put up tents for a large portion of my men. We had no floors to our tents. When we removed to other quarters we had to build barracks there. We had some tents. We cut down timber for the materials for our barracks. We cut it down with our own men. I made application for tools and could not get them... I furloughed some men at one time on that ground. I asked that a furlough should be granted for men to go home and bring their tools. Some of the men lived in the neighborhood, and they went and bought tools for that purpose."[45] "The four regiments Georgia reserves have been newly organized, and without any effort being made to assign the old and young men to separate regiments, as should have been done. A large number are evidently within the ages of eighteen and forty-five, and I respectfully recommend that a reliable conscript officer be sent among them. These troops are entirely without discipline, and their officers are incapable of instructing they being ignorant of their own duties. I recommend that one competent officer from the Invalid Corps be assigned to each regiment as drill officer and instructor. I found their arms in serviceable order, but many are lacking bayonets, cartridge boxes and accouterments. Furlow's battalion of Georgia militia, temporarily serving here, is armed with muskets without bayonets and accouterments. Of the whole force there are 452 men entirely without arms."[46]

On June 18th, General Winder wrote to General Bragg that the guard force numbered 2,867; all were members of the Georgia Reserves except 371. He was of the opinion that the guard force should be doubled.[47]

On Monday, June 20th, "The old guard [left] this morning, probably for the front, we have a new set on."[48] Two guards were reported hung that same day for having attempted an escape, a few days beforehand, with a group of prisoners.[49]

Thus, after the 26th Alabama had left, the guard forces were under the immediate command of Colonel Henry Forno, P.A.C.S., and were composed of Captain Dyke's company of Florida light artillery, the Fifty-fifth Regiment Georgia Infantry, the First, Second, Third, and Fourth Regiments Georgia Reserves, and Lieutenant Colonel Furlow's battalion Georgia militia, an aggregate of 3,600 men, of whom 647 were on the sick report.[50] "The men were in commotion, and evidently manifested concern about something. They went busily to work planting artillery to command the camp and railroad, an effort that was understood when we found that Kilpatrick was operating with a cavalry force in the vicinity of Augusta."[51] In the third week of June, the guards "... were on the alert being in constant expectation of an attack, as it was reported that our cavalry were in the immediate vicinity. Nearly all the forces about the prison were sent away, leaving scarcely none but the guard on the stockade."[52]

"The rebels were using all their available time for the strengthening of their position. The result of their labor soon became apparent in the long line of fortification which appeared a little way from the stockade, and directly in front of it. Evidently, it was the intention of the enemy to use us as a shield for themselves in case of an attack, for an assault could not be made on them without exposing us to the fire of our own men."[53]

"The number of men detailed for guard duty each day is: Commissioned officers, 7; non-commissioned officers, 16; privates, 280; total, 303, exclusive of artillery. The guard is posted as follows: One man in each sentry box at the top of the stockade, forty men at each gate in the day and eighty at night. The remainder are posted in a line around and fifty yards distant from the stockade. The reliefs not on duty are required to remain at or very near their posts.

"All the officers in command are of the opinion that the prison is secure as at present guarded, but all ask that I will suggest to the department that they believe it would be hazardous to the safety of the prisoners to make the contemplated change in the guard by substituting for one of the regiments now present a regiment of the reserve

[44] Boggs, p.38.
[45] *Wirz Trial*, p. 446.
[46] *O. R.*, VII, p. 549.
[47] *O.R.*, VII, p. 378.
[48] Northrop, p. 77.
[49] *Ibid.*
[50] *Ibid.*, p. 548.
[51] Kellogg, p. 129.
[52] *Ibid.*, pp. 145, 146.
[53] *Ibid.*, p. 186.

forces of the State, who are entirely unaccustomed to guard duty and liable to the numerous diseases that are incident to the commencement of camp life."

The above was taken from a report of Walter Bowie, Captain and Inspector in the Adjutant and Inspector General's Department to his Superior, Brigadier General R. H. Chilton, on May 10, 1864.[54] W. M. Hammond, Captain and Assistant Adjutant-General, wrote from Macon, on June 21, after his inspection of Andersonville the previous day: "The guard, commanded at present by Col. J. H. Fannin, First Georgia Reserves, consist[s] of four regiment State reserves, a detachment from Fifty-fifth Georgia Volunteers, and Dyke's Florida battery, the aggregate effective strength being 1,588. The reserve troops are poorly instructed and without discipline."[55]

Maile, an uninformed prisoner, described the placement of the guards thus: "The day guard at the stockade consisted of one hundred and eighty-six men; the day reserve of eighty-six men; the night reserve consisted of one hundred and ten men; the outlay pickets of thirty-eight men."[56] A soldier of the guard at Andersonville had to serve every third day, two hours on and four hours off, for that twenty-four hour period.[57]

General Winder described, on July 21st, the minimum number of guards required every day to secure the prisoners at Andersonville. At the stockade, there were 52 guard posts, which, with the three shifts, required 166 enlisted men including the 10 extras or supernumeraries. These were under the command of two commissioned officers.

Around the two unenclosed hospitals, the smallpox hospital being the second, there were 23 guards on each of three shifts. Sixty-nine guards were needed, plus 4 supernumeraries, all of whom were overseen by one commissioned officer. The pickets around the perimeter away from the stockade numbered 206 and were necessary to prevent tunneling. There were also 43 "... outlying pickets" and railroad-bridge guards. These were commanded by six commissioned officers.

One hundred guards were necessary to watch those men who were out gathering wood; another 25 supervised various working parties in the surrounding environs.

Not included in this total of 613 were the "accidental" guards and the men who were guarding the Confederate camps.

The guard force numbered 2,421 including 517 sick, on daily duty 227, and the artillery company 126 leaving 1,551.[58]

The guard was gradually being enlarged by means of retaining prisoner guards whenever new "fish" were brought to the post

Colonel Chandler said, after his inspection near August 1st, that there were required to be posted 784 men as guards plus any needed for the many details.[59] General Winder said, on September 17, "The troops at Andersonville who come off guard in the morning have to go on at night."[60]

Colonel Chandler said, "The Fifty-fifth Georgia is composed of men who were absent from their command at the time their regiment proper was captured at Cumberland Gap. They are thoroughly demoralized, mutinous, and entirely without discipline, and should be at once removed from this point and their places supplied with better troops. The colonel of this regiment, C. B. Harkie, though armed at the time, permitted his men to drag him from a railroad car and march him up and down the platform of the depot, and to take him from his tent, place him on a stump, and compel him to go through the manual of arms with a tent pole, and to sign and forward his resignation to the War Department. This last he recalled by a telegram from Fort Valley. He has recently rejoined the command, but dares not assume command of the regiment."[61] General Winder rationalized this occurred more than a year ago and at or near Cumberland Gap.[62]

---

[54] *O. R.*, VII, p. 138.
[55] *Ibid.*, p. 392.
[56] Maile, p. 31.
[57] *O. R.*, VIII, p. 620.
[58] *O. R.*, VII, p. 480.
[59] *Ibid.*, pp. 548, 549.
[60] *O. R.*, VII, p. 837.
[61] *O. R.*, VII, p. 548.
[62] *Ibid.*, p. 757.

On August 1st, the guard at Andersonville consisted of the following troops commanded by Colonel Henry Forno:

| Unit | Commanding Officer | Ready For Duty | Sick | AWOL, Spec. Duty Arrested, etc. | Pres. & Abs., Aggregate |
|---|---|---|---|---|---|
| 1st Ga. Reserves | Lt. Col. .J. J. Neely | 312 | 202 | 206 | 736 |
| 2nd Ga. Reserves | Lt. Col. C. M. Jones | 385 | 75 | 139 | 611 |
| 3rd Ga. Reserves | Lt. Col. John L. Moore | 553 | 144 | 304 | 1,016 |
| 4th Ga. Reserves | Maj. J. H. Burkes | 376 | 126 | 183 | 704 |
| 55th Ga. Regiment | Capt. J. M. Griffin | 91 | 37 | 93 | 230 |
| Fla. Lt. Artillery | Capt. C. E. Dyke | 114 | 24 | 24 | 162 |
| Furlow's Ga. Bat. | Lt. Col. T. M. Furlow | 371 | 39 | 108 | 516 |
| | **Totals** | 2,202 | 647 | 1,057 | 3,975 [63] |

| DUTY | OFFICERS | NCO'S | ENLISTEDMEN |
|---|---|---|---|
| Day guard at stockade | 2 | 10 | 156 |
| Day reserve at stockade | 2 | 8 | 80 |
| Night reserve at stockade | 2 | 8 | 110 |
| Guards with wood squads | 1 | - | 100 |
| Guards at batteries | - | 6 | 30 |
| Provost guards | 4 | 10 | 75 |
| Outlying pickets | - | 8 | 38 |
| Bridge guards, &c. | - | 2 | 10 |
| Men on duty in stockade | - | - | 45 |
| Hospital guard | 1 | 4 | 69 |

| | OFFICERS | NCO'S | ENLISTEDMEN | AGGREGATE |
|---|---|---|---|---|
| Present for duty | 132 | 282 | 1,788 | 2,202 |
| Required daily for duty | 15 | 56 | 713 | 78 |
| | 117 | 226 | 1,075 | 1,418 |
| Unarmed guards | | | | 452 |
| Number of guards that could be armed in an emergency | | | | 966 [64] |

On November 26th, 1862, Major Edmund A. Deslonde wrote to General P. G. T. Beauregard, Commanding the Department of Georgia and South Carolina, recommending James H. Fannin of Troup County, Georgia, for an appointment in the quartermaster or commissary department. Major Deslonde described Fannin in this manner: "Mr. Fannin was a planter and thoroughly acquainted with the state, with its people and resources. He was a man of in-

[63] *Ibid.*, p. 552.
[64] *Ibid.*, p. 553.

telligence and integrity and I am satisfied would make a zealous and competent officer. He was for several years an engineer on the Vicksburg and Shreveport Railroad in charge of construction. He would before this have been in service, but being physically weak could not endure the hardships of the field." As of March 12, 1863, no official action had been taken on this request.

He, evidently, had been captured for the Amnesty Oath was administered by Adjutant Carl Reiss, 68th New York Volunteers on December 8, 1863, at La Grange, Troup County, Georgia.

At the camp of the Georgia Reserves near Atlanta, an election was held for colonel, lieutenant colonel, and major on May 5, 1864. James Fannin was elected colonel of the First Georgia Reserves by a unanimous vote. He was ordered to report to Andersonville, was there in the summer of 1864, and was listed on a requisition as "Commanding Prison Guard." He was absent beginning August 14th, "... by order of General Winder for 20 days." He was with a brigade of troops commanded by Colonel Henry Forno, Acting Brigadier General on September 1st.

He was captured at Fort Tyler by scouts of Gartrell's Second Brigade on April 16th and transferred to Captain J. C. Samson (Company B, 17th Indiana)who commanded prisoners at Macon Armory April 23, 1865.

He was paroled in Macon on April 25th by Captain G. H. Knowland, Provost Marshal. He was subpoenaed by Colonel Chipman as a witness in the trial of Wirz.[65]

"In the after part of the day I went up for medicine for the sick men in our 'mess,' and while waiting for my turn to be served, I had a good confidential talk with one of the guards, whom I found to be a true Union man. He had been driven from his home into the Confederate army about four weeks before, although for a year and a half he had managed in one way and another, to keep out of the service. He was a very intelligent man, bout middle age, and gave it as his opinion that the C.S.A. was about 'played out.' The heavy rains had destroyed the wheat crop, and it was doubtful in his mind if the Confederate government could subsist us three months longer. He was looking for a speedy change in his own condition, for 'as soon as your army crosses the Chattahoochee river,' he said to me, 'I shall turn away from these things and seek my home.'"[66]

"About the first of June they told us that the 51st Virginia regiment was at Andersonville for the purpose of guarding us to the place of exchange."[67] In the third week of June,"... the rebel regiment about us, it was said, had an order read to them at dress parade, announcing to them that in about three weeks they would be allowed a furlough, as the prisoners were to be sent away. This rumor was perpetrated for reasons best known to our enemies themselves."[68]

General Winder wrote, on June 24th, to General Samuel Cooper, in Richmond. He thought the guard force should be reinforced. He felt that, in the event of a raid on the post, the prisoners would, by the force of numbers, be able to overcome the small guard at the post at that time. General Winder feared the raid would be successful. He thought, "If successful, the result to the country would be much more disastrous than a defeat of the armies; it would result in the total ruin and devastation of this whole section of country. Every house would be burned, violence to woman, destruction of crops, carrying off negroes, horses, mules, and wagons."[69]

He also thought, "There has been, and I am satisfied that there is now going on, a correspondence in the prisons with disaffected persons outside, and I have every reason to believe that just before my arrival an agent of General Sherman had been here tampering with the prisoners. From the information I have been able to collect since I have been here I am satisfied that there is a portion of the population around here who ought to be looked after, and who actively sympathize with the prisoners.

"In order to enable me to watch and counteract this influence I respectfully ask that Capt. D. W. Vowles, with a detailed man by the name of Weatherford, on the police at Richmond, and two other well-selected detectives, be ordered to report to me immediately. It is difficult for those at a distance to realize the great responsibility of the command of this post and the great danger of a successful outbreak among the prisoners."[70]

General Winder seemed almost paranoid in his belief " ... there were sinister forces at work in the vicinity of the prison." By July 9th, he said, "The guard is raw and dissatisfied." He was still anxious to receive the detectives he had asked for. "There is treason going on around us, even to depositing arms in the adjacent counties to arm the prisoners... I am obliged to commit the investigation to incompetent hands and I fear it will fail. We are in a critical situa-

---

[65] Military records of Colonel James Fannin from the National Archives.
[66] Kellogg, pp. 141, 142.
[67] *Ibid.*, p. 121.
[68] *Ibid.*, p. 150.
[69] *O. R.*, VII, p. 411.
[70] *Ibid.*

tion. Do send me the assistance I ask. Believe me there is very great danger here."[71] The authorities in Richmond were apprised of the lack of an adequate guard force. As late as July 25th, Seddon said the force was "alarmingly small." The guard at Andersonville was never increased significantly in number or quality, which indicates that the authorities in Richmond felt that the more efficient and well-trained regiments best served the cause of war by being assigned to the front lines.

There were a few soldiers present in the Confederate contingent with some, though limited, musical ability. The Federal prisoners soon tired of hearing the antiquated instruments on which Southern patriotic songs were played repeatedly. McElroy described the prisoners' reactions to these music-makers. "One fife, played by an asthmatic old fellow whose breathings were nearly as audible as his notes, and one rheumatic drummer, constituted the entire band for the post. The fifer actually knew but one tune - *The Bonnie Blue Flag* - and did not know that well. But, it was all that he had, and he played it with wearisome monotony for every camp call - five or six times a day, and seven days in the week. He called us up in the morning with it for a reveille; he sounded the 'roll call' and 'drill call,' breakfast, dinner and supper with it, and finally sent us to bed, with the same dreary wail that had rung in our ears all day...The Rebels were fully conscious of their musical deficiencies, and made repeated but unsuccessful attempts to induce the musicians among the prisoners to come outside and form a band."[72]

After completion of the pen, some blacks continued to work on the fortifications from sunrise to sunset, even on Sundays. In the early part of July, when Sherman was within three miles of Atlanta, the prisoners noticed a great commotion taking place, in regard to the fortifications around the pen, which could be seen from the inside of the prison. A great number of men were busy building entrenchments and forts.

In addition, on July 27th, General Winder appealed to the citizens of the nine counties surrounding the post to furnish labor to complete the work. The prominent citizens suggested they could best spare the farm laborers at that time rather than at a later date. Winder said that the engineer-in-charge, Captain T. Moreno, estimated that 2,000 Negroes with proper implements could complete the job in ten days. Winder asked that the owner furnish implements with each Negro sent. Also needed would be fifty wagons and teams. Since provisions and forage were scarce, Winder requested that food for the hands and forage for the horses be sent, too. Winder said this appeal would be the last made on the hard-pressed populace and, though he had the power to impress the needed labor, he was sure the patriotic sympathies of the people would not necessitate its use.[73] The engineer officer-in-charge told Doctor T. S. Hopkins, the engineer department surgeon, that he had 1,000 to 1,200 Negro men working on the fortifications around the pen.[74] The trees that interfered with the field of fire of the artillery were cut down. The prisoners seemed to sense that the Confederates were in a state of alarm or panic. The direction in which the trees had been cut indicated they expected an attack, probably by way of the railroad. That is, the trees were cut down between the batteries and the station. Several Confederates came into the pen to entice men to go out and help with this work. On Saturday night, July 23rd, they worked all night.

"They threw up a line of rifle pits around the Stockade for the infantry guards. At intervals along this were piles of hand grenades, which could be used with fearful effect in case of an outbreak. A strong star fort was thrown up at a little distance from the south-west corner. Eleven field pieces were mounted in this in such a way as to rake the Stockade diagonally. A smaller fort, mounting five guns, was built at the northwest corner, and at the northeast and southeast corners were small lunettes, with a couple of howitzers each."[75]

"At the time they expected Stoneman's raid down there, soon after the capture of Atlanta, I saw from 500 to 1,000 negroes chopping wood to the westward, so as to make a range for the use of their artillery. They also at the same time put up two stockades around the main stockade of the prison and made a place for the artillery to work around the prison."[76] "The rebels posted their men about the prison, as if in readiness of some expected attack. They were busy as bees in throwing up earthworks, in plain sight of us. Trains were coming up from below, loaded with troops, and a large number of new tents were pitched near the railroad station. They worked away busily their breastworks, making them as formidable as they could. As a train came in at eleven o'clock at night, and the whistle was heard; the Rebs greeted it with loud cheers, but there was a sudden cessation when they halted, which we attributed to the reception of news that was not very welcome to them."[77] "The negros were made into a squad by

[71] *Ibid.*, p. 451.
[72] McElroy, p. 337.
[73] *O. R.*, VII, pp. 503, 504.
[74] Chipman, p. 122.
[75] McElroy, pp. 192, 193.
[76] Chipman, p. 173.
[77] Kellogg, pp. 183, 184.

themselves, and taken out every day to work around the prison. A white Sergeant was placed over them, who was the object of the contumely of the guards, and other Rebels. One day as he was standing near the gate, waiting his orders to come out, the gate guard, without any provocation whatever, dropped his gun until the muzzle rested against the Sergeant's stomach, and fired, killing him instantly."[78] This incident was corroborated by Northrop.[79]

The prisoners' inducement was extra food and good shelter, but only a few men went out. There was much discussion among the men as to whether or not going out and building fortifications should be construed as aiding the enemy. Most thought they should not strengthen a fort whose purpose was to kill their comrades. John E. Gilbert, called "Shorty" by his friends, was especially vocal in his arguing against their working for this purpose.[80] "They felled an immense number of pine trees, so the landscape about us began to present quite a barren appearance, and this seemed to indicate the fact that they wished uninterrupted range for their artillery."[81]

Around the stockade, seven artillery forts were built whose guns, when loaded with canister and grape, were very effective as a deterrent to mass escape. Clavreul said a battery of six guns was on the eminence guarding the entrance.[82] "Upon two sides of the stockade, and some two to four hundred yards distant, were two earthworks, one upon either side, and each mounting four cannon."[83] The actual type of cannon present is not known and varied as the conditions of the war necessitated. Some authors described them as "sixteen guns,"[84] "twenty four twelve-pound Napoleon Parrots,"[85] and "three six gun batteries."[86] The largest of the forts that surrounded the pen was called the Star Fort and was located on the southwest corner. Within these forts were 17 cannons which "... were mounted in barbette and embrasures. Lunettes and redoubts covered all approaches to the two great gates."[87]

Colonel D. T. Chandler, Assistant Adjutant and Inspector General, said, on August 5th, there were sixteen pieces of artillery at Andersonville, but only a part of these were in position. The rest would be placed in position as soon as the fortifications were completed. In addition, six more pieces of artillery were en route to that post.[88]

He also said that the powder magazine had not been completed at that time and that the post's ammunition was being kept in the commissary store and in a canvas tent.[89]

All summer there was a continual strengthening of the fortifications of the post. This construction increased to nearly fever pitch, especially as the fighting approached Atlanta and the threat of a raid by General Stoneman surged into nearby localities.

The newly-arrived prisoners soon learned the guards could be counted on for supplemental supplies. Commercial intercourse between the prisoners and guards was strictly prohibited by the officers. Colonel Persons ordered, on May 23, through his adjutant Captain R. D. Chapman, Acting Adjutant of the Post by General Orders No. 37, that no one should communicate with any paroled prisoner.[90]

However, since bartering was beneficial to both parties, it flourished. The men learned the sentinels would sometimes negotiate when the Officer of the Day was on the other side of the prison. Things got so bad that, on June 30, General Winder issued General Orders No. 58, "Trading by commissioned officers with the troops and prisoners at this post is positively prohibited, and violation of this order will subject the officer to a trial by court-martial."[91]

"The ignorant young Georgians, would be at the gates with sticks of wood, twists of tobacco, or a cow horn full of soft-soap, ready to trade with the prisoners who were carrying out the dead."[92]

Tobacco was always desired by the prisoners. "Smoking was indulged in by those who could afford it. The tobacco used was nearly all plug. It was first chewed, then dried in the sun and afterwards smoked."[93]

Even if no money was available, "... the guards would trade for any kind of tricks we had, such as comb, knife, pocketbook, looking-glass, finger ring, brass button, or anything. They had to trade, peanuts, potatoes, turnips, cab-

---

[78] McElroy, p. 163.
[79] Northrop, p. 62.
[80] Urban, pp. 347-351.
[81] Kellogg, p. 192.
[82] George Robbins, ed., *Diary of Rev. Henry P. Clavreul* (Waterbury, Conn.: 1910), p. 15.
[83] T. H. Mann, "A Yankee in Andersonville," *Century Magazine* (July, 1890), p. 455.
[84] Maile, p. 29.
[85] *Sanitary Commission*, p. 77.
[86] Fosdick, p. 37.
[87] Hamlin, p. 24.
[88] *O. R.*, VII, p. 548.
[89] *Ibid.*
[90] *O. R.*, VII, p. 159.
[91] *Ibid.*, p. 426.
[92] Boggs, p. 46.
[93] Lyons, p. 64.

bage, sometimes bread, that had been sieved and salted."[94] One prisoner had a good scheme for staying healthy. He would make sour beer by letting the corn meal ferment and sour overnight and sell it by the cupful. He would trade it for brass buttons and postage stamps. These items were then traded to the guards for sweet potatoes.[95] The guards especially desired buttons because most of them had only leather or wooden buttons on their homespun butternut uniforms. "One of the eagle staff buttons was worth five dollars in confederate money."[96] "The order that Captain Wirz gave to prevent the trading in clothing was never carried out to my knowledge. Trading was carried on in clothing, and rebel soldiers wore our uniforms... The fact is that every man down there wore our blouses, from the highest to the lowest, with the exception of Captain Wirz. I never saw him wear anything but a colored shirt and white pants. He had a gray uniform with eagle buttons on, but he seldom wore it."[97]

"Our brass buttons especially were prized quite highly among our enemies, and they were almost all the time ready for a trade for them."[98] Sometimes the exchange was made by tossing the bartered goods up to the guard in the tower; at other times string was used to facilitate the exchange. "I know that the prisoners used to trade with my regiment, the fifty-fifth Georgia, while they were on duty. The men of the fifty-fifth Georgia would try to get on the same post near each other in order to trade. They would get together in guard-mounting (I have seen them do it and heard them talk about it) in order to get on the same post to trade, and to prevent the reserves from interfering with them in trading with the prisoners."[99]

"Gilbert and Fralich were both showing symptoms of getting scurvy, and we began to anxiously consider what we could do to prevent it from getting worse...We hailed several of them in regard to a trade for our buttons, but were unsuccessful until a guard came on post who wanted a dozen of New York State buttons. The rebels appeared to value that kind of button very highly, and would pay more for them than for the common United States Regulation button. We did not have any of the former kind; but as our necessity was great, and believing that the end justified the means, we concluded to play a trick on the rebel by giving him United States buttons in place of the ones he wanted. After some little bargaining, he promised to furnish us with two quarts of corn meal, three pounds of pork, three potatoes, and three onions, providing that we got him one dozen New York State buttons - the exchange to be after dark. Watching that he did not notice what we were doing, we cut off a dozen of our buttons, and after rubbing them until they shone like gold. we strung them on a string, and held them up for his inspection. He was pleased, and remarked, 'All right, boys; I will be ready for you when I get on post to-night.' ... We were heartily glad when the guard made his appearance and informed us that he was ready for the trade. He requested one of us to cross the dead-line, and come to the stockade and throw up the buttons. As a guard was but a short distance on each side of him, we felt a little suspicious about doing so, and asked him what guarantee we would have that they would not fire on the one crossing. He then told us that he had made arrangements with the other guards about that, and we would be in no danger... We hesitated for a few moments, and talked the matter over among ourselves, when Fralich, who was getting impatient, grabbed the buttons, and stepping over the dead-line, ran to the stockade with them. He threw them up to the guard, and catching the bag that the guard dropped containing the victuals, he safely returned to us... We watched him examining the buttons, but as he said nothing, we supposed he could not discover the difference in the dark. In the morning when he came on post he told us that we had cheated him. He did not appear to care much, and laughed over the matter, saying that we were up to all kinds of 'Yankee tricks.'"[100]

One prisoner, Francis Curtis, described an interesting contract he made to obtain food from the guards. "About this time, the last of January, 1865, a soldier from a New York regiment, an Irishman, came to me and said he was trading with a guard, and could get me some flour, little biscuits and occasionally an egg; and when I reached home I was to pay him twice in value what he was getting there. I was from Massachusetts, sick, with little prospect of getting home, and a total stranger, I accepted his kind offer, and have the account at home today. Finally I persuaded him to give my companion, Davis, food on the same terms. Davis was able to get home in May, and, stopping in New York, paid both bills."[101]

Kellogg felt he needed to vary his diet and so decided to trade his gold pen. He succeeded in selling it to a rebel lieutenant for three bars of soap. He then sold the soap for five dollars and twenty-five cents in greenbacks. With this

---

[94] Clifton, p. 7.
[95] Berry, p. 340.
[96] *Wirz Trial*, p. 676.
[97] *Ibid.*
[98] Urban, p. 393.
[99] *Wirz Trial*, p. 484.
[100] Urban, pp. 393-395.
[101] *Massachusetts Monument*, p. 35.

he went to the rebel sutler and invested in beans and salt.

The guards realized they could make a fast profit by re-selling various commodities. This speculating was called "dickering" by the prisoners.[102] The guards began to buy items with an eye towards wheeling and dealing with the prisoners. This was strictly prohibited. Even some ladies in the surrounding area, left at home while their loved ones were away at war, learned they could earn extra household money by selling near the stockade. Thus, every day there would gather around the pen "... hucksters with barrels and baskets of vegetables, meat, and poultry. Ladies deprived themselves and families of flour, sugar, and molasses, to bake cakes and pies for the thriving Andersonville market."[103]

Andrew J. Spring, of the 16th Connecticut, testified: "I procured vegetables after I was outside in the bakery. I procured all that I needed, and also sent quantities in to our boys by smuggling them by the guards. I procured them mostly from the 55th Georgia boys, and the 3rd Georgia regiment's sutler furnished me with a supply that I had. I think there was plenty of green corn to be had there; there was a large cornfield about a quarter of a mile the other side of the big stream, below the 55th Georgia regiment; I should think there was quite a large field there, 75 to 100 acres, I should think. I purchased vegetables of citizens. Citizens would very frequently smuggle things down there by the bake-house on their wagons, pretending that they had business there. They would stop and sell provisions to us for the sake of getting greenbacks; they would rather trade with us than with their own men, because they could get hold of greenbacks; there were strict orders prohibiting trading of that kind. The orders were issued by Captain Wirz. That was a peach-growing country. I procured great quantities of peaches there and smuggled them into the stockade to our boys. I should judge the supply was good from the way they came in; almost any of the confederate troops had peaches there in any quantity. When such things were taken into the stockade to our boys, Captain Wirz, if he discovered it, would confiscate them, and take them to his headquarters; and he also gave orders to the sergeants at the gates that of all the things which they could confiscate from our boys, they should have one-half for getting it away from them. That applied to vegetables, peaches, sweet potatoes, onions, and all such things as that that we get."[104]

Another commodity that was the object of "dickering" was Federal currency; the greenback. Confederate currency had a blue field on the reverse of most bills and so was called a "blueback." No Yankee dollars were allowed, officially, within the prison. This presented a problem for the Confederate administrators. Any one of about four things could happen concerning greenbacks. They could be confiscated as contraband. Any time more than one hundred dollars was found, the Confederates considered it was Federal government money and subject to confiscation. Some money was stolen by the inspecting "Examiners" when the prisoners were admitted. Some prisoners were given worthless receipts which could not be redeemed and others were given bluebacks in compensation at the official rate of exchange. This was always less than the "going" rate set in the market place.

The official rate was about four-and-a-half to one, but the unofficial rate varied by how many rich "fresh fish" had recently entered the pen. The men from Plymouth were especially well-off because they had been allowed to keep their personal belongings. Most of them arrived in good health with their knapsacks intact. Thus, money was then more plentiful and the rate of exchange dropped. During the hard times in the fall of 1864 with the high rate of inflation as the value of the currency of the Confederacy in its twilight plummeted, the rate was forty bluebacks to one greenback. As the inflation hit the Confederacy, the depreciation of money continued until "... a soldier paid a darkey two hundred dollars to hold his horse while the soldier ate his dinner."[105]

The possession of a large sum of money was not permitted within the prison because, if it were to be offered to a guard for a man's freedom, it might be too tempting. Many guards were bribed in this fashion. Several men made their escapes by having the guards turn their heads as the prisoners sneaked off into the surrounding woods.

"There was a man inside who made greenbacks. He made them out of paper, with a lead pencil and green pencil. That is all that he used that I know of. I could not say what kind of paper he used... at twilight, at the time when these bills were generally passed."[106]

A Unionist [probably Spencer], who lived in the vicinity of Andersonville, wrote, in a newspaper article, after the war; "The writer of this was the foreman of the last grand jury which was impaneled for Sumter County, Georgia, and, in the performance of his duties, he had to investigate a large number of presentments for dealing in the forbid-

[102] Stevenson, p. 20.
[103] Spencer, p. 41.
[104] *Wirz Trial*, p. 111.
[105] Smith, p. 15.
[106] *Wirz Trial*, p. 583.

den currency, which was brought against poor Union men in every instance. Struck by this fact, he resolved to examine, as his position gave him a right to do, into all the circumstances; where money originally came from, who did the selling of it, indeed the whole modus operandi, and he elicited the fact above stated, how the money was obtained, that the Winders and Wertz [sic] were the principals, acting through subordinates, in gathering bushels of plums, in the way of premiums, etc. Meanwhile the prisoners were left to the tender mercies of their jailer and commissary for their food, which might have been improved in quantity at least, if their money had been left in their own possession."[107]

Spencer said the hierarchy at Andersonville made money by entrapping speculators in greenbacks at the post: "If any unfortunate purchaser of the prohibited currency was suspected of using it for remittance to the North, to pay his debts contracted before the war, the same men who had sold him the funds, and who had received their pay for them, would enter a complaint in the form before a justice of the Superior Court of the county, who resided conveniently near the post, and the unlucky operator was arrested under the law, torn from his family, and turned over to the tender mercies of the provost marshal...

"Cases like this were a daily occurrence; if the business became dull, the detectives who General Winder brought out with him were set to work, and some ignorant subject was inveigled into the snare which was artfully contrived for him, and while engaged in a bargain for the denounced money, would be arrested and marched off for punishment, by using mulcted in black mail, or confinement until the next grand jury of the county met to investigate his case, and probably indict him. If he proved to be made of pliable stuff, and sought to escape farther annoyance, he compromised the matter with W. S. Winder, the adjutant, by paying him a round sum, besides forfeiting into his lenient hands the greenbacks which he had obtained from his cousin; but if the accused was obstinate, he was at once arrested by a warrant granted by the convenient justice above referred to, and, under heavy bonds, awaited the issue of his trial.

"The records of the court of Sumter County yet exhibit numerous indictments which were found for violating this law of the Confederacy, when the defendants had proved too contumacious for the manipulations of the adjutant.

"One case may be cited as an instance of proof of all others. An Israelite, not entirely 'without guile' on the question of good money, was approached by one of these detective harpies of General Winder's, and induced to go up to Andersonville, where the victim was told in great confidence that he could purchase any quantity of the coveted greenbacks from the sutler. Arrived there, they enter the store, the door was closed and locked, and the transaction began. Twenty-five for one was asked and given; the national currency safely deposited in the purchaser's pocket, the loyal money placed in the sutler's till. Just at this critical moment a signal cough was given, a body was projected through an open window, the Jew was in the grasp of a detective, and marched off to the provost marshal's, and by him sent to the guard-house. For three days the prisoner suffered durance, when he at last succeeded in gaining an interview with Adjutant Winder. The result of the conference was he gained his liberty, but he paid into that officer's hand the three thousand dollars of disloyal money which he had purchased from R. B. Winder's sutler, with two thousand five hundred dollars of Confederate currency in addition, and then went his way to his home, a poorer but certainly a wiser man. He had been taught a lesson in cent. per cent. by a Gentile which excited his wonder, if it did not arouse his envy at the skill displayed,"[108]

It must be remembered that Ambrose Spencer, a biased Unionist, relayed this incident.

Some prisoners accidentally stumbled into the deadline and were shot. Some reached under the fatal line to reach for a root or to get the purest water upstream and were shot. Others were so depressed and or insane they took their own lives, intentionally.

"One day I saw a prisoner who had become insane rush inside the deadline, and baring his breast call on the guard to shoot him. Ordinarily this would not have needed a second invitation, but the guard happened to be humane, and called to the comrades of the man to take him back to his tent. Another day a prisoner who was sleeping in his tent alongside the deadline, and whose foot in his sleep protruded within the limit, was fired at and wounded."[109]

"That unoffending men were shot down without warning, there is no doubt whatever; that men, weary of torture, staggered to the deadline, and calmly, joyfully received the fatal shot, there is positive evidence."[110] Boggs said

---

[107] Author's library.
[108] Spencer, pp. 51-53
[109] Miller, p. 16.
[110] Hamlin, p. 53.

that the number of men who were shot after intentionally having walked into the deadline "... could be counted by scores."[111] Northrop said that "... from three to six shots [were] fired nightly by sentries."[112]

"In justice to the old men, I will say that all the shooting was done by the boys, and at least a few of those old men denounced the shooting as an outrage. I remember hearing one who was on guard, and was speaking to some prisoners on the inside, say that 'God would not prosper a nation or people who used human beings as we were being treated.'"[113] After one man stepped inside the deadline, the sentinel fired and, missing his target, wounded two men innocently lying down in their tent.[114]

In the third week in June, "One poor fellow was shot through the body just for reaching inside the 'line,' to get a root for the purpose of making a little fire to do some cooking. The one who thus shoots a soldier, it is said, receives a 'furlough,' as a reward for the very virtuous deed he has done. The absolute truth of this I can not vouch for, but I have noticed that almost invariably the man who performs such an act is relieved from duty by another person, and he is not seen."[115]

"I very well remember, one case, - that of one of those nude men who had been wandering around the grounds in the broiling sun all day until late in the afternoon. When he came up to the deadline on the west side near the South Gate, observing the shade of the stockade, he deliberately crawled under the deadline and started for the shade. When about half way, men who were trying to call the poor fellow back saw the guard raise his gun, and called out to him, 'Don't shoot! Don't shoot! The man is crazy.' He gave no heed to their entreaties, but fired. The man fell mortally wounded. There he lay for hours writhing in agony, but the authorities did nothing to relieve him, and about sunset he breathed his last. No comrade dared go to his assistance."[116]

James K. Davidson testified, "I saw two men shot there by the guards; I do not know the names of either of them; it was down on the east side of the stockade near the branch; the man had been washing his clothes and was hanging them on the guard line to dry; one of the garments blew over the dead-line; he reached through to pick it up, when the guard fired and shot him; I think it was the last of March or the first of April, 1864. The other case happened on the north side of the stockade; the men reached through the dead-line to pick up some crumbs of bread that had been thrown out there, and he was shot; he was killed. The other man was killed instantly; he was shot in the breast; the second man was shot in the head; I do not know his name."[117]

John Burns Walker, of the 141st Pennsylvania infantry, testified about a prisoner who was killed in his sleep at about 10 o'clock on the night of September 4th. He heard a gun shot, went out of his tent and to a near-by tent, where a man had received a head wound which caused his brains to be scattered around the vicinity. Walker testified, "I know the man's name was Prendiville, because I wrote it on a paper and pinned it on his breast; I wrote the cause of his death - that he was shot by the guard - and I pinned the paper on his shirt bosom. I made a memorandum at the time for myself, and I have it here. I wrote this on the morning after the man's death.

> 'Morris Prendiville, Co. H, 7th Indiana regiment, infantry; shot through the head on the night of the 4th of September, 1864, by the rebel guard. He was asleep in his tent, directly opposite the post. The guard had no cause to commit the crime.'

The Judge Advocate later stated, in reference to this death: "I desire to call the attention of the court to the following extract from the hospital register:

> '11,230, Prendiville, M., private 7th Indiana, Co. H, complaint unknown; admitted September 6th; died in quarters.'"[118]

W. W. Crandall, of the 4th Iowa infantry regiment testified: " I buried dead at Andersonville. I assisted in burying the dead from June 23, 1864, until September 8. I was detailed for that duty. It would be pretty hard to tell the number of prisoners that I buried who had been shot, because it became so common a thing that we did not fix the number. I should say at least thirty, possibly forty, and it may be more. I cannot tell the exact number."[119]

There were at least three reasons for a sentry to shoot a prisoner: he had a legitimate reason; a prisoner crossed

---

[111] Boggs, p. 40.
[112] Northrop, p. 85
[113] Urban, p. 358.
[114] Kellogg, p. 143.
[115] Kellogg, pp.146, 147.
[116] Lyons, p. 62.
[117] *Wirz Trial*, p. 142.
[118] *Ibid.*, p. 350.
[119] *Ibid.*, p. 257.

the deadline in a suicide attempt; or just for pure "sport," as in Yankee hatred.

An incident at about noon on Sunday, May 15th, illustrates the diverse descriptions given by some authors of a soldier and the fate he met within the prison. This interesting, one-legged character, crippled since he had lost his leg at the Battle of Chickamauga, roamed the pen. His name was Hubbard; he was probably from Chicago, Illinois, and had served in the Thirty-eighth Illinois Infantry Regiment.

**The Death of Chickamauga** - This depicts the death of a crippled prisoner who was suspected of betraying a tunnel to the Confederate authorities. He committed suicide by stepping across the deadline when threatened by his fellow prisoners. (Goss)

Because of his facial features, this hook-nosed man was known by some authors as "Pol Parrot," "Hook-Nose" and "Pretty Pol." Others called him "Chickamauga" because of the place of his capture. One of the few times Chickamauga was identified as being the same person as Pol Parrot was in the testimony of a prisoner: "I saw a one-legged man;' they called him 'Chickamauga,' and sometimes 'Pretty Polly,' at the front gate."[120] Another, Ambrose Henmen, a private in Co. L, 4th United States cavalry, testified: "I saw a man shot at the South Gate, about the last of May, 1864. The man had several names - 'Pretty Polly,' 'Fortune Teller,' and 'Chickamauga.' Captain Wirz was present at the time he was shot. Pretty Polly, as I called him, went up to the gate. Wirz was at the wicket gate, having the gate open. Pretty Polly asked him to let him out. Captain Wirz drew his revolver and told him that he could not get out. Pretty Polly seemed to be afraid of the raiders inside, as they called them. Wirz drove him back from the dead-line and closed the gate and walked out. Chickamauga walked inside the dead-line and sat down, saying he would rather be shot by their men than be killed by our own men. Wirz ordered the sentinel to shoot him. The sentinel hesitated, and before the sentinel fired, Wirz went up to the sentry box with his revolver drawn. But before he got there the sentry fired at the man and shot him down, the ball striking him in the chin and passing through the breast. I heard nothing about furloughs. I spoke to Captain Wirz at the time, after the man was shot, and asked the privilege of taking him from the dead-line. He gave me permission, telling me to take him and go to hell with him.

"I picked him up and carried him back about four rods from the deadline. He lay down there and died. The men crowded around there so much to see him, that Captain Wirz ordered the sentinel to fire again. I saw Captain Wirz up in the sentry box. I did not see him before he went to the sentry box. I could not see over the stockade. I saw him at the gate before the man was shot. He drew his revolver and ordered him back. There was some crowd. Captain Wirz went to the sentry box. He gave orders to the sentinel, before he went up, to shoot the Yankee son of a bitch. The sentinel was only a few feet from where the crowd stood."[121]

Others called him "mutton-head" because he was slightly dim-witted. Others called him "Frenchie" because most of the men in the prison who were neither American nor German were called by this name. Some thought he was a Canadian by birth. "In our intercourse with fellow-prisoners we were known often to each other by the State from which we came, and by our service, more than by our real names."[122]

Some said he was a member of the 38th Illinois Regiment, 84th Illinois Regiment, or the 8th Missouri Regiment. A prisoner, Thomas Walsh, testified he had been confined in the same prison building in Richmond and that they had

[120] *Ibid.*, pp. 297, 298.
[121] *Ibid.*, p. 373.
[122] Hugh Moore, *Journal of the Illinois State Historical Society*, Clifford H. Haka, Assoc. Ed. (Springfield, Illinois: Winter 1972), Vol. LXV No. 4., p. 459.

come down together on February 29th.

Hubbard had been suspected of betraying several unsuccessful attempts to tunnel to freedom. Finally, the frustrated tunnelers decided to capture Pol Parrot and punish him. He pleaded his innocence and, since this fell on deaf ears, he decided to commit suicide. He crossed the deadline, pulled open his shirt, and implored the guard to shoot, saying: "If I have lost the confidence of my comrades I want to die." The guard fired and the buckshot and ball tore away the lower jaw of Pol Parrot and entered the lower part of the neck.[123]

Belcher said the cripple stayed in the deadline 15 or 20 minutes and 150 to 200 prisoners gathered around the deadline at the time of this incident.[124]

There was a rumor among all the prisoners that, if a guard killed a prisoner, the guard would be rewarded with a sixty-day furlough. If the prisoner were only wounded, the guard would only receive a thirty-day furlough. "So whenever the report of a gun was heard, the boys would call out 'Furlough!' 'Furlough!'"[125]

At Wirz' trial, there was some discussion as to whether Captain Wirz had the authority to issue 30- and 60-day furloughs. Captain James H. Wright, quartermaster of the 55th Georgia regiment, testified: "After General Winder came there he had authority to give thirty days' furloughs, and I suppose when Captain Wirz was acting in his place he could give such furloughs, but when Colonel Persons was there he had authority to give only seven days' furloughs, and when Captain Wirz was acting in his place he could only give seven days' furloughs...I do not think the commander of the post had any right to give furloughs for longer than seven days."[126]

Wirz' clerk, Benjamin F. Dilley, whose desk was right beside Wirz', testified: "I do not think Captain Wirz had authority to give a 30 days' furlough. He gave furloughs for eight days, when the colonel commanding the post was absent. It was about harvest time, and the men wanted to go home and attend to their grain when these furloughs were given. There was not any other time that I know of that furloughs were given by Captain Wirz. I never heard tell of such a thing as a furlough being given for shooting a Union prisoner."[127]

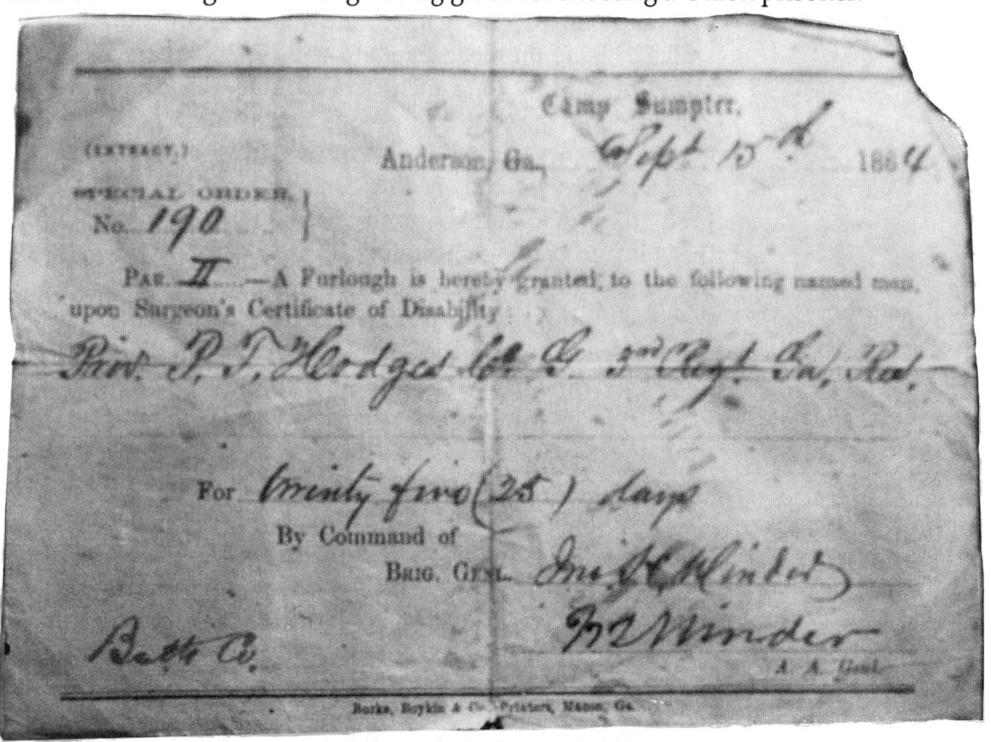

Camp Sumpter,
(EXTRACT.) Anderson, Ga., Sept 15th 1864
SPECIAL ORDER, No. 190
PAR. II —A Furlough is hereby granted, to the following named men, upon Surgeon's Certificate of Disability
Pvt. P. T. Hodges Co. G. 3rd Regt. Ga. Res.
For twenty five (25) days
By Command of
Brig. Gen. Jno. H. Winder
Bath Co. W S Winder
A. A. Genl.
Burke, Boykin & Co., Printers, Macon, Ga.

**Furlough Granted upon Surgeon's Certificate of Disability** - given to Private P.T. Hodges, Co. G., 3rd Regt., Ga. Reserves for 25 days by command of Brig. Gen. John H. Winder, signed by W.S. Winder, A.A.Gen'l. (Author's Collection)

One prisoner testified that he knew of one instance of a furlough being granted: "I was out on parole most of the winter, from the 21st of November, 1864, until the time I left. My duties outside the stockade was writing for Captain Wirz. I had no particular duties assigned to me, but to assist in writing... I made out a furlough once for a man who killed one of our own men; he received the furlough for thirty days. His name was Scott; he belonged to the fourth Georgia reserves. The man he killed was Henry Lockmire, belonging to some Pennsylvania regiment. It was in the latter part of February, 1865. The soldier came there and claimed his furlough, saying that he had earned it by killing a man. I don't recollect what Captain

---

[123] Boggs, p. 33.
[124] *Ibid.*, p. 135.
[125] Helwig, p. 25.
[126] *Wirz Trial*, p. 407.
[127] *Ibid.* , p. 673.

Wirz said to him, only he ordered me to make out a furlough for him for thirty days...I know it was for that cause, because the men said it was, and it was known that the men were receiving furloughs for killing our men. Captain Wirz gave furloughs to the troops who were guarding the prison... I believe General Gartrell had command of the troops during the latter part of the time "[128]

The prisoner continued: "That is the only instance I know of... He said he shot the man two days before he applied for the furlough. He stated that he was on duty, at the time he shot him, on the east side of the prison hospital and outside the hospital. There was no question asked then about what kind of a man he had shot; the day he killed the man he was questioned about it... I understand that Captain Wirz had questioned him. Captain Wirz told me to write out the furlough and he signed it."[129]

One Confederate soldier, a private in the First Georgia Reserves, wrote a letter to President Jefferson Davis, protesting the illegal shooting of prisoners by young, trigger-happy sentinels.

*First Regiment Georgia Reserves,*
*Camp Sumter, June 23, 1864.*
*President Jefferson Davis:*

*Respected Sir:*

*Being but a private in the ranks at this place, consequently if I see anything to condemn (as I do) I have no power to correct it. Yet as a humane being and one that believes that we should 'do as we would be done by,' I proceed to inform you of some things that I know you are ignorant of, and in the first place I will say I have no cause to love the Yankees (they having driven myself and family from our home in New Orleans to seek our living amongst strangers), yet I think that prisoners should have some showing. Inside our prison walls all around there is a space about twelve feet wide, called the 'dead-line.' If a prisoner crosses that line the sentinels are ordered to shoot him. Now, we have many thoughtless boys here who think the killing of a Yankee will make them great men. As a consequence, every day or two there are prisoners shot. When the officer of the guard goes to the sentry stand, there is a dead or badly wounded man invariably within their own lines. The sentry, of course, says he was across the dead-line when he shot him. He is told he did exactly right and is a good sentry. Last Sabbath there were two shot in their tents at one shot. The boy said that he shot at one across the dead-line. Night before last there was one shot near me (I being on guard). The sentry said that the Yankee made one step across the line to avoid a mud hole. He shot him through the bowels, and when the officer of the guard got there he was lying inside their own lines. He (the sentry) as usual told him that he stepped across, but fell back inside. The officer told him it was exactly right. Now, my dear sir, I know you are opposed to such measures, and I make this statement to you knowing you to be a soldier, statesman, and Christian, that if possible you may correct such things, together with many others that exist here. And yet if you send an agent there he will of course go amongst the officers, tell his business, and be told that all is well, but let a good man come here as a private citizen and mix with the privates and stay one week, and if he don't find out things revolting to humanity then I am deceived. I shall put my name to this, believing that you will not let the officers over me see it, otherwise I would suffer, most probably.*

*"Yours, most respectfully,*
*James E. Anderson,*

[This letter was endorsed:]

*July 23, 1864.*
*Respectfully referred, by Direction of the President, to the Honorable Secretary of War*
*J. C. Ives,*
*Colonel and Aide-de-Camp.*[130]

From the endorsement, it can be seen that the President of the Confederate States received it and forwarded it to the Secretary of War. The disposition of this appeal for justice was never made apparent.

About the 24th or 25th of June, meetings were held in the pen and six men were appointed to be a committee of prisoners to go to Washington to meet with Lincoln to entreat him to exchange prisoners. They were sent away with the blessing of Captain Wirz and General Winder. In fact, General Winder forwarded a copy of the resolutions and the petition to Lincoln. The original was given into the hands of Colonel Hall, at Hilton Head, with a letter from Major General Stoneman. The paper was taken by Lieutenant Prescott Tracy and given to Colonel Hall, who was deputy

[128] *Ibid.*, p. 299.
[129] *Ibid.*, p. 300.
[130] *O. R.*,

provost marshal under General Foster. There was some discussion at the trial as to whether the petition was received by the authorities.

The committee of six was composed of Prescott Tracy, Sylvester Norrit, Dennison, Johnson, Higginson, and Edward Wellington Boate. Twenty-one prisoners, including the six commissioners, left Andersonville and went to Macon; from Macon, they went to Augusta, then down to Charleston; from there, they traveled to Beaufort, and from there to a place in the vicinity called Pocotaligo, where nine of the twenty-one were exchanged. Two of the committee of six were detained. The remainder went to New York and Tracy took the delivery of the paper into his own hands. He applied to General Dix for transportation to Washington, but he was refused and he came to Washington with the aid of the Sanitary Commission. They were refused an audience with the President and the Secretary of War. After this, a proposition was made to the Federal government to send 15,000 prisoners home without asking any equivalent. This, too, was refused.[131]

On the 22nd of July, 1862, a cartel of exchange was drawn up and agreed to by General John A. Dix of the U.S.A. and by General Daniel H. Hill of the C.S.A. It stated that all prisoners of war were to be discharged on parole in ten days after their capture. The prisoners were to be taken to points mutually agreed-upon, at the expense of the capturing side. The surplus prisoners on one side who were not exchanged were not permitted to go back into service until declared exchanged.

Alkin's Landing, on the James River, about thirty miles south of Richmond and Vicksburg, on the Mississippi, were chosen as the points of exchange. General Lorenzo Thomas was chosen the first Federal Commissioner of Exchange, and Judge Robert Ould was chosen Confederate Commissioner of Exchange.

**Judge Ould** - Confederate Commissioner of Exchange who had the very difficult job of trying to swap prisoners. The Federal government was reluctant to receive very weak and debilitated prisoners in exchange for relatively healthy Confederate prisoners who had been given new uniformas. The problem of captured former slaves who had joined the Federal army was another obstacle.

For about a year, the cartel worked smoothly with very little friction between the two belligerents. During that period, there were slightly more captures by the Confederates than by the Unionists. This advantage was lost after the captures made by the Union forces at Gettysburg, Vicksburg, and Port Hudson in July of 1863. Many minor disagreements and petty arguments that were not resolved finally culminated in the total suspension of the exchange.

A few of the causes of friction between the belligerents are shown in the following incidents and situations. In the spring of 1863, Colonel A. D. Streight, with a cavalry brigade, went on a raid through northern Alabama. He had been ordered on the raid by General Rosecrans. This group of raiders did much damage by destroying military targets until forced to surrender near Rome, Georgia, to General N. B. Forrest. In the course of the raid, a large group of Negroes from Alabama had sought refuge within the raiding party. Streight and his officers were to have been paroled and exchanged "... as soon as practicable."

The higher-ups in Richmond informed Colonel Ludlow, who had become the Federal Commissioner of Exchange, that Colonel Streight and his officers would be turned over to the authorities in Alabama. Alabama Governor Shorter requested they be brought to his state so that they might be tried in the state courts there "... for abducting slaves."

Also, by special order of the President, the Confederates refused to release the officers of General Milroy's command who had been captured at Winchester on about the middle of June in 1863. Another point of disagreement

131 *Wirz Trial*, pp. 692-696.

was caused by the paroling of captured Yankee prisoners at the places of capture by "... independent commands under Mosby, Imboden, Ferguson, McNeil, Morgan, and Quantrill." These independent raiders were not equipped to handle and transport captured prisoners to the points of exchange as specified in the cartel. The Confederates wished to charge these prisoners off on their side of the ledger, but the Federal authorities thought their exchange illegal and promptly ordered the released men back to duty.

When the men of Confederate General Pemberton were captured at Vicksburg, the whole group was restored to active duty immediately by the Confederate army. This was thought by the Federals to be in direct violation of the cartel.

Another violation, according to the Federals, was the retention of "... citizens, army surgeons, and chaplains" as prisoners when captured by Lee in the Pennsylvania campaign.

The Federals were also very upset over the treatment of captured white officers who had been in predominately black units. President Davis issued an order which stated that, when Negroes who had been runaway slaves enlisted in the Northern army and were captured, they were to be returned to their former masters. The officers of these "black" regiments were treated with the utmost indignity and cruelty by their Southern captors.[132] Some were treated as non-entities and were kept months after their fellow officers in predominately white units had been exchanged. They were made to eat and sleep with their black enlisted men and none of the social advantages or privileges of rank were extended to them. In fact, Secretary James A. Seddon said, "As to white officers serving with negro troops, we ought never to be inconvenienced with such prisoners."[133]

Lieutenant-General U. S. Grant wrote to Major General B. F. Butler on April 17th, 1864: "No distinction whatever will be made in the exchange between white and colored prisoners...Non-acquiescence by the Confederate authorities to these propositions will be regarded as a refusal on their part to agree to the further exchange of prisoners, and will be so treated by us."[134]

The Confederate authorities were often cited for their lack of supplying clothing and barracks for their Federal prisoners. Of course, it is well-accepted now the South could not do so, because it could not even clothe its own troops.

At one time, the South petitioned Secretary Seward to send clothes for the Federal prisoners. The reply was the Federal government would not supply clothing to prisoners of war. A society in New York volunteered to send several bales of clothing and cases of shoes which were forwarded to Richmond. There, the clothes were divided and distributed in proportion to the number of men in the various prisons.[135]

Boxes of goodies from loved ones sent down by the *Flag of Truce* boat to City Point, were "... stored, thousands in number and for months, in Kerr's warehouse, in full sight and within fifty feet of Libby Prison, from whose east windows the famishing owners could plainly read their names on the covers."[136]

"General Hayes learned that in a building, not far from our quarters had been stored a number of packages sent through the lines for our prisoners, and he directed me to visit the building and to give him a report. I found some thousands of packages which had accumulated for years and many of which had crumbled almost to dust. The sight was really pathetic when one bore in mind the loving thought with which the little parcels had been prepared in Northern homes and had been sent forth as a greeting to the soldier member of the family. It is difficult to understand just what the idea of the prison authorities had been in regard to these packages. They had received them by flag of truce with the understanding, if not with the promise, that they would be delivered as far as the men to whom they were addressed were within reach. No trouble, however, appears to have been taken to look up the owners. The fragments of many opened packages indicated that things which gave any appearance of value had been appropriated by the guards, while the thousands of packages that remained had simply been thrown into a corner of the tobacco warehouse to rot. The contents of such of the parcels as were still intact were naturally varied. I remember, among the things that remained, testaments, locks of hair, packs of cards, and reading matter of one kind or another, from hymns to melodramatic romances. With these articles were in most cases loving short signatures which gave no clue to the full name of the writer. Not a few of the packages had contained food and these had naturally decayed with the damp or had been eaten by rats and by insects. The traces of food could, however, still be noted on the wrappers.

---

132 Moran, pp. 1-6.
133 *O. R.*, VII, p. 204.
134 *Ibid.*, pp. 62, 63.
135 Stevenson, p. 454.
136 Moran, p. 29.

"I made out lists of the names and addresses that could still be deciphered on the wrappers of the parcels which were not too much decayed and the contents of which could still be of value for the prisoners. These lists I compared with the rosters of the prisons and in the chance that some of the roster names might not have been correctly entered, I took pains more than once to call out the names at the roll-call of the prisoners. I recall but one or two instances in which I was able to connect the men with the parcels. The accumulation had been going on for such a period of months and of years that the men had very largely disappeared, either by exchange or by death. The general finally told me to give up the task as not worth further labour."[137]

Dr. M. M. Marsh was in charge of United States Sanitary Commission matters in the states of Florida, Georgia, North Carolina, and South Carolina. He was employed in this capacity from January of 1863 until the end of the war. His headquarters was at Beaufort, South Carolina. One of his jobs was to send clothing and provisions and sanitary stores through the lines for the benefit of the Federal soldiers held in Southern prisons. When the Sanitary Commission was out of a certain article of clothing, Dr. Marsh would buy that article from the United States quartermasters. It was his particular job to forward the supplies to Andersonville. The sanitary stores were sent through the lines to five other prisons.

The following is a list of the supplies that were sent to Andersonville only:

| | | | | | |
|---|---|---|---|---|---|
| 5,052 | wool shirts | 46 | cotton pants | 4,092 | pounds condensed milk |
| 6,993 | wool drawers | 534 | wrappers | 4,032 | pounds condensed coffee |
| 3,950 | handerchiefs | 69 | jackets | 1,000 | pounds farina |
| 601 | cotton shirts | 12 | overalls | 1,000 | pounds corn starch |
| 1,128 | cotton drawers | 817 | pairs slippers | 4,212 | pounds tomatoes |
| 2,100 | Blouses | 3,147 | Towels | 24 | pounds chocolate |
| 4,235 | wool pants | 5,431 | wool socks | 3 | boxes lemon juice |
| 1,520 | wool hats | 50 | pillow cases | 1 | barrel dried apples |
| 2,565 | Overcoats | 258 | bed sacks | 111 | barrels crackers |
| 5,385 | Blankets | 122 | Combs | 60 | boxes cocoa |
| 272 | quilts | 100 | Tin cups | 7,200 | pounds beef stock |
| 2,120 | pairs shoes | 2 | Boxes tin ware | | Paper, envelopes, &c. |
| 110 | cotton coats | | | | Pepper, mustard |
| 140 | vests | | | 1 | box tea, 70 pounds [138] |

Dr. Marsh testified that a pound of beef stock was supposed to equal about seven pounds of beef. The condensed milk and the condensed coffee were equal to five pounds of the real thing. A small portion of these articles were sent in the month of July. He began to send them quite regularly from about the 10th or the 15th of August up until about the 1st of November. He testified that he had no evidence any of those articles ever reached the prisoners at Andersonville.

On two of three occasions, he personally passed the stores over to some agent authorized by the Confederate government to receive them. At other times, the supplies were sent by his agent and received by an agent of the Confederate government. This agent of the Confederate government usually, but not always, gave a receipt for the articles with a promise, on Dr. Marsh's part, that he would return the receipt when he obtained it from the persons who took final delivery of the packages. If the things were sent to a single prisoner, then this prisoner's receipt was to be returned. Once or twice, some of the Confederate agents who were sent to receive the goods refused to give receipt. A Colonel Waddy, on one or two occasions, refused to give a receipt.

Augustus Moesner, of Company G, Sixteenth Connecticut Volunteers, arrived at the prison on May 3rd and, on May 24th, was detailed as a clerk in Wirz' office. He testified that he never saw any provisions sent by the Sanitary

---

[137] George Haven Putman, *A Prisoner of War in Virginia* (The Knickerbocker Press, 1914), p. 74.
[138] Chipman, p. 158.

Commission and, since he visited the cookhouse every day, he probably would have seen them if they had been there.[139]

Augustus Moesner further testified: "As far as I recollect we got boxes from the north three times. The first boxes we received came in May, 1864. Those boxes were boxes sent from the friends of prisoners and not from the Sanitary Commission. The boxes were brought into the stockade and every one who received a box had to sign a receipt...A few days afterwards I was paroled and came out, and we had close to our office a shanty where some provisions for the hospital were kept. I saw many boxes in there. I asked one of the clerks 'what kind of boxes those were,' and he told me that those were boxes for prisoners who could not be found or who had died. The things in those boxes were turned over to the hospital and the confederate hospital steward divided them... The second time we got boxes was in August. We got at this time only a few boxes. Lieutenant Davis was in command of the camp. We got about sixty or seventy pairs of pants, about 100 blouses, 100 caps, and fifty pairs of shoes... The third and last time I recollect that we got some boxes was in the first part of November, 1864. We got about 300 blankets and 300 pairs of pants. They were what are known as citizens' pants, brown and gray, a mixed color, and we got gray shirts and gray drawers and stockings, but only fifty pairs of shoes...There were no prisoners in the stockade then, only those in the hospital and the men who were paroled. Captain Wirz sent down for all the paroled men, about 150, and they were brought to our office and every one of those paroled men got a whole suit, except shoes, because we had only fifty pairs of shoes. Our chief clerk, Martin, called the roll and I had a sheet of paper and wrote down the names of the men as they were called, with their rank, regiment, and company; there were several columns in which I marked down what each man received, and after he had received it he had to sign his name, or if he could not write he made a cross and I put my name down as witness...The other things were turned over to the confederate hospital steward; he came over and the things were counted off all together and he signed a receipt for them and they were brought over to the hospital or Dr. Stevenson's office."[140]

The Unionist Doctor Bates testified: "I saw some sanitary commission goods which had been received at the prison from the north for the prisoners - nothing like provisions, though - clothing and blankets. I do not recollect in what quantities. I thought it was quite a genteel little present, under the circumstances, but far too short to supply their wants. I saw the boys wearing the clothing afterwards; I saw some with pants, some with drawers, some shirts, some with blankets. I know of no misappropriation of supplies of that character, which arrived from the north."[141]

"Captain Wirz gave orders that if he caught any rebels wearing our uniforms he would have him court-martialed; those were his words. He said it had been done at Belle Island, but it should not be done at Andersonville."[142]

A prisoner, Benjamin F. Dilley, who was detailed as a clerk in Wirz' headquarters, testified; "We found the addresses of some of the men from the book, and the boxes were sent to them into the stockade. Those that were not sent to the hospital. So far as my knowledge goes that applies only to the boxes sent to Belle Island. The sanitary goods were distributed to the hospital. I do not know of any of them being distributed in the stockade. There were thirteen blankets, some shirts, and several pairs of pants distributed in my ward, in which we had 80 men. The robbing of the boxes was done by Wirz' sergeants - Duncan, Ritchie, Kerr, and those men. Duncan frequently came up in the mornings and took whiskey and provisions of every kind out of that hospital commissary building. It was notorious that he did that; many of us knew it, but Captain Wirz did not know it. I knew it. I was in Captain Wirz' headquarters. Martin knew something about it. He was Captain Wirz' head clerk. If he had a confidential friend, Martin was the man."[143]

Dilley said the hospital commissary building was a small building about 50 yards behind Wirz' office. The hospital steward and "Wirz' sergeant" had a key.

Another prisoner testified: "I saw boxes of clothing and other articles sent by the sanitary commission; I saw them at the depot and at Captain Wirz' headquarters; I saw mostly dried beef and dried apples, fruit of almost all descriptions; I saw clothing; I never saw either clothing or rations of that kind issued to the prisoners; I have seen rebels wearing the clothes; I have seen them using our blankets and shirts, and also shoes that I knew were ours; I never saw them using the rations; I have seen Captain Wirz make use of some of those articles; I have seen him use some of the crackers and cheese and dried beef at his office; I saw boxes lying there containing sanitary stores that

---

[139] *Ibid.*, p. 41.
[140] *Wirz Trial*, pp. 537, 538.
[141] *Ibid.*, p. 41.
[142] *Ibid.*, p. 672.
[143] *Ibid.*, 697.

were not good; I saw them in August or about the 1st of September; they had been there all summer, I believe; I saw the same boxes previously; I think I have seen at the depot as high as four or five hundred boxes of different sizes from the sanitary commission; I knew that those boxes contained sanitary goods because they were marked "U.S.'"[144]

Doctor A. V. Barrows, the U. S. acting assistant post surgeon at Plymouth, testified: "At the dispensary, which was a small log building, there was also another small building, and in that there were supplies, I think, which I was told came from Richmond, from our lines. I can enumerate some of the articles; there was dry beef - perhaps two or three hundred pounds; Bologna sausages, and some such articles of diet. I think I never saw any clothing there. I have seen once, when visiting the depot, boxes marked to different soldiers; but I do not know what became of them. Nobody in my ward got any matter of clothing. Once or twice a small piece of dry beef was brought in there, but not enough to allow each man half an ounce of it. I do not know who used the dry beef and Bologna sausages... I never received it in my ward but once or twice and did not see it in the hospital. I have asked the confederate hospital steward several times for it. I think I got some once."[145] What happened to these many stores can only be imagined. Very few of these supplies were ever distributed to the prisoners, a possible indication of embezzlement.

After Doctor Head left Andersonville, he told his wife about the suffering he had witnessed. His wife and several of her friends decided to ride throughout the county and gather items to relieve the prisoners. The Rev. Mr. Davis, a Methodist minister and presiding elder, lived in Doctor Head's house in Americus. Mr. Davis said it would be good to get permission from General Winder for this undertaking and he did so. Two loads of relief supplies were carried to the prison by servants and given to the hospital. The ladies decided to accompany the third lot of supplies on the train from Americus. The doctors at the hospital sent over a wagon to the railroad depot to receive the provisions. A nasty incident occurred when the third convoy of wagons trudged up to the prison. Doctor Head testified as to the content of the wagons: "I don't know what it all was; I did not examine it; there were tomatoes, biscuits, sweet cake - I don't think there was any flour. There was some coffee and sugar and a little of everything that could be had in that part of the country."[146]

The rabid Unionist, Ambrose Spencer, who lived near-by, told what happened to these good Samaritans: "At length the Rev. Mr. Davis saw General Winder, and told him what some of the ladies of the county had done and what they wished to continue doing, and Winder apparently entered cordially into their views, and gave his consent that provisions and clothes could be sent to the hospital patients. Two lots were sent and distributed, and active exertions were made by the few ladies before referred to prepare another and a larger supply. A third stock was accumulated, and several ladies, with three gentlemen, proceeded up to Andersonville with them to superintend their proper distribution. The gentlemen were Dr. B. J. Head, Messrs. Stephen Daniels, and Wills C. Godwin. The last named had been particularly requested by the doctor to accompany him.

"When they reached the post, the supplies were left in the charge of Mr. Daniels to be unloaded, while the doctor and Mr. Godwin proceeded to the office of the provost marshal for a permit to carry the things through the line of sentinels. With an oath, Lieutenant Reed, the provost, swore 'he would give no pass for any such d----d traitorous purpose.' He was told that it was by authority of General Winder. 'I don't believe it,' said he; 'he's not such a d----d fool as that.' Sitting in his office were several rebel officers unconnected with the post - some prisoners of war on parole. One of these swore that the doctor 'ought to be hung for his Yankee sympathies, and he was ready to put the rope on his neck then and there.' Another threatened to shoot him, as 'he was no better than a Yankee.'

"Driven from the offices by such and other menaces, he proceeded to General Winder's quarters, and stated to him his object and that of the ladies, and requested a pass to take the things to the Federal hospital.

"'I'll see you in hell first!' returned the general. 'You are a d----d Yankee sympathizer, and all those connected with you.'

"'You are mistaken, general,' said the doctor. 'You know that I am no Yankee sympathizer, sir. I do sympathize with suffering humanity, and this is a mission of mercy.'

"'God d--n your mission of mercy!; cried the general. 'I wish that you and every other d----d Yankee sympathizer, and every G-d d----d Yankee to, were all in hell together!'

"'But general,' rejoined the doctor, 'we are here by your express permission given to Mr. Davis.'

"'It's a d----d lie!' replied he. 'I never gave him or any one else permission to keep the d----d ------ from starving, and rotting too, if they choose.'

"'Well, general, will you allow the provisions to go in this time, now that they are up here?'

---

[144] *Ibid.*, p. 141.
[145] *Ibid.*, p. 54.
[146] *Ibid.*, p. 365.

"'No, by God! not the first d----d morsel shall go in,' returned the general.

"At this moment the little provost marshal, Reed, entered the office hastily, and said,

"'General, give me an order to have these goods confiscated?'

"'I don't think I've got the power to do that, Reed,' replied he, 'but I have got the power to prevent the d----d Yankees from having them, and, by God! they shan'n't.'

"Seeing that he could not procure the requisite pass, and fearing, from the threatening language of Winder, the scorching looks and oaths of other officers, that the ladies and himself might be subjected to personal restraint, if not to personal abuse, he reluctantly advised them to give up the attempt and to return home, which they did.

"The load of necessaries which was carried up on this occasion filled a four-mule wagon. They were taken and used at the post...

"After such a repulse, it is not surprising that these kind-hearted women ceased in their efforts to mitigate the sufferings of the patients, or were unwilling to expose themselves to another so gross affront."[147]

Doctor Head testified about this same incident: "The third time my wife rode over in the country as well as about town, and that got up a large quantity of provisions, clothing, and one thing and another that was appropriate, and it took a good many servants to carry them up. Several of the ladies concluded that they would go up themselves on that occasion, and my wife among them. They insisted that I should go along with them and I told them that I would do so. We went up, and when we arrived at Andersonville the doctors had sent a wagon over to meet us. I told the negroes to put the things in the wagon as quick as they could and carry them over to the hospital and distribute them and get back against the down train came along, so that we might all get home that night. As soon as they started to lead the wagon this Lieutenant Reed, whom I have heard spoken of here, ripped out a very profane oath, and asked where the provisions were going, as though he were very mad, and I observed that they were going over to the Yankee hospital, and he swore that they should not go there. There were several other confederate officers present, colonels, and majors, and captains, and some of them got cursing about it and one man in particular told me that I ought to be hung; others said I ought to be shot, and I don't know what W. S. Winder or, R. B. Winder may have been present. I could not say if they were. I never was intimately acquainted with them, and I do not recollect. Well, I thought I would get into the hospitals independent of the officers, having had the permission of General Winder, and I said but little more, that we would settle our difficulty. I went over to General Winder's headquarters myself, leaving the ladies at the depot, and told him the circumstances; that we were there in accordance with the permission given by himself, and that I wanted to get an order from him to carry the provisions over to the hospital. I saw he was very much excited; he go up from his chair and turned round, using very profane language. He said, 'He did not know why in the name of hell and damnation everybody was turning Yankee sympathizers, or that there were so many sympathizers with the damned Yankee,' and then he ripped out an oath and said, 'Are you all scared by the Yankees?' I said to him, 'General, I do not suppose that the donors of these things are scared; this is a mission of mercy and charity, and I do not suppose they ought to feel alarmed in any way.' That seemed to irritate him worse, and he expressed a wish, according to the best of my recollection, something like this, 'That every damn Yankee sympathizer and that every damned Yankee upon the continent was in hell.' He wound up by saying, 'You cannot carry those things in; they shall not go; they shall not have them.' About this time this little fellow Reed came round and said, 'Oh! general, will you give me an order to have these provisions confiscated?' And the general said, 'I do not know if I have authority; I cannot do it.' I got away as quick as I could. I thought it was an unhealthy place for me. I went back to the depot and saw the ladies and told them to say no more about it; that I thought it very doubtful if I would be permitted to leave the place alive as it was, and that if they said anything more they do doubt would be arrested, and that we had better get away as soon as possible. In a few minutes there came along a train with some of our soldiers in it who had been out some time, and were hungry, and the ladies gave them the provisions. As soon as the passenger train came along we got on board and went home. That is the whole story."[148]

This is another incident that, if it took place (and it seems to have), it illustrates the psychological profile of a few of the higher-up Confederate officers at Andersonville. It also illustrates that the prison's neighbors were made aware, by Dr. Head, of the alleged injustices being perpetrated against the helpless prisoners. Would-be Good Samaritans, in their attempts to help their fellow man, were thwarted and were considered a nuisance by the officers who intervened. This vignette is corroborated by both Head and Spencer.

Every night very large fires were lit made of torchwood or "lightwood" as the men called it.[149] (Torchwood was

[147] Spencer, pp. 92-94.

[148] *Wirz Trial*, p. 364.

[149] Mann, p. 455.

any of the various resinous woods suitable for making torches and is the wood of the rutaceous tree, Amyris balsamifera, of Florida") Lightwood was also called "fat pine" by some Southerners.[150] These fires were set about 30 to 40 feet away from the stockade to light up the exterior wall. "Slaves and teams were employed to build piles of pitch-pine along the cleared space beyond the outer stockade. At night, when these were lighted, a line of fires was made which illuminated a wide arc. In the edge of the gloom beyond the fires, patrols paced to and fro until the dawn."[151] "Outside of and around the stockade were numerous piles of pine knots, from which bright fires were kept burning dark and foggy nights to light up the surroundings."[152] A requisition slip for July indicated Wirz received from Dick Winder 620 cords of word for the "... bakery, cookery and guard fires around the stockade."[153]

These fires caused areas of brightness and darkness to criss-cross within the pen. There was security and haven within the shadow especially when one's intention was to tunnel or to commit mayhem.

When Wirz first arrived at Andersonville, his headquarters was located on the high ground which rose up to the southwest of the South Gate. For some period of time, he was in a tent. In fact, in the O'Dea print, two walled tents adjacent to each other are designated "Wirz' Quarters."

These were later replaced by a crude wooden cabin. Attached to the cabin was a sign that designated the occupant as "Commandant of the Prison Interior."[154] It was a rather large cabin in front of which was a flag pole. "I have often wondered why they had no Confederate flag floating over us. They had a very nice flagstaff, but during my seven months' sojourn there I never saw the flag once; nor do I remember seeing any regimental flags."[155] "About twenty rods southwest from the South Gate, on high ground, overlooking the prison, was the large log-house wherein quartered the Rebel officers. The Confederate flag floated from a pole in front of this house. Near this pole were two cannon, or signal guns, used to warn the whole Rebel force in case the prisoners attempt to break out. At various places between this house and the South Gate were the different instruments of torture, viz: the stocks, thumb-screws, a barbed-iron collar, shackles, balls-and chains, etc."[156]

McElroy told of his being taken to Wirz' office when he was offered a temporary detail outside to assist in making up some rolls. "I was taken up to Wirz' office. He was writing at a desk at one end of a large room when the Sergeant brought me in. He turned around, told the Sergeant to leave me, and ordered me to sit down upon a box at the other end of the room.

"Turning his back and resuming his writing, in a few minutes he had forgotten me." While his back was turned McElroy felt in the box and found it loaded with soft soap. He loaded all his pockets with the soap and wiped his hands on the back of his shirt. During a five- or six-hour wait, he endured horrible pain from the caustic blistering of

**Hopkin's drawing of McElroy** - stealing some soft soap from a supply box while he waited for an interview with Wirz about a possible parole to work outside the stockade. The very alkaline soap burned the thighs of McEroy, but soap was a precious commodity at Andersonville. (McElroy)

[150] Stevenson, p. 21.
[151] Maile, p. 33.
[152] Boggs, p. 22.
[153] Military records from the National Archives.
[154] Chipman, p. 122.
[155] Hyde, pp. 234, 235.
[156] Boggs, p. 21.

his thighs and back which had come in contact with the soap. He was not detailed by Wirz but did return to the pen with a couple pockets full of precious soap.[157]

"In the latter part of November Captain Wirz' office was removed near to the commissary building..."[158]

Blacks in Southern prisons usually fared worse than their white comrades. Homer Sprague, a Union officer imprisoned at Danville, stated, "The negro soldiers suffered most. There were 64 of them living in prison when we reached Danville, October 20, 1864. Fifty-seven of them were dead on the 12th of February, 1865, when I saw and talked with the seven survivors."[159]

Any discussion of blacks at Andersonville must be separated into blacks who were Federal prisoners there and those civilian blacks who worked for salaries. "There were several negroes of both sexes employed around the hospital headquarters in various capacities, one of whom, an old negress whom they called 'Aunt Sue,' whose gray head and wrinkled features indicated an age not less than sixty years..."[160] Civilian blacks were employed to go down to inspect the wells within the prison to search for lateral shafts off to the side heading for the palisade and freedom.

Black prisoners were detailed to the burial detail to put their dead comrades on the cart at the Dead House and carry them to the cemetery. Black and white prisoners as well as civilian blacks worked at the construction of the fortifications surrounding the pen. "When a negro was placed in a squad among white men, it was usually accompanied with the injunction addressed to the sergeant of the squad, 'Make the damned nigger work for and wait upon you; if he does not, lick him, or report him to me, and I will.' I never knew an instance, however, where a sergeant required of the black any service not usually allotted to others, and that in drawing and distributing rations."[161]

The first new group of men brought into the prison after the armies had been dormant for the winter, were the 700 prisoners captured on February 20th, at the battle of Olustee, Florida. These prisoners, about 500 white and 200 black, were brought in about the middle of March. The whites belonged to the Seventh Connecticut, and the Seventh New Hampshire, and "Sherman's regular battery." The blacks were from the Eighth United States Colored Troops, and Fifty-fourth Massachusetts. The prisoners related the battle this way: "In this instance, a bungling Brigadier named Seymore had marched his forces across the State of Florida, to do he hardly knew what, and in the neighborhood of an enemy of whose numbers, disposition, location, and intentions he was profoundly ignorant. The Rebels, under General Finnegan, waited till he had strung his command along through swamps and cane brakes, scores of miles from his supports, and then fell unexpectedly upon his advance. The regiment was overpowered, and another regiment that hurried up to its support, suffered the same fate. The balance of the regiments were sent in at the same manner - each arriving on the field just after its predecessor had been thoroughly whipped by the concentrated force of the Rebels. The men fought gallantly, but the stupidity of a Commanding General is a thing that the gods themselves strive against in vain. We suffered a humiliating defeat, with a loss of two thousand men and a fine rifled battery, which was brought to Andersonville and placed in position to command the prison."[162]

The two hundred blacks of the 8th U.S. Colored Troops captured at the battle of Olustee were placed within the pen in March. Among the number of wounded was one very pathetic black. "One fellow had a hand shot off, and some enraged brutes had cut off his ears and nose, and otherwise mutilated him. The doctors refused to dress his wound, or even amputate his shattered arm; he was naked in the prison, and finally died from his numerous wounds."[163] Miller described this man by saying, "One poor fellow was said to have sixteen wounds on his body, and could only crawl on his hips, being denied even the privilege of going to the hospital."[164]

Within the hospital depicted in the informative print entitled *Let Us Forgive, But Not Forget* by Felix La Baume, was drawn a tiny figure with the following explanation in the legend at the bottom. "A colored soldier of the 7th U.S. Colored Troops, who lost his arm by grapeshot and had been captured in the battle of Olustee, Fla. The Rebels had cut off his nose and both ears and taken all clothing from him. He was literally naked up until the time of his death in March 1865. Died from exposure and starvation, hastened by the mortification of his numerous wounds."[165]

"The negroes were put in a squad by themselves, and a white union sergeant appointed over them. They would be taken outside, and made to do work. One day a 55th Georgian, without a word or act of provocation, put

[157] McElroy, pp. 210-212.
[158] *Wirz Trial*, p. 669.
[159] Author's library.
[160] Hyde, p. 300.
[161] Ross, p. 160.
[162] McElroy, pp. 160, 161.
[163] Boggs, p. 33.
[164] Miller, p. 33.
[165] Felix La Baume print in author's collection.

his gun to the sergeant's breast and fired, murdering him instantly, simply because he was in command of the negroes."[166]

"The negroes were mostly wounded and mutilated; when there had been a case of amputation, it had been performed in such a manner as to twist and distort the limb out of shape."[167]

It was interesting that one prisoner did not notice the blacks who had been within the prison for at least three months. "It was in July that I first noticed negro prisoners among us, though they were, doubtless, there previous to that time. Scarcely any of them but were victims of atrocious amputations performed by rebel surgeons. Most of the blacks were New England men."[168]

"Some that came in on June third were from a colored regiment. A number of the 54th Mass. regiment, and some others, were already of our number, and they were universally treated better than we white soldiers. They were taken outside everyday to perform some labor, and allowed double rations, and also the privilege of buying things outside and bringing them into the prison at evening, and selling them to such as had any money, for a good round price in 'greenbacks'."[169]

"During the occupation of Andersonville as a prison, it was a punishable offense for a colored man or woman to feed, shelter, aid, or even converse with a prisoner on parole. To others they had no access. I have been informed that they were not allowed about the prison grounds; and so great was their superstitious horror of the cruelties perpetrated upon the prisoners that only a comparatively small number had ever found the courage to visit the cemetery up to the time of our arrival [in the summer of 1865]."[170]

Not only were the Federal blacks not treated by some of the Southern doctors, they were not treated by some of their own doctors as is related by the following anecdote.

Just after the Battle of the Crater in Petersburg, there were five Federal surgeons who were part of Wilson's cavalry raiders taken at Reams Station and kept at the Central Park Hospital in Petersburg. This was the way Major John Herbert Claiborne described the situation. "On reaching the place I was shocked beyond expression to find about a hundred and fifty wounded negroes, who had been brought in since I left, and were lying about on the grounds, most of them naked; and with every conceivable form of wounds and mutilation, were shrieking, praying, and cursing in their agony and delirium, their wounds undressed and festering under a summer sun.

"The Federal surgeons whom I had engaged the day before were lounging in front of their quarters, doing nothing. Their spokesman replied that they '... were sick, and tired, and disgusted, and they were prisoners of war, and were not in duty bound to do any work.' 'Very well,' I replied, 'but you should have said this yesterday when I approached you. As prisoners of war I know very well what to do with you,' and calling an orderly directed him to go to Major Bridgeforth, General Lee's provost marshal and ask him to send me a sergeant and a guard to take away five medical officers. One of them asked immediately, 'Major, where are you going to send us?' 'To the prison at Andersonville, Georgia, to-morrow morning.' I replied. They all joined in, 'Give us another opportunity.' The next morning everything was in ship-shape order."[171]

Thus, banishment to Andersonville was often used as a threat. When Sumner U. Shearman, Captain, Fourth Rhode Island Volunteers, was captured at Petersburg, he was told, "They are going to take you down to Andersonville. They are dying down there three or four hundred a day; you will never live to see home again."[172]

"Soon after the arrival of the colored troops, an old southern planter came in, and looking over the camp, saw a colored man among the rest whom he believed was one of his slaves escaped from his plantation in 1856. The old planter talked with him, but he denied all knowledge of slavery, saying he was born in Massachusetts, which statement was vouched for by his comrades. After questioning and cross-questioning him, and receiving no satisfactory reply, the old planter retired, saying that in all probability he had 'mistook' his man. But the next day... he returned with two of the oldest slaves on his plantation. The planter's name was Samuel Johnson. Arriving at the prison, he, with one of the old negro slaves, was admitted by Captain Wirz, and at once proceeded to the quarters of the colored troops. As they were near our own quarters, and we thought it strange to see a citizen walk into camp, followed by Capt. Wirz and a guard, many of us followed them to see what was going on. Walking in among the negroes, the planter said to the old slave, "'Sam, look these men over sharp, and tell me if you know any of them.'

[166] Miller, pp. 33, 34.
[167] Goss, p. 160.
[168] Goss, p. 159.
[169] Kellogg, pp. 124, 125.
[170] Walker, p. 69.
[171] John Herbert Claiborne, *Seventy-Five Years in Old Virginia* (New York and Washington: The Neal Publishing Co., 1904), pp. 208, 209.
[172] Sumner U. Sherman, *Battle of the Crater and Experiences of Prison Life* (Providence: Snow & Farnham, Printers, 1898), p. 17.

"The old man at once assumed all the dignity requisite for the imaginary honor conferred upon him,... He devoted some time to rubbing some old brass-bowed spectacles,... he slowly looked from one to another until his eyes rested upon the man whom the planter claimed as his own. Slowly raising his hand, and pointing his finger at him, he said,

'"Dat am Sam Johnson's nigger, sure.'

"The officer in charge asked for no further proof in the matter, and the Massachusetts colored soldier who had for eight years been at liberty, again found himself in bondage. A rebel soldier was called in, and at the point of the bayonet the man... was marched out of the prison gate."[173]

"Another colored soldier belonging to the same regiment, who was captured at the same time, was struck in the forehead by a spent ball which just crushed the skull, leaving the minie wedged in the bone. I heard him ask a Confederate physician if he would try and extract the ball, or in some way alleviate the terrible pain. The dashing young Doctor, whose well-fitting new grey uniform, covered with brass buttons, and well polished boots and sword bespoke the self-imagined aristocrat, made some abusive remark to the poor sufferer, and left him. A few days later, as I stood looking at the dead, who were brought to the South Gate previous to their removal to the dead house, I saw the body of the colored soldier who had so piteously begged aid of the young rebel Doctor. In two other cases where men were hit in the head by spent balls, they recovered when the balls were extracted. One of these men, Henry Crow, Company C, 5th Vermont Infantry, recovered from his wound, but was not of a sufficiently strong constitution to stand the hardships to which we were subjected, and on August 26th he died, his grave or number, being 4883."[174]

The "Senate Executive Document 62 Showed 111 marked burials of black prisoners who died at Andersonville."[175] Northrop said that, on May 26th, there were 125 Negroes left out of the 200 that were brought in from the battle of Olustee in March.[176]

Major Archibald Boyle was a major of the 12th U.S. Colored Troops. He was captured at the Battle of Olustee at Ocean Pond, Florida, on the 20th of February while commanding the First North Carolina Volunteers. McElroy said "the nigger officer" was a Major Albert Bogle and that he was a member of the Eight United States regiment. At a station between Macon and Andersonville, the car in which Major Boyle rode was fired into twice by a Confederate officer.[177] McElroy also said, "Once a Rebel officer rode up and fired several shots at him, as he lay helpless on the car floor."[178]

Boyle arrived at Andersonville on the 14th of March. He was severely wounded but had been refused admittance into the hospital and been refused all medical treatment. Boyle had received a flesh wound in the body and a very severe wound in the lower part of the right leg, which had fractured both bones. His wound was full of gangrene and he went on crutches to the hospital then inside the stockade. "I went in, and one of our own men, who was acting hospital steward, commenced to bind up my leg, and was binding it when Surgeon White came in and ordered him to desist, saying at the same time, 'Send him out there with his niggers.' or something to that effect, and using an oath at the same time. The steward finished the dressing of my leg, and it was cared for by our own men afterwards. I was in full uniform then. At the time I was captured I had on sword, sash and belt. "

A few weeks later, Major Boyle went up to the hospital again. "While there the hospital steward, Robinson, who was the right hand man of Dr. White, came in and asked if I was the major of a negro regiment; I told him I was an officer in the United States military service. He asked me what regiment, and I told him. He said, 'You are the man. Now I want you to go out of this.' I asked him who he was, and he told me that was none of my business. A little while afterwards Mr. Burns, one of our own men, who was acting as hospital steward, came in and said to me, 'This man Robinson says that if I do not persuade you to go out, he will ball and chain you.' I afterwards learned, that the language he used to Burns was, that if I did not go out he would shoot me and ball and chain him. Robinson was a Confederate hospital steward; I think he was the chief steward of the post."[179]

Major Boyle testified about how the officers of colored troops were refused recognition as officers. "While I was there I demanded to have my rank recognized. I made several demands. I was used to every respect the same as private soldiers, only worse. I made a demand on Colonel Persons, when I was in the stockade; I think so, but I will not state positively. However, after I was refused treatment in the hospital, in June or July, I made two demands on

[173] Dufur, pp. 109-111.
[174] *Ibid.*, pp. 111, 112.
[175] Walter L. Williams, "Again in Chains," *Civil War Times* (May, 1981), p. 38.
[176] Northrop, p. 62.
[177] *Ibid.*, p. 63.
[178] McElroy, p. 162.
[179] Chipman, pp. 177, 178.

Captain Wirz. The first time he said he would see me about it. This was about October, 1864. The next demand I made, he sent in after me and I went out and saw him. A day or two afterwards he sent me with a letter, under charge of an officer, to see General Winder. Captain Wirz said that he could not do anything, as he was merely a subordinate under General Winder. When I got to Millen an officer came to me and got my name, rank, and regiment. The officer commanding at Millen, Captain Bowles, put me in the stockade again and refused to put my name on the register, saying at the same time that I should never be exchanged... I left Andersonville on the 18th of November, 1864, and arrived at Millen on the 20th."[180]

In a letter from Wirz to Colonel Fannin at Millen, dated November 28th, he wrote: "I have the honor to forward to you under guard, in charge of Detective Weatherford, eight prisoners of war, to wit:

"A. Boyle, major 35th United States, He was captured at Ocean Pond, Florida, while in command of a negro regiment; he has not been recognized as an officer, although he has made several attempts to be recognized and exchanged. I forward him to you to enable him to see the general commanding."[181]

The "code of silence" displayed towards Major Boyle was typical of the harsh treatment rendered Federal officers of the so-called "colored troops." The officers were thought of as the leaders of the ex-slaves in an insurrection against their former slave-owners in the South. The residents of some Southern states wanted the officers to be returned to those states so that they could be tried for leading slave insurrections.

Southern forces were always seeking Federal officers to exchange for their own, badly-needed, Southern officers. A round-up of Federal officers from the pen was made in the summer for a prisoner exchange and to eliminate the leadership in the possibility of an uprising by the enlisted men.

"Along in the last of August the Rebels learned that there were between two and three hundred Captains and Lieutenants in the Stockade, passing themselves off as enlisted men. The motive of these officers was two-fold: first, a chivalrous wish to share the fortunes and fate of their boys, and second, disinclination to gratify the Rebels by the knowledge of the rank of their captives. The secret was so well kept that none of us suspected it until the fact was announced by the Rebels themselves. They were taken out immediately, and sent to Macon, where the commissioned officers' prison was. It would not do to trust such possible leaders with us another day."[182]

Northrop said that, on August 24th, "There have been commissioned officers in the prison. Today eighteen were taken out to be sent to Charleston. I know of two who have not gone; Colby, of a New Hampshire regiment and one of a regiment of the 6th corp."[183]

Northrop mentioned knowledge of a "Major Oberly."[184]

One of the very few reported acts of compassion performed by General Winder involved one of his friends who was also an officer from the old days prior to the war.

One of the older Plymouth prisoners had been the chief clerk of the Post Quartermaster at Plymouth. His name was Captain Everett and, in the former days, he had been captain in the regular army. At one time, he had held a position upon General Winder's staff. Almost everybody in Plymouth knew and respected Captain Everett. He was put into prison with the rest of the Plymouth Pilgrims, and was finally taken sick, the hardships of confinement proving too much for his age. When General Winder learned the condition of the man who had once been associated with him, Winder took him out of the pen and gave him good care, provided medical assistance and better food. Captain Everett was too debilitated and he died. Winder allowed him to have one of the very few Christian burials. This convinced Everett's comrades there was at least one soft spot in the heart of the gray-haired general.[185]

There were some fraternal organizations represented among the prisoners within the pen. There were some Odd Fellows, who lived in a good-sized house which was made of logs and which was located near the southwest corner. Some Odd Fellows on the outside of the prison supplied these fellow members on the inside with food and clothing and so they were much better off than the balance of the prisoners.[186] "In April one thousand tents arrived... When the tents were finally issued great favoritism was shown by those in authority and we were not long in discovering that Free Masons and Odd Fellows were first served. Further observation soon convinced us that the same distinction was made in issuing daily rations, and that the members of these two world-wide organizations received

[180] *Wirz Trial*, pp. 326, 327.
[181] *Ibid.*, p. 162.
[182] McElroy, pp. 378, 379.
[183] Northrop, pp. 117, 118.
[184] *Ibid.*, p. 63.
[185] Kellogg, pp. 238, 239.
[186] Miller, p. 31.

much greater attention and consideration than any of the others."[187]

Members of another fraternal organization which flourished within the pen, and who received preferential treatment, were the Freemasons. The Masonic Temple inside the pen was described as "... an extensive enclosure of evergreen boughs and brush" with "... the square and compass suspended over the door."[188] "Rebel Masons interested themselves in assisting their brother Masons in presents of medicine, food, tent material, reading and writing material, vegetables and in many ways not known to those not familiar with Masonry."[189]

"The Lodges at Thomasville and Albany were conspicuous in their efforts to seek out and aid the Masons in prison and hospital. Delegations from these bodies went to Andersonville, and, not without difficulty, found the names of many who required their fraternal assistance. Money, clothing, and food was provided by the Albany Lodge, and the destitute brothers were cheered by the kind attention of their friends, relieved by their bounty, solaced by their care, or buried with the mystic ceremonies of the order. The Lodge at Macon contributed clothing, and rendered such other services as their means permitted, while individual members of other Lodges exerted themselves in the cause of humanity, and rescued many from their undeserved suffering."[190]

"I know there was one prisoner buried there with Masonic honors - from the stockade. I saw the procession coming from the stockade."[191]

Lieutenant Hyde of Dufur's Company B of the 1st Vermont Cavalry passed as a sergeant after having been captured at Brandy Station on October 11, 1863. After being a prisoner for eight months and suffering from diarrhea, he was in a very debilitated condition. "He was a Free Mason, and from a piece of bone I had made him a small scarf pin representing the order - the square and compass; as the poor fellow was so very destitute of anything pertaining to the comforts of life, I borrowed from him the scarf pin, and going to the gate, I handed it out to a rebel sergeant whom I had seen wearing the same symbol, I said; 'The man who wears this is lying in a critical condition, and I wish you would kindly call upon him.' He bowed assent, and during the day came in. Being on the watch for him, I at once guided him to where the sick man lay. He talked with him an hour or so and went out, saying he would call again. The next morning he walked hurriedly into the Lieutenant's tent, threw down a parcel, and walked out. It contained one pair of drawers, one shirt, and a pair of feeting, some medicine and food. We were encouraged by the kindness the rebel Sergeant had shown the poor fellow, as the Lieutenant was beloved by all his company...Aid came too late; in a few days Lieut. Hyde had become so very low that he was taken out to the hospital; and a few hours later a man came in bearing the sad intelligence that our comrade was dead, and saying that with farewell messages to ourselves, he had requested that his dying love be conveyed to his young wife, with his wish that she would meet him in heaven. When the Lieutenant fell into the enemy's hands he was not recognized as an officer, so passed as a private, believing he would be better treated."[192]

"The Rebel Masons interested themselves in securing details outside the Stockade in the cook-house, the commissary, and elsewhere, for the brethren among the prisoners who would accept such favors. Such as did not feel inclined to go outside on parole received frequent presents in the way of food, and especially of vegetables, which were literally beyond price. Materials were sent inside to build tents for the Masons, and I think such as made themselves known before death, received burial according to the rites of the Order. Doctor White, and perhaps other Surgeons, belonged to the fraternity, and the wearing of a Masonic emblem by a new prisoner was pretty sure to catch their eyes, and be the means of securing for the wearer the tender of their good offices, such as a detail into the Hospital as nurse, ward-master, etc."[193]

Little did some men know that, by joining fraternal organizations in their hometowns, their lives would be spared or made less ardurous in a prison camp in southwest Georgia. There is no question that favoritism and nepotism flourished at Andersonville among the prisoners and guard officers.

If a Confederate soldier deserted, went over to the enemy, joined the Federal army and was later captured by his former Confederate comrades, he was bitterly hated. These re-captured turncoats were called "buffaloes." At Andersonville, many buffaloes and their fellow prisoners did all they could to conceal their identity from the authorities. The buffaloes assumed false names and passed themselves off as members of northern regiments.[194]

---

[187] Bates, p. 33.
[188] Hyde, p. 213.
[189] Author's library.
[190] Spencer, pp. 141, 142.
[191] *Wirz Trial*, p. 482.
[192] Dufur, pp. 98, 99.
[193] McElroy, p. 377.
[194] Kellogg, pp. 243, 244.

Vawter had a buffalo in his unit when it was captured by some Confederates led by a major. "We had in Company A of our regiment a man who deserted the rebels at the battle of Perryville, and enlisted with us. As the rebs came down, he recognized his old comrades, and knowing he would be shot anyway, he resolved to sell his life for all it would bring. So, as they came up, he shot the Major through the heart, killing him at once. The next instant he fell among us riddled with balls, and his rash deed came near causing the death of every one of us.

"'Kill every ____ ____ ____ ____!' cried a rebel officer in excitement.

"Just then we saw Wheeler and staff, and called to him. The Johnnies pointed to their dead officer and claimed treachery. But the General ordered them to guard us as prisoners, and not to shoot any one who surrendered."[195] Thus, a possible slaughter was narrowly averted by the timely arrival of Confederate General Wheeler.

There were a few Indians in the pen, who had been used as scouts in the conflict west of the Mississippi. "They were well formed, vigorous looking men, but how long they endured is unknown."[196] "A few Indians belonging to a Western regiment were captured and brought into Andersonville. I think there were ten or fifteen of them, and in less than ninety days, not one was living. The confinement was what they could not stand."[197] Helwig said there fifteen Indians there and one died.[198] "I found that the Indians confined there were not enduring as well as the whites. They stayed very close to their quarters, however, and were not given to exercise as much as the whites, which might possibly account for their lack of stamina."[199] The survival statistics of the Indian population is mostly anecdotal; they probably fared as well as their white counterparts.

Another minority within the prison was a group of young boys, some of whom had been drummer boys for their regiments. They would signal orders to the rest of the regiment by various drum rolls and cadences. These boys varied in age from about twelve or thirteen upwards. These pathetic boys were made to endure the rigors their older comrades did until Wirz became commandant. He ordered that all the very young who wished to could be removed from the prison. Most stayed with their friends within the prison. "Captain Wirz took about thirty boys out of the stockade; there was one of those little boys at Captain Wirz' house and another at the headquarters, and another at hospital headquarters, and another in the hospital. There were some two or three more going about there. I do not know where they belonged; I heard Captain Wirz remark to one of the prisoners that he took the boys out of the stockade because it was not fit for them. Captain Wirz said that he did not take out the boys to work, but that it was too miserable a place for the boys to live in."[200] "I know that about seventy, or probably eighty boys were paroled - brought out and put on nominal detail duty connected with the hospital. I know that they were permitted to go and pick black-berries, and Captain Wirz ordered them to be given tin pails to pick blackberries in."[201] "He took them out for the purpose of having them gather blackberries for the hospital. They would gather some; but they would sell more than they gave to the hospital."[202]

"There were in the camp a good many little boys who were supposed to have been drummers in the army; one day Captain Wirz came in and took one of them out; the next day he came in again and took out about thirty; at that time a man asked to be taken out and Captain Wirz said that he took the boys out because they could not stand the miasmas in there, and that he would not take him out; I saw about thirty boys taken out that day and I know there were others in the hospital; some of the boys were in the hospital, some were engaged at one headquarters and others at the other headquarters; others were sent out for blackberries for sick men; they were sent out for blackberries several times. I heard from some of my friends that the nurses made wine with the blackberries for themselves - I know that few of the sick ever received it - and that they were sent into camp to make pies. Those nurses were our own men...I saw nurses who were acting as clerks at the doctors coming round the stockade, coming near the South Gate, bringing haversacks full of blackberries; those blackberries were taken into the camp, and as there were several bakers in the camp they made pies of them. I cannot say that they were the blackberries that the boys had gathered."[203]

On the night of August 6,th one of the younger inmates, who was 15 years old, died. He was too young to have legally been in the service and was "... very proud that he had endured his imprisonment" as well as most of the

195 Vawter, pp. 29, 30.
196 Miller, p. 33.
197 Dufur, p. 109.
198 Helwig, p. 26.
199 Hyde, p. 236.
200 *Wirz Trial*, p. 522.
201 *Ibid.*, p. 696.
202 *Ibid.*, p. 674.
203 *Ibid.*, p. 514.

men.[204]

"There was a drummer boy, whose smooth face and childish voice called for sympathy. He was rapidly wasting away, and his friends were anxious to save him. The beans were brought in barrels, which were set on the ground to be emptied, and the empty barrels taken out in the last wagon that came in. One day a barrel was turned over on its side to scrape out all the beans; the boy squatted at its mouth, and when the Quartermaster's back was turned, it was turned bottom-upward over him. When the last load came in, two men set that barrel up in the wagon without turning it over. The boy got out all right, but was caught and brought back the next day. He didn't last long after that. Three or four weeks later, he was put in a wagon at the other gate. That time we knew that he would never be sent back."[205]

About one of the little boys: "We had one at our headquarters. He carried water, and sometimes he was sent off with messages... The little boy that we had at our office was a short time at Captain Wirz' house - perhaps a week or two."[206]

"Mrs. Wirz took a great liking to one of our little drummer boys. She took him out and dressed him in a nice fitting suit of gray. The boy was only eleven years old, and very handsome. The little fellow put on his suit of gray, and Mrs. Wirz said, 'How do you like your clothes?' 'I do not like them at all.' replied the boy. 'Why, what is the matter?' 'I do not like the color.' Mrs. Wirz liked him all the better for the bold spirit he manifested. She then made him a suit of blue, and also a nice red cap, and thenceforth he went by the name of Red Cap.

**Little Red Cap** - Name given to a drummer boy who was an aide to Wirz. He was one of about eighty removed from the prison by Wirz. Wirz felt that the rigors of the prison were too great for the 12- to 15-year-old boys. They were given soft jobs on the outside. (McElroy)

"Red Cap would come in every day or two and tell us what was going on outside. He told us Mrs. Wirz quarreled with Wirz every day because he did not try to prepare some kind of a shelter for the prisoners. She wished him to let a few of us out at a time to cut timber to make our own shelter with. No, he would not do that. Finally Mrs. Wirz told him if he didn't do something for the relief of the prisoners, she would poison him; 'For,'said she, 'I cannot sleep nights; my dreams are one continued nightmare, and I will stand it no longer.' Mrs. Wirz was a true southerner, of the kind called 'creole' but for all that she had a great deal of humanity about her. She continued her threats and pleadings, but they were of no avail. She finally did give him a dose of poison. He had been threatened so much that when he did get it he knew what was the matter, and took something to counteract it. After that 'Old Wirz' let us out oftener for wood."[207]

"One of the best purveyors of information was a bright, blue-eyed, fair-haired little boy, as handsome as a girl, well-bred as a lady, and evidently the darling of some refined, loving mother. He belonged, I think, to some loyal Virginia regiment, was captured in one of the actions in the Shenandoah Valley, and had been with us in Richmond. We called him 'Red Cap,' from his wearing a jaunty, gold-laced crimson cap. Ordinarily, the smaller a drummer boy is the harder he is, but no amount of attrition with rough men could coarsen the ingrained refinement of Red Cap's manners. He was between thirteen and fourteen, and it seemed utterly shameful that men, calling themselves soldiers should make war on such a tender boy and drag him off to prison.

"But no six-footer had a more soldierly heart than little Red Cap, and none were more loyal to the cause. It was a pleasure to hear him tell the story of the fights and movements his regiment had been engaged in. He was a good observer and told his tale with boyish fervor. Shortly after Wirz assumed command he took Red Cap into his office as an Orderly. His bright face and winning manners fascinated the women visitors at headquarters, and numbers of them tried to adopt him, but with poor success. Like the rest of us, he could see few charms in an existence under the Rebel flag, and turned a deaf ear to their blandishments.

---

[204] Kellogg, p. 296.
[205] Vawter, pp. 82, 83.
[206] *Wirz Trial*, p. 553.
[207] William N. Tyler, *The Dispatch Carrier and Memoirs of Andersonville Prison* (Port Byron, Ill.: 1892), pp. 37-39.

He kept his ears open to the conversation of the Rebel officers around him, and frequently secured permission to visit the interior of the Stockade, when he would communicate to us all that he had heard. He received flattering reception every time he came in, and no orator ever secured a more attentive audience than would gather around him to listen to what he had to say. He was, beyond a doubt, the best known and most popular person in the prison, and I know all the survivors of his old admirers share my great interest in him, and my curiosity as to whether he yet lives, and whether his subsequent career has justified the sanguaine hopes we all had as to his future."[208]

McElroy received a letter from Red Cap while McElroy was in the process of publishing his book. Red Cap wrote, in part, from "Eckhart Mines, Alleghany County, Md., March 24, [1899?]. I was a drummer boy of Company I, Tenth West Virginia Infantry, and was fifteen years of age a day or two after arriving in Andersonville, which was in the last of February, 1864. Nineteen of my comrades were there with me, and, poor fellows, they are there yet... I was the little boy that for three or four months officiated as orderly for Captain Wirz. I wore a red cap and every day could be seen riding Wirz' gray mare, either at headquarters, or about the Stockade. I was acting in this capacity when the six raiders... were executed. I believe that I was the first that conveyed the intelligence to them that Confederate General Winder had approved their sentence. As soon as Wirz received the dispatch to that effect, I ran down to the stocks and told them... The world will never know or believe the horrors of Andersonville and other prisons in the South. No living, human being, in my judgment, will ever be able to properly paint the horrors of those infernal dens... Yours truly, Ransom T. Powell."[209]

There were several young boys, aged ten to fifteen, who were members of the crew of some of the ships of the United States Navy. These young fellows were called "chickens" and were usually befriended by an "old barnacle-back" who took care of the youngsters and assumed responsibility for their safety and welfare. McElroy told of one young boy who arrived at Andersonville after having been captured on board the United States' sloop *Water Witch* in Ossabaw Sound. He had lost one of his arms and his gentle nurse was allowed to accompany him to the hospital to bring him back to health. The old salt shaded him, fed him, dressed his wound and washed his clothes.

Since, for some reason, the naval prisoners were allowed to come in with their duffel bags intact, and most sailors were good at sewing, this youngster had nice clothes made from white, naval duck material.[210]

At least three or four women were known to have been imprisoned at Andersonville. One was taken prisoner when Plymouth, N. C., surrendered. "Margaret Leonard, - wife of a private of Company H, second Massachusetts heavy artillery. During the battle, she was engaged making coffee for the men in a building exposed to heavy fire. At one time a solid shot passed through the building, taking with it one of her dresses, which hung on a nail by the wall. Another carried away the front legs of her cooking-stove. Yet when the fight was over, on the evening of the 19th, she had coffee for the men, and supper for the officers. She was in Fort Williams during the remainder of the fight, and subsequently went through with a long and severe imprisonment at Andersonville, Macon, and Castle Thunder, Richmond."[211]

When Florena Budwin's husband joined the army, she decided to follow him into service. It was not uncommon for determined women to try to accompany their husbands or boyfriends into the military service. A lady could wear her hair short and with the very cursory physical examinations in vogue, it was not difficult to pass herself off as a male. Both Florena and her husband were captured and shipped off to Andersonville where they lived together until he was killed, probably by a guard. She continued living in her disguise and, in September, she was transferred, as were most other prisoners, to the new prison at Florence. While at Florence, she was taken sick and, in the process of being treated, she was given a thorough examination by the doctors. After her discovery, this lady soldier was given a private room and the ladies of Florence donated nutritious food and women's clothing for her. This special treatment was unable to rejuvenate her and she died from pneumonia on January 25, 1865. In February, all sick prisoners were paroled and exchanged to the North.[212] John W. Northrop wrote in his diary on August 23rd, "An interesting gossip was afloat when I came here that there were two women in prison disguised as Union soldiers. It was accepted as a fact by many who gave plenty of reasons for believing it, and it was a topic for talk among them which I was curious to hear. In June two sprightly persons were shown me as the alleged women. Many times after I saw them, always together, always by themselves. There was nothing in their appearance to discredit the story except male attire; nothing to suggest to me, under the circumstances, that they were women, in the absence of the story that

[208] McElroy, pp. 290,, 291.
[209] *Ibid.*, pp. 292, 293.
[210] *Ibid.*, pp. 361, 362.
[211] Goss, p. 60.
[212] G. Wayne King, "Death Camp at Florence," *Civil War Times Illustrated* (January, 1974), p. 38.

they were women. They looked like beardless boys, feminine of stature and of features, with an air of shyness. The story could not be traced to an origin, nor was it denied except by ridicule. Its believers said their appearance was prima facie evidence, and accounted for their presence in several ways. For three weeks they have not been seen. This morning believers in the rumor are on to the fact that three weeks ago they left their dugout at sunset and passed the South Gate. Where they went, how and why, is a mystery, but the story is now more than ever believed. They were called by some, 'camp angels.'"[213]

Dr. W. J. W. Kerr of Corsicana, Texas, wrote an interesting article in a Confederate Veteran magazine titled, "Sad Ending of a Wedding Trip": "In the summer of 1863 Capt. Harry Hunt, of Buffalo, N. Y., captain of a coasting vessel running out of New York City, married Miss Janie Scadden, daughter of Thomas L. Scadden, of Chicago, Ill. After the wedding Captain Hunt took a number of his invited guests to New York and went aboard his vessel for a little pleasure trip at sea. They had been out only a few hours when a United States revenue cutter ran across them and forced Captain Hunt to go down on the coast of North Carolina for a load of corn. While loading Johnny Reb ran in on him and captured the vessel, wedding party and all; but after finding out that the party was composed of non-combatants, all were turned loose except Captain Hunt. His wife, thinking he would be released in a few days, refused to leave him; but instead he was finally sent to Andersonville Prison and both were held as prisoners of war.

"In July, 1864, I was ordered to duty at Andersonville to take charge of the dispensary and to superintend the building of a hospital and other government buildings connected with the prison. On the night of my arrival I heard a very small infant crying near my office, which was in the 'Star Fort' just outside the southwest corner of the prison. Upon inquiry one of the guards informed me that it was the infant of Captain Hunt and his wife, only three days old. Next morning I went down to see Mrs. Hunt and infant and found her in a tent in the most abject poverty I had ever seen. While she was inside of the prison one night the Federal prisoners cut the back of the tent that had been furnished her and Captain Hunt and stole her trunk, with nearly all of her clothes and some $5,000 in greenbacks that was in the trunk. She had been in the prison thirteen months when her baby was born, and all she had to dress it in were some little wrappers that she had made out of an old calico dress, and her own clothing was hardly sufficient to cover her. I found on talking to her that she was a cultured, very intelligent woman.

"I went back to my office and drew up a petition to General Winder (who was in charge of the post) and got all of the surgeons at the post to sign it to have her boarded out in the neighborhood as soon as she was able to go. I presented the petition to General Winder, and he asked me what it meant. When I explained he said he had forgotten that there was a lady prisoner there, but it would be against the rules of war to board her out, though he would like to do so if he could. I remarked to him that oft times things came up in this world that we had to shut our eyes to. He turned his face toward me, shut his eyes closely, and said: 'Doctor, I don't see anything at all.'

"I left him and went out about a mile and a half from the prison to old Farmer Smith. He would not consider it at first, but finally told me to get the consent of his wife, and it would be all right with him if I would make it all right with the Confederate authorities. This I agreed to do, and I then told Mrs. Smith what I wanted. She also refused, but I finally secured her consent.

"That evening I went by train to Macon, Ga., and asked a friend of mine, who was merchandizing when the war broke out, for some goods to make clothing for a lady and her baby in prison at Andersonville. We went to his store and found a lot of remnants of flannels, calico, domestic, etc., enough to relieve her necessities until the war released her. When I got back to the prison I sent the goods to Mrs. Hunt.

"I had Captain Hunt paroled when I first went there and appointed him a ward master in the hospital, so he could be with his wife. After they found out that I sent the goods, Mrs. Hunt wrote me the most beautiful and touching letter I ever read and with it sent a beautiful diamond scarf pin that Captain Hunt had worn for several years, which she begged me to wear as long as I lived. I wrote in reply that in her impoverished condition I could not and would not accept it. Two days after that Captain Hunt came to my office and told me that little Harry was very sick, and they wanted me to go to the house to see him at once. I said: 'O no, Captain, you can't fool me. You are only wanting me to go to the house so Mrs. Hunt can persuade me to wear the pin, and I am not going to do it.' But finally I took the pin, because I could not reconcile Captain and Mrs. Hunt otherwise."[214]

A prisoner testified that he knew of ladies within the pen: "Yes, sir; two ladies came there in that way. As to the first lady who came with her husband, (I did not know her name). I understood...that Captain Wirz sent her to his own house, and that, she having insulted the family, he removed her. The other lady was in a very delicate condition,

[213] Northrop, p. 116.
[214] Kerr, p. 318.

and Captain Wirz gave her and her husband a tent at headquarters - one of the best tents he had - until her illness was over, and he had her kindly treated...He had a tent ordered for herself and husband, and paroled her husband - detailed him in connection with the hospital during her illness."[215]

Solon Hyde, one of the druggists, described the Hunt family. "Occupying a wall-tent near our dispensary was a lady with a young child. I at first supposed that she was the wife of one of the officers in charge, but soon learned that she was a prisoner, having been captured in company with her husband, who was a steamboat captain and a civilian, though at the time of his capture he was engaged in transporting government troops or supplies somewhere on the coast of North Carolina. His name was Herbert Hunt, and their first child, who was named Frank, was born in that tent, - an experience that perhaps has not a parallel in all history...

"The mother bore her trials with considerable fortitude, though only a prisoner nominally, as she was permitted to go where she pleased and spent a great deal of time at Mr. Smith's about a mile south of the prison. Mr. Hunt was acting as ward-master in the hospital, and was 'hail fellow well met' with everyone. One of the Confederate attaches, a Mr. Robertson, had his wife with him, and the two ladies seemed to enjoy themselves together very much. We found them to be a cheerful part of our hospital association, and very estimable ladies, and we had the pleasure, when we became acquainted, of spending some very pleasant evenings at their quarters, after they had taken possession of two vacant shanties deserted by some of the batterymen."[216]

The Forty-eighth New York Regiment's members were called L'Enfants Perdue (the Lost Children), but the prisoners anglicized it to mean the Lost Ducks. They were mostly composed of Italians, Spaniards, Portuguese with a predominance of Frenchmen. "It was believed that every nation in Europe was represented in their ranks, and it used to be said jocularly, that no two of them spoke the same language...They wore a little cap with an upturned brim, and a strap resting on the chin, a coat with funny little tales about two inches long, and a brass chain across the breast; and for pantaloons they had a sort of a petticoat reaching to the knees; and sewed together down the middle. They were just as singular otherwise as in their looks, speech and uniform. On one occasion the whole mob of us went over in a mass to their squad to see them cook and eat a large water snake, which two of them had succeeded in capturing in the swamps, and carried off to their mess, jabbering in high glee over their treasure trove. Any of us were ready to eat a piece of dog, cat, horse or mule, if we could get it, but, it was generally agreed, as Dawson, of my command expressed it, that 'Nobody but one of them darned queer Lost Ducks would eat a varmit like a water snake.'"[217]

Another description of this incident was given by Hyde. "During the hard rain that caused a breach in the palisade he was standing near the break on the east side and saw something swim in from below. Seizing a piece of driftwood he plunged into the flood and succeeded in killing and securing it. He said its skin was like an eel's, but it had no fins and a suspiciously snakelike though blunt tail. Having nothing else to do he skinned it, and the flesh looked so tempting, and the pangs of hunger were so great, that he concluded to cook and eat it. So he dressed it nicely, cut it into thin slices, and fried it, eating heartily of it himself and giving part to his chums, telling them it was an eel. They praised it highly and soon cleared the platter. From his description I suppose it was a water-moccasin, a venomous snake abundant in the swamps and streams of the South."[218]

When Sally Hemings died at the age of 62 in 1835, she had had two sons as a result of her relationship with Thomas Jefferson. One, Eston Hemings, moved to Wisconsin. The other, Madison Hemings, moved to Ohio and had a son, Thomas Eston Hemings, who fought for the Union and died at Andersonville.[219]

There was a man in McElroy's company that was over six feet tall who, after losing all his excess fat, was called "Flagstaff" for obvious reasons. His comrades "... cracked all sorts of jokes about putting an insulator on his head, and setting him up for a telegraph pole, braiding his legs and using him for a whip lash, letting his hair grow a little longer, and trading him off to the Rebels for a sponge and staff for the artillery, etc."[220]

"A native Georgian who gave the name of Ann Williams arrived at Andersonville on the morning of January 15. Two days later, Wirz reported as a fact 'beyond doubt' that she had 'sexual intercourse with at least seven prisoners.' But she was not a prostitute, Wirz continued, for 'on every occasion [she has] refused to take money, saying to them that she was a friend of theirs and had come for the purpose of seeing how she could help them.'"[221]

---

[215] *Wirz Trial*, p. 696.
[216] Hyde, pp. 248, 249.
[217] McElroy, p. 162.
[218] Hyde, pp. 305, 306.
[219] Fawn M. Brodie, "Thomas Jefferson, An Intimate History," *Southern Living*, August, 1982, p. 469 and p. 474.
[220] McElroy, p. 339.
[221] Futch, pp. 114, 115.

Besides the three or four known female inmates in the pen, many times female visitors were seen in the guard towers. These were mostly wives and girlfriends of the guards. "Some Southern ladies, who later viewing the interior of Andersonville from the stockade platform, turned away their faces weeping."[222] On June 4th, a "... great lot of ladies came to the stockade to see the prisoners. Some seem to be union at heart."[223] "Even women and young girls came from distances to view the spectacle. They climbed the parapets of the earthworks, and gloated and made merry over the scene of suffering. They threw crusts of bread over the palisades to see the starving wretches struggle for the morsel of life."[224]

"One day when there was a large crowd of curious visitors, a young miss of sixteen, 'followed by a diminutive specimen of female Africanism,' ascended one of the guard towers and beckoning her small black companion to her side, yelled out to the inmates within the prison, 'Look here, Yanks!'

"Startled at the fair apparition, they all gazed up at her.

"'Do you see this nig?' she shouted, pointing to her follower.

"'Well, she's your sister; do you know it?' and exclamations of delight at this unexpected display of delicacy and wit resounded through the throng of outside admirers as the refined exhibitor slowly descended from her conspicuous perch."[225]

Five or six hundred paces from the stockade, on the bank of Stockade Creek and near the Andersonville Depot was the officers' stockade called "Castle Reed." This pen was used to hold officers before it was abandoned after a few weeks. All known officers were sent on to the officers' prison at Macon. Castle Reed was abandoned because of the "... fear of revolt in keeping officers near so great a number of rank and file of the army, and partly from the unfortunate selection of the locality."[226] It never held over 250 prisoners and most all of the inmates were southern offenders.[227] "The confederate guard-house was Castle Reed."[228]

It was a miniature of the big pen. Its palisade was "... fifteen feet high, and measured 190 feet in length by 108 feet in width, and was provided with a shed in the interior 45 feet long by 27 feet wide, and also with a walk, suspended on the outside of the palisade, for the use of the sentries. The location and the provisions of this stockade were worse and more dangerous than even the main prison."[229]

Captain Wilson French of the 17th Connecticut Volunteers, was captured in February of 1865, in the southern part of Florida; he arrived at Andersonville in the middle of February and placed in Castle Reed with sixty-four other officers.

"It was a building formerly used for a guard-house, as I understood."[230] Captain French testified: "Had we not been allowed to buy provisions we would have starved there. We never had any difficulty in getting vegetables; we used to buy almost anything that we wanted of the sergeant who called the roll mornings and nights. His name was Smith, I think; he was Captain Wirz' chief sergeant; we were divided into messes, eight in each mess; my mess used to buy from two to four bushels of sweet potatoes a week, at the rate of fifteen dollars Confederate money per bushel. Turnips we bought at twenty dollars a bushel. We had to buy our own soap. We bought meat and eggs and biscuit. There seemed to be an abundance of those things. They were in the market constantly. That sergeant used to come down with a wagon-load of potatoes at a time, bringing twenty-five bushels at a load sometimes."[231]

Captain French stayed in Castle Reed for about five weeks. "We had to do our own cooking in the building, and when first I went there we were not allowed to go outside unless to go to the sink. They were giving us from thirteen to fifteen dollars in Confederate money to one in greenbacks, and the latter part of the time they gave us twenty dollars for one. According to my observation, produce raised in the Southern states was cheaper than that of the North... The wood was issued to the detachment. It was then subdivided among the nineties, and then again subdivided into thirty pieces. The piece for each man was in thickness and length about the size of my arm, and it was to last for three days."[232]

As the days of spring lengthened, Andersonville began to flourish and mature. The fortifications surrounding

---

[222] Maile, p. 26.
[223] *Ibid.*, p. 45.
[224] Hamlin, p. 186.
[225] Spencer, p. 30.
[226] Hamlin, p. 63.
[227] Walker, p. 67.
[228] *Wirz Trial*, p. 500.
[229] Hamlin, p. 64.
[230] Chipman, p. 180.
[231] *Ibid.*
[232] *Ibid.*, p.181

the pen were strengthened in order to repulse any attack from without or within. The confusion and disorder of the first few months were ameliorated. Confederate officers learned ways to accomplish their assigned tasks more expeditiously. Sources of supplies were discovered or created. It was a time of consolidation. The trauma of the birth of the prison eased, and things began to improve slightly.

With the coming of summer, however, the plight of the prisoners became worse. The men sought solace among themselves and were visited by the representatives of many religions. The number of escape attempts increased and more tunnels were found. The heat and the desire for potable water forced many to dig wells.

## *Chapter Eight*

# Prison Life in the Summer of 1864

***"The small, medium-sized, and spare men stood it better than those given to corpulency, and single men better than the married ones, on account of the latter worrying over thoughts of their families."***

Hyde, p. 236

Men have always sought divine intervention when in trouble and the men at Andersonville were no different. For the first few months after the establishment of the prison, the spiritual needs of the prisoners were met by fellow prisoners who had been elders and lay preachers in their hometown churches. They led their comrades in prayer and conducted informal services around crude altars. Most men had a Bible or New Testament in their knapsacks when captured and were allowed to bring them into the stockade. These two books were, by far, the most popular reading materials in the prison.

There was a turn around at the east end of the street which led from the North Gate. It was used by the wagon that brought in the rations each day. Inside this circle was a tree stump used by those who wished to hold prayer meetings. These religious gatherings were usually held at about sunset. "These men were desirous of forming some system of holding religious meetings, but the terribly crowded condition of the prison had prevented much action being taken in the matter. A few would sometimes get together and have a prayer-meeting, but it was only after the enlargement of the stockade that much attention was paid to this important movement."[1]

Furguson said, "Sergeant Benjamin N. Waddle, of Ohio, an old college friend, must receive the honor of being the first man to gather his dying comrades together to seek consolation at the throne of grace in worship and prayer. This noble and pure-minded man died at Annapolis on his way home."[2]

There were two main leaders of the "Praying Band," as the more devout were called. One leader was Thomas J. Shepherd, a native of Ohio and a member of the Ninety-seventh regiment of Ohio Volunteers. He had been a minister prior to the war and was known as Elder Shepherd. Frank Smith said ten or fifteen men were mostly responsible for conducting the religious services "... which consisted of preaching, prayer meeting, short talks, singing, bible classes and regular Y.M.C.A." The Rev. Shepherd was sometimes known as the "Andersonville Chaplain" and, in 1884, was the Financial Secretary of the Ohio Baptist Educational Society. He resided in Granville, Ohio.[3]

The other leader was Sergeant Boston Corbett, who was a native of New Jersey, and who would later become famous as the man who killed John Wilkes Booth, the assassin of President Abraham Lincoln. Corbett was known around the interior of the pen for his religious fanaticism. Andersonville was certainly not a healthy environment for someone with a personality disorder. If someone went into the horrors of Andersonville with a psychiatric problem, that person would certainly leave in deeper trouble. Corbett's highly neurotic behavior deteriorated from his imprisonment and, after returning home and becoming psychotic, he was committed to an insane asylum.

"He believed he took orders directly from the Almighty. Thus, he marched to a different drummer, gorily so, one might add. In 1858, Corbett, a hat maker in his pre-military days, was accosted by a pair of streetwalkers. It is unclear whether he succumbed to their blandishments or simply feared in the future that he might. A conversation with the Creator showed him the way to salvation: Corbett castrated himself, thus foiling lust's temptations. At the onset of the Civil War, Corbett enlisted in the Union Army. According to his military comrades, he was an odd sol-

---

[1] Urban, p. 338.
[2] Furguson, p. 81.
[3] Frank Smith, p. 78.

**Sergeant Boston Corbett** - One of the leaders of the religious groups at Andersonville. He would, after the war, gain fame for killing John Wilkes Booth, assassin of President Lincoln. Later Corbett was doorkeeper for the Kansas legislature, became insane, was placed in an asylum from which he escaped, and disappeared. (Sergeant Kirkland's Museum)

dier indeed, given to suddenly erupting in religious hymns or else spending hours staring at lights in the sky, which others developed eyestrain trying to see. In combat, however, Corbett proved to be a fighting machine. In the engagement at Culpeper Courthouse, he was said to have held more than two dozen Confederates at bay single-handedly before finally being taken prisoner. Five grueling months at the Confederate prison at Andersonville probably did little to improve his rationality, and when he was involved in a prisoner exchange, one must assume the Rebels felt they had struck a good bargain indeed."[4]

After his exchange, Corbett was with the troops which trapped Booth in the tobacco barn in Bowling Green, Virginia, twelve days after the assassination of Lincoln. "After testifying at the assassination trial, Corbett took to the public appearance circuit, billing himself as the Avenger of Blood. However, his lectures proved less than a total success; he often digressed from the stated subject, the pursuit of Booth, to impart to his audience caustic messages and insults from God.

In the 1880s he was pensioned off by the Kansas legislature, which named him a doorkeeper. Corbett soon came to see these politicians as rogues disobeying the will of God. One spring day in 1886, he fired two revolvers into the crowded assembly. Somehow, no fatalities resulted and Corbett was hauled off to the Topeka Asylum for the Insane. It did not take long for Corbett to escape from the asylum, leaving behind a letter addressed to the American public, complaining of their ingratitude for the services he had rendered. Nothing more was ever heard of him."[5]

Boston Corbett and Thomas J. Shepherd spent a large part of their time at the side of the prisoners who were dying and in pain away from home and loved ones. They led the Praying Band and preached the sermons each evening at dusk.[6] Futch said that these Sermons occurred on alternate nights. The circle of prayer meetings was very popular and so, by the first of July, the praying prisoners would be seen somewhere in the pen each night at twilight. "A Reverend Mr. Gardner of the 135th Ohio Regiment conducted religious meetings and held short services over the bodies of some of the men."[7]

After the prison was enlarged, the leaders of the Praying Band succeeded in obtaining a small area of ground on which to hold the evening services. The services were very informal and commenced when enough men had gathered together. They sat on the ground awaiting the opening prayer. Then, one of the leaders preached a short sermon and led the singing of hymns; he concluded with a benediction. Sometimes an invitation was extended to any who desired to come forward to be prayed for. They were asked to come forward into the circle and kneel in a row on the ground. Sometimes five or six penitents would come forward.

Kellogg described one evening meeting. "Just after one of our quiet sunsets, we gathered together and the elder gave us a splendid discourse upon the text, 'Fight the good fight of faith'... At the close of the meeting four came forward for prayers - one backslider, one new convert, and two who were just beginning to feel the infinite importance of eternal things..."[8]

It was not until about the middle of May that the first representative of a formal religion visited the prison. At

[4] Carl Sifakis, *American Eccentrics* (New York, New York: R. R. Donnelley and Sons, Co., 1984), pp. 107,108.
[5] *Ibid.*, p. 109.
[6] Urban, p. 340.
[7] Boggs, p. 339.
[8] Kellogg, pp. 180, 181.

that time, the Reverend William John Hamilton, a Catholic priest who was over sixty years old, arrived. Reverend Hamilton was priest at the Assumption Church in Macon and his diocese included the prison in southwest Georgia. "The train left Macon at half-past eight in the morning, and got to Andersonville at about half-past one in the afternoon..."[9] He only stayed three or four hours. The purpose of his visit was to find out the number and condition of Catholic prisoners so an appropriate number of priests could be sent. "I saw Captain Wirz the first time I went there. He received me with all kindness and politeness, and seemed to be pleased at my going there when I stated my purpose...He said that he was very well pleased to see me, and that he had expected priests would have gone there before that time...I met him always in his office. There was no restriction upon me whatever in regard to my taking with me anything I chose into the stockade."[10] Captain Wirz gave him a pass valid for the one day only. Wirz walked down to the stockade with him and showed him the entrance.

The next week, Father Hamilton returned and spent three days visiting the stockade and hospital. He then wrote a full report of his findings to his bishop. He spent two days in the stockade and one in the hospital, giving solace to the suffering and administering the sacraments to the dying an average of twenty or thirty times per day. This was how a priest ministered extreme unction to a dying man: "Placing a long purple scarf about his own neck and a small brazen crucifix in the hands of the dying one, he would kneel by the latter's side and anoint him upon the eyes, ears, nostrils, lips, hands, feet and breast, with sacred oil, from a little brass vessel, repeating the while, in an impressive voice, the solemn offices of the Church."[11]

After Father Hamilton's second visit to the pen, he wrote to his bishop, Bishop Augustin Verot, in Savannah, and told him there were large numbers of men dying daily. The Bishop sent Father Peter Whelan to Andersonville about June 1st, and soon sent the French priest, Father Clavreul, to assist him there.

"Peter Whelan was born in 1802 in County Wexford, Ireland. From 1822 to 1824 he attended Birchfield College in Kilkenny, where he received a sound classical and mathematical education before coming to America. He was ordained in Charleston on November 21, 1830. For the next two years he served as secretary to the bishop before beginning his duties in communities throughout North Carolina, including New Bern, Washington, Long Creek, and Raleigh. He was said to have celebrated the first Mass ever offered in Raleigh, at the boarding house of Mathew Shaw, a Presbyterian. He was summoned to Savannah when the bishop succumbed [to yellow fever]. There the Irish priest was stationed for the rest of his life. Soon Whelan became administrator of the whole diocese.

**Father Peter Whelan (1802-1871)** - The only known photograph, probably taken just after the Civil War. (Meaney)

Fort Pulaski, manned by five companies of Confederates, guarded the port of Savannah. When Bishop Verot asked for a volunteer priest to go to Fort Pulaski and serve the needs of all the Catholic troops stationed there, especially the Montgomery Guards composed almost exclusively of Irish Catholics from Savannah, the sixty-year-old Whelan answered the call. The Federals slowly severed Pulaski from Savannah as part of their planned blockade of all Southern ports. On April 13, two days after Pulaski surrendered, the captured Confederates were divided into groups for transportation north. Whelan, then a prisoner of war, endured the rigors of the voyage with the men and, after arriving at Governor's Island, New York, he shared their prison life as well.

After suffering immensely in "Castle William," he was transferred to Fort Delaware, which was called "Starvation Island" because of the poor provisions. After staying there about four weeks or so, Whelan was taken down to Aiken's Landing where, on August 12th, he was unconditionally released. He returned to Savannah where Bishop Verot assigned him to the job of ministering to the Confederate military posts.[12]

When Father H. Clavreul left France for America in September of 1860, he was presented a chalice by a fellow priest. He ended up in Florida at the start of the war and was assigned to minister to the Confederates at the garrison at Fernandina, Florida. He was there in November of 1861 when the

---

[9] *Wirz Trial*, pp. 291, 292.

[10] *Ibid.*, p. 292.

[11] McElroy, p. 216.

[12] Peter J. Meaney, *The Georgia Historical Quarterly*, Vol. LXXI, No. 1, Spring 1987, pp. 1-24.

two thousand-man garrison, both infantry and cavalry, surrendered to the U. S. Naval forces, "... after a short and desultory resistance." Clavreul was allowed to cross the lines a few weeks later, thanks to the courtesy of the Federal officer in command at Jacksonville. He was sent to Savannah, where he had charge of orphan boys, and where he ministered to the Confederate soldiers stationed at Thunderbolt and at other posts and forts on the Savannah river.

In July of 1864, Father Clavreul left Savannah for Andersonville to assist Father Peter Whelan. Clavreul mistakenly said that Father Whelan had been at the prison since March. Clavreul kept a diary while at the prison from July 15th to August 20th, a total of thirty-six days. There, he administered the sacraments of penance and extreme unction to 390 prisoners; interestingly, about 320 of these men were foreign-born. In his daily diary, Clavreul listed the recipient's name, his age, and his birthplace like this: "John Brown, 30 yrs, England." The list does not include those prisoners who were attended by Father Whelan yet Clavreul felt they would have been just as numerous.

Near the end of July, Bishop Verot, with his Vicar General, Father Duncan, came to Andersonville. They stayed two days and shared, with Father Whelan and Father Clavreul, the work of attending to the dying.

Clavreul lived in a small shack or hut that measured about 8 by 12 feet, located about a mile from the stockade. After a restless night on a bunk in his hut, he would eat a hurried breakfast and be at the entrance of the stockade every morning at 5 o'clock.

When Clavreul left the hospital at about midday to go to his shack to eat, he always stopped at the dead house. At his hut, his lunch would be about the same the prisoners ate, i.e."... corn bread, cow peas, and parched corn coffee." He worked until sundown with only a "... one hour recess at midday."

On the 20th day of August, Clavreul became sick "... with continued vomiting." Father Whelan decided he should leave on the morning of the 20th for Savannah. He spent that day and the following night on board the train completely unconscious, lying under the car seat. He revived when he arrived at Savannah.

By the 24th of September, Clavreul had sufficiently recovered. He again began to administer to the prisoners in Savannah who, just a few days beforehand, had arrived from Andersonville. From the 21st of September to October 6th, he administered the sacraments to seventy more prisoners at Savannah.

**Father H. Clavreul** - He administered the sacraments to hundreds of prisoners at Andersonville and Savannah. (Robbins)

Most of the prisoners were exchanged in November and, on December 21st, Savannah surrendered. In April of 1865, Clavreul administered to the white and black refugees who had come down with smallpox and who had been sent to Fort Boggs, one-and-a-half miles from the city of Savannah. Later, after the war, he was called back to Florida and assigned to eastern Florida around St. Augustine and Jacksonville. He helped in the publication of his diary, from which the above sketch was taken, in July, 1908, while in St. Augustine.[13]

Father Hamilton went to General Cobb and described the condition he had witnessed. General Cobb asked Father Hamilton what he would recommend be done to alleviate the suffering, as he intended to write to Richmond concerning the conditions at the prison. General Cobb said the conditions were unavoidable because of the blockade. Father Hamilton then recommended the prisoners be released at Jacksonville into the hands of the Federal troops there. Father Hamilton saw Cobb again when he introduced Father Whelan to Cobb on about the first of June. At that meeting, Cobb gave Father Whelan a letter of introduction to General Winder, which he wrote in their presence. Father Hamilton's final visit to Andersonville was in February or March, 1865.

Father Whelan arrived at Andersonville on June 16th and stayed four months. He left in October, after most prisoners had been sent to Millen and other points. Father John Kirby, of Augusta, came to take over the void left by the departure of Clavreul, but he remained there only two weeks. After Father Kirby left, a Jesuit from Spring Hill College near Mobile arrived, but he, too, stayed only two or three weeks. His name was Father Hossanah or sometimes he was called Father Anselm Usannez.[14] He was especially valuable because he spoke three or four languages. One of the priests from Savannah became completely prostrated, and went to Macon where Father Hamilton resided; he lived with Hamilton a few days while he regained his strength.

Father Whelan was "... middle-aged, tall, slender, and unmistakably devout."[15] He described how he ended his

---

[13] George Robbins, ed.,*Diary of Rev. Henry P. Clavreul*, Published by the Conn. Association of Ex-Prisoners of War (Waterbury, Conn.: April 1910), pp. 1-18.

[14] Meaney, p. .

[15] McElroy, p. 216.

days. "When I leave the prison in the evening, full of sorrow at what I have seen here, I find that the best use I can make of my time is in studying the Word of God, and especially the Psalms of David."[16]

All the priests at Andersonville were very dedicated and were often seen crawling on their hands and knees into the shebangs to give succor and extreme unction to the dying. They were followed by a small crowd of admirers and the curious.

"In late August, as Sherman was about to enter Atlanta, a transfer of prisoners to Savannah and Charleston began. By late September, Whelan decided that he could leave, but his ministrations to the prisoners were not over. The priest contacted Henry Horne, a well-educated and devout Catholic as well as a successful restaurant owner in Macon. From him Whelan borrowed $16,000 in Confederate money, the equivalent of $400 in gold, and went to Americus, in January, to purchase ten thousand pounds of wheat flour. Baked into bread and distributed at the prison hospital, this much-needed food soon became know as 'Whelan's bread.' It lasted several months."[17]

Reverend Whelan testified: "I borrowed $16,000 and went down to Andersonville. I spoke to Captain Wirz and he freely gave me permission to purchase flour for the prisoners. I gave the money to a gentleman in Americus of the name of Wynne, and he purchased the flour and sent it to Captain Wirz. I think that he wrote a letter to Father Hamilton stating that he did so. When I applied to him about it he mentioned to me that he would have to take the flour in his own charge and see that it was cooked and distributed in bread to the prisoners. I could not say whether it was distributed."[18]

"In the fall of 1864 Father Whelan came to me and asked me if my name was Dr. Bates. I said 'Yes.' Said he, 'You are the man I want; I want you to have Hennesey and Delaney appointed for the distribution of the bread. I have bought 10,000 pounds of flour, and I will put it in the hands of Captain Wirz, and I want you to see to the proper distribution of it.' I told him I would do so whenever I had an opportunity."[19]

Dr. John C. Bates testified: "I saw some few instances of neglect on the part of the nurses... On one occasion I detected fourteen loaves of bread that were being kept from the prisoners. It was what was known as Father Whelan's bread, which he had placed under my direction. Two men named Delaney and Hennesey had been selected by Father Whelan to distribute the bread. They appropriated on one occasion fourteen loaves. It was in the spring of 1865, and I was officer of the day. I went to every wardmaster and inquired the number of loaves he had for his ward. I then went to the head distributor and found out the number of loaves issued to each ward, and the returns corresponded. 'Now,' said I to Delaney and Hennesey, 'I have the returns from headquarters and I find there are fourteen loaves missing. Those loaves must be accounted for. You cannot wrong the patients out of their rations in that way; I will step out for a moment, and the loaves must be produced.' I absented myself for a moment, and when I came back the fourteen loaves were produced and were distributed among the sick."[20]

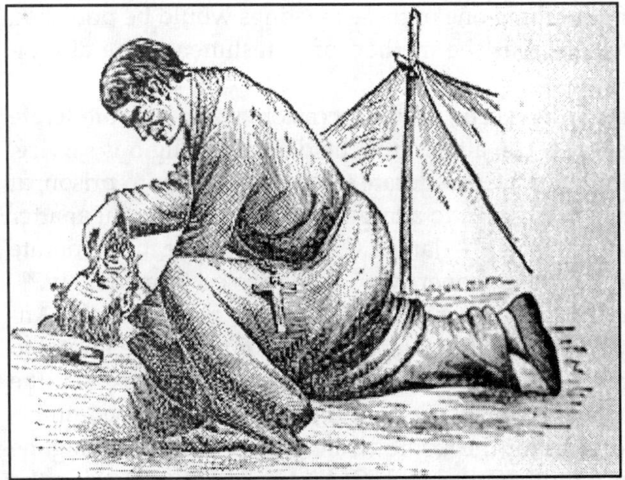

Catholic Priest Administering the Last Rites

The prisoners were starved for information about the progress of the war since few prisoners were admitted during the latter part of the summer. They also desired to know the status of the exchange talks. The priests were not allowed to discuss either of these two subjects or they would be forbidden to enter the pen. "The Catholic priest was in almost daily, visiting the sick of his own order, and giving a word of good counsel to all. We sometimes tried to draw out from him some information of matters in the world outside, but we could seldom gain anything, as he was not allowed to make any communications to the prisoners under penalty of being forbidden admission to the prison."[21] The priest about whom Kellogg wrote was Father Whelan. "Captain Wirz, commanding the prison, was a member of the Catholic church, and it was said that he would allow none but Catholic

[16] *Ibid.*, p. 217.
[17] Meaney, p. 19.
[18] *Wirz Trial*, p. 427.
[19] *Ibid.*, p. 663.
[20] *Ibid.*, p. 662.
[21] Kellogg, p. 163.

priests to enter the prison for the purpose of administering spiritual consolation to the dying."[22]

Almost all prisoners were aware of the visits of the Catholic priests but few were aware of visits by religious counselors of any other denominations. "The churches of all denominations, except one solitary Catholic priest, ignored us as wholly as they would dumb beasts."[23] Miller said, "A catholic priest was the only minister who was ever known to come into the prison. He did not hold any public services."[24] Priests "... are said to be using their doctrinal influence to get men to swear allegiance to the Confederacy. I do not accept this as true, though one of Erin's sons frequently visited, who said to me that he refused to renounce Uncle Sam yesterday went out with the priest and had not returned."[25] "Among the new arrivals in June was Chaplain Saul Hathaway of an Indiana infantry regiment. He had been in Belle Isle and Pemberton prisons at Richmond and was sent away from there on the plea of being insane, but in reality to remove to a safer place such an irrepressible patriot...Hathaway came to our division and said he would preach next day, which he said was Sunday. The whole camp turned out to hear him. A sergeant came with a squad of men to see and hear what was said and done, and informed Hathaway that he might preach and pray provided there was no objectionable language used, but that singing would not be allowed. Hathaway replied that he would preach, pray and sing as long as the Lord gave him breath, and the whole Confederacy could not prevent it while he was alive. The meeting was not dispersed. At its close Hathaway was marched to headquarters but was soon returned. He started around the next day, announced a prayer meeting for Wednesday night, and kept up regular services till his sickness and death. We arranged for celebrating the Fourth of July that year and had chosen Hathaway as the orator of the day. But he was taken violently ill on the second of the month and died on the eighth. He lay on his back in his dugout and sent for the boys and talked with and prayed for them for days after he was unable to stand on his feet. We could often hear him singing his favorite hymn: *Jesus, Lover of my Soul*."[26]

On Sunday, July 26th, Northrop went to a "... meeting this morning near the big pine trees in the southeast part of the pen, preaching by Sergeant Benjamin N. Waddle, of 126th Ohio. Some of those active in carrying on the meetings are Rev. T. J. Shepherd, B. N. Waddle, M. H. Miller, 22nd Mich. Cavalry, and Robert H. Kellogg, of 16th Connecticut Regt., Thomas A. Cord, U. S. Infantry, also Boston Corbett.There is often a chorus of nearly a hundred voices, some evenings, of fine singers."[27] "There were four or five places where these ragged, scurvied, filthy, vermin-eaten wretches met twice a week and tried to worship God."[28] Vawter said the most favorite hymns were *O Thou Fount* and *Rock of Ages*.

There were some men in the prison who annoyed and disturbed these religious meetings. The leader of the Regulators issued an order which stated any one found guilty of disturbing one of these meetings would be punished by a number of lashes on the bare back. Whipping on the bare back was the method of punishment generally inflicted by the Regulators.

Most men said no Protestant minister ever came within the prison except, on one occasion, when a Confederate chaplain came in and read an extract from some Northern newspaper. He, afterwards, held a short religious service. This occurred near the first of August, when "... a man, professing to be a Confederate Chaplain, came into prison, at the request of General Winder, and read an extract from the *New York Herald*, to a large crowd, regarding the matter of exchange, (i.e., that an immediate exchange was more than probable)."[29] James C. Melvin said a Confederate preacher was in the pen on Monday August 1st, and this minister said the prisoners would be paroled immediately.[30]

"A Methodist missionary to Florida troops in the Confederate army, Reverend E. B. Duncan, addressed the Andersonville prisoners on two occasions. Visiting the post in early August for the purpose of expounding the gospel to the company of Florida artillery stationed there, Duncan delivered a sermon in the stockade from atop a box near the sutler's stand. Again in January, 1865, when only about 5,000 captives remained at Andersonville, he stopped on his way to Florida and spent three evenings conducting religious services for the Confederate troops. Before leaving, he preached to the stockade inmates and, briefly, to the patients in the prison hospital. Of his second adventure in the stockade, Duncan wrote to a fellow minister: 'They stood up round me, while I stood on a box and declared to them the Gospel. I had unusual liberty, and they listened with most profound attention. At the close, I invited them to seek

[22] Urban, p. 345.
[23] Boggs, p. 55.
[24] Miller, p. 30.
[25] Northrop, p. 74.
[26] Bates, pp. 37, 38.
[27] Northrop, p. 93.
[28] Vawter, p. 61.
[29] Kellogg, p. 195.
[30] Melvin, p. 125.

religion and come to God, when the ground was literally covered with them that prostrated themselves. But few in that vast assembly remained standing... They treated me with the greatest respect, thanking me kindly and begging me to return, and followed me when leaving as if loath to let me go. Many came to shake hands, until, like the Indian, I said, 'I shake hands in my heart.'"[31]

The Rev. E. B. Duncan, testified: "I have lived for the last few years in Florida. Previously to that time I lived in Tennessee; I am a Tennesseean by birth. I am a minister; a Methodist. I have been preaching in Florida for the last two years to the confederate camps in Florida; I was a missionary. I have been in northern Alabama during this war, and also in the neighborhood of Fort Donelson. I had a circuit which embraced Fort Donelson and Fort Henry. I was at Andersonville, Georgia. My object in going there was to preach to the Florida troops at Andersonville. My mission was to the Florida army. I preached to the prisoners in the stockade. My pass, I believe, dates the 31st of July , 1864. I preached in the morning to the Gamble artillery, from Tallahassee. I was to preach that evening at 4 o'clock in the stockade. I went to General Winder, who was then in command, to get a pass, and he referred me to Captain Wirz. Captain Wirz had gone home, which was about two miles off, they told me. Next morning, the 1st day of August, at 10 o'clock, I called at Captain Wirz' office; I told him that I wished permission to preach in the stockade. He granted me permission, and gave me a pass to go in at will. He told me what would be the best time to go in, and mentioned the roll-call, the sick-call, and the rations. He told me it would suit me better at that hour. I went in that morning and preached to the prisoners. I took in a paper which I was permitted to take in, a Macon paper, which had in it a piece respecting the exchange of prisoners. I went in with a great deal of pleasantry and met a good many of them at the gate. They had come out to sick-call. Said I, 'Men, I have some good news for you in this paper, and I have some better news to tell you after you hear this.' They said they would hear both. I told them I wished to preach to them. I did so, and they stopped me every ten steps to have the piece read respecting the exchange. I was very much broken down myself. My lungs were weak and I called on several of the prisoners to read it. At last I got to the middle of the stockade, where Captain Wirz told me it was most suitable to preach. It was near the sutler's shanty, I think. They put me out a box, and I told them that if they would gather around, I would preach as loud as I could. They did so, a larger congregation than I could see. I could not see the extent of my congregation. It rained upon me twice while I was preaching, but no man left. I had great liberty in preaching. I would say further that my pass was given to go in at will; and last February I preached again at the stockade and in the hospital on my old pass. Captain Wirz' manner towards me at that time was very gentlemanly. He gave me every assistance. I only spent a moment in his office. He was a businessman, and I was also of the same order.

"I preached to the Union soldiers at Andersonville on the 1st day of August, 1864, and also in February, 1865. I was there about a week each time. The last time I was there it was very cold weather. I did not go into the stockade until Saturday, which was the first warm day suitable for me to preach. I did not circulate around much; it was very cold weather. I was with our Florida troops and preached to them every night. When I was there in August I circulated all the time. While I was at Andersonville I did not know or hear of Captain Wirz shooting, killing, kicking or otherwise injuring a prisoner; I heard nothing on that score."[32]

Confederate Captain Samuel B. Davis described the religious leaders at Andersonville, "They were in the stockade day after day for nine months, holding the closest relations to those to whom they were indeed ministering angels, who had opportunities, if any one had, of seeing and hearing everything that took place in and around the stockade; they swore that Captain Wirz gave them every facility to attend the sick and dying; that he welcomed them to the stockade when they first came there, and they swore they never heard or knew that Wirz shot, or beat, or maltreated a single prisoner at Andersonville.

"At the trial five or six of the most intelligent and respectable men that had entered Andersonville gave similar testimony - Brooklyn Eagle, July 27, '66"[33]

Each morning would be heard a drum roll announcing dead-call, the time the dead were to be brought to the South Gate. "The same drummer thumped away at a certain hour each morning to summon the camp to deliver up its dead."[34]

"Some of the prisoners died so suddenly that we could hardly realize that they had passed away. They appeared to be as well as the rest of us up to within a few hours of their departure, when they would expire, sometimes without a groan.

[31] Futch, pp. 60, 61.
[32] *Wirz Trial*, pp. 609, 610.
[33] Boyer Davis, p. 36.
[34] Fosdick, p. 41.

"An Irish soldier died in this manner close to us, on the day the Maryland boy died. He and an Englishman kept close together, and were evidently intimate friends. On the day he died we received molasses instead of meat, and the Englishman was offering his friend his portion and urging him to eat; but finding that he made no effort to take it, he sat down and rested his friend's head on his lap. He, however, soon after again commenced to urge him to eat his rations, holding the molasses to his lips and telling him to take it, saying it would do him good. Sergeant Bradbury and myself were passing them at the time, and noticing the deathly appearance of the sick man, we went close up to them, and Bradbury told the Englishman that his friend was dying, to which he replied, 'Oh, I guess not.' but immediately made an effort to lay him down. He died, however, before he could do so."[35]

Many soldiers woke up in the morning to find their tentmate dead and the body would become the possession of this friend. Sometimes a few words were said over the body, appealing to a divine being to bring peace to this friend. If the prisoner had died during the night when the pen first opened, the body would be placed in front of the shebang until morning. The bodies of a few men were buried after being sewn into burlap sacks while others had the luxury of clothing. Later most were buried naked, the clothing being needed by the living.

In the morning, the bodies would be collected by the men who had been detailed to collect all the bodies within the pen. The deceased would be taken and lined up adjacent to the deadline between the South Gate and the little bridge which crossed Stockade Creek.[36] These men "... would peep down into the gopher holes as we called them and hollow,' are you dead?' If they didn't speak they would reach down and pull him out. Sometimes they couldn't speak but were not quite dead and they would roll them back, by the next time they came in they were pretty sure to be dead."[37] There, just inside the South Gate, the fallen comrades were thrown on an army wagon by Negro prisoners detailed for this purpose. Everyone said the bodies were thrown on in a random, calloused fashion. Only one man, the Southern surgeon, Doctor Bates, testified the corpses were laid on the carts in an orderly manner. He said the dead "... were laid in the wagon, I believe, head foremost, one on another, regularly along in layers."[38] After the wagon had been loaded, it was driven to the cemetery. "Oftimes the dead were not drawnout for two days. I have counted two hundred or more dead men at one time; and as they lay exposed to the hot sun, the effect can better be imagined than described. Thus the dead who died inside the stockade were disposed of for the first two months; after that they were carried outside to the dead house."[39] "In the early morning the dead-cart came for the bodies. This was an army wagon without covering, drawn by four mules and driven by a slave. The bodies were tossed into the cart without regard to regularity or decency, being thrown upon one another as logs or sticks are packed in a pile. In this manner, with their arms and legs hanging over the sides, and their heads jostling and beating against each other, they were hauled to the cemetery."[40] "During the first part of the season the dead were taken from the prison direct to the place of burial, but later on a dead-house was erected outside; and each afternoon the dead were carried out to this, where they remained until they would be taken to the burying ground."[41]

**The dead being swung up on the Dead Wagon** - About 24 of the dead were carried out at a time in wagons that, later that day, would be used for hauling rations to the prisoners. (Boggs)

Sometime in May or June, the dead house was erected just inside of the second palisade southwest of the South Gate. This depressing mortuary was visible from the north slope. It consisted of little more than four poles with pine boughs arranged so as to cover the cadavers from the hot Georgia sun. The dead house was usually depicted with pine boughs on three of the four sides. After the erection of the dead house, the dead were first carried to the South Gate and then on to the dead house. After resting in this abode for varying lengths of time, the army wagon would arrive and the dead were then placed on the wagon for transport to the cemetery. "The 'Dead House' was constructed of insufficient dimensions to contain the bodies of all that died. Sometimes forty, often thirty were placed

[35] Urban, p. 406.
[36] Dufur, p. 178.
[37] Clifton, p. 10.
[38] Chipman, p. 132.
[39] Dufur, p. 78.
[40] Frank Smith, pp. 51, 52.
[41] Dufur, p. 127.

upon the ground outside its limits, where they lay in the open air."[42]

When a friend died, sometimes his death would not be reported at roll call so that the decedent's rations could be eaten until the deception was discovered by the authorities. When Dowling's comrade died, Dowling buried him under their underground hut and told the sergeant of his squad this comrade was sick and couldn't attend roll call. He lived for several weeks on double rations. When the secret was discovered, Dowling received nine lashes at the whipping post.

Thomas H. Horne testified: "One man died and lay there so long that he could not be taken out, and they had to bury him where he died."[43] After a few weeks, as wood became more scarce, the bodies became more valuable. They were a means to get to the outside of the pen. They would not be placed in front of the shebangs because they would be stolen during the early morning. Instead, they were kept within the shebang sometimes under the blanket with their tentmates. Some prisoners actually tied the bodies to themselves; sometimes this tether would be cut during the night and the body stolen .

Fosdick told about the preparation of one of his comrades, C. B. Bartshe of Rossville, Iowa, for burial after his death on May 23rd. "He seemed to weaken down gradually, until one night I awoke and found him dead, with his arm lying across me as when we lay down. I brushed back his matted hair, felt to see if he had any pulse, then lay down beside him until morning. When dead-call sounded we carried him to the gate, pinned a slip of paper to his shirt bearing his name, company and regiment, tied his toes together, wrapped his tattered garments about him, then took our last look at one we loved as a brother."[44]

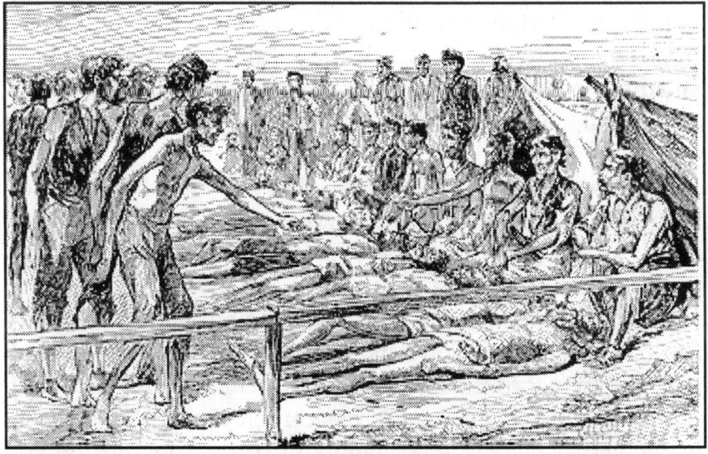

**Prisoners selling their dead friends** - to other prisoners who could go out and, possibly, bring in food and wood. Thus the dead became a commodity to sell, worth about $5 each at the time. (Grigsby)

In time, the men recognized that the carrying out of a fallen comrade to the dead house was a very valuable task. The cadaver itself took on a monetary value. "It came to be considered a privilege to assist in this work, so that men would contend for it. It even came to be a matter of trade, and from one to three dollars in United States money was the price for being permitted to carry out a dead body. In doing this work, the bearers would not only have the opportunity of breathing God's free air for a short time, but they often obtained admission to the hospital for a few moments, where they were likely to find some untasted portion of food that had been given to the sick, and this they would obtain to appease their hunger. They were allowed by the guard to collect any wood that lay along the roadside; and often two fellows who had given two dollars for a dead body, would bring in wood that they could sell for five."[45]

"They were then carried on litters to the inside of the outer stockade, and from there they were hauled away in wagons - sometimes two-horse, sometimes four-horse wagons."[46]

"Our orders were to go into every ward in the morning and take the dead out. I have seen 128 bodies and 135 bodies lying in the dead-house at one time, lying there before the wagons came after them to move them out. The dead bodies were allowed to remain over a day without being taken off, so that when loading them up the bodies often bursted. A major there ordered us every evening to get six ounces of liquor, because he imagined we ought to have that on account of our business."[47] "As soon as breath left the body it became a piece of merchandise, exchangeable for rations of food, or even for money. The dead man's nearest friend claimed the corpse, and was generally as proud of his property as a boy is of his first pantaloons. The secret of their value was this: we did not get half enough wood to cook our food, and we were allowed to carry the dead bodies of our comrades to the dead house outside of the prison; on our way back we could gather as much wood as we could carry, and this extra allowance would insure

[42] Frank Smith, p. 50.
[43] Chipman, p. 177.
[44] Fosdick, p. 48.
[45] Dufur, p. 79.
[46] Chipman, p. 132.
[47] *Wirz Trial*, p. 348.

us well cooked victuals for two weeks. But the great trouble was to keep the body from being stolen until the time came for carrying it outside, for we could only go out with the dead from ten o'clock in the morning until four o'clock in the afternoon; as if a friend should happen to die in the night, ten chances to one but his poor tenement of clay would be stolen by daylight. To prevent this many of the boys fastened a strong piece of cord to the corpse, and tied the other end around their own wrist, and then the body could not be removed without waking them; but for all their watchfulness, many a hungry, half-starved man who went to sleep at night with bright visions of well-cooked food on the morrow, has awake in the morning to find that the friend who was so near and dear to him, dearer when dead than he was in life, has been removed forever from his sight, and the profit of his removal gone to another."[48]

This taking out of the deceased provided a unique method of escape. It was sometimes called the "dead dodge." "Each morning all the dead were gathered and taken over to the south side before being removed to the dead house. Often some of the boys would play dead, and the comrades understanding the 'dodge' would tie the big toes together with a rag, label the body and take it to the 'dead house,' then upon the tricky 'yank' himself depended the completion of the efforts to reach 'God's country' as we always called the north."[49]

Another description of this method of escape follows: "One was to feign death, and to be laid out; this laying-out consisted of having a string or piece of cloth tied around the head under the throat, to keep the jaws from dropping, and the two big toes were tied together, to keep the legs from spreading apart. A person who wished to try this mode to escape was laid out in this manner by his friends, and carried by them, accompanied by a Rebel guard, to the dead-house, which was outside of the prison. Here he had to lay all day, with a dead man on each side of him, and if the deaths were very numerous that day, perhaps one or two dead men would be laid on top of him; all this he would have to bear with patience until nearly midnight, and then, when all was still, steal carefully by the guard, perhaps to wander for a day or two in the surrounding swamps, or, more likely, to be recaptured next morning by Turner and his blood-hounds, and be turned into prison again with a ten pound ball and six inch chain riveted to the ankle, as a punishment for trying to escape."[50]

After this was tried several times, the authorities placed a guard at the dead house so that the "dead" would not get up and run away. "After the death of a prisoner, his comrades would write his name, company, and regiment on a piece of paper, and then pin it on his clothing. If his name was not known, as was sometimes the case, the single word 'Unknown' was written on the paper. They were then carried to the Dead House, and laid side-by-side on the ground. Sometimes more than one hundred bodies would be lying in a row at one time, awaiting burial."[51]

Sometimes the paper with the information was tied to one of the toes or wrists when the "body" was carried out. Just outside the gate, a clerk was stationed whose duty it was to record the names, company names and regiment numbers of the unfortunates. "Within the large Court beyond the Wicket Gate, was a desk upon which was the Andersonville 'Death Register.' One of our own number was detailed as clerk. He received an extra ration and the liberty of remaining outside, under oath not to make any attempt to escape. When the prisoners, with their dead comrade reached this desk, the clerk would copy upon the register what was placed upon the slip... (i.e. the next higher number sequentially)."[52] "On a card attached to the wrist of the deceased was written by the detachment sergeant, his name, regiment and date of death. These names were taken by the enumerator, who verified the record as the bodies were carried through the gate."[53] A better name for the enumerator was the "death register clerk." "If the name, company and regiment were known, they were given to the death register clerk, who recorded the name on his record, and duplicated that number on the body. This enabled the burial squad (our own men) to mark on a stake the location of each body."[54]

"One day a prisoner by the name of John L. Ransom, being outside the gate, and too weak for his task fainted. The rebels thought him dead, chucked him in the dead pile, where after lying in the hot sun for some time, he came to, sat up, and said, 'For God sake! give me some water:' A rebel officer said, 'Lookey heah, Yank, if you hain't dead yet, you get back inside to die and thet putty darned quick."[55] This prisoner survived Andersonville and became the author of *The Andersonville Diary*.

This was one of the better descriptions of the funeral process: "Every morning the dead were gathered up and

[48] Brownell, pp. 22, 23.
[49] Frank Smith, pp. 31, 32.
[50] Brownell, p. 18.
[51] Urban, p.305.
[52] Frank Smith, p. 53.
[53] Maile, p. 37.
[54] Maile, p.  .
[55] Boggs, p. 46.

carried to the South Gate and there laid in rows until all were brought there. The gate would open and we would carry out our friends. Immediately outside of the gate one of our men was stationed whose duty it was to make a complete record of the dead. He would first give the corpse a number, you would then give him the man's name, the company and regiment he belonged to, when he died and the State he was from. We then carried the body to the dead house. When they were all carried out a wagon with four mules and four negroes would drive up and the loading process would commence. Two negroes on the ground and two on the wagon. The two on the ground would take a corpse by the knee and arm and throw it up on the wagon; the two on the wagon would take it in the same manner and throw it up front, piling them on top of one another until it was full. They would then fill up the hind part in the same manner; I think 24 was a load."[56]

Several different wagons were used at various times to carry the dead to the cemetery. "Every morning a large army-wagon would be driven up to the dead-house, and twenty or thirty bodies would be loaded in like so many logs of wood, one top of another, some with an arm hanging out at the side, and others with their limbs protruding at the sides, for there was no covering at all. The rebels finally became ashamed of their own want of decency, and provided a covered wagon."[57] "They were all placed in the dead house, where they lay until three o'clock in the afternoon, when the dead wagon, which was a large box drawn by mules, was brought around and the bodies thrown in."[58]

James K. Davidson, of the 4th Iowa cavalry testified: "We would go by way of the depot sometimes and get rations in the same wagon in which we carried dead bodies; those were the orders, I believe, from the quartermaster or the man who had charge of the teams; I believe his name was Duncan; I think he was an officer; he had charge of the cook-house." He said that the wagons were pulled by two teams and that 20 to 25 bodies constituted a load of dead.[59]

"The dead wagon had either two or sometimes four horses."[60] One author described the wagon as a "... common field cart."[61] "Two six-mule teams were kept busy drawing the dead to the burying-ground, and, in August, when the death rate was so great, three hundred bodies were lying unburied at the dead-house. It was necessary to employ the whole team-force of the prison, including bread and wood teams, to draw them away."[62]

This privilege of carrying out the dead, evidently, was discontinued later in the summer. "In the early summer prisoners were occasionally detailed under guard to carry the dead some distance from the gate. On the return they were allowed to gather up chips which had accumulated from the hewing of stockade timbers The quantity a man, weakened by hunger and disease, could bring in would sell for five dollars, U. S. currency. Competition to get out on one of these details became so intense that the privilege was discontinued."[63] Besides the competition to get detailed to take out a body, the large number of escape attempts also influenced this discontinuance.

The heavily-laden wagon ambled up the single-lane path the few hundred yards from the dead house. About two hundred yards past the kitchen, the wagon would be unloaded of its gristly cargo under the watchful eyes of "countless " buzzards that almost continually circled the cemetery. "From the prison we could see the buzzards lazily flying in circles over and around the last resting place of our companions."[64] The bodies were recorded by a paroled Federal prisoner, Dorence Atwater, in a book called the "dead list." Atwater secretly kept a second copy, which became invaluable after the war to help identify the graves.

The actual grave was nothing more than a "... trench running due north and south," two to three feet deep, dug by Federal prisoners. Ira Petit, mistakenly, said, "Our men carry out the dead, the rebels buried them."[65] Kellogg said that, when the prison first opened, the Confederates supplied simple wooden coffins but this was quickly discontinued. Urban also said, "When the prison was first established, the rebels furnished plain pine coffins for the dead; but that was soon abandoned."[66] This supplying of the caskets by the Confederates may only have been rumored. As early as April the 11th, Dick Winder said, "I am burying the dead without coffins."[67] He also said, "Materials were too scarce and I considered it much more important to alleviate the suffering of the living than to use these materials

[56] Walker, p. 35.
[57] Kellogg, p. 278.
[58] Brownell, p. 23.
[59] *Wirz Trial*, p. 141.
[60] Clifton, p. 10.
[61] Author's library.
[62] Frank Smith, pp. 26, 27.
[63] Maile, p. 37.
[64] Brownell, p. 24.
[65] Ray, p. 203.
[66] Urban, p. 367.
[67] *O.R.*, VII, p. 40.

with the dead."[68]

The next method of burial utilized by the Confederates was to dig a trench with a ten-inch dirt step or shelf at the corpse's head and feet. Across the deeper portion of the trench containing the body was placed a slab of wood resting on the two steps to keep the dirt off the body. "About 9 A. M. we were sent to dig graves, with a guard of forty men placed over us. We dug trenches about one hundred and sixty feet long and three feet deep, and at the bottom of this we dug a vault of one foot in depth. Jake Helamaker, of Ohio, and myself split slabs and placed one over each of our dead. We also, as far as could be done, placed a board with regiment, company and name."[69] "Many of the diggers did escape, and finally the rebs released us from our parole and placed a guard over us."[70] "The rebs had formed guard lines around the grave-yard; but covered wagons were used to bring dead bodies from the prison. Two of the diggers were placed in each wagon upon its return to the stockade, and the curtains being tied down, two of us would slip out while on the road on the first trip, and hid in the swamp near by until the next trip, when another comrade and a fellow-prisoner followed us, and we immediately took up our line of march for 'God's country.'"[71] "When they first took their prisoners to Georgia, they furnished coffins, but the mortality became so great that they finally neglected to do that, and dug a trench about two and a half feet deep, with a kind of shelf of dirt ten inches high, on which they placed slabs of wood to keep the earth from them. In a little time they died too fast for even this, and they then dug a trench that would hold about one hundred and twenty five bodies in which they placed them close together and covered them up."[72]

"By the large prison gate there lay ten dead men ready to be carried out for burial. They were to be taken just as they were, placed in an army wagon, one upon the other, until it was filled, and driven off to the place of burial, like so many animals, without coffin, or even a winding sheet. Then they were to be placed side by side in long, shallow trenches, a few boards placed over them, a covering of earth thrown in, and the burial of the patriot was ended."[73] "At first the bodies were covered with boards but when men were dying at the rate of a hundred or more every day the boards were dispensed with."[74] As the bodies began arriving more rapidly, the step and board were eliminated. Lye was sprinkled on the decedents to hasten decomposition.

At the head of each grave was placed a small, wooden slab about a foot wide and a couple of feet high. On this head board was branded a number. The dead were serially numbered from number one upward. These numbers were recorded in the "dead book," which was kept by the office of the Chief Surgeon. "Books and a tent" were provided by the authorities for the use of the burial detail.[75] "For the care observed in the burial of the dead after the carts arrived at the cemetery, and the preserving of the records of the victims, and the place, we are indebted to our own men, who were paroled especially for the purpose."[76]

There were accusations made against the Federal prisoners paroled on the burial detail that they had desecrated the dead. After his inspection in August, Confederate Lieutenant Colonel D. T. Chandler reported the dead prisoners' "... hands in many instances [had been] first mutilated with an ax in the removal of any finger-rings they may have [had]."[77]

Because the handling of the bodies was so traumatic, those men detailed to bury the dead were issued a ration of whiskey to fortify them. "Large quantities of whiskey were given to the men who attended to the burial of these."[78]

A prisoner testified: "I was on duty as a grave-digger. The prisoners were buried in trenches 180 feet long, 7 feet wide, and 3 ½ feet deep. That was the order we had from Captain Piggot, superintendent of the graveyard. They were laid side by side on their backs; and we generally covered them with some pine slabs or puncheons as they were called, until these got so scarce that we could not get enough to cover the bodies, so we just put them in without anything covering them but the ground. The bodies when they came there for internment were about half mortified. We could hardly touch them to pull them out of the wagons on to the old stretcher without their skin remaining in our hands; and they were full of vermin of all descriptions. Two teams drawn by four mules each, were employed in

[68] *O.R.*, VIII, p. 732.
[69] Compton, p. 63.
[70] *Ibid.*, p. 57.
[71] *Ibid.*
[72] Kellogg, p. 279.
[73] *Ibid.*, p. 69.
[74] Lyons, p. 102.
[75] Stevenson, p. 452.
[76] Hamlin, p. 57.
[77] *O.R.*, VII, p. .
[78] Kellogg, p. 276.

bringing the dead to the graveyard. They were covered wagons like our army wagons. They were hauling steadily from morning till night almost...

"I saw Captain Wirz in the graveyard very often, because his residence was just beyond the graveyard, and he passed on his old gray horse every morning. He never did anything in the graveyard... we had to hand in our report every evening to him. He gave us directions how deep we should dig the graves. We dug them in accordance with his orders, three and a half feet deep. He gave no orders in anything else about the burying-ground. We once made application for another stretcher. He said we should go to Dr. White, and Dr. White said that we should go to Captain Wirz. The old stretcher had such a big hole in it that the dead would sometimes fall through as we were carrying them from the wagon to the grave. We made application to Captain Wirz, as he passed one morning, to get us a new stretcher. He said we should go to Surgeon White. We went to Surgeon White and he told us we should go to Captain Wirz; that he was the proper officer."[79]

W. W. Crandall, a prisoner of the 4th Iowa Infantry Regiment, testified: "When I was engaged in the burying ground I worked with those who dug the graves. A man by the name of Byron had charge of digging those trenches. I think he belonged to the second Georgia reserves - either the second or third. He was detailed to take charge of us. I never heard him give any orders in relation to the digging of those graves. We were never restrained from digging to any depth we chose, but we were expected to dig a certain depth. We might dig deeper if we chose. I never heard anybody order us not to dig deeper. I don't remember that I ever saw or knew of any indecencies ordered or directed towards those who were buried. I have seen them robbed of their clothing. I have seen the rebel soldiers rob the bodies of their clothing, and I have seen our own men do it. I never saw any corpses with their fingers cut off or mutilated in any way. The bodies were not kicked or cuffed about, or handled indecently in any way in the burying-ground. There were two different teams that assisted in drawing; that is, there were two drivers...

**The Graveyard at Andersonville** - This depicts the unloading of the dead off the Dead Wagon onto stretchers which were then carried to the prepared slit trenches. (Dowling)

"We cut pine trees, varying from eight to fourteen inches through, and split them into slabs from three to four inches thick; that is what we called puncheons. They were seven feet long, just long enough to lie across the trench. We used these puncheons until near the middle of August. I commenced to work in that burying-ground the 23rd of June. We discontinued the use of puncheons because we had not help sufficient to bury the dead and to continue splitting the puncheons. There were not colored men at work with me in the burying-ground. There were no colored men at work in connection with the burying-ground at the time I had anything to do with it, so far as I knew. I think there were about thirty Union soldiers at work there, digging, covering, making stakes, bringing water, &c."[80]

W. W. Crandall, also testified. "We buried the bodies in trenches about seven feet wide. I don't remember the length, but we put 150 bodies in each trench. The trench was dug about seven feet wide and nearly three and a half feet deep; then for a foot or a foot and a half deeper it would be six feet wide, leaving a six inch shoulder upon each side; then as long as we had sufficient help, there were men splitting pine puncheons seven feet in length. They were laid over the bodies, and then the grave was filled. The bodies were laid upon the ground side by side as close as they could be laid. We covered them in that way until, I think, the middle of August, when some of the men detailed were taken sick, and there were so many more to be buried that we were short of help, and after that no puncheons were used. We then merely dug the trench, six feet and a half wide and three and a half or four feet deep, and buried the bodies that way. Sometimes we were so crowded with work and so short of help that we could not dig the trench that deep. I think three feet was the least depth that we ever dug."[81]

---

[79] *Wirz Trial*, pp. 316-319.
[80] *Ibid.*, pp. 260, 261.
[81] *Ibid.*, p. 257.

A black soldier, captured at Olustee, testified: "White soldiers were burying the dead before we went there. There were no white soldiers so engaged at the time we were there. There was a gang of confederate colored; about twenty. We all worked in the same burying ground, but they did not allow us to have any conversation with them...They buried none there but our own Union men...There were forty or fifty at work burying...The men were laid in, side by side, and the dirt was thrown right in on them...They were laid in decently and respectfully. The sergeant was over us, and he told us how he wanted them put. He was a confederate sergeant. He told us to be particular to lay them in as straight as we could, and as close together as we could get them...We lay them on their backs...There were no coffins there, and no boards to make them. We didn't even have boards to put over them after we put them in. For two pits or trenches we had boards to lay over them, but after that they gave out."[82]

In William Tyler's *Memoirs*, he related how he was detailed by Wirz to the burial detail for a few days. "We heard that the rebels intended to take some of us out to shoot, for the Yankees had been shooting the rebel prisoners, and the rebels were going to retaliate. One day a rebel sergeant came in and commanded about one hundred of us to fall in to go for wood. We formed a line and marched out. After they had marched us about half a mile from the pen they formed us in a line, with one Reb in front of each Yank, then old Wirz gave the command to ready, aim. You may be sure my heart came up into my mouth, and for a fact I thought the rebels were going to retaliate; but instead of shooting they searched us, to see if we had any arms concealed. Finding nothing of the kind, they put us back into the prison.

"The next day the same sergeant came in and inquired for men by the names of Root and Tyler. Tyler being my name I knew it was me he was after, but having the retaliation in my head you may be sure I kept still; but one of our own men pointed me out. The Johnnie came up to me and said, 'You are wanted outside;' and looking around he found Root, and told us both to follow him. Our comrades, supposing we were to be shot, escorted us to the gate and bade us good-bye for the last time, as they thought. The truth of the matter was we were taken out to help bury the dead.

"Well, we were taken before Wirz. 'Now,' said he, 'if youans' wont run away you can stay out here and bury the dead.' We took the oath, and were told to go to a small log cabin, where we found twenty of our men who had already been taken out for the same business.

"It did seem nice to get into a house which contained a fire-place and a crane where the kettle hung. One of the men swung the crane out and hung a kettle of beans over the fire. That night I lay as near the fire-place as possible. The bubble of the bean-pot was music to my ear. I kept quiet until I thought my comrades were asleep, then raising myself in a sitting posture, swung the crane back and took the pot of beans off. With much difficulty I succeeded in finding a spoon; I then sat as close to the kettle as possible, with one leg on each side of it, and went in for dear life.

"The next day the men concluded to leave me to take care of the cabin, being too weak to be of much service. The provisions were locked up in a big box, and the men went to work. I swept out the cabin and walked out to see what could be seen. Walking along I saw an old colored woman and her little boy, hanging out clothes. He sat on the bank of the creek throwing crumbs from a good-sized piece of corn bread to the fish. I went up to him and snatched the bread from his hands. He jumped up and ran to his mother crying, 'That man has got my bread.' 'Never mind, honey; that man must be hungry.'

"The following day three more men were brought out to bury the dead. Our cook as usual hung up the kettle of beans to cook for breakfast.

"The next day the men took me out to help bury the dead. Upon arriving at the place of burial I was yet so weak that I was of no service. So they set me to bringing water for the men to drink. The way the graves were dug was to dig a ditch six feet wide, about one hundred yards long, and three feet deep. They then laid them as close as possible, without box, coffin, or clothes. I have counted three hundred and sixty lifeless skeletons of our boys that had died in one day. As I was going to the well for water, the third or fourth day of my stay outside, I met Wirz and two confederate officers. Wirz said, 'What are you doing here?' I told him I was carrying water for the men who were digging graves. 'Well,' said he, 'if you don't get inside of that gate, double quick, I will have a grave dug for you, and prepare you to fill it.' You may be sure I went in, and was a prisoner inside again."[83]

"During the months of July and August the Rebels experienced no little trouble in obtaining enough well prisoners to bury the dead properly, and as they understood that office, this duty was always devolved on prisoners, as the work was intensely painful and laborious under the hot Southern sun, and many a Union soldier lost his life in it.

---

[82] *Ibid.*, p. 179.

[83] William N. Tyler, *The Dispatch Carrier and Memoirs of Andersonville Prison* (Port Byron, IL:1892) pp. 32-37.

The Rebels would not allow negroes to be detailed for that purpose, as they could use them to better advantage in other ways.

"One warm morning, as I was standing by the prison gate, Captain Wirtz [sic] approached and accosted me, asking if I would not like to come outside on parole of honor and dig graves. Seeing no chance of immediate escape, I agreed to his proposition, to hold good for a time, but at the same time I told him I was not very strong, and I feared I could not sustain the labor and hardship of a grave digger, for any great period, though I would do my best as long as my strength sustained me. He said I need do only what my present strength allowed, and I thereupon agreed to commence work next morning.

"There were about forty of us at this work of digging graves and we often were compelled to toil until ten or eleven o'clock at night, in order to be able to bury all the dead who would be brought from the dead house in the coming morning. Occasionally we buried in one morning not less than two hundred men, the average number of burials was about sixty per day, out of a population probably not exceeding twenty thousand at this time.

"Our mode of digging the graves was very simple and is easily explained. We dug large trenches, about four feet deep and six feet wide, long enough to contain about two hundred men, and in one instance we buried in one trench four hundred men. After laying the bodies in these trenches, without any coffins, as close together as we could pack them, we covered them up with dirt, and put at the head of each man a stake with a number on it."[84]

Many of the Union dead were already such "... masses of utter corruption" that they were "... unfit for any man to handle and could only be placed in the trenches by the use of pitchforks with which two men would lay hold of a body, dump it into the trench."[85]

Because the bodies were brought in such a decomposed condition due to the August heat, the burial detail petitioned Wirz, asking that they be relieved from their job and their place taken by the Negro prisoners. Dowling reasoned, "They usually did not seem much to mind being engaged in work of this sort, as it was not usually very hard, and did not compel them to labor very rapidly, both of which circumstances partially suited the cases of most of the negro laborers whom I met at the South."[86]

The commander of the camp said the Negroes could be better utilized raising corn and hogs for the army. He threatened the recalcitrant prisoners, who said they might be driven to attempt to escape. He placed guards around the grave detail "... with orders to kill the first 'God damned Yankee' that made an attempt to get away." Wirz threatened to bury the detailed men under a pile of Union dead. "He further swore that if we did not do the work and inter the dead properly he would with his own men pile up the dead bodies above the surface until they fell over upon us... a mass of rotten, decaying humanity."[87]

"We lived in little log huts, outside of the stockades, and in the immediate vicinity of the railroad station. The evenings were always our own, save when the number of dead bodies was occasionally so extreme that we were unable to get through with the work of burying them during the day, and in such events we were obliged to work at night, and sometimes until very late, so that we might be ready to commence upon a fresh lot of bodies early on the next morning."[88]

"The next morning I went to Captain Wirtz, as did also quite a number of my companions, and told him I was sick and totally unfit to perform work such as digging graves, but he refused most positively to release me from the duty.

"Having in this brutal manner refused to grant us leave to return within the camp and relieve us from our parole, all the men engaged in grave digging determined to escape, and, accordingly, that night the whole crowd, numbering forty in all, made their escape. They got off, however, with but little start before their absence was discovered and pursuit commenced, bloodhounds, cavalry and infantry all joining in the pursuit. The consequence was that the next day every man was retaken and severely punished. For myself I was placed in the 'Spread Eagle Stocks' for twelve hours, during which period I very nearly perished. It will be obvious that after a few hours this torture became frightful, and it is a pitiable fact that many Union soldiers died while undergoing this horrible barbarity. At the end of twelve hours, and when nearly dead, I was released, and by Wirtz' order sent back into camp."[89]

Although coffins were, possibly, utilized during the first couple of weeks, the only mention of the use of a coffin

---

[84] Dowling, pp. 133-135.
[85] *Ibid.*, p. 135.
[86] *Ibid.*, p, 136.
[87] *Ibid.*
[88] *Ibid.*, p. 247.
[89] *Ibid.*, pp. 262, 263.

in the later months was the following, pathetic incident involving two Kentuckians who were father and son. "The son, about nineteen, had been feeble all summer and the special object of his father's care. They struggled hard to realize the hope of seeing home. The father did every way possible to obtain food adapted to his case, carried him to the sick call in his arms, begged doctors to give him the best treatment possible that they might not be separated. The other morning the boy died, the father kneeling by him fanning his brow and wetting his parched lips. He laid him out as well as possible, went to the gate and begged for lumber and tools that he be permitted to make a coffin. His request was granted. Lumber and tools were placed inside the gate; the coffin was made, the corpse deposited in it, a prayer offered, and the father bade farewell."[90]

There were a few ancillary buildings up in the area of the depot. One was a blacksmith shop or ax factory where axes and other hand tools were made and repaired. They also made horseshoes for the horses and mules of the post. "There were several other buildings at the depot, a church, a blacksmith shop, and a post office. I believe the axe factory was a wooden building. I should judge it was about sixty feet long and forty feet wide; it was a two-story building. I was inside of it. I do not know how many men were at work inside of it. They had no machinery, only the common blacksmith tools. I don't recollect how many forges there were in it. I think there were five or six. These men were at work making axes, some of them, and some of them were shoeing mules and horses. They shoe mules and horses in a blacksmith shop; that was where they made their axes; that is what I mean by axe factory."[91]

Colonel Chandler testified: "I visited the quartermaster's establishment; I visited the workshops; they were west of the railroad. I cannot say how many buildings or tents were inside of the quartermaster's establishment. There was an old shed where they had the carpenter's shop, a small place for the blacksmith's shop, and a small storehouse. The old shed for the carpenter's shop was not larger than from this partition to the door (about fifteen feet). There were three or four men at work there. I saw a small quantity of lumber there; as far as I recollect I do not think there were more than eight or ten pieces of plank there. Captain Winder told me about the great difficulty he experienced in getting lumber, and showed me by the requisitions in his letter-book the efforts he had made to get this lumber. I read his whole letter-book in reference to the entire business. I saw the building which contained the quartermaster's store it was up towards the depot; I do not think the quartermaster's storehouse was one-third as large as the commissary's storehouse."[92]

Major George M. Proctor, a resident of Barren county, Kentucky, was a major and commissary of subsistence. "I applied to the quartermaster for teams and he did not furnish them to me. I then went to the commandant of the post, General Winder, and said that if he did not furnish the teams or have it done I would not stay there; that I was only on duty there temporarily, and that I would not remain at the post unless I got proper facilities. He made requisitions upon the quartermaster to furnish me with teams. I was furnished with eight teams, with which I was able to get along."[93]

Andrew J. Spring testified: "I was detailed to bake bread there; I am not a baker by trade, but it is not much of a job to learn to bake this corn-bread; I cannot tell where the meal came from; it was brought from the storehouse to the depot and from the depot to the bake-house; I have been in the storehouse at the depot; there were plenty of rations there. The storehouse was so filled there that one could scarcely get through it; it was a very large warehouse; I should think it must have been three or four hundred feet long and forty feet wide; it was generally full. I believe it was a story and a half high. These five or six times that I was there, I should judge it was half full of different stores, meal, bacon, flour, and other stuff; I should think two-thirds of the supplies there was meal and flour. I would not testify to how much flour there was, but I should think that about two-thirds of the supply was corn-meal; at one time when I was there I saw a large pile of flour at one end of the building; they said it was flour. I went up and felt it, and saw it was flour."[94]

"I inspected the commissary building; it consisted of one long building; I think there was no other place where they kept commissary supplies; it was a long building alongside of the railroad; one end of it was devoted to offices - there were two offices, I suppose it was considerably over a hundred feet long, and about twenty-five feet wide; I found very little in that building besides worm-eaten peas, which I condemned as unfit for use; they were not what we call 'beans;' they were black peas."[95]

---

[90] Northrop, pp. 124, 125.
[91] *Wirz Trial*, p. 146.
[92] *Ibid.*, pp. 246, 247.
[93] *Ibid.*, p. 668.
[94] *Ibid.*, pp. 116, 117.
[95] *Ibid.*, pp. 246, 247.

Major Proctor was commissary of subsistence from August 21st until the last of November, while Captain Armstrong was sick. Major Proctor testified, "A clerk took the requisitions up, as soon as they came to the office, to headquarters and had them approved...We issued a day ahead...There were only two ovens there...I had eighteen or twenty placed there...I turned the ration over to the quartermaster sergeant who went with them to the cookhouse with the wagons." Major Proctor said that the sergeant was responsible for the rations and the lieutenant, who belonged to the Georgia reserves, was named James Allman and was placed there by order of General Winder.[96]

W. W. Crandall testified: "During the winter I was in the commissary there was a barrel - I don't remember the amount, but it was about a barrel - of stinking pork brought to the commissary; it was turned over by the men who were at work for Captain Wirz, and through his orders, and issued to the Yankees. The next day, or the next day but one, I had orders to weigh off the same number of pounds of beef, and had orders to select the best there was in the commissary and turn it over to Captain Wirz. He came to me particularly himself and said, 'I want you to take particular pains and get me the best there is; it is for my own eating.' I know that the pork came from his hands from this fact; he came there and said there was some pork coming from his house, and it was brought over by men who were at work for him. I was in the commissary and had the handling of all the meat there."[97]

"The exchange of meat was made, I think, in January, 1865... I was then at the commissary. My duties were to weigh and load into the wagon all rations sent from that commissary, to weigh the commissary stores into the commissary as they came there, and out of it when they went out. I went in the commissary the 1st of November and staid there all the time till I was sent away for exchange, on the 18th of March... The long building, when I first went there, was occupied, the most of it, for the commissary, and one room for the quartermaster, and the other building on the opposite side of the railroad was occupied for the commissary also. During the winter the quartermaster removed his stores into the building across the railroad, and the commissary occupied the whole of the long building. That was the winter of 1864-1865 - I think in the month of January, 1865. Up to that time the commissary used the most of the long building, and all of the other building. After that the quartermaster used the small building, and the commissary used the whole of the long building. I worked at both buildings when they were occupied. Whenever they issued from the short building I went there. The quantity in the two buildings varied. We handled them over when Captain Armstrong took command as post commissary. He relieved Major Proctor. I think it was in December, 1864. There were then about one thousand five hundred sacks of peas, about eight hundred sacks of meal, and quite a quantity of rice. I cannot tell the quantity. I believe there were between one hundred and twenty-five and one hundred and fifty barrels of molasses. There was a little bacon, but very little. I am speaking now of the month in which we took an inventory. We handled them all over. I think it was in December."[98]

**Prisoners returning into the pen with a trophy** - This drawing depicts prisoners bringing in a coveted wood supply. (Abbott)

Besides food, the second most precious commodity at Andersonville was wood. There were fallen trees and wooden debris littering the grounds around the pen. Anytime a man was allowed out for any detail, he would usually gather as much wood as he could carry when he returned. "Thousands of cords of dry pine lay just outside the gate, but we were not permitted to gather it except in very meager quantities."[99]

A man could carry enough wood to last about two weeks or enough for about a dozen men to cook for one day. "I was on the north side, and no man was allowed at any time to go out, even on the south side, unless he paid three dollars in Federal money to the guards. On paying that money we could go out and get wood."[100] "They would not

[96] *Ibid.*, p. 670.
[97] *Ibid.*, p. 258.
[98] *Ibid.*, pp. 259, 260.
[99] Lyons, p. 40.
[100] Chipman, p. 180.

allow more than six or eight outside the gate at one time."[101]

Imprisonment with little wood, sometimes that being wet, was very frustrating. "I remember one incident. A young fellow was trying to cook his dinner. He couldn't make the fuel burn, so he gave way to a fit of swearing. The fire blazed up for a short time and then went out. Then he had another fit. He would jump up and down, pouring out oaths like water. Finally he had a desperate attack, and after dancing and swearing for a while, he kicked over his dish and jumped on the fire. He cursed the fire, the fuel, the cornmeal, the Southern Confederacy and everything he could think of. After a while he cooled off."[102]

Northrop told about another incident, which illustrated how everyday life within the pen was dominated by the need to have a fire. He told about a fracas between two men. One of the men was assaulted by the other, clubbed over the head, and killed. The argument arose purely because they could not decide who would cook on their fire first. The assailant was bucked and gagged by the resulting crowd, the club used for a gag.

"No wood was issued to us. The only way of getting it was to stand around the gate for hours until a guard off duty could be coaxed or hired to accompany a small party to the woods, to bring back a load of such knots and limbs as could be picked up. Our chief persuaders to the guards to do us this favor were rings, pencils, knives, combs, and such trifles as we might have in our pockets, and, more especially, the brass buttons on our uniforms. Rebel soldiers, like Indians, negros and other imperfectly civilized people, were passionately fond of bright and gaudy things. A handful of brass buttons would catch every one of them as swiftly and as surely as a piece of red flannel will a gudgeon. Our regular fee for an escort for three of us to the woods was six over-coat or dress coat buttons, or ten or twelve jacket buttons. All in the mess contributed to this fund, and the fuel obtained was carefully guarded and husbanded."[103]

In a letter to the *New York Evening Post* on August 3rd, 1965, Spencer said, "Squads were permitted, to the number of thirty, to go out under guard daily for one hour, without axes or any cutting tool, to gather the refuse and rotten wood in the forest; and if they outstaid their time they were tried by a drumhead court martial, charged with violating their parole, and, if found guilty, were hung. I, myself, saw three bodies hanging who were thus executed."

No cooked rations were issued at Andersonville until the completion of the bakery on May 10th. Prior to that date all rations were issued raw and had to be cooked by the individual prisoners. "I have often seen men with a little bag of meal in hand, gathered from several rations, starving to death for want of wood and in desperation would mix the raw material with water and try to eat it."[104]

The men made rather elaborate stoves out of mud or, more correctly, clay. The clay at Andersonville was fine-grained, very cohesive and appeared to be a bright, brick-colored red. When molded and sun-dried, it hardened into a very serviceable stove. Later, besides the every-man-for-himself gathering of wood, there was some sort of organized gathering by predetermined squads of men. Exactly how it was determined which thirty sent a man outside or at what frequency is not known. At times, there were over one thousand groups of thirty.

Wood also had to be supplied to the hospitals. The logistics of providing wood for 35,000 men was a tremendous undertaking. Some authors said a piece of wood about the size of a man's forearm was the average daily ration; on many days, no wood ration was issued. If this was, indeed, the daily ration, then some ingenuity must have been necessary to cook the meager rations and to generate enough heat to warm the body when there was ice on the puddles or snow on the ground. "The order was, in every wood guard, to allow one soldier to each three prisoners. A guard of one hundred men would take out three times that number. There was no guard to carry out prisoners for wood that I remember, until after the prisoners came back from Thomasville; that was in the latter part of the summer. There was wood hauled in wagons - not much, but some - before that time."[105]

Kellogg confirmed that there were organized details of men constituting wood squads. He said that once he waited at the gate for a long time, when "... it was our turn to obtain fuel." He was finally told by the rebel sergeant he could not go, and he went back to his tent.[106]

The Confederate authorities feared that, with so many men out of the pen on their honor not to escape, this privilege would be abused by the prisoners. This was the case with the wood details. Sometimes the men would overpower their guards and flee into the woods, heading north. This could be accomplished in several ways. A pris-

[101] Boggs, p. 46.
[102] Lyons, pp. 66, 67.
[103] McElroy, p. 153.
[104] Sanitary Commission, p. 77.
[105] Author's library.
[106] Kellogg, p. 138.

oner could hit his guard and flee; he could bind the guard to a tree and flee; he could bribe him to look the other way; or he could, nonchalantly, stroll out of the guards' field of vision or duck under a bush and hide until dark. This was the most common method of escape and it was surprising this privilege of going out on detail was allowed to continue as long as it did. As time passed, the wood details had to travel further from the pen to find wood. This gave an even greater opportunity for escape. No axes were ever issued to the details to help in their harvest of firewood. "Sometimes the rebel soldiers, for a consideration from the prisoners, would get permission to take a squad of them to the woods for fuel. This was working nicely and we were getting a supply of wood through that source, until some of the prisoners abused the privilege by tying their guards up to trees and running away, which stopped the going out for wood. When going to the woods in this manner we filled our stomach with leaves and weeds, in order to get something green."[107] "Often the ration of wood was, ironically, called a 'tooth-pick.' It would be split into small short splinters. Water in a quart tin cup setting on small blocks of clay could be brought to a boil before the wood under it was consumed. Then into this was stirred the corn meal."[108]

Several prisoners were allowed to go to the adjacent woods on the 11th of June. One sergeant and one corporal from Kellogg's squad "... came back in greet glee, bringing with them some beautiful flowers, and what was of more use to us, a good supply of wood."[109]

Walter Bowie, Captain and Inspector in the Adjutant and Inspector General's Department after his inspection, wrote to Richmond on the 10th of May. He reported that, until a few days beforehand, prisoners had been allowed out to gather boughs, "... but owing to too great an intimacy which sprung up between the prisoners and their guard, the exchanging of clothes &c., the commander found it necessary to withhold this privilege."[110]

On June 9th, in the morning, there was issued an order allowing the prisoners to go for wood only if they would take an oath not to escape. Melvin said that the order started with the phrase, "... wishing to do all in our power to alleviate the suffering of prisoner's life."[111] This did not seem to deter the prisoners, for, on June 17th, "... fourteen prisoners ran away from the wood squad in the evening, taking nine guns along."[112]

No wood was issued for the six weeks following June 30th. "We were allowed, several times, to go out under guards, - six men from a squad of ninety, or eighteen men from a detachment of two hundred and seventy - to bring in what we could find in the woods. The squad of ninety men of which I was sergeant went from the 30th of June to the 30th of August without any issue of wood from the authorities."[113]

"Soon after roll-call, on the morning of the 16th, a rebel Sergeant came in with an order from Captain Wirz, for the Sergeant of our ninety to come out and rectify a mistake which had been made in the roll of names. On my way back to the prison from the Captain's office, I quietly shouldered a pine log, which lay invitingly near the road-side, and carried it in. For a wonder, the rebel officers made no objection to it, and we really exulted in our valuable prize, for our ninety had had no wood given them by the rebs since the 30th of June, or nearly a month, and uncooked rations had been distributed to us many times. About the only variety we had in those days was a little sorghum molasses with our corn meal. Salt, we concluded, was a scarce article in the confederacy, since we would pass four whole days in succession without seeing any."[114] "Wood was issued to us about the end of the second week in August, the first time since the 30th of June, and then we were only given two sticks for the whole ninety."[119115]

Once, when Tyler went out for wood, the following incident occurred. "As our little squad marched out, about fifty yards from the stockade I saw a good sized log lying there. It was about eight feet long and two feet in diameter. I saw that the rebel guard was a kind looking old man, and asked him if he would be so kind as to help me get the log inside of the stockade. 'Now,' said he,' if youans won't try to run away, I will help you.' I gave him the desired promise, and he laid down his gun and helped me to roll the log in. That was the second time I had received a kind act from one of the rebel guards. I got a couple of railroad spikes from one of my comrades, and split the log all up in small strips, and then we fixed our cave up with a good roof, and I must say it was really comfortable."[116]

What was the amount of firewood needed for the prisoners? Major-General John H. Wilson testified: "The

---

[107] Boggs, p.47.
[108] Maile, p. 40.
[109] Kellogg, p. 136.
[110] *O.R.*, VII, p. 137.
[111] Melvin, p. 106.
[112] Miller, p. 46.
[113] Chipman, p. 165.
[114] Kellogg, pp. 179, 180.
[115] *Ibid.*, p. 220.
[116] Tyler, pp. 51, 52.

quartermaster's monthly allowance for wood, in summer time, or from May till October, is a cord for every twelve men; that would require about 1,250 cords to 15,000 men. A man can cut two cords of wood a day. About thirty men per day would cut all the wood required for 15,000 men, and a guard of ten, fifteen, or twenty men would be ample to protect that number of men in the work. The winter allowance would be just double."[117]

James H. Fannin was asked by General Winder to respond to the allegation made by Chandler, after his inspection in August, that the prisoners were in dire need of wood. Fannin said that he was in command of the guard at the post from about the middle of May until about the 12th of July. During that period, he lived in the cabin nearest the pen and in full view of it. He said that, at all times of the night, there would be seen a thousand campfires flickering. It was part of Fannin's duty to detail, every day, 100 men to guard those men who were allowed to go out to scrounge for fire wood. He said that, when the pen was enlarged, there was such a large supply of limbs and brush the wood detail was suspended, temporarily. The prisoners took down the old north wall in one night that Fannin felt showed that they had plenty of axes within the pen. He said, "... small piles of wood could be seen at almost every tent." C. M. Jones, Lieutenant-Colonel, Second Regiment Georgia Reserves, swore that the statement of Fannin was true.[118]

To a soldier in the field, and, especially, to a soldier who was a prisoner of war, nothing was dearer than receiving something from a loved one at home. Several boxes of letters were received at Andersonville and, a few times, parcels from the North were brought on the post after having passed through the lines. Mail through the lines from the North passed from Old Point Comfort, the nearest post office, to Fortress Monroe, then was carried via the "Flag-of-Truce Boat" *New York* to City Point, Virginia, the point of entry into the Confederacy. From this point, the mail was forwarded to Andersonville.

The individual letter would be enclosed in an inner, unsealed envelope with Confederate postage attached; sometimes a silver dime would be attached. This inner envelope was enclosed in an outer envelope addressed to the Commanding General at Fortress Monroe with the Federal postage attached to get it to that point. There, the outer envelope was opened and destroyed, and the inner placed in the nearest post office for points south. Thus, all mail from the North arrived at Andersonville post-paid and deliverable. Because of some regulation known only to Wirz, he would allow no letter to be delivered unless a ten-cent duty or bounty was paid to him first. This was inexcusable since all postage on through-the-lines letters had been paid-in-full to the satisfaction of the postal examiners at City Point.

**Mail Call** - This was a rare occurrence. There was a mail box at the South Gate for outgoing mail. It was alleged that incoming mail was stolen and that prisoners had to pay a ten cent toll to receive any piece of mail even though all incoming mail was pre-paid by the sender. (Abbott)

"Packages of letters came to the prison by flag of truce, but under the regulations of Captain Wirz every prisoner was compelled to pay the Captain 10 cents in silver before receiving his letter. The Captain knew very well that the greater number of men had no money and those who were so fortunate as to possess greenbacks must buy their silver from his sutler paying an enormous premium. These letters had been prepaid, and the stamp bore a 'worthless' photograph of Jeff Davis, but the Captain must have hard cash or he would keep the letters. And he kept them. These letters were worthless to him, but when he knew that kind words from home and love ones had come so near and were withheld. Yet this man gloated over their misery and became profane in his delight at their tears."[119]

Incoming letters were mentioned in a few books about Andersonville. "Letters from home very seldom reached us, and few had any means of writing. In the early summer, a large batch of letters - five thousand we were told - arrived, having been accumulating somewhere for many months. These were brought into camp by an officer, under orders to collect ten cents on each - of course most were returned, and we heard no more of them. One of my companions saw among them three from his parents, but he was unable to pay the charge. According to the rules of transmission of letters over the lines, these letters must have already paid

[117] Chipman, p. 186.

[118] *O.R.*,

[119] Antrim, p. 121.

ten cents each to the rebel government."[120]

"About the middle of August, the prisoners became very excited when they learned that a large quantity of letters from the North were in the office of Captain Wirz and that they would probably be distributed soon."[121] "Quite a number of letters came in on the 1st of September."[122]

Lewis Dyer, a black soldier in the 12th U. S. Colored Troops, testified: "I was at work a part of the time I was there inside the fort digging a well; I stayed inside the fort, I guess, very near a month; I went from there back to the stockade and was working outside, and then I went to the hospital, and from there I went to Dr. White's house as a servant; I was Dr. White's servant about two months...

"I have seen three thousand letters that came there; Captain Wirz brought them up to Dr. White's office for Captain Reed's wife to read over; she was to take out everything in the letters, and then the letters were burned; this was while I was a servant at Dr. White's; I have seen money, postage stamps, writing paper, needles and thread, and pictures taken from letters; I assisted in burning the letters; they ordered me to burn the letter and I did so; Mrs. Reed conducted herself as near right at the time as she could, I believe; she made fun of the letters; she read the Yankee letters and said she was going to burn them all up; Dr. White was present sometimes."[123]

"I saw about three hundred or four hundred dollars in money taken from the letters at Dr. White's house. The money was greenbacks and silver. Mrs. Reed kept it there in a box until the prison was broken up. There was no memorandum made of what letters the things came out of; she just opened them, took the things out, and threw the letters aside."[124]

There was a letterbox attached to the wall near the South Gate for the reception of letters written by the prisoners. To this box were attached notices to communicate important ideas to be read by the prisoners.[125] "There was a letter-box at the South Gate; it was about a foot square. I saw it full of letters at one time. When it contained letters there was a list posted up on the post to which the box was nailed, and during such time as it contained letters a sergeant came in every morning and unlocked it and called off the letters. If the men to whom the letters belonged or any of their friends were there the letters would be delivered to them. I saw one very small lot of boxes come for the prisoners."[126] Hyde said that, when he was let out on parole, he was able to observe "... the letters seldom got farther then Wirz' quarters, where they were thrown into a box, and when it got full they would send them heavenward in the form of smoke. Occasionally they would sent a lot off - I suppose to keep up an appearance with our government; but the greater portion were burned, and I was really glad the boys inside did not know this, as writing letters seemed to cheer them up and to bring them into communion with home."[127]

"The order was for any person who wanted to see Captain Wirz to drop a note in the letter-box, and it would go up through a regular channel and be examined by his clerks, and if his clerks thought it of any importance they would keep it and show it to him, and then the man would be granted an opportunity of seeing him. This was done, to some extent."[128]

Writing paper and writing utensils were at a premium within the pen. These were articles that were usually stolen by the guards when the prisoner was searched upon his arrival at Andersonville.

Most letters were of one page. If they consisted of more than one page, each page had to have been signed by the writer. The writer had to give his detachment and ninety and to request that the recipient write to him in care of this detachment. He was allowed to speak in positive terms about the kind treatment he had received but, of course, he could not complain of cruel treatment or insufficient rations.

James C. Melvin wrote home on June 3rd and he came into the Federal lines at City Point in early July. The letter was not delivered to his home in Massachusetts until January of 1865, long after he had arrived safely.[129] Melvin said that letters could not be sent out after June 26th, but he did not give any reason for why this was.[130]

As expected, the mails were not very reliable in the war-torn South. Ira Petit wrote dozens of letters home, yet only two ever arrived at their destination. Early in June, Miller wrote a letter to his sister, and placed it, unsealed, in

[120] Dowling, pp.171-172.
[121] Kellogg, p. 225.
[122] *Ibid.*, p. 236.
[123] *Wirz Trial*, pp. 408, 409.
[124] *Ibid.*, p. 410.
[125] Kellogg, p. 224.
[126] *Wirz Trial*, p. 562.
[127] Hyde, pp. 213, 214.
[128] *Wirz Trial*, p. 500.
[129] Melvin, p. 104.
[130] *Ibid.*, p. 113.

the box at the South Gate as he had been instructed to do. On the 17th of January, 1865, about seven months after writing it, the letter arrived at and was postmarked at Old Point Comfort, Virginia. It arrived at its destination in Pennsylvania on about the first of February. Unfortunately, he had been home a month before his letter arrived. In his letter he said, "We are treated pretty well. Get enough to eat."[131] Of course, he knew the letter would be read by Confederate censors.

For more information about Prisoner of War and Flag of Truce covers, see Dietz' *Confederate States Catalog and Handbook*.[132] For almost all known Andersonville-related covers, see Volume 28, No. 3 *of The Confederate Philatelist*, published by the Confederate Stamp Alliance.[133]

Once Stockade Creek became so contaminated by the offal from the bakery and the guard camp upstream, Wirz encouraged the digging of wells to supplement the water supply. He distributed shovels and other implements to help the men seek better water. The men used canteen halves, sharpened sticks, and pen-knives to dig into the Georgia clay. The loose dirt was hauled to the surface in meal-sacks, knapsacks, haversacks, buckets or pants legs (with one end tied). "The excavated dirt was put in a 'meal sack' which we stole from the ration wagon for the purpose. Every morning a line of bright red earth could be seen along the edge of the swamp, the nightly result of the labors of earnest seekers after freedom."[134]

"It was Duncan who once made a report that the prisoners complained about the water... Captain Wirz gave Duncan some tools, picks and shovels, so that the prisoners could dig some wells, and also he gave Duncan orders to provide the prisoners, as far as he could, with barrels to put around the wells to prevent men from falling in - what we call curbs. It was Duncan and Humes to whom those orders were given... There was a well close to the cook-house No. 1; I do not know if the water was good or what kind of water it was, but I saw that there was a well there... When the prisoners complained about the water, that it was dirty, there was an order given to Duncan to put the slops in some barrels, and to carry them off with teams, but Duncan could not get teams; they could not be furnished by the quartermaster… Duncan came into the office and reported to Captain Wirz that it was impossible to carry off those slops, because he could not get teams; that he had been to the depot to the quartermaster and the quartermaster told him that he had none on hand."[135]

"We at last succeeded in getting a spade, an old rope, and a common wooden water-pail, and with these implements commenced operations. The ground, with the exception of a few feet of soft soap stone, was of a soft, loose, sandy nature, and we made considerable progress in sinking it. We had succeeded in digging about forty feet when we came to water, but of so small a quantity that it did not amount to much; so we dug down about six feet more when we struck a good stream of water. I was in the well digging about the time it was finished, and I noticed that at the place where we first found water, small quantities of sand would be continually working out of the wall or side of the well, and fall to the bottom. Great was our disappointment, however, when we looked down the well in a few days after, and discovered that it had caved in in such a manner as to make it useless for us to think of working at it any longer... Several of these wells were used by the prisoners as a screen to cover their attempts to tunnel out. Under the pretence of digging a well for water, they dug into the earth for a considerable distance; and then, abandoning it, would start a few feet from the top, and commence tunneling for freedom. This work had to be done entirely after night, as the rebels were always on the watch; and even among us there were a few who, for a paltry amount of victuals or tobacco, were willing to betray their comrades."[136]

"In the early summer, Captain Wirtz [sic] issued to the prisoners picks and shovels, with which to dig wells for increased water supply. From some of these wells the men started tunnels through which to escape. Discovering this, the commander withdrew the tools, and ordered the wells to be filled up. Permission to keep one of them open was purchased by a group of prisoners. It was sunk to a necessary depth, covered with a platform and trapdoor, and supplied about one thousand men."[137]

After Wirz took away the shovels and had ordered the wells filled in, the men began to suffer terribly from thirst. Maile said one particular well and the stream were the only two sources of water for part of the summer. The weak ones could not get to the little, 12-foot space between the bridge and the deadline to get water.

"Sometimes the wells were in the tents. That was the case very often; with the big wells, it was the case about

[131] Miller, p. 28.
[132] August Dietz, Sr., *Confederate States Catalog and Handbook* (Richmond, Va.: The Dietz Press, Inc., 1959), pp, 184-191.
[133] Patricia A. Kaufmann, ed., *The Confederate Philatelist,* Vol. 28, No.3 May-June 1983, pp. 63-69.
[134] Kellogg, p. 119.
[135] *Wirz Trial*, p. 540.
[136] Urban, pp. 359, 360.
[137] Maile, pp. 55, 56.

half the time... about half the wells were covered, and were used at night for sleeping purposes."[138] "The prisoners began digging wells along the base of the hill, near the edge of the swamp. Here much better water was found , and encouraged by their success, others began sinking wells on higher ground, with varied success."[139]

Water could be reached after digging ten-to-twenty-feet down when the well was sunk near the creek. Good water was found at the twenty-three feet level when dug near the South Gate.[140] By experience, the men found they obtained better and colder water when they dug further away from the stream. After the pen was enlarged, one could dig down 65 feet in the new part without hitting water.[141] "It is difficult on the north side to reach water by wells. The south side had, several weeks ago, reached water by digging 20 to 30 feet. In the 36th detachment, on the north side, they have sunk 80 feet and the water is red, hard and impure."[142] Helwig said that, to get water on the south side, the well must be 15 to 20 feet deep whereas, on the north side, the well must be 30 to 40 feet deep.[143] Lyons said that some wells were 80 feet deep. Stevenson said that over 200 wells were dug within the pen.[144] One prisoner testified: "I found one hundred and five wells in the camp when I left the place."[145]

While the men were digging down a well or tunnel, they did not have ladders so they used any tree trunk or heavy pole to ascend and descend the shaft. "As digging proceeds men go down on poles, where one can be obtained, bracing against the bank and ascending the same way."[146]

The following story of "stealing the deadline" must have brought smiles at each retelling. "Yesterday I noticed a deadline board laying on the ground inside, one end about three feet from the post, blown, I suppose, by the wind. We have been troubled about getting in and out of the well we are digging, and cannot find anything to put down to climb on. I conceived the idea of capturing it to obviate the trouble. It got pretty dark near midnight. I approached the place cautiously, and lay flat and crawled to the board and tied a string to the end farthest in and sitting on the ground 25 feet away, drew it cautiously until out of danger from being shot by sentinels, when I picked it up and brought it to our place. Thompson watched the guard while I pulled it away, to warn me if they were likely to shoot, but the other boys didn't know when I stole the 'dead line.' We covered it with sand when Rebel sergeants came in the morning, and after the well was finished, broke it up for wood to cook our rations of meal."[147]

Several men were killed by cave-ins. On June 28, "... a man who was quietly sleeping in his little blanket tent near the edge of one of these deepest wells, was instantly buried alive by the falling in of the earth."[148]

The men became very possessive of their wells. "I have known prisoners to dig and claim a well and refuse to give a drink of water therefrom to one of their suffering comrades unless he paid for it."[149] "At our feet lay one begging for water groaning with pain. It was conjectured, because of his hoarse cough, that he had mumps, or measles or small pox, by some persons. Some dare venture but little here to aid suffering strangers when it is all one can do to keep alive. All the assistance we could offer was to give a cup of water. This I gave at arms length."[150] "A dying man might ask a dozen for a drink before he would find one to bring it to him, unless he had comrades who had known him before he got into the pen."[151]

Immediately after the fish arrived and got a place to lay their heads at night, they began to think about getting out. It can be assumed that, within days of the organization of the prison, tunnels were started under the palisade. Though the Confederates condoned well digging, they did not allow any wells to be started anywhere near the deadline, to discourage any tunneling. The prisoners, however, always wanted to start as near the deadline as possible so less digging would be necessary. They would start it in the shadow of the palisades caused by the nighttime guard fires burning between the main palisade and the second palisade. Usually, a prisoner with a shebang near the deadline, would be approached by a small group of potential diggers who would ask to use his shebang to begin a tunnel. It took twenty men about a month to dig a tunnel.[152]

[138] Wirz Trial, p. 574.
[139] Fosdick, p. 43.
[140] Dufur, p. 75.
[141] Kellogg, p. 167.
[142] Northrop, p. 117.
[143] Helwig, p. 34.
[144] Stevenson, p. 448.
[145] *Wirz Trial*, p. 521.
[146] Northrop, p.65.
[147] *Ibid.*
[148] Dufur, p. 84.
[149] Davis, p. 26.
[150] Northrop, p. 68.
[151] Vawter, p. 60.
[152] Brownell, p. 18.

They would dig straight down for at least seven or eight feet and then let the tunnel take off to the palisade. The sand in the horizontal tunnel was pushed backwards "… until the well was reached, where it fell to the bottom. This 'well' was ostensibly a well - its real use was to dispose of the sand dug at night and during the day it was taken out giving the appearance of digging for water."[153]

At other times the tunnel would be thirty or forty feet down below the pen's surface. To conceal the opening, a ledge was usually made across the top, boards were laid on this ledge, and six or eight inches of dirt were placed on top. A layer of soil specifically saved to match the surrounding soil was sprinkled around to camouflage the tunnel in case of quick cover-ups. Frustrating cave-ins, caused by the sandy Georgia soil, were ever-present. On many mornings, the prisoners were saddened to wake up and see a couple logs of the palisade at a level two or three feet lower than the rest of the palisade. They knew that one of their comrades had, possibly, lost his life by having the logs fall on the back of some hapless digger who was then trapped like a mole in a dead-fall. "In one instance, the log slipped down after the digger had got beyond it. He immediately began digging for the surface for life, and was fortunately able to break through before he suffocated. He got his head above the ground, and then fainted. The guard outside saw him, pulled him out of the hole, and when he recovered sensibility hurried him back into the Stockade."[154] In another tunnel, a large German soldier of the 2nd Minnesota, got stuck within the tunnel and the man's friends finally had to ask aid of the Confederates to get him out.[155]

The dirt from the vertical shaft would be piled up near the well entrance but any from the horizontal shaft had to be scattered around the pen or into the sink area in order not to arouse suspicion. Sometimes the excavated dirt would be disposed of by dropping it down the legs of a man's trousers as he nonchalantly strolled around the pen.

"These men would dig their tunnels with knives, tin pans, and an instrument that was made out of a shovel. A shovel would be taken from the working party and the handle burnt out of it. The iron which lapped over the wood of the handle would be then turned up at right angles, and the blade of the shovel would be rounded off.

"They would work with it by lying flat in the tunnel and just shoving it forward as hard as possible. It was not very dark there at night-time; he had candles. We got them from the post adjutant, the post sutler, who would get them in very small quantities. They were a contraband article in the camp, and we were not allowed to have them. Whiskey was a contraband article. Candles were contraband on account of the tunneling operations having been discovered. The adjutant was forbidden to bring any more into camp, as he stated himself."[156]

The first tunnel McElroy helped dig illustrated the natural tendency, when digging with the right hand, for the tunnel to veer off to the left. McElroy and his friends had dug for several days and had not reached the stockade though the length of the tunnel indicated that they should have passed under it. They double-checked the length with a piece of string. The next day, the earth gave way under a man fifteen feet away from the tunnel entrance although the men had dug several times that far. This indicated the tunnel had been dug in the shape of a horseshoe because of too much digging with the right hand. Diggers always feared the tunnel would be discovered before it was used or "opened." They selected only trusted comrades to help them dig. The location of a tunnel being dug was also kept secret in order to keep weak comrades from informing the Confederate authorities of its location in exchange for a morsel of food or a twist of tobacco.

The prisoners felt there were informants within the prison who were telling the authorities when a tunnel had been started and where its entrance was located. Often the authorities would walk into the pen and walk directly to the shebang containing a tunnel entrance.

"The rebel quartermaster... came in, and counting the sentry posts so as to get the right location, came direct to the well and inquired who was digging it. At last he got a ladder and went down, and, taking a stick, commenced jabbing around and soon found the tunnel. He very kindly offered us picks and shovels if we wanted to start another. The well was filled up, and that ended our attempts at escaping by the underground route."[157]

"To escape being detected at our work, we had to commence digging at least ten feet from the dead-line, then from the dead-line to the stockade that formed the wall was fifteen feet, and from the stockade to the outside picket was twenty feet, so that we had to dig under ground about forty-five or fifty feet. When a tunnel was commenced, twenty or thirty men clubbed together to dig by turns; the work was all done at night, and the mouth of the tunnel covered over by day with old pieces of clothing and dry sand. One man dug, and the rest carried the dirt off to a

---

[153] Hopkins, p. 102.
[154] McElroy, p. 176.
[155] *Ibid.*
[156] *Wirz Trial*, p. 561.
[157] Williams, p. 12.

distance, and scattered it around, so as not to excite suspicion. After digging a hole about five feet deep, and four feet in diameter, we commenced tunneling toward the stockade. Our tunnels were about three feet wide and four feet high. Only one man could work in the hole at a time. To get the dirt out we tied a pantaloon-leg to the middle of a piece of rope, and the man inside, by pulling the rope, drew the bag to him and filled it, and then it was drawn out and emptied. The digging of these tunnels was very hard on our clothing; we had to use our pantaloons for dragging out the dirt, and the ropes were made of strips of cloth braided together."[158]

After completing a tunnel, the diggers usually waited until there was no moon or until a hard rain concealed their movements. "We then had to wait for a dark or stormy night, and then one by one we entered the tunnel. The man who had worked in the hole last went first to open the other end, and slowly and carefully we crawled out, though rain, and mud, and darkness."[159] After a tunnel was opened, the escapees would go directly to the creek to attempt to foil the dogs.

The usual punishment for one who had betrayed a tunnel was to have a "T" branded on his forehead, hand, or chest. Sometimes the "T" would be tattooed into the forehead by scratching the letter into the skin and then spitting tobacco juice to render it brown permanently. At other times, half of the traitor's head would be shaved to make him very conspicuous and subject to the ridicule and scorn of his fellow inmates.

One day in May a tunnel traitor was caught red-handed in such a way that there was no doubt as to his guilt. The unruly mob was going to hang him, when someone suggested that "Captain Jack," the tattoo artist, tattoo a letter "T" on the traitor's forehead. They held the man down on the ground while Captain Jack alternately pricked the skin across the forehead and down the nose and spit brown tobacco juice onto the tiny wounds. It was afterwards learned he was a Confederate plant placed within the pen to learn of tunnel locations.[160] Vawter described another man with a "T": "There was a fellow (he died at Savannah) who wore a large 'T' on his forehead. He informed on a tunnel company when they were nearly through, and they made the 'T' with a hot railroad spike. After that, when a sneak reported on his fellow prisoners, the rebs took him out of the pen, and we saw him no more."[161]

On July 21, a prisoner told the Confederate quartermaster, James Selman, Jr., about a tunnel in the process of being dug. He was given a plug of tobacco as a reward. The prisoners learned the identity of the informant and tattooed "Traitor" on his forehead after half of his head had been shaved. The next day, the prisoners were informed that that day's rations would not to be distributed until those men who had assaulted the informant gave themselves up. It was not known if anyone went forward, but the rations were, finally, distributed that day.[162]

The Confederates almost became obsessed with the thought of discovering tunnels. "The intervening space between the wall and the dead line was overgrown with weeds, and was occasionally tested by workmen with long drills to ascertain the existence of tunnels."[163] "Workmen would make the rounds of the prison, next to the dead line, with sharp pointed poles, to discover any tunnels by pounding on the ground or running the sharp point down."[164] "The confederates used long poles with sharp iron points, which they would punch into the ground.... to see if any of the tunnels were near completion, if so, of course they could find it out by the spike striking through into the hole."[165]

"Every day squads of men explore the ground inside and outside of the stockade with feeling rods which they punch into the ground."[166] "They discovered the tunnel on the afternoon of the thirteenth of May, and Captain Wirz swore that no more rations should be issued until the place was filled again with earth... The 'reb' quartermaster came in with men and the necessary implements, and filled up the place."[167]

McElroy said, at Savannah, that Lieutenant Davis, once tried to discover tunnels by driving a weighted, two-wheeled cart around the deadrun in hopes the weight of the cart would cause the tunnel to cave in. Frank Smith corroborated the use of the cart: "A two-wheel cart was loaded with boulders and large stones and driven about between the 'dead line' and stockade in order to see if they could not break through some tunnel."[168]

The actual officers in charge of pen security seemed to be Duncan, Ritchie, and Humes. A clerk in Wirz' office testified: "Duncan acted as a detective; all his work was done at night... I know that he and Ritchie and Humes re-

---

[158] Brownell, pp. 18, 19.
[159] *Ibid.*, p. 19.
[160] McElroy, pp. 179, 180.
[161] Vawter, p. 79, 80.
[162] Northrop, p. 92.
[163] Maile, p. 31.
[164] Miller, p. 21.
[165] Frank Smith, p. 33.
[166] Northrop, p. 64.
[167] Kellogg, p. 87.
[168] Frank Smith, pp. 33, 34.

ported tunnels... 84 tunnels were reported before August."[169] "Ritchie was with him. Ritchie was an assistant of Duncan; Humes also was an assistant. Ritchie was with Duncan when Duncan did these things; he drove the wagon that went into the stockade and carried the goods in and out of the stockade... Duncan and Ritchie reported these tunnels; they were the principal men who reported tunnels or anything going wrong in the stockade... Duncan and Ritchie would go round the stockade. They had their men inside, at least we judged that they had."[170]

Where the tunnel openings emerged was sometimes a surprise. "One fellow, after he and his comrades had worked for weeks, dug up through to see where he was, and was somewhat surprised to see two rebel soldiers playing cards! He was under the guards' tent, and later when one of the 'Rebs' fell into the hole, it led to discovery."[171] Northrop told about what some other tunnelers found when they opened a tunnel: "It had been completed to the point where they wished to come out. The head man was pulling down the dirt when suddenly it broke away covering him, and down came a gray jacket with a Rebel in it, gun and all. The relief guards were just being mounted and one of them stepped upon the exact spot where they were to escape."[172] He also told on Friday, June 3rd, that nine men had tunneled out and one guard escaped with them. The authorities, after finding the tunnel, filled it in. Once, when some men were digging a tunnel, the men dug into an old, buried kitchen sink, which was impenetrable, and they had to start over.

General Winder, on June 22nd, said, "We have this morning discovered a tunnel under the pickets 14 feet deep and from 90 to 100 feet long."[173] "Tunneling cannot be successfully done more than sixty or eighty feet horizontally, the air becoming insufferable."[174] The prisoners rigged various, ingenious, ventilation systems that allowed at least one tunnel to be 140 feet long. Kellogg said that one tunnel caved in after having been dug 90 feet.[175]

In the third week of July, Kellogg and his friends had dug a tunnel which was ready to break through that night. Just before sunset, the tunnel was discovered by the rebels. "Four of the boys were at work in it at the time, and of course were caught; but instead of meeting with punishment, the rebel Quartermaster gave each a double ration for the skillful manner in which they had constructed the tunnel."[176]

Sometime in the month of April, a large group of prisoners formed a conspiracy to free the entire prison population in a mass escape. "The plan was to weaken the stockade by tunneling under at five or six places, and then make a rush against it and push it over. They then intended to charge the rebel batteries, and try to capture them and turn the cannon on the rebels. The plan was well arranged, and as a large number of the most desperate men had organized and sworn to break out and get their freedom or die in the attempt, it might have been successful, at least so far as the overthrowing of the stockade was concerned, had not a traitor disclosed the plot to the enemy, who came in and had the tunnels shut up, and took the most vigorous measures to prevent an outbreak. The miserable traitor was taken out of the prison, and no doubt received a reward for his treachery."[177] Compton told about this near-mass escape: "We came near all getting out one day; we had organized into regiments and divisions; officers were elected; we all had clubs. We had worked until one whole side of the prison was ready to fall; we intended to charge the battery the first thing, but when we were about ready to make a break, we found that one of our soldiers had divulged our plans. The traitor was taken out of prison, and that saved his life, for we would have killed him if we could have found him."[178]

The following was taken from Kellogg's description of the conspiracy. Kellogg "... learned there was a secret organization in progress for the purpose of attempting an outbreak and escape on a grand scale. The plan was to recommence tunneling, and in this way undermine the stockade at several different points. At a pre-concerted signal the men were to rush upon it in a body sufficient to overturn it, and still another body were to seize the artillery and turn it upon the rebel camps, leaving us to pursue the way we had chosen, towards Pensacola, Fla., as the most feasible, from whence we could join our lines. Under pretense of digging for water we would sink a well in some chosen spot, and after getting down several feet, abandon it and commence in another place, which was really the point of attack all the while, but which could be better worked by the ostensible object of the other. Reaching the requisite

[169] *Wirz Trial*, p. 682.
[170] *Ibid.*, p. 681.
[171] Dufur, p. 133.
[172] Northrop, pp. 107, 108.
[173] *O.R.*, VII , p. 396.
[174] Northrop, p. 103.
[175] Author's Library.
[176] Kellog, p. 185.
[177] Urban, p. 360.
[178] Compton, p. 44.

depth in the second, the tunnel was to proceed out from it to the desired place. Of course the work must be done at night, and with just such instruments as could be obtained. There were old knives, spoons, broken canteens, in short anything that could scoop out a handful of earth. This in one part of the camp was of a reddish color, while in others it was so sandy as to defy all attempts to make a way through, as it would fill in as fast as we might dig. To dispose of this as fast as it would be taken out, we obtained an old sack, and this was to be filled and passed along to men who were to be stationed at proper intervals between the point of working and the first well, which it was found to be very convenient to fill up just then, as a well without water was of no account. Beyond this it was conveyed to the marshy places, and to the brook itself, and left there. As nothing could be done except under cover of the friendly shadows of night, it must be comparatively slow.

"While we were contemplating the best method of action in our proposed endeavor, they were having a pic-nic, or something of the sort, among themselves, being regaled by a band of music with such airs as the *Bonnie blue flag*, and *Southern Marsailles*. A great crowd of ladies were discoverable, who were probably present to applaud and admire the men who thought it a brave deed to shoot a defenceless prisoner."[179]

Kellogg described the ringleaders of the plot: "They were a bold set of fellows, most of them those who had been prisoners for a long time, and had tried to escape several times before."[180] On May 16,th "... very strict orders in regard to attempts to escape were read in the camp at morning roll-call. We thought it very poor policy for them to do this, for the penalties were only what we expected, as a matter of course, and the issuing of the order only proved that they were 'on the scare' a little. The punishment assigned for the violation of such orders, was the wearing of a heavy cannon ball, attached to the ankle by a chain. This had already been awarded to some, but Yankee ingenuity had found a way by which they might be unfastened, so that freedom could be enjoyed through the day, and the thing put on to appear in due form before rebel majesty at the hour assigned."[181]

On May 24th, the stockade, "... being undermined in five or six places, and we looked with the greatest interest for the hour to arrive, when at the sound of the trumpet, the walls, Jericho-like, would fall and let us go free. The men were all ready for a general rush upon the artillery, and imagination already pictured the dismay of the rebels, and our own triumph as our exulting hosts should pass on beyond the boundaries of oppression towards their native land of freedom. The night was auspicious, being dark and rainy, and we ardently hoped everything would favor our darling scheme. Just before the hour for action had arrived we found the whole plot was disclosed. One of the ring-leaders had given the minutiae of the affair to Capt. Wirz. He was at once taken out of prison and probably richly rewarded for his villainy, and it was well for him, for his long continuance on earth might have been a matter of doubt if he had remained in his accustomed quarters. Vigorous measures were quickly taken to prevent any further attempts on our part. A large reinforcement of rebel troops arrived to make the guard doubly sure. The stockade was strengthened in such a manner as to resist a like onslaught in the future, and things generally indicated a determination on their part to make sure their hold upon us a while longer.

"The evening after the disclosure we found the following posted near the prison gate:

## NOTICE

*'Not wishing to shed the blood of hundreds not connected with those who concocted a mad plan to force the stockade, and make in this way their escape, I here-by warn the leaders and those who formed themselves into a band to carry out this, that I am in possession of all the facts, and have made my dispositions accordingly, so as to frustrate it. No choice would be left me but to open with grape and canister on the stockade, and what effect this would have in this densely crowded place need not be told.*

*May 25th, 1864*
*H. Wirz*

"On the day following the sensational notice of Capt. Wirz, he took several men into his employ for the purpose of digging a trench around the camp inside the 'dead line', for the more ready discovery of any 'tunnels' that might have been dug, and also to render it more difficult to attempt any more in the future. Doubtless he thought he was

[179] Kellogg, pp. 88-90.
[180] *Ibid.*, pp. 95, 96.
[181] *Ibid.*, pp. 98.

doing a smart thing, accomplishing that which would effectually put an end to all similar working, but even then Yankee ingenuity was busy in solving the problem - how this could be made void - and the result was a conclusion to dig under the trench, although it involved a greatly increased amount of labor."[182]

Another description of this same conspiracy follows: "First a secret society was organized, bound by the most stringent oaths that could be devised. The members of this were divided into companies of fifty men each, under officers regularly elected. The secrecy was assumed in order to shut out Rebel spies and the traitors from a knowledge of the contemplated outbreak. A man named Baker - belonging, I think, to some New York regiment - was the grand organizer of the scheme. We were careful in each of our companies to admit none to membership except such as long acquaintance gave us entire confidence in.

"The plan was to dig large tunnels to the Stockade at various places, and then hollow out the ground at the foot of the timbers, so that a half dozen or so could be pushed over with a little effort, and make a gap ten or twelve feet wide. All these were to be thrown down at a preconcerted signal, the companies were to rush out and seize the eleven guns of the headquarters fort. The Plymouth Brigade was then to man these and turn them on the camp of the Reserves who, it was imagined, would drop their arms and take to their heels after receiving a round or so of shell. We would gather what arms we could, and place them in the hands of the most active and determined. This would give us from eight to ten thousand fairly armed, resolute men, with which we thought we could march to Appalachicola Bay, or to Sherman. A traitor revealed everything to Wirz. One day a guard came in, seized Baker and took him out... we never heard of him after he passed the inner gate.

"Immediately afterward all the Sergeants of detachments were summoned outside. There they met Wirz, who made a speech informing them that he knew all the details of the plot, and had made sufficient preparations to defeat it. The guard had been strongly reinforced, and disposed in such a manner as to protect the guns from capture." After the sergeants returned, Wirz posted his threatening notice on the gates.[183]

Kellogg told of a rumored, non-existent outbreak on a grand scale, "The Sergeants in charge of messes were all ordered outside, in obedience to orders from Capt. Wirz, who informed them that he had discovered an organized body of six thousand men who had planned a new outbreak, and he threatened if the attempt was made, to open with his artillery upon the prison, and 'fire as long as there was a man kicking.' Somebody had humbugged him in fine style, for no such thing was in contemplation, much less in process of working."[184]

**Guard being overpowered by prisoners out on parole** - This was one of the easier ways to initiate an escape attempt. (Dowling)

On Thursday, July 14th, just after the Raiders were hung, the sergeants of the detachments were called out and told that an escape plot had been discovered; if it was attempted, Wirz would kill every man in the pen. The cannon fired two shots and Rebel soldiers formed a line at double-quick. It scared the prisoners at first until they realized that it was only a practice skirmish. Several volleys of musketry were fired.[185]

Wirz said that, from the first of April to the 8th of May, there had been 13 escapes.[186] For the month of June, he said 47 had escaped and 44 had been recaptured.[187] The lucky ones had escaped by various methods. Some had hid in the ration barrels, some clung to the bottom of the ration wagons, some were carried out pretending to be dead, some tunneled, while others scaled the wall on foggy nights. The most popular method and the most likely to succeed was to walk away from a detail. Dowling crossed the deadline, threw a plank on the palisade wall, shimmied up the plank and escaped over the wall.

Wirz boasted that only 27 men had escaped and not been recaptured from the 1st of April through the 31st of July.[188] On August 1st, Captain Wirz said there had been "... 83 tunnels, some 20 feet under ground, and varying in

---

[182] *Ibid.*, pp.103-109.
[183] McElory, pp. 193, 194.
[184] Kellogg, pp. 177, 178.
[185] Northrop, pp. 91, 92.
[186] *O.R.*, VII, p. 169.
[187] *Ibid.*, p. 438.
[188] *Ibid.*, p. 517.

length from 10 to 140 feet, have been discovered and filled up."[189] At that time, he was still able to assert that only one prisoner had escaped since April 1, by way of a tunnel and that 11 others had walked away from a work detail while outside the pen.[190]

Wirz told, in his monthly report for August, that 30 men had escaped, 4 of whom had been recaptured. At the end of the report Wirz lamented, "Of the thirty prisoners eleven escaped while on parole of honor not to escape as long as they would be employed to work outside. The balance of nineteen escaped, some on bribing the sentinel with greenbacks, some simply walking off from the guard while returning from the place where the tools were deposited at night that are used in the stockade in daytime. Perhaps twenty-five more escaped during the month, but were taken up by the dogs before the daily return was made out, and for that reason they are not on the list of escaped nor recaptured.

"That only four were recaptured is owing to the fact that the guard nor the officers of the guard reported a man escaped. The roll-call in the morning showed the man missing, but he was too far gone to be tracked. As we have no general court-martial here all such offenses go unpunished, or nearly so.

"The worthlessness of the guard forces is on the increase day by day."[191]

In early August, Henry Damon of the 7th Michigan, escaped by disguising himself as a Confederate sergeant with a fake rollbook in hand; he left with the genuine Confederate sergeants after roll call.[192] McElroy said, "Only three hundred and twenty-eight succeeded in getting so far away from Andersonville as to leave it to be presumed that they had reached our line."[193]

Charles M. Smith told in his book, *From Andersonville to Freedom,* the particulars of his escape. At the hospital, Smith had made the acquaintance of Dr. A. W. Barrows, of Amherst, Massachusetts, a member of the Twenty-seventh Massachusetts Infantry, and of A. A. Crandall, of Ulysses, Pennsylvania, a member of the Fifty-third Pennsylvania Infantry . Their plan of escape was, "We decided to go west to the Chattahooche River, cross into Alabama, find the headwaters of the Choctawhatchee River, and follow it south through Alabama and western Florida to its mouth, where it flows into the Choctawhatchee Bay, and where we expect to find the United States gunboats. We collected medicine, matches, salt and food, the latter consisting of biscuit and bacon. The most important article to be obtained was turpentine, for with this applied to our shoes we could baffle the bloodhounds. It counteracts the scent of the man, and prevents the hounds from following the track."[194]

They decided to leave by way of the main entrance of the hospital in the daytime, when many people were coming and going. The guard and Confederate officers, Confederate surgeons, and wagons, which brought supplies to the hospital, were passing in and out during the day. October 9th, 1864, the day they left with blouses and trouser legs tucked in, filled with biscuits. A slab of bacon was tucked in the small of one of the men's back. They traveled all night, walking very fast, sometimes running, taking the precaution to keep the soles of their shoes wet with turpentine. This device to deceive the dogs must have worked. Once they overheard one of the trackers, who was only a few feet away, say, "I think they must have had something on their feet."

The escapees scrounged dry corn, squashes, pumpkins, watermelons, persimmons, and, in Alabama, sugar cane. They ate the meat of guinea hens, goats, and opossum after coming upon one which feigned death. They used the seven stars, Pleiades, as their guide at night. Matches were kept dry in a bottle. For 33 days, they traveled about 400 miles through Georgia and Alabama. Charles M. Smith boarded the flag-ship of the gunboat fleet on November 11th, 1864.[195]

After men escaped, they ate anything they could find that was nourishing, such as parched corn, raw beans, wild grapes, sumac berries, blackberries, cantaloupes, watermelons, etc. Vawter described eating a frog he caught while on the outside: "To divide him with our thumb nails was the work of an instant; to eat him took but a minute more."[196] He also described an interesting companion. "Here we felt safe, for on a log, not more than fifty feet away in the swamp, lay an alligator about ten feet long, and we knew no hound would care to hunt along the shore of that swamp. The reptile lay there for two hours about the middle of the day, and we regarded him as a friend."[197]

---

[189] *Ibid.*, p. 522.
[190] *Ibid.*, p. 439.
[191] *Ibid.*, p.708.
[192] Northrop, p. 173.
[193] McElroy, p. 175.
[194] Charles Smith, pp. 29, 30.
[195] *Ibid.*, pp. 27-71.
[196] Vawter, p.94.
[197] *Ibid.*, p.89.

**The Kennel** - This was where the Bloodhounds were kept on post. It was located northwest of the pen. The O'Dea print calls this kennel the "Bloodhound Cabin." (Gross)

**Hero** - This dog was a Russian Bloodhound, and was used during the war at Libby Prison and Castle Thunder, Richmond, Virginia, to guard Union prisoners and to recapture those who had escaped. Weight, 198 pounds; height, three feet and two inches; length, from tip to tip, seven feet, one-and-one-half inches. (Goss)

**Spot** - This dog was a Cuban Bloodhound, and the only survivor of a pack of hounds (some of them, however, being the common Southern hounds) used by Captain Wirz at Andersonville Prison, for recapturing escaped Union prisoners. Weight, 159 pounds; height, three feet; length, from tip to tip, six feet, four-and-one-half inches. (Gross)

Invariably, when escapees sought aid in making their way to the Union lines, they would seek out the help of blacks who were more apt to be trusted not to betray them. The escapees trusted the black field hands but were sometimes betrayed by the Southern house servants. The blacks already had their "underground railroad" in operation to points north, using secret hiding places within their cabins and adjacent wooded areas. There were white Unionists, usually known to the blacks, who were sympathetic to the plight of the Yankee escapees. The blacks would also warn the escapees to skirt around the farms of rabidly loyal Southerners.

Some blacks were, however, very wary of aiding unknown, thin, white men in ragged clothing because the blacks' loyalty had been sometimes tested by thin, bony-looking Southerners disguised as escaped Union prisoners. If found to have aided one of these bogus Yankee escapees, the black would be subject to excruciating punishment, usually lashes to the back with a wide leather strap. This threat of possible punishment would make blacks very cautious in aiding true fugitives in need.

"They displayed an incredible amount of cunning and intelligence in secreting the escaping prisoners, or piloting them, in relays, to the Union army. From the oldest mammy to the little pickaninny, would solemnly assert that 'they did not know nuffen about any Yankee dat runned away,' and express their fear and utter horror of a Yankee soldier, while perhaps beneath the rude floor of that cabin lay a trembling fugitive, hearing the slave drivers using threats and persuasions to extort a betrayal from the poor slaves, but they could find no Judas there."[198]

The small hut or kennel where the bloodhounds were kept was beside the one lane path to the cemetery in plain view from the south side of the interior of the pen. The official count of the number of dogs housed in this shack is unknown, but was given by various authors as "nine,"[199] "five or six,"[200] "twelve,"[201] and "twenty-two."[202] "A large pack of bloodhounds, which consisted of two enormous Cuban bloodhounds, [were] said to be the best scented dogs in the world, and about 40 [were] half-bloods."[203] "There were three packs of hounds; ten in each pack, one blood hound and nine fox hounds, which were as ferocious as the blood hounds. They were in charge of a Sergeant Turner, who was as ferocious as his dogs, and whom we afterward sent to the Dry Tortugas for ten years, for his cruelties. And he deserved a worse punishment, for he sat on his horse and allowed the hounds to tear their victims almost to pieces before interfering."[204]

Andrew J. Spring of the 16th Connecticut testified the dogs drew rations at the bakery. "I frequently saw hounds about there. They used to draw rations for these hounds at the bakery. They drew the bread which I supposed was cooked for the men inside; they issued for these hounds there about twenty-five or thirty loaves."[205]

It was rumored there were more than fifty dogs kept at various intervals between Andersonville and Macon, about sixty miles distant, along the route taken by most fugitive prisoners. Most towns in the South had men who made supplemental incomes by recapturing fugitive slaves with dogs. These dogs, trained prior to the war, were used to chase down escapees. The dogs housed on post were fed scraps from the cookhouse and were under the direct supervision of Sergeant Wesley W. Turner and a civilian named Benjamin Harris.

Turner purchased a piece of land in the district near Americus before March or April of 1864. Ambrose Spencer met him one day in Americus and asked him if he was going to settle the land. He said he was not; he was making more money than anybody in the area. He said the Confederate government paid thirty dollars for the recapture of each prisoner; this sum was paid by Captain Wirz.[206]

"The first dogs that were used there belonged to a man by the name of Harris. This Harris lived some five or six miles, I suppose, from Andersonville. He had a pack of eight hounds, besides a dog which they called a 'catch-dog.' Harris did the hunting there for a long while before they got the regular prison hounds. He used to be there every day, and always in the morning he would make a circuit around the stockade to see if any had escaped, and if any had, he would of course follow them; and then he would always scour the country all around. And then they had some dogs which a man by the name of Turner tended. Those dogs did not come there, I think, until May. Turner tended about fifteen dogs, which were kept exclusively for hunting down prisoners. I have seen Turner draw rations for them many a time. He had a young man about eighteen or twenty years old who assisted him, and that young

[198] Author's library.
[199] Spencer, p. 75.
[200] Chipman, p. 251.
[201] Dufur, p. 134.
[202] Spencer, p. 76.
[203] Fosdick, p. 37.
[204] Way.
[205] *Wirz Trial*, p. 112.
[206] Chipman, p. 153.

man used frequently to draw rations for the dogs. He would usually, I think, present a paper. I know that he did so once, because I showed it to several prisoners in the bakery, with Captain Wirz' name to it. All it said was, 'Give this man all the bread and meat he wants for the dogs.'"[207]

"My impression is that Turner did have two packs; I think he did. He kept the packs together - that is to say, he kept both packs near his headquarters. I think Turner had about 15 dogs, and the old man Harris had 8, I think, in his pack. I saw 17 dogs at one time; that was about the 1st of September. Those 17 dogs had been out on a hunting excursion. Harris had his pack there; whether Turner had all his there or not, I do not know, but there were 17 in all."[208]

Colonel James H. Fannin of the First Regiment Georgia Reserves testified: "Sergeant Turner, the owner of the dogs, belonged to the 1st regiment Georgia reserves, my regiment, company H; I was not personally acquainted with all the men in the different companies; I do not know that I ever saw Turner till an order came from General Winder, in June or July, 1864, requiring this man Turner to report to him in person; I recollect sending for the man, and his reporting to me; I sent him over to General Winder, and he came back and reported to me that General Winder had given him a furlough to go home; I said that was something rather irregular, I thought; and I asked him on what business he had been ordered; he said that the general had ordered him to go home and get a pack of negro-dogs he had, and bring them there in order to capture prisoners; I told him that I should object to anything of that kind; I was needing all the men I had at the time, as the guard duty was very heavy; but I was overruled. He was sent for his dogs, and returned with them, I think, in the latter part of June, or about the first or the middle of July; I did not know the man personally until he reported in pursuance of that order...He was detailed by General Winders's order; I should not have respected the order if Captain Wirz had detailed that man. Dogs were used to catch confederate soldiers; some men deserted; the dogs were put on the track, and overtook them; they were brought in by this man Turner; they were used for capturing Union prisoners and confederate soldiers; I believe; I know of but one instance of their overtaking confederate soldiers; I think some eight or nine were pursued at that time; they were pursued about ninety miles."[209]

**Wirz with his pack of dogs.** Taken from the O'Dea print.

Every morning, one or two of these men would be seen with the pack of hounds, searching the space between the inner and middle palisades for evidence a tunnel had been opened during the night. The keeper of the dogs blew a "dog horn" to command the dogs as he circled each morning.[210] "Every morning at daylight the dogs were called together, and with their master, who was mounted on a large bay horse, they made a circuit of the prison, outside of the picket"[211] "Each morning about six o'clock the Andersonville pack of twelve bloodhounds, led by 'old Spot.' encircled the prison walls."[212] "To frustrate night break outs, which would inevitably be discovered at roll-call the following morning, man-tracking hounds were led by mounted men on a wide circuit around the prison, with the well-nigh universal result that the trail was struck and the fugitive taken."[213]

There were two types of dogs kept at Andersonville: "tracking hounds" and "catch dogs." The tracking hounds were scent hounds and did the actual tracking. Since the weak prisoner was no real threat, the inclusion of fierce "catch dogs" was seen as evidence of the deliberate attempt to harm the escaped prisoners.

These catch dogs were used to follow the pack of scent hounds and then to attack the weakened fugitive and hold him with claw and fang until the pursuing hunters could catch up and apprehend the escapee. These two types of dogs were the subject of much debate. Some said they were ferocious, man-killing hounds; others said they were simple, docile, fox-and-deer hounds. "The ordinary bloodhound of these regions is cowardly from degeneration, and dare not face the look, nor disregard the voice of man, and until the catch-dogs arrive and dash in, and lead the way, they bay and show their teeth from safe distances; but the victim once disabled, they tear and rend the living limbs

[207] *Wirz Trial*, p. 321.
[208] *Ibid.*, p. 322.
[209] *Ibid.*, pp. 434, 435.
[210] Northrop, p. 93.
[211] Brownell, p. 20.
[212] Dufur, pp. 133, 134.
[213] Maile, p. 32.

without reluctance."[214] "The bloodhounds here used appear to have been of a degenerate breed, and to have lacked the great strength, the invincible determination, which the true race possesses. The bloodhounds introduced into Cuba, to exterminate the Indians, were ferocious and powerful animals. From these the present stock in Southern Georgia were probably descended, and during three centuries of change, have gradually lost their nobler qualities."[215]

**Prisoners being treed by a pack of hounds** - Many tricks were tried to try to foil the ability of the dogs to track the prisoners. The trick the men thought most reliable was to place turpentine on the soles of the shoes. It seemed to work with some success. (Abbott)

Wirz had a favorite tracking dog in Richmond named "Spot," a "Cuban Bloodhound" used to capture escaped prisoners who had been transported from Richmond.[216]

The Southern surgeon, R. R. Stevenson, described Spot and the other dogs of Andersonville. "The writer has often seen this formidable animal, which certainly in his youth must have been as fine a specimen of the kind as could be met anywhere; but, unfortunately for the thrilling portion of the account of his doings at the time of the war, the poor beast, worn out from old age, and with hardly a tooth in his head, wandered about, a harmless, inoffensive creature. He was the property of the Commandant of Libby, who kept him because he was a pet dog of his father's, and there the brute lived, a pensioner in his old age. As to his worrying men, he could not, had he even tried, have worried a child. The other prisons had none, not even as pensioners... The writer does not deny that when a prisoner got out of the stockade trying to escape, a few mongrel or half-breed fox-hounds were used to track him, but the worrying was all done in the correspondent's own brain."[217]

G. F. Elliott, formerly of the 1st Marine Artillery, and an Andersonville prisoner, described Spot. "I have a pretty lively recollection of a Cuban bloodhound named 'Spot' at Andersonville; weight, one hundred and fifty pounds; height, three feet four inches; length from tip to tip, six feet five inches. Rather a queer kind of a fox or deer hound."[218]

"The first pack was organized under the superintendence of Wesley W. Turner, a citizen of Sumter County, and numbered nine. For the use of his dogs and managing them, taking them to track and catch prisoners, he was paid by Wirz seven hundred and fifty dollars per month. During the month of May, however, the control of the hounds was transferred to Benjamin Harris, who managed them during the remainder of the time that they were required. There were other volunteer packs within a distance of twenty or thirty miles, whose services were occasionally used by their owners, and who were paid fifteen dollars a head for all captures returned to the prison. At one time Harris' pack attained the number of twenty-two, and among them were dogs of pure Cuban blood.

"The constitution of a pack of hounds is somewhat peculiar. It is requisite to assort them in such a way that every advantage may be taken of their different abilities and powers of endurance. Some are needed to trace the steps of the fugitive and point out the course he has taken; their scent must be keen and their muscle good. To supply any failure on the part of these, others are needed, who will take up the scent and 'keep it warm.' After these come the 'catch dogs' - the real bloodhounds, who, following at a more leisurely pace, keep within hearing of those who head the course, and when the quarry comes to bay, or 'is treed,' are generally up in time to take the prey. These

214 Hamlin, p. 65.
215 *Ibid.*, p. 66.
216 Goss.
217 Stevenson, p. 455.
218 Moran, p. 156.

dogs are naturally very ferocious, and require no other stimulus to display their savage characters than a sight of the chase which they have been pursuing."[219]

Joseph R. Achuff, of a Massachusetts regiment, escaped when he and two companions overpowered his guard when outside gathering wood. They tied him up and set off when he was soon set upon by the dog pack. He was mangled and repeatedly bitten before being taken before Wirz, who put him in the stocks for thirty-six hours.

Wirz often would join the drivers in their pursuit of an escapee. Sometimes the chase would last for twelve hours at a stretch. "When notice was given him that a prisoner has escaped, word was passed to Harris, and the animating sounds of yelping hounds and braying horns gave signal that 'game was up.' With canteen well filled with hospital whisky, and haversack stuffed with meat and biscuit, his pouch of tobacco dangling from a button-hole, and his revolver buttoned in its holster, the jailer would mount his pony and hurry away to the exciting sport."[220]

One prisoner, after having been caught by the dogs, described what took place. The keeper "... immediately called the dogs off and told me that I would have to go back with him. He put up his pistol and talked pretty clever to me. He said, 'The old captain told me to make the dogs tear you, but I have been a prisoner myself and know what it is to be a prisoner, and I would not like to do that.' Speaking kindly to me, he took me back to headquarters. The first question of Captain Wirz was, 'Why did you not make the dogs bite him?' evidently showing that he had given the order which the man told me he got. The answers of the man showed me that he was under the command and inferior to Captain Wirz. He replied, 'I guess the dogs hurt him enough,' and that seemed to satisfy Captain Wirz, who ordered me to be taken back to the stockade."[221]

One soldier saw a victim of a dog attack. "I went over there and found Dr. White there and handed him over the written request, and as I came there I saw a man lying on the ground; his clothes were literally and practically all torn to pieces, and you could see the marks of the teeth of the dogs right in his throat all over, and the blood was running and he was almost dead. He was not torn in any other parts of the body that I know of; I know that his clothes were all in rags, all torn to pieces. I don't know if his body was hurt in any other part or not. Captain Wirz, Dr. White, Dr. Stevenson, Humes, and several others were there. They were all talking about it, and they did not seem by the way they spoke to have any compassion on the man at all. I heard Captain Wirz make the remark that it served the damned dog right, meaning of course the man lying on the ground. That man died the same day. He never was brought to the hospital. He died right on the spot."[222]

Tyler and some comrades started a tunnel by branching off from a sixty-feet-deep well which had not struck water. About eighteen feet down from the surface they struck out for the palisade seventy-five feet away. From this tunnel, on a dark, rainy night, filed less than a dozen men when a rather plump escapee became stuck ; while being pulled up, he let out a cry. Tyler fled through the swamps of Georgia with the aid of friendly blacks. After seven days, he was treed by dogs after travelling only about twenty-five miles.

"'Come down, you damned Yanks, or we will fill your carcasses full of cold lead.'

"'Gentlemen,' said I, 'if you want to shoot, shoot; for I would rather be shot than chawed by them dogs.'

"One of the Rebs spoke to the captain and said, 'Let's make them Yanks come down and see how quick the dogs will get away with them.'

"'No,' replied the captain, 'they look as though they had had trouble enough.'

"They muzzled the dogs and tied them together. Then we surrendered. The old gentleman treated us kindly, giving us something to eat and also presented each with a quilt. At noon the next day we got back to prison. Wirz told the guards they were damned fools for bringing us back and told us we should be thankful to get back alive. After relieving us of our quilts the gates were opened and we were marched into Andersonville again."[223]

Dowling told of an escape which caused the death of some of the tracking dogs. "Another plan of escape was devised by us, in which a Rebel sergeant was to play a conspicuous part. It was arranged by several of the prisoners with one of the sergeants on guard outside the prison, that he and prisoners engaged in the scheme should, on a given day, make their exit together, and all push for the Union lines. The plan could not be carried out without the pretty manifest co-operation of the sergeant, and he therefore determined to be off too, as his position would no longer be an enviable one at the South, especially with Captain Wirtz, whose temper was fast getting worse. The guard had engaged to furnish to each man of the Yankee squad a gun and sixty rounds of ammunition....A strong

---

[219] Spencer, pp. 75, 76.
[220] *Ibid.*, pp. 78, 79.
[221] *Wirz Trial*, pp. 72, 73.
[222] *Ibid.*, pp. 182, 183.
[223] Tyler, pp. 27, 28.

pack of bloodhounds and a squad of well-armed men were dispatched in pursuit of them as soon as their escape was discovered, but their expedition was attended with very disastrous results. About twenty miles beyond Andersonville, and on a Northern route, they came up with the fleeing prisoners and their Rebel guide, on the Flinch River, and making an assault upon them and an attempt to capture them, were completely driven off, all of the dogs but two being killed, one man killed and three of them badly wounded...The whole party, led by the Rebel sergeant, succeeded in gaining the Union lines in safety."[224]

An interesting anecdote involved one of the dogs kept in Richmond. "A most important part of the protection, however, was given by the addition to the prison guard of a magnificent blood-hound. The sergeant marched in front of the guard and the hound in the rear, and looking from the prison windows we could see him cock up his eye at us as he passed, as if he very fully understood the nature of his responsibilities. From time to time, the hound would also, either under orders or possibly of his own notion, make the circuit of the building, sniffing around its foundations. There would have been no chance of an undiscovered tunnel while that dog was within reach. I had trouble with that dog some months later when I was on parole in Richmond. I had been told that the intelligence of the blood-hound enabled him to be taught all kinds of things, but that it was very difficult, if not impossible, to unteach him anything. This hound had been taught 'to go for' anybody wearing blue cloth. At this later time, I had secured clean clothes from home and blue was, therefore, really blue instead of the nondescript colour of my much-worn prison garments. I had occasion from time to time to go to Castle Thunder, where the dog was kept, and the sergeant of the prison guard amused himself by putting the dog on a long leash to see how near he could get to the little Yankee adjutant without quite 'chawing' him up. I complained in due form to the captain of the guard that the jaws of the hound did not constitute a fair war risk. He accepted my view and had the dog put on a shorter leash so that I was able to get past him into the prison door. I was told that when Weitzel's troops entered Richmond, the dog was captured and was later brought to New York and sold at auction on the steps of the Astor House. If the buyer permitted any of his home circle to wear army blue, there must certainly have been trouble."[225]

**Prisoner being "Bucked" for a very minor offense.** After a few minutes in this position, the prisoner would not be able to walk for hours. (Abbott)

There was at least one dog kept within the pen by the prisoners. On the 15th or 16th of June, 2,300 prisoners entered the prison. Among those were several of the wounded from Plymouth and those left behind to care for them. Accompanying them was Trip, the little dog that had been the mascot of Company B of the 16th Connecticut Volunteer Regiment, who was welcomed enthusiastically by members of that regiment who had arrived earlier.[226]

Perhaps the usual and customary punishments meted out by the armies of the Civil War to maintain discipline should be reviewed. Extra work, confinement in the guardhouse, or being made to walk extra guard duty were the usual punishments for most minor offenses. Some examples of minor offenses were drunkenness, being discourteous to an officer, or unsoldierly conduct. A slightly more severe punishment was being ordered to walk extra duty while carrying a log over the shoulder for a few hours. The greater the offense, the heavier the log, or the longer it was shouldered.

Flogging was prohibited in both armies by acts passed by their respective legislatures. Another punishment for rather minor offenses was to be made to ride the "wooden horse." This was a piece of lumber on which the person had to straddle with weights attached to his feet to give a greater downward tug to his legs. The square edges of the lumber dug into the thighs, causing excruciating pain after a few minutes. For a slightly more severe punishment for say, insubordination, being "bucked and gagged" might be in order. "Bucking" was the tying of a man's arms around his bended knees through which a pole had been stuck. This could be sometimes accompanied by "gagging' which entailed having a stick forced back-

[224] Dowling, pp. 128-130.
[225] Putnam, p. 28.
[226] Kellogg, p. 139.

ward into the mouth by its being tied behind the head. It was said that the recipient of this punishment could not walk for some time after being in this position for two or three hours.

For those in the artillery, a man found guilty of some minor offense was strapped, spread-eagle, with his wrists and ankles tied to the rim of the extra wheel of a caisson. After an hour of this, the recipient had usually learned his lesson.

Branding with a hot iron or tattooing with indelible ink was punishment used in both armies. The first letter of the offense, "D" for deserter, "C" for cowardice, "T" for thievery, was stamped into the hip, hand, forehead or cheek.

The old stand-by of attaching a ball and chain was used in both armies. The graver the offense, the heavier the cannon ball attached and the longer the time the ball was attached. Stealing from the living or the dead of a battlefield might cause this to be levied.

Cursing an officer might cause a man to end up hanging by his thumbs. A variation was to hang with the hands behind one's back and another was to be hanging so only the tips of the toes touched the ground. This was particularly excruciating and usually caused the person to black out.

In both armies, a prison term was reserved for more severe crimes. Armed robbery, cowardice, or sleeping while on sentry duty might cause such a long sentence.

Of course, death by the firing squad or by hanging was reserved for the gravest capital offenses, such as killing an officer, rape, mutiny, spying, or homicides in general. The defendant would sometimes be made to dig his own grave and then stand before it to be shot while the whole regiment watched. Sometimes he sat on his coffin while waiting to be shot.

At Andersonville, men absent from the morning roll-call were punished by not being issued their rations that afternoon. Other minor offenses were punished by putting the men on work details, not to exceed two hours.

**Vignettes, Outer Border of O'Dea's Print, *Andersonville Prison*** - This shows various prisoners being bucked and gagged, wearing a ball and chain, sitting in the stocks, and hanging by his thumbs. (O'Dea)

If a man escaped and was recaptured, he was supposed to be punished by having a ball and chain attached until he was either exchanged or released from prison. This was the punishment to be rendered, according to the Confederate regulations. "Men caught in attempting escape are unreasonably punished by wearing ball and chain, bucking and gagging, putting in stocks, hanging by thumbs, by lash and close confinement."[227] "Every day or two there would be prisoners brought back that had tried to make their escape. They were brought just inside of the gate and there bucked and gagged for a half of a day at a time."[228] There were several punishments for the offenses prevalent at the camp. The area of punishment or the location of the instruments of torture was southwest of the South Gate and near the cabin of Wirz. "There was a sort of guardhouse very near the stocks."[229]

"There was a fellow known as Jim Malloy, who was a great sleight of hand performer; he had three assistants. It seemed that bolts and bars would not hold him. One night Jim and his three assistants were fastened to an iron bar by means of clevices. Malloy was quite a ventriloquist, and during the night the ignorant guard who stood over them, was startled by a solemn voice from the clouds, warning him of the vengeance to come upon the rebels for their cruelty to the Union prisoners, and while the guard stood trembling, behold the bars fell from their limbs, and they made their escape without hindrance.

"Jim Malloy was supposed to [have been] a spy; he escaped ten or twelve times, but was always recaptured. I

[227] Northrop, p. 72.
[228] Steven Payne's diary in private hands.
[229] *Wirz Trial*, p. 320.

think he a made his way to our lines and reported, when he would allow himself to be retaken."[230]

At one time the stocks were dismantled and brought within the pen; two men were put in them after being recaptured following a tunneling escape attempt. The men were in relatively good condition before being placed in the stocks. They were placed in the stocks at about 11 o'clock one morning and were kept in them until the next morning. They were kept in the stocks two hours and then two hours out of the stocks as was the custom at Andersonville. "A portion of the stocks were at one time inside the stockade. I could not tell exactly when it was. It was just for the time being. The original stocks were outside the stockade, between Captain Wirz' office and the stockade. They were inside the latter part of July. They appeared to be brought in for that occasion, because they were not there afterwards. They were about the length of that table (about twelve feet), and about four or five inches wide. The stocks were about five feet ten inches long, and there was a space for the neck and a space for the feet, so that they could close over and keep the men in, and there they lay. The men were spread out in the stocks full length, with the arms stretched out at right angles with the body. The stocks were situated right opposite the gate; the north gate. It was where we hung the men... The stocks were never empty... They were put in there for a show, as a guarantee to the balance of the prisoners what they would get if they attempted to get away." One of the men died the next morning in his shebang. The stocks were then dismantled and immediately taken out.[231]

One man, after having been recaptured, was "... led bleeding, and torn to the stocks, fastened in the infernal machine, the maggot flies deposit[ing] their eggs in his wounds. He is punished for ten or twelve hours and then turned into the prison with wounds uncared for. A few days later we see him a working mass of maggots."[232]

"Some of the punishments that were inflicted on them for any offense such as trying to get out or saying bad things against the rebels, were, we were tied up by the thumbs whipped with a raw-hide, put in the stocks, which was a frame, two posts set in the ground, between the posts was a heavy plank with a hole in it to fit the neck, another piece slipped in to hold the neck in. It was made to raise or lower to suit the height. Then your hands were tied behind you then raised till your toes would touch the ground, left there for two hours with hot sun beaming down in your face. They were often taken down dead, and then they had other cruel ways of torture, such as they had to punish their slaves."[233]

**Prisoners on the Chain Gang** - Ten to twenty men were joined by painful iron anklets on a chain. Each of the members had to move in a synchronized manner. When one member needed to visit the sink, all had to go. Sometimes an individual would have a large cannonball attached to his ankle for several days. (McElroy)

W. W. Crandall, testified about Duncan, who "... had charge of the cook-house there. During the first time I was there he used to come into the stockade with rations. During the later part of the time they said he was acting as detective. In the first days of October, 1864, I was in the ball-and-chain-gang. I saw him and another man named Barr bring a man to put in the stocks. His name was James Armstrong. He belonged to an Ohio regiment; the number of the regiment I cannot tell. They put him in what they called the 'spread-eagle stocks,' and after putting him in they took from him his money and a picture. I heard Armstrong plead with Duncan for the picture, saying either that it was the picture of his sister or of his mother. He did not get it. He was left there three or four hours, when Duncan came back alone and took him out, saying that he was going to send him away on the cars. I heard Armstrong at that time ask

[230] Compton, p. 41.
[231] *Wirz Trial*, pp. 214-216.
[232] Boggs, p. 32.
[233] Clifton, p. 11.

Duncan if he could not give him back that picture. The answer was, 'You may consider yourself damned fortunate to get away at all, and that you are not put in the ball-and-chain-gang with those other boys.' I did not notice anything that he took except the money and picture. I do not know how much money. The man told me the amount while he was still in the stocks. I think he stated the sum was about eight or nine dollars in greenbacks."[234]

"At one time seven men, sitting in the stocks near the Star Fort - in plain view of the camp - became objects of interest to everybody inside. They were never relieved from their painful position, but were kept there until all of them died. I think it was nearly two weeks before the last one succumbed."[235]

"Another contrivance was a small log, perhaps six inches in diameter, with long legs attached after the fashion of a saw-horse, and about four feet high. The victim would be placed astride of this, his hands fastened behind him, his feet tied together underneath, and gagged by trying a stick in the mouth. As it was difficult to keep in balance in this position, without the use of hands and feet, the poor fellows would often slide around the pole and hang head downward, the feet being securely tied."[236]

Andrew J. Spring testified men in chain gangs were not required to perform any duty and were kept about ten or fifteen rods outside of the stockade near the stocks. "They merely went down to the bake-house in the morning and washed themselves. Our boys there they would feed them with the best they had, and consequently they fared better in regard to rations than if they had been inside the stockade."[237]

**Prisoner Being Whipped with Flat Shingle** - The Chief Regulator would, many times sentence a prisoner to be spanked for minor offenses. Turner, the keeper of the hounds, would sometimes administer the punishment if ordered by Wirz. (McElroy)

"I believe as many as sixty men were chained together at one time, and, as all had to move when one did, these were kept in almost constant motion in order to attend the necessary calls. The ankles around which were fastened the iron bands would become a raw sore, by having to drag the ball and chain, and in many instances flies would get in and blow them. In a short time they would be filled with maggots, and later be afflicted with gangrene, which necessitated amputation, and finally resulted in death."[238]

If "... one of the number having died while thus hobbled, the services of a blacksmith with cold chisel and hammer was required in order to remove his shackles and separate the dead from the living."[239]

"One man who was whipped was a soldier belonging to the eighth United States colored troops. He was a colored man named Isaac Hawkins. He was ordered by Wirz to receive five hundred lashes. The sergeant miscounted and he received two hundred and fifty. He was whipped for carrying onions to the hospital; to the sick men in the hospital, I believe. Wirz gave the order for the application of five hundred lashes. I believe he was not present when they were given. A man named Turner, who used to run the hounds, was I believe, the man who whipped him."[240]

"One day they caught a man stealing from a sick man. They tied him to a post and stripped his back and whipped him with a cat o'nine tails. I witnessed the whipping and it was terrible."[241]

W. D. Hammack, of the 55th Georgia, testified for the defense: "Confederate soldiers were treated in the same way as federal prisoners, with the exception of their being chained together. I know that confederate soldiers have had on ball and chain, but I have not seen them chained to one another. I never saw confederate soldiers in a chain-gang, but I have seen them with ball and chain on. I have seen them in the stocks. I do not know how long they were kept in them; I saw them in what they called the "spread eagle" stocks. I saw confederate soldiers there very often; there was one fellow put in there because at the dress parade one day in August, when the adjutant ordered the

[234] *Wirz Trial*, pp. 367, 368.
[235] McElroy, p. 376.
[236] Fosdick, pp. 44, 45.
[237] *Wirz Trial*, p. 116.
[238] Fosdick, p. 45.
[239] Leonard, p. 60.
[240] *Wirz Trial*, p. 174.
[241] Helwig, p. 34.

officers to the front, this fellow stepped out and went to the front of the regiment with the officers. He belonged to the 4th Georgia reserves. He was put in the stocks on that occasion, and I have seen him in the stocks a dozen different times...They took a barrel, knocked out one head of it, cut a hole in the other large enough for a man's head to go through, and put it on them. That punishment was inflicted by order of court martial."[242]

**The Vertical Spread Eagle Stock** - This is a very reliable rendition of the stock. One prisoner describes it as having a roof to shade the prisoner; it was made out of nicely finished planks.

Andrew J. Spring testified that a black Confederate soldier was lashed. "I can speak of one of them in particular; one of them was sick and refused to go to work. The man who had charge of the gang at that time - I forget his name - reported the matter to Captain Wirz. Captain Wirz came along and ordered the negro to be taken up to the stocks and whipped; I forget the number of lashes the man got; I saw them given to him. I believe that the man who whipped him was named Humes; he was generally called quartermaster, but was nothing but a private soldier, as I understood, to issue rations from the bakery to our men in the stockade. He used to go in with the wagon and issue the rations."[243]

There were swallows that lived in the cracks between the logs of the palisade. They could be seen, especially at dusk, skimming and darting about, feeding on the maggots, flies and mosquitoes. The men tried to kill these swallows with "... long willow or cane poles," being careful not to risk instant death by leaning over into the deadline to retrieve their quarry. On the 23rd of May, for some unknown reason, a large flock of birds alighted inside the pen. This caused a frenzy as the men attempted to stone or knock down these birds. That day, many small sparrows were killed, plucked and eaten, some raw.

Northrop said, on August 10th, "... no bird have I yet seen in this foul realm."

As the number of prisoners constantly grew, the Southern guard became increasingly aware of how tenuous the security of the prison was becoming. Therefore, the guard held practice alerts every few hours.

On July 13th, late in the day, "... we were a little excited by hearing the rifled pieces, bearing on the prison, very suddenly discharged. They were loaded with blank cartridges, as it proved. Immediately following these discharges, a great commotion was visible in the rebel camps. The regiments fell in at the double quick, and formed in line of battle around the stockade. All the pieces of artillery were manned, and we thought our forces must surely be in the vicinity, but we learned that it was merely an attempt on the part of the Confederate authorities to see how quick they could get their troops out in case we really should try to force the stockade."[244]

On July 14th, the sergeants of the detachments were taken out and told the men must stay away from the area near the gates, especially when they were open for the admittance of new fish. That evening, the guard fired two blank cannon shots as well as many muskets.[245] Hopkins said that, on that day, the garrison was, also, called out.[246] The purpose of this demonstration was not known but perhaps it was to reinforce their edict.

On July 28th, one thousand new prisoners were brought into the prison. "Just before they came in at the prison-gate, the rebs in the fort around the Captain's quarters fired a solid shot across the prison, directly over our heads. A large crowd of us had gathered near the gate, to watch the new-comers, and the Johnnies, thinking we might possibly seize upon the opportunity to make a break and get out, had fired over us in this manner to intimidate us. Soon after this, a line of poles was planted through the prison, to which were nailed white flags, not as a sign of surrender, but as a warning to us, that no crowd should approach nearer the gate than those, under penalty of being fired upon with artillery, - that is, when prisoners were being marched in."[247]

---

242 *Wirz Trial*, p. 510.
243 *Ibid.*, p. 114.
244 Kellogg, p. 178,and Urban, pp. 351, 352.
245 Miller, p. 46.
246 Hopkins, p. 93.
247 Kellogg, p. 191.

**Killing Chimney Swallows at Twilight** - For food, prisoners took long willow or cane poles and swatted at swallows that skimmed around the pen at dusk. The swallows built their mud nests in the cracks between the posts of the stockade. At another time, a large flock of birds alighted within the pen and many were struck and killed. (Grigsby)

"As the prisoners who were captured in Maryland came into the prison, we crowded toward the gate for the purpose of getting a talk with them, when the rebels, who, I suppose, thought we intended making an attempt to escape, fired a cannon-ball directly over our heads, we at first believed that they intended to open fire on the prison, and some of the prisoners threw themselves in terror on the ground; but from the throats of thousands of the doomed men inside of the prison arouse such a howl of derision and defiance as was perhaps never before heard on the face of the earth.

After the gates were closed, several rebels came in and planted a line of poles through the prison on which were placed small white flags. This was intended to warn us not to approach or gather in crowds nearer to the gate than the poles when prisoners were being marched in. Captain Wirz declared that if we did he would open fire on us, and fire away as long as any one was 'left kicking.'"[248]

On July 29th, a line of four poles, to which were nailed small white flags, were placed along the lengthwise center of the pen.[249] The men in the pen were informed that, if they gathered in unusually large groups between these poles and either the North or South Gates, then the cannons in the surrounding forts would open fire. This warning to prevent crowding was tested almost immediately because several hundred prisoners came in the same day the flags were put up.[250] Soon after the poles were erected, "... some were moved nearer to the stockade, while others were left remaining on the old line."[251]

"The next day a line of tall poles, bearing white flags, were put up at some little distance from the Dead Line, and a notice was read to us at roll call that if, except at roll call, a gathering exceeding one hundred was observed, closer to the Stockade than these poles, the guns would open with grape and canister without warning."[252] "Captain Wirz planted a range of flags inside the stockade, and gave the order , just inside the gate, 'that if a crowd of two hundred (that was the number) should gather in any one spot beyond those flags and near the gate, he would fire grape and canister into them.'"[253]

---

[248] Urban, pp. 373, 374.
[249] Miller, p. 46.
[250] Kellogg, p. 191.
[251] *Ibid.*, p. 200.
[252] McElroy, p. 194.
[253] *Wirz Trial*, p. 345.

## *Chapter Nine*

# Some Successful Remedies to Some Problems

*"No effectual remedy for all these evils seems available so long as the numbers are in such excess over that for which the prison was designed."*

B. R. Wellford, Jr.
Confederate War Dept.

The rapid influx of new prisoners in the late spring necessitated the enlargement of the prison. Kellogg said that, on the 24th of May, nine hundred prisoners came in and "... we were getting frightfully crowded. There was no circulating about the camp except with the greatest inconvenience."[1] "We thought when there were ten thousand in the pen that it was crowded to the last degree; but now it contained eighteen thousand."[2] Just before opening the new addition, Northrop said, "At night when we lay down every passage, every space is covered, thousands sleeping without the least covering or shelter."[3]

The measurement of the prison was 1,010 feet long by about 787 feet across the north wall and 779 1/2 feet across the south wall. Captain Wirz wrote, on May 8th, to Major Thomas P. Turner, who had been ordered by General Winder in Richmond, on April 30th, to inspect the prison: "The necessity of enlarging the stockade is unavoidable, and I shall commence as soon as I can gather a sufficient number of negroes."[4]

Captain James H. Wright, of the 55th Georgia Regiment, volunteered to superintend the enlargement ordered by Colonel Persons. The actual work was done by about 100 white and about 30 black prisoners.[5] Wirz used extra rations and "... better treatment in every respect" as inducement to get the men to work. There was a heated discussion by the prisoners as to whether or not working on the enlargement constituted aiding and abetting the enemy. Most men thought it was not right to help the Rebels and yet it was not as bad as working on the fortifications around the prison which might increase the danger to Federal troops on some future rescue mission. Some men rationalized that, since increasing the size of the prison was to decrease the discomfort of the entire prison population, the workers should not be the subjects of the wrath of their fellow prisoners. All the work was done with axes, spades, and shovels. Captain Wright said there were plenty of tools on hand.[6]

During most of the month of June could be heard the chopping and falling of the trees to be used to make the addition to the northern portion. Why the prison was enlarged only in a northerly direction is unknown. If the south wall had been pushed further southward, it would have brought it into closer proximity to Sweetwater Creek proper. In fact, one prisoner testified, "I heard one of the rebel sergeants say that the stockade was about being enlarged on both ends, north and south; that is, if it were enlarged on the south side it would bring it down toward the large creek down there."[7]

---

[1] Kellogg, p. 103.
[2] Boggs, p. 37.
[3] Northrop, p. 80.
[4] *O.R.*, VII, p. 169.
[5] Chipman, p. 158.
[6] *Wirz Trial*, p. 374.
[7] Chipman, p. 180.

The new addition was laid out by Sid Winder, who had laid out the original prison. The stockade was now 161 yards shy of being a mile in circumference. "The peculiar singing of hundreds of slaves" on the outside, who helped in the labor was heard from inside the prison.[8] The prisoners learned from the Rebel sergeants there was a new addition being added to the north end of the prison.[9] It took a little over three weeks to complete the job.[10]

The habitable area was increased from 740,520 square feet (17.0 acres) to 1,176,120 square feet, (27.0 acres). An acre equals 43,560 square feet. The prisoners made very poor estimates of the size of the prison. For instance, Vawter estimated that the "... North side contained about seven and a half acres, South side about three and a half."[11] The habitable area was the area enclosed minus the area between the dead line and the palisade, the swamp, the streets, and paths. The number of square feet per man jumped from 33.2 square feet to 40.5 square feet per man in July.

**Over Crowding at Andersonville [12]**

| Month 1864 | Mean Strength Federal Prisoners | Area of Stockade in Sq. Feet | Average Number of Sq. Ft. per Prisoner |
|---|---|---|---|
| March | 7,500 | 740,520 | 98.7 |
| April | 10,000 | 740,520 | 74.0 |
| May | 15,000 | 740,520 | 49.3 |
| June | 22,291 | 740,520 | 33.2 |
| July | 29,030 | 1,176,120 | 40.5 |
| August | 32,899 | 1,176,120 | 35.7 |

In the late spring, the density was equivalent to more than 1,600,000 people per square mile.[13] By comparison, Belle Isle held 10,000 prisoners on six acres. The density of a Federal prison might be interesting for comparison. Elmira contained 6,000 men and was within a 40 acre enclosure. The Confederate prisoners at Chicago, Johnson's Island, Point Lookout, and Fort Delaware were provided with spacious exercise grounds, and were furnished with crude barracks.

United States Army Captain James M. Moore was sent, in the summer of 1865, to Andersonville, accompanied by Clara Barton, "... by the Quartermaster-general, upon order of the Secretary of War, to take possession of the cemetery and initiate the necessary steps for its permanent improvement."[14] "Captain James M. Moore, in his official report to the war department, gave the dimensions of the prison as 1,540 feet long by 750 feet wide. This was, no doubt, by actual measurement. He gave the trip taken off by the Dead-line as 17 feet, which reduced the prison to 1,506 feet by 716 feet, or 1,078,296 square feet. The evidence showed that the swamp covered about two acres and the necessary passageways another acre, or 131, 880 square feet, which would leave 946,416 square feet. At times there were 35,000 prisoners at Andersonville Prison, each of whom had 27 square feet, or a space 3 by 9 feet. When there were 30,000 the space would be 31 feet, or 5 by 6.2 feet."[15]

On July 1st, the 610-foot addition was completed, the guards were withdrawn from their guard towers on the north wall, and a 10-foot opening was made in the old north wall. All detachments that numbered above 48 (i.e., those near the swamp) were ordered to proceed within 2 hours into this new position. At that time, those detachments numbered 49 through 98 prepared to move immediately to the new quarters.[16] Wirz made the threat that, if any man failed to be in the new addition in the allotted time, all of the prisoners' personal property would be confiscated.[17] This requirement, that hundreds of weak, debilitated prisoners rush through a ten-foot space, was thought to

---

[8] Boggs, p. 51.
[9] *Ibid.*
[10] Chipman, p. 158.
[11] Vawter, p. 37.
[12] Breeden, p. 181.
[13] Hamlin, p. 49.
[14] Chipman, p. 464.
[15] *Ibid.*, p. 140.
[16] Melvin, p. 115.
[17] Kellogg, p. 157.

have been just another of Wirz' cruel directives. Urban said Wirz ordered this mad rush because he "... wanted a little amusement." To comply with this order was difficult in the prisoners' weakened condition, whereas, to healthy men, it would have been a very reasonable order. There was no record of any men failing to be through the opening by the appointed time.

In two hours, 13,000 men of the 22,000 within the pen crowded through the 10-foot opening.[18] They were obliged to jump a trench 5 feet deep and 3 feet wide, with a bank of dirt on the other side. Twenty fell into the trench. Pieces of tree trimmings remained on the ground of the new annex when the men went in.[19] "Thirteen thousand men must crowd through an opening eight or ten feet in width, in this short space of time, or lose their little property."[20] Since the new land was very desirable, there was a "perfect stampede" into the newly-opened portion.[21] The tenants of the old portion were very elated with the new improvement in their condition. Kellogg said the prisoners became "beautifully less." Those entering the new land felt fortunate not to have had the filth and excrement with which to contend.

"Every green weed and herb was plucked and devoured, the wood and stumps were gathered and stored for scarce times."[22] Because of the scarcity of wood, on the night of July 1st, men came from all sections of the prison to help themselves to the old north wall. They dismantled it with axes and pocket knives "... working until nearly morning in pulling down and carrying it off for fuel, so that at daylight but a very small portion of it was left standing."[23] The next day, a rumor circulated about the interior of the pen to the effect that Captain Wirz had ordered that no more rations would be issued until the stolen timber had been replaced. Northrop said, "On July 2nd, Capt. Wirz directed that no rations be issued until every stick was replaced. He was heard to say on the 3rd, at the gate, that he would 'learn the G-d d--n Yankees' that he was in command and if the sons of bitches died like hell there would be enough left.'"[24] This directive proved to be only a rumor and the rest of the old wall soon disappeared.

In the new annex the men found "... a very limited supply of red root and white gum bark can be found, on our new lot, and pine bark, which are used to check the almost universal complaints, diarrhoea, dysentery and urinary troubles. I observed several men today had buried their limbs to the knees, as a remedy for scurvy."[25]

Urban described how he and his tent-mates made their shelter in the new areas. "Some of the soil close to us was composed of brick clay, and we found that by mixing it up with water, and letting it dry, it would get almost as hard as a stone...We gathered a lot of this clay, and built a wall about six inches high around out lot. After ... a few days, we gathered more clay, and at first only for amusement and pastime, commenced to build our wall higher and stronger. We then discovered that when exposed to the sun for several days it would become very hard, and we commenced to think that we might secure some kind of a shelter by raising the wall higher and arching it part way in. We built the two sides and one gable end of our house about three and one-half feet high, and taking Gilbert's blanket for a roof, we had a pretty good protection against the heavy dews so prevalent after night in that part of the country."[26]

Because one rain lasted 10 hours on Sunday July 3rd, there were 2 to 4 inches of standing water all over the newly-opened addition. The weak prisoners died by drowning; the strong stood up all night to keep out of it.[27]

"For a short time after we had occupied the new part of the prison, we had succeeded in keeping our corner pretty clean, and the number of deaths was not as large as in some parts of the prison, but it was now getting to be almost as bad as the old part of the prison. A number of prisoners from the vicinity of the swamp, in their desire to get away from that place, had commenced to move among us; and as they were all in the most horrible condition, some of them being compelled to crawl on their hands and knees, it greatly added to the unpleasant condition of our quarters.

"Close to us on our right was a small piece of ground a few feet square, and on this could be found almost all the time one of these poor beings, who had crawled there to die. They belonged to that class who had no special friends or companions, and consequently were the most unfortunate class of all in prison. When a few who belonged

---

[18] Dufur, p. 96.
[19] Northrop, p. 82.
[20] Kellogg, p. 157.
[21] *Ibid.*, 158.
[22] Boggs, p. 152.
[23] Kellogg, p. 158.
[24] Northrop, p. 85.
[25] *Ibid.*, p. 83.
[26] Urban, p. 337.
[27] Northrop, p. 83.

to one company, or became intimate friends, kept together, and endeavored to cheer and help each other, they always got along much better than the unfortunates who were without friends or close companions

"As mentioned before, the prisoners who crept to this spot to die belonged to the first-named class; and as they were in the most wretched condition, it of course was very unpleasant to us, but they had no place to go to, and it was certainly unkind to ill-treat them, as several German Wisconsin soldiers did. These men had their quarters close to the spot, and it was a source of great annoyance to them; but they displayed a want of feeling for their companions that was contemptible. They often ordered them away when the poor fellows were beyond the power of obeying. One who was thus spoken to, asked, 'Where do you expect me to go to?' 'To where you came from; you are too filthy to be here,' was the brutal reply. The dying man told them that he would not trouble them long; and so it proved, for on the following morning he was carried to the Dead House.

"On another occasion, a soldier belonging to a Maryland regiment crawled to this spot to die. He was a mere boy, and his emaciated body and pain-pinched face did not altogether hide the fact that he had been remarkably handsome; and not only his physiognomy, but his conduct, gave strong indication of a pure moral character. Being very sick, and unable to keep himself clean, he of course was very filthy; and his general appearance was in strange contrast to his gentle pure-looking face. One of these Wisconsin soldiers, who, as Gilbert expressed it, had as little humanity as the rebels, ordered him to move away; and weak as he was, he would have made an effort to do so, had some of us not interfered and told him to stay. His look of gratitude was surely enough to compensate for the short time we were annoyed by his presence. A few hours after, as gently and quietly as falls the autumn leaf, his pure spirit left his tortured body, and winged its way to a better land."[28]

Dick Winder, on July 9, requested "... ten small, compact saddle horses that should not affect the supply of artillery horses." On the same day, General Winder wrote to Richmond requesting, for the second time, the detectives for whom he had previously sent. "There is treason going on around us, even to depositing arms in the adjacent counties to arm the prisoners." Without the ones he asked for, he was "... obliged to commit the investigation to incompetent hands and I fear it will fail. We are in a critical situation. Do send me the assistance I ask. Believe me there is a very great danger here."[29]

On July 21st, Colonel Persons requested the Southern Telegraph Company put up a telegraph line between Fort Valley and Andersonville, a distance of about 30 miles. He felt it would be advantageous to have it for three reasons: to announce the arrival of additional prisoners, to inform the post of the approach of any Federal raiding party riding with the intent of freeing the prisoners, and to allow the post to summon help in case of a prisoner revolt within the pen.[30]

The difficulty of Dick Winder in feeding the prisoners was echoed by General Winder on the 25th day of July when he wrote to General Sam Cooper: "There are 29,400 prisoners, 2,650 troops, 500 negroes and other laborers and not a ration at the post."[31] The next day, General Winder was assigned to the command of the military prisons in the States of Georgia and Alabama. General W. M. Gardner, was assigned to command of the military prisons in the other states east of the Mississippi River.[32]

It is interesting to note that, even with the expansion of the prison, General Winder, on August 4th, in a letter to Lt. Col. Chandler, stated, "The present and constantly increasing crowded state of the stockade will, I fear, compel me to occupy the space between the present stockade and the stockade now being erected for defense for prisons. This will be a serious inconvenience, but I see no help for it."[33]

Many of the prisoners incarcerated at Andersonville were from the streets of the larger cities of the North. They were members of street gangs, bounty-jumpers, thieves, and petty gangsters. "They called themselves the New York Bummers."[34] They banded together at the prison and were the perpetrators of chaos and mayhem on the sick and weaker prisoners. These ruffians were called "Raiders " by the other prisoners.

The Raiders had been at Belle Isle before coming to Andersonville. One author said there was a group of deserters described variously as "bounty-jumpers" and "desperadoes" at Salisbury who attacked and robbed the new fish. "At their own request their status was changed, and they were sent as prisoners of war to Andersonville, Georgia. There the Union prisoners, detecting them in several robberies and murders, organized a court-martial, tried them,

[28] Urban, pp. 403-405.
[29] *Ibid.*, p. 451.
[30] *Ibid.*, pp. 480, 481.
[31] *Ibid.*, p. 499.
[32] *Ibid.*, p. 501.
[33] *Ibid.*, p. 541.
[34] Tyler, p. 30.

and hung six of them upon trees within the garrison, with ropes furnished by the Rebel commandant."[35]

They stole from their fellow prisoners and, on occasion, killed during the commission of robberies. They concentrated their attacks on the traders who were relatively rich. On many mornings, men would wake up to find a fellow prisoner with his throat slit and his personal belongings missing. The prisoners were terrified by these roving gangs who became bolder and did not hesitate to commit their crimes in daylight. Several prisoners mysteriously disappeared without a trace, murdered by the Raiders. The men feared the Raiders much more than the authorities or Wirz' wrath. The size of the band increased daily in size and, by June, it "... seemed that half the prisoner population were members of the raiders." The hard-core Raiders numbered probably about 100 but, if one includes the several hundred sympathizers and opportunists, the total band numbered about 700, according to Brownell. McElroy said they numbered 400 to 500 men.[36]

McElroy said many members of the 7th New Hampshire regiment were Raiders because they had been drawn to that state by the large bounty offered there.

"Decoys ('bunk-steerers' at home) would be on the lookout for promising subjects as each crowd of fresh prisoners entered the gate; by kind offers to find them sleeping places they would lure them to where they could be easily despoiled during the night... All men having money or valuables were under continual espionage, and when found in places convenient for attack, a rush was made for them. They were knocked down and their persons rifled with such swift dexterity that it was done before they realized what had happened."[37]

The Raiders were armed with slingshots, brass knuckles, billy clubs, and "... several of them had succeeded in smuggling bowie-knives into prison."[38]

McElroy told of one of the first major clashes between the general prison population and the Raiders, whom he called "N'Yaarkers." "We had in our squad a little watchmaker named Dan Martin, of the Eighth New York Infantry. Other boys let him take their watches to tinker up, so as to make a show of running, and be available for trading to the guards.

"One day Martin was at the creek, when a N'Yaarker asked him to let him look at a watch. Martin incautiously did so, when the N'Yaarker snatched it and sped away to the camp of his crowd." Martin gathered 200 of his friends and they vowed to go to the South Side and get back his watch. They went over and met the Raiders who, at that time, numbered over 300; they were soundly whipped by the Raiders. It was from that time that the Raiders had, more or less, free run of the camp.[39] The chief, or leader, of the Raiders was William Collins. The organization got so large it was subdivided into smaller bands, each led by an experienced thief. They were known as the "Curtis Raiders," "Delaney's Raiders," "Collins' Raiders," etc.[40] Collins was called "Mosby" by most of the prisoners and his men were called "Mosby's Marauders" or "Mosby's Raiders."[41]

The names of the Raiders who, later, were hung were: Cary "Terence or Terrence" Sullivan, of the 76th N. Y. Regiment; William Collins, alias Mosby, 88th Pennsylvania Vol. Inf.; Charles Curtis, 5th Rhode Island artillery; John Sarsfield, 144th New York Infantry; Patrick Delaney, 83rd Pennsylvania Infantry; and A. Muir, alias Jack the Sailor, U. S. Navy. Northrop's company had a strange relationship with the Raiders in return for their silence after he "... learned that one of the dealers, or 'raiders' bore the name of Cary. He was at Belle Isle and is charged with being the cause of several deaths. Today he was pointed out to us and we recognized Sullivan of our company (the 76th New York) who deserted October 10, 1863, near the Rapidan River south of Mitchell, Va. He was a substitute from Buffalo, a gambling, fighting, bad tempered fellow, feared in the company. He thinks we suspect him, and tonight sends word by Nooney, who knew him in Canada, that if we do not expose him, Company F shall never be disturbed by raiders."[42]

"Sullivan's given name announced by the regulators as Terrence, was carried on the company roll as Cary. We know Sullivan deserted our regiment while it was forming for expected battle, on the night of October 10th, 1863, and was captured by Rebel cavalry that was flanking our infantry a few hours prior to the beginning of Meade's great retreat to Centerville, Va."[43]

---

[35] Albert D. Richardson, *The Secret Service, The Field, The Dungeon, and The Escape* (Hartford, Conn.: American Publishing Company, 1865), pp. 409, 410.
[36] McElroy, p. 222.
[37] *Ibid.*, pp. 221, 222.
[38] *Ibid.*, p. 222.
[39] *Ibid.*, pp. 149, 150.
[40] Boggs, p. 36.
[41] *Ibid.*, p. 44.
[42] Northrop, p. 76.
[43] *Ibid.*, p. 87.

It was rumored that Muir had been acquitted of a crime in Dublin, Ireland, and that he had confessed his guilt to his priest.[44] He was captured in the Albemarle Sound of North Carolina, from the *Water Witch*.[45]

"They say one of the prisoners killed his own brother for his money and then dug a hole under his bunk and buried him there and he layed on him for a week or two before the rest of the boys found it out and when they found it out, they hung him and five others."[46]

On the night of June 15th, the Raiders fought all night on a rampage. Almost every night the sound of clubs and fists landing on flesh could be heard with an ensuing chase by friends of the victim. Northrop said the threat of attack was so frightening he did not feel safe to go to sleep unless someone in his tent kept watch. He felt the Raiders were very friendly with the Confederate authorities. "Raiders are on the good side of our keepers. They sell articles they steal, or exchange them for food and things which help to keep them in strong physical condition. They are allowed favors not accorded others, are continually fawning to Wirz and his subordinates."[47]

The prisoners sometimes would punish the Raiders individually. "It was not infrequent that one of the camp thieves or raiders would be arrested in his prowling operations at night, carried to the brook, to endure the process of 'gagging' and 'bucking,' having one side of his head shaved, and this not being considered sufficient punishment, he would finally be thrown into the swamp, there to consider the propriety of discontinuing his raids for a time."[48]

The Raiders were located on the high ground near the clump of pine trees in the southeast corner of the pen. "They spliced their tent stuff together, and getting some poles, made what they called a 'big shebang' which afterward became known as 'Raider headquarters.'"[49] "Raiders occupied the southwest corner of the prison, a space about 100 feet square. This was known as the 'raider's corner'."[50] The Raiders' "… headquarters was a large, roomy tent, with a circular top, situated on the street leading to the South Gate, and capable of accommodating from seventy-five to one hundred men. All the material for this had been wrested away from others."[51]

The Raiders signaled orders and commands to each other by whistles. Thus, in the pen at night would be heard their whistle calls followed by cries from their victims. From this area would be heard fighting and then a rush as the Raiders ran to escape from the scene of a crime.[52]

One of the few times wheat flour was issued instead of corn meal, Dufur decided to get a larger quantity of food; he sought to trade his wheat flour ration for a larger quantity of corn meal. "As I passed down the street shouting; 'Who will swap meal for flour?' a man opened the door of the largest tent in the prison and beckoned me to enter. I was very thoughtless in going so near this tent, knowing it to be a rendezvous of the Raiders, six or eight of the leaders owning the tent together. Seeing I hesitated a moment, two other men stepped out and told me to walk in, if I wished to trade. I dared not do otherwise, and entered, thereupon a pug-nose, pugilistic ruffian, took from a shelf a small box, already containing six or eight quarts of flour, and told me to empty my own into that. I did so, and then waited two or three minutes, thinking they might not rob me, relying a little upon my lameness in eliciting their sympathy. But no; they were the wrong men to sympathize with suffering humanity. One of them at length said; 'What are you waiting here for?' 'For the meal I expect you to give me,' I said. 'Oh, get out of this,' he said taking me by the arm. I was knocked down and brutally kicked out of the tent. I could show no resistance, as I was weak and lame. Such were the characteristics of the Andersonville Raiders."[53]

About 350 new fish came in on Wednesday, June 29th, and were immediately introduced to the cruelty of the Raiders. Kellogg said that one man was severely beaten and cut about the head and robbed of his watch and $175 in money.[54] Northrop said that one of Sherman's soldiers, at about 3 p.m., was violently assaulted while asleep, and robbed of $85 and a watch. With blood streaming down his face from a gash on his forehead, he went to the gate where he reported the attack to the Confederate authorities. Some sergeants of detachments went to verify to the truthfulness of the plaintiff.[55] That man was John W. Urban who, in his own book, said that the watch was a friend's and he was only carrying it because his friend's clothes had no pocket. Urban said that he had no money but

[44] *Ibid.*, p. 90.
[45] Hopkins, p. 82.
[46] Blessing Diary.
[47] Northrop, p. 64.
[48] Kellogg, p. 113.
[49] Boggs, p. 27.
[50] Lyons, p. 67.
[51] McElroy, p. 223.
[52] Miller, p. 22.
[53] Dufur, pp. 87, 88.
[54] Kellogg, P. 156.
[55] Northrop, p. 80.

vouched for the correctness of everything else about the incident in Kellogg's book.

Urban related his robbery in his own book thus: "In the afternoon I went to the brook to get a drink of water, when noticing that some rebel soldiers were drilling on the ground outside of the stockade, I went to the south end of the prison, where I could get a better view of them. Having been but a short time in the prison, I knew nothing about the locality where the raiders had their quarters, and so, unconsciously, got right in among them. I was looking at the rebel soldiers drilling, when I noticed a stranger who had come close to my left side, and was apparently looking at the same object. Directly after a second came to my rear, and another to my right side. The three coming so close, aroused my suspicions, and I was thinking about moving away from the place, when I felt a hand lift the watch from my pocket. Turning suddenly, I grasped the thief by the throat; I succeeded in getting a very good hold, and as he was quite a small man, I soon had the best of him. In the scuffle some one tripped me and I fell to the ground. I, however, kept my hold on his throat, and was giving him a severe choking when some one, to compel me to let go, commenced to give me a terrible beating. Being now thoroughly alarmed, I cried 'Murder!' as loud as I could. Some one then, to stop my cries, commenced to choke me; and I have no doubt that they would soon have finished me, had my cries not been heard by the Regulators and my friends, who came to the rescue. The fellow whom I had taken by the throat was a New York ruffian by the name of Crowly. He was a small, villainous-looking, pock-marked fellow, and was no doubt one of the light-fingered gentry who are so numerous in that city."[56]

The disturbance attracted the attention of the Confederate authorities, and a sergeant, with several guards, came into the prison to investigate. Crowly then pled pitifully to them, even shedding tears, and charged Urban with attempting to kill him. Urban then told the Confederate sergeant Crowly had taken his watch, and it was he who was the aggrieved party. Urban felt the Confederates expected to gain a watch by the search when they took them both out side. After they got outside the prison, the sergeant proceeded to search Crowly, but no watch was found. They were then taken back into the prison.

Immediately upon entering it, they noticed that a roundup of all the Raiders had begun. James Madison Page, among others, had approached Captain Wirz and had voiced complaints about the Raiders, but it was probably the attack on Urban that was the straw that broke the camel's back. Crowly and about fifty of his comrades were soon under arrest. Urban was of German descent; he asked Wirz, in German, to send in the troops and Wirz accompanied Urban while they searched for the culprit.[57] "The rebel quartermaster, rebel sergeants and guards" came in and, assisted by the Regulator Chief, Jim Limber, began three days of arrests.[58]

"Limber Jim was one of the Cahaba prisoners. He was a tall, slim, wiry man, good-looking, good-hearted, full of energy, a lover of fun, and was at Cahaba, as at Andersonville, the best known and most popular man in the prison. He had, it was said, traveled with a circus before the war, and it is very likely that as clown or actor in a circus he acquired not only his nickname, Limber Jim, but also the inexhaustible fund of anecdote and glibness of tongue that enabled him to be so entertaining and rendered him so well-known and popular. Soon after we entered Andersonville, 'Limber,' as we called him for short, invented 'root beer.' He obtained in some way a large barrel, filled it with water, sorghum, molasses, and corn meal. This mixture soon worked and acquired a sourish, sharp taste, similar to, but not nearly so pleasant, as the taste of the old-fashioned metheglin, made of honey and water.

"The sassafras tree abounds in that portion of Georgia, and Limber had obtained by digging them from the ground in the prison, a lot of sassafras roots. These he boiled, and with the tea, flavored this beer, and called it 'root beer.' Mounted on his beer barrel, or on a box, Limber would draw a crowd by telling jokes or stories, or by singing a song, and then he would expatiate on the health-giving, disease-curing properties of his 'root beer.' It was, according to his talk, a panacea for all the ills that prison life was heir to. It was good for scurvy, and that was the disease that scourged us most. When the Plymouth men came in, Limber got rich. He sold hundreds of barrels at 5 cents a glass that cost less than that many cents per gallon. Then he went into trade generally, and besides beer kept everything to see that could be obtained. I have heard that he won money at poker, and ran a faro bank with great success. I did not see him do either. I do know that he acquired a large amount of money - several thousand dollars. He secured for his mess a large tent that would hold twelve or fifteen men, pitched it on the South side, where the raiders were mostly congregated, had all of his mess-mates armed with knives and clubs, and had two of the largest and strongest men of the whole prison employed to stand guard over this tent at night. Here Limber and his guards and friends lived like kings. "At first the raiders let Limber alone, probably because he was such a favorite and had so many friends. Afterward they were kept off by his giant guards.

---

[56] Urban, pp. 328, 329.
[57] Hopkins, p. 80.
[58] Kellogg, p. 156.

"One evening, however, Limber went down to the creek alone, and three of the boldest of the raiders saw him. This was the opportunity that they long had sought, but a sad day for them was the day they tackled Limber Jim. One big burly Irishman caught him from behind, put an arm around his neck, under his chin, drew him back and held him nearly choked, while the other searched his clothes. The day after the robbery of Limber Jim a plan for an organization was agreed upon by the leading men throughout he prison." (Grigsby said the robbery of Limber Jim was the incident which caused the organization of the regulators and the subsequent hanging of the six raiders.)[59]

"On the 29th of June three hundred prisoners came in from West Virginia... One of their number - a German - was at once seized upon by the mob and his watch that he had saved and one hundred and twenty-five dollars were taken from him. In cutting his pocket, they inflicted a serious wound upon the man's leg... at once the injured man proceeded to the gate, where he came face to face with Capt. Wirz... All at once the old Captain motioned the man back into camp, and as fast as the Captain could walk he proceeded to the ration wagon that had just passed through the gate loaded with cooked meal... He ordered the wagon out before it was unloaded and, stepping upon a box, made the following remarks:

"'Men, listen to vat I say! Py Got I will never issue any more rations to you, till you tell who dese men be dat ish robbin' you!' "... The heads of the institution offered to any man who would come out and give the names of all he knew of these men, and point them out to the officials, - that he should at once be taken out and given a parole of honor; - that he should have the limits of a mile around the prison, ten dollars in greenbacks, and should be the first to go home...

"In about an hour from the time of the robbery, eight rebel sergeants walked into the gate, each with revolver in hand, and proceeded direct to the large tent headquarters. The commander in a stern voice, ordered the inmates to come forth... Eight men were taken from this tent and marched out of the gate. Upon this, the prisoners saw that the 'Rebs' were going to aid us in earnest, and all arose as one man and pointed the guilty parties out to the rebel sergeants as fast as we could discover their whereabouts. Thus, about seventy-five Raiders were marched out of the gate in less than two hours; and during the remainder of that day and the following forenoon the number was swollen to one hundred and twelve."[60] "They sent in twenty or thirty of their best men, armed with revolvers, to assist us in hunting out the desperadoes."[61]

There were about 25,000 men within the pen at that time, and almost all were of equal rank, being privates with a few sergeants. Pandemonium reigned as would be expected since "... the Rebels never made the slightest attempt to maintain order in the prison."[62]

The Plymouth Pilgrims "... established guards around their squads, and helped beat off the Raiders when their own territory was raided, but this was all they would do. The rest of us formed similar guards. In the southwest corner of the Stockade - where I was - we formed ourselves into a company of fifty active boys - mostly belonging to my own battalion and to other Illinois regiments - of which I was elected Captain. My First Lieutenant was a tall, taciturn, long-armed member of the One Hundred and Eleventh Illinois, whom we called 'Egypt,' as he came from that section of the State. He was wonderfully handy with his fists... We made a tacit division of duties; I did the talking, and 'Egypt' went through the manual labor of knocking our opponents down. In the numerous little encounters in which our company was engaged, 'Egypt' would stand by my side, silent, grim and patient, while I pursued the dialogue with the leader of the other crowd. As soon as he thought the conversation had reached the proper point, his long left arm stretched out like a flash, and the other fellow dropped as if he had suddenly come in range of a mule that was felling well...

"In spite of our company and our watchfulness, the Raiders beat us badly on one occasion. Marion Friend, of Company I of our battalion, was one of the small traders, and had accumulated forty dollars by his bartering. One evening at dusk Delaney's Raiders, about twenty-five strong, took advantage of the absence of most of us drawing rations, to make a rush for Marion. They knocked him down, cut him across the wrist and neck with a razor, and robbed him of his forty dollars. By the time we could rally, Delaney and his attendant scoundrels were safe from pursuit in the midst of their friends."[63]

On June 29, the robbery of Urban took place and Northrop said that, on that same day, "... steps are taken to or-

---

[59] Melvin Grigsby, *The Smoked Yank* (Chicago: Regan Printing Company, 1891), pp. 116-118.
[60] Dufur, pp. 90-93.
[61] S. B. Davis, p. 32.
[62] McElroy, p. 225.
[63] *Ibid.*, pp. 226, 227.

ganize a police force."[64] The next day, the rowdies were forced to run the gauntlet and, on the following day, July 1, the prison leaders met to form a vigilance committee known as the Regulators. Dufur said that, after the running of the gauntlet, "... the following day officers were chosen, and a regular police organization was the result."[65] "The organization was made up of western men, from Illinois, Iowa, Indiana and Ohio; comparatively few from each of these states. He seemed to have some distrust of laying his plans before eastern men generally..."[66] "Some of the regulators were looked upon as distasteful as the raiders. The biggest part of the camp were down upon them. Some of the speculators joined the regulators. The speculators, regulators, and raiders were about the same thing."[67] A regular police force was organized which would, later, number 1,200 honest men. These were divided into companies, each commanded by an enlisted man designated as its officer. These men would soon criss-cross all parts of the pen in an attempt to quell the mayhem that had run rampart. Signals were transmitted by the use of whistles so any policeman within earshot could immediately summon help in an instant, if needed.

McElroy gave the best insight into the Regulators. "This state of things had become unendurable. Sergeant Leroy L. Key, of Company M, our battalion, resolved to make an effort to crush the Raiders. He was a printer, from Bloomington, Illinois, tall, dark, intelligent and strong-willed, and one of the bravest men I ever knew. He was ably seconded by 'Limber Jim,' of the Sixty-Seventh Illinois, whose lithe, sinewy form, and striking features reminded one of a young Sioux brave... Though fearfully reduced in numbers, our battalion had still about one hundred well men in it, and these formed the nucleus for Key's band of 'Regulators'... Our best man was Ned Carrigan, Corporal of Company I, from Chicago - who was so confessedly the best man in the whole prison that he was never called upon to demonstrate it... He had fought in the ring, and on one occasion had killed a man with a single blow of his fist, in a prize fight near St. Louis... Key proceeded with the greatest secrecy in the organization of his forces. He accepted none but western men, and preferred Illinoisans, Iowans, Kansans, Indianians and Ohioans. The boys from those States seemed to naturally go together, and be moved by the same motives. He informed Wirz what he proposed doing, so that any unusual commotion within the prison might not be mistaken for an attempt upon the Stockade, and made the excuse for opening with the artillery. Wirz, who happened to be in a complaisant humor, approved of the design, and allowed him the use of the enclosure of the North Gate to confine his prisoners in.

"In spite of Key's efforts at secrecy, information as to his scheme reached the Raiders. It was debated at their headquarters and decided there that Key must be killed. Three men were selected to do this work. They called on Key, at dusk, on the evening of the 2nd of July. In response to their inquiries, he came out of the blanket-covered hole on the hillside that he called his tent. They told him what they had heard, and asked if it was true. He said it was. One of them then drew a knife, and the other two, 'billies' to attack him. But, anticipating trouble, Key had procured a revolver which one of the Pilgrims had brought in his knapsack, and drawing this he drove them off, but without firing a shot...

"Whether Key had originally fixed on the next day for making the attack, or whether this affair precipitated the crisis, I know not, but later in the evening he sent us all orders to be on our guard all night, and ready for action the next morning...

"The Raiders... threw out pickets to all the approaches to their headquarters, and provided otherwise against surprise. They had smuggled in some canteens of a cheap, vile whiskey - made from sorghum - and they grew quite hilarious in their Big Tent over their potations... "Morning at last came. Our companies mustered on their grounds, and then marched to the space on the South Side where the rations were issued. Each man was armed with a small club, secured to his wrist by a string...

"The Rebels - with their chronic fear of an outbreak animating them - had all the infantry in line of battle with loaded guns. The cannon in the works were shotted, the fuses thrust into the touch-holes and the men stood with lanyards in hand...

"The whole camp gathered where it could best view the encounter. This was upon the North Side... The Raiders' headquarters stood upon the center of the southern slope, and consequently those standing on the northern slope saw everything as if upon the stage of a theater...

"When all was ready we moved down upon the Big Tent, in as good order as we could preserve while passing through the narrow tortuous paths between the tents... The prison was as silent as a graveyard. As we approached, the Raiders massed themselves in a strong, heavy line, with the center, against which our advance was moving, held

[64] Northrop, p. 80.
[65] Dufur, p. 95.
[66] Northrop, pp. 80, 81.
[67] *Wirz Trial*, p. 606.

by the most redoubtable of their leaders... Not a blow was struck until the lines came close together. Then the Raider center launched itself forward against ours, and grappled savagely with the leading Regulators...One - perhaps two - endless minutes the lines surged - throbbed - backward and forward a step or two, and then, as if by a concentration of mighty effort, our men flung the Raider line back from it - broken - shattered. The next instant our leaders were striding through the mass like raging lions... In five minutes after the first blow was struck the overthrow of the Raiders was complete. Resistance ceased, and they sought safety in flight."[68]

As the mass of spectators on the other slope realized the Regulators had been victorious, they let out a tremendous shout. Soon it became time to receive the rations. "Wagons containing bread and mush had driven to the gates, but Wirz would not allow these to be opened, lest in the excited condition of the men an attempt might be made to carry them. Key ordered operations to cease, that Wirz might be re-assured and let the rations enter. It was in vain. Wirz was thoroughly scared. The wagons stood out in the hot sun until the mush fermented and soured, and had to be thrown away, while we went rationless to bed, and rose the next day with more than usually empty stomachs to goad us on to our work."[69]

The Regulators thought the Raiders, with their spies and hangers-on, never totaled more than 500 men. They continued to arrest Raiders all day on the Fourth of July. "The Raiders' tents were torn down and pillaged. Blankets, tent poles, and cooking utensils were carried off as spoils, and the ground was dug over for secreted property. A large quantity of watches, chains, knives, rings, gold pens, etc. - the booty of many a raid - was found, and helped to give impetus to the hunt. Even the Rebel Quartermaster, with the characteristic keen scent of the Rebels for spoils, smelled from the outside the opportunity for gaining plunder, and came in with a squad of Rebels equipped with spades, to dig for buried treasures... It was claimed that several skeletons of victims of the Raiders were found buried beneath the tents... By evening Key had perhaps one hundred and twenty-five of the most noted Raiders in his hands. Wirz had allowed him the use of the small stockade forming the entrance to the North Gate to confine them in."[70]

George W. Fechtner testified: "I was prison sutler part of the time, and I was chief of regulators and magistrate for the southwest part of the camp. My duty as magistrate was to punish men for stealing; I punished some by flogging, some by setting them to work, and some by sentencing them to be washed. They were so very dirty that they had to be washed once in a while, and it was a punishment to them... In the southwest part of the camp all the men guilty of stealing were brought before me for trial; they were prosecuted by the men from whom they had stole; they would steal tin cups, clothing, food and anything they could get their hands on. The police there were organized for the defence of the camp; they were composed of companies, thirty men to a company. They were organized for the regulation and defence of the men in the camp... Eleven of them were tried, six were hung, and five sentenced to wear a ball and chain. There were sixteen companies of police; they were organized by the chief of police; a man named Keese was the first chief; he was appointed by the regulators themselves; the regulators elected their own captains, and these captains elected the chief; complaints were made daily concerning robberies; I would dispose of them to the best of my ability. For stealing a tin cup if the man was healthy, he was flogged; if he was not healthy he was made to sit in a tent all day long, or he was taken down to the creek and washed; the men of the regulators executed my orders - the police."[71]

Fechtner continued: "I was magistrate there from about the 1st of July until I left. I was chief of regulators for a short time - about a week. I held quite a number of investigations as a magistrate. My duties as a magistrate did not occupy much of my time. I had my office in my tent. Men were not tried in the tent but in the street. I did not impanel a jury. I decided the cases myself. I heard the evidence and decided the cases; sometimes, when the case was complicated, I asked the advice of others. And I imposed the sentence. Sometimes a sentence was that a man should be washed. If a man had stolen a tin cup or committed a slight offence, and he was too sickly to be flogged, that punishment was inflicted. I would flog him if he was a well man for stealing a tin cup. A man would get from one to thirty lashes. I cannot say how often I imposed that sentence upon a soldier; some dozen times. I did not whip soldiers myself for stealing a tin cup, but I had it done. When a soldier was sickly he would be sentenced to be washed or to sit in his tent. Washing a man was a punishment. I cannot tell why, but men would refuse to be washed. The water was clear and good during the last two months. The man was taken down to the creek, put upon the platform

[68] McElroy, pp. 227-233.
[69] *Ibid.*, p. 233.
[70] *Ibid.*, pp. 237, 238.
[71] *Wirz Trial*, p. 558.

there, and washed. Not with brushes and towels, with hand and soap… "[72]

Northrop described the roundup by saying that, two hours after Urban had been assaulted, at "… about 5 p.m. an order came from Capt. Wirz that if we wished to take them outside, he would furnish a guard, we to point them out, and he would 'clear the stockade.' Sergeants with revolvers, guards with bayonets fixed, enter, and Rebel and Union soldiers walk side by side in a good work. Our boys lead the way to the den of thieves, murderers and traitors, point them out, and put them under their charge as fast as found. Outside the gate was another strong guard who received them… Near us one of the leaders, a strongman, was overtaken, but swore he would never be taken alive. He fought desperately, but one of our men struck him with a stake, knocking him senseless. One or two others were badly hurt. We saw Sullivan marching under three bayonets… At dark the work ceased; nearly sixty had been taken out… The boys shouted, 'Bully for the Captain,' for the men who took the initiatory step, and for the guard. With the work of catching raiders began a search for money and lost property. In one place two stockings filled with greenbacks, another with watches (two gold), and other things were found buried, preparatory to being sold to the Rebels. Two men were found buried near the southwest corner. One had his throat cut, the other had the appearance of having been beaten and strangled. Bones of others were reported found."[73]

On the following morning, Thursday, June 30, the roundup of the Raiders continued but, on that day they did it without the help of the Confederate guards. The Raiders were marched to the gate through crowds of shouting, jeering men. They were then turned over to a lieutenant and a guard after being prodded by kicks and clubs.[74]

"The next day… twelve of these men were returned to the prison with a ball and chain upon their legs that they were to wear during the remainder of their imprisonment; they were also to be tried for robbery in our own lines, if the Federal Government saw it. The remainder of the gang - excepting six of its leaders - were turned back into the camp and compelled to run the gauntlet; two ranks of men, facing each other extended from the gate back into the camp, perhaps two hundred feet. These ranks were probably fifty deep, as the exciting scene brought thousands of men to the spot. The two ranks were armed with sticks, clubs and everything with which they could inflict a blow. At first, one man ran through at a time, until fifteen or twenty had passed, whereupon the gang standing in the gate, awaiting their time, made a rush through as one man, thereby escaping many blows that would have justly fallen upon them had they passed through singly. One man, small in stature, and a sailor, drew a dirk knife, as he started upon this perilous race, and swinging it to the right and left, as he broke through the ranks, badly wounded quite a number by the thrusts he so dexterously executed; but he was quickly overpowered and so badly injured he lived only a few hours. Two others also lost their lives through this mode of punishment."[75]

Another description of the arrests of the Raiders was given by Brownell. Wirz "… listened with patience to the story of our wrongs, and told the committee to bring every one of the rascals that we could catch to the prison gate. In less than an hour our committee had caught one hundred of the most desperate of these thieves and cut-throats, and delivered them to the guard at the gate. 'Now,' called out Captain Wirz from the top of the high gateway, 'let every man who has ever been injured by these men, and also the friends of the dead, whom these men have murdered, prepare for revenge. Get each of you a club, and form a double line, and I will turn them loose, one by one, and make them run the gauntlet. One by one, at the command of Wirz, the victims were driven by the Rebel guards into the space between the two lines. But see, a bold and daring thief is about to take the run, and clubs are held by firmer hands, for he was the leader of the gang, and had been a bold, a desperate and daring man. A smile, or more properly a ghastly grin, played around the ugly mouth of Capt. Wirz, as he saw the anxiety of these revengeful men to have their victim; such a scene as this was just suited to his brutal nature, and with a laugh that seemed to come from the infernal regions, he gave the order; 'Drive him out.'

"Like a gladiator entering the arena to battle with the enraged beasts of the forest, came that desperate thief to face five hundred of his fellow men, nearly all of whom he had personally wronged, and whom he knew were thirsting for his blood. He took one look along the line, then started on a wild run, but was met by many blows given by revengeful hands. With savage desperation, he drew a knife that he had concealed about his person, and laying about him to the right and left like a madman, he wounded five men, two of them mortally. In a moment, all was consternation and dismay; the double line was broken, and the friends of the champion gave a cheer of triumph. But their momentary triumph was soon at an end, for Wirz ordered every one of those who had just been released to be again brought to him.

[72] *Ibid.*, pp. 583, 584.
[73] Northrop, pp. 80, 81.
[74] *Ibid.*, pp. 81, 82.
[75] Dufur, pp. 94, 95.

"When this was done, he told us to appoint a Judge and twelve Jurymen, and examine the case of each one of them separately... After ten days spent in trying their cases, six were found guilty of murder and sentenced to be hung. The proceedings of the trial were all copied and sent to Macon, where our Union officers were imprisoned, and submitted to the examination of General Stoneman, who signed the papers, saying that he highly approved of hanging any who had abused their fellow prisoners as these had done."[76]

Well over 100 prisoners were taken out and kept in the porch, or rectangular pen, between the outer and inner doors of the South Gate.[77] Miller said it was rumored that two Raiders were killed during this roundup while resisting arrest.[78] On June 30, "... our rations were stopped until the raiders were taken out."[79] Eventually, 175 men were arrested and turned over to the guards at the South Gate on July 2, 3, and 4.[80]

Wirz, following the orders of General Winder, emphasized that the prisoners themselves should hold the trial with witnesses being called, with men assigned as the Raiders' prosecutors, and others assigned as their defenders. Spencer said there were three judges presiding; the jury consisted of 18 prisoners.[81] Northrop said the jury consisted of 13 men from the western states.[82] Newly-arrived prisoners were asked to serve on the jury because they had not been prejudiced by things they had seen; nor had they heard of acts committed by the Raiders. Lieutenant Samuel Boyer Davis gave Northrop permission to go out with the witnesses to "... take the evidence." Frank Smith said the Raiders were tried "... outside the stockade in a shed granted by Captain Wirz."[83] "We chose a judge and jury - several lawyers volunteered for the prosecution; Mosby had some money, and hired the best counsel in the camp for his defense. Each man was tried separately. The court was in session several weeks. The jury found six guilty, and the judge sentenced them to be hung until dead. The papers were then sent to Washington, and came back signed by Abraham Lincoln."[84] "The pleading was as good as was ever heard in a trial of this kind. The rebel officers and privates would come and listen for hours to the speeches, and examination of witnesses. General Winder was present one whole day, and seemed to have his curiosity aroused by the legal lore displayed by Uncle Sam's private soldiers."[85]

The official court reporter at the trial of the Raiders was Edward Wellington Boate. He testified, one morning, that a man named Dowd had been brought out after having been beaten and, as the result of his complaint to Wirz, General Winder authorized a trial and the court was established.

*Camp Sumter*
*Andersonville, Ga.*
*June 30, 1864*

*General Orders No. 57*

*A gang of evil-disposed persons among the prisoners of war at this post having banded themselves together for the purpose of assaulting, murdering, and robbing their fellow-prisoners, and having already committed all of these deeds, it becomes necessary to adopt measures to protect the lives and property of the prisoners against the acts of these men, and in order that this may be accomplished, the well-disposed prisoners may, and they are hereby authorized to, establish a court among themselves for the trial and punishment of such offenders.*

*On such trials the charges will be distinctly made with specifications setting forth time and place, a copy of which will be furnished the accused. The whole proceeding will be kept in writing, all the testimony will be fairly written out as nearly in the words of the witnesses as possible.*

*The proceedings, findings, and sentence in each case will be sent to the commanding officer for record, and if found in order and proper, the sentence will be ordered for execution.*

*By order of Brig. Gen. John H. Winder.*

*W. S. Winder*
*Asst. Adjutant General.*[86]

---

76 Brownell, p. 16.
77 Miller, p. 23.
78 *Ibid.*, p. 22.
79 *Ibid.*, p. 46.
80 James Page, p. 113.
81 Spencer, p. 131.
82 Northrop, p. 82.
83 Frank Smith p. 58.
84 Compton, p. 42.
85 *Ibid.*
86 *O.R.* VII, p. 426.

Twenty-four prospective jurors were selected from the sergeants of squads who had been brought that morning to Captain Wirz' headquarters and, from these 24 men, 12 jurors were elected. Greacen said the Raiders "... were tried by a court martial composed of twelve of our own officers, who were brought from Macon Prison for that purpose."[87]

Colonel James H. Fannin, of the First Regiment, Georgia Reserves, witnessed the jury selection and testified, "I was one day about 150 yards from Captain Wirz' headquarters, and I heard a whooping, as if from a crowd of men. I looked and saw that they were federal prisoners standing in front of his door. I walked in that direction, and went up the steps. I judge there were about 120 sergeants standing there together. I think there were four ranks doubled - eight ranks - to get them into a small space, right in front of the house. Captain Wirz seemed to be making a speech to them. I walked between the house and the men and stepped up on the floor, near Captain Wirz, and I inquired of some men who were standing there. They told me that these men had petitioned to be allowed to do as they pleased with some men inside the stockade who had been committing outrages - robberies and murders upon others of their number. About the time I stepped near Captain Wirz, he took a hat in his hand - a black, tall hat; he held it out, and one of the prisoners stepped forward, (I did not know him by name,) and took from the hat small slips of paper, and in that way selected a jury from the number, to try these men. Captain Wirz made a few remarks to them, and, using some profane language, said that he would turn the damned rascals over to them, or something of that kind, and let them do as they pleased with them; they could try them. They went back then with expressions of gratification. They hurrahed. The jury were selected, and marched out as their names were called. They formed a line, and were counted out just before me; I was within about three yards of them. They were all marched inside the stockade. There a court was convened; a guard was furnished them, and went in and brought out the men whom they desired to have tried."[88]

"Key organized a court martial composed of thirteen Sergeants, chosen from the latest arrivals of prisoners, that they might have no prejudice against the Raiders. I believe that a man named Dick McCullough, belonging to the Third Missouri Cavalry, was the President of the Court. The trial was carefully conducted with all the formality of a legal procedure that the Court and those managing the matter could remember as applicable to the crimes with which the accused were charged. Each of these was confronted by the witnesses who testified against him, and allowed to cross-examine them to any extent he desired. The defense was managed by one of their crowd, the foul-tongued Tombs shyster, Pete Bradley ... Such was the fear of the vengeance of the Raiders and their friends that many who had been badly abused dared not testify against them, dreading midnight assassination if they did. Others would not go before the Court except at night. But for all this there was no lack of evidence; there were thousands who had been robbed and maltreated, or who had seen these outrages committed on others, and the boldness of the leaders in their [height] of power rendered their identification a matter of no difficulty whatever.

"The trial lasted several days, and concluded with sentencing quite a large number to run the gauntlet, a smaller number to wear balls and chains, and the following six to be hanged:

John Sarsfield, One Hundred and Forty-Fourth New York,
William Collins, alias 'Mosby,' Company D, Eighty-Eighth Pennsylvania
Charles Curtis, Company A, Fifth Rhode Island Artillery
Patrick Delaney, Company E, Eighty-Third Pennsylvania
A. Muir, United States Navy
Terence Sullivan, Seventy-Second New York

"Those sentenced to ball-and-chain were brought in immediately, and had the irons fitted to them that had been worn by some of our men as a punishment for trying to escape... "It was not yet determined how punishment should be meted out to the remainder, but circumstances themselves decided the matter. Wirz became tired of guarding so large a number as Key had arrested, and he informed Key that he should turn them back into the Stockade immediately. Key begged for little farther time to consider the disposition of the cases, but Wirz refused it, and ordered the Officer of the Guard to return all arrested, save those sentenced to death, to the Stockade. In the meantime the news had spread through the prison that the Raiders were to be sent in again unpunished, and an angry mob, numbering some thousands, and mostly composed of men who had suffered injuries at the hands of the marauders, gathered at the South Gate, clubs in hand, to get such satisfaction as they could out of the rascals. They formed in two long, parallel lines, facing inward, and grimly awaited the incoming of the objects of their vengeance.

---

[87] Greacen, p. 9.

[88] *Wirz Trial*, pp. 437, 438.

**Some Raiders** - who were not guilty of murder were sentenced to have to run the gaunlet composed of fellow prisoners arranged in two columns. They struck the prisoners with sticks and billy clubs. One man, a sailor, pulled a knife and broke out of the gauntlet. He was struck down and killed by a man with a large timber who happened to be nearby. (McElory)

"The Officer of the Guard opened the wicket in the gate, and began forcing the Raiders through it - one at a time - at the point of the bayonet, and each as he entered was told what he already realized well - that he must run for his life... They did this with all the energy that they possessed, and as they ran blows rained on their heads, arms and backs. If they could succeed in breaking through the line at any place they were generally let go without any further punishment. Three of the number were beaten to death. I saw one of these killed... While the gauntlet was in operation, I was standing by my tent at the head of a little street, about two hundred feet from the line, watching what had been done. A sailor was let in. He had a large bowie knife concealed about his person somewhere, which he drew, and struck savagely with at his tormentors on either side. They fell back from before him, but closed in behind and pounded him terribly. He broke through the line, and ran up the street towards me. About midway of the distance stood a boy who had helped carry a dead man out during the day, and while out had secured a large pine rail which he had brought in with him. He was holding this straight up in the air, as if at a 'present arms.' He seemed to have known from the first that the Raider would run that way. Just as he came squarely under it, the boy dropped the rail like the bar of a tollgate. It struck the Raider across the head, felled him as if by a shot, and his pursuers then beat him to death."[89]

Because of the crowding in the porch and the need to use the gate, Wirz decided that the main body of Raiders should be returned to the pen. A couple of authors have said that the Raiders were sentenced to run the gauntlet the day after the trial. A few Raiders were allowed to re-enter the pen without having to run the gauntlet and after only having to bear the cold stares and derisive shouts of their fellow inmates. Twelve Raiders were sentenced to wear a ball and chain until exchanged. The six sentenced to die remained outside until the time of their trip to the gallows.

"A few against whom positive proof could not at once be brought, were sent into prison again, where they had to run the gauntlet between a long line of enraged men, who armed with heavy clubs, dealt blows at the miscreants as they ran past."[90] Urban said that the gauntlet was formed "... outside of the Prison."[91] Both Dufur and Miller said that three of those who ran the gauntlet were killed.[92]

Some authors have said that the trial took 10 days; others have implied that most men used the 10-day period from trial to hanging to write to various Federal authorities in order to get their permission to hang the six Raiders. Dufur said, "The Confederate Government at once sent word to our Government stating the facts of the situation, and asking what was to be done with these men. Our Government ordered that they be tried by a jury of our own

[89] McElroy, pp. 238-240.
[90] Kellogg, p. 157.
[91] Urban, p. 331.
[92] Dufur, pp. 94, 95; Miller, p. 23.

men, and punished as their reason dictates."[93] Lyons said the transcript of the six Raiders' trial was sent to Washington, "... where it was approved by the Government."[94] "We sent a report through to General Sherman, explaining the matter. He sent back word to string them up."[95] Brownell said the Federal officers in Macon were informed of the situation and had "... approved of the whole thing."

Colonel Fannin testified about the independence of the trial. "The confederate troops or officers had not anything in the world to do with that matter. I heard General Winder speak of it. I think he wrote to Richmond to know what to do about the matter. After these men were sentenced by the court, he would not allow them to be hung until he received orders; I don't know from where or from whom. I know he waited some time before they were hung."[96]

On Sunday night, July 10, it was announced within the pen that six of the Raiders had been convicted, condemned to death, and were to be hanged the following day just after noon.[97]

On Monday, July 11, the construction of the scaffold was begun at 9 a.m. Wirz had timbers and tools brought in the South Gate and the crude scaffold was erected within 100 feet or so of the gate by carpenters secured by the Regulators. Regulators with billy clubs had to guard the timbers from marauding prisoners seeking wood. "The scaffold consisted of two pieces of 4 X 4 joists as uprights, and another 4 X 6 framed into the top of these, from which the six fatal ropes were suspended. On the inside of each upright was a cleat, nailed about six feet from the ground, and from one cleat to the other ran a plank, fourteen feet long. This plank was sawed apart in the middle, and a prop placed under each end, near were it had been sawed apart. A rope was attached to the foot of each prop; by pulling on the ropes, the plank would break down where it was split. On this plank the culprits were to stand, while the executioner, standing upon another plank just in the rear of the trap, was to perform the awful work."[98]

**Hanging of the Raiders** - On July 11, the prisoners hug six fellow prisoners for their participation in organized robberies and murders in the pen. They were tried and found guilty by fellow prisoners. This drawing depicts the last Raider being led up the ladder to the deadfall after he had fled to the swamp. (Kellogg)

The Reverend Peter Whelan testified: "I administered to five of the prisoners who were hanged. There was one of them who was not a Catholic... They were put in the stocks. I visited them the evening before they were hanged and gave them all the consolations of religion that it was possible for me to do. The next morning Captain Wirz came down to carry them to the stockade to be delivered to the prisoners there. I asked him to delay their execution for another day. He said to me that it was out of his power."[99]

That morning, "... some time was employed in attaching halters to the beam and adjusting nooses."[100] Six men were selected to act as the hangmen. Before the hanging, they busied themselves, "... trying the strength of the ropes, and arranging the dead fall."[101] "There was much canvassing as to where they should be executed, and as to whether or not an attempt to hang them inside of the Stockade would not rouse their friends to make a desperate effort to rescue them, which would precipitate a general engagement of even larger proportions than that of the 3rd... Some five thousand or six thousand new prisoners had come in since the first of the month, and it was claimed that the Raiders had received large reinforcements from those, - a claim rendered probable by most of the new-comers being from the Army of the Potomac."[102]

McElroy was ordered, by Key, to gather his company of Regulators and to guard the carpenters who were to

[93] Dufur, pp. 93, 94.
[94] Lyons, p. 71 or 171.
[95] Tyler, p. 30.
[96] *Wirz Trial*, p. 438.
[97] Northrop, p. 87.
[98] Dufur, pp. 101, 102.
[99] *Wirz Trial*, p. 428.
[100] Northrop, p. 88.
[101] Brownell, p. 16.
[102] McElroy, p. 241.

erect the scaffold. He was assured that, if attacked by the Raiders, the entire force of Regulators would come to their rescue. McElroy, with his friend, Egypt, got his group of Regulators together and went to the site designated for the construction of the scaffold. It was "... an open space near the end of the street running from the South Gate, and kept vacant for the purpose of issuing rations. It was quite near the spot where the Raiders' Big Tent had stood, and afforded a good a view to the rest of the camp as could be found."[103]

"Key had secured the loan of a few beams and rough planks, sufficient to build a rude scaffold... The carpenters sent by Key came over and set to work. The N'Yaarkers gathered around in considerable numbers, sullen and abusive. They cursed us with all their rich vocabulary of foul epithets, vowed that we should never carry out the execution, and swore that they had marked each one for vengeance... by noon the scaffold was finished."[104] "A stout beam was fastened on the top of two posts, about fifteen feet high. At about the height of a man's head a couple of boards stretched across the space between the posts, and met in the center. The ends at the post laid on cleats; the ends in the center rested upon a couple of boards, standing upright; each had a piece of rope fastened through a hole in it in such a manner, that a man could snatch it from under the planks serving as the floor of the scaffold, and let the whole thing drop. A rude ladder by which to ascend completed the preparations."[105]

After the carpenters finished, the rest of the Regulators joined the group with McElroy. They formed a hollow square around the scaffold with McElroy's company making up the line on the eastern side of the square. About one third of the 30,000 men in the prison packed around the formation. The others were on the north side.

"Outside, the Rebel infantry was standing in the rifle pits; the artillerymen were in place about their loaded and trained pieces, the No. 4 of each gun holding the lanyard cord in his hand, ready to fire the piece at the instant of command. The small squad of cavalry was drawn up on the hill near the Star Fort, and near it were the masters of the hound, with their yelping packs.

"All the hangers-on of the Rebel camp-clerks, teamsters, employees, negros, hundreds of white and colored women, in all forming a motley crowd of between one and two thousand, were gathered together in a group between the end of the rifle pits and the Star Fort. They had a good view from there, but a still better one could be had a little farther to the right, and in front of the guns. They kept edging up in that direction, as crowds will, though they knew the danger they would incur if the artillery opened.

"The day was hot."[106]

"Key took up his position inside the square to direct matters. With him were Limber Jim, Dick McCullough, and one or two others. Also, Ned Johnson, Tom Larkin, Sergeant Goody, and three others who were to act as hangmen. Each of these six was provided with a white sack, such as the Rebel brought in meal in. Two Corporals of my company - 'Stag' Harris and Wat Payne - were appointed to pull the stays from under the platform at the signal."[107]

"A little after noon the South Gate opened, and Wirz rode in, dressed in a suit of white duck, and mounted on his white horse - a conjunction which had gained for him the appellation of 'Death on a Pale Horse.' Behind him walked the faithful old priest, wearing his Church's purple insignia of the deepest sorrow, and reading the service for the condemned. The six doomed men followed, walking between double ranks of Rebel guards.

"All came inside the hollow square and halted. Wirz then said:

"'Brizners, I return to you dese men so goot as I got dem. You haf tried dem youselves, and found dem guilty. I haf had notting to do wit it. I vash my hands of eferyting connected wit dem. Do wit dem as you like, and may Gott haf mercy on you and on dem. Garts, about face! Vorwarts, march!'

"With this he marched out and left us."[108]

"One of them gasped out;

"'My God, man, you don't really mean to hang us up there?'

"Key answered grimly and laconically:

"'That seems to be about the size of it.'

"At this they burst out in a passionate storm of intercessions and imprecations, which lasted for a minute or so, when it was stopped by one of them saying imperatively:

"'All of you stop now, and let the priest talk for us.'

---

[103] *Ibid.*, p. 242.
[104] *Ibid.*
[105] *Ibid.*, pp. 242, 243.
[106] *Ibid.*, p. 243.
[107] *Ibid.*, pp. 243, 244.
[108] *Ibid.*, p. 244.

"At this the priest closed the book upon which he had kept his eyes bent since his entrance, and facing the multitude on the North Side began a plea for mercy.

**Hanging of the Raiders** - This shows the two boards supporting the deadfall with ropes leading from them to be pulled by the two executioners. Notice Father Whelan reading the Bible after pleading for their lives to be spared. (McElroy)

"The condemned faced in the same direction, to read their fate in the countenances of those whom he was addressing...

"The whole camp had been as still as death since Wirz' exit. The silence seemed to become even more profound as the priest began his appeal. For a minute, every ear was strained to catch what he said. Then, as the nearest of the thousands comprehended what he was saying, they raised a shout of

"'No! no!! No!!'

"'Hang them! hang them!'

"'Don't let them go! Never!'

"'Hang the rascals! hang the villains!

"'Hang 'em! hang 'em! hang 'em!'

"This was taken up all over the prison, and tens of thousands throats yelled it in a fearful chorus.

"Curtis turned from the crowd with desperation convulsing his features. Tearing off the broad-brimmed hat which he wore, he flung it on the ground with the exclamation:

"'By God, I'll die this way first!' and, drawing his head down and folding his arms about it, he dashed forward for the center of my company, like a great stone hurled from a catapult.

"'Egypt' and I saw where he was going to strike, and ran down the line to help stop him. As he came up we rained blows on his head with our clubs, but so many of us struck at him at once that we broke each other's clubs to pieces, and only knocked him on his knees. He rose with an almost superhuman effort, and plunged in the mass beyond...

"As Curtis broke through, Delaney, a brawny Irishman standing next to him, started to follow. He took one step. At the same instant Limber Jim's long legs took three great strides, and placed him directly in front of Delaney. Jim's right hand held an enormous bowie-knife, and as he raised it above Delaney he hissed out:

"'If you dare move another step, you --- --- ---, I'll open you from one end to the other.'"[109]

"When Wirz saw the commotion he was panic-stricken with fear that the long-dreaded assault on the Stockade had begun. He ran down from the headquarter steps to the Captain of the battery shrieking

"'Fire! fire! fire!'

"The Captain, not being a fool, could see that the rush was not towards the Stockade, but away from it, and he refrained from giving the order.

"But the spectators who had gotten before the guns, heard Wirz' excited yell, and remembering the consequences to themselves should the artillery be discharged, became frenzied with fear, and screamed, and fell down over and trampled upon each other in endeavoring to get away. The guards on that side of the Stockade ran down in a panic, and the ten thousand prisoners immediately around us, expecting no less than that the next instant we would be swept with grape and canister, stampeded tumultuously. There were quite a number of wells right around us, and all of these were filled full of men that fell into them as the crowd rushed away. Many had legs and arms broken, and I have no doubt that several were killed.

"It was the stormiest five minutes that I ever saw.

"While this was going on two of my company, belonging to the Fifth Iowa Cavalry, were in hot pursuit of Curtis...

"Curtis ran diagonally down the hill, jumping over the tents and knocking down the men who happened in his way. Arriving at the swamp he plunged in, sinking nearly to his hips in the fetid, filthy ooze. He forged his way through with terrible effort. His pursuers followed his example, and caught up to him just as he emerged on the

[109] *Ibid.*, p. 247.

other side. They struck him on the back of the head with their clubs, and knocked him down... Their success was announced with a roar of applause from the North Side. Both captors and captured were greatly exhausted, and they were coming back very slowly. Key ordered the balance up on to the scaffold. They obeyed promptly. The priest resumed his reading of the service for the condemned. The excitement seemed to make the doomed ones exceedingly thirst. I never saw men drink such inordinate quantities of water. They called for it continually, gulped down a quart or more at a time, and kept two men going nearly all the time carrying it to them.

"When Curtis finally arrived, he sat on the ground for a minute or so, to rest, and then, slowly and painfully climbed the steps. Delaney seemed to think he was suffering as much from fright as anything else, and said to him:

"'Come on up, now, show yourself a man, and die game.'

"Again the priest resumed his reading, but it had no interest to Delaney, who kept calling out directions to Pete Donnelly, who was standing in the crowd, as to disposition to be made of certain bits of stolen property: to give a watch to this one, a ring to another, and so on. Once the priest stopped and said: 'My son, let the things of this earth go, and turn your attention toward those of heaven.'

"Delaney paid no attention to this admonition. The whole six then began delivering farewell messages to those in the crowd. Key pulled a watch from his pocket and said:

"'Two minutes more to talk.'

"Delaney said cheerfully:

"'Well, good by, b'ys; if I've hurted any of yez, I hope ye'll forgive me. Shpake up, now, any of yez that I've hurted, and say ye'll forgive me.'

"We called upon Marion Friend, whose throat Delaney had tried to cut three weeks before while robbing him of forty dollars, to come forward, but Friend was not in a forgiving mood, and refused with an oath.

"Key said:

"'Time's up!'

"[He] put the watch back in his pocket and raised his hand like an officer commanding a gun. Harris and Payne laid hold of the ropes to the supports of the planks. Each of the six hangmen tied a condemned man's hands, pulled a meal sack down over his head, placed the noose around his neck, drew it up tolerably close, and sprang to the ground. The priest began praying aloud.

"Key dropped his hand. Payne and Harris snatched the supports out with a single jerk. The planks fell with a clatter. Five of the bodies swung around dizzily in the air. The sixth - that of 'Mosby,' a large, powerful, raw-boned man, one of the worst in the lot, and who, among other crimes, had killed Limber Jim's brother - broke the rope, and fell with a thud to the ground. Some of the men ran forward, examined the body, and decided that he still lived. The rope was cut off his neck, the meal sack removed, and water thrown in his face until consciousness returned. At the first instant he thought he was in eternity. He gasped out:

"'Where am I? Am I in the other world?'

"Limber Jim muttered that they would soon show him where he was, and went on grimly fixing up the scaffold anew. 'Mosby' soon realized what had happened, and the unrelenting purpose of the Regulator Chiefs. Then he began to beg piteously for his life, saying:

"'O for God's sake, do not put me up there again! God has spared my life once. He meant that you should be merciful to me.'

"Limber Jim deigned him no reply. When the scaffold was re-arranged, and a stout rope had replaced the broken one, he pulled the meal sack once more over 'Mosby's' head, who never ceased his pleading. Then picking up the large man as if he were a baby, he carried him to the scaffold and handed him up to Tom Larkin, who fitted the noose around his neck and sprang down. The supports had not been set with the same delicacy as at first, and Limber Jim had to set his heel and wrench desperately at them before he could force them out. Then 'Mosby' passed away without a struggle.

"After hanging till life was extinct, the bodies were cut down, the meal sacks pulled off their faces, and the Regulators formed two parallel lines, through which all the prisoners passed and took a look at the bodies. Pete Donnelly and Dick Allen knelt down and wiped the froth off Delaney's lips, and swore vengeance against those who had done him to death."[110]

Kellogg said Wirz entered at about half-past four.[111] Miller said Wirz entered with the Raiders when, "... a little

---

[110] *Ibid.*, p. 251.

[111] Kellogg, p. 170.

after noon the South Gate opened."[112] Northrop said that, shortly after 1 o'clock, "… the gate opened and Capt. Wirz, dressed in a white duck suit, upon his gray horse, accompanied by a Catholic priest, followed by the guard with the doubly doomed prisoners. They were six dressed only in undershirts and drawers and heads uncovered."[113]

At 12 o'clock, Brownell said, the Raiders were brought in and marched to the scaffold; there, Wirz made the following speech: "Here are your fellow prisoners, as fat and as healthy as they were before they were arrested. They have been tried by a Judge and Jury selected from among yourselves, found guilty of murder and sentenced to be hung. Your officers at Macon have approved of the whole thing. Now to me it is a matter of no interest. Hang them, or release them; trust yourselves again to their mercy, or, by hanging them, relieve yourselves forever from their oppression." - and ten thousand voices cried; "hang them! hang them as high as Haman!"[114] Urban, not recognizing Wirz, said that an officer and a squad of Confederate soldiers were sent into the pen to maintain order at the execution.[115] Another author described Wirz' speech as saying, "These men have been tried and convicted by their own fellows, and now return them to you in as good condition as I received them. You can now do with them as your reason, justice, and mercy dictates. And may God protect both you and them."[116]

Northrop said Wirz made this lengthy speech. "Prisoners, I deliver these men to you in as good condition as I found them. I have had nothing to do in convicting them of crime of which they are accused, except to lend my assistance for their and your protection; nor do I charge them or believe them guilty, and shall have nothing to do with the execution of your sentence. You have tried them; I have permitted it. You have convicted and sentenced them; if they are hung, you, not I, will be responsible for it. I deliver them to you; do with them as you please, and may God be with them and you. Guards about face; forward march."[117] Northrop said that the speech was read from a piece of paper held in Wirz' hand, and that it had been written by Lieutenant Samuel B. Davis or some other officer of the post. Wirz and the guard left immediately but Father Peter Whelan stayed with the condemned Raiders.

Northrop described how the crowds appeared: "Looking from my position near the scaffold to the north of the sloping ground I beheld the most densely packed crowd I had ever seen. The south side if possible was more densely packed. They came from every extreme portion of the stockade until they could get no further. The regulator squads, armed with clubs, formed a square around the scaffold to keep back the crowd."[118]

Wirz made a rather serious mistake by not binding the Raiders' hands outside the pen. Northrop said their arms had been "pinioned." Accompanying the six, the Catholic Priest, Father Whelan, beseeched the Regulators to spare the lives of the condemned. Finding that his pleas fell on deaf ears, he turned his attention to their spiritual needs.

"They themselves seemed strangely unconcerned, apparently thinking it was simply an affair got up thoroughly to frighten them, and they appeared to cling to the idea, even until they had ascended the platform erected for their execution."[119] Each seemed to be accompanied to the scaffold by two men. They walked up the few steps. One man was responsible for putting the meal-sack over the prisoner's head and the noose around the neck of his charge. As they were ascending the two or three steps up to the platform of the scaffold, Curtis broke free and fled northward into the swamp, sometimes getting hip-deep in the mire. Two pursuers recaptured him before he reached the north side.

There was a great commotion and swirling of the masses of prisoners at this time. Some prisoners were, inadvertently, knocked into some of the scattered wells with the result that some prisoners broke limbs. Some of the weakened men were trampled as were some flimsy shebangs. The spectators on the parapets cried out in near panic, thinking there was an outbreak in progress. Seeing the Confederates move to their cannons panicked the prisoners even more. The artillery had been put on alert for just such an event.

Wirz had the entire guard force put on alert the day of the hangings. All cannon were loaded with grape and canister, and were aimed at the prison interior. The artillery batteries had been ordered not to open fire unless they were instructed to do so by means of the firing of one of the two signal cannons located in front of Wirz' headquarters. Leonard said Wirz mounted a sentinel box and, from there, he witnessed the executions. This event caused a gathering of about 1,000 or 2,000 curious spectators, both black and white, to gather on the parapets of the forts so

[112] Miller, p. 24.
[113] Northrop, p. 88.
[114] Brownell, p. 16.
[115] Urban, p. 335.
[116] Kellogg, p. 170.
[117] Northrop, p. 88.
[118] *Ibid.*
[119] Kellogg, p. 171.

that they could see better.[120] Other men, women and children had gathered on the high ground between the principal fort and the prison to get a better view of the grim proceedings.[121]

When Curtis fled from his guard and the mass of men swarmed, Wirz thought it was a mass break-out. "He ran to the signal battery yelling, 'Fire! fire! shoot! shoot!' The captain of the battery, being a man of cool judgment, did not obey Wirz, but the citizens and guards, who were in the way of the cannon, stampeded into a regular panic, injuring many of the citizens. Had the captain of the battery obeyed Wirz there would have been forty-four cannon, loaded with grape and canister, opened on that human mass in the prison. The thirty-five thousand lives in our prison hung on the firing-cord of that signal gun."[122]

Curtis was quickly returned to the area where the other five still stood on the ground and then all six were rushed up the steps of the scaffold. Father Whelan was asked by the Raiders to seek mercy for them. He then addressed the Regulators and the gathered crowd who shouted him down, demanding that the execution proceed.

Northrop said that this was the dialogue that transpired immediately before the hanging.

When a Regulator was beseeched by a Raider for mercy, the usual response was, "No you must die."

"Then said Collins, to the priest:

"'Then do pray for us, pray long and hard!'

"He prays but Collins breaks in vehemently.

"'I am guilty, but not of this; I have been an awful man! I have not had a fair trial, ' and many other sentences, and all shout together, 'Yes, yes!' Sullivan broke in"

"'Neither am I guilty, but' - and he groaned, 'I did not expect ever to come to this.' 'Nor I,' all shouted in concert.

"Their exclamations were so loud, continuous and distressing, that I heard nothing of the prayer. Several times the sack was removed from their heads as they feelingly urged to be prayed for, until the executioners had decided not to repeat it, when Curtis asked for one moment. Speaking loudly, he asked:

"'Have I a friend within hearing?'

"A voice answers, 'Yes, it is me, Curtis.'

"'Is it you Tony Ryan? Come up here.'

"Executioner - 'No, he can't come up.'

"Curtis - 'Then I have one request, Tony, it is my dying request. I want you to keep my watch and send it back to my father-in-law in New York City.'

"Tony - 'I will do it, Curtis.'

"Curtis - 'I am ready. This is a hard sight, boys,' and he groaned.

"Sullivan and Muir both said; 'May God bless our souls.!'

"The executioners stepped from the platform, the props were pulled, the traps fell."[123]

Dufur said that Curtis asked that his friend give his watch to his wife in New York, should his friend live to be exchanged, and that she not be told how he had died.[124]

Five of the six were "launched into eternity." Collins, or "Mosby," at one end of the scaffold, being a large man, broke his rope and fell to the ground bleeding from his nose and ears.[125] Tyler said he was the only fat man in the pen. Tyler, incorrectly, said Collins fled into the swamp at that time. He said Collins then jumped "... to his feet, [struck] out right and left with his fists, and lay out fifteen or twenty men, and finally [fought] his way through the crowd to the creek, but he got mired in the mud, and was captured and brought back. He looked up and saw the five swinging to and fro, and said, 'I will soon be with you.'"[126] He begged piteously for his life but was rushed up the scaffold; a noose was put around his neck and he was shoved off the platform where he joined his comrades dancing at the end of the ropes. All six drew their knees up in an involuntary movement in a partially-kneeling position.[127]

George Conway, of the 3rd New York artillery, testified: "One of them had formerly been in my regiment. While on the scaffold he bid me good-bye, and told me that there was a watch of his in the hands of Captain Wirz, and he told me to get it and keep in remembrance of him. I sent out two notes to Captain Wirz about it, but received no an-

---

[120] Northrop, p. 90.
[121] Boggs, p. 43.
[122] *Ibid.*, p. 44.
[123] Northrop, pp. 89, 90.
[124] Dufur, p. 103.
[125] Author's library.
[126] Tyler, p. 31.
[127] Northrop, p. 90.

swer to them. One day the captain was riding around between the stockade and the dead-line; my tent was near the dead-line; the back of it was hanging on the dead-line, and I spoke to him and asked him - said I, 'One of those men that was hung requested me to get a watch of his which you have.' He looked at me, and said he, 'I know nothing of your watch; all the damned Yankees ought to be hung.' He started on, and I thought it would be of no use for me to ask any more for it."[128]

After about a half-hour, the men were taken down and the bodies given to their Raider friends who cursed and threatened the Regulators. Dufur said they were taken down an hour later and taken to the Dead House.[129] Then the timbers of the scaffold were taken down.

These excerpts are from a diary of James H. Buckley, Co. K, 53rd Illinois: "They were delivered up at a little before five in the afternoon. All mounted the Scaffold at five... At eight minutes past five o'clock the trap was sprung... Collins' rope broke and he fell through. They took him up immediately adjusted the rope. It was all done by Thomas Goodman, a citizen formerly a lieutenant in the 3 months service. When he took him up, the leader asked... if he had any friends. An answer. Then he turned to beg mercy. The hang man held a knife to his throat saying 'shut up you tried to murder me but you did not accomplish it.' After adjusting the rope, he was pushed off. He was launched into Eternity at 9 minutes after 5. They struggled some. They remained hanging 27 minutes."[130]

The tents of the Raiders were searched and "... beneath their tents were found knives, pistols, watches, money, etc., and it is said that buried beneath one tent was the body of a man who was supposed to have been murdered by them."[131] Urban said watches, money, and different kinds of weapons were found under the shebangs. He also said that the body of a man was found. He said the Confederates took possession of the valuables.[132]

The bodies of the raiders were buried a few paces away from the other Federal prisoners, it being thought that they did not deserve to be buried with those who had died honorably for their country.

"From that time on every man ate his own rations."[133]

"After the executions Key, knowing that he, and all those prominently connected with the hanging, would be in hourly danger of assassination if they remained inside, secured details as nurses and ward-masters in the hospital, and went outside. In this crowd were Key, Ned Carrigan, Limber Jim, Dick McCollough, the six hangmen, the two Corporals who pulled the props from under the scaffold, and perhaps some others whom I do not now remember."[134]

"One of the Raiders - named Heffron - had, shortly after his arrest, turned State's evidence, and given testimony that assisted materially in the conviction of his companions. One morning, a week or so after the hanging, his body was found lying among the other dead at the South Gate. The impression made by the fingers of the hand that had strangled him, were still plainly visible about the throat. There was no doubt as to why he had been killed, or that the Raiders were his murderers, but the actual perpetrators were never discovered."[135]

Sergeant Leroy L. Key, who had presided over the hangings of the six Raiders, on July 11th, related how he fared after that event. "On the 12th day of July, 1864, the day after the hanging of the six Raiders, by the urgent request of my many friends... I sought and obtained from Wirz a parole for myself and the six brave men who assisted as executioners of those desperados. It seemed that you were all fearful that we might, after what had been done, be assassinated if we remained in the Stockade; and that we might be overpowered, perhaps, by the friends of the Raiders we had hanged, at a time possibly, when you would not be on hand to give us assistance, and thus lose our lives for rendering the help we did in getting rid of the worst pestilence we had to contend with.

"On obtaining my parole I was very careful to have it so arranged and mutually understood, between Wirz and myself, that at any time that my squad (meaning the survivors of my comrades, with whom I was originally captured) was sent away from Andersonville, either to be exchanged or to go to another prison, that I should be allowed to go with them. This was agreed to, and so written in my parole which I carried until it absolutely wore out. I took a position in the cook-house, and the other boys either went to work there, or at the hospital or grave-yard as occasion required. I worked here, and did the best I could for the many starving wretches inside, in the way of preparing their food, until the eighth day of September, at which time, if you remember, quite a train load of men were removed, as

[128] *Wirz Trial*, p. 323.
[129] Dufur, p. 103.
[130] James H. Buckley diary, in private hands.
[131] Kellogg, p. 156.
[132] Urban, p. 331.
[133] Tyler, p. 30.
[134] McElroy, p. 252.
[135] *Ibid.*, p. 257.

many of us thought, for the purpose of exchange; but, as we afterwards discovered, to be taken to another prison. Among the crowd so removed was my squad, or, at least, a portion of them, being my intimate mess-mates while in the Stockade. As soon as I found this to be the case I waited on Wirz at his office, and asked permission to go with them, which he refused, stating that he was compelled to have men at the cookhouse to cook for those in the Stockade until they were all gone or exchanged. I reminded him of the condition in my parole, but this only had the effect of making him mad, and he threatened me with the stocks if I did not go back and resume work. I then and there made up my mind to attempt my escape, considering that the parole had first been broken by the man that granted it."

He did escape, with a few fellow workers, and, after having spent several days eluding patrols, was captured. He spent several weeks in various rural jails and military prisons. Luckily, he was eventually sent, not to Andersonville, but on to Savannah on the 21st of November. Two days later, he was asked to sign a parole before being sent down the river on a Flag of Truce boat and being placed on board one of the exchange ships lying in the harbor.[136]

After Key was taken outside for his safety, he appointed Sergeant A. R. Hill, of the 100th Ohio Volunteer Infantry, to succeed him. Hill was a large man, about 39 years old. He was captured at Limestone Station, in east Tennessee, in September, 1863, and was taken to Belle Isle. There he fought and beat the champion prizefighter. Hill became the chief administrator of the police department and often sat at the door of his tent to listen to both sides of an argument and to dispense justice. He would summon the suspect in a petty theft case and, if the perpetrator were found guilty, he would order that the culprit be made to bend over until he could grab his ankles; Hill would apply a split shingle to that part of the anatomy then most prominent, having been made bare by dropping his pants to his feet. This shingle was called a "shake" in the South and was over 3 feet long.

Those Raiders who had had iron applied while in the custody of the Regulators begged Hill almost daily to have those instruments of pain removed. Hill refused, stating those criminals would wear their irons until they were exchanged.[137]

After these hangings, there was an amazing decrease in the amount of crime within the pen. The Regulators then gained unchallenged control of the prison population. The hangings and the threat of swift punishment applied by the lawful peacekeepers were, thus, a remedy for the rampant terror within the pen. Though this remedy had been initiated by the prisoners themselves, the roundup, detention, and executions took place through the joint efforts of the prisoners and Confederate authorities.

In July, General Samuel Cooper, Adjutant and Inspector General in the War Department, sent Lieutenant Colonel Daniel T. Chandler, a West Point graduate, to inspect Andersonville. Colonel Chandler, accompanied by Major W. Carvel Hall, was ordered, on July 25th, by Colonel R. H. Chilton, Inspector General in Richmond, to go to Andersonville on an official inspection visit of the prison and post. He was told to give special attention to four areas of concern: first, the shelter, police, prison discipline, and proper security of the prisoners; second, the prison hospitals and their management; third, the strength and character of the guards; and fourth, the advantages of that site.[138] They arrived there on the 29th, 30th, or 31st, and stayed about 4 days.

One morning, near the 2nd of August, the two of them entered the prison with Wirz and rode "... from one part of the stockade camp to the other," with Wirz acting as guide. The Colonel paid little attention to Wirz but was very attentive to the tales the prisoners told of their tribulations. Chandler testified: "The ration was the same as was issued throughout the confederate service to troops in the field - the same exactly as to troops engaged in active service. I do not know whether the men in the stockades actually received that allowance. I do not pretend to say they did; I endeavored to ascertain, but I could not get the commissary's abstract of issues. I asked the men what they got and they showed me their ration. It looked small to them, but it seemed to me to be the amount. In quality it was the same as I had been in the habit of eating myself."[139]

Colonel Chandler and Major Hall wrote a "report of inspection" on August 5th and sent it to Richmond. Extracts of this report were sent from Richmond back to General Winder on September 3.

The letter sent to General Winder by the direction of General Samuel Cooper on September 3, told him the measures to take to correct the abuses cited in Chandler's report. These were: "... the want of proper attention, provisions, medicines, and accommodations." General Winder, on September 13th, asked Colonel Forno, Major Proctor, Doctor White, Captain Wirz, and Captain R. B. Winder to prepare answers to this letter as related to their respective

---

136 *Ibid.*, pp. 471-473.
137 *Ibid.*, pp. 252-257.
138 *O.R.*, VII, p. 429.
139 *Wirz Trial*, p. 249.

departments.

In General Winder's reply, on October 8th, to General Cooper, he said he knew what the tenor of the report would be before he saw it because the inspectors' sympathy for the prisoners was so great and apparent it attracted the attention of prison officers and citizens, and caused them to remark about it.

General Winder explained away the prisoners' digging for roots with their hands in the swamp by saying they were just acquiring a commodity to sell or an article of trade. He explained away the impossibility of obtaining anti-scorbutic vegetables by saying he had had long consultations with the chief commissary of the district and the commissary of the post and they had decided peas and rice were the only vegetables obtainable in sufficient quantities to be issued and then only with irregularity. Chandler had asked why easily obtainable green corn was not issued. The general said there were 100 ears per bushel, but if 2 ears were needed per man per day, this would require 640 bushels for the 30,000 men. Corn ripened at various times and large numbers of men were needed to pick it; this made its issue prohibitive. Green corn would also exacerbate the men's diarrhea.[140]

Colonel Chandler, in his report, made a statement about several of the officers of the post. The following was his recommendation with regard to General Winder: "My duty requires me respectfully to recommend a change in the officer in command of the post, Brig. Gen. J. H. Winder, and the substitution in his place of some one who unites both energy and good judgment with some feelings of humanity and consideration for the welfare and comfort (so far as is consistent with their safe-keeping) of the vast number of unfortunates placed under his control; some one who at least will not advocate deliberately and in cold blood the propriety of leaving them in their present condition until their number has been sufficiently reduced by death to make the present arrangements suffice for their accommodation, and who will not consider it a matter of self-laudation and boasting that he has never been inside the stockade, a place the horrors of which it is difficult to describe, and which is a disgrace to civilization; the condition of which he might, by the exercise of a little energy and judgment, even with the limited means at his command, have considerably improved."[141]

Chandler's report was sent up the chain of command in the War Department until it was sent by Judge J. A. Campbell, Assistant Secretary of War, to Secretary of War Seddon with the endorsement, "These reports show a condition of things at Andersonville which calls very loudly for the interposition of the Department in order that a change may be made."[142]

On September 24, Wirz wrote to General Winder, rebutting the three or four points raised by Chandler relating to his command such as the lack of wood, the poorly-managed sick-calls, and the inadequacy of the cooking facilities. Wirz said Chandler and Hall toured the prison in 3 hours when he thought it would have taken a week to do it properly.

In regard to the lack of wood for the prisoners, Wirz stated: "Out of the thirty-odd thousand prisoners confined in the stockade (not including the patients at the hospital), only 8,000 uncooked rations were issued and these 8,000 prisoners always received either the bread or the meat in a cooked state, having only the one or the other to cook for themselves. These men were furnished daily with ten cords of wood for cooking purposes, which was to be equally divided amongst the detachments by sergeants appointed from their own numbers. Besides the wood thus furnished, and at the time of Colonel Chandler's inspection tour, the prisoners received over 1,000 posts 23 feet long each which had been removed by them upon the occasion of enlarging the stockade. It is a notorious fact that over fifty yards were in existence at one time within the stockade, the prisoners lending wood one to the other by the stock or other quantity. Colonel Chandler did not ask me a single question in regard to wood. From the fact that he saw one prisoner digging small pieces of wood from a mud hole I presume he thought the statements of prisoners in regard to the wood question were to be believed. If Colonel Chandler had asked me I would have presented the matter to him in an entirely different light. This man, gathering wood, in common with many others, did so for the purpose of selling the same to cake bakers and restaurant keepers, who, drawing their rations cooked, had no wood issued to them, and in order to carry on their business, were obliged to buy wood from whom they might."[143]

Wirz, in his response to the Chandler inspection, stated, in regard to the ovens and cooking facilities: "It took weeks before a sufficient number of bricks could be obtained; the kettles, after a delay of over two months, were finally received, but lime, a very necessary article, could not be procured from any quarter. General Johnston had taken all the trains upon the Atlanta and West Point railroads, thereby butting us off from Opelika, the only point

---

[140] *O.R.*, VII, pp. 755-758.
[141] *Ibid.*, p. 552.
[142] *Ibid.*, p. 551.
[143] *Ibid.*, p. 759.

from where we could likely obtain the article required. About three weeks since the post quartermaster received a small supply, but from whence he obtained it I did not ascertain. I had in the meantime finished setting the kettles in the clay, and also put up a bake-oven with the same material. In putting up bake-ovens, of which we should have three more, a great many difficulties were to be surmounted, the worst of which is to obtain the necessary castings. Patterns for doors and other things have been sent to Macon for casting over two months ago. We are told they cannot be cast unless we furnish the coke, which can only be obtained in Montgomery. Up to this moment we have not procured any, consequently we have been unable to set the bake-ovens. Large sheet-iron pans are indispensable to bake the large quantity of bread required. We cannot obtain them but in lieu thereof are furnished with tin pans, which are burnt out and rendered useless in two weeks. When the quarter-master of the post applied to Major Dillard, in Columbus, Ga., for sheet-iron for pans, the major remarked that the sheet-iron should be used for our army, and not for Yankees. The above are some of the reasons why Colonel Chandler found the cooking apparatus insufficient. We were well aware of the fact, and needed not to be reminded thereof by him..."[144]

Before Chandler left, he said, "This beats anything I ever saw; it is, indeed, a hell on earth."[145] Wirz also said Major Hall remarked about the prison, "... that it was about on a par with the Federal prison at Johnston's Island, which is represented as being the best prison in the North."[146] Major Hall, in a letter to Chilton on November 22, denied he ever made the above statement: "I did not express any such opinion, nor did I ever use any language, which the utmost ingenuity could pervert into such a misrepresentation of my conviction."[147]

When General Winder wrote to Richmond the rebuttal of the charges made by Chandler, he characterized the statements of Chandler as being false, "... but in no instance is a single statement satisfactorily controverted; on the contrary, they are sustained..." The report forwarded to Richmond contained no report by Colonel Forno nor Major Proctor even though they had been asked to write one by General Winder. Colonel Chilton, to whom the rebuttals had been sent in Richmond, said that, by General Winder "... characterizing the statements 'as false' he imputes to Colonel Chandler 'conduct unbecoming an officer and a gentleman ...'" Chilton recommended that action be taken to relieve Chandler from the imputation of falsehood and the rebuke of an officer who seemed to be careless and indifferent with respect to the honor of another officer's reputation.[148]

Chandler testified: "On my return to Richmond in October, I spoke to Colonel Chilton, chief of the bureau, with reference to my report, and he told me that it had not been acted upon. The former secretary of war had been relieved and General Breckinridge appointed secretary. At my insistence, Colonel Chilton urged the department to take the matter up, for the reason that General Winder had rather decried the correctness of some statements that I had made, and I made a counter report, furnishing evidence of the accuracy of my report. I went to Judge Campbell and asked him to take it up, and he promised that he would do so. I do not believe it was ever taken up; that is to say, I do not think it was ever decided. Judge Campbell might have been considering it at the time of the evacuation."[149]

It was at that point (i.e., after the Chandler report reached Richmond) that many wondered why General Winder was not removed instead of being given a promotion. Within a few weeks, he was given a broader scope of authority. On November 21st, General Winder was made commissary general of prisoners east of the Mississippi.

After Colonel Persons had relinquished the command of the post to General Winder, Persons sought an injunction from the judge of the Southwestern Circuit to close the public nuisance at Andersonville. He prepared the case for trial and drew up the specifications of the bill. He acted in response to the complaints from some near-by residents who feared that the effluvium given off by the stockade and cemetery was injurious to their health. He went to see the judge of the district court and read the bill to him. The judge appointed the day for the hearing. Persons obtained the injunction but was warned by the judge that he would be subject to possible bodily harm if he persisted in his undertaking for an inquiry and hearing.

General Howell Cobb, at Macon and in command of the Military District of Georgia, soon learned of the injunction. Word of the impending litigation was also forwarded to Richmond to the War Office and a party was sent down to examine the pen. General Cobb sent an inspection party from his headquarters 60 miles away. General Cobb would be held responsible for any mismanagement or corruption at the pen in his district. This inspection party,

144 *Ibid.*, pp. 758-760.
145 *Ibid.*, p. 759.
146 *Ibid.*
147 *Ibid.*, p. 1156.
148 *Ibid.*, p. 756.
149 Chipman, p. 74.

headed by Cobb, included the surgeon on his staff, Surgeon Eldridge; they sent back a rather favorable report concerning the post.

Before Colonel Persons could appear before the court, he received a communication from General Cobb in which the general implied that, if Colonel Persons continued with his pursuance of the bill against the government, the general would consider this to be inconsistent with the Colonel's duty as a Confederate officer. Though never stated per se, Persons got the distinct feeling that he would be court-martialed if he continued. He, of course, dropped the whole matter.[150]

Maile mentioned this incident. "The people of Macon petitioned General Howell Cobb, the military governor of Georgia, for the removal of the prison located sixty miles away, lest an awful pestilence sweep over their county."[151]

During the first nine days of August, the weather was oppressively hot, with little or no rain for relief. Moreover, the stream had become so contaminated it was not fit to drink from. "The water had now become so impure that it was almost impossible to get a drink of it that was palatable inside of the stockade. Not only the stream and spring along its banks were impure, but even the few deep wells had become so from vermin dropping into them. I have walked along the stream, and examined spring after spring to get a cup of water that was a little better than the rest, and would at last be compelled to dip it from some spring, the bottom of which would be white with maggots."[152]

"On the 7th, 8th, and 9th, the weather was so awfully hot that it really appeared as if the heat would kill us all; those were the most terrible days in the history of our prison. On the 9th, one hundred and seventy-five prisoners died, and the mortality in the three days was nearly five hundred. I have not the least doubt that had not a kind Providence interfered and sent the great rain-storm on the 9th, death would have swept all of us away inside of sixty days."[153]

**The Flood Opening the Palisade** - The guard was called out in force and no one escaped. Prisoners were not allowed to keep the recovered timbers, though wood was very precious. (Kellogg)

On Tuesday, August 9, before noon, there commenced a very hard rain, which continued most of the afternoon. The run-off from this torrential rain made the creek swell so that it tore six holes in the stockade after it had been undermined. One sentinel box fell into the stream on the west side. "In about an hour this stream, which was originally ten feet wide, had spread out until it was three hundred feet wide and six feet deep."[154]

"The brook began to rise, and was soon too large to get through the vents made for it in the stockade. It dammed up at both walls til it almost reached the top. The upper wall gave way, and a flood eight or ten feet deep and fifty wide was rushing through the pen. When it struck the lower wall, it, too, fell with a crash. A hundred brave men rushed into the boiling flood to ride out on it."[155]

The long roll sounded from the South Gate. The guards came double-quick from their quarters and took their positions at the east and west breach. "The alarm was given in what the rebels would call 'right smart quick,' for two of the guns in the fort about the head-quarters of Captain Wirz, were at once discharged as a signal for them to rally and instantly their whole force outside fell in under arms, and took positions in front of these gaps, to keep the yankees in."[156] The large logs that had made up the stockade came floating down the stream. The men waded out and retrieved the logs but they were not used by the men; an order was issued requiring that the logs be returned under the penalty of having rations cut off for five days. After the rain stopped, the guards could only affect temporary repair before darkness. They built fires by which to work. Extra guards were kept on duty all night. The Confederates

150 Spencer, p. 96.
151 Maile, p. 54.
152 Urban, p. 390.
153 *Ibid.*, p. 407.
154 Lyons, p. 53.
155 Vawter, p. 65.
156 Kellogg, p. 210.

worked through the night to repair the damage done by the rain; by morning, the repair was complete.

"Directly after noon on the 9th, the rain-storm already spoken of commenced, and this event will be remembered by those who witnessed it as long as their memory lasts. The large ink-black clouds approaching from the West, the constant vivid flashes of lightning, and sharp, quick claps of thunder, which reminded us of a heavy cannonade, all indicated that a fearful storm was approaching, and we watched its approach with a great deal of interest and anxiety. It soon burst over us with a fury that was appalling, and the rain poured down as if all the flood-gates of the heavens had opened. The deluge of water, the terrific flashes of lightning, the crashes of thunder and roaring of the storm, made a scene awful and grand. The lightning struck into the stockade, and several times into the trees that surrounded our prison in rapid succession. Consequently we did not notice that the small stream through our prison had become a raging torrent, and was threatening to sweep away part of the stockade, when the boom of a cannon from one of the forts announced the fact that the rebels were alarmed about something, and getting on our feet we discovered that the stockade was being swept away at both sides of the prison. The greatest excitement now existed among the rebels, who were falling into line, and marching to the place where the break in the stockade had occurred, for the purpose of preventing us from making our escape.

"Although the storm was still raging with great fury, and the rain pouring down in torrents, we commenced to crowd toward the stream, hoping some chance of escaping would present itself. The rebels had, however, formed a strong line to prevent this; but it was some satisfaction to us to know that our enemies had to leave their snug quarters and be exposed to the storm as well as we. After the storm subsided, some of the prisoners jumped into the still raging stream, and caught some of the wood floating down; but Wirz, with the devilish cruelty so characteristic of the man, ordered them not to use it, threatening that if we did he would stop our rations for five days. No rations were issued on this day, and hungry and wet, we passed a most miserable night.

"The rebels worked like beavers all night and the following day, to replace the stockade washed away. It was also weakened at different places, and a large number of blacks were sent inside of the prison to fix and strengthen it. These poor people were very friendly to us, and would watch every opportunity to show their sympathy in some substantial manner. They would keep a close watch on the guards, and at every opportunity slip to the prisoners tobacco or some articles of food. A squad of these people were at work close to us, and we were watching them working, when one of them suddenly slipped his hand in his pocket, and taking out a piece of tobacco, flung it to us; the next instant he had resumed his work. This was repeated several times by the generous fellow, who had no doubt amply supplied himself with the weed for the purpose of sharing it out to us. He was, however, at last caught in the act, and a stop put to it. As he threw the last piece the guard saw the action, and yelled out, 'Look out thar, or I will blow your brains out!' The poor fellow was almost frightened to death; but the guard no doubt only intended to give him a good scare."[157]

"On the 10th, the day after the great flood, it was very warm until noon, when it again rained until night. The next morning it was clear, cool and pleasant, and we had a chance to dry off. The entire prison, including the swamp, was swept in such a manner as to be quite clean compared to its former condition. Almost all the filth and vermin on the ground was swept away, and the atmosphere was quite pure."[158]

On that day, a Wednesday, soldiers and Negroes were busy repairing the walls. They were taunted by the prisoners with shouts such as "That's the way your Confederacy will fall," "Grant and Sherman are making bigger holes than these," "Ho, Reb, what are doing with dat nigger dar; 'pears to us you're reduced to the level of the nigger,'" etc.[159]

By August 12th, the post was secure, "... after three days of constant labor of the whole command."[160] On August 13th, General Winder wrote to General Samuel Cooper, detailing the damage done to the palisade by the rains. "On the morning of Tuesday, the 9th, we had a shower of rain, which did no material damage, but about 3 'clock it commenced to rain, and I have not seen such a rain in many years. In less than an hour the stream running through the prison rose between four and five feet and carried away about 100 feet of the stockade, and the rain washed ditches inside and out, parallel to the stockade, from three to eight feet deep, and broke through and carried away about thirty feet of the stockade in another quarter. The alarm guns were fired and the troops were on the ground promptly, the militia first. There was no escape, nor was there any attempt to escape on the part of the prisoners; their own self-constituted police kept order within the stockade. No doubt sixteen guns bearing on them had a

[157] Urban, pp. 408-410.
[158] *Ibid.*, p. 411.
[159] Northrop, p. 103.
[160] *O.R.*, VII, p. 586.

wholesome influence... If we had not had a large negro force working on the defenses I think it would have been impossible to have saved the place. I enclose a sketch of the damage done."[161]

"Immediately after the washing away of our prison walls, the 'Rebs' commenced another stockade outside the old one and at a distance of about ten rods from it. We watched them, wondering what they were about, and only found out when we saw all around us a double enclosure. The logs to this second stockade were not hewn, but put up rough, and in some places there would be three or four inches space, through which we could see them still at work outside, and it was not long until a third stockade was completed, and stood about thirty feet distant from the middle one. We were now completely nonplussed, what could induce them to erect a third stockade, was a problem we could none of us solve. We naturally supposed the second one was to effectually prevent our tunneling, but what could be the intention of a third one, and so close to the second, we did not understand. We learned afterwards that the two outer stockades formed a lane or alley, in which the rebs could pass from one fort to another, and transfer their guns, ammunition, &c., without being exposed to the fire of an enemy, in case of an attack. Earthworks and small forts had been thrown up on each corner of the stockade, and the only entrance to them was from this alley or lane."[162]

On the stump at the end of North Street one evening in early August, sat an emaciated cavalry sergeant, T. J. Shepherd, of Columbus, Ohio, formerly an honored preacher of the gospel. Around him was a small group of men whom he led in the doxology, which is a hymn used to start some services. It begins, "Praise God from whom all blessings flow." Some 25 starving men gathered around and joined in the singing. Said Brother Shepherd: "I have today read in the book of Numbers of Moses striking the rock from which water gushed out for the ample supply of man and beast. I tell you God must strike a rock in Andersonville or we shall all die of thirst. And if there is no rock here, He can smite the ground and bring forth water to supply our desperate needs. Of this I am sure; let us ask Him to do this."[163] He successively called on the men gathered and asked them to pray for water. They prayed about an hour and then closed with the doxology. He asked that all the men pray vehemently for water and to meet each evening to do so again. They did this from Monday to Thursday evening.

"For a month previous we had noticed that a number of the stockade timbers near the north gate had been loosened by the percolating of the copious rain and they were sagging considerably and had settled out of line. We wondered why they had been allowed to remain so long in this unsafe condition. Was it a coincidence that after prayer began to be offered the quartermaster of the prison notified Capt. Wirtz [sic] that stockade timbers were out of line and should be set right? He was ordered to take a gang of slaves and make the necessary repairs. About fifteen stalwart negroes were marched through the main gate and turned into the twenty-foot space between the dead-line and the wall. With pike poles the closely adjoining posts were heaved into position and the earth was closely tamped.

"Then the workers faced about and commenced digging a trench up the hill nearly as wide as the space between the dead-line and the stockade. A part of the gang swung their picks into the red clay which was shoveled against the timbers. Another set followed with heavy rammers and pounded the whole into a smooth, sloping surface which was tamped closely to the base of the wooden wall, making a perfect watershed, and thus preventing the further loosening of the earth at the base of the stockade. By Thursday evening the broad trench with rounded bottom was completed from the swamp up the dead line space to the north gate."[164]

After the rains had come from the west and knocked over the palisades, the Confederates fired a solid shot over the prison to warn against any attempt at escape. "The down-pour may have continued twenty minutes, perhaps half an hour, or possibly longer."[165] Then the sun burst forth and soon a voice was heard from near the north gate yelling, "A spring! A spring! A spring has broken out!" In the center of the space between the stockade and the dead-line, at the point where the earth had been most deeply excavated, a large spring about "as thick as a man's arm" arched into the air.[166]

"... On Saturday morning, to our delight, we saw the quartermaster again enter the gate with a gang of slaves, bringing fence boards, hammers, nails, axes and stakes. A double row of the latter was driven, so that the direction crossed the dead-line at a slight angle down the hill. A strip was nailed across each pair of stakes, and in the aperture rested a trough made of two fence boards nailed together. At the lower end of this chute in an excavation was set a

[161] *Ibid.*, p. 589.
[162] E. L. Clapp, Andersonville: *Six Months A Prisoner of War* (Milwaukee: Daily Wisconsin Steam Printing House, 1865), pp. 13, 14.
[163] Maile, p. 62.
[164] *Ibid.*, pp. 63, 64.
[165] *Ibid.*, p. 67.
[166] Roach, p. 218.

sugar hogshead, around which clay was tamped so as to aid in making it watertight. When all was ready the upper end of the chute was thrust under the falling column of water, which swiftly ran down and filled to overflowing the large barrel. From this the men by crowds dipped freely of the refreshing, life-giving water."[167]

"The food-famished prisoners feasted their eyes on it for days...

**Providence Spring** - This stone pavilion was built by the Women's National Relief Corps to enshrine and protect the Providence Spring. It was built over the fountain, which to this day still yeilds cool water. In the marble above the spring is written: "With charity to all and malice toward none."

"[The water being] out of reach, all sorts of devices were invented to get some of it... mustard cups, tied to strings, obtained somehow, even to robbing the mealsack of an inch or so, to unravel and make a line, then the 'casting' was equally the performance of our expert, as for fish, in order to land the cup, with mouth upstream and on its side in the little water line, where, at best, but a few drops could be obtained at each cast, often all was spilled before landed. The art of recovering the cup with contents was quite a trick. Some were successful; the majority failed to get enough to satisfy the slightest thirst. The fishing process was very dangerous as the fisher dared not reach over or under the dead line. The stream grew a little stronger and to some extent nullified the bad effect of the water obtained at the usual place at the brook...Wirz sent a force of negroes into camp to stop the flow of water of this Providence Spring. Their efforts were in vain - fruitless, but Oh! how fruitful to us poor wretches as the stream of life resented the brutal interference of Wirz, and in its wrath burst forth a torrent compared to its original flow... We now could get water from near the dead line, by an extra reach... Wirz went so far as to lead it out of reach, yet its flow of pure water into the former reekings and seepings for the rebel sink was still a vast improvement, for it purified the stream and increased the flow.

"This condition of things stood for a few weeks when a committee of seven were appointed to meet the 'Devil' at the South Gate to bid him 'good day' and induce him to allow the water of Providence Spring to be led into camp by the method of sinking several rice tierces or barrels at intervals with a trough from each to the other, also from each of them inside the dead line to one inside the camp so that the long single line of waiting men could be cut into several lines, thus preventing waste of water and the long tedious wait to get it. By appointment Wirz met the committee. The committee was so arranged that four were chosen to speak. When halted and formed in front of his 'Satanic Majesty' the speaker nearest him when the halt came, was to open negotiation for the water supply. When ranged in front, it fell to my lot, being directly in front, face to face, to make known our request, and we thought it a reasonable one under the circumstances; but you can imagine our surprise as well as my colleagues' when Wirz ripped out a sulphurous oath, accompanied by 'reinforcements' - a brace of navy revolvers, aiming them at us, we mean both singular and plural - for we imagined that we would see the points of each bullet in both guns, though they were aimed in different directions. Then followed this most exquisite language, 'No, the water of the creek is good enough for you God-damned Yankee sons of --------. [No man gets it.] Go back, or I will blow your damn brains out and sent you to Hell!!!'... We 'right faced' and quickly moved off without music...

"Wirz fell sick and went home to Macon... Our next "Boss" was Lieutenant Davis, who was not much improvement over Wirz... The Committee tried Davis on the water question but he would not work with us... Wirz recovered and returned to us... We once more met him on the water question... Wirz consented at once and sent some slaves into camp, lumber and other material and the committee was the 'Boss' of the work, known as 'The Water Works Contractors.'"[168]

The Regulators immediately took charge of the spring to keep order.

---

[167] Maile, p. 70.

[168] Hopkins, pp. 99-101.

Most times, there would be a line of about 1,000 men waiting to fill their cups or canteens. "Falling into files of four, a column is often formed which it takes two hours to pass to the end of the spout."[169] Once this spring opened, there was never any want for clean, cool water.

Was the spring a "new" spring or was it an old spring that, once its debris had been scraped off its surface by the rain, just sprang forth again? "Natives of the area say that the spring had been there years before the War, that it had been a favorite deer stand for local hunters and that when the breastworks for Camp Sumter were hastily thrown up, dirt and debris covered the watering place and closed the spring."[170]

Indeed, the prisoners had noticed that, after digging for roots for fuel in the swamp at night, the next day, their footprints would be flooded with pure water. This phenomenon was more easily explained after Providence Spring opened up. In the neighborhood of the spring was lots of sub-terranean water near the surface, with artesian pressures at work.

Lieutenant-Colonel T. M. Furlow, replied, on August 16th, to a query by General Winder as to the propriety of having so many men out of the pen on parole. Furlow said that, in the month he had been connected with the post, he had never seen anything to cause alarm or suspicion. He had noticed, many times, that the men spoke to the Negroes, but this was only to purchase peaches or watermelons; soon the work of the Negroes would be completed and they would be leaving. Furlow had never heard of any pillaging. Their responsibilities as nurses and on burial details were duties the garrison troops did not want. Using these prisoners was cheap and cost only slight ration increases since they got double rations. In case of a raid by a cavalry party, enough notice would have been had to put the parolees back into the pen.

Boredom within the pen was always a problem. The men spent most of their waking hours just thinking of ways to survive the harsh conditions. When not thinking about basic survival, such as the attainment of food, water, shelter, warmth in the winter and coolness in the summer, they sought to keep their minds busy. Some sought relief in gambling in such ways as by playing cards or dice, by lice-racing, prize-fighting, or by playing board games such as chess, checkers or chuck-a-luck.

Of the card games, poker was always the most popular with euchre, pinochle, whist, rummy, seven-up and bluff also being very popular. Men made cards by tearing up any handy paper. Minie balls were pounded flat and embellished by having the Roman numerals V or X carved in them. Some men would pound the imprint of a five- or ten-dollar coin into the soft lead.

"An attempt was ostensibly made to issue us cow-peas instead, and the first issue was only a quart to a detachment of two hundred and seventy men. This was two-thirds of a pint to each squad of ninety, and made but a few spoonfuls for each of the four messes in the squad. When it came to dividing among the men, the beans had to be counted. Nobody received enough to pay for cooking, and we were at a loss what to do until somebody suggested that we play poker for them. This met general acceptance, and after that, as long as beans were drawn, a large portion of the day was spent in absorbing games of 'bluff' and 'draw,' at a bean 'ante,' and no 'limit.'

"After a number of hours' diligent playing, some lucky or skillful player would be in possession of all the beans in a mess, a squad, and sometimes a detachment, and have enough for a good meal."[171]

"It is a superstition of soldiers that it would not be well with them to go to battle with cards on them. If killed, it would be evidence of sin unrepented; so they fling them pell-mell when trouble is ahead. But when again settled in camp they beg passes and tramp miles to find a sutler where they can be bought at for ordinary prices, and play all day and after tattoo for stakes, often pledging their next pay. That is a way they have of keeping a clean record to go before the Great Judge."[172]

Various board games were played such as chess, draughts, checkers, or cribbage. Some boards had been brought into the pen, while others were made from available material, such as a top to a ration box. Other players simply drew in the dirt and used sticks made into individual pieces or checkers. "Some whiled away the hours playing chess. We marked out a place on the ground for a board, and made our set of men by nitching sticks so that we would know them. When we moved a piece, we stuck it in the ground so it would stand. Though there were a few who had boards of their own making."[173] McElroy made a chess set from a soft, white root from the swamp. He carved crude men with a pocket knife and blackened one set with pitch pine soot. A piece of plank was marked ap-

[169] Northrop, p. 117.
[170] Sheppard, p. 12.
[171] McElroy, p. 151.
[172] Northrop, pp. 147, 148.
[173] Vawter, p. 61.

propriately and he was ready to play. Minie balls were often carved into chess pieces.

Shooting dice has been popular with soldiers for over 2,000 years. Some prisoners hammered Minie balls into cubes to make lead dice.

During the warm summer months, prize fights were held for the entertainment of the prisoners. Northrop said that, on June 23, a number of very brutal fights were fought. One man was knocked down eleven times before the end of the fight. "For amusements we had about every day an amateur prize fight near the lower end of the sinks, in which one or both of the contestants were pretty sure to have on one of the red caps of the Brooklyn Fourteenth."[174]

McElroy told of a prize-fight which took place a few days after the first prisoners had arrived. "One afternoon a number of us went across to their camp, to witness a fight according to the rules of the Prize Ring, which was to come off between two professional pugilists. These were a couple of bounty-jumpers who had some little reputation in New York sporting circles, under the names of the 'Staleybridge Chicken' and the 'Harlem Infant.'

"On the way from Richmond a cast-iron skillet, or spider, had been stolen by the crowd from the Rebels. It was a small affair, holding a half gallon, and worth to-day about fifty cents. In Andersonville its worth was literally above rubies. Two men belonging to different messes each claimed the ownership of the utensil, on the ground of being most active in securing it. Their claims were strenuously supported by their respective messes, at the heads of which were the aforesaid Infant and Chicken...

"When we arrived a twenty-four foot ring had been prepared by drawing a deep mark in the sand. In diagonally opposite corners of these the seconds were kneeling on one knee and supporting their principals on the other. By their sides they had little vessels of water, and bundles of rags to answer for sponges. Another corner was occupied by the umpire, a foul-mouthed loud-tongued Tombs shyster, named Pete Bradley. A long-bodied, short-legged hoodlum, nick-named 'Heenan,' armed with a club, acted as ring keeper, and 'belted' back, remorselessly, any of the spectators who crowded over the line...

"At Bradley's call of 'Time!' the principals would rise from their seconds' knees, advance briskly to the scratch across the center of the ring, and spar away sharply for a little time, until one got in a blow that sent the other to the ground, where he would lie until his second picked him up, carried him back, washed his face off, and gave him a drink. He then rested until the next call of time.

"This sort of performance went on for an hour or more, with the knock-downs and other casualties pretty evenly divided between the two... A bunch of blood soaked rags was tossed into the air from his corner, and Bradley declared the Chicken to be the victor, amid enthusiastic cheers from the crowd."[175]

Another of the ways that the soldiers passed the time away was to hold lice races. With minor variations, this was conducted by dropping lice on a hot tin plate and betting which louse would reach the edge of the plate first. "We would get a tin plate from some one and make a small ring in the center of the plate then make a ring around the cut edge of it, then heat it in the sun, drop the two lice in the center of the plate, bet on the one getting out of the ring first. Someone would say 'drop' and as soon as they struck the plate they would start and it was fun to see them run."[176]

"There were two kinds of lice, some were dark, some slimmer and more round and lighter color. One fellow had one that was the best. That fellow could have bet any money on it if he had it. I seen poor fellows crawl up to look at the lice race that would be dead in thirty minutes, and I have seen them sitting up on the ground, their head between their hands, and fall over dead, lay there till the dead wagon came and hauled them out."[177]

Others played musical instruments or sang to while away the time. "Some might think that a prison would be barren of music. It was not so at Andersonville. There were few instruments, as I remember. But singers were there in plenty, and every evening the strains of the *Star Spangled Banner*, *America*, and other patriotic songs were heard throughout the camp. Mingled with these would be the hymns and sacred songs sung at the prayer meetings. And now and then a cultured voice would sing a song of love, or of home. I often recall a night in July, a clear, manly voice near me sang *The Sword of Bunker Hill*. When he ended the guard near him called out, like Oliver Twist, for 'more.' I seldom heard any of the southern soldiers singing, and believe they were not as given to music as our boys. Their favorite and almost only tune for the little drum corps was *The Bonnie Blue Flag*, and they played it over and over again, until everybody grew heartily sick of it. Whenever any of the negro slaves were working near the prison

---

[174] Williams, p. 14.
[175] McElroy, pp. 146-148.
[176] Clifton, p. 12.
[177] *Ibid.*

we would hear their weird, sad and monotonous songs."[178]

Even the Confederate Colonel Fannin testified, "All the music we had at Andersonville was made by federal prisoners who were paroled. I made application to Captain Wirz one day, just before a train of cars arrived, for the detail of a man by the name of Johnny Griffiths, a fife-major in one of the federal regiments who was captured in northern Georgia; Captain Wirz remarked to me that he had no authority to detail the man, but that he would make an effort to have it done for me; the man was paroled, and acted as fifer of my regiment until he was sent away to be exchanged; there was quite a number of such men paroled."[179]

"The three songs most popular at the South, and generally regarded as distinctively Southern, were *The Bonnie Blue Flag, Maryland, My Maryland,* and *Stonewall Jackson Crossing into Maryland.*. The first of these was the greatest favorite by long odds. Women sang, men whistled, and the so-called musicians played it wherever we went. While in the field before capture, it was the commonest of experiences to have Rebel women sing it at us tauntingly from the houses that we passed or near which we stopped... All familiar with Scotch songs will readily recognize the name and air as an old friend, and one of the fierce Jacobite melodies that for a long time disturbed the tranquility of the Brunswick family on the English throne. The new words supplied by the Rebels are the merest doggerel, and fit the music as poorly as the unchanged name of the song fitted to its new use... Next in popularity was *Maryland, My Maryland.*. 'The air is old, and a familiar one to all college students, and belongs to one of the most common of German household songs; *O, Tannenbaum!*

"*Stonewall Jackson Crossing into Maryland*... Its air was that of the well-known and popular negro minstrel song, *Billy Patterson.*

"We heard these songs with tiresome iteration, daily and nightly, during our stay in the Southern Confederacy. Some one of the guards seemed to be perpetually beguiling the weariness of his watch by singing in all keys, in every sort of a voice, and with the wildest latitude as to air and tune...

"We revenged ourselves as best we could by constructing fearfully wicked, obscene and insulting parodies on these, and by singing them with irritating effusiveness in the hearing of the guards who were inflicting these nuisances upon us."[180]

Reading materials within the pen were always at a premium. Many men brought in their own personal prayer books, Bibles, or New Testaments. These were, by far, the most abundant books within the pen.

Kellogg said, "One of my comrades, by some means became the possessor of *Woodbury's Shorter Course in German,* and I began to study that language. This book was a perfect treasure, and with it I passed many an otherwise dull hour, agreeably and profitably."[181]

"In the middle of May a rebel publication fell into our hands, printed at Richmond, and called *The Second Year of the War.* It was a very one-sided affair, full of misrepresentations, making everything Southern about perfect, and all action on the corresponding side unworthy and barbarous. It spoke of the robbery of shoes and clothing from the dead and wounded, at the second Bull Run battle, as a very commendable act on the part of their soldiers."[182]

In the middle of May, "... a copy of the *Macon Telegraph* was brought into camp, giving an account of the battle between Grant and Lee."[183] The *Macon Confederate* was in the prison at the end of May.[184] "The Macon *Telegraph and Confederate,* only the day before the surrender of the city to the Federal forces, justified the atrocities at Andersonville..."[185] "Copies of the *Charleston Mercury* of June 6th and 7th found their way to our hands, giving an interesting account of a naval conflict between the iron ram *Albemarle* and several Federal wooden gunboats."[186] Some Macon newspapers came into the pen on the 11th of August. [187] A Macon *Telegram* was in the stockade in the middle of August.[188] Many times an Atlanta paper that had originated in Memphis made its way into the prison. It was facetiously called the *Memphis-Corinth-Jackson-Grenada-Chattanooga-Resacca-Marietta-Atlanta Appea,"* denoting the cities falling in the advance of Sherman's army from the time of Memphis' fall in 1862.[189]

---

[178] Miller, p. 30.
[179] *Wirz Trial,* p. 434.
[180] McElroy, pp. 333-337.
[181] Kellogg, p. 232.
[182] *Ibid.,* p. 92.
[183] *Ibid.,* p. 79.
[184] *Ibid.,* p. 116.
[185] Author's library, p. 186.
[186] Kellogg, p. 130.
[187] *Ibid.,* p. 217.
[188] Kellogg, p. 78.
[189] McElroy, p. 264.

Northrop mentioned that in the prison was a copy of an 1861 *Atlantic Monthly*, a Milton's *Paradise Lost*, and a copy of Victor Hugo's *Les Miserables*.[190] McElroy often read a copy of the massive medical textbook, Gray's *Anatomy*.

On Monday, the 15th of August, "... some photographic artists came from Macon, and taking their position in sentry-boxes at different points around the stockade, they proceeded to engrave our wretchedness by art. It might have been by order of the authorities, or simply a private enterprise, but we thought we would have liked one of the pictures to show to our friends, and to look at, if we should ever be away from the miserable scenes themselves."[191] This is the only mention of the visit of a photographer to the prison written by an ex-prisoner. Kellogg described the visitors as "artists." It is assumed, therefore, that the photographer brought an assistant as would be expected because of the heavy baggage necessary to ply his trade.

**Brigadier General John Henry Winder** - Proably taken at Andersonville on August 15, 1864, by photographer, A. J. Riddle. (Dave Mark Collection, Linthicum Heights, MD)

All the prisoners who died at Andersonville could have saved themselves by simply going to a guard or Confederate sergeant at roll-call and asking to take the oath of allegiance to the Confederate government. Of course, that same option was open to all the Confederate soldiers who died in Northern prisons. It is a tribute to all Northerners and Southerners who died in prison that they did not ask to be saved.

Those prisoners at Andersonville could ask to go out, to be given uniforms of gray, to be fed better rations and sent off to serve in the Confederate Army. They would be assigned to some post, usually in the rear, where they would not be tempted to flee to their own lines. A few accepted this offer. Some went out only to facilitate their escapes. Those who did go out risked their lives if they returned to the pen on a recruiting mission.

"At Andersonville there was a standing offer of immediate release to any prisoner who would take the oath of allegiance to the Confederacy and engage in non-combatant service. Officers who entered the prison with these proposals were shunned by our men. I recall a prisoner who thus enlisted. When he re-entered the prison in Confederate uniform as a recruiting officer, his reception was such that he fled to the gate for his life; shouting to the guard to protect him."[192]

"Often overtures were made to us to enlist in the Confederate service. These were received with derisive jeers, and though the prisoners were surrounded by the horrors I have described, they would strike up the *Star Spangled Banner*, *Yankee Doodle*, *John Brown*, and other Union army airs."[193]

"Strange to relate, that out of the seventeen thousand registered sick, there is record of only about twenty-five who accepted the offers to save their lives, and took the oath of the rebels."[194]

"In November, 1864, Colonel O'Neil of the Tenth Tennessee Confederate Infantry, came to the general hospital at Andersonville, and asked the privilege of addressing the Irish hospital attendants. They were marched outside the hospital enclosure, surrounded by a circle of guards, and Colonel O'Neil addressed them. He told them it was evident there was no hope of exchange, they could see the fate that awaited them. If they would enlist in the Confederate service they would receive food, clothing, and comfortable quarters. They would not be required to go to the front and be exposed to death and capture by the northern army, but would be used to do camp, guard and garrison duty, [and] to relieve Confederate troops which would be sent to the front. The Irish Union soldiers listened - turned and went back to the misery and wretchedness of prison life. Every man went back."[195]

When the 2nd New Jersey Cavalry opposed the 10th Tennessee Confederate regiment at Egypt Station, Mississippi, on December 28th, 1864, they were met by a withering fire from the skirmish line, which killed 3 Federal officers and 20 men and which wounded 74 others. When they charged, the "rebels" threw down their guns and surrendered. They immediately alleged they had been ex-prisoners of Andersonville and had joined the Confederate forces to avoid starvation and death. They claimed they were going to cross the lines at their first chance. They said they

190 Northrop, p. 77, p.59, p. 123.
191 Kellogg, p. 223.
192 Maile, p. 122.
193 Smith, p. 21.
194 Hamlin, p. 33.
195 Smith, pp. 21, 22.

had not been given arms and ammunition until the night before the engagement and surrendered at their first opportunity. Major A. A. Hosmer, Judge-Advocate, recommended the Government not recognize the propriety of prisoners escaping by this means and, because they had fired with such deadly precision, they should not be shown any clemency and should be held and tried as deserters.[196]

Since receiving a wound at the Battle of Seven Pines in 1862, Wirz had suffered with an inflammation, or osteomyelitis, of one of the bones in his right forearm. After the war, at his trial, Wirz argued that he was so weak and infirm during his tenure at Andersonville he did not have the strength to kill anyone by shooting, pistol-whipping, stomping or kicking him to death. By August, his health had deteriorated so badly that he had to leave for several weeks. Descriptions of his health problems seem to indicate that he had other problems in addition to the infection in his arm. He seemed to have suffered a generalized physical as well as mental exhaustion. Wirz had hoped the wound would improve if he went to an area away from the prison, with all its miasmas. Some prisoners thought that, by Wirz' leaving, *their* condition might improve. This did occur to a small extent, thereby showing that Wirz was but one factor in their suffering.

**Riddle's photo shows the burial detail at the cemetery.** In the shallow trench that was to hold one to three hundred is the body, on a crude stretcher, of the next prisoner to be buried.

Joseph Adler, a prisoner, testified: "I do not recollect ever seeing Captain Wirz strike or kick any of the sick or anything of that kind; I have heard him use very abusive and insulting language."[197] Kellogg testified: "I have seen Captain Wirz in the prison frequently. He usually came in more often than otherwise mounted on horseback. He would ride inside the dead line and examine the prison. I cannot say that I ever saw him perpetrate any acts of cruelty on the men."[198] "... A man ... showed Capt. Wirz his ration of corn bread, and asked whether better could not be furnished; he was met with the response, 'Damned you; I'll give you bullets for bread.'"[199]

"The chances of escape were very small, for the pickets were very watchful, and often we were discovered before one man had escaped. Of those that did get out not more than one of every ten ever got more than ten miles before they were recaptured and sent back to prison, with the additional curse of a ball and chain.

"The only way to get rid of this ornament was to watch for Wirz when he came into the prison, and beg of him to have it removed; sometimes he would relent, but more often the only answer would be 'Get out, you damned thief of a Yankee.'"[200]

D. H. Stearns, a steward, testified about a request he had made for poles and pine boughs to make the hospital patients more comfortable. "I asked if poles and boughs could not be procured, as wood was plenty around there; they told me in that case that the commandant, Captain Wirz, would not allow the men to go out for that purpose. I asked Captain Wirz, myself, for passes to permit the men, who had already given their parole not to attempt to escape, to go outside the hospital for that purpose. He refused me, calling me some one of his pet epithets, a God-damned Yankee son of a bitch, and told me that, if I said anything more to him about it, he would take my pass away and put me in the stockade."[201]

Samuel M. Riker, one of Wirz' clerks, testified: "I never saw Captain Wirz commit any acts of cruelty to the prisoners... I never came in direct contact with Captain Wirz until some time in November, 1864, about the 15th, when I was detailed to report to his headquarters. I stayed there from then till I left the prison, which was on the 23rd of March, 1865. I was a clerk at his headquarters; I kept the squad books of the stockade, principally."[202]

Did Wirz actually murder any prisoner in an outright, premeditated manner in front of one or more eyewitnesses? One author described an interesting incident. From his own observation, Doctor T. H. Mann, of the 18th Massachusetts Volunteer Regiment, stated; "On one occasion he rode into the stockade accompanied by two or three

[196] *O.R.*, VII, p. 554.
[197] Chipman, p. 175.
[198] *Ibid.*, p. 65.
[199] Ferguson, p. 84.
[200] Brownell, pp. 19, 20.
[201] Chipman, p. 176.
[202] *Wirz Trial*, p. 369.

attendants also on horseback; the object of his visit was to demand that the chief of the Union League be delivered up to him... Of the crowd that collected about him not one in fifty knew that such a league existed, and of the actual members of the league but few knew who the chief was. Wirz was very soon informed to that effect, which seemed to rouse the demon within him, so that he swore fearfully at the crowd that gathered about him.

**Riddle's photo taken from the North Gate down Broadway.** The mule-drawn ration wagon can be seen with its stacks of cards of cornbread. The slant-roofed sutler's shed can be seen in the background. (Author's Collection)

"He soon turned to retire from the prison, and while nearly within the gateway drew his heavy revolver and shot the whole six barrels into the crowd of emaciated, starving wretches who had collected about him. Without stopping to discover the effects of his shooting, he put spurs to his horse, sprang out through the gate, and galloped away from the stockade. Two men were killed outright by his shots, and several others were wounded."[203]

Captain Davis repudiated this story. "The date of this alleged shooting is not given, Wirz was not accustomed to be accompanied by mounted attendants, and if on any special occasion he was so attended it was in all probability by officers of Gen. Winder's staff or artillery officers, these would certainly have reported such an action on the part of Wirz or anyone else. I cannot believe any such improbable statement. I never heard of it and I was in a position to know of it, had it occurred while I was at Andersonville or temporarily absent. I have written, however, to Capt. W. S. Winder to ask if he ever heard of such an occurrence, and the following is what he says: 'Such a thing could not have occurred without some of the officers of the guard knowing it, and they never would have been willing to have approved of it by their silence.'

"... For such an act to have occurred in such a public place and in such a public manner would have attracted the attention of hundreds of people outside the stockade.

"I can and do most positively assert that I never heard of that case; and I do not hesitate to denounce this charge as a most outrageous and wicked one; and, I do most positively say, that I never heard of Capt. Wirz shooting any prisoner as was charged at his trial."[204]

Jacob D. Brown testified he saw Wirz, in side a sentry-box with a guard, order the guard to kill a man dipping fresh water under the dead-line on about July 27th. He testified that he saw the same incident repeated on or about the middle of August.[205]

**Capt. Wirz Stomping to Death Sergeant S. H. Nelson, of Co. I, 4th Vermont, Dec. 13, 1864**. He was buried in Grave No. 12,283. This vignette was taken from the print by O'Dea.

John A. Cain testified: "He shot a young fellow named William Stewart, a private belonging to the 9th Minnesota infantry. He and I went out of the stockade with a dead body, and after laying the dead body in the dead-house Captain Wirz rode up to us and asked by what authority we were out there or what we were doing there. Stewart said we were there by proper authority. Wirz said no more, but drew a revolver and shot the man. After he was killed the guard took from the body about twenty or thirty dollars, and Wirz took the money from the guard and rode off, telling the guard to take me to prison."[206]

Thomas C. Alcoke testified, according to Spencer: "On one occasion a sick man asked Captain Wirz to let him go outside for some fresh air. Wirz inquired what he meant. Then turning round and saying to him, 'Any air is too good for a damned Yankees,' pulled out his revolver and shot him down. The man died in two hours afterward, and he spoke in condemnation of this act to Wirz, who told him 'he

[203] Mann, p. 610.
[204] S. B. Davis, p. 34.
[205] *Wirz Trial*, p. 79.
[206] *Ibid.*, p. 398.

would put him in the same fix;' he replied that he was not afraid of it. Wirz then called a corporal and two guards, who put a ball and chain upon him. The man who was shot was named, Wright, and belonged to the Eighth Missouri.

"James H. Davidson also saw this deed. He says that 'Wright was sick, and lying upon the ground. He asked Wirz to let him go out for some purpose, when Wirz cursed him and shot him with his revolver, and said 'he was killing more Yankees at Andersonville than Lee was at Richmond.'"[207]

Alcoke, of the 72nd Ohio, testified, in part, that he saw Wirz kill a man. "One day there was a man sitting down, a kind of weakly man. Captain Wirz passed in the stockade, when this man got up and asked him if he could go out to get some fresh air. Captain Wirz asked him what he meant by that. The poor fellow 'wormed' around and said he wanted air. There was some thing said, when Captain Wirz wheeled again, pulled out a revolver and shot him down. This was some part of the summer, two months after I got there. The ball took effect in the breast; he died in about two or three hours afterwards...The man that was shot belonged to the eighth Missouri; they called him 'Red' in the regiment; I could not say what his name was; I knew him at Memphis; I saw the man fall, and I saw the boys look at him; I saw the man drop and he never got up any more. He lay there till the next day; some of the boys went to Captain Wirz and asked him if they could not carry the body out; he said they could. I saw the pistol in the hands of Captain Wirz; I saw him pull it out; they were about four and a half feet apart. This occurred in February, I think; February or June or along in there. I cannot say for certain in what month it was."[208]

Another witness against Wirz was an ex-prisoner from Nashville, Tennessee, who had been sent to Washington by General Thomas. He stated, "I have seen him often at Andersonville, but I know him as the man who shot my comrade, William Stewart." He told of the circumstances surrounding the shooting: "Stewart and I had brought a dead body out to the dead-house without being ordered to do so, when Wirz came up and asked what we were doing there. Stewart replied that we had brought out a dead body. Wirz said it was a lie, that we were trying to make our escape. Stewart said it was not so; we had come out for the purpose he had stated; when Wirz told him if he said that again he would blow his damned brains out. Stewart repeated what he had said before, when Wirz drew his revolver and shot him." He testified that Wirz had been about eight feet from the victim; the bullet struck him in the breast and he survived for less than half an hour.[209]

Spencer told of a couple more murders allegedly committed by Wirz:

"William Harrington was lying upon the ground one day sick, when Wirz [passed by;] Harrington asked him for some materials with which to make a tent. As he proffered his request, Wirz jumped upon him with his heavy-heeled boots several times, and stamped upon his breast, while the poor invalid screamed with agony. 'There, God Damn you! ask me for tents again!' cried Wirz, as blood and froth poured from the wan prisoner's mouth. He was taken to the hospital, and left it only in the dead-wagon."[210]

"On one occasion, as the men were being divided into squads, one of the prisoners, from extreme exhaustion, did not or could not fall in, when Wirz told him, with the usual oath, if he did not 'get into line and stay there, he would beat his brains out!' The man replied that he could not stand up. ''Then lie there, God damn you!' and repeatedly struck him over the head and face with the butt of his revolver. His skull was broken, the dark tide flowing out from an aperture over the right temple, and he died just where he lay."[211]

"It finally came my turn to go for wood. There were six of us picked out to go. One of the six was a very sickly man, and could hardly walk, without carrying a load. He could not be persuaded to let some stronger man take his place, so out we went, sick man and all. We went about half a mile from the pen, and every man went to work picking up his wood. Finally, we started for the stockade; but the sick man could not keep up; he had more wood than he could carry. We went as slow as our guards would let us, in order to give him a chance. Just then Wirz came riding along on his old white horse, and seeing the sick man some twenty yards behind, said, 'Close up there, close up there, you damned Yankee.' The sick man tried to hurry up, but stubbed his toe and down he went, wood and all. Wirz sprang from his horse and ran up to the poor sick soldier and kicked him in the stomach with the heel of his big riding boot, and left him a dead man. 'That is the way I serve you damned Yanks when you don't do as I tell you.' The rest of us went back to the prison pen, sick at heart."[212]

---

[207] Spencer, p. 110.
[208] *Wirz Trial*, p. 67.
[209] Spencer, pp. 111-113.
[210] Spencer, p. 113.
[211] *Ibid.*, pp. 113, 114.
[212] Tyler, pp. 49, 50.

"One day, when the Rebs brought in our meal, an old prisoner managed to steal one of the meal sacks. He stole the sack to make him a shirt. He cut a hole in the bottom for his head, one in each side for his arms. It made the old gentleman quite a shirt. Wirz missed the sack, and refused to issue any more rations till the sack and man were found. He found the man and took him out, and put him in the stocks and left him there all night. In the morning when he went to let him out the man was dead."[213]

William Willis Scott testified as to the cruelty of Wirz: "In the latter part of August, a sick man sitting on a bank, asked Captain Wirz to be sent to the hospital, when the latter cursed the invalid and struck him a violent blow over the head. The man went into his tent and died a day or two after."[214]

Martin E. Hogan testified that he "... saw Captain Wirz take a man by the collar because he could not walk faster; the man was so worn by disease that he could not; throwing the man on his back he stamped upon him with his feet; he saw the man bleeding, and he died a short time afterwards... when the prisoners were being removed from Andersonville to Millen."[215]

Lieutenant Samuel Boyer Davis was ordered, on July 21st, to take charge of the prison at Macon where 1,200 officers were confined. He had been there about 2 weeks when the following incident occurred: "After I had been at Macon a short time, some of the officers who were paroled came to me and said that they had heard that a friend of theirs (a colonel), who was with Stoneman in his raid, and who had been mortally wounded, was in a hospital in Macon, and was very anxious to see one or two of the officers confined in the prison, in order to send his last messages to his wife and family. Upon inquiry, I found the case to be a bona fide one, and I sent the prison Adjutant with the two officers to visit the wounded colonel. The officers were under parole, and I sent no guard, save the adjutant; he to act more as a guide and as protection than anything else. They returned in an hour. The next morning I was relieved by the Colonel commanding the post and returned to Andersonville.

"On my arrival there I asked for a court-martial, but after hearing from the officer commanding at Macon, Gen. Winder refused to call a trial, and he said I had only done what any kind and humane man would have done under the circumstances...

The next day, after the above matter was settled, I was ordered to assist Capt. Wirz, in charge of the prison at Andersonville. This was brought about by Wirz being quite sick. I had only been on duty as above stated for a day or two, when he (Wirz) was taken seriously ill, and I was put in charge in his place... I think it was on the 13th or 14th of August that I relieved Capt. Wirz."[216]

Colonel Fannin testified: "I know that Captain Wirz was sick at Andersonville last summer, and for a time was confined to his house, and did not come to the post. The house at which he was living was, I think, about two miles from Andersonville. I was out once, in company with Dr. White, and Captain Wirz was then confined to his bed. I was going to another place, and was passing Captain Wirz' house with Dr. White; he and I stopped... Captain Wirz was absent from the post at the time the stockade was washed down, and I think that was on Tuesday, the 13th of August..."[217]

Though Wirz' wound in his right forearm continued to ooze through the summer with spicules of bone working their way out, it is unknown what sickness caused Wirz to request a furlough. He seemed to be "out of his head." General Winder, on August 13th, said, "Captain Wirz is very sick, produced entirely by overwork for want of assistance. He ought to have gone to bed two weeks ago, but kept up because he had none to whom the command could be turned over."[218]

Kellogg said, "Capt. Wirz, our inhuman prison commandant, was taken sick about this time, and went to Macon. Various were the wishes of the men as they heard it, but the mildest form they took was, that he might never recover. He was succeeded, temporarily by Lieut. S. B. Davis, and from all that we could learn of him, we thought the change might be much to our advantage, as he would probably be more humane in his treatment of us. He had the reputation of being a good officer among the men who knew him, and the rations which followed his inauguration were certainly larger and better, and indicated a heart little larger than that which dwelt in the bosom of his predecessor. The day before, we only had a little corn-bread, without meat or salt, and now came fresh beef, bacon, beans, bread and molasses."[219]

---

[213] *Ibid.*, p. 53.
[214] Ferguson, p. 85.
[215] *Ibid.*, p. 83.
[216] S. B. Davis, pp. 21, 22.
[217] *Wirz Trial*, p. 437.
[218] *O.R.*, VII, p. 589.
[219] Kellogg, p. 228.

"Lieut. Davis, our new commandant, did institute a better order of things. Our food was better every way, and beside, he issued an order, requiring the prison to be kept clean. The order was posted in different parts of the prison, so that all could see it, and avail themselves of its privileges. He furnished us with the requisite tools to perform the work assigned to us, and it was something so unusual to see our enemies taking even a slight interest in our comfort. We ardently hoped that Capt. Wirz would never make his appearance again, for he would never do as much for us as we were having done then. With his second advent we knew would come anew, misery and starvation, for his active mind would probably devise new methods, while he was lying by, to enhance our sorrow, if he should return."[220]

W. D. Hammack of the 55th Georgia regiment, testified: "I don't remember whether it was just before Davis took command or just after Captain Wirz came back, but he was very weak and we would help him on his horse of evenings when he would start; we would get him on a chair and then help him on his horse...

"I never knew Captain Wirz to shoot or beat a prisoner so that he died while I was there. I never heard of it while I was at Andersonville.

"I know something about Wirz being absent for a time. He left there some time about the last of July; Davis took command some time about the last of July, and Captain Wirz did not return till perhaps the last of August; I will not be positive about the dates; it was the last of July, though, that Davis took command - I think about the last days of July. I saw Captain Wirz in September; he looked feeble and bad. He was in a feeble condition before he gave up as sick. I saw him at his headquarters frequently. He would sit up and attend to his business, and then he had a cot there on which he would lie down; he would lie there some time and then perhaps he would get up and proceed with his business. When he first returned to the stockade after his illness and the prisoners were being removed in September he would sit in a chair and let the prisoners march along, keeping their files dressed so that he could count them; he would sit out in front of his office and count them as they would march by. He would go home in the evening; by evening, I suppose, I mean what you call afternoon here. He would go off about four o'clock. Prisoners would leave after he went away. He came and went in an ambulance for a while. I think it was in September; I cannot say for how long a time; I don't remember. I reckon it was one or two weeks."[221]

Captain J. H. Wright, who was quartermaster of the 55th Georgia, testified about the illness of Wirz: "I know that in September he was feeble, and I had to send him backwards and forwards in an ambulance; the first part of September I think it was. I think he used the ambulance two or three weeks… In September, when Captain Wirz was so feeble, he would generally go home tolerably early in the afternoon; about 3 or 4 o'clock, I suppose."[222]

"I cannot swear certainly what day in the middle of September Captain Wirz was sick and confined to bed. It was when the sailors were sent off. I went out to Captain Wirz' house and saw him in his bed with his wife in the room near him. I asked him in French if he would allow me to go away with the sailors. He told me he could not do it; that he had orders only to send away sailors, white and colored. At that time Captain Wirz was on duty, but Sergeant Smith attended to his duty when Captain Wirz could not come. Captain Wirz was sick two or three days; I think for near three days he did not come to headquarters."[223]

Lieutenant Davis was well-liked by the prisoners and they took advantage of his humanity. "We asked Lieutenant Davis, and he gave us passes so that we could go and bathe in a creek that was there. After Captain Wirz got well he took away those passes from us, and told us that he would allow no Yankee to have any privilege whatsoever. Those were his words."[224]

Eventually the inevitable happened: "The clerk in the office of the Prison Commandant, came in on a pass, bringing with him the unwelcome intelligence that Captain Wirz, our old tormentor, was back again from Macon."[225]

Besides the insinuations of his alleged robberies of newly-arriving prisoners, a man testified about the possible theft of some of the prisoners' rations. Samuel M. Riker, Wirz' clerk, testified: "I know of rations being exchanged. Once in February, I think, Captain Wirz laid down a lot of pork of his own. It spoiled in the curing, and he sent it to the commissary, and received in return an equal amount of good beef, which was the prisons' rations. I ate some of it myself, and it made me sick, it was so much tainted."[226] Riker continued: "Duncan's full name was, I think, James W. Duncan. He was on duty there in more than one capacity, I suppose. He had first charge of the bakery and cook-

[220] *Ibid.*, p. 232.
[221] *O.R.*, VII, pp. 502, 503.
[222] *Wirz Trial*, p. 483.
[223] *Ibid.*, p. 528.
[224] *Ibid.*, p. 348.
[225] Kellogg, p. 236.
[226] *Wirz Trial*, p. 369.

house. He had charge of issuing rations there and cooking them, and issuing them to the prisoners. He was also a government detective at the post of Andersonville, under the direct control of Captain Wirz. Duncan and Bowens [sic] and Humes, who were all connected with that duty, lived a short distance from the cook-house, and the rations used by them were taken from the prisoners' rations to a great extent. I know that meat was taken to their house in large quantities, and I have heard that there were quantities of it found in the cellar after they left the place. I saw the meat taken there myself. Fresh beef was not always issued, and he could have better quality for his own use by preserving it. I never knew him to take anything but rations. I have known a number of instances where he has been bribed to let men go away from the prison in squads, leaving on parole for the north, for a certain remuneration, taking watches and money, and such like valuables."[227]

Captain James W. Armstrong, a resident of Macon, Georgia, was stationed twice at Andersonville; the first time was from the 31st of March until he left on the 1st day of August. He was there again from the 10th of December until the end of the war. His duties were to receive stores and to issue them to the prisoners and garrison troops. "I issued those rations until July 14th to Captain R. B. Winder, quartermaster; after that time to Captain Wirz. The requisition from Captain Wirz to me was the ordinary provision return, known as form 13. Captain Wirz would generally furnish me with the number of rations… In fact it took nearly all day, and very often quite all day, to get it out - I mean to haul it away from the commissary building. The requisitions were generally made by Captain Wirz between 11 and 12 o'clock in the morning… I was troubled very much for storage room and could not accumulate a stock on hand. At first I occupied a room some 70 feet by 30, until some time in July; after that I occupied a house, I suppose 130 by 30." Captain Armstrong left there, sick, on the 1st of August. Major Proctor took over his duties at that time. Armstrong came back on the 21st of August, but soon left again and remained away until the 10th of December, when he took charge of the commissary department again.[228]

General Winder, on June 22nd, in a letter to General Cooper, described Dick Winder's chief assistant, Private W. F. Butler: "This man is detailed for the quartermaster at this post and his services are utterly indispensable here. The quartermaster must have some confidential man in his office; otherwise, he could do no outdoor work. Having charge of the prison at Macon, as well as this post, he must have some one in the office he can trust. The place of Butler cannot be supplied here, as there is no population in the vicinity, and a haphazard detail will not answer, as the quartermaster must necessarily sometimes trust him with money. I am absolutely obliged to detain this man until you can be heard from, and I earnestly request that the detail be indefinitely made… Butler is the only detailed man in the quartermaster's department at this post."[229]

The following incident, related by S. Boyer Davis, occurred in August and is self-explanatory: "Some of the prisoners came to me one morning and said that one of the distributors, Staunton by name, had badly beaten one of the prisoners, because he had attempted either to steal an extra allowance or had terribly abused him (Staunton) about the distribution of provisions. They assured me it was not Staunton's fault, that he had only done his duty; but they also said it would be very unsafe for him (Staunton) to be left inside the prison, as the worst element of the men had threatened to kill him if possible. I was unwilling to act in the matter unadvisedly, or, I should say, without first knowing the whole state of each side of the case, and at the same time I did not care to investigate it myself. At that time the better class of prisoners had arranged a court for trial of such offences; a court similar to the one which in June had tried, convicted and executed six of their comrades for murder and robbery. I therefore told the prisoners they must try Staunton themselves, and if they cleared him I would see he was not injured; while if, after a fair trial, they found him guilty, I would stand by the findings of the court. In order that the man (Staunton) might not be injured before trial, I took him outside of the prison and kept him under guard until next morning, when he was returned to the custody of the prisoner's court for trial. After a day's sitting the court sent me word that they had fully investigated the trouble and that Staunton had only done his duty. The feeling, however, of the rough element of the prisoners was decidedly against him, and it was asserted that if he was cleared by the court that he would be killed by the prisoners. After his being cleared, the court was afraid to make public their finding, less a riot be brought about, and I was sent for to come to the gate of the prison, and told of the finding of the court, and requested to take Staunton out, as the court and its officers, while they could protect the prisoner for the present, were unwilling to take the risk of keeping the man in the prison after night, and when it should be known that he had been cleared of the charge. This risk was increased, as the man who had been beaten was badly hurt, and his friends were hourly growing more and more clamorous about the matter. I went into the stockade myself, against the advice of my in-

---

[227] *Ibid.*

[228] *Ibid.* pp. 659, 660.

[229] *O.R.*, VII, pp. 395, 396.

formant, rode to the court tent, and placing Staunton in front of my horse started for the gate, I was forced several times to stop and demand of the surging crowd passage-way for the prisoner. Finally we got to the gate, and Staunton was afterwards kept outside."[230]

The following was an interesting incident of a wife's visit to the pen to see her husband, who was a prisoner. There was one man in the prison who was a pro-Union Georgian. In 1861, the man, named Hirst, went North, leaving his wife in Georgia, and joined a western regiment. In one of the battles between Sherman and Johnston, he was captured. After having arrived at Andersonville, he was recognized by one member of the Georgia Reserves while carrying out one of the dead. From this friendly guard Hirst learned about his wife after 3 years. It was arranged this guard would help get a letter to his wife, telling her of his imprisonment. A few days later, this guard tossed a letter to the man from his wife by hiding the letter in a ball of clay. Two days later, the woman came and asked Wirz to let her see her husband. Wirz allowed her to stand 30 paces outside the gate, where her husband stood, but neither was allowed to speak. They did, however, speak each others' names lovingly when they first sighted each other. Then the visit was abruptly ended with the wife being sent away and the husband sent back into the pen. The next day, she came again with clothing and some provisions to ease his stay. Wirz refused to allow her to give him these items and she was ordered never to come back again. She was escorted to the edge of the post. The husband was then brought before Wirz, who tried to entice him to join the Confederate army. When he refused to do this, he was bucked and gagged and "... locked in the dungeon, being brought out and maliciously punished at intervals for several days." On the recommendations of the surgeons, he was returned to the pen. During the dispersal of the prisoners in September, he escaped from a train for parts unknown.[231]

As early as June 7th, the prisoners asked for permission and for materials with which to construct shelters for their sick. They were refused. However, three weeks later the authorities said that they were in the process of constructing more sheds for the sick prisoners. Five sheds were built near the north wall, commencing in the latter part of June, in an attempt to ameliorate the prisoners' plight. Though crude, consisting only of a roof supported by poles, they were at least an attempt to remedy one of the many factors causing the prisoners' suffering.

On the 7th of June, Northrop and 29 others went to the gate and asked permission to go out under guard to bring in poles and wood for making shelters for the sick and dying, who were lying in the streets and swamp. "We were refused, harshly cursed and ordered away by Captain Wirz."[232]

As early as June 30, Doctor White said that barracks for the prisoners were being constructed. He did say it was "... an immense task and will not soon be completed."[233]

Five two-story barracks, or sheds, were built within the pen on the north portion parallel to the north wall. "They were merely roofs on boards, placed upon posts, at the distance of seven feet from the ground."[234] They were built just before the dispersion of the prisoners, beginning in September. Kellogg said that, near the 8th of August, the first barracks' frame was brought into the prison, after having been assembled outside, "... ready to be put up very soon."[235] They measured 134 feet by 20 feet. These sheds had no sides, no floor on the ground floor, and no partitions within. Each shed would, later, sleep about one detachment of 270 sick men when the prison held only the sick. There was a pit adjacent to each shed for use as a latrine.

Hamlin said the sheds were, "... not commenced until late in the term of its occupation, too late to render much service."[236] Northrop said, on August 10th, "... for several days barracks have been in course of erection in the north part, the work being done by our men on parole who bring the lumber in on their shoulders. They are allowed an extra ration and occasionally opportunities to trade for their benefit."[237]

"On the north side of the prison, good and substantial barrack accommodations were begun, and the sheds were nearly completed when the work was stopped on account of prison gangrene and scurvy attacking the prisoners, resulting in such great mortality that the post was afterwards abandoned, that is, for the regular reception of prisoners."[238] "The authorities brought in lumber and erected five sheds, each one about fifty feet long and twelve feet wide. These consisted of a frame eight feet high, above which was a roof. There were two floors in each of these, the first

---

[230] S. B. Davis, pp. 29, 30.
[231] Northrop, pp. 100, 101.
[232] *Ibid.*, p. 73.
[233] *O.R.*, VII, p. 427.
[234] Hamlin, p. 57.
[235] Kellogg, p. 209.
[236] Hamlin, pp. 56, 57.
[237] Northrop, p. 103.
[238] Stevenson, p. 21.

floor eighteen inches from the ground and the second three feet above the first.

These sheds were divided into wards, each ward containing sixty men, it was the duty of the ward master to direct and assist the nurses in drawing rations and distributing to the sick and to do all that he could to relieve their suffering until death came."[239]

Doctor Stevenson, Surgeon-in-charge of Post, sent a report for the month ending October 31st, through Doctor White, who then was "... chief surgeon and inspector of hospital, Georgia and Alabama" to General Winder. In this report, Doctor Stevenson said he had "... succeeded in establishing a receiving and distributing division inside the stockade. By this plan a great many cases are disposed of without sending them to the general hospital. I am completing the sheds as rapidly as circumstances will permit - some difficulty has been experienced in obtaining lumber and bricks, but by sufficient energy this will be obviated. The buildings for drugs, commissaries, bedding, &c., is about completed... Wells are being rapidly sunk in the prison hospital. A good and sufficient supply of water is obtained about forty feet from the surface of the ground. I would respectfully urge the necessity of putting a stockade around the hospital buildings.[240]

As the summer of 1864 concluded, many dynamic changes had taken place at Andersonville. The intolerable heat, accompanied by mosquitoes, flies, and maggots, made the pen a death trap. The advancement of Federal cavalry in Georgia was relentless. The trains bringing "fresh fish" arrived daily. Wagonloads of the dead left the pen with cargoes to fill the gaping, slit trenches. Support from Richmond, minimal at best, diminished further. The care of prisoners was never very high on the Confederate list of priorities. Richmond's energy was channeled towards feeding and supporting the ever-shrinking war machine. It became obvious, to the authorities in Georgia, that they must either expand the prison or, better yet, build a new prison that was remote from Federal pressure. This latter alternative was to become the remedy of choice.

---

[239] Lyons, pp. 72, 73.
[240] *O.R.*, VII, p. 1076.

## *Chapter Ten*

# The Fall of 1864 Including The Dispersal of the Prisoners

*"For God's sake send me $100,000 for prisoners of war and $75,000 for pay of officers and troops stationed here... I have only had $75,000 since 1st of April."*

Captain Richard Bayly Winder
July 18th

As the war progressed, it became increasingly clear to the Confederate authorities that a successful outcome to the war would not be attained. The burden of the growing number of prisoners started to take its toll as the limited resources of the Confederacy became exhausted. The South had barely enough food to feed its own soldiers; the dwindling food supply was distributed by Commissary-General Lucius Northrop, who thought that the necessity of feeding Yankee prisoners ranked just slightly above that of feeding livestock. General Winder, by the middle of the summer, became aware that, with the encroachment of the Federal troops, he would soon need to move the prisoners under his care at Andersonville. General Winder sent a small contingent of officers, headed by his son, Sid Winder, to find a suitable location for a new prison and to supervise its construction. The money required to pay for the establishment of this new prison and for the maintenance of the other prisoner-of-war camps was always reluctantly appropriated.

The post at Andersonville always seemed to have a very low priority for funding. Captain Richard B. Winder was almost continually begging for funds from Richmond to run the post. Lieutenant J. H. Wright, quartermaster of the 55th Georgia regiment made a requisition, in April, for $75,000 to pay the troops that were at Andersonville. In the Confederate army, it was the quartermasters who also served as paymasters. The money was sent through Dick Winder for Captain Wright, but Dick Winder used the money for expenses incurred in the early operation of the post. Dick Winder was told, by the Quartermaster-General, that all quartermasters in the vicinity had been ordered to fill any orders he might requisition. Dick Winder wrote, on July 18th: "For God's sake send me $100,000 for prisoners of war and $75,000 for pay of officers and troops stationed here... I have only had $75,000 since 1st of April."[1]

He said, on September 3rd: "On May 27, pay fund, $73,000 has been received; on August 1, quartermaster's funds, $75,000 has not been received; on August 15, quartermasters funds, $10,000 has been received and devoted to purchase of greenbacks per order of Quartermaster-General, and the greenbacks forwarded by express; on August 3, $50,000 has not been received, and when it is, is to be turned over to Henry De Veuve, bonded agent for the establishment of a shoe shop at Oglethorpe, Ga., so you will perceive that I am still without any funds whatever, and my credit is gone...Two hundred and fifty thousand dollars would relieve me for a time, and my estimates cover that amount and more. Of course I am speaking of this in addition to the $75,000 quartermaster's funds of August 1, which I am expecting. If I do not get this money I really do not know what I shall do, except to ask to be relieved from this post. You must recollect that I am in a strange country, only relying on myself, and can get no assistance... I

[1] *O.R.*, VII, p. 473.

would willingly purchase the greenbacks for you, but as the Commissary-General has fixed the price at $4.50 for $1, I cannot get them for less."[2]

On several occasions, the Confederate authorities told the prisoners, falsely, that release was imminent. The reason for doing this was to keep the prisoners calm and placated. General Winder always, almost to the point of being paranoid, feared an uprising, especially when the ratio of prisoners to guards became very large. Of course, just the nature of the exchange negotiations would explain some of these disappointments of the prisoners. "The rebel Quartermaster told us on the 7th of August, that he had seen a dispatch from the Confederate Government to General Winder, ordering him to commence paroling the prisoners at once."[3]

Near the 1st of September, while Sherman was in the process of capturing Atlanta, the Confederates decided to remove all ambulatory prisoners from Andersonville to a safer locale and to turn it into a prison hospital camp. They had just built five sheds near the north wall; each of these was capable of holding a whole detachment of sick prisoners. All prisoners not sick were ordered out of the barracks so the sick could be placed in them.

Andrew J. Spring testified about General Winder: "I saw him at one time come down there about the 1st of September with an order; he went into a sentry-box and read the order to our men. It was to the effect that there was a general exchange to commence… They were exchanged from one stockade to another, that was all."[4]

On Tuesday, the 6th of September, a Confederate officer came inside and, calling all the sergeants of the detachments together, made the following announcement. He said, "Prisoners, I am instructed by General Winder to tell you that a general exchange of prisoners has been agreed upon; your vessels are now waiting for you at Savannah and Charleston. Detachments, from one to ten, will leave tomorrow morning."[5] In fact, they were told to be ready to leave anytime after midnight.

The thought of finally going home caused great excitement and joy throughout the pen. Some fainted. "One man who had pined to almost helplessness, on hearing the news leaped to his feet, shouted, clapped his hands and fell dead."[6] "Some of the sick felt so joyfull that they died fore joy. The excitement was to great fore them. They could not stand it."[7] Those too sick to travel, pathetically, had to be left behind. Tearful farewells were heard throughout the prison. The sick would tell their comrades who were leaving to look up their families when they returned to the "Land of the Free." Those leaving gave all their valuable belongings to those remaining behind, in the mistaken belief the pans, eating utensils, and blankets would not be needed.

General Winder said his guards at Andersonville had to pull double shifts as a result of Generals Samuel Jones and Lafayette McLaws keeping his guards. He was having difficulty moving the prisoners as instructed by the Secretary of War.

"Close to our quarters twelve of them, belonging to one regiment, quartered. They dug a hole in the ground about eighteen inches deep, and banked up the loose earth to keep the water from flowing into it. They had been left in possession of a few blankets, and with these they formed a roof. After it was finished it looked comfortable compared to some of the lodging places which the other boys had, but it was undoubtedly a mistake to them to dig in the ground as they did. Death soon came among them, and one by one they fell victims to the fell destroyer, until only one remained of the twelve stout, hearty men, who less than three months before had entered the prison; and he was so sick when we were removed to Millen prison that he could not go along. Thinking we were going home, he made frantic efforts to get up and accompany us, but all in vain; he was too far gone.

"The name of this poor unfortunate, I think, was William Langdon, and he was from the interior of New York State. He had been in the army but a few short months when he was captured and taken to Andersonville. In conversation with him one day, he informed me that he had received a letter from home a few days before his capture, informing him that he was the father of twin daughters; and he often talked about them, and told us how anxious he was to get home to see them. When we left he wept and begged piteously to be taken along, but we were obliged to leave him."[8]

The men gathered their few belongings and soon lines formed within the pen near the South Gate, the Gate of Death, and expectant whispers were heard to the effect that the lines were moving. Some men succeeded in "flanking out" by taking the identities of the dead or of those unable to make the trek who were from the lower-numbered de-

---

[2] *Ibid.*, p. 762.
[3] Kellogg, p. 208.
[4] *Wirz Trial*, p. 114.
[5] Boggs, p. 55.
[6] Northrop, p. 124.
[7] Blessing diary.
[8] Urban, pp. 371, 372.

tachments. Ross said his detachment was formed into 4 companies or 4 car loads to a detachment. It can be assumed some of the more well-off prisoners bought or attempted to buy their way out with these first few detachments. Outside, the men were allowed greater freedom than usual on the short, quarter-mile march to the railroad station. "Just before we got to the depot, the train stopped and there were fifteen or twenty women lined up with baskets of provisions. That incident I will never forget. The women came to the cars with their baskets saying, 'Men divide it up. We can't feed all, we wish we could'"[9] "As we were waiting for the train a boy came along selling biscuits. I asked him how he would trade his biscuits for a button, so I gave him five buttons for five biscuits."[10]

Since the men had been falsely told, on other occasions, that an exchange agreement had been reached, they were dubious even on their way to the trains. A Confederate officer assured them they were, indeed, on their way home. That they were on their way to freedom at last was reinforced by the fact that there were assigned only two guards on each car of the train. The men thought they would have placed a larger guard over them if they were only going to transfer them to another prison.

Kellogg described the actual embarkation this way: "As we marched out of the gate, we were divided into squads of sixty men each, and marched over to the depot. The sick ones were placed between the strongest of us, who bore them up, and in this manner we wended our way slowly along the road. When we were passing the headquarters of Captain Wirz, he cried out to us, 'You'll never come back there again!' Upon our arrival at the depot, we were immediately loaded into the cars, a squad of sixty in each one, with two guards upon the top. We found placed for us inside, some corn-bread and bacon, which we were told was our allowance for two days, and also one or two wooden buckets in which we were to get our supply of water at the different stopping-places. We immediately divided and distributed the ration, and had barely time to fill one of our buckets with water when the cheering sound of the locomotive's whistle was heard, and we were off."[11] Kellogg said over twelve hundred men went out before sunset. Urban said on the 7th of September, six detachments or about 2,000 men left, supposedly for home.

On the 8th, at midnight, a "large number" of prisoners were removed from the pen. Later that day, some men were returned because of a lack of space in the box-cars, to await a later train. On the 9th, 10th, 11th, 12th, and the 13th, more men were taken out and, by then, the North slope was beginning to thin out rapidly and looked "quite bare."

On September 12th, the Surgeon-General, Samuel P. Moore, sent a letter to Surgeon White at Andersonville and ordered him to assign medical officers to accompany the prisoners as the prisoners were relocated. All the sick who could safely be moved, should be so moved. The medical officers were to accompany the sick and Doctor White was to visit each place and see that the sick were properly cared for. He was to "... use all the means for their comfort that the Government can furnish."[12]

After arriving at Andersonville on July 28th, Blessing left, on September 13th, for exchange. He arrived at Rough and Ready, Georgia, on the 22nd after having been given only a small piece of cornbread and a small piece of bacon the night he left Andersonville. Blessing and 468 others were exchanged there near Atlanta.

One of the trains which left on the 13th, "ran off the track," killing and wounding a large number of men.

On the 13th of September, Vawter flanked out by "... going out on a dead man's name." "At about four o'clock p. m., a heavy guard marched down to the South Gate, and called for the detachments that had been notified that morning. Nine hundred and sixty men were taken out and marched to the depot. There we waited till sundown, when our train backed in. We were put in twelve boxcars - eighty men to a car!

"Two days rations of corn bread and bacon were put in each car; three companies of guards were distributed over the train, most of them on top of the cars. The officers that were detailed to go to the caboose, and the train started out just as twilight deepened into night.

"We ran six or seven miles... ...running down grade in a cut, when, suddenly, the car seemed to be lifted several feet high and dropped. It came down with a crash. Part of the timbers of the floor broke upward into the middle of the car, hurling its mass of living freight toward the ends. At the same time two corners were crushed in and two burst outward. For a few seconds there was a loud crashing of timber; then groans, shrieks and wails, and the noise of escaping steam, were the only sounds.

"The engine lay in the ditch, with its head buried in the bank. The first three cars lay over against the bank just behind it, and were not much damaged. The fourth lay with one end against the rear of these, and the other end on the track; it having stopped the momentum of the train in that position was what crushed it in the peculiar manner

[9] Clifton, p. 13.

[10] Lyons, p. 78.

[11] Kellogg, pp. 283, 284.

[12] *O.R.*, VII, p. 817.

described. The fifth was the worse wreck of all, the sixth having telescoped it from end to end. The forward end of the sixth was crushed in; the rest stood on the track undamaged. The guard were all in confusion and out of place. The moans of the dying and shrieks of the wounded sounded a good distance off.

"Men were getting out of all the cars. The guard recovered from its panic, and had formed a line around the wreck. We took out ninety-eight Yanks and twenty-four rebs, who were badly wounded, and twenty-six Yanks and eight rebs, dead; a total of thirty-four killed, and one hundred and twenty-two badly hurt.

"Rebels and Yanks worked together till the wounded were all out of the wreck, which was probably about midnight. We did not get all the dead out till daylight next morning. A construction train came down next morning, unloaded its gang of men, took up the wounded, and returned to Andersonville. It returned about noon, and getting the debris out of the way, and getting all the cars that could be run on the track, they took us back to the pen.

"When the train came back after taking the wounded, they brought the bloodhounds and took a circuit around the wreck before we left."[13]

Doctor Jones arrived the day after the wreck, which occurred about 3 miles from the prison and less than 2 hours after the prisoners had left the stockade heading for Millen.[14] Jones noted: "The ratio of mortality continued to increase during September; for, notwithstanding the removal of half the entire number of prisoners during the early portion of the month, seventeen hundred and fifty-seven deaths were registered from September 1st to the 21st, and the largest number of deaths upon any one day occurred during this month, on the 16th, Viz., one hundred and nineteen."[15]

On the 14th, the men in the pen received the unwelcome news that the prisoners who had belonged to Sherman's army were to be sent away before any of the prisoners who had been held longer. Thirty men belonging to Sherman's army left on the 17th for that army. Word was sent in, on the 18th, that 1,100 more men were to leave on the 19th. The shipments of prisoners were stopped for a few days for no apparent reason. The prisoners were then also beginning to hear rumors that a new prison was being built 5 miles from Millen, toward Augusta.

The first frost of the year occurred on the 25th of September. On the 27th, three more detachments left and the following day "some more" left. About Sunday the 25th, "... 4 detachments and all marines and sailors [were] taken out."[16] By the middle of October, there were only about 5,000 men left at Andersonville within the stockade and these were ordered to move to the south side of the pen.[17] "None but the sick and wounded, together with the attendants, nurses and medical officers, and a small guard, were left at Andersonville. The post was then placed in the command of Colonel Gibbs, with R. B. Thomas, A.A.G., Major G. M. Proctor, and Captain J. W. Armstrong having charge of the commissary department. Captain Henry Wirz had the same control over the discipline of the hospital that he had formerly held over the prison; Surgeon R. R. Stevenson was placed in chief control of the medical department, with some thirty assistant-surgeons and contract doctors."[18]

After Captain R. B. Winder left with General Winder, he was succeeded by Lieutenant J. H. Wright of the 55th Georgia regiment as acting post quartermaster. He was on duty at Andersonville from February, 1864, to February, 1865. Dick Winder left Captain Wright a few old horses, ambulances, and wagons, but Captain Wright had to secure transportation for hauling through his own ingenuity. "I got a few old broken-down mules from the convalescent camp; they generally commenced dying in a few days. I had no difficulty in getting axes when I made requisition for them. Captain Wirz made requisition on me for axes, and I had no difficulty in getting them. I think I left seventy-five axes there."[19]

Captain J. H. Wright testified: "I went to Captain R. B. Winder every week, and made effort to get lumber from him and General Winder. The millers would not let him have any lumber, because they said they had furnished the post with a great deal of lumber that had never been paid for, and they could not carry on their mills unless they got pay for their lumber. They would not let him have it. I had a quantity of nails on hand, but they were tens and twelves; they were all too large for nailing boards. I made efforts to get some of smaller size, and I tried to swap these large-sized nails for smaller ones; but I could not find smaller nails anywhere. I used the tens for building the hospital. I never tried to obtain any other kind, I had plenty on hand of these sizes, tens and twelves."[20]

---

[13] Vawter, pp. 72-78.
[14] *O.R.*, VIII, p. 619.
[15] Dowling, p. 218.
[16] Stephen, p. 22.
[17] Stevenson, p. 25.
[18] *Ibid.*
[19] Chipman, p. 158.
[20] *Wirz Trial*, p. 480.

"The nineteenth of October we received orders to leave Andersonville… we hobbled over to the station. Those that were not able to walk were hauled on lumber wagons. While we were waiting for the train, a rebel amused himself by throwing yams into the crowd of prisoners, to see them scramble and fall over each other in trying to get one. That was fun for the rebels but was life for us, and he kept it up for quite a while. Finally, the train arrived; we were put on board..."[21]

Because of the colder weather, when the men moved across to the south side, they almost invariably dug into the ground to conserve heat. On the 1st of November, some of these were ordered out of the prison, into cars, and were taken to the newly-completed prison at Millen.

Thus, during the fall evacuation, most of the prisoners were sent to Charleston, but others were sent to Millen, Savannah, and Florence. Some were sent to Macon for a few hours, then on to Millen and Augusta. There, they were given food and water by the men, women, and children of Augusta. The humane efforts of the family of Mrs. J. B. O'Donnell was especially helpful to the men.[22] The prisoners left the next day for Charleston and the "race-course" just outside of that city.

Dufur was a member of one of the first six detachments which left Andersonville and sent to Savannah. They arrived at about midnight and were taken from the cars and marched about 100 yards to a small, ploughed field. There they were kept until morning. The next day, they were again loaded into box-cars and taken to the old race course at Charleston.[23] Brownell was one of about 1,000 prisoners who were put into the jail yard at Savannah. "The ground within the jail wall had been used during the summer for a garden, and some cabbage stumps were left standing; these, with half the weeds and grass in the garden, we cooked for greens. A large rat was seen to run under a pile of lumber in the yard, and a dozen men soon had the lumber pulled over, and they caught ten fine large rats; these were dressed, and our native-born Yankees indulged in a dish of rat soup. A few days after this a large dog came into the yard with some of the visitors, and he was killed and concealed until night, then cooked and eaten. I did not eat any of his flesh, but those that did said it was as good as mutton."[24]

Another group of prisoners, which included John Urban, left Andersonville in early September and was taken to Macon at about 10 o'clock that night; they stayed there 5 hours until the train left for Savannah at 3 in the morning. The prisoners arrived there at about 6 o'clock the same evening and marched the short distance to the new, 10-acre "bull-pen," as some of the prisoners called it.[25] Lieutenant Samuel Boyer Davis, then commandant at Savannah, initiated an interesting method of detecting tunnels. He had a heavily-laden cart drawn by a mule around the deadline so that a wheel of the cart or a mule's leg would drop into the tunnel. The people of the city lined both sides of the street to watch this grim procession. The rations were rather skimpy the first day but, on the second day, they received the best rations some of the men had ever received, consisting of "… one-half pint of good corn-meal, one-half pint of boiled rice, one-fourth pound beef, salt, molasses," and a most welcome, small piece of soap, the first in four months.[26] The pen was rather small compared to Andersonville and contained only a few thousand men. It rained on the 2nd, 3rd, 4th, 5th, and 6th of September. Urban thought there was a rather large group of Unionists in Savannah. The weather became a lot colder after the 7th. Yellow fever was also raging in Savannah and soon attacked those within the pen. The temperature changes would soon begin to cause that disease to diminish. The doctors did not know this was due to the death of the carrier, the *Aedes aegypti* mosquito.

Just after noon on the 12th of October, the prisoners marched down to the depot and were loaded into box-cars. It was during this march to the depot that a Confederate officer, probably Lieutenant Davis, began to beat the sick who could not keep up the pace. It is not known if this was Samuel Boyer Davis, but it probably was. He used a large stick or club of wood, and "… commenced to beat the lingering men in a most brutal manner over the head and shoulders, in several cases knocking them down with such violence that they could not get up. A number of citizens who witnessed the brutal act, and even a few of his own men, commenced to cry 'Shame!' and the cowardly scoundrel, intimidated I suppose by them, stopped his beating, but kept cursing us until we were loaded in the cars.

"A large crowd had gathered around the train and we soon found that the blacks, and also a considerable number of the whites, sympathized with us; and had the brutal officer who had charge of the train let the people help us, we would have received substantial aid before we left the city. Just before our departure a beautiful lady, accompa-

---

21 Helwig, p. 44.
22 Kellogg, p. 286.
23 Dufur, p. 135.
24 Brownell, p. 26.
25 Tyler, p. 43.
26 Urban, p. 428.

nied by a black woman, who was carrying a large bundle of clothing, came to the car for the purpose of giving it to the prisoners. The brutal, pompous officer mentioned before, came riding up to put a stop to it. The lady seeing the officer approaching, and knowing she would not have time to distribute the clothing, ordered her servant to throw them into one of the cars. The colored woman trembled with fear, and appeared to be in doubt as to what to do - no doubt wishing to obey her mistress, and yet too much afraid of the rebel officer to do so - when the lady seized the bundle and threw it into the cars. The enraged officer called on one of his men to fire on the determined woman; but the guard made no effort to obey the brutal order, and the noble woman, who was as cool and collected as if in her reception-room at home, gave the officer a look of contempt and defiance, which said as plain as words, 'Fire if you dare!' and walked away."[27] The prisoners were loaded into common box-cars with a guard at each door and four or five of them riding on the top; they proceeded to Millen.

The men became very depressed and despondent when they ended up at Savannah and not on their way to freedom.

At a mass meeting held September 28th, 1864, by the Federal prisoners confined at Savannah, Ga., it was unanimously agreed that the following resolutions be sent to the President of the United States, in the hope that he might thereby take such steps as in his wisdom he may think necessary for our speedy exchange or parole.

> "*Resolved,* That while we would declare our unbounded love for the Union, for the home of our fathers, and for the graves of those we venerate, we would beg most respectfully that our situation as prisoners be diligently inquired into, and every obstacle consistent with the honor and dignity of the Government at once removed.
>
> "*Resolved,* That while allowing the Confederate authorities all due praise for the attention paid to prisoners, numbers of our men are daily consigned to early graves, in the prime of manhood, far from home and kindred, and this is not caused intentionally by the Confederate Government, but by force of circumstances; the prisoners are obliged to go without shelter, and, in a great portion of cases, without medicine.
>
> "*Resolved,* That, whereas, ten thousand of our brave comrades have descended into an untimely grave within the last six months, and as we believe their death was caused by the difference of climate, the peculiar kind and insufficiency of food, and lack of proper medical treatment, and whereas those difficulties still remain, we would declare as our firm belief, that unless we are speedily exchanged, we have no other alternative but to share the lamentable fate of our comrades. Must this thing still go on? Is there no hope?
>
> "*Resolved,* That, whereas, the cold and inclement season of the year is fast approaching, we hold it to be our duty as soldiers and citizens of the United States, to inform our Government that the majority of our prisoners are without proper clothing, in some cases being almost naked, and are without blankets to protect us from the scorching sun by day or the heavy dews by night, and we would most respectfully request the Government to make some arrangement whereby we can be supplied with these, to us, necessary articles.
>
> "*Resolved,* That, whereas, the term of service of many of our comrades have expired, they, having served truly and faithfully for the term of their several enlistments, would most respectfully ask their Government, are they to be forgotten? Are past services to be ignored? Not having seen their wives and little ones for over three years, they would most respectfully, but firmly request the Government to make some arrangements whereby they can be exchanged or paroled.
>
> "*Resolved,* That, whereas, in the fortune of war, it was our lot to become prisoners , we have suffered patiently, and are still willing to suffer, if by so doing we can benefit the country; but we must most respectfully beg to say, that we are not willing to suffer to further the ends of any party or clique to the detriment of our honor, our families, and our country, and we beg that this affair be explained to us, that we may continue to hold the Government in that respect which is necessary to made a good citizen and soldier.
>
> P. Bradley
> Chairman of Committee on Behalf of Prisoners"[28]

When the prisoners were being transferred from Savannah to Millen, one man jumped through an open box car door and made off through the countryside. "He came to a large sweet-potato patch, and after digging out as many as he could eat, he moved on until daylight, when he hid himself in a wood. Sometime in the afternoon, he discovered that he was being pursued by bloodhounds; and now, thoroughly alarmed, he made off. He climbed a tree and

---

[27] *Ibid.*, pp. 432, 433.
[28] *O.R.*, VII, p. 889.

waited for the appearance of his pursuers. The dogs soon reached his hiding-place, and directly after their owners, who were mounted. They commanded him to come down, and he obeyed, not knowing what was in store for him.

"He had, however, fallen into better hands than he had expected, and they treated him kindly. On the way going to the railroad station, from where he was sent to prison, they let him dig up as many sweet-potatoes as he could carry; and when he came into prison he had a string tied around his pantaloons and his shirt filled with them."[29]

Lyons stayed at Savannah for 13 days and was then carried to Millen, about 70 miles northwest from Savannah.

**Lieut. Samuel Boyer Davis devised this method of detecting tunnels** - This was used at Savannah but not used at Andersonville. A heavily-laden mule cart made a daily circuit of the deadline to find any tunnels. (McElroy)

The prisoners were told that, because the people of Charleston were so incensed by the shelling of their beautiful city, extra guards would be necessary to protect them from the population. The prisoners were, for the most part, not greeted with the wrath of the people, but by their friendly gestures, especially by the women. They secretly passed vegetables, clothing, and Confederate money to the prisoners. The prisoners disembarked from their trains in the center of the city and marched a half-mile to the outskirts to an old racetrack called Washington Park, by the side of the Ashley River. They were kept inside of a deadline which had been marked off by a Confederate soldier driving a horse, which plowed a single furrow.

Dufur said: "The first three days we were in Charleston we camped at the water's edge, and could plainly see Fort Sumter and the Island from which our men were bombarding the city... While occupying a vacant lot as our temporary camping ground we were allowed to go into the water, and there was not one minute during the daytime that there were not from twenty-five to two hundred men wading in the water hunting for oysters. They would wade nearly to their arm-pits, and when their bare feet came in contact with the coveted prize, and it was too far below the surface to reach with the hand, then down went the man out of sight, and up came the oyster... I found 23 which I kept in a hat... At night, we fell back from the water's edge and a guard was posted between us and the water. One day, a piece of square timber, some three feet long and 12 or 14 inches square, was floating around... the boys pushed it through the water at play. A man from Wisconsin hid his head behind it and struck out for Morris Island that night."[30] Whether he reached his destination is unknown.

There, 7,000 or 8,000 prisoners were guarded by the 5th Georgia regiment. Kellogg said "... over six thousand." The guard force was commanded by Lieutenant Colonel Iverson. "The race-course upon which we were camped, was a broad, grassy flat, just outside the city, but commanding a view of its houses and buildings. The track was grown over with grass, and the judges' stand looked very rickety, indeed, hardly able to stand by itself. The large building formerly used as a stand for spectators, was now occupied by Col. Daniels, of the 5th Georgia regiment, and Lieut. Col. Iverson; the latter in command over us."[31] They were a more intelligent and better-equipped guard force than any at Andersonville. They had seen combat and veterans usually showed mutual respect for their combat-seasoned captives. They bragged that they had "... always been at the front, until within four weeks."[32]

The rations were slightly better than those at Andersonville; one day's ration was three-and-a-half large, hard-bread, crackers and bacon. Some of the messes were even issued salt and soap. Abundant water, of poor quality, was obtained by digging numerous wells only about 4 or 5 feet deep. "A saltish kind of mineral water" was brought up to the prisoners from an artesian well located down in the city.[33] The prisoners were organized into "thousands," "hundreds" and "twenties." Kellogg was in a squad designated 3rd "hundred," 1st "thousand." No shelter whatsoever was issued. Some men had the foresight to have not left their shelters at Andersonville.

A Confederate officer came to the prison one afternoon and called for volunteers to work upon the fortifications in and around Charleston harbor. He promised that those who went out would have all they wanted to eat, and, in addition, would be issued tobacco and whiskey. Several hundred accepted the invitation.

During the 11 days Dufur was at the racetrack, five of the prisoners were quite badly wounded by shells from

---

[29] Urban, pp. 434, 435.
[30] Dufur, pp. 137, 138.
[31] Kellogg, pp. 290, 291.
[32] *Ibid.*, p. 291.
[33] *Ibid.*, p. 293.

their own guns.[34] "A great many of the women and children came over, bringing with them wheat bread, sweet potatoes, and clothing, which they would throw over the line, when the guards were turned with their backs toward them. They had orders to stop anything of the kind they saw, and some of them were so accommodating they would not see if they could, and kept their faces turned away purposely."[35]

A couple of days after arriving, 15 of the 100s were given one day's rations and were told to be ready to leave the next day for an unknown destination, probably Florence. A few days after this and every day afterwards, two or three Sisters of Charity would ride over from the city in a two-horse ambulance with scarce supplies for the prisoners. These were passed around to Catholic and Protestant alike. Sometimes the Sisters were accompanied by a "... dapper-looking little Priest."[36]

On September 17th, Kellogg and two other prisoners stood by the prison gate awaiting the arrival of a young physician named Yarmony, who had come from the city to call on the prison. He had been a medical student in New York City. Yarmony wore a smart-looking Confederate uniform and was thought by the prisoners to have been truly sympathetic to their plight. He visited every afternoon and would sometimes bring Kellogg "... a few diarrhea powders in his pocket or a few drinks of whisky in a little stone jug. We very much needed acids, for the scurvy, but these, he declared, it was impossible to obtain."[37] Kellogg was admitted to the hospital for the possible amputation of a gangrenous hand. Three of the four surgeons thought amputation was not necessary. He treated himself with fresh vegetables bought from the rebel sutler with money sent to him from his Major and Adjutant, who were being held in prisons in the city. This could have been their personal money or money obtained by signing notes giving speculators the power of attorney to be reimbursed by one of the prisoners' friends in the North.

A rebel sutler drove up every day from town, with one or two wagonloads of food and other articles. These he sold at quite reasonable rates. Lieutenant Colonel Iverson, the commanding officer, forbade him from charging more than would be charged for the same items in the city. "His price for bread was fifty cents for a small loaf, and twice the amount for one a little larger. Sweet potatoes were $10.00 a bushel; cooking soda $10.00 per pound; pepper, in the berry, $20.00 a pound; radishes, ten for $5.00, and other articles in the same proportion."[38] These prices were in Confederate currency, which traded at the rate of seven for one greenbacks at that time. "At Andersonville it had been five to one."[39]

Kellogg described an interesting incident he witnessed at the racecourse. "I never saw but one instance of disobedience of orders by a rebel soldier, and that was at Charleston, when the men had crowded rather too closely upon the 'dead line,' at the prison entrance. Colonel Daniels, of the 5th Georgia regiment, seeing it, stepped up to one of the guards and ordered him to fire into us. He replied, 'I can not do it, Colonel.' 'I order you to fire into those men,' repeated the Colonel, sternly, and again the soldier said, 'Colonel, I can not do it.' The Colonel said no more, but turning on his heel, he walked rapidly away."[40]

"An order was issued from head-quarters, for the hospital camp to be moved at a greater distance from the camp of the 5th Georgia regiment, and in the midst of a drenching rain, the sick men had to strike their blanket tents, and put them up again as best they could. We were told by an officer of the guard that there was considerable yellow fever in the city, and that we were moved from fear of contagion."[41] "Yellow fever is caused by a virus which enters the body as an infected *Aedes aegypti* mosquito withdraws a blood meal. Once within the bloodstream, the virus causes vascular congestion with frequent small hemorrhages throughout the body, and severe destruction of the liver. At the outset, fever and headache are the most common signs, but soon backache, joint and abdominal pains, jaundice, multiple hemorrhages, and, in malignant cases, vomiting of blood (black vomit) intervene."[42]

The epidemic continued and first attacked the guards. Many of the officers and men of the 5th Georgia regiment died of it. None of the prisoners were victims until about the 1st of October. When two of the hospital attendants were struck down with it, they were removed to a special area reserved for yellow fever patients. The Confederate authorities decided to send the prisoners as rapidly as possible to the newly-built prison at Florence. The men were transferred at a rate of about 1,500 a day and all the enlisted men had left by the 8th of October. Those who were well

---

[34] Dufur, p. 138.
[35] Kellogg, pp. 293, 294.
[36] *Ibid.*, p. 298.
[37] *Ibid.*, p. 301.
[38] *Ibid.*, p. 306.
[39] *Ibid.*, p. 307.
[40] *Ibid.*, pp. 307, 308.
[41] *Ibid.*, p. 302.
[42] Savitt, p. 240, footnote.

were transferred first, followed by those who were sick and in the hospital.

During this final transferal, the men devised a rather ingenious method of escaping. They huddled in the bottoms of the abandoned wells, had their comrades cover them with brush and debris, and waited for nightfall when the camp would be deserted. Two of those hidden prisoners were discovered by chance to the amusement of both Confederates and Yankees. This discovery caused a meticulous search with sharpened poles by which several other groups of hidden prisoners were detected.

At one of the stations between Charleston and Florence, the men had a chance to buy "pones" from a black woman for $2 in Confederate money.[43]

General Winder recognized the need for a new prison in the early part of the summer and conveyed this to the Secretary of War on July 25th.[44] He dispatched his son, Sid, to again select the site for a new prison. Captain Sidney Winder, with Captain D. W. Vowles, found a site 5 miles from Millen, toward Augusta.[45] General Winder wrote to Richmond from Andersonville, on August 7th, and asked General Samuel Cooper for the "... authority to impress negroes, teams and wagons, lumber and saw mills. We are full here to overflowing."[46] The selection of this site, located near the plantation of a widow in Burke county, prompted a physician to write a futile letter of protest, on August 10th, to Secretary Seddon. He stated the reasons the local inhabitants of the county did not like the prospect of a prison being located there. First, he said, the water to be enclosed within the stockade sprung from "... unhealthy, rotten limestone." He said the local folks never "... ever thought of drinking it." The doctor's second reason was that the land selected was close to a large working plantation with about 150 Negroes employed there. "Her tithe alone last year was 1,300 bushels of corn, 2,500 pounds of bacon, &c."[47] Despite these objections, work began on the new prison as soon as laborers and equipment could be gathered at the site. Dick Winder sent ahead all the tools and implements which could be spared.

On the 18th of September, General Winder wrote General Cooper from Millen and said he thought the stockade would be ready the following week. He asked General Cooper, "Shall I remove my headquarters to this place?"[48] Because Generals Jones and McLawshad borrowed some of the guard force from Millen, General Winder wrote to General Cooper again on September 21st, saying "... we are much delayed for want of labor. We will be brought to a standstill if funds are not furnished. We have not one cent and no materials or tools. Please sent $250,000 at once to Captain R. B. Winder, prison quartermaster."[49]

General Winder was at Camp Lawton on September 26th and said he would leave the following day for Andersonville to pack up his office and move his headquarters to Millen.[50] He would carry his staff, composed of Captain W. Sidney Winder, A.A.G., Captain Richard B. Winder, A.Q.M., and Surgeon Isaiah H. White.

Dick Winder said that, some time in September, he had been assigned to duty as Chief Quartermaster of Prisons in Georgia and that his headquarters were ordered to be moved to Camp Lawton; he remained at Andersonville until the 1st of October. On that day, he assigned Captain James H. Wright, his assistant quartermaster, to take over his old position at Andersonville. Captain L. L. Varnadoe, assistant quartermaster, had already been assigned by the Quartermaster General to duty at Millen. The pen at Millen was enclosed on about the 1st of October, but the baking and cooking facilities were not completed on the 8th because of the difficulty in obtaining transportation.[51]

Dick Winder suggested the baking and cooking facilities be put inside of the prison and there be one cook house for every 1,000 men. This suggestion was adopted.

General Winder finally moved his headquarters to Millen on Tuesday, the 11th of October. He left Col. Gibbs as Commandant of the Post at Andersonville. On the 15th, General Winder said that all prisoners from Savannah were at Millen except for the very sick. Seven hundred sick prisoners had been sent before the hospital was completed. The crews had been working vigorously on it, and expected to have one ward finished the same day. The guard at Millen consisted of the 1st and 2nd Georgia reserves. "They are the most unreliable and disorganized set I have ever seen. They plunder in every direction and are creating a very bitter feeling against the Government. It is impossible to prevent it or identify them, as the officers will not exercise any authority, and some of them even encourage it.

---

43 Kellogg, p. 315.
44 *O.R.*, VII, p. 546.
45 *Ibid.*
46 *Ibid.*, p. 565.
47 *Ibid.*, p. 579.
48 *Ibid.*, p. 841.
49 *Ibid.*, p. 854.
50 *Ibid.*, p. 881.
51 *O.R.*, VIII, p.733.

"If they could be substituted by the Second Regiment Georgia State Troops, raised in this and the adjoining counties, it would be a great benefit to the country. The First and Second Reserves should be where there are other troops to control them."

General Winder also told Cooper, "We can with great convenience accommodate 32,000 prisoners, and could without inconvenience increase it to 40,000."[52]

Dick Winder would later describe his trip from Andersonville to Millen: "When I left Andersonville six of the prisoners that had been paroled and under me, and to whom I had become much attached, made petition to be allowed to go with me, which petition was granted them. Four of these I took and kept with me at my own private quarters, about three miles from the prison, and allowed them all sorts of privileges. The other two went on duty with Captain Varnadoe. The four who were with me at my quarters drew their rations with mine, one of them always superintending the receiving of them. After this several teamsters and others made similar petitions, and one or two *nolens volens* ran off from Andersonville, caught up with the wagon train, and came on to Millen. These men were never punished for this, and were put on duty with Captain Varnadoe, and I take occasion here to remark that for any act of kindness that I ever showed a prisoner while I was connected with the prison department, upon my honor I was never paid or received anything whatever, and not one can be found who can say such a thing about me, except in some little act of kindness to me afterward - one of them, for instance, at his own request, covered a saddle beautifully for me, another made me some shoes and boots. These are the only returns that I now recollect ever to have received from them, and for these acts of kindness to me, knowing their necessities, I paid them afterward."[53]

The Confederates had chosen to place the prison a short distance from the Georgia Central Railroad within a large pine forest. Forty-two acres were cleared and included with the enclosure.[54] The outside dimensions were 1,398 feet by 1,329 feet, and the deadline was located 30 feet inside the palisade.[55]

Luckily for the prisoners soon to arrive, the Confederates left the wood scraps and branches upon the ground which would be used to make the prisoners' shebangs and to be used as fuel. General Winder said he had brought eleven guns from Andersonville and would bring the rest of the armament from there soon.

No shelter of any sort was supplied the prisoners. The suffering continued as at Andersonville, with the same diseases prevailing. Through the center of the camp passed a clear creek. It was comparatively pure because there were no guard camps located above the pen. There were left about three acres of timber for shade through which the creek murmured. After the creek followed its own channel for about half the width of the pen, the Confederates created an artificial, straight channel about four feet wide. This increased the swiftness of the flow and enabled the water to carry off all the filth of the prison. At the beginning of this straight part was built a sturdy bridge.

The prisoners were all kept on the west side of the creek, and used the grove of trees and the east side as a kind of public park or promenade.[56] In October, the weather became cooler with several heavy frosts.

John Urban first arrived at Millen, about ninety miles northwest of Savannah, on October 13th. He felt "... the food was slightly better than at Andersonville, and consisted of one pint of corn meal, six ounces of uncooked beef, six spoonfuls of cooked rice, and a little salt. Beans were sometimes substituted for the rice. The rations were soon after cut down, and were about as bad as at Andersonville."[57] Lyons said they were sometimes given sweet potatoes.

By the first of November, about 10,000 prisoners had been confined there, some coming directly from Andersonville. Vawter stayed overnight at Macon and then was brought to Millen. As was done at all the prisons, when prisoners arrived too late in the afternoon to be formed into detachments, they were kept outside the gate in a grove of trees until the following day.

On November 2nd, the weather became stormy and turned cold. During the night of the 22nd of November, "Among the number that perished during the night, was one of our comrades by the name of John W. Mathias, a native of Carlisle, and a member of company C of our regiment. Sometime during the night he crept up to where several members of his company stayed, and on his knees begged for the help it was impossible for them to give him. In the early part of the night we heard him praying that God would relieve him of his sufferings, and daylight revealed the fact that his prayers had been answered."[58]

Urban, while exploring his new home, found an "... old friend William Rinear, a neighbor in our Northern

---

[52] *O.R.*, VII, p. 993.
[53] *O.R.*, VIII, pp. 733, 734.
[54] *O.R.*., VII, p. 870.
[55] *Ibid.*, p. 882.
[56] Vawter, pp. 130-133.
[57] Urban, p. 438.
[58] Urban, p. 441.

home. We had left him in Savannah prison, then apparently in good health, and did not again see him until one morning I was walking through the prison, when I noticed a sick man who I thought resembled some one I knew. I went close to him, and found it to be Rinear. He was in a dying condition, and could only make out to talk to me a little. I asked him what I could do for him, and he said that some one had given him a brier root to make tea with, for the purpose of stopping his diarrhoea, and that if I wished to I might make him some tea; but that he did not think it worth while, as he knew that he was dying. He also said that he had made his peace with God, and was anxious to go. After staying with him for a short time, I went for Gilbert, and soon returned with him to see what we could do for our dying comrade. We looked for the brier root, but it was gone - some one had, no doubt, in my absence, picked it up. But it could not have helped poor Rinear anyhow; he was fast sinking away, and soon after passed to his eternal home."[59] "Instead of carrying the dead to a dead-house outside of the stockade, as was the custom in Andersonville, at this place they were carried to the gate, where they were laid inside of the prison until the arrival of the mule-team, when they were taken away to the burial-ground."[60]

"With as little feeling or respect for the poor victims of their brutality as if they were logs of wood, the rebels threw them on the wagon until it was full - their arms and legs in some cases dangling out over the wagon - and then drove off."[61]

On the 3rd of November, about 1,000 prisoners arrived from Andersonville. These men were some of the sick men who had been left behind when the others were scattered to other prisons. They reported that the pen at Andersonville was now "about empty."[62]

"On the 8th of November, the day that the loyal states reelected Abraham Lincoln to the chief magistracy of the Nation, we concluded also to have an election. The rebels, who had worked hard to convince us that it was the fault of Lincoln's administration that we were not exchanged, had greatly encouraged the idea. Black and white beans were furnished to vote with - the black ones representing the Republican party, and the white ones the Democratic party. A ballot-box was placed inside the prison, and men stationed there to see that all voted fairly. All them that wished to vote fell into line, and marching up, quietly deposited their votes. In the evening after sunset the votes were counted, when it was found that 3,014 had voted for Lincoln, and 1,050 for McClellan."[63]

"The rebels had counted us in companies of one hundred, for the purpose of issuing rations to us. Each company had a mess sergeant, whose duty it was to call up his hundred, to be counted in the morning, and to draw and divide the rations in the afternoon. We voted by these company hundreds in this election. Rebel officers were in the pen nearly all the day, watching for the result."[64]

The prisoners at Millen were offered the same two options, in order to get out of the prison, they had been previously offered at Andersonville. These options were to join the Confederate army or to take the non-combatants' oath and work for the Confederate war effort. "Calls were made for shoemakers, machinists, blacksmiths, etc. The rebel authorities offered to furnish food and clothing and pay good wages to any one who would go out on parole and work in their shops. It was a great temptation to mechanics who were starving in filth and rags; and a good many yielded to it and went out. I will say, though, that but few native Americans were among them. They were generally foreigners who did not fully understand the war and its issues."[65]

"It was also intimated that if any one would enlist in their army, he would receive rations and pay as a soldier, but while in Andersonville I saw no strong effort to induce any one to enlist. But in Camp Lawton, soon after the Presidential election, rebel recruiting officers came into the pen and openly and boldly tried to hire men to join the rebel army. They offered any one a good suit and fifty dollars (Confederate) at once, and would take him out and put him on full rations, as soon as he would sign his name to their muster roll"[66]

Sergeant W. Goodyear, company E, 7th Regiment Connecticut Volunteers, said, in the book by Kellogg, that the inducements offered were "... three bushels of sweet potatoes, a suit of clothes and one hundred dollars in Confederate script."[67]

"After their names had been obtained, a drum beaten at the gate called them out. As they went over the creek

---

[59] *Ibid.*, p. 443.
[60] *Ibid.*, p. 444.
[61] *Ibid.*
[62] *Ibid.*, p. 448.
[63] *Ibid.*, p. 449.
[64] Vawter, pp. 136, 137.
[65] *Ibid.*, pp. 138, 139.
[66] *Ibid.*, p. 139.
[67] Kellogg, p.

toward the gate, thousands - almost the entire camp - crossed over to see them go out; and the miserable wretches had to run a gauntlet of the fiercest hisses and blood-curdling curses that ever saluted mortal ears! And only the presence of a strong rebel guard prevented that vast mob from falling upon them, then and there."[68]

"During the latter part of our imprisonment in Millen, the rebels had again commenced to give us molasses instead of beef. It was at this time that we struck upon an idea which was the means of helping us considerably. It was to take our ration of molasses, make candy, and sell it to the new prisoners who were coming in almost every day, and almost always had a little money. Gilbert was quite a good hand at making candy after he had transferred our rations into it, I went out to try my luck. I was fortunate enough to get among a squad of new prisoners who had just come from Sherman's army, and soon made a sale of it all. We determined to carry on the business on a more extensive scale. We took the money we had thus obtained, and with it purchased molasses from some of the prisoners who could not use it, and then with our next day's rations we made quite a lot of candy, and I soon had sold all of it, realizing quite a profit. With the proceeds we purchased sweet-potatoes and beans from the rebel sutlers, and what we did not use for ourselves we would trade off for molasses with the other prisoners. We also added to our stock of bedding by purchasing an old blanket, for which we paid four dollars and seventy-five cents. We also purchased a little tobacco for Fralich. He kept a monopoly of the candy business because he bought some soap, washed his hands and advertised 'nice clean candy.'"[69]

On the 13th of November, a physician came into the prison to select 75 sick men out of each "thousand" to, supposedly, be sent home. Since those prisoners in the worst shape were to have been selected, there was a definite increase in the number of sick men. There probably was a large amount of feigning illness as well as attempts to bribe the doctors to win a place in the group of those leaving. This first group left on the 15th, but, for some unknown reason, they returned to the pen the next day. They left for good on the 18th.

Phillip Cashmeyer told about a problem at Millen with prisoners who had enough cash or valuable possessions to bribe Confederate authorities to place them on the exchange list. "As well as I can recollect, I was at Camp Lawton Prison, near Millen, Ga., in September, 1864. While I was there orders were received to select a number of the sick prisoners to be exchanged. I heard many of the sick complain that such of the prisoners, sick or not, who had money could have their names put upon the list for exchange, to the exclusion of the more afflicted who had not money to bribe the officers with that had the making of the selections for exchange, so that many of the sick who would have otherwise been exchanged and living were left in prison to suffer and die. Upon making inquiry relative to their complaints I found that it was true and reported the same to General Winder, under whom I was acting. He at once instituted means to recover from the officers of the prison the money they had thus obtained. When making my inquiries into the matter the prisoners would refuse to testify to having given it. Notwithstanding, I found means to establish the truth of the complaints, and General Winder succeeded in recovering a portion of the money from the officials in whose possession it was."[70] This same incident was repeated in a letter of Phillip Cashmeyer, written on October 12th, to N. P. Chipman, Judge Advocate of the Commission which tried Wirz: "The only instance of improper treatment I heard of here was that when an exchange of sick prisoners was agreed upon Captain Vowles (commandant), was said to have placed the names of such persons as paid for the favor on the list of those who were to be immediately forwarded to Savannah for exchange to the exclusion of some of the sick, who complained bitterly of it. Upon hearing of it General Winder instituted inquiry, but the evidence of the prisoners not being acceptable, the charge was not sustained, although $60 paid by a prisoner was recovered from a clerk in Captain Vowles' office. The suspicion was so great against this officer that General Winder declared he should have no such command in the future."[71]

The following was taken from the personal diary of a Confederate officer high in command at Andersonville and other Southern prisons: "At one time an order came to Camp Lawton to prepare 2,000 men for exchange. The order from Richmond was to select first the wounded, next the oldest prisoners and the sickly, filling up with healthy men according to date. This party went first to Savannah, as arranged; but by some mistake the ships were at Charleston, and the poor wretches had to be taken there; and every one who knew the Southern railroads in those days, and the difficulty, or rather impossibility to procure food for such a crowd along the road, will know what those poor fellows suffered. At Charleston they were refused, the commissioner declaring that 'he was not going to exchange able-bodied men for such miserable specimens of humanity' (The term [actually] used was more brutal).

[68] Vawter, p. 140.
[69] Urban, pp. 444-448.
[70] *O.R.*, p. 754.
[71] *Ibid.*, p. 765.

Finding him obdurate, Colonel Ould requested him to take them without exchange. This he refused with a sneering laugh, and the crowd was ordered back. Never did the writer of this witness such woe-begone countenances, in which misery and hopelessness were more strongly painted, than shown by those poor fellows on their return. And the curses leveled against the rulers who thus treated the defenders of their country were fearful, although certainly well deserved. As the stockade gate closed upon them, the surgeon in charge said to the writer: 'Poor fellows! the world has closed upon more than half of them: this disappointment will be their death-knell.' His words proved true. Who murdered those men? Let history answer the question."[72]

The men taunted their captors with "How do you like Sherman's marching orders?", thereby reminding them that they were being transported as a direct result of the movements of General Sherman.[73] Urban said, "Sherman commenced his march from Atlanta on the 14th of November - six days before our removal - and that the situation of our prison was directly in the line of his march toward Savannah."[74]

On Sunday, November 20th, and on the following day, a large number of prisoners was taken out of the prison, loaded into box-cars, and sent in the direction of Savannah. Lyons at Millen said, "... as we were going from the prison to the train I saw piles of boxes filled with blankets and clothing. Upon inquiry I found that these had been sent there by our Sanitary Commission to make us comfortable, but they were not delivered to us, notwithstanding men were chilled to death while these comforts were just outside the prison stockade."[75] When he left for Savannah, Lyons observed from his railroad car that, "... all along this route we saw baskets of rolls and sandwiches, which the loyal people had sent to us, but the guards kept them from us."[76] After reaching Savannah, Lyons was marched to the river, where he signed a ledger, was put on board a former cotton-carrying boat, and then was conveyed to a United States vessel. Once on board, Lyons was given hardtack, boiled pork, and tin cups of delicious chocolate.

The detachment which included Urban left for Savannah at 12 noon; it arrived at 9 p.m. They stayed in Savannah overnight, and, the next morning, some were put into box-cars and others onto open platform cars and taken south. The next morning, Urban's group stopped at a station near Blackshear, Georgia.

By the 2nd of December, the vanguard of Sherman's army had possession of Millen. When all the Confederates had left Millen, it was turned over to a Mrs. C.M. Jones, who bought it from the Confederate States. General Winder wrote, from Columbia, at his Headquarters of C. S. Military Prisons East of the Mississippi, on January 21, to Mrs. Jones: "The occupation of Savannah by the enemy renders it inexpedient for the Confederate States to continue to occupy the stockade at Camp Lawton. It is therefore given up to you, and I will take the earliest opportunity to send an agent to arrange and settle the account between yourself and the Confederate States."[77]

Urban described the station where he and his comrades stopped near the town of Blackshear. There, they had a couple of hours' layover until they left for Blackshear. "It was a wild, desolate-looking place, only one house being in sight. We were then told to get off of the cars, as the train would stop for an hour or two, and we would have the privilege of warming ourselves. The men on the open platforms were in a sorry condition. I was in the act of getting out of the car, when a prisoner, who had been on one of the platform cars, came to inform me that a member of our regiment was dying in the cars he had left. I hastened forward, and found the poor fellow to be William Dutton, a member of Company C and a native of Chester, Pa. He was in a dying condition. I went and told Gilbert and Fralich and they helped me lift him from the cars. Some of the men had built fires, and we were going to carry him to one of them, when a rebel officer told us not to do so, as that would kill him. We tried to bring him to, but poor Dutton was past recovery. After his death Gilbert went to one of the rebel officers and requested permission to bury our dead comrade. The rebel officer procured a spade for us, and a few steps from the railroad track we dug a grave and buried him.

"After we left the station I was informed that McCoy, a member of Company G of our regiment, has also frozen to death on one of the hind cars, and his body was left lying on the ground near the railroad track."[78] After a few hours, they were placed back in the boxcars and the train headed to Blackshear proper. "Just as the guards had got us loaded a handsome lady came riding on horse-back and began talking very earnestly to one of the confederate officers. Our guards told us she was pleading with the officer to make us a New Year's present. She finally got the officer's consent, and two large wagons drove up to the cars, and each prisoner got a good half pound of pork, and it

[72] Stevenson, pp. 453, 454.
[73] Urban, pp. 450, 451.
[74] *Ibid.*, p. 451.
[75] Lyons, p. 86.
[76] *Ibid.*, p. .
[77] *O.R.*, VIII, p. 111.
[78] Urban, pp. 454-456.

was good pork, too...

"We lay in boxcars all night, and the next morning went through to Andersonville."[79] Urban's group arrived at Blackshear at 3 p.m., and they were told that, on the following day, they would be exchanged at either Charleston or Savannah. The men would not have been so gullible as to believe this but for the fact that, the next morning, the guard started making preparations for their parole. They did not leave Blackshear until 6 o'clock that evening. They arrived at Savannah at 3 o'clock that morning and left for Charleston at 8 o'clock after a 5-hour lay over on the 26th. All that time, few, if any, guards accompanied the prisoners. None were necessary because the prisoners thought they were on their way to freedom. Immediately after they reached Charleston, they were surrounded by a strong guard and the prisoners guessed the truth. They were marched to another train depot in the northern part of the city. On that trek, they were the objects of abuse and vicious taunting. Some of the women of the city threw dirty water at them as they marched through town. They left Charleston at midnight, having had nothing to eat on the 27th and 28th. Urban and his fellow prisoners were given only a pint of wheat flour outside of the Florence stockade at 5 p.m. and were marched in at 8 o'clock.[80]

Vawter related his experiences at Blackshear: "We had been in this place but a few days when we were informed that a special exchange of ten thousand sick and wounded prisoners [was] ordered to take place immediately, and that two thousand were to be taken from our pen." They were taken to Savannah, where a part of them were exchanged in about the middle of December. The remainder were sent back within a few days.

"We stayed at Blackshear about two weeks. We were then loaded on the cars and taken to Thomasville, which is near the southwest corner of the State. Here we were corralled and guarded in the same manner as at Blackshear."[81]

Vawter described where he was kept, "... in the pine woods, about a mile from Blackshear; we were corralled on about five acres of ground.

"There was no wall or fence to enclose us. A dead-line was staked off, and outside of it another row of stakes marked the line of sentinels, who stood about ten or fifteen steps apart, all around us, ready to shoot any one who passed the first row of stakes. The fact that they built no wall around us, and no quarters for themselves, made us think they did not intend to keep us there very long...

"We drew raw rations, about the same as at Millen...

"Because of flanking, when we were counted onto the train to take us away, it was found that the number of men reported for rations exceeded the actual number in the pen about seven hundred."[82]

Some of the sick prisoners left Savannah after a rather short stay and were taken south in boxcars with guards riding on the top. They were taken, at about 20 miles per hour, to the small town of Thomasville, about 200 miles southwest of Savannah. It was the impression of the prisoners that they were being taken to a place inaccessible to General Sherman's army. They marched the prisoners about three miles back into the woods from the railroad tracks. There was no stockade there and a small ditch was dug which delineated the outer perimeter of the prison area. While they were there, four of the prisoners attempted to escape. Three of these were successful, but one was shot and died two days later. They stayed in Thomasville about 2 weeks; those who were able marched across the country to the prison at Blackshear. "We were forced to march in the cold biting wind, there were a good many of the prisoners died on the road. Most of the men were without shoes. Their feet looked more like big bloody pieces of meat than like human feet. They could easily be tracked by their poor, bleeding feet."[83]

About 10,000 soldiers went to Blackshear and 7,000 returned to Andersonville on two or three trains. "When we first started from Thomasville one of the guards came up to me and said, 'Yank, I want you to carry this knap-sack!' I told him I was not able to carry myself. 'It don't make no difference to me whether you can carry yourself or not but you will carry this knap-sack as far as you go, or I will blow your brains out.' So I was forced to carry his knap-sack, which weighed about forty pounds.

"Some of the time I thought I would fall, but I managed to keep along until the first day noon, when we made a halt, and the rebel gave me a small piece of meat. 'Now,' said the Johnnie, 'I have given you a good ration, and I hope you will carry my knap-sack without grumbling.' We started on, but had not gone over five miles when I gave out. I could not go any farther; so down I went my full length on the road. 'Get up, you damned Yank, or I'll run thou through with this bayonet.' A confederate officer made him take the knap-sack , and he put it on another prisoner.

---

[79] Tyler, pp.45-48.
[80] Urban, pp. 454-462.
[81] Vawter, p. 150.
[82] *Ibid.*, p. 152.
[83] Tyler, pp. 44, 45.

We finally did get through to Blackshire (sic), more dead than alive."[84]

As at Andersonville, prisoners began to arrive at Florence before the workers had the stockade completed. Northrop left Andersonville on Monday, the 12th of September, after taking a very meticulous bath in anticipation of a long trip to the North. Two days' rations of corn bread were given to the prisoners as they were placed in cattle cars. Northrop's train passed Macon that evening and there was a short layover in Augusta, just before nightfall. There, a couple of ladies distributed two baskets of small bread loaves and then the train left for Kingsville, South Carolina. At Orangeburg, a few of the prisoners were permitted to leave the train, go to a wayside inn, and buy bourbon drinks for $2 Confederate apiece.[85]

At one South Carolina town, a large "... quantity of resin ... [had] waited so long for the blockade that the barrels have burst and scattered it as free as water. The boys eat as much as they please and put as much as they please in their pockets; they pick it up as children gather shells on the shore, for several reasons, first, ravenous hunger; second, as a medicine for urinary difficulties; third, it will make a fire."[86]

Near nightfall on the 15th, the train stopped in a desolate area. Soon a group of Negroes carrying "beetle axes" and led by an officer came down a road and went off into a wooded area. Six men from each car were ordered to follow them, to tote out the wood cut by the Negroes, and to stack it in the tender of the train. This procedure was repeated a few hours later and, in the morning, the train was in Florence, South Carolina.

Small squads from each car were allowed to go the 350 yards to a swamp for water, but, because the containers used to carry the water were so small, thirst still prevailed.[87]

Northrop said Florence was the junction of four railroads coming together from Columbia, Charleston, Cheraw, and Wilmington. He said he was "... told that the country near is noted for savage gangs of marauders who have been known to fight to the death when attempts by civil authorities have been made to break them up."[88]

Northrop's group was inspected by three men on horseback and then again by a group of ladies. Then came a woman driving a cart loaded with turnips she "... wished to exchange for a ring."

Before noon, they were ordered back on the train, and were carried one mile down the tracks towards Charleston, where they were again ordered off. On the 16th, they were marched off through some woods to "the old field" about a half-mile away. There, they halted; several hundred prisoners rushed past their guards to gather grass and weeds for food and bedding. There was great excitement in the camp because they also took down a nearby rail fence. They were stopped in this endeavor by the objections of their guards, but a kind-hearted Confederate officer intervened.

There in "the old field," there were 2,000 more prisoners camped on the ground who had made the trip from Andersonville previously by way of Savannah and Charleston. On the 17th, it began to rain; it continued for 9 days. The field was covered with from 1 to 3 inches of water; the depressions in the field were covered by 3 to 18 inches of water. The men tried to stay and sleep on the high ground.

On the 15th and 16th, large groups of Negroes with spades and axes passed through camp on the way to build the stockade.

On the 16th, after the first confrontation, about 500 men made another rush past the guards and headed for the woods about 350 yards away. Soon a "heavy line" of Confederate veterans arrived who were deployed smartly at the double-quick. There was a small skirmish and about ten prisoners were killed. The starving prisoners gathered nuts and wild berries, which they brought back when recaptured. "Before this excitement was over, rations were announced. All got a small piece of Indian pone, a few spoonfuls of corn meal an hour later, largely gathered from citizens."[89] Northrop said, on the 16th, "... the issue consisted of three spoonfuls of flour, three ounces fresh beef, one-half pint of meal, the same of brown beans, with the proclamation: 'This ration is for two days."[90]

"Two or three months ago some 6,000 Federal prisoners of war were sent there, from whence or by whom I did not know. The number of guards to receive them was about 125 South Carolina reserves, totally inadequate for the duty. The prisoners broke through the lines, and from 400 to 600 made their escape and plundered the citizens in the vicinity of the camp."[91]

---

[84] *Ibid.*, pp. 45, 46.
[85] Northrop, pp. 125-128.
[86] *Ibid.*, p. 129.
[87] *Ibid.*, pp. 129-135.
[88] *Ibid.*, p. 135.
[89] *Ibid.*, p. 137.
[90] *Ibid.*, p. 138.
[91] *O.R.*, VII, p. 1086.

"The rebels telegraphed in different directions, setting forth the fact that there were hundreds of live Yankees running at large in the neighborhood of Florence. Cavalry and infantry were sent in pursuit, and the patrolling parties redoubled their diligence until within a few weeks nearly all the prisoners were brought back."[92]

Another prisoner said that, while the stockade in Florence was being built, there were two rows of guards with a line of fires which completely encircled the camp of prisoners. Even with this extra vigilance, the men vowed to chance death by being fired at rather than by starving to death. On the night of September 28th, soon after dark, several men began a rush past the guard. Many were wounded and one was killed in the breakout. As an inducement for calm and order, the quartermaster promised rations at dawn the next morning. The meal was issued early; then, a little past noon, they got a piece of sweet potato, rice, and molasses.[93]

Brownell stayed in Charleston ten days before he was sent to the unfinished pen, where he received no rations for the first two days. James Miller was, also, one of the first to arrive at Florence. He left Andersonville by "flanking out" in a lower-numbered detachment on September 12th. The next morning, they reached Augusta; the morning after, they were in Charleston. After an hour's stopover, they were heading for Florence. They arrived at the depot "some distance" from the town at about noon. They stayed in the boxcars overnight and, the next morning, marched about a mile to a temporary holding pen while the Florence prison was being completed. Then occurred one of the few truly humanitarian acts by Confederate prison guards. The next day, all of the sick men in the camp were allowed to roam the vicinity to ask for food. Some scoured the neighboring forests, looking for indigenous herbs or berries to help their scurvy and other deficiency diseases. Miller found help from some women who shared with him some vegetables from their meager food supplies.[94]

Fosdick left Andersonville on October 2nd, using a tent pole for a cane. Carrying his "mush kettle," Fosdick left Andersonville on the 3-day trip to Charleston, thinking he would be exchanged. He and his comrades were placed in freight cars with the doors secured with 4- or 5- inch openings. "When the train stopped for wood or water the boys would stick their cans out of the cars, and beg the guards to dip up a little water from the ditches alongside the railroad track. They would give them bone finger-rings, brass buttons, or anything they might have in their possession, for a can of water dipped out of a stagnant pool, covered with green scum an inch thick, with hundreds of wigglers and infant tadpoles in it. This was both victuals and drink...

"About three men died each of the three days; when they reached Charleston, about forty comrades, bloated and smelling, were removed and buried with no record made of their names or regiments."[95]

Fosdick and his comrades were taken a few miles outside of Charleston and kept for about a week. He was then taken to Florence where, "... in the whole place there was not one respectable dwelling."[96]

While the prisoners were in this temporary camp, Confederate officers came into the enclosure and offered the prisoners their freedom if they would enlist in the Southern army. They were told they would be used to guard installations and perform other services in the rear and would not have to fight at the front. This offer was accepted by a "large number" of starving prisoners, most of whom privately vowed that, at the first opportunity, they would head for their lines. Evidently, enough men took the Confederate oath of allegiance to fill a sizeable camp. "Over at our left was a camp which we were told was occupied by those prisoners who had taken the oath."[97] Boggs said a group who had been Raiders at Andersonville went out and enlisted. "In all there were, perhaps, three hundred who joined the Rebels. These men ... went out dressed in Rebel uniform and, after a few days, were marched through the prison carrying Rebel guns and the Rebel flag and inviting their former comrades to join them."[98]

Dufur arrived at Florence on the evening of the 17th of September. They were marched about a mile in the direction of the new stockade, which was nearing completion. There were about 150 slaves doing the work. The 600 men were halted about a half-mile away; two acres of ground were marked out in a square and a heavy guard was thrown around them. They were near a large forest and one side of the square extended within about 100 yards of the woods. Two pieces of artillery were placed by the authorities to guard that side of the square.

After the men had been there three days, the stockade was rumored to be complete. The 20th was a cloudy day with a cold, drizzling rain. Just before night, Dufur heard a musket shot on the side of the camp nearest the woods. There was heard a couple more shots in rapid succession and the entire camp surged and stormed the artillery posi-

---

[92] Fosdick, p. 82.
[93] Author's library.
[94] Miller, p. 35.
[95] Fosdick, pp. 75-77.
[96] *Ibid.*, p. 80.
[97] Kellogg, p. 319.
[98] Boggs, p. 65.

tions. In less than five minutes, the camp was empty. The men fled by way of the woods and made their way as best they could in their weakened condition. By raiding farms without the knowledge of the owners and, at other times with the aid of friendly Negroes, Dufur stayed free for six days before being recaptured. In three more days, Dufur rejoined his comrades inside the newly-completed Florence prison.[99]

On Sunday, October 2nd, 1,500 men arrived in the early morning from Charleston. Later, at about 9 a.m., orders were issued that the prisoners were to break camp and enter into the just-finished pen. A cavalry guard trooped into camp to aid in the transfer. The men packed up all the gear and marched one mile over a field covered with weeds and grass. Off in the distance, they could see the cultivated plantation and houses belonging to a Doctor Garrett, "a noted planter." On this short trip, the men picked up sticks and pieces of wood, which would be useful in the construction of shebangs and for the cooking of rations. "But ere we reached the gate the order came to throw down every stick; guards with bayonets enforced the orders."[100] "On the morning that they were put in the stockade all the citizens from the surrounding country were assembled, with such arms as they could get, as the prisoners had threatened that they would not go into it."[101] On Sunday, October 9th, 1,500 more prisoners arrived from Andersonville via Charleston.

Some groups, when they had arrived past late afternoon, too late to be organized in detachments, were ordered to spend the night nearby in what had once been a cornfield, sleeping between the furrows. One group, which had arrived on a cold, frosty night, was not allowed to approach the fires of the guards nor to gather any wood to make fires for themselves. Urban's group left Charleston at midnight and arrived at 5 p.m. Each man was issued a pint of wheat with which most men mixed water and which they ate as a bland paste. They were then were marched into the pen at 8 o'clock.

The prison at Florence was, basically, of the same design as that at Andersonville. The palisade was made of tall, unhewn pines placed upright in a ditch and standing about sixteen feet above ground.[102] "The logs were not hewn, as at Andersonville."[103] The area of land enclosed was about 15 acres but about five acres were unavailable for habitation because they were so swampy.[104] Boggs said they had 12,000 prisoners on about seven acres of habitable land.[105] "The prison was longest east and west, and contained twelve or thirteen acres, with a gate on the west side."[106]

Instead of the sentry boxes or "pigeon roosts" as at Andersonville, the earth was piled up around the outside, making a ledge on which the guard detail could pace back and forth. The dirt was obtained from a large ditch surrounding the ledge, which also made tunneling much more difficult. The top of the palisade reached about chest-high on the average guard. On Monday, October 3rd, the Negroes were still packing the dirt up around the palisade.[107]

There was a small stream of clear, cold water flowing from north to south between two hills with a swampy area adjacent to the stream. It was cleaner and its volume of flow was about six times the stream at Andersonville. The creek ran "... north to south, two or three feet deep by six feet wide."[108] For a part of the winter, there was ice on the stream, sometimes an inch thick. "The swamp is forty to sixty rods wide, black, and covered with prickly vines. A brook, larger than that at Andersonville, runs through it, which is to supply water which cannot be obtained without going half knee deep in mud. The stockade contains twenty acres."[109]

"The swamp is said to be filled with snakes. I saw a large rattlesnake, dead, killed by negroes. These in the swamp and stream are called moccasins. Two men were bitten yesterday by these while in the water washing, and have died. I saw these men; they were bitten in the heel. Several of the snakes have been killed. A gang of negroes are working in the swamp; mule teams are passing back and forth, keeping the water constantly black with mud. We are forced to drink it. Three men have been shot within two days, near the north part of the stockade, where we get water."[110]

---

[99] Dufur, pp. 199-202.
[100] Northrop, p. 153.
[101] *O.R.*, VII, p. 1086.
[102] Boggs, p. 57.
[103] Fosdick, p. 83.
[104] Kellogg, p. 317.
[105] Boggs, p. 58.
[106] Fosdick, p. 84.
[107] Northrop, p. 154.
[108] Fosdick, p. 84.
[109] Northrop, p. 153.
[110] *Ibid.*, p. 156.

"There were forts at the corners, mounting two pieces of field artillery each, and one gun before the gate, all arranged to rake the interior of the prison."[111] "A line of breast-works had encircled the stockade in a short time, with a small place at each corner, in which to run the artillery."[112] "At all hours of the day and night, a man stood by these guns, ready for action in case of any attempted outbreak on our part."[113] "Beyond this was still another, and outer line of works, with a deep ditch. The slaves would commence their work early in the morning, and continue until sunset, stopping only a short time for dinner. Their overseers, or drivers, were black like the rest, and stood with whip in hand directing and hurrying up the work. If they chanced to see one of the men slack at all, they would sing out, flourishing the whip at the same time, 'Sharp dere, boy; sharp dere.' It seemed their disposition to avoid work if it were possible. Sundays all work was suspended upon the fortifications, and they sported about in their best clothes, which were none of the finest at that, however."[114]

"A few rods from the north side of the stockade, was a large camp occupied by slaves, several hundred in number, all under the command of Lieut. De Loyle, an engineer officer. This man had the sole charge of laying out the fortifications, and the slaves performed the labor upon them."[115] "The slaves employed to build the stockade, erect barracks for the rebel soldiers, cut wood for the prison, etc., passed our camp going out in the morning and back at night, accompanied by two or three overseers who rode on horseback and each carried a large whip. These masters compelled the slaves to strike up a chant and sing at the tip of their voices, going and coming, which probably was to make us think they were happy, but which we knew to be otherwise. The master of the hounds, with his yelping pack, brought up the rear, to see that all were safely corralled at night."[116]

Northrop, while wandering within the pen one night, discovered what turned out to be an old slave cemetery. "In making my way, I stumbled in the darkness over what I was impressed was a grave, falling directly across another. This morning I go there. I find several graves, mostly new. Three old ones are small. There are no names, the only indices being the mound; the sticks at head and foot. Several beautiful pines are left standing near. Probably it was a negro burial ground, as negroes (slaves) go into back lonely places in the woods to bury their dead."[117]

On Wednesday, October 5th, the camp was organized by being laid out in squares, with all streets meeting at right angles. The men were divided into thousands and were put through the agonies of two roll calls with no rations issued that day. "We were here arranged into detachments of a thousand, with a Sergeant in charge of each detachment. There was also a Sergeant in charge of each hundred, and one to each mess of twenty. The camp was laid off in squares, each detachment occupying a square, with the hundreds arranged in regular order, with a small alley between where we could get in ranks and to have roll-call. There was one main street, running from the gate through the center to the east side, to which these alleys ran at right angles, and there was also a bridge over the creek, on the main street...The first groups occupied the west side of the creek."[118]

When prisoners were first brought into the prison, a large number of trees were still standing, but they were soon cut down to make rather comfortable shebangs. A typical shebang was like the one Urban took over when its original occupants died. "Two of the first inmates of the prison had erected a shelter by digging about twelve or fifteen inches into the ground, and over this they formed a roof with limbs, brush, and earth. A fire corner and mud chimney were at the one end, and the entrance at the other. It was a warm nest during dry weather, but when it rained the water soaked through, and made it of course a very unhealthy place. Both of the occupants had taken sick and died."[119]

Near November the 20th, Dufur and his tent-mate went to work on their winter quarters. "We went to the brook and with our hands and the half of a canteen, managed to dig clay from the bed of the stream, and with the aid of a small wooden trowel, converted this soap clay, as it was called, into bricks about three-fourths the size of an ordinary brick. They were of a reddish gray color, and after we had dried them in the hot sun for three or four days, they became quite hard. By carefully laying them closely together and two deep, we erected the body to our house, size 5 X 7 feet, and about 4 feet in height. The tops of the walls were slightly drawn in and on a stick raised above the walls for a ridge pole, our blanket was stretched, thus forming quite a respectable roof. We then built a little fire-place, and our

[111] Fosdick, p. 84.
[112] Kellogg, p. 337.
[113] Kellogg, p. 328.
[114] *Ibid.*, pp. 337, 338.
[115] *Ibid.*, p. 337.
[116] Fosdick, p. 89.
[117] Northrop, p. 154.
[118] Fosdick, 84.
[119] Urban, p. 464.

winter quarters were completed." This abode was great for a week or 10 days until the rains came.[120] No shelters or tents were ever issued by the Confederates.

Wood for fuel was no real problem at first at Florence for there was plenty of scrap wood, stumps, and limbs. Later, when fuel became scarce, "... one hundred and fifty men were detailed to supply fire wood for the men. They were divided into about fifty choppers and one hundred carriers."[121] In about the middle of November, wood was brought in by the choppers and stacked in piles at the gate. This wood was distributed to the men by measuring a certain amount per thousand men; that averaged out to about a "small green stick" per man. "Hundreds of naked feet not recovered from sun burn and scurvy, and now inflamed by a touch frost."[122] On Thursday, November 17th, Colonel [G.P.] Harrison let a few men from each thousand go to the woods to gather poles and brush to make a small shed for each thousand for those that have no shelter."[123] Colonel Harrison was the Commandant at Florence and was well-liked by the garrison and its prisoners.

The deadline was marked by a shallow ditch or furrow, with no wooden rail put up, which ran only part way round the interior. "The balance of the line was just where the guards chose to claim it."[124] "The dead line here at Florence is simply a furrow made with a plow about twenty feet from the wall."[125]

A small bridge, allowing the passage of but one prisoner at a time, was built over the small stream dividing the prison into two, almost-equal parts. Every Sunday, all the ambulatory men would be taken to the east side and made to cross this bridge; they were counted, one at a time, to get a more accurate accounting. This was called "taking a census;" once, 160 more rations were issued than there were men in the prison. The men were then consolidated into the lower-numbered hundreds to take the place of those who had died, had been taken to the hospital, had escaped, or had been detailed outside. Dufur's tent mate sold his old camping ground for "... five buttons and four chews of tobacco" when he was consolidated to a lower-numbered hundred.

Northrop told of the rage Lieutenant Barrett, of the Fifth Georgia Regiment, exhibited on Thursday, December 1st, when he accompanied a column of men to be counted. The prisoners were marched across the bridge from one side to the other and back again, in order to get an exact count and to prevent flanking. "The column was moving over the long corduroy road across the marsh, when Lieut. Barrett came running toward the stream with the pomposity of a brigadier. Attempting to cross, he slipped and tumbled in. The boys laughed. He no sooner got on the bank, wet, and daubed with the black mud, than he drew his revolver and snapped it. It missed; shouts increased; snapped again; again it missed. Pulled again the cap went, but missed fire. The crowd became tumultuous and provoking; he drew excessively mad. Fired with passion, he leaped the stream, ran through the swamp to one of his guard, seized his musket and fired quite at random, though he intended to hit, for his bullet whistled along the line, grazed a man's arm, and entered the dirt roof of a shanty, but seriously injuring none that I know of."[126]

Miller also recounted this incident: "Barrett was a young man, well built, erect, active, fairly intelligent, with red hair, a typical southern blood. He realized to the fullest extent the great importance of his office. He was always fully armed, his pants stuck into his boots, a jaunty uniform, and an air of bravado that only party concealed a really cowardly heart. Woe betide the luckless wretch who got into his pathway. A curse and a kick were the lightest he could expect to receive. One day he had ordered all the prisoners to one side of the camp for the purpose of counting them. Barrett was standing on the other side of the brook, and ordered a company of prisoners to move on. They did not hear, or did not obey, and he drew his revolver and fired at them. The shot fell short, and the boys yelled in derision. Seizing a gun from a guard, he again fired, but without effect, and another yell greeted him. In his rage he gave the gun back to the guard, and started toward his quarters, swearing, and evidently intending to return with a force and take summary vengeance, but for some reason, he did not come back. Wirz was mad most of the time, but Barrett was always mad."[127]

Lieutenant Barrett was described by several other prisoners. "Captain Wirz surpassed him in cruel inventions to enhance our misery, but he did not equal him in coarse brutality. Like Capt. Wirz, he constantly used the most profane and blasphemous language, and delighted in drawing his pistol and firing it over the heads of the crowd."[128]

---

[120] Dufur, p. 219.
[121] Mann, p. 619.
[122] Northrop, p. 171.
[123] *Ibid.*, p. 175.
[124] Boggs, p. 57.
[125] Northrop, p. 165.
[126] *Ibid.*, p. 180.
[127] Miller, p. 37.
[128] Kellogg, p. 341.

Urban said Barrett was "… one of the most cowardly and brutal wretches that ever lived," and that he "… frequently came into prison and fired a pistol over the heads of the prisoners, to see them dodge around to get away, and their fright appeared to give him intense delight."[129]

Northrop said, "Lieut. Barrett, 5th Georgia, having immediate charge of prisoners, sports a sanitary hat on his red pate. The 'red-headed Lieutenant' he is called. He is the scum of Georgia. One of the most despicable, insignificant, fire-weed characters; phosphoric, ill-tempered, hell-infused images of man that ever served a worthless, wicked cause! He will stand at the gate for hours with a revolver in hand, occasionally pointing and snapping it, swearing practically, calling them 'dirty sons of bitches,' 'lousy hell devils,' laughing fiendishly. He often snatches clubs and throws them with all vengeance into crowds of prisoners who come to look at the brute fool, attracted by his loud oaths... He is meaner than Wirz, but can't carry it out so logically with a tyrant's grace... Wirz did not care so much to look on the ruin he wrought, the misery he caused, but knew his plans. 'Red-head' likes to invite the ladies and go up with them and look down from the wall and hoity toity and simper and giggle, ordering us, fustian style, to do some insignificant thing. At some furtive remark, like 'Where did you get your hat?' he will go into a spasmodic rage… Presenting his revolver, cocked, with assumed dignity will say: 'Who said that? I dare the son of a bitch, the damned Yankee, to say that again!"[130]

Lieutenant Barrett caught one man "flanking," ordered him stripped, tied across a barrel, and "… with a leather whip with five or six hard lashes (called the 'cat'), he cut the miserable man's back into shreds, and he was dead before they got him untied."[131]

Boggs said, "Barrett was a low, ill-born wretch of the most brutal type. He seemed to delight in being present when a slave was to be tied up by the thumbs and whipped, and he took pride in showing the guards how he could knock down and kick the poor helpless imbecile prisoners, who were so idiotic that they could not understand him, and would stand and stare vacantly when he spoke to them. He practiced the most brutal and barbarous cruelties on this class of helpless prisoners. Barrett continued in command of the interior of the prison until March, when the few survivors of his cruelty were sent to our lines. We never knew what became of Barrett until about two years ago a comrade living at Augusta, Ga., stated through the 'National Tribune' that Barrett was living at that place."[132] Northrop described Barrett. "The man who has immediate charge of prisoners has been disgustingly in evidence for three days. He seems a cross between an idiot and a lunatic. His name is Barrett. Before his name was learned prisoners dubbed him 'Red Head,' for his hair being the color of red sand and coarse as horse tail. He is a lieutenant in the 5th Georgia that served as guard at Andersonville until in the summer. The first thing he did was to show his disorderly temper... In camp, a Rebel soldier told me Barrett is hated. He had not been in charge a day before he ordered up several detachments, one after another, and damned them vehemently with a flourish of his revolver for no conceivable reason. His savage antics are outrageous. He has no gentlemanly qualities like the first officer in charge."[133]

Miller said, "… fortunately, this inhuman wretch died near the close of the war."[134]

Prior to being assigned as Commandant at Florence, Colonel George P. Harrison, Jr., had command of the 32nd Georgia Infantry Volunteers and of one of the two Confederate brigades at the Battle of Olustee. Harrison promised the prisoners that any letters or boxes sent through the lines would be given to their rightful recipient. He encouraged the men to appeal to the Federal government to send packages of goods for their relief.

The following exchange supposedly took place between Colonel Harrison and one of the men in the pen: "Col. Harrison, late from Charleston, was standing by one of these guns today, making us fair promises and kindly answering questions about corresponding with friends. One of our men came up, whom we thought green, or who had forgotten where he was and who he was talking to said:

"'Colonel, does a letter need a Reb stamp on, to go through?'

"'A what stamp? Reb!, Young man, you call me a Rebel? What do you mean by Reb?'

"'A Rebel stamp, one of your stamps,' replied the man.

"'You call me a Reb, you puppy! Young man, I do not stand here to be insulted, I'll learn you all not to call the South Rebels! I will fix you.'

"Our voices all rose to apologize for the indiscreet act. The Colonel turned, and his agitation having somewhat

---

129 Urban, p. 466.
130 Northrop, pp. 161, 162.
131 Boggs, p. 60.
132 *Ibid.*, p. 62.
133 Northrop, p. 148.
134 Miller, p. 38.

subsided, said in an earnest way:

"'We are not Rebels, we will have you to understand. The people of the South are honorable, besides I claim to be a gentleman, myself, and I am not a Rebel; neither will I suffer such epithets to be used in relation to my people. I exact from all of you proper respect. If I ever hear another man use such language I will take him out and teach him what I can do. I will show him a Rebel in a way he never thought of, by Heavens!'

"'Well, I suppose I ought to have said your stamps, or Confed stamps.' replied the man.

"'Our Government is the Confederate Government. No, I reckon you don't need a Confederate stamp,' said the Colonel."[135]

As at Andersonville, there was a roll call or, more correctly, a counting every morning; rations came in that afternoon and its sufficiency was based upon that morning's count. "The rules of the prison were such, that any man being absent at roll-call, and thus throwing the thousand out of their rations, should be tied to the whipping-post, situated in the central part of the prison, and there receive as many blows - of the cat-o'-nine-tails - as the chief of police saw fit to inflict."[136] On a few occasions, Boggs would count the newly-dead so that an extra ration would be sent in that afternoon. Sometimes extra rations could be gained by "flanking," which involved rushing to different detachments to be counted more than once. Sometimes eight or ten rations would be gained by failing to subtract those who had died between the time of the counting and the time the rations were issued.

Just as there had been an interest in the newly-built prison on the part of those people who had lived near Andersonville, so was there a similar interest on the part of those who lived near Florence. Ladies would often ascend the guard platform and peer into the squalor. The officers sometimes would bring their lady friends to the pen, probably just for casual entertainment or for something to do in a small town.

While the men were being dispersed from Andersonville to various other prisons, they were subject, even while in transit, to the authority of the Regulators. This authority was re-established immediately at each new prison site, and the same individuals who had wielded power at Andersonville continued to do so at Florence. The Regulators were there with the same brutal "Chief of Police," Stanton, who had been head of security at Andersonville for the previous six months. Police regulations were strictly enforced and violators were usually punished by a shingle spanking to "... that portion of the body best fitted by nature." Sometimes, for a major offense, the prisoner was tied to a stake and whipped on his bare back.[137] Concerning Stanton, "All knew his record as a soldier had been won during his incarceration, as he came too direct from the place where he was drafted to the prison pen to receive any war record worthy of note."[138] They had a site designated as Police Headquarters at Florence, as well.

While Colonel G. P. Harrison was the commandant of prisoners and the guard troops at Florence, the overseer of the prison was Lieutenant Barrett of the 5th Georgia Regiment. "The garrison of this post consists of five battalions of 'reserve troops' (about 1,200 effective men), the Fifth Georgia Regiment, detachments from artillery companies stationed around Charleston, and one small company of cavalry; in all about 1,600 effective men. There is also one battery of light artillery. The artillery detachments have been ordered back to their commands. I think the Fifth Georgia Regiment should remain a short time until the 'reserve forces' can be somewhat instructed in guard duty; they are as yet very badly instructed."[139] At least one prisoner noticed this while he was kept in the open field: "Two sentinels would pace their beat facing each other until just in time to avoid a collision, when they would halt, about face, and march back. Old soldiers would have known better. The proper way would have been for all the sentries on the line to march one way, and the turn at the same time and march back. In that way no portion of the line is left unguarded."[140]

Evidently, Lieutenant Barrett was given a promotion because Phillip Cashmeyer said that Captain Barrett and Lieutenant Wilson had charge of the prison interior. He also stated that a Lieutenant Cheatham, Adjutant, had charge of the searching of the prisoners upon their reception into the pen.[141]

Lieutenant Colonel John F. Iverson assumed command on the 10th of October. From the time of his arrival, "... the deaths [had] decreased from thirty-five to forty per day to one single demise."[142] Colonel Iverson vigorously tried to maintain the best conditions for his charges. He wrote to Sid Winder, the Assistant Adjutant-General, saying that,

---

[135] Northrop, pp. 154, 155.
[136] Dufur, pp. 204, 205.
[137] Miller, p. 41.
[138] Dufur, pp. 209, 210.
[139] *O.R.*, VII, p. 973.
[140] Williams, p. 16.
[141] *O.R.*, VIII, p. 766.
[142] *O.R.*, VII, p. 979.

if he could only increase the rations, then "I will have the satisfaction of knowing that the prisoners under my charge are well housed, plenty of fuel, good hospital accommodations, and in as good a condition as they could reasonably expect."[143]

From his headquarters in Columbia, General Winder forwarded this request with the following endorsement: "The prisoners never will be properly fed until commissaries are ordered for prison duty. I never have been able to get anything from staff officers not on duty with the prisons. I hope that assistant commissaries will be ordered to report to me for duty, and that they be not, as heretofore, young men with no experience; the duty requires experience."[144]

Iverson furnished shovels with which the prisoners could dig wells. He had issued soap for the first time on Saturday, October 22nd. Northrop used the soap, but kept an eye out for snakes down at the creek.

The garrison troops did not receive full rations. Northrop said he "... asked a guard yesterday if it is necessary to stint us on rations. He answered; 'I don't know; I recon 'tis; we'ns don't get the fo'th part we want; we buy of the people. It's mighty tough on yo'ns fellers; so it is on we'ns; we'ns have to do duty."[145] Miller said, "... the guards at the prison were living on short rations."[146]

W. D. Pickett, Lieutenant-Colonel and Inspector General, inspected the prison camp at Florence and reported, on October 12th, to Lieutenant-General William Joseph Hardee, commanding the department. Lt. Colonel Pickett said Colonel Harrison has "... used commendable energy in constructing the stockade and in improving the condition of the prisoners. The stockade in which most of the prisoners are confined ... on the whole, is a healthy one.

"The total number of prisoners is 12,362, in which are included 860 sick in hospital and 20 men out on parole. This number does not include 807 men who have taken the oath of allegiance and enlisted in the service of the Confederate States. The stockade... will be finished in about one week.

"The condition of these prisoners has not been much mis-represented. The great majority of them look emaciated and sickly and are full of vermin, and filthy in the extreme. Three-fourths of them are without blankets and almost without clothing. Few have a change of underclothing...

"For the improvement of their condition I would made the following suggestions:

"First. The Federal authorities should be informed of the condition of their men in regard to clothing and blankets, and they be requested to supply this very urgent demand. I understand there are 5,000 suits now in Charleston for them... They should receive at least one blanket and one suit of clothes for each man.

"Second. The requisite amount of medical officers and medical supplies should be at once furnished - say nine additional surgeons with proper supplies of medicine.

"Third. There is an entire want of cooking utensils...

"Fourth. Shelters of a permanent character should be at once constructed... I have directed Colonel Harrison to construct shelters out of clapboards...

"The quartermaster's department is very deficient in supplies. Eight or ten wagons are urgently required for hauling wood and supplies for the post."[147]

General Hardee endorsed the report of Colonel Pickett: "... everything in my power will be done to alleviate the condition of Yankees in my possession."[148]

This report also had the endorsement of Secretary of War Seddon. "Make extracts of the various portions of this report applicable to the different bureaus, with instructions to take immediate measures to alleviate the suffering stated."[149]

On the morning of Sunday, November 20th, the prisoners received three gills of flour. (One gill equals one-fourth of a pint.) Little did they know this ration was to last for four days. On Monday the 21st, a cold and rainy day, Lieutenant Barrett discovered what he thought was freshly-dug dirt that had been thrown on the ground near the creek. He thought it was evidence a tunnel was being dug and decreed no rations would be issued until the tunnel diggers surrendered. Barrett "... sent in some men with an iron rod about eight feet long and sharpened at the end. Commencing at once corner of the dead line, they ran this into the ground at every two or two and one-half feet, un-

143 *O.R.*, VIII, p. 160.
144 *Ibid.*, p. 161.
145 Northrop, p. 156.
146 Miller, p. 40.
147 *O.R.*, VII, pp. 972, 973.
148 *Ibid.*, p. 974.
149 *Ibid.*

til they went around the whole prison."[150] No one came forth on that day nor on the next day. It was cold and depressing those two days with over an inch of ice on the puddles. The men had to endure over 60 hours with no rations issued.

**Prisoner Being Hung by His Thumbs Behind His Back** - This was an especially brutal punishment that several prisoners were made to suffer on the direct orders of Lieutenant Barrett at Florence.

The starving men decided a few must surrender themselves in order that the rest might draw rations. Twenty men volunteered to take the punishment and four were selected by drawing lots. These four said that they would start a tunnel and then confess they were the ones digging out. This satisfied Lieutenant Barrett, for rations were issued on Wednesday afternoon. He put the "culprits" into irons and said, "I appoint tomorrow as a day on which you will remember me." He then issued two-thirds of a pint of rice to each man but, since there was little or no fuel within the pen, many of the men ate the rice raw. This, in itself, was difficult because most of the men had only a few loose teeth due to scurvy. In the next few hours, hundreds were in agony because of "cramp colic" caused by the raw rice swelling up and absorbing body fluids. Many died horrible deaths that day. On the next morning, the Lieutenant, "... after hardening his heart with villainous whiskey," had the four men's hands tied behind them and then a small rope tied to their thumbs and passed over a log on the roof of the two cabins which were occupied by him. He and his assistants hauled the four up until their feet were off the ground. "The poor fellows screamed with pain and begged the guards, 'for God's sake, to shoot them' Barrett all the while showering from his tongue the most bitter invectives he could master. After a time, three fainted away, and their heads hang limply forward, the fourth sets his teeth hard together, his muscles contracted and his body and face take on a horribly set appearance.

"When Barrett is satisfied the men are taken down; one is dead, two recover and the other is incurable with lock jaw, from which he died the next day. All this is done under the eyes of John H. Winder, Jefferson Davis' friend and counselor."[151]

It was on the previous day, Wednesday, that more dead were carried out than on any other day in the four-month existence of the prison.[152] Dufur said that, on the third day of a fast, extra guards were placed on duty and, at 4 p.m., one pint of meal was issued.[153]

Steward Brown, paroled to work in the hospital as he was at Andersonville, told Northrop the fate of the four who volunteered as tunnelers. "They were put in the guard house the first night and given a supper. In the morning, Lieut. Barrett, half drunk on sorghum whisky, ordered the heroes brought out and strung up. A strong hemp cord was looped around their thumbs, then drawn over ends of poles projecting from the guard house roof, three guards to each of the victims, pulling them clear from the ground. They shrieked in frenzy. The agony was so apparent that a couple of the guard involuntarily protested and were ordered arrested by Barrett. The men begged to be shot. Barrett laughed, sneered, and swore in fiendish delight; answered their agonized supplication with vile ridicule, vulgar boasting, savage denunciation, murderous threats, swaggering about with drawn sword, saying it pleased him best to let them die in their present plight; that he had authority and proposed Yankees find it out." They were cut down after fainting and carried to the hospital.[154]

Miller said he witnessed a prisoner hanging by his thumbs, on November 12th, from the area near the gate. He had gone there to investigate the source of some horrible screams.[155]

There was also a "working squad" to help clean up or to police the prison interior. A person serving on this squad received an extra ration. "It was about this time that I witnessed one of the saddest and most brutal acts I had

---

150 Fosdick, p. 88.
151 Boggs, pp. 60-62.
152 Miller, p. 38.
153 Dufur, p. 227.
154 Northrop, p. 179.
155 Miller, p. 38.

yet witnessed in my prison life. It was a rule of the prison that all the inmates, in obeying the calls of nature, would go to the part of the prison set apart for that purpose. This was of course right and proper, so far as it applied to men who could go there; but in the following case the attempt to enforce the rule was as senseless as it was brutal.

"Among the inmates of our prison-pen was a small, tender-looking drummer boy, about thirteen years of age. He had been a prisoner but a short time, but his health soon gave way, and he commenced to suffer with the diarrhoea. Weak and faint, he got up and proceeded to go to the water-closet arrangement of the prison; but had proceeded but a short distance, when he found that he could not go any farther. A brutal guard, with a malignant spirit that would have disgraced an imp from the infernal regions, and who it is hard to believe was human, deliberately raised his rifle and fired at the child. The bullet sped on its deadly mission, passed through the body of the demon's innocent little victim, and he fell dead on the ground. A cry of horror rang out from those who had witnessed it, and the poor little corpse was tenderly lifted from the ground and borne to a tent.

Strong men wept like children, others raved and swore vengeance, and all expressed it as the most dastardly, cowardly outrage they had yet witnessed.

The companions of the dead boy washed his body, and after fixing him for burial, all who wished had the privilege of seeing him. His beautiful curly hair hung in ringlets around his brow, and his pure white face looked as peaceful as if he were sleeping."[156]

The men became more depressed when exchange talks were discontinued. The possibility that they would see their loved ones left at home became more remote. Daily, the effects of disease and infirmity took their toll. With the passage of time, the prisoners' need for religious solace and consolation increased.

The same lay religious leaders at Andersonville were transferred to Florence where they continued to aid their fellow prisoners. The clergy associated with the garrison troops occasionally visited the prison. "The chaplain of the 5th Georgia regiment preached to the prisoners occasionally and he also sent a great many tracts to be distributed among the patients in the hospital. "[157] The Reverend Mister Gardner was one of several clergy who stayed with their fellow comrades when captured and endured the hardships of the prison. "Rev. Mr Gardner, of the 135th Ohio regiment, died in the early part of November. He was one to conduct the religious meetings at Andersonville, and also frequently held short services over some of the poor boys who died there. His illness was a severe and protracted one..."[158]

The rations were issued raw. During the first two weeks after the prison at Florence was established, meat was issued on alternate days. This was stopped and no meat was ever issued afterwards. The rations, about three-fourths of the time, were eight ounces of corn meal. Occasionally "cow peas," turnips, corn on the cob, or rice would be substituted.

"The food we received was of the worst description, and hardly enough to keep any one alive. It generally consisted of one pint of cornmeal, or wheat flour, and sometimes a few raw beans. Sometimes we received salt, but as often none; and when we did get this article there was so little of it that we could hardly taste it when mixed with the food. Fralich and I discovered that by putting our salt together and dissolving it in water, we could get a better taste of it by dipping our mush into the water. In this way we dined together until we were separated. It was certainly more social than elegant looking to see us with little wooden spoons dip each mouthful as we ate it into the same cup, which contained the precious salt.

"I did not see any meat of any kind while in this prison."[159]

"... when we first came to Florence our rations consisted of a little over a pint of corn meal, two or three small sweet potatoes, and a little meat once a day. In place of potatoes, we would get a few peas or a gill of rice. The meal was brought in two-bushel sacks, the highest number of sacks to the thousand men being ten sacks in any one day, or twenty bushels to the thousand men. As there were thirty-two quarts to the bushel, each thousand received 640 quarts of unsifted meal, or a little over a pint to a man. As December and January came in, the sweet potatoes, meat and rice were things of the past... until when January came we received only eight bushels, or 256 quarts of meal to the thousand men."[160] "We scraped the inner bark off of our scanty rations of green pine wood and eat it, made gum of the pitch pine and chewed it, to keep our jaws going. On one occasion I saw a man of the 111th New York and a company comrade of my two hut mates cook some *scraps of old boot legs*, stir in meal until it was thick gruel, and eat

---

[156] Urban, pp. 466-468.
[157] Kellogg, pp. 339-340.
[158] *Ibid.*
[159] Urban, 465.
[160] Fosdick, pp. 98, 99.

it!"[161]

"When the rations would be brought in, he would gather up an armful of clubs, and after the prisoners had collected in considerable crowds he would rush in and throw his clubs into the crowd, with all the force he could muster. Men had arms broken, and others were crippled in various ways by these fits of Barrett's insane rage."[162]

Smith, in his book, *From Andersonville to Freedom*, related a very pathetic tale about the scarcity of food supplied to the prisoners at Florence. "I will relate one amusing incident connected with prison life. I know a Connecticut man, John Chapman, Company B, Sixteenth Connecticut Volunteers. His home was in Suffield, Conn., and Chapman told me the story. Chapman took into Andersonville a little dog, which had been with him since his enlistment, two years before, with him at the battles of South Mountain and Antietam, and which was with him when he was captured at Plymouth, North Carolina. From Andersonville, Chapman with his dog, went to Charleston, then to Florence, South Carolina, all the time guarding jealously his dog, but one morning, at Florence, the dog was not. Chapman barely lived to reach home. One day, after the war, at a dining-room in Hartford, he overheard a man say, 'The sweetest morsel I ever tasted was a little yellow dog I stole, and cooked and ate in Florence prison.' Chapman at once said to the man, 'Friend, that was my dog.'"[163]

A man named Armstrong from Charleston was commissioned sutler by Colonel Iverson. Iverson set the prices and they were very reasonable, with sweet or Irish potatoes going for $20 per bushel.[164]

A short time after the men had been in the prison, they learned most of their comrades who had been left at Andersonville because they were so sick, now were in the hospital which was located about a mile from the pen.[165] The hospital had armed guards around it and was surrounded by a deadline. The hospital was composed of "... nine long sort of sheds, made of a frame-work of poles overlaid with pine boughs, which afforded some protection from the sun, but none at all from the rain.

"There were ward divisions, eleven in number, and each one was in charge of a ward-master, assisted by from eight to ten nurses. There were also seven stewards, whose business it was to receive the medicine from the dispensary, and see that it was faithfully administered to the sick, of whom there were about sixty in each ward."[166]

This was how John A. Reed said this first "stable hospital" came to pass: "Our condition evoked the sympathy of the major in command of the prison at Florence, and he being short of supplies, made an appeal to the surrounding planters for provisions temporarily, and it was not long until their negro slaves had prepared for us the most nourishing meal we had had since we had been captives. Having no guard of any consequence, the major permitted us to roam around pretty much as we pleased. I once heard the major say, 'No guard is needed; they are too damned weak to run away if they wished to do so.'

"The following day, after our arrival, negroes began building a stockade, which we knew was intended for our future prison. The attention of the major being called to the condition of the sick, he replied, 'What can I do? The only hospital we have here is now overcrowded with sick and wounded.' Some unoccupied, dilapidated stable were pointed out to him, and he said with feeling.

"'Take any stable you find unoccupied and do what you can to make them comfortable, and I will render you all the aid I can.'

"A barn, the property of a railroad engineer, was selected and among those assisting in getting it ready and looking after the sick were Sergt. James Gilmore, Corp. John Sheaffer, Private Jerome Sheaffer and myself, (George W. Bumbaugh) all of Co. A, 101st (P.V.I.) Regiment, and James Dunlap, of Co. G, 103rd Penna. By nightfall, we had the sick all under cover of beds of clean straw. Evidently, the major in charge had too much heart for the position, for in the course of a few weeks he was superseded by a captain more of the type of our Andersonville jailer. The new commandant instituted a change immediately after he took control. The day after his arrival he made it obligatory on all the attendants at the stable hospital to sign a parole not to attempt to escape. The parole was such that, after discussing it among ourselves we decided that there was no such a thing as a Confederate government, and that there was no moral obligation on our part to observe it."[167] Having been told that they would be put into the prison on October 6th, the five attendants, plus two others guided by a Negro, Uncle Pete, set out for freedom. They had a compass and a railroad guide. Uncle Peter told them to rub their feet and legs thoroughly with pine straw which would

161 *Ibid.*, p. 99.
162 Fosdick, pp. 111, 112.
163 Smith, pp. 22, 23.
164 Northrop, p. 159.
165 Kellogg, p. 320.
166 *Ibid.*, p. 321.
167 Reed, pp. 59, 60.

confound the pursuing dogs. After several weeks of heading in the general direction of Wilmington, they were captured and sent back to Florence. They knew to use fictitious names which was lucky because, after their return, "... an order was read in prison that in the event of our capture we were to be shot without trial." Because of his swollen feet and high fever, he was selected to be released on parole the next day with a group examined by the doctors and chosen for exchange.[168]

At about 4 o'clock every afternoon, the young Surgeon in charge, Dr. Strother, would come to the prison and examine all those men who were at sick call. He would determine who was sick enough to warrant being admitted to the "stable" hospital. The sick who were able walked to the hospital, and those too weak or debilitated rode in an army wagon drawn by a span of mules. Near the middle of October, Dr. Strother caught yellow fever and nearly lost his life. His place was taken by the Assistant Surgeon, Junius O'Brien, a Kentuckian, and a "rabid secessionist."

**Interior of a Hospital Shed at Florence** - Several sheds were built within the pen and prisoners were laid out on each side of the shed with a walkway down the center. Each was considered a "ward." (Boggs)

On about the 20th of October, the prisoners were ordered to clear the northwest corner of the pen of all shebangs so the hospital could be moved inside the stockade. A police guard was put around this space. The reason for moving the hospital inside the pen was never stated, but it was probably for security or convenience. At first, there were no structures in the stockade for the shelter of the sick, but, by the first of November, one shed had been completed and preparations for others were being made. "Two of them were seventy-five feet long, and thirty-one in width, without a nail in them. The frames were made of timber, cut in the swamp near the prison, and fastened together with wooden pins. The roof was made of 'shakes,' or shingles held on by heavy poles for weights."[169] "After we had remained there six or eight weeks, the rebels erected three sheds, forty or fifty feet in length. They were erected in one corner of the stockade and used for a hospital. There were no walls to these sheds."[170]

The sick were carried in and laid out in two double rows under each shed. Each double row was called a ward. "Wards are being built on hospital ground from poles and lumber, by men on parole. The work is slow. Medical supplies received from Columbia, South Carolina, from the medical purveyor, are less than half the requisitions of Surgeons, Junius O'Brien, David Flood and Strather."[171] The hospital had no beds, floors, nor straw, "... though it could be easily had." "A short distance from the prison are stacks of old straw and acres of wild grass, which men would have gladly pulled had they permitted."[172]

"Dr. O'Brien was now relieved of his duties as Surgeon in charge, by Dr. David Fludd, who was one of the original signers of the Secession Act which placed South Carolina out of the Union. He was very kind and gentlemanly, however, with us, and won the respect of all who knew him."[173]

"A bakery was also established, and a small loaf of wheat bread issued to the patients daily. The surgeons in charge seemed to do as well as possible with the small resources and means which they possessed. Indeed they were very kind to us, and manifested considerable interest in our welfare."[174] There was a steady increase in the number of patients until there were nearly 800 crowded within the hospital.

Kellogg was made a hospital steward after he went to Lieutenant Colonel Iverson's headquarters and signed the following parole:

---

[168] *Ibid.*, pp. 60-63.
[169] Kellogg, p. 326.
[170] Dufur, p. 213.
[171] Northrop, p. 165.
[172] *Ibid.*
[173] Kellogg, p. 326.
[174] Abbott, p. 206.

*Head-Quarters, Military Prison*
*Florence, S. C., Oct. 19th, 1864*

*I, R. H. Kellogg, Sergeant Major 16th Connecticut Vols., a paroled prisoner of war, do hereby pledge my word of honor that I will not violate my parole by going beyond one-half mile from the hospital limits.*

*Witness, C. H. Moody*
*Signed, R. H. Kellogg*[175]

Kellogg was assigned to the 5th ward, and had over one hundred and fifty patients under his care. He, with the help of a few nurses, had to give medicines, sometimes three times a day, to these one-hundred-and-fifty needy patients. In about the middle of November, the rations of the ward-masters, and other hospital attendants, were greatly reduced. "Before this, we had received plenty of flour, beans, corn meal and salt, with an occasional issue of fresh beef, and now a bakery and cook house were constructed outside, and we received what we had, already cooked, but greatly reduced in quantity. At this time, our comrades in prison were only getting a pint of coarse corn meal, with the smallest modicum of salt occasionally. We were not allowed to carry any of our food to them..."[176]

There was one secure area at Florence where prisoners were placed in close confinement. This dungeon, called the "Bastille," was dreaded by all because it was dark, damp, and cold. "The Bastille... was a small stockade built of logs closely planted, about twelve to twenty feet or two hundred and forty square feet, floored above with logs and planking to hold a cannon and other paraphernalia, for readiness in case of a 'break' by the prisoner. Under this, was the 'Bastile' with its log door and no daylight, except such as sifted through the slight crevices, banked by earth, six or more feet high, outside (the stockade was banked the same and was the 'promenade' of the guards) which made it literally a cellar into which the poor devils seeking escape, trading for food, and were caught, were thrown, to suffer as none can imagine."[177]

About that time a load of stores arrived at Florence for the hospital from the Sanitary Commission. Among the stores was a large quantity of sheets, "... some of them entirely new, and of fine quality."[178] Though the patients were lying upon the bare ground, the principal surgeon decided that the sheets should be exchanged for sweet potatoes, which would be of more benefit to those with scurvy. "A notice to this effect was posted in several different places, and soon the ladies, young and old, were flocking in from all the surrounding country, anxious to make the exchange. In this way quite a large quantity of potatoes was gained and issued to the men in the hospital. The old sheets were used for bandages, and were invaluable for this purpose, as many amputations of limbs, affected by gangrene, were almost constantly taking place. Many of the ladies who came to the Dispensary to examine the goods, were dressed to the height of fashion, wearing clothing of the most costly material. It was difficult to see where the war had cost them much personal suffering."[179]

The medicines prescribed for the prisoners at Florence were obtained from Doctor Chisholm, the medical purveyor at Columbia, South Carolina. The doctors were limited in both the quantity of the medicines that they could give the men and in the variety available for them to prescribe. The supply that was ordered from Columbia for a month was usually used up in a couple of weeks. When this happened, the doctors would have to resort to using barks and roots of the Southern forests to make medicinal decoctions. One of the treatments for diarrhea was the use of one of the decoctions or teas steeped from oak, sweet gum, or persimmon bark.[180] The dispensary was outside the stockade and only a few yards from the guard house.

"Nearly all the packages of herbs in the dispensary, bore the label of the 'C.S.A. Laboratory,' but the quinine, and valuable drugs, had on a foreign label, English, I think, and undoubtedly found their way into the country by way of the blockade runners."[181] On Friday, December 2nd, Northrop went to sick call and got a decoction of wild cherry bark. The steward gave it out to whomever came with a tin cup, or bottle, until it was gone. About half of those who came got some of the elixir. The steward had two pails and would ask what the patient wanted, either decoction of wild cherry or one of white oak bark and sweet fern.[182]

All the diseases at Andersonville were present at Florence. The rations were slightly more abundant, varied,

[175] Kellogg, p. 322.
[176] *Ibid.*, p. 340.
[177] Styple, ed., p. 175.
[178] Kellogg, p. 327.
[179] *Ibid.*, pp. 327, 328.
[180] *Ibid.*, p. 324.
[181] *Ibid.*
[182] Northrop, p. 180.

and, therefore, more nutritious. On September 17th, Northrop said he had a "very pronounced" case of scurvy that had again manifested itself in his legs. In his diary he entered: "Press the swollen flesh and it does not return to shape. It is yellow, dark in spots. On one ankle, the flesh girds tightly about the bone. Every step taken seems like tearing it loose. We buy miserable apples and fine sweet potatoes. I ate them raw. It was the greatest happiness I had experienced from eating, though blood ran from my gums, inflamed with scurvy, and some of my teeth tore loose."[183]

As at Millen, the dead at Florence were laid by the gate side-by-side, heads to the wall, to await the dead wagon. "The dead would be brought to the gate and there be left for twenty-four hours before they were drawn away, instead of being picked up and carried outside each morning, as the rebels had previously been in the habit of doing."[184]

The dead had their big toes tied together with a cotton string, and their arms folded on their breasts. Taken in the carts, into ditches they were "... tumbled in like so many dogs; a few pine tops were thrown upon the bodies, a few shovelsful of dirt, and then haste was made to open a new ditch for other victims."[185] The dead were buried "... on the plantation of Dr. Garrett, a wealthy landholder, and an owner of many slaves but who was said to be a Union man. He offered to enclose the ground used as a place of burial, by a railing, to preserve it from desecration. The dead were carted away from the hospital every morning, in an army wagon drawn by mules. The deaths amounted to twelve per cent per month of the whole number."[186] This dead wagon was filled to overflowing each day; it carried the dead to the gaping slit trenches where the Union prisoners buried their own. Three thousand died in the four months of the prison's existence.

The people in the South hoped McClellan would defeat Lincoln in the election of 1864 because he would soon bring peace whereas Lincoln's election would just bring a continuation of the war. In order to find out the sentiment of the prisoners, the authorities at Florence held a mock election on Tuesday, November 8th, within the pen, similar to those held in several prisons throughout the South. "On the day of election, a quantity of white and black beans were given to Sergeant Kemp of the 1st Conn. Cavalry, by the Rebel Quartermaster, with the understanding that they be used as ballots, whereby the political opinions of the prisoners might be ascertained; the white beans representing McClellan, and the black ones President Lincoln. Two empty bags were hung up on the stockade, inside the dead line,' and the 'thousands' were ordered to fall in, in succession, and all who wished to vote, to march in line to the spot. Beans were given them, and one by one they stepped up and deposited their vote as they chose, a man standing by, the while, to see that no fraud was committed. I have not the exact figures, but I think the proportion was two and a half for Lincoln to one for McClellan. This was an expression of feeling and opinion among men who were ragged and half famishing with hunger, yet were not in favor of any peace gained by disgraceful compromise."[187]

Miller said the results were never announced; Barrett discontinued the mock election when he found the results were running ten black (Republican, War, Lincoln) beans to one white (Democrat, Peace, McClellan).

Northrop said, on the day of the sham election, that, by 8 o'clock in the morning, the guard walk was swarming with spectators, both men and ladies, to watch the election. The men were marched to the polling places in squads. Sometimes whole squads went to the bag to deposit black beans. When a man separated and went to the Democratic bag, the Confederates would clap their hands and shout a "rebel yell." The prisoners would taunt the Rebels shouting, "Colonel, give us another bag of your black beans." Where there were 12,000 in the pen, about 1,800 voted. To say it another way, about five-sixths decided not to vote because doing so was only for the enjoyment of the Confederates.[188]

On several occasions, the prisoners were offered their freedom if they would come out and cooperate with the authorities. Confederate recruiting officers sought men to take the "oath of treason" as some of the prisoners called the oath of allegiance. Those willing to go out would yell to a guard, "When can you take us out? I have starved long enough."[189] The men who went out were considered traitors by their fellow prisoners and were subject to their wrath. They would be stripped of their blankets and cooking utensils when they were making the long trip to the gate. These attacks became so frequent that Confederate guards were stationed inside the pen to protect those going out.

---

[183] *Ibid.*, p. 138.
[184] Dufur, pp. 217, 218.
[185] *O.R.*, VII, pp. 976, 977.
[186] Kellogg, p. 424.
[187] *Ibid.*, pp. 329, 330.
[188] Northrop, p. 172.
[189] *Ibid.*, p. 157.

Brigadier-General W. M. Gardner wrote, on November 2nd, to General Samuel Cooper, Adjutant and Inspector General in Richmond: "Lieutenant General Hardee, without my knowledge, has given permission to Colonel Daniel, of the Fifth Georgia Regiment, to fill up his companies with such prisoners as should take the oath of allegiance and enter our service. About 1,100 of them enlisted, and have been carried away to some place unknown to me by one of General Hardee's inspectors."[190] On November 5th, 270 prisoners went forward and took the oath of allegiance to the Confederate States of America.[191] On the 17th of November, many of the Yankee prisoners who had taken the oath began to return to prison.[192] They were found to be completely untrustworthy by the Confederates, deserting at their first opportunity. They had been at Charleston, doing duty. They did seem to have put on some weight, and had haircuts and shaves. They had been given uniforms of a gray color similar to galvanized tin, and so were derisively called "galvanized Yanks." They were met with a very cold reception by their comrades who had remained true to their government and to the rule about giving aid and comfort to the enemy. These "galvanized Yanks" soon rid themselves of the gray clothing in order to blend back into the prison community and to lessen the stigma of their unfaithfulness.[193]

One Confederate officer attempted to enticed the prisoners to enlist in the Confederate army in this manner: "A large dry goods box was rolled into prison and one or two smaller ones, and when all things were in readiness, the rebel officers came in with their enlistment rolls, which were spread on the smaller boxes preparatory to taking names. Then our Charlestonian mounted the larger box and addressed us at length, asserting that our government had thrown us aside, and cared not what we had suffered nor what our fate might be... He dwelt a short time on the grand achievements of the Confederate army, and gave it, as his firm belief, that the South would soon be a free and independent nation, winding up by offering us an opportunity of enlisting in what he termed the 'most powerful army on earth,' which in a few months would march to final victory, and by joining them we with the rest, would become the happy recipients of a large bounty, and a land warrant for one hundred and sixty acres of good land, in a warm climate, where we could become prosperous farmers.

"... we grew so indignant at his audacity that we all rushed at him with one impulse, dumped him and his goods box the other side up, and he barely escaped with his life. The enrolling papers were captured and destroyed by our loyal boys. Several who had become nearly starved and almost destitute of clothing, made their wishes known to the rebels and were taken outside - about 300 in number."[194]

Northrop said that, on Thursday the 17th, about 300 prisoners who had gone out and taken the "Rebel oath" were returned into the pen again. They were from Sommerville, South Carolina, and were dressed in full Confederate uniforms. They were stripped of all property except the clothes on their backs. They were despised yet, at the same time, they were pitied by the loyal men who had turned down the offers. The galvanized Confederates said they were turned back in because they had stolen a bull and some chickens with which to feed themselves. "Knowing the boys were coming, Col. Harrison had the loyal prisoners working for the 'Rebel poor,' as the boys call them, building shanties on the pretense of sheltering the sick; and now these 'galvanized Rebs' come pouring in, enough to four times fill the huts he has let us build, and the shelterless for whom we intended them, get no relief."[195]

At other times, officers came in, recruiting for a pioneer corps. The men were promised plenty to eat and that they would never need to shoulder a gun. They were to go with the army to build roads and earthworks, to clear fields of fire, and to do other construction.

On Thursday, the 24th, the Confederates came in and sought bookkeepers to go to Charleston and other cities in the South. Those wishing to go were to appear at the gate and volunteer in the presence of an officer. Large wages were offered as an inducement.

After the war, President Cleveland would veto a bill extending a pension to those who took the oath while prisoners of war.[196]

One prisoner at Florence devised a clever method for sneaking food into the pen. Northrop related how a man named Slick Brown had "... left his home to escape Rebel rule, and joined the army of the Cumberland; had been a prisoner ten months; had an interview with a sister at the prison gate last August, when Lieut. Davis was in command, during Wirz' sickness, and received a few articles of apparel and food."

---

[190] *O.R.*, VII, p. 1086.
[191] Miller, p. 47.
[192] *Ibid.*
[193] *Ibid.*, p. 39.
[194] Fosdick, pp. 94-96.
[195] Northrop, p. 175.
[196] Miller, p. 39.

At Florence, Slick Brown was allowed to go out and chop wood. When the choppers returned at sunset, they were searched and not allowed to bring anything in except wood or a bundle of wild grass, unless they had bought it from the sutler. Slick Brown would take one of the logs that he had cut and hollow it out so that he could bring in a peck of beans or potatoes concealed in the hollow cavity.[197]

Later in November, word was sent into the pen to make out a list of all prisoners who were born outside of the United States. Included on this list were to be also those prisoners whose terms of enlistment service had expired. The prisoners concluded that some kind of partial exchange had been agreed upon and that it would be in their best interest if they fit into one or both of the categories. When the Confederates read the roll, it must be assumed that they thought all the prisoners were foreign mercenaries.

"The next day, an order came in for all those whose names appeared on the roll to appear at the gate. They were marched out and stood around a stump from which a Rebel officer gave the following speech:

"'Prisoners, you can no longer have any doubt that your Government has cruelly abandoned you; it makes no efforts to release you, and refuses all our offers of exchange. We are anxious to get our men back, and have made every effort to do so, but it refuses to meet us on any reasonable grounds. Your Secretary of War has said that the Government can get along very well without you, and General Halleck has said that you were nothing but a set of blackberry pickers and coffee boilers, anyhow.

"'You've already endured much more than it could expect of you; you served it faithfully during the term you enlisted for, and now, when it is through with you, it throws you aside to starve and die. You also can have no doubt that the Southern Confederacy is certain to succeed in securing its independence. It will do this in a few months. It now offers you an opportunity to join its service, and if you serve it faithfully to the end, you will receive the same rewards as the rest of its soldiers. You will be taken out of here, be well clothed and fed, given a good bounty, and, at the conclusion of the War receive a land warrant for a nice farm. If you '

"But we had heard enough. The Sergeant of our division - a man with a stentorian voice - sprang out and shouted:

"'Attention, First Division!'

"We Sergeants of Hundreds repeated the command down the line. Shouted he:

"'First Division, about - '

"Said we:

"'First Hundred, about - '

"Second Hundred, about - '

'"Third Hundred, about - '

"'Fourth Hundred, about - ' etc., etc.

"Said he -

"'Face!!'

"Ten Sergeants repeated 'face!' one after the other, and each man in the hundreds turned on his heel. Then our leader commanded -

"'First Division, forward! March!' and we strode back into the Stockade, followed immediately by all the other divisions, leaving the orator still standing on the stump.

"The Rebels were furious at this curt way of replying. We had scarcely reached our quarters when they came in with several companies, with loaded guns and fixed bayonets. They drove us out of our tents and huts, into one corner, under the pretense of hunting axes and spades, but in reality to steal our blankets, and whatever else they could find that they wanted, and to break down and injure our huts, many of which, costing us days of patient labor, they destroyed in pure wantonness."[198]

This rebuttal of the overture put forth by the Confederates was typical of the responses of most prisoners. Overwhelmingly, the prisoners followed the motto of the Ex-Prisoner of War Association: "Death Before Dishonor."

Commerce between the prisoners and the guard force continued at Florence as it had at Andersonville. The guards still hoped to acquire U. S. Staff and New York State buttons for $10 each.

This was how one guard had been flimflammed out of some money. "The rebel soldiers belonging to the different battalions were frequently granted passes by Lieut. Col. Iverson, which allowed them to come into the prison and trade for gold pens, rings, pocket-books, knives, buttons, or anything that they could get, giving in return sweet po-

[197] Northrop, pp. 175, 176.
[198] McElroy, Vol. II, pp. 467, 468.

tatoes or Confederate money. A 'Johnnie' came in one day, with a great desire to obtain some New York State buttons, which being very showy, were in great demand and high in price. It was quite plain that he had traded for them before, as he had a full row upon the gray coat he wore, and also four of them on the back. While he was bargaining with two or three of the prisoners, one of the boys stepped softly up behind, and with a sharp knife cut off the four upon the tails of his coat. Then presenting himself in front of the 'reb,' he said, 'I have a few New York State buttons that perhaps I'll sell you.' 'Have you?' exclaimed he, with evident joy upon his countenance, 'Let me look at them.' Taking them in his hand, and carefully examining them, he remarked, 'They are just like those on my coat.' so paying a good round price for his own buttons, he departed, greatly pleased that he had found some 'more of that same kind.'"[199]

There was a prisoner at Andersonville named Stanton who was out on parole, detailed to dispense food from the ration wagon. He was a very dark-skinned Irishman who had "... a bulldog face and build, hair, strange in such men was short and kinky - so much so that he was named the 'Irish nigger.'" Once he assaulted one of the "ever-present 'shadows'" following the wagon, begging for a bone. Stanton kicked him with his boot, lacerating his lip and knocking out 8 or 10 teeth.

Later, at Florence, Stanton was Assistant Chief of Police to Big Pete the Canadian Frenchman who was the Chief of Police. After Big Pete fell ill, Stanton assumed command. Another incident involved a Pennsylvanian who used, without permission, a cup to cook in and returned it to its owner. A cup was a most precious item in prisons. Though the cup was returned, this man was sentenced by Stanton to be lashed 150 times, until the offender's back was shredded.

A Sergeant Edmund English was sentenced by Stanton to an indeterminate number of lashes for, allegedly, calling Stanton an "Irish nigger." "Trial at the Bull Pen Court was denied him by Stanton, though that made little difference to Stanton as he intended to whip this man most brutally... On the 21st of October the hearing of English was to take place before Lieutenant Barrett... A dozen more men were mustered who had agreed to do their best to save English, though it cost their lives and the life of Stanton was to be taken, at the first stroke of the lash... He was brought to the post and tied, with Stanton standing close by, his fiendish eyes feasting upon the form he thought he had in his power and would kill, if he was allowed, and the victim failed to survive the ordeal... The brave, defiant English, with flashing eyes stood and answered the charges of his tormentor. When Barrett said 'We will now hear the prisoner in his own behalf.' Without a tremor of fear, in a clear, plain but thrilling, convincing argument, did English state his case; and while doing so, was struck by the end of Stanton's club in the mouth, accompanied with vile epithets. Further outrage was stopped by Barrett. Pointing his revolver close to the face of Stanton, he said, 'Another move, and I'll blow your damn brains out!' Barrett stock rose in our esteem, slightly - English was not ordered free. Stanton foamed and gnashed his ugly teeth, and made most awful threats until Barrett closed his tirade by a movement of his pistol to the very mouth of the brute - so close it left its imprint..." The ruthless grip of Stanton was broken. Stanton was exchanged in December and sent to Camp Parole, Annapolis, Maryland. There, Stanton was met by the Pennsylvanian whom he had lashed so unmercifully in Florence. Stanton was shot dead. Conveniently, no witnesses came forward and "... no one shed tears over the 'Irish Nigger.'"[200]

It was implied, by several authors, that some U. S. Sanitary Commission goods were used by the garrison troops, but most agreed that they were more fairly distributed at Florence than at Andersonville. On Thursday, October 20th, Northrop said Sanitary goods from the North had been at Florence for several days. "Yesterday blankets were issued, about five to one hundred men. Names of the worst cases taken; blanks and prize tickets were placed in a hat, from which we drew. I saw the sentry on post this morning with a blanket on in lieu of an overcoat. Lieut. Barrett, 5th Georgia, sports a sanitary hat on his red pate."[201]

On Saturday, "... several hundred suits or pieces of suits, of clothing" were issued. This averaged out to about four pieces to a hundred men. Shirts, drawers, pants and hats were issued... No man got more than one piece of clothing except some of men paroled outside the pen received whole suits. Those on parole were usually scorned and envied by those inside the pen who would have preferred to have been given their discarded clothing. .[202]

On Thursday, November 17th, another load of Sanitary goods was distributed to paroled men outside, to the police, and to some for hospital usage.[203]

---

[199] Kellogg, pp. 335, 336.
[200] Styple, ed., pp. 127-152.
[201] Northrop, p. 161.
[202] *Ibid.*, p. 164.
[203] *Ibid.*, p. 175.

In November, a large load of stores was received at Florence from the U. S. Sanitary Commission, "... consisting of shirts, drawers, hats, shoes, stockings, slippers, dressing gowns, blankets, bed-quilts, besides things for the comfort of the sick, such as condensed coffee and milk, extract of beef, tomatoes in tin cans, etc. These articles were stored in the log house used as a dispensary, and one of the prisoners placed in charge of them. They were drawn from this place as they were needed, by the stewards, and by them given to the ward-masters, who issued them to the sick men in their respective wards ... keeping an account of them as they were expended. The Surgeon and other officers acted very honorable, allowing nothing to be stolen or wasted."[204]

When the sanitary commission clothing was distributed, Dufur received a "... tall, light colored wool hat." Not needing that hat, and, since the men would not trade for the pants or shirt he did need, he traded it to a Confederate sergeant for a peck of sweet potatoes. He and his tent-mate ate a few of them; then he dug a hole in the ground and buried the remainder. They slept with their heads on top of the potato bin, but, the next morning, they found someone had dug into the potato bin and all but two or three had been stolen.[205]

"While it was gratefully received there was not enough to supply very many of the needy ones. My one suit of clothing was in fair condition, but I was of course anxious to secure a new supply, not knowing how much longer my imprisonment would continue. So taking my shirt, tore several rents in it, and giving it to a comrade whose detachment was called before mine, told him to wear it when he went before the distributing officer. He did so, and came back with a new shirt. When my detachment was called I put on my torn shirt, and appeared before the officer who was giving out the clothing. When he saw me, he asked me if that was my shirt. I promptly replied that it was. 'Is it the only one you have?' 'Yes, sir.' 'Well, I am sorry for you, my boy, but I have given out one new shirt on that today, and cannot give another.'

"Can you imagine how I felt? I went back to my tent chagrined and crestfallen, to bear the badinage of my comrades, and procuring a needle and thread sewed up my torn shirt as best I could."[206]

Two days after Thanksgiving, on the 26th of November, the long-awaited time of parole finally arrived for the men in the Florence hospital. They were only told their parole was imminent about an hour before the actual proceedings began. At about 1 p.m., a group of Confederate officers, accompanied by several clerks and a small group of soldiers, came into the hospital. Two tables were brought out; on these tables the rolls of the hospital were spread out. "The masters of the different wards, in turn, called off the names of the patients as they stood on the roll-book, until fifty from each ward had been paroled; making three hundred and fifty in all. One well man was then paroled to each company of ten sick ones, as attendants. These were selected by the rebel Surgeons, from the hospital nurses, &c. No man was allowed to go, who could not walk up to the table and sign the parole papers, and for this reason scores of poor fellows were left behind, while their comrades who were stronger, passed out before them. The paper to which we signed our names, as nearly as I can recollect, read as follows:

> *We, the undersigned, do solemnly pledge our sacred word of honor, that we will not take up arms again in any garrison, fortification or field work of the United States, or do any police or constabulary duty, or any duty usually performed by soldiers, until we shall have been duly declared exchanged.*[207]

They were told they should be ready to leave for Savannah on Monday. The nurses, on Sunday, prepared their charges to leave by giving them haircuts, shaves, and by scrubbing off their accumulated grime with soap which had been requisitioned by the surgeon-in-charge.

Shortly before sunset on Monday, they were marched out of the stockade, and encamped for the night near the cook-house; there, two day's rations were issued to the men for the journey home. For the first time in months and months, no guard was placed around those soon to leave.

The men were aroused at about 2 o'clock in the morning, and they were marched over to the railroad track about a half mile away. There, the roll of the entire group was called and the men were then loaded into the box-cars. Each car was loaded with 55 prisoners and two guards. A large tub was placed inside of each car to be filled by men especially detailed for that purpose. A Doctor Orme, of Milledgeville, Georgia, accompanied the men on the train. At about sunrise, the train pulled out; it arrived in Charleston after dark, having taken the entire day to travel 103 miles. They stayed about two hours in Charleston and then left on another train for Savannah. While on their way, they

---

[204] Kellogg, pp. 323, 324.
[205] Dufur, pp. 229-231.
[206] Miller, pp. 39, 40.
[207] Kellogg, pp. 342-344.

passed a trainload of prisoners that had been confined at Blackshear, Georgia, which was heading for Florence. In Savannah, with Sherman only 45 miles away, the men were kept in a vacant lot at the corner of Liberty and East Broad streets. The next morning, just after sunrise, they marched down to the dock where three steamers were waiting. Before boarding, the men haggled over the price of a piece of pie from a group of women, either $100 in Confederate money or three cents in silver. The names of the three steamers were the *Beauregard*, the *General Lee*, and the *Jeff Davis*. The first carried the officers, and flew the flag of truce. The latter two carried the enlisted men.[208]

Kellogg and his group left the dock at about 9 o'clock in the morning and, after an hour, the transfer was completed in the Savannah River. They boarded the "receiving ship" the *New York*, and then moved as rapidly as feasible to a "clothing ship" by the name of the *Crescent*. It was on the "feeding ship" that they received a welcome home feast and a new blue uniform. On the *Crescent*, they were taken to the transport *General Lyon* which transported them up past Hatteras to Fortress Monroe and then on to Annapolis. There, they received two-months' pay and a 30-day furlough.[209]

This was how James Greacen was paroled from Florence: "The morning of the 26th of November, 1864, three rebel officers came into the hospital part of the stockade, saying they were going to parole 500 of the sick. The hospital was divided into wards of 100 men each, each man numbered. The officers informed us that they would parole the first fifty of each of the first two wards... When the hospital steward commenced calling the roll of my ward, No. 9, I anxiously awaited my name... Next the steward said, 'No. 48, James Greacen, Co. I, 22nd Mich. Inf'ty.' I then stepped forward to the table, signed my parole, swearing that I would never take up arms for the U. S., until legally exchanged and notified thereof... The next morning we were placed on flat cars, reaching Savannah about four o'clock in the afternoon, where we were permitted to camp in an open field adjoining the city... furnished with white bread, sweet potatoes, and coffee.

"The next morning... three transports lay at the dock which conveyed us down the Savannah river to a point opposite Fort Pulaski. About three o'clock that afternoon, we stepped off the rebel flagship onto the *General Lyon*.

"The union officers shook each by the hand as we stepped on board... When taken prisoner, I weighed 180 pounds, I now weighed 96 pounds. Bath tubs and soap were at once furnished us, our rags, vermin and all, floated down the river, new suits throughout, were furnished us, after which we were furnished with coffee, bread, butter, beef, potatoes, and a gill of vinegar.

"The *General Lyon* weighed anchor the next morning, and the next day, on our way to Annapolis, nearly went to the bottom in a storm off Cape Hatteras, where two months later she did sink to the bottom with 500 paroled prisoners on board. Here, our clothing, which we had drawn but four days before, was destroyed, and we were again supplied with new clothing, the government paid us four months pay and gave each of us a 60 days' furlough."[210]

On Sunday, November 27th, orders were received by Lieutenant Barrett to parole 1,000 of the sickest of the prisoners. Since there were about 10,000 inmates, this meant about 1 man in 10 would be leaving. There was the expected sudden increase in the number of sick prisoners; those who were already sick suddenly got worse, hoping to become part of the lucky 10 percent.

The first thousand was called before the surgeon so that one hundred of the sickest could be weeded out. "The commanding officer came in and ordered the first thousand to fall in near the gate and between the dead line and the stockade. This ground was selected because it afforded ample room and because the dead line prevented the other prisoners from approaching those who were undergoing an examination. It was at first reported that three men were to be chosen from each hundred, thirty from each thousand, making four hundred from the camp of twelve thousand, there being about that number at this time. But seeing that this was going to be too much work, and require too much time, only four or five thousand were formed from which to select the required number."[211]

On the next day, the second thousand were examined. On the third day, none went out; however, a new group of fish came in. They had gone from Andersonville to Savannah, had been paroled, but then had been sent, inexplicably, to Florence. Nothing happened the next two days, but, on December 2nd, those sick men sent out from the second thousand were brought back. Nothing happened until the 5th, when the sick of the second thousand were again taken out for exchange. During the early part of December, the weather was quite pleasant. On the 7th of December, when the third, fourth, fifth, sixth, and seventh thousands were examined and the lucky ones sent outside, the weather became quite cold and unpleasant.

---

208 *Ibid.*, pp 344-348.
209 *Ibid.*, pp. 351, 352.
210 Greacen, p. 11.
211 Dufur, p. 214.

The process of selection was done approximately according to the following format. The thousand would be called up to the gate and formed into a line inside the deadline. The surgeon would walk down the line of men and, by observation and interrogation, select those men who were the sickest. Men whose terms of enlistment had expired were also given preference. "At the time of our parole, the rebel officers had taken, as far as practicable, those men whose time had expired, evidently intending to cheat the Government as much as possible; and one of the examining Surgeons also took out some of the men for bribes, obtaining in this way gold rings, greenbacks, &c. Two of my own comrades succeeded in making their escape in this way."[212] For some unknown reason, the surgeon would approve for release the sergeant in charge of each thousand, whether he was sick or not. Once outside, the men were marched into an open field where the oath of parole was administered and "... our descriptive lists taken."[213]

This was very time-consuming and so it was usually the next evening before they were placed in boxcars and taken to Charleston. A few would die on their way to freedom. Miller left on the 9th of December, in the evening, and arrived at Charleston the next morning. He was marched to the shore, and put into a boat which had a white flag flying from its bow; they steamed out past Fort Sumter, where this boat rendezvoused with another boat which was flying a white flag and a United States flag. A plank was placed between the boats and the men marched to freedom. The men laughed, wept, danced, and celebrated in their own way. This boat carried them out to the large steamship, *United States* where they were given a bath and their rags were traded for new clothes. They threw the old ones overboard; the rags tended to float back towards shore. The men laughingly said that it was the graybacks heading back to Florence. It is ironic that the rations issued after the men had endured months in rebel prisons were coffee, some hard tack, and a piece of pork.

Miller's boat started north on Monday, the 11th of December, after loading more men on board on Sunday. On Wednesday, they were at Fortress Monroe and, on Thursday, they arrived in Annapolis. Some men died in transit and others died at Annapolis. There, they were given back pay and a furlough to spend time with their families.

Urban, being very ill, was taken out of the prison, paroled, and put on a train for Charleston. There, Urban and his group were marched to the wharf and put on a Confederate steamer. It took them to the steamship *New York*; they tied alongside it. They were then taken to the steamship *Star of the South* taken to Fortress Monroe (for a day), and then on to Annapolis. Urban arrived on Monday, December 19th. He was admitted to the St. John's College Hospital. Finally, on the 7th of July, 1865, after almost 7 months of medical treatment recuperation, Urban was discharged from the hospital and sent home.

This was how Northrop spent his last few days at Florence. "My thousand was marched inside the dead line early this morning, and examined by hundreds, - Standing at open ranks, the surgeon passed down the front rank, feeling the arms of men, sometimes examining their breasts, sending the most feeble to the gate. He passed down the rear rank the same way till near me, then passed several of us without noticing us at all. The truth was prima facia, for I was bowed, and one side of my face was bloated, one eye closed, and mouth inclined to one side. With a side glance he said sharply, motioning with his hand, 'Go out'. A look of good-bye to friends and comrades in distress, and I hobbled away."[214] On Tuesday, November the 29th, men came into Florence from Blackshear, Georgia. As Northrop was waiting for a train to leave Florence, he witnessed the arrival of 170 men just captured from Sherman's army. This was in the cold of November and there was a good chance of parole any day. "They were forced to undress, stripping off even their drawers. Tents, overcoats, blankets, all extra clothing was thrown in piles, and then they were roughly ordered to dress hurriedly, and marched into the prison from which we had just escaped, leaving blankets and charges of clothing. It seemed to us that nothing but a merciless, hellish feeling of revenge could have prompted such an inexcusable action on the part of the Rebels."[215]

Besides enduring the cursory examination by the physicians, Dufur was asked some rather interesting questions. He was asked how long he had been a prisoner, when he was captured, if his term of service had expired, and if he would be willing to go to Canada and stay there if he got his freedom?[216]

Dufur told about his leaving Florence headed for Charleston, "It was about 3 o'clock P.M. when we left the prison; near the gate were two or three log cabins and a large window in the end of one of these, sat some Confederate officers with the books. As we passed the window in single file, each man was asked his name, company and regiment, and as soon as they were registered the man touched the pen and he was a paroled prisoner. It was nearly

---

[212] Kellogg, p. 351.
[213] Miller, p. 42, 43.
[214] Northrop, p. 182.
[215] *Ibid.*, p. 183.
[216] Dufur, p. 234.

dark before this work was completed. Some wood was then given us and fires were built and we were told to gather around and make ourselves as comfortable as possible.

"We had not drawn our rations for a day when we left the stockade, therefore the officers in charge issued a small ration of hard tack (four, I think) to each man. Just before daylight, the following morning, a freight train drew up and we boarded it - about fifty men in a box car - and started for Charleston, S. C., a distance of one hundred and three miles. We were eighteen hours on the road and arrived at Charleston about midnight."[217]

No shells were falling on the city, so the men reasoned this was a genuine exchange. They were given a breakfast of hard tack and molasses and taken to the wharf after being warned "... that if one of our number spoke impertinently to a man, woman or child, who might gather to look at us as we passed through the streets, the offenders should be at once returned to the bull pen."[218]

Dufur and his friends could see "... eight or ten of those large ocean steamers, together with the mammoth receiving ship, the *New York*," out in Charleston harbor. Each bore a white flag but, due to a gale, they were forced to march in two ranks to the Marine Hospital, about 1 and 1/2 miles away. Then they were taken to the South Carolina penitentiary about a mile distant, for 3 days and nights. They were given new clothes to wear. At noon on the 4th day, 600 were transported to the *New York*. When they threw their old clothes overboard, "... there was never recorded so great a loss of life as when these garments were committed to the waves."

Double rations were given, causing two or three to die as a consequence. It consisted of six hard tack, a half-pound of boiled bacon, and a large cup of coffee. Many had the common sense to throw away part of the ration.

After a 3-day trip up the coast on board the *Crescent*, they docked at Annapolis. Amid band music, they marched to Parole Camp after receiving hair cuts, shaves, and taking baths in Annapolis. There they got a new set of clothes and the old ones were sent back for the newly-released to wear on their homeward journey.

There they drew 2-months' pay, plus 27 cents per day for each day in prison, and given a 30-day furlough.[219]

Of all the books written about Yankee prisoners in the South, one which stands out among them was a tale of romance between a boy from Detroit and a girl from a plantation near Florence. It was titled, *Josie, Heroine of Florence* and was written by Morgan E. Dowling.

In November of 1863, Morgan E. Dowling, of the 17th Regiment Michigan Volunteers, was captured near Knoxville and taken to a prison in Atlanta called the Deserter's Home, probably so-called because it had been used chiefly for the confinement of deserters. It was divided into two living areas, one for Confederate deserters and convicts and the other for Union prisoners. The commander there was a Captain George Walker who was a kind and courteous gentleman who tried to ameliorate the men's sufferings. The quarters were crowded, filthy, and infested with vermin. The food was poor in both quality and quantity. There Dowling met a prisoner who gave his name as Frank Holmes and who said he was a member of an Indiana regiment. It was discovered by the prison surgeon that Frank Holmes was really a girl who had clipped her dark curls closely and passed as a soldier. Her name was Emma Grosvenor, and she had fought in many great battles for over 2 years. She was immediately removed from the prison and introduced to a female friend of Captain Walker, Josie Seymour, who took her under her charge. Dowling at once became infatuated with Josie and for the next few days was able to catch fleeting moments with her. Josie was the beautiful Unionist daughter of a wealthy secessionist plantation owner who lived about 12 miles from Florence. Dowling was shipped off to Richmond where he became an inmate on November 25th of Belle Isle.

Dowling stayed at Belle Isle until taken out to go to Andersonville on about the 1st of April when he boarded cattle-cars in Richmond. He and a comrade cut through the back of the car with a knife, fell to the tracks outside Raleigh, and set out westward for East Tennessee. They were captured in western North Carolina by Indians of the Creek nation employed by the Confederates to guard the passes of the mountains. On their way to a Confederate headquarters, they passed a distillery where they bought enough "fire-water" to make the Indians sleepy. Dowling and his friend, were, later, captured again and taken to Atlanta. Here, on the railroad station platform, he saw again his friend, Josie Seymour. He was taken to Andersonville where Wirz had a 32-pound ball and chain attached to his ankle for three months. He said he was assigned to a hundred subdivided into messes of twenty men each. Some of the men called the encumbrance a "watch and chain." He got a file and bullet from a guard and filed out the iron rivet which held it on and used the bullet to make a removable lead rivet so he could remove his shackle except at roll-call and when observed by the guards. Every morning at roll-call they checked the chain. He wore it about 2 hours each day and it was taken off after 10 days. Dowling again escaped by overpowering his guard who was ac-

[217] *Ibid.*, pp. 237-239.
[218] *Ibid.*, p. 240.
[219] *Ibid.*, pp. 241-249.

companying him to get wood. He fled, was recaptured, and put in the stocks. The rebel laid the victim flat on his back, stretching his arms about his head until they were almost out of the socket and then put them in holes in a bar. Then the legs were stretched and pulled so the man was in a "spread eagle" position. Here he was left for 24 hours; Dowling endured this "three times in succession."[220]

Dowling's next attempt to escape occurred when he had himself carried to the dead house. A Confederate came in and commenced to take Dowling's shoes off. Dowling tried to sneak a peek and their eyes made contact. The Confederate thief ran, terrified, from the shed. He returned with a guard, captured Dowling, and took him again to Wirz, who ordered that a sixty-pound ball be put on his leg. He was put in a guard house on rations of bread and water until he would promise not to escape again. He was, however, taken in three days to the pen after being threatened with death by hanging or by being shot if he tried to escape again.

Dowling next went to work on a tunnel. The rebels gave shovels out in the pen to dig wells and collected all the tools each night. By using various ruses such as in telling the Rebels they had only given out, say, 20 shovels when they had really given out 22, the prisoners amassed a small quantity of shovels.

Dowling told of a plan involving the conspiracy of a Confederate sergeant who furnished each of the tunnelers a gun and sixty rounds of ammunition. Due to the sickness of one of his friends, Dowling decided not to go. When the men were discovered missing, a strong pack of dogs and a squad of pursuers took off after them. About 20 miles from Andersonville, on a northern route near the Flint River, the pursuers attacked the escapees and their rebel sergeant guide. The Yankees drove off the assault, killed all the dogs but two, killed one pursuer, and wounded three others badly. This was one of the few successful mass escapes from Andersonville.[221]

Dowling was, at that time, asked out by Wirz to do a stint as a grave-digger. Dowling gradually put on weight and gained back his health. He obtained some respectable clothes from a newly-made acquaintance who was one of the Confederate guard. "There being no danger that any one would dare to molest me in them or strip me of them while I was engaged in my present occupation, being expressly under the care and protection of Captain Wirtz (sic), whom his own men feared to provoke, just as fully as did any Union prisoner in his hands."[222] This friend invited Dowling to accompany him to the elegant home of a family who lived near Andersonville. Here he was surprised to find his old friend, Josie Seymour. Every evening Dowling had free, he spent with Josie. Their relationship deepened into love. They walked in the gardens of the plantation and talked many times about the feasibility of both fleeing to the Union lines about 160 miles away. After Dowling's attempt at escaping with the grave diggers, he was returned to the pen.

It will be remembered that Josie was from a plantation near Florence and so, when the prisoners were, supposedly, being shipped there, Dowling "flanked" into the second hundred and boarded the train. Sadly, he learned they were being shipped to Savannah, but then, he learned that they would be forwarded to his hoped-for destination, Florence. He soon learned the location of the Seymour mansion and, on the very next day, he escaped. Near the 1st of August, he made his way to the Seymour plantation 14 miles away.

He was hidden by Josie in a Negro cabin on the plantation. Here he courted Josie for several weeks, almost oblivious to the war. They rode on nocturnal, romantic, moonlight rides and visited friends loyal to the Union who were members of the Union League. Dowling was, finally, discovered by Josie's father who forbade any marriage between his daughter and Dowling. He ordered Dowling to leave and to go to other Union League families. At that time, Josie, begged on bended knee for her father's blessing. Her father, Colonel Seymour, relented and let Dowling move into the big house. They were married in a church and he was recaptured, literally, at the altar on Monday, September 5th. He was captured by a band of Confederate soldiers gathering up all able-bodied men to press into service. He was taken back to Florence where he told them he was from Macon; he was sworn into Confederate service. The next night he deserted, went back to Josie for a quick visit, and then, on horseback, enjoyed a few days' freedom before being captured again.

On the return trip he again escaped, and was recaptured by a party of men from Florence seeking escapees. He was asked how he had just escaped from Florence and he, thus, was kept from a possible appointment with the firing squad. Dowling returned to Florence on September 23rd, where he was hung by his thumbs for his escape. "The guard took me to the front of the main gate, where was a large frame erected similar to that for a large swing. I was placed upon a small stool under the crossbeam, my thumbs were tied by two small ropes depending from it, the stool was then knocked from under me, and I was swung off into the air. There I was left swinging for nearly half-an-hour

---

[220] Dowling, pp. 114, 115.
[221] *Ibid.*, pp. 129, 130.
[222] *Ibid.*, pp. 248, 249.

enduring indescribable anguish, when the prisoners who had assembled near the main gate - which was always left standing open during the day, but was very strongly guarded - maddened by this horrible spectacle, and evincing a disposition to break out into open mutiny at all hazards, induced the commanding officer to order me to be taken down. I had lost all feeling, was almost senseless, and it was only with the greatest care from the Rebel surgeon that my life was saved. For two days thereafter I was kept in the guard house and then sent into camp."[223]

In October, Dowling made an escape in a most daring way. He waited for two sentinels to approach each other on the ledge around the palisade, salute, turn about face, and march away from each other. Dowling then crossed the deadline, placed a 6-foot plank against the wall, and climbed up and over the palisade.

He went to one of his Union League friend's home; from there he fled, after spending a few moments with Josie. He was captured by the hounds again and returned to Florence where he had attached a ball and chain for three months. In two hours, he had a lead replacement for the iron rivet.

On October 17th, the commander came in and told Dowling that he had a visitor at the gate. It was Josie and, through her intercession, she had obtained a parole by appealing to Captain Walker, who had come to visit her and her father. Captain Walker, not knowing Josie was married, had asked the commander of the prison to let Dowling out to cut wood minus the ball and chain. After a few days, he was again restricted to the prison interior and given his "watch and chain." Of course, Captain Walker had learned Josie and Dowling were man and wife. Dowling decided not to attempt any more escapes but to await the defeat of the South. He had made six escapes, averaging about 50 miles each time from the point of departure.

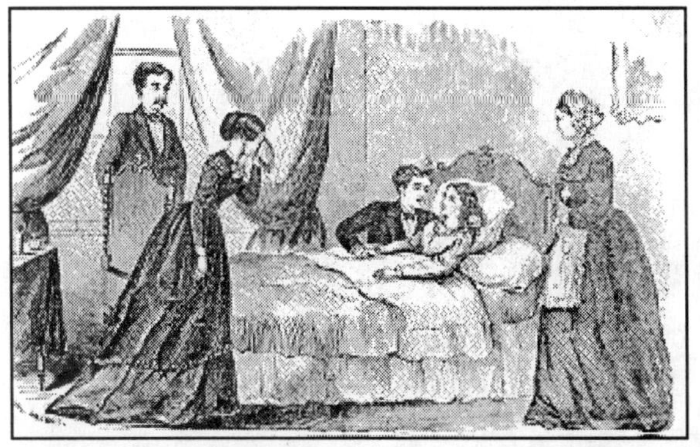

**The Death of Josie** - This beautiful young girl in South Carolina became the lover and, finally, the wife of a Yankee prisoner in Florence. After their marriage, she became very sick. He took her north for medical treatment and she died in New York immediately after reaching that city. (Dowling)

On December 13, 1864, Dowling was taken to Charleston and exchanged. He went by steamer to Annapolis where all the ex-prisoners were photographed to show what rebel imprisonment had wrought. He was given his back pay and a 30-day furlough. At the end of the furlough he reported to Camp Chase near Columbus, Ohio, where he received another 30-day furlough because of his condition. At the end of that time, he was reassigned to his unit, which was doing duty as a provost guard and which was encamped on Beasley's Farm near Petersburg. On April 7th, he was again with his regiment but only about 100 men of the original 1,000 men were still with the unit. He was mustered out on June 3rd at Detroit. He left immediately for Florence, and soon arrived at the house where Josie was staying. After a joyful reunion, Dowling stayed there about a week; then he and Josie headed north. While in Richmond, he noticed how thin, pale and weak she was getting. They stopped over a little while in Washington where she said she felt a little stronger and then they continued on to New York City. Here he called in the best medical doctors available. She held on for about a month longer, but died of a lung ailment.

On October 1st, he had a white marble monument erected on her new grave in Greenwood Cemetery in New York City with the one word "Josie" on it.[224]

In the latter part of the fall of 1864, all prisoners at Andersonville who were physically able to withstand the rigors of a short trip were moved to one of the five or six minor prisons or holding pens along the crude railroad lines. After being in one of the several holding pens for various lengths of time, the prisoners were, usually, taken to one of the bigger prison camps, such as those at Florence or Millen. After the dispersal, Andersonville, then filled only with the very sick and infirm, was strictly a medical facility.

[223] *Ibid.*, pp. 325, 326.
[224] *Ibid.*, pp. 327, 505.

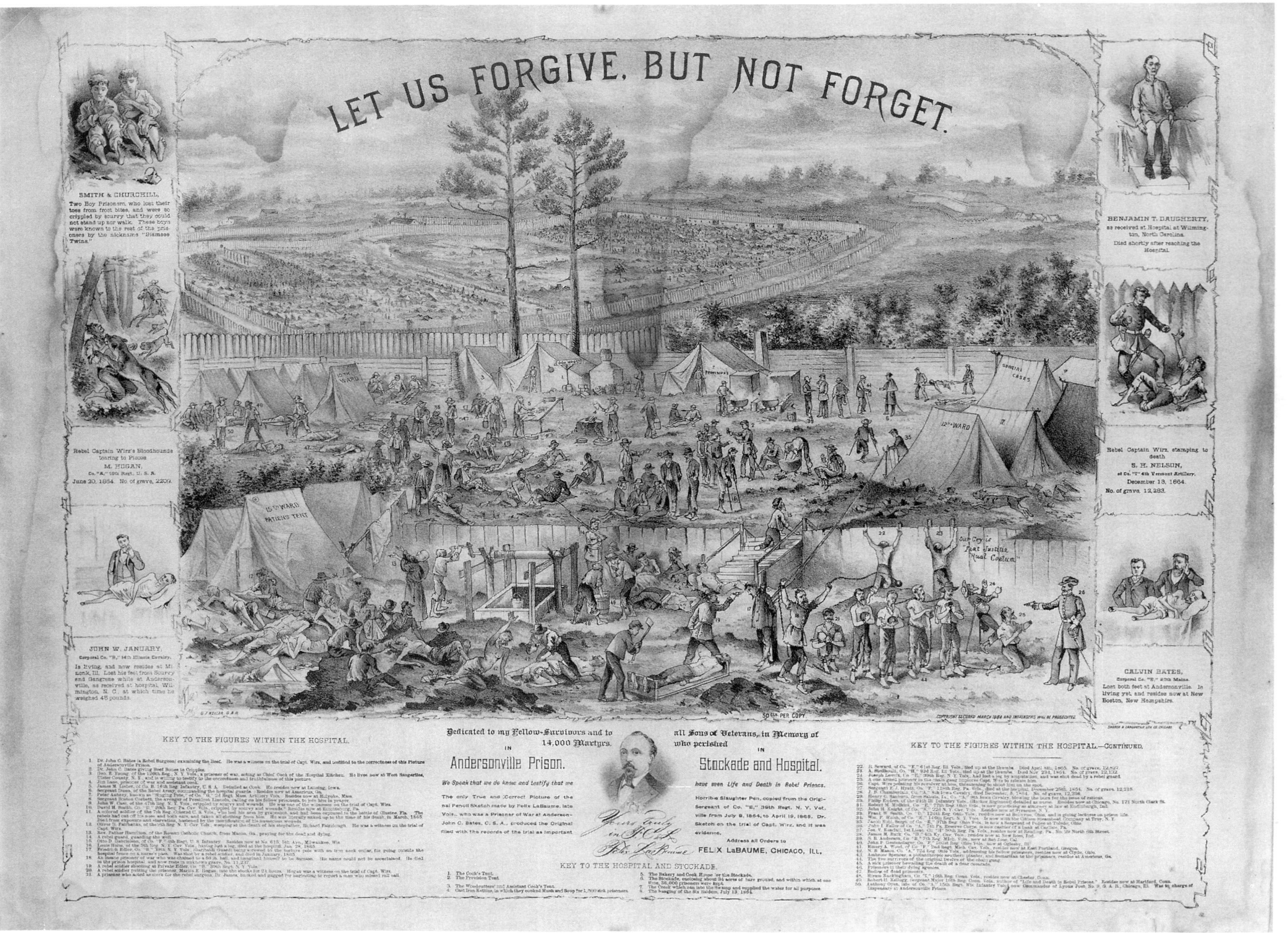

LET US FORGIVE, BUT NOT FORGET.
SMITH & CHURCHILL.
Two Boy Prisoners, who lost their toes from frost bites, and were so crippled by scurvy that they could not stand up nor walk. These boys were known to the rest of the prisoners by the nickname "Siamese Twins."
Rebel Captain Wirz's Bloodhounds tearing to Pieces
M. HOGAN,
Co. "A," 19th Regt. U. S. R.
June 20, 1864. No. of grave, 2209.
JOHN W. JANUARY,
Corporal Co. "B," 14th Illinois Cavalry.
Is living, and now resides at Minonk, Ill. Lost his feet from Scurvy and Gangrene while at Andersonville, as received at hospital, Wilmington, N. C., at which time he weighed 45 pounds.
BENJAMIN T. DAUGHERTY,
as received at Hospital at Wilmington, North Carolina.
Died shortly after reaching the Hospital.
Rebel Captain Wirz, stamping to death
S. H. NELSON,
of Co. "I" 4th Vermont Artillery,
December 13, 1864.
No. of grave, 12,283.
CALVIN BATES,
Corporal Co. "E," 20th Maine.
Lost both feet at Andersonville. Is living yet, and resides now at New Boston, New Hampshire.
15th WARD PATIENTS TENT
12th WARD
SURGICAL CASES
Our Cry is "Fiat Justitia Ruat Coelum"
50cts. PER COPY
KEY TO THE FIGURES WITHIN THE HOSPITAL.
Dedicated to my Fellow-Survivors and to all Sons of Veterans, in Memory of 14,000 Martyrs who perished
IN
Andersonville Prison.
IN
Stockade and Hospital.
We Speak that we do know and testify that we have seen Life and Death in Rebel Prisons.
The only True and Correct Picture of the Horrible Slaughter Pen, copied from the Original Pencil Sketch made by Felix LaBaume, late Sergeant of Co. "E," 39th Regt. N. Y. Vet. Vols., who was a Prisoner of War at Andersonville from July 9, 1864, to April 19, 1865. Dr. John C. Bates, C. S. A., produced the Original Sketch on the trial of Capt. Wirz, and it was filed with the records of the trial as important evidence.
Yours Truly in F. C. L.
Felix LaBaume
Address all Orders to
FELIX LaBAUME, CHICAGO, ILL.
KEY TO THE HOSPITAL AND STOCKADE.
KEY TO THE FIGURES WITHIN THE HOSPITAL.—CONTINUED.

## *Chapter Eleven*

# The Winter of 1864-1865 After the Disbursement of The Prisoners

*"When all was arranged, Col. Iversons sent an Orderly to tell his chief that things were in readiness and he was invited to dine with him. Gen. Winder assented, and as he stepped to the tent door he fell prostrate on the ground, and immediately expired."*[1]

Through the year 1864, Andersonville had been the largest prisoner-of-war camp the world had ever known. After the disbursement of the prisoners, Andersonville became, for all practical purposes, a hospital camp. All prisoners able to walk were placed on trains, leaving only about 7,000 to 7,500 invalids and very sick prisoners. As the year closed, Andersonville prison experienced the death throes felt throughout the Confederacy. Some prisoners who had spent six or eight months in Andersonville and who had been sent away, supposedly for exchange, found themselves being sent back there before the year's end. Later, some would be sent back a third time after having been rejected for exchange by their own troops. With the decrease in the number of prisoners, conditions improved for those remaining.

One improvement was that the deadline was taken down. "After the removal of the prisoners had commenced, on or about September 10th, the prisoners immediately commenced the removal of the dead-line; first the top rails, and afterwards the posts supporting the dead-line proper. They converted the material into fuel generally. This dead-line continued down for several weeks, I don't remember exactly how long, but until probably about the middle of October. During the abolition of this dead-line, the prisoners had unrestricted intercourse with the guard in conversation, trading, &c.; not only with the guard, but with the officers of the guard and the officers of the day. This was done with the full knowledge of Captain Wirz; [he] was aware of the fact; he could see it."[2] "After that time there was no shooting on the dead-line until the it was reconstructed... It was reconstructed in about the middle of October. There was no shooting to my knowledge after the dead-line was put up. I never saw any man shot; I never knew a man to be shot after the 10th of September on the dead-line."[3]

Other improvements were increases in food and wood rations. "After the number of prisoners had been reduced by transfer and exchange, I believe to about 7,000, the camp was reorganized into detachments of 500, subdivided into squads of 100 each. They were all moved then on the south side, and the camp was thoroughly reorganized. Captain Wirz sent for the sergeants of these hundreds; they went to his headquarters, and he told them, me amongst the others, that the camp had been reorganized, and that, owing to the decrease in the number of prisoners, he was in hopes the provisions would be more abundant, of better quality and more regular in their issue. They were increased, in fact, the same afternoon. He also increased the ration of wood. Wood was hauled in wagons, so as to furnish a sufficient quantity for cooking, and in addition to that, he permitted squads to go out to the number of 20 from each hundred, every day, under guard, and they were furnished with axes at the South Gate, to chop wood and bring it in; sometimes they went two miles from the stockade.

[1] Fosdick, p. 104.
[2] *Wirz Trial*, p. 588.
[3] *Ibid.*, p. 598.

"Those who had blankets used them as coverings or tents. Of course those who had no shelter tents or blankets were permitted then to go out and chop pine tops, and they made a pretty good shelter. They used them for bedding also. After that there was abundance of wood in the camp.

"There was abundance of fuel, both for cooking and heating purposes."[4]

Near the first of October, the regularly-appointed sutler of the post, James Selman, Jr., left Andersonville for a thirty-day sick furlough. Captain Wirz said he did not wish to appoint anyone to take the place of Selman but, because of the continued flagrant trading between the guard force and the prisoners, he appointed Private James Duncan as a temporary sutler. Wirz felt the illegal traffic would completely demoralize the troops at the post. He appointed Duncan, knowing Selman would be back at the post in thirty days after regaining his health.

Wirz said the reason he appointed James Duncan was he "... could not get a stranger who would have been willing to undertake the job for such a short time and because I did not know of any one. Duncan in his capacity as employee at the prison has free access to the prison. If he cannot be trusted he ought to be dismissed altogether. In his capacity, not speaking of his being sutler pro tem., he has all the opportunities to do any amount of rascality if he sees proper to do so. Not having been yet informed by any one that he ever did anything wrong, and not having seen anything wrong about him myself, I gave him the sutlership in charge during Selman's absence.

"I have never been bought by Mr. Selman nor Mr. Duncan either to give either of them the appointment, but acted solely with the view of promoting the interest of the prison under my charge."[5] Evidently, General Winder heard about this temporary appointment and promptly caused the following letter to be sent:

> *Camp Sumter, Andersonville,*
> *October 25, 1864*
>
> *The temporary authority given to Private James Duncan to act as sutler for the prisoners is hereby withdrawn, by order of General Winder, and he will no longer suttle for the prisoners.*
>
> *Geo. C. Gibbs,*
> *Colonel, Commanding.*[6]

Within minutes of receiving the above letter, Captain Wirz wrote to Captain Sid Winder, Assistant Adjutant General of General Winder at Camp Lawton with his father. Wirz wrote, "It was never my intention to deprive Mr. Selman of his position, which, if due bills which I have seen in his possession, and from what he has told me himself, has been equally beneficial to himself as well as to some of his friends.

"I have suspended Mr. Duncan unless you should see proper to countermand your order to Colonel Gibbs.

"At the close of this lengthy communication allow me to say most respectfully that it has made me feel badly that the general commanding should see proper to interfere in such an unimportant matter, knowing, as he well knows, that I would rather lose my life than do anything wrong, or suffer wrong to be done by others under my control, being aware that their actions were wrong."[7]

"There were numerous sutlers in the stockade - one chief sutler. About the middle of October there were great complaints made against this sutler, who was a Jew, in regard to his practices of extortion. Captain Wirz one day came in, and gave him a few moments to remove his effects of a purely personal nature, and after the sutler had done so, Captain Wirz told the boys to go and help themselves, which they did, reserving only some vegetables, some potatoes and onions, I believe, which he had there for sale, for the use of the sick in the hospital. Captain Wirz said to the sutler, 'I will give you five minutes' (I think that was the time specified) 'to remove your personal effects, your books and clothing,' and then he said, 'get out of this;' and the contents of his store were distributed among the prisoners. Captain Wirz reserved something for the sick... Captain Wirz reserved some potatoes; whether the sick got them I could not say, but they were reserved for that purpose."[8]

"The sutler was a Jew; I don't know his name. He was not the one who had been there all summer; that was another one. The Jew had been there ever since the time the first sutler left - the sutler who was there all summer. A man by the name of Selman was sutler all summer. Selman may have left with the first detachment that went down towards Savannah. If you narrow me down to the point I will say that it was on or about the 10th of September that Selman went away and this Jew succeeded him. I do not know who appointed the Jew as sutler. He was not in the

---

[4] *Ibid.*, pp. 589, 590.
[5] *O.R.*, VII, p. 1041.
[6] *Ibid.*, VII, p. 1041.
[7] *Ibid.*, p. 1042.
[8] *Wirz Trial*, p. 588.

stockade as sutler during the time Selman was there; I do not know in what capacity the Jew was in the stockade...Captain Wirz reserved a few bushels of potatoes at the time he cleaned the sutler out. There were onions, red paper and so on. Captain Wirz reserved only the potatoes - about four or five bushels, I should judge."[9]

"In the fall of 1864, General Imboden was appointed Inspector of Prisons West of the Savannah River and made a personal inspection of Andersonville prison. He was led to make the inspection by the report of Colonel Bondurant, who had been sent by him to make an examination of affairs at that prison, and on written application from Wirz, suggesting measures for the amelioration of the condition of the prisoners there, which were strongly approved by Colonel Gibbs, an old U.S. Army officer, a cultivated, humane and urbane gentleman, in command of the post.

"At this time there were 7,500 prisoners at Andersonville and the guard consisted of the First Brigade of Georgia troops, under Brigadier General Gantrell. The commandant of the whole post was Colonel Gibbs."[10]

General John D. Imboden "... found the prisoners badly off for clothing, shoes, etc., and that there was no clothing to give them. Many of our guards on duty were in rags and were barefoot, and in lieu of overcoats many had to protect themselves with a tattered blanket drawn over their shoulder...

"I investigated particularly the food and found no discrimination was made in the issue of rations to guards and prisoners alike. In quantity, quality and kind, the daily rations were the same. One-third to one-half pound of meat per day, one pint to one pint-and-a-half of corn meal, and occasionally wheat, flour and potatoes."[11]

On January 2nd, General Winder assigned Brigadier General John D. Imboden, to have command over all military prisons in the states of Georgia, Alabama, and Mississippi. He was ordered to establish his headquarters at Augusta. General Winder still had assigned, to his headquarters at Columbia, South Carolina, Chief Surgeon Isaiah White, Captain Richard Bayly Winder, Chief Quartermaster; and Captain Samuel T. Bayly, his assistant Adjutant-General.[12]

It must have been extremely depressing to the prisoners when many of them were returned to Andersonville in December and January. Most had been told, when they had left in the early fall, that they were headed for freedom; they then ended up at Millen. Many of those same prisoners were being re-assigned to their old pen at Andersonville. Spencer said, in December and January, "The severest weather was experienced that ever visited that region of country."[13]

"When we came to Andersonville the second time, about the 21st of December, 1864, and when we were being arranged into detachments, or after we were arranged, Captain Wirz came to each detachment and read the rules which he had adopted for the government of us as prisoners of war. The rules stated that we would be shot if we entered into the dead-line, and that any prisoners speaking to the guard would be shot by the guard without halting. He went on to explain that a little. He said that if any of the Yankees traded with the guards and if the guards took their money and did not give them anything for it, and if afterwards, the Yankee came to him to complain, he should punish the Yankee and say 'bully' to the guard. He also stated in the rules that if we committed any mischief, such as taking up boards or disturbed anything, our rations would be cut off until the perpetrators were found and punished."[14]

Asbery Stephen was brought back to Andersonville on December 23rd from Millen. Francis C. Curtis said he was returned to Andersonville from Blackshear after General Sherman had taken Savannah. He arrived back at about dark on Christmas Eve. He noted quite a change had taken place since he had left. The Confederates had leveled and ploughed the south side of the pen and filled in all of the wells that had been dug. That day, there was a very cold rain falling and the shivering men could only lie down in the soft, muddy furrows. They were allowed to go out and gather wood and pine needles to build new shebangs. They received typical Andersonville rations.[15]

Tyler left Blackshear on New Year's Eve, rode in the box-car all night, and arrived back at Andersonville at about ten o'clock on the morning of New Year's Day, 1865. He was taken, with his fellow comrades, to the area just outside the pen where the men huddled close to keep warm against the cold north wind. It was at that time a rather pathetic incident took place when one of the men tried to warm up by moving close to one of the many fires the guards had built to keep warm. "One of our little drummer boys stepped up to the fire to warm, when old Wirz came along and ordered him back. The boy started back, but seeing Wirz going away went back to the fire again. Wirz

[9] *Ibid.*, p. 598.
[10] Ashe, p. 10.
[11] *Ibid.*, p. 11.
[12] *O.R.*, VII, p. 12.
[13] Spencer, p. 136.
[14] *Wirz Trial*, p. 173.
[15] Mass. Monument, p.

turned, and seeing the boy, drew his revolver and shot him dead. The little fellow fell in the fire. I could not hear what the rebel guards said to Wirz, for the wind was blowing the other way, but this I do know, he took their arms away and put them in irons."[16]

Tyler and other men were then counted off into detachments and marched into the sparsely-populated prison which contained about seven thousand at the time. "We had no shelter of any kind, so four of us clubbed together and dug a hole seven feet deep, and then widened it out at the bottom so as to accommodate four of us. It was all open at the top, but it kept the cold winds from us."[17]

"It finally came my turn to go for wood. There were six of us picked out to go. One of the six was a very sickly man, and could hardly walk, without carrying a load. He could not be persuaded to let some stronger man take his place, so out we went, sick man and all. We went about half a mile from the pen, and every man went to work picking up his wood. Finally, we started for the stockade; but the sick man could not keep up; he had more wood than he could carry. We went as slow as our guards would let us, in order to give him a chance. Just then Wirz came riding along on his old white horse, and seeing the sick man some twenty yards behind, said, 'Close up there, close up there, you damned Yankee.' The sick man tried to hurry up, but stubbed his toe and down he went, wood and all. Wirz sprang from his horse and ran up to the poor sick soldier and kicked him in the stomach with the heel of his big riding boot, and left him a dead man. 'That is the way I serve you damned Yanks when you don't do as I tell you.' The rest of us went back to the prison pen, sick at heart."[18]

Captain Wright testified that he, as Post Quartermaster, and Colonel Gibbs, as Commandant of the Post, were served with an injunction obtained by Benjamin B. Dykes in December or January. They retained Samuel Hall of Macon, an attorney and judge, to represent them. This bill sought to prevent the government from using the cemetery and from cutting wood and timber from Dykes's land. Dykes contended that he had not been compensated for wood cut off his land and the graveyard was a nuisance.

"There was an injunction served on me and Colonel Gibbs in December, 1864 or January, 1865, by Mr. Dykes, to stop our getting wood or timber off his land for the use of the prison, and to stop burying the dead on his land... The people in the neighborhood were very much dissatisfied at having this lumber used and not being paid for it, and they grumbled a great deal about it, and were constantly threatening the men who were at work getting wood. It finally resulted in this injunction."[19] "When the bill was presented to the judge for his sanction, he wrote an order on the back of it, requiring the defendants to show cause why an injunction should not issue. I answered the bill for them, procuring affidavits, appeared before him and showed such cause, as I was able to show. The hearing of it was postponed to enable me to get the testimony of some other witnesses, the affidavits of some other witnesses, and after it was postponed, Dykes dismissed his bill voluntarily. It was stated that there were other parties concerned in it with Dykes. I went to those parties and they denied it. I took proof to the effect that that field in which the prisoners were buried was a burying-ground before the war, and that citizens had been buried there, and that the ground had been dedicated to the public use. I went out there to that ground and I saw signs of graves that must have been there before the stockade was put up. I think the confederate dead were buried in the same field, at some distance apart, however; by themselves; it was pointed out to me. I know the circumstances with regard to the termination of that suit. The officer at the post, Wirz among the number, urged me to get the government to pay those claims, and let them go on getting wood. I went to this man, Dykes, and promised - and not only promised him but promised men by the name of Colman and Hobart, who owned land around there - to use my endeavors to get their pay from the government. I wrote several letters on the subject, but got no answers to them. I wrote to General Winder, and I wrote to the quartermaster general in Richmond."[20]

Judge Samuel Hall further testified, "Captain Wirz applied to me to arrest... a man named Duncan - the same Duncan that has been in court. The charges made against him were appropriating supplies that were sent there for the use of the prisoners - molasses, sacks, and grease."

Hall was then asked by the court, "Was not that application on the part of Captain Wirz made after a detective by the name of Weatherford had come there and investigated the circumstances?"

Hall answered, "I think he spoke to me prior to Weatherford's arrival. Weatherford went there and made this discovery. My recollection is that Captain Wirz spoke to me about it before Weatherford went there; I know after he

---

[16] Tyler, pp. 48, 49.
[17] *Ibid.*, p. 49.
[18] *Ibid.*, pp. 49, 50.
[19] *Wirz Trial*, p. 480.
[20] *Ibid.*, pp. 490, 491.

went there, Captain Wirz spoke to me about it... A man named Humes was also complained of..."[21] No injunction was ever granted.

In the fall, all prisoners on the north side of the pen were moved to the south side. In an attempt to improve the sanitary conditions within the pen, the north side was plowed over after all the wells had been filled in. Vawter, after he had returned to Andersonville, said the south side was thickly-settled but that it was not as crowded as when he had been there previously. "We all settled on the south side of the brook. The north side contained but a few stragglers on the 1st of January."[22]

The prisoners at that time heard some very depressing news from some "fresh fish." "About the first of January a few prisoners were brought in, who told us that Sherman had reached the sea, at Savannah, and had turned northward into Carolina. So the last lingering hope that he would rescue us died within us."[23]

The men suffered terribly from exposure during the cold January, because it rained almost constantly that month. "Many of the men lying on the wet ground by night, and sitting on it by day, had contracted colds, that settled on their lungs. Hundreds had that peculiar cough and that brightness of the cheek and eye, that told us that consumption had set in and that if they were not soon exchanged they would be beyond the reach of cartel."[24]

Of course, the men used the few sunny days of January to hang their clothes and blankets out to dry. It also afforded a time to take off their clothes and skirmish for vermin. To sleep on the dry sand was a welcome relief.

"It rained about four days of a week, and was cloudy and damp nearly all the time. Heavy east winds prevailed. We seldom saw the sun shine.

"The rebel authorities allowed a detail of three men from each hundred to go out - under guard - to woods to pick limbs and such other pieces of wood as we could find, for fuel. We had no axes and had to content ourselves with scraps. The best of it was where pine logs had rotted and left the knots. These, being full of tar, burned freely in the dampest weather."[25]

"In this way about two hundred men went out every day, and returned with an armful or a shoulder-load of wood. I think most of our wood was carried three-fourths of a mile.

"When we got our wood home, with a railroad spike for a wedge, and a pine knot for a maul, we split it; and broke it up fine so as to make it go as far as possible. If you went out today, it will be thirty-three days - or nearly five weeks, - before your turn comes again." It would take a strong man to carry wood enough to keep himself dry and warm for five weeks.[26]

"One way we had to keep warm those damp, chilly days, was to dig a funnel shaped home in the sand, about four feet in diameter, and two feet deep. Four of us would sit in this hole. Our feet would be together in the bottom; our knees together in the center; then leaning forward till our heads were almost together, we would spread our blanket over the pile, and draw it down close to the edges - thus keeping in the heat of our bodies and the warmth of our breath. I sat in such a hole frequently all day, except time enough to draw and eat my rations. Some dug these holes larger and deeper and eight or ten would get into them."[27]

"During the winter the guard relaxed much of its sternness and rigor, and many of the men who composed it were willing to enter into conversation and traffic with us, when their officers were not in sight. This gave rise to several manufacturing industries. One was carving pipes. Some of the boys, when they got out for wood, would dig greenbria-roots, and from these and other kinds of wood, finely-carved pipes were made. Frequently two or three weeks' labor was expended on a single pipe, which was then sold for a half gallon of 'nigger peas,.' a quart of meal, or three dollars 'Confed.'

"Another branch of business was carving toothpicks. These were made from the bones of meat that we drew, and, like the pipes, they were valuable in proportion to the amount of labor bestowed on them.

"Bob Mc---- made toothpicks. His kit of tools consisted of a piece of an old case-knife, one side of it cut full of notches for a saw; a brick bat, which he used for grindstone, file, and polisher; and a piece of coarse needle fastened into a bone handle, and ground flat-pointed, which served as a drill or boring machine. With such a set of tools, if he had favorable weather, he could turn out two good toothpicks per month."[28]

---

[21] *Ibid.*, pp. 494, 495.
[22] Vawter, p. 156.
[23] *Ibid.*, p. 161.
[24] *Ibid.*, p. 167.
[25] *Ibid.*, p. 158.
[26] *Ibid.*, p. 159.
[27] *Ibid.*, p. 160.
[28] *Ibid.*

Still another branch of business carried on at that time was "raising" Confederate notes. Confederate money was poorly-made, both in design and in execution. The "ones," "twos," "tens," and "twenties" were almost alike, except in the figures that told their denomination. If a man could get a one- or two-dollar bill, he knew where to take it and have it converted into a ten or twenty. "All work done in the best style of art and warranted to pass." In buying beans or meal with this money, we always aimed to trade so as to get one or two small bills in change so that we could make another "raise."[29]

On January 24th, General Winder said there were more troops than were necessary to guard the prison at Andersonville since most of the prisoners had been exchanged. He wanted to send the Second Regular Georgia Reserves to other prisons in South Carolina, but could not, by law, transfer them out of the state of Georgia.[30]

The report of sick and wounded at Andersonville for January was as follows:

| | | |
|---|---|---|
| Remaining last report: | Sick | 742 |
| | Wounded | 71 |
| | Total | 813 |
| Taken sick or wounded during the month | | 589 |
| | Aggregate | 1,402 |
| | Returned to duty | 267 |
| | Died | 199 |
| | | 466 |
| Remaining; Sick, 869; wounded, 67; total | | 936 |
| Mean strength, enlisted men | | 5,000 |
| Average number on sick report daily in hospital | | 890 [31] |

"During the month of February the rebels furnished material, and detailed a lot of prisoners - giving them extra rations - and had three sheds erected.

"These sheds were about twenty-five feet wide, by one hundred and fifty long; about five feet high at the eaves, and ten or twelve feet high in the center - roofed with boards, and left open on all sides. They were designed for a shelter for those who had no blankets or tents of any kind; and during a hard rain one thousand men would crowd under each shed."[32]

"... When it was not raining most of the men preferred to remain outside, on account of the vermin - especially fleas - which were so much worse in the dry sand under these roofs than in other parts of the prison.

"I am glad to give to the notorious Winder and Wirz credit for this much humanity. Perhaps the reader thinks it was no great thing to build such sheds. Had they been built in the fall, they would have saved many lives."[33]

"Two men were buried inside the stockade after the men began to go away. There was one dead man who lay in the barracks about four days. He became putrid and was not carried out. Whose fault it was I do not know. He was buried there.

"Another man was buried there very near the raider's tent; I saw his grave. I am not able to state why these men were buried inside the stockade."[34]

Sometime later, two more sheds were built in the southeast corner, perpendicular to the south wall and parallel to each other. The exact date they were built is unknown. Stephen said they were being worked on February 10th.

This was how Captain Richard B. Winder spent his first few weeks of 1865: "When General Sherman made his march through Georgia, the prisoners were necessarily squandered in every direction. At that time I was ordered to take charge of the prison wagon train and save it from the enemy. I had with me, to the best of my recollection, some twenty odd prisoners as teamsters, ambulance drivers, &c., and only five of our own men, including two wagon-masters, and no arms, except private arms. We were within a few miles of the fighting, and so close that I lost much baggage that was stored in a house close by. Two of these prisoners that morning (not knowing the proximity of the enemy) I had given permission to go fishing, and we had to decamp so suddenly that I could not wait for them - in fact, supposed they had gone to their own men - and was very uneasy lest they should give information of the whereabouts of my train, and made on that account a very long march; yet soon after we encamped at night on the

[29] *Ibid.*, p. 163.
[30] *O.R.*, VIII, p. 126.
[31] *Ibid.*, p. 161.
[32] Vawter, pp. 165, 166.
[33] *Ibid.*, p. 166.
[34] *Wirz Trial*, p. 171.

banks of the Savannah River these two men came up, each one toting a bag of sweet potatoes. Not one of these prisoners deserted me. They all said, as I was told, that I had treated them so well and so kindly that they felt in honor bound to respect their paroles. The next morning we commenced crossing the Savannah River and encamped at Barnwell District, S. C. We remained in camp for some time, when I received an order to send a portion of the wagon train to Columbia, S. C., a portion of it to Augusta, Ga., and to hold the balance subject to orders. A portion of the prisoners remained with me; the balance went to Columbia. I remained there in camp some six weeks; sent to Augusta; got some powder and shot, and, as game was very plentiful, frequently allowed several of these prisoners my double-barreled shotgun and a small rifle to go off on horseback and amuse themselves in their own way." He was then ordered to Columbia, S. C., and immediately assigned to duty as Chief Quartermaster of All Prisons East of the Mississippi River.[35]

On January 20th, General Winder, from Columbia, wrote to General Cooper, asking what to do with the prisoners at Florence. "I am at a loss to know where to send prisoners from Florence. In one direction, the enemy are in the way. In the other, the question of supplies presents an insuperable barrier. I again urge paroling the prisoners and sending them home... The guard is very weak and insufficient to take care. At once give full instructions."[36]

On January 26th, General Winder asked the Federal Government be told of the suffering of the prisoners and their great need for clothing.[37]

Colonel H. Forno, Inspector of Military Prisons in South Carolina, said, after he had made an inspection of Florence on January 23rd, "There has been but two issues of meat in the last two months and scarcely ever sirup." Col. Forno also said that there was little or no transportation at the post and prisoners were compelled to carry the timber, for the construction of the buildings necessary for the public use, on their shoulders a distance of one mile. He said that there had been a few cases of smallpox and typhoid fever. He observed the guard force was "... inefficient and without proper discipline, and composed of reserves and about ninety men of the 55th Georgia Volunteers."[38] There were seven endorsements on Forno's report. One, from Commissary-General L. B. Northrop, advised that, unless he received more money, they would get less food, not more. It was forwarded up to the Secretary of Treasury, G. A. Trenholm, who said his funds were limited and that "... no provision has yet been made by Congress for the replenishment of the Treasury."[39]

Colonel Forno said, on January 23rd, that Florence had 6,845 men in the stockade; another 156 were paroled to work and 537 more men were in the hospital for a total of 7,538 prisoners.[40]

Lieutenant Colonel Iverson reported to Colonel Forno that the following were issued at Florence, "One pound of meal, one-third pound of peas, three pounds of salt per 100 rations per day. No soap, tobacco, or meat is issued, except one-half pound of beef per day to men who do duty as laborers on Government work... I urge the rations be increased."[41] Colonel Iverson reported this also to General Winder and added "... if a change in the ration can be made I will have the satisfaction of knowing that the prisoners under my charge are well housed, plenty of fuel, good hospital accommodations, and in as good a condition as they could reasonably expect."[42] General Winder endorsed, "Respectfully referred to the Adjutant-General and most earnestly request that a remedy be immediately applied. The prisoners never will be properly fed until commissaries are ordered for prison duty. I never have been able to get anything from staff officers not on duty with the prisons. I hope that assistant commissaries will be ordered to report to me for duty, and that they be not, as heretofore, young men with no experience; the duty requires experience."[43] Also, later endorsed on this letter by L. B. Northrop, Commissary-General of Subsistence, was this comment: "The state of the commissariat will not allow the issue of a full ration to our own troops in the field, much less to prisoners of war. It is just that the men who caused the scarcity shall be the first to suffer from it... Present appearances indicate the prospective necessity of a still greater reduction of the ration."[44]

For several months, there were negotiations between General Grant and Colonel Ould to allow each side to provide medicines and clothing to alleviate the suffering of their men held in the other's military prisons. The South al-

---

[35] *O.R.*, VIII, p. 734.
[36] *Ibid.*, p. 96.
[37] *Ibid.*, p. 135.
[38] *Ibid.*, p. 737.
[39] *Ibid.*, pp. 138, 139.
[40] *Ibid.*, p. 137.
[41] *Ibid.*, p. 139.
[42] *Ibid.*, p. 160.
[43] *Ibid.*, p. 161.
[44] *Ibid.*

lowed and even encouraged this procedure. The South invited the North to send its medical doctors to come south to treat their own men. This was never done.

Brigadier-General Wm. N. R. Beall, C.S.A., was a paroled prisoner and was made the agent to supply Confederate prisoners of war. The South sent cotton to New York City near the 1st of February to be sold; the money collected was to be used to buy supplies for the Confederate prisoners. With 830 bales of cotton sent north, the Confederate agent bought "... 16,983 blankets, 16,216 jackets and coats, 19,888 pair of pants, 19,000 over shirts, 5,948 pair of drawers, 10,140 pair of socks, 17,000 pair of shoes."[45]

**Prisoners Lined Up So that Doctors Could Pick the Ones That Were the Most Debilitated -** At Florence, it was well established that the authorities took bribes to be put on the list of those to be released. General Winder was at Florence to investigate this practice when he died. Those prisoners who had an acting ability were at a definite advandage.

General H. W. Halleck wrote and complained to Grant that "... all the proceeds of the rebel cotton are devoted to supplying the rebel prisoners with new clothing, shoes, and blankets. Not a cent is expended for provisions. The result is that we feed their prisoners and permit the rebel Government to send cotton within our lines, free of all charge, to purchase and carry back the means of fitting out their own men for the field. Under these circumstances the Secretary of War is not disposed to sanction the admission of any more cotton on the same terms."[46]

Early in February, the Confederates at Florence ordered all the prisoners who were able to be transported to be taken to Goldsborough, North Carolina. The sick from the rest of the prison were brought into the sheds. The Confederates told these men that, if they would take an oath not to go beyond the stockade, they would not actively guard them. The prisoners agreed. They were then made to swear not to talk with the Negroes or slaves. The men detailed to work in the hospital were tempted to leave, but decided to stay with their helpless comrades.

General Winder was told, on February 4th, by General Cooper, that General Beauregard had advised moving all the prisoners in Florence back to Andersonville, if General Winder agreed. J. A. Campbell, Assistant Secretary of War, wrote General Braxton Bragg, on February 12th, that it was necessary to move the prisoners at Florence to the vicinity of Wilmington as they were to be exchanged there within the following two weeks. Forno asked Gen. Bragg, at Wilmington, if he could spare 500 men for temporary duty as guard for the transfer. Beauregard then changed his mind and agreed that sending the men to Wilmington was the best solution.

Phillip Cashmeyer recounted on September 22, 1865, the incidents preceding the death of General Winder in a letter to Colonel N. P. Chipman, Judge-Advocate at the Wirz trial. "...As well as I can recollect, I was at Camp Lawton Prison, near Millen, Ga., in September, 1864. While I was there, orders were received to select a number of the sick prisoners to be exchanged. I heard many of the sick complain that such of the prisoners, sick or not, who had money could have their names put upon the list for exchange, to the exclusion of the more afflicted who had not money to bribe the officers with that had the making of the selections for exchange, so that many of the sick who would have otherwise been exchanged and living were left in prison to suffer and die. Upon my making inquiry relative to their complaints I found that it was true and reported the same to General Winder, under whom I was acting. He at once instituted means to recover from the officers of the prison the moneys they had thus obtained. When making my inquiries into the matter the prisoners would refuse to testify to having given it. Notwithstanding, I found means to establish the truth of the complaints, and General Winder succeeded in recovering a portion of the money from the officials in whose possession it was. I visited the prison at Florence, S. C., in the later part of the year 1864, and fore part of 1865, and while there heard a general complaint from the prisoners of the bad treatment they received, and of their being robbed of their moneys and jewelry. On making inquiry into the nature of their complaints I found that upon the prisoners being received into the prison it was the practice of those in charge of the prison to take from them their moneys and other valuables, and from such as they got small amounts they would give receipts to, but to those from whom they obtained large amounts no receipts were given. The same practice prevailed there as at the

[45] *Ibid.*, p. 241.
[46] *Ibid.*

other prison in relation to the selection of the sick to be exchanged. They were on leaving the prison refused the moneys and other valuables which had been taken from them, upon the plea that the officer having them in charge was absent and that they were not responsible. The treatment in other respects at this prison was of a similar character to the others. Some of the officers having charge of the prisons I had visited I found to be extremely corrupt and were constantly practicing toward the prisoners such treatment as did not come within the range of their duties, thereby causing death and suffering among them..."[47]

At Florence, "The prisoners complained greatly of the harsh and brutal treatment they received from Captain Barrett and Lieutenant Wilson, who had charge of the interior of the prison. They charged these officers with cruel and undeserved punishments, such as lengthened confinement upon bread and water in the guardhouse for trivial offenses. Some deaths were reported as the result of their brutality. Lieutenant Cheatham, adjutant, had charge of the searching of the prisoners at their reception, performing this often indecently; was charged with often refusing a receipt for any sums he took from the men excepting small ones, thereby causing the loss of money due many of the prisoners at their departure, at which time Lieutenant Cheatham was absent upon a furlough for thirty days. Colonel Iverson declared, in reply to the indignant demands of the losers, that Lieutenant Cheatham alone was responsible. The prisoners made a report of the above facts to and appealed to General Winder for protection, which application I forwarded to him. He thereupon came to Florence, on the route declaring his determination, if he found the statement true, to remove and punish the parties complained of, and bringing other officers with whom to fill their places. Unfortunately, just as he reached my tent with his staff he was attacked with disease of the heart and died instantly.

"I left Florence immediately after this, having charge of the body of General Winder, since which time I have had no connection or communication with the Confederate prisons."[48]

Monday, February 6th, was very cold as General Winder left Columbia for Florence with his small party consisting of Lieutenant Colonel Henry Forno and Captain Phillip Cashmeyer, then acting sutler at Florence. Sidney Winder had remained at Columbia. General Winder was on his way to investigate the rumors of cruelty and thievery at Florence. After Winder's fatal heart attack, Cashmeyer was ordered, by Forno, to accompany the body to Columbia. "General James Chesnut made the funeral arrangement, and the services were held on Thursday, the 9th of February, in Columbia. After lying in state at city hall, the general's remains were taken to Trinity Church by an impressive escort. A detachment of cavalry was in the lead, then came the family and the pallbearers (including Generals Joseph E. Johnston, Mansfield Lovell, and Wade Hampton), followed by a regiment of infantry, various Confederate officers and officials, and several thousand citizens bringing up the rear... Only cemetery employees witnessed the actual burial, for Winder's body was placed in an unmarked grave. Sherman's army would reach Columbia within a week....It seemed likely that the remains of the commissary general of prisoners would be desecrated if found, so the family decided to take no chances."[49]

A corroborating account of Winder's death was given by Fosdick. "It appears that the rebel officers had prepared a dinner and laid in a supply of sorghum whisky, and were preparing to have a 'big time' with what they had saved by cutting down the rations of the prisoners. When all was arranged, Col. Iverson sent an Orderly to tell his chief that things were in readiness and he was invited to dine with him. Gen. Winder assented, and as he stepped to the tent door he fell prostrate on the ground, and immediately expired. This put an end to the festivities of that day, and no doubt saved gallons of villainous whisky for future use, as but few had got drunk when the above event took place."[50]

Pasted in an old scrapbook was found a small portion of a column, from an unknown newspaper, describing General Winder. It said, "As he entered and stooped to put down his satchel, he fell forward upon his face, and when raised was dead." "He never touched stimulants of the grosser kind, and rarely tasted even a glass of wine."

"The 8th of February we first heard of Winder's death, which caused great joy through all the prison camps - joy that he could no longer torture Union prisoners.

"He was directly and the immediate cause of all the unnecessary suffering among us. He was the commissary general of prisoners, and he had it in his power to say what they should have to eat, where and what kind of quarters they should occupy, and what they should have to minister to their comfort. In all the prisons there as great rejoicing over his death."[51]

---

[47] *Ibid.*, p. 754.
[48] *Ibid.*, p. 766.
[49] Arch Fedric Blakey, *General John H. Winder, C.S.A.* (Gainsville: University of Florida Press,1990), p. 5.
[50] Fosdick, p. 104.
[51] Abbott, pp. 172, 173.

"The Confederate authorities removed his body from Florence to Columbia. Here, they placed the body in state in the City Hall. At half-past three in the afternoon of February 9, a procession comprising a military escort and a large number of citizens accompanied Winder's corpse through the streets to Trinity Church. The rector interred the body in the church cemetery. Winder's remains rested there until March 28, 1878, when his relatives moved them to the family vault at Greenmount Cemetery in Baltimore, Maryland, where they inscribed on the gravestone, 'Blessed are the pure in heart'."[52]

George L. Marshall related a story about the re-interment of General Winder in *Confederate Veteran* magazine as told by his grandfather, Colonel Jackson Marshall, who had been General Winder's secretary. "At his burial my grandfather and my uncle, C.O. Marshall, were among the few who officiated. He was secretly buried, for fear that his grave would be desecrated. After the interment, the fresh earth was leveled off and a heap of brush piled on the new[ly]-made grave and burned into ashes to destroy the trace. Many years after, this son, living in Baltimore, Maryland, wishing to remove [Winder's] remains to his native land, procured the services of Colonel C.O. Marshall, who was then living in Columbia, South Carolina, to locate the grave. So well did he remember the exact spot and from measurements and bearings taken from a close-by tree, it was located with exactness. Fearing that the corpse was in no condition to be seen, my uncle requested Mr. Winder to retire until he could first investigate its condition. Upon opening the casket [he found] the remains were in a perfect state of preservation, his gray uniform almost spotless, and his Confederate buttons still shining."[53]

"Greenmount Cemetery Records, Baltimore. Winder's step-daughter, Caroline 'Carrie' Eagles, requested the return of the remains on 26 March 1878. The inscription was originally meant to read 'Blessed Are The Pure in Heart.' I have been unable to determine why the change was made [to 'Blessed Are The Good and Brave']... Winder, his wife, Caroline, Carrie, and Sidney are all buried next to each other in Beach Area 1, lot 13."[54]

On February 14th, Brigadier General Gideon J. Pillow, was assigned as Commissary-General of Prisoners after the death of General Winder. Brigadier-General Gardner was given control of the prisoners east of the Savannah River.

On February 16th, General Samuel Cooper announced a general exchange had been agreed upon. The prisoners were to be exchanged as quickly as possible. This was conveyed to the commandants of the prisons at Florence, Charlotte, and Salisbury.[55] The Federal Secretary of War directed all Confederate prisoners were to be sent to the exchange point at City Point on the James River east of Petersburg. Those prisoners not wishing to be exchanged could be sent to New York.[56]

General J. M. Schofield, Major-General at Wilmington, on the 21st of February had not received the order and so refused to accept the first 2,500 prisoners sent by Major-General R. F. Hoke. Lee wrote to Grant and asked that, for the sake of the poor prisoners, he should accept them because they had been on a long, tiresome journey with no food. The officers not accepted at Wilmington were sent to Danville.

Finally, on the 22nd of February, Grant told Schofield to accept all prisoners and to forward them to Annapolis. After they were sent to the Wilmington area, Grant felt "... should they fall into our hands by the fortunes of war, we should still be in honor bound to regard them as delivered to us by the enemy."[57] The Federals sent out provisions to be cooked by the Confederates and to be fed to the prisoners. Lee said that the prisoners should be marched, if practical, because they tied up the railroad. The officers should be separated and should ride on the trains.

Brigadier General W. M. Gardner advised General Bradley T. Johnson, on February 16th, that the 7,000 would be sent to Salisbury. In about the middle of February, a general exchange was agreed upon. The Florence prisoners were to be sent on to Wilmington. General Bragg in Wilmington ordered that all prisoners of war, not officers, were to be exchanged at Wilmington as soon as they arrived. There should be duplicate lists of the prisoners with a signed receipt given by the receiving Federal officer. On the next day, February 19th, all, including officers, were to be sent. The Federals refused to accept them and the Confederate railroad authorities refused to send trains to Wilmington. Major-General R. F. Hoke, said "... in the name of humanity, consent to their delivery." A couple of days later, through the intervention of General Grant, they were accepted.[58]

About the last of February, a Confederate officer came in and ordered that all the remaining prisoners were to

[52] Duffy, pp. 164, 165.
[53] W.H. Graber, "Pathetic Story of Captain Wirz,' *Confederate Veteran* (Nov. 1990), p. 490.
[54] Blakey, p. 5 note 13.
[55] *O.R.*, VIII, p. 238.
[56] *Ibid.*, p. 266.
[57] *Ibid.*, p. 289.
[58] *Ibid.*, p. 290.

go to the railroad depot, which was about a quarter-mile away. Some of the men walked, some hobbled, some crawled, and the very debilitated rode in wagons. "We took all but those thought to be dying; they were left without help of any kind; there were perhaps thirty or forty in this condition." After about two days' ride on the boxcars, still immediately behind the Confederate lines, the Confederates began to excitedly back up the train as fast as it would go. Soon the train stopped, the men were ordered off the cars, and they camped in the woods. Boggs said that the Confederate acted as if they expected an attack; some rebel cavalry helped guard them that night. The next day, they were returned to their old quarters at Florence. They found some of the dying men still in pretty good shape after the four days they had been neglected. On about the 1st of March, they were again ordered into the boxcars and started over the same route. Whenever the train would stop, the men would lay the dead beside the tracks. They knew then that they were headed for Wilmington, which was in Federal hands. The train flew a white flag from its engine as it sped along. They soon spied Union soldiers acting as pickets and then they were behind the Yankee lines in Wilmington. The rebel officer in charge of the prisoners saluted a Union major and the exchange was initiated. About thirty Yankees and some of their surgeons advanced to the train and aided the men in getting off. "The Rebel guards now move a few yards away, and look ashamed, and sneaking."[59] The Yankees helping unload had tears in their eyes at the sight of their emaciated comrades. They shared their clothing, giving the weak men shirts, stockings, and all they could spare. These troops were on picket and part of Schofield's corps. Some wagons came over from Wilmington loaded with rations. Coffee was made, boxes of hard tack were opened and passed around freely, vinegar and onions were distributed. The men were warned by the surgeons not to eat too much too rapidly, but they could drink all the coffee they wanted. The next morning, they were given soap; they went to a small creek nearby and bathed off prison grime. They then marched into Wilmington and boarded ships for home.

Hopkins told, in his diary, about his trip home from Wilmington: "Finally, we were carried - those who could, walked - to the wharf and placed in the hold of the *John C. Leary*. We lay like herring across the floor, on cots or mattresses. The vessel had only been cleaned after the unloading of horses to replenish the worn Cavalry, and the horse smell was very distinct and not pleasant to the hundreds of weak and sick mortals in the hold.

"Three ships left Wilmington on the same hour - two sister ships, that had brother names - *John C. Leary* and *William Leary* and the third was the *General Lyon*. The two last went ashore at Hatteras Cape, in a rough storm and blow.

"Almost the total number was lost (including the crew) of fifteen hundred prisoners on the *General Lyon*, escaped prison to die on the ocean... This was the night of February last...

"We reached our goal, Annapolis, on a cold morning in a slight snowfall, practically naked, we were carried from the hold, in the arms of strong men, who wept as children at the condition of their comrades... Immediately wrapped in warm and soft blankets, carried through lines of hundreds of soldiers, where there was not a dry eye..."[60]

Often, the prisoners who were well would bribe Confederate officers and medical personnel to get themselves placed on the list of sick prisoners due to be exchanged. Never blatant at Andersonville, it was so at Millen. It was described by Phillip Cashmeyer, General Winder's "special agent:" "The only instance of improper treatment I heard of here was that when an exchange of sick prisoners was agreed upon. Captain Vowles was said to have placed the names of such persons as paid for the favor on the list of those who were to be immediately forwarded to Savannah for exchange to the exclusion of some of the sick, who complained bitterly of it. Upon hearing of it General Winder instituted inquiry, but the evidence of prisoners not being acceptable, the charge was not sustained, although $60 paid by a prisoner was recovered from a clerk in Captain Vowles' office. The suspicion was so great against this officer that General Winder declared he should have no such command in the future."[61]

It was this robbing of prisoners and bribery which prompted General Winder to come to Florence, the place of his death.

After the death of General Winder, Colonel Forno, being the senior officer present, was left in charge of the prison at Columbia and Florence. Forno telegraphed the railroad superintendent at Wilmington to prepare to furnish transportation for 5,000 prisoners to be transferred from Florence to Columbia. There, he received several conflicting orders and found that there was little subsistence to be found there. It was decided to try to forward the officers numbering about 1,200 to Charlotte and the 7,000 enlisted men to Raleigh.

An agreement was also arranged, about the first of February, which released and delivered all prisoners of war held in close confinement or irons.

---

[59] Boggs, p. 71.
[60] Styple, ed., pp. 169, 170.
[61] *O.R.*, p. 765.

After General Winder died in February, Colonel Forno was made Commandant of all prisons east of the Mississippi River. General Bradley T. Johnson was assigned, near February 12th, to command all prisons in South Carolina. The Secretary of War ordered that a large prison, to hold about 15,000 men, be built at Killian's Mills, about eleven miles from Columbia; it was scheduled to be finished in the third week of February. It, of course, was never completed.

**Statistics of Andersonville Prison, Georgia**
From February, 1864 to March, 1865*

| | Month | No. of Prisoners | No. in Hospital | Av. No. of Deaths Daily |
|---|---|---|---|---|
| 1864 | February | 1,600 | 33 | |
| | March | 4,603 | 909 | 9 |
| | April | 7,875 | 870 | 19 |
| | May | 13,486 | 1,190 | 23 |
| | June | 22,352 | 1,605 | 40 |
| | July | 28,689 | 2,156 | 56 |
| | August | 32,193 | 3,709 | 99 |
| | September | 17,733 | 3,026 | 89 |
| | October | 5,885 | 2,245 | 51 |
| | November | 2,024 | 242 | 16 |
| | December | 2,218 | 431 | 5 |
| **1865** | January | 4,931 | 595 | 6 |
| | February | 5,195 | 365 | 5 |
| | March | 4,800 | 140 | 3 [62] |

The greatest number of deaths on any single day was on the 23rd of August, 1864, and was 127, or about one death every eleven minutes.

The following table relating to the deaths at Andersonville was made from hospital records:

**Deaths at Andersonville**
From February, 1864 to March, 1865

| | Mouth | Deaths in Hopital | Deaths in Stockade | Deaths in Small Pox Hospital | Total |
|---|---|---|---|---|---|
| **1864** | February | 1 | - | - | 1 |
| | March | 262 | 15 | 5 | 282 |
| | April | 471 | 71 | 34 | 576 |
| | May | 633 | 65 | 10 | 708 |
| | June | 1,041 | 150 | 10 | 1,201 |
| | July | 1,119 | 614 | 5 | 1,738 |
| | August | 1,489 | 1,592 | | 3,081 |
| | September | 1,255 | 1,423 | | 2,678 |
| | October | 1,294 | 301 | | 1,595 |
| | November | 494 | | | 494 |
| | December | 166 | 2 | | 168 |
| **1865** | January | 191 | 8 | | 199 |
| | February | 147 | | | 147 |
| | | 100 | | | 100 |
| | TOTAL | 8,663 | 4,241 | 64 | 12,968 |

Hung in stockade for crime ........ 6
Total deaths as registered ........ 12,974 [63]

[62] Hamlin, p.245
[63] Hamlin, p. 246

The hospital records show that 17,873 patients were registered; 823 of these were exchanged, and about 25 took the oath of allegiance, leaving 17,048 to be accounted for, giving a mortality of seventy-six per cent. Besides the registered dead, there were some who perished due to the falling of the excavations in the stockade; others were destroyed by hounds and hunters in the forests.

The actual disassembly of the post that once had a combined population of prisoners and garrison troops totaling over forty thousand beings, would take several weeks. Some of the problems that had plagued the prison for its entire lifetime, continued and, indeed, intensified, as the prison folded. Contact with Richmond became very tenuous. As the Confederacy collapsed, the care of prisoners of war warranted only the lowest priority. Little food and supplies were needed at Andersonville in its latter days. The disruption of the railroad service by Federal troops brought hardship to their confined comrades.

As the conditions of the Federal prisoners improved with the closing of the prison doors, conversely, the conditions of some of the Confederate personnel took a turn for the worse. Several would soon see themselves confined and one would pay the supreme penalty for their involvement in the treatment of Federal prisoners at Andersonville.

Several times the Confederate authorities gathered prisoners into trains, carried them to Federal lines, and tried to send them through the lines. At others times in March and April, they were rebuffed and returned to Andersonville or some other holding pen. Finally, in disgust, the authorities took the prisoners to Federal picket lines and told the men they were free and to make their way as best they could.

By the end of February, 1865, Andersonville was only the shell of the post it had been six months earlier. There was a reduction in the size of the garrison which was necessary to guard the smaller number of weakened prisoners. There were a few fresh fish still arriving for their first imprisonment while others were returning for their second and third visits to this infamous prison.

Soon, the final death-gasp of this post would be heard in the gentle forests of southwest Georgia.

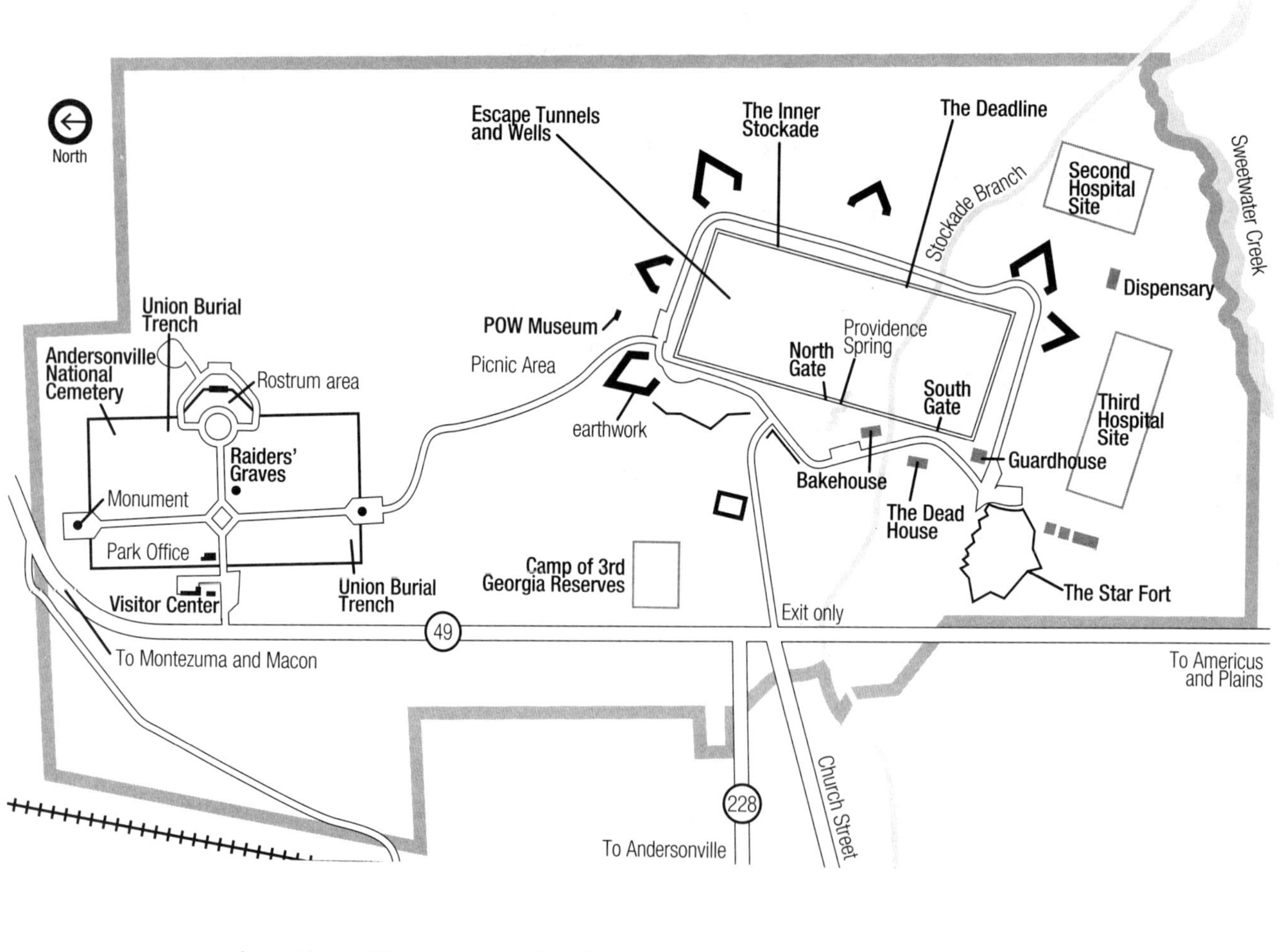


Andersonville National Historic Site

## *Chapter Twelve*

# The Spring of 1865 Leaving Andersonville

*"Finally on the 17th of April, 1865, the old South Gate was thrown open... and when safely out I turned and looked back and not one living soul remained within the enclosure."*

John M. Tate, pp. 10, 11.

It would take several weeks to actually disassemble the post that had once held a total population of over forty thousand beings. Some of the problems that had plagued the prison during its entire lifetime continued and, indeed, intensified as the prison folded. Contact with Richmond became very tenuous. As the Confederacy collapsed, the care of prisoners of war warranted only the lowest priority. Little food and few supplies were needed at Andersonville in its latter days. The disruption of railroad service by Federal troops brought hardship to their confined comrades.

There were many interesting escapes and releases from the prison at Andersonville. One of the most interesting escapes was when Billy Bates and his friend, Dick King, escaped on March 2, 1864, via a tunnel, which took them 7 months and 8 days to dig. Bates incorrectly thought he had arrived there on February 11, 1863. Little did they realize the surprise awaiting them. On March 28th, they were ordered to advance and be recognized by a Yankee picket near Bridgeport, Alabama. A couple of days later, they were taken by ambulance to be presented to General Sherman who ordered that they be taken immediately to Washington to relate their experiences to President Lincoln. They were not allowed to bathe or to change their lice-ridden clothes. They were escorted by a guard named Collins and a physician named Ross to ensure that they arrived safe and sound.

"We arrived at Washington about 6:30 A M., April 28, 1864. Collins left us in care of Doctor Ross at a sort of a soldiers' home or hospital near the depot, and reported to President Lincoln immediately. He soon returned with orders to convey us to the White House at once. We were accordingly loaded into an omnibus and driven under the famous portico at the main entrance to that historic building and carried into a reception room on the first floor, where we remained an hour or more. The guard then beckoned to Collins and took him directly to the President by virtue of the orders, which he bore from General Sherman.

"He returned in a few minutes followed by President Lincoln. The President came striding across the room, took each of us by the hand, saying, 'Come along, boys; come along,' and undertook to lead us into an adjoining room.

"Our feet had become so swollen and sore that we had scarcely borne our weight on them since leaving Cincinnati, but we did manage, by the aid of Collins and Doctor Ross, to hobble along to the next room. The effort, pain and excitement took away our speech for a minute.

"Mr. Lincoln wheeled a couple of fine tapestried chairs into position for us, but we demurred to soiling them He kindly pushed us down into them, saying, 'There is nothing in the White House too good for my boys,' and sat a moment looking at us with one hand on my head and the other on Dick's shoulder.

"'Now, boys, tell me all about it. I want to hear your story. General Sherman has asked for a patient hearing of all you have to say. So tell me all about it.'

"We were still unable to speak. His considerate kindness broke us down. We burst into tears and were almost hysterical. Seeing our condition, the President continued in a kindly tone of voice, 'Don't break down now, boys.

Cheer up and remember that you are almost home. We are all friends here, and I want you as friends of mine to do me a favor and tell me all you can about Andersonville.'

"Recovering in a measure our self control, we began, and as we warmed up to the work we forgot the wounds, bruises, sores and filth of our starved, emaciated bodies - forgot for the time the horrors of imprisonment and the deadly perils of escape - forgot even that we were at the seat of our great nation, in sight of its magnificent capitol and in the presence of the greatest living ruler, and the noblest, grandest man on earth.

"We talked on and on with a perfect abandon. When one grew too weak for speech the other continued the tale.

"The President listened with close attention and until we finished our long and rambling story, and rarely interrupted us by a word or a question...

"The President sprang to his feet and started toward the door, saying, 'My God, when will this accursed thing end?'

"He and General Cary excused themselves for a few minutes, as I afterwards learned, to transmit the following telegram to my father:

> *Executive Mansion, Washington, D. C.,*
> *April 28, 1864.*
>
> *Calvin Bates, Mansfield, Ohio:*
> *Your son, Ralph Bates, of Troop H, Ninth Ohio Cavalry, has made his escape from Andersonville prison. He is in my care. I will send him home. Don't let him die.*
>
> *Abraham Lincoln*
> *President.*

"He returned in a few minutes and said: 'Now, boys, just keep quiet; we will soon have your affairs all right,' and commenced to question us anew.

"'Did the guards take good care of you? Who is the other man you have alluded to, boys?'

"Collins replied that it was Doctor Ross, of Ecnia, Ohio, who came with us at his own expense.

"'Where is he? Bring him in immediately.'

"He then questioned Doctor Ross closely concerning our condition when he first saw us at Cincinnati, and finally, turning to Collins, ordered him to have us washed and supplied with suitable clothing and returned at once to the White House...

"On our return to the hospital we were taken to the bathroom and stripped of our rags, when the work of cleaning up began. We were rubbed, scrubbed, scraped and doused until we could endure it no longer, and our hair and beards were shingled as close to the skin as possible. Brandy was administered once or twice to strengthen us for the ordeal, but it came near being too much for us in spite of all. We actually collapsed until the doctor was alarmed.

"A free use of stimulants rallied us for a time and the working of donning new suits of blue commenced. Our new clothes hung on us like the covering of a scarecrow. Our novel appearance at once aroused Dick's vein of humor and remarked: 'Collins, you are the most extravagant man I ever saw.'

'"Why so?' asked Collins.

"'Don't you see we could just as well both be put into one suit and thus be more economical?'

"After this transformation we were re-conveyed to the White House and put to bed.

"The President came in to see us, and finding us in bed, limp, white and speechless, said:

"'Has it come to this? Never mind, you will soon be walking about.'

"Just then a lady came into the room when Mr. Lincoln turned to us and said:

"'Boys, this is the other half of this administration.' He seemed to be in a jovial mood, made a number of humorous remarks and told stories to provoke our sense of mirth, and gave us several pretty severe pinches, as he said, 'Just to see if there was a pinch of flesh on either of us.'

"Mrs. Lincoln was for giving us 'something good to eat,' but Doctor Ross forbade it peremptorily.

"Mr. Lincoln said Doctor Ross was medical director of that department and must be obeyed accordingly. We were then left alone for a much needed sleep.

"On waking Doctor Ross took us to another room to be weighed. Here we found President Lincoln, General Cary and several other gentlemen assembled to witness this operation and certify to its correctness. Mr. Lincoln was weigh master and directed Dick to be put on the scales. He seemed to distrust his own senses the first time and had him put on again to be sure he was right.

'"Cary, this man weighs sixty-four and a half pounds.'

"I was next put on the scales, when he called out: 'Cary, this one weighs only fifty-nine and three-fourths pounds.'

"The President returned with us to our bedroom and sat some time, asking additional questions about Andersonville, as they occurred to him... The next day was one of glorious, unbroken rest...

"The following morning we were carried into a large dining-room and propped up in chairs in front of the table, when President Lincoln came in and seated himself between us. Our breakfast consisted of beef, tea and boiled milk; there was nothing else in sight on the table...

"Another day and night passed without interruption. On the following morning we were much improved. On the eleventh morning President Lincoln came to the room to say goodbye and told us to be of good cheer for we were to start for home that day."[1]

One diarist said he got out of Andersonville by bribing a Confederate sergeant. "There was a sergeant belonging to our company that had a watch and he gave it to a Rebel sergeant to take thirty of us out and we paid the sergeant three dollars apiece after we got to St. Louis."[2]

Another prisoner told of his journey, in about the middle of March, through Georgia to Florida for exchange. They were taken in railroad cars to Albany and then marched the 60 miles to Thomasville, some of the sick being hauled in wagons. In the afternoon, word came that the exchange had been called off and so again came the long, 60-mile trek; in a few days, they were returned to Andersonville for the third time. "In a few days all were taken out of the stockade, down the same route, and set at liberty to find the Union lines as best they could."[3]

The following was, in part, how a correspondent for the *New York Times* described the exchange of prisoners from Millen on November 18th and as it was written in the *Bangor Jeffersonian* on December 6th. "The rendezvous for the exchanges is at Venus Point on the Savannah river whence the spires and many of the houses of the city of Savannah are visible. Our boats are invariably the first at the rendezvous, anchored in mid-river awaiting the rebel vessels, whose tardiness proceeds from the fact that it is only at the proper tide certain obstructions of the channel above can be crossed. Finally they appear over the low marshes, and in half an hour their uncouth, grotesque, towering ships are puffing and wheezing near us. Colonel Mulford immediately goes in a yawl boat to the *General Beauregard*, a small steamer used by Captain Hatch the rebel agent, as the flagship of his transport squadron, and after a few moments consultation, the rolls of the prisoners are transferred. The rebel ship is at once laid alongside a neat Union vessel, and the poor fellows are transhipped. Those of them who are able to move without aid pass to the protection of the old flag first; then come those who hobble on crutches, and last the few whose helplessness require that they should be carried on stretchers. In all this operation the greatest formality is observed. A number of rebel civilians, with bands round their hats, labeled 'Committee for the wounded' whose position corresponds with our own Sanitary Commission, accompany the boats from Savannah to attend on the sick, and assist in the transhipment; but seldom on either side is a word spoken except on the subject of the matter in hand. A different course is forbidden, and if on either side there happen to be a disposition to engage in conversation, watchful guards step up and ask that the conversation shall cease. When the rebel boat moves off and the men are huddled together on the decks of our own vessels, then rises hearty shouting and cheering. Three cheers and a tiger for the old flag; three more and a tiger for Colonel Mulford; then comes a burst of song, most often the words being, 'Rally round the flag boys, from near and from far; down with the traitor and up with the star.' Then vermin infested rags, are rudely torn off and flung into the water, or cast with glee into the flaming furnaces of the steamers, and new clothes are issued, and a general cleaning-time inaugurated. The steamer *Eliza Hancox* has a spacious deck, affording room for dancing, and Terpsicore finds her votaries. As soon as possible, barrels of hot coffee are prepared, and hams are cooked, and boxes of hard bread opened for the refreshment of these men.

"Remember, too, that the men thus returned are the best specimens of the suffering. Only those are forwarded to us whom the rebel medical authorities decide to be strong enough to bear the fatigue of transportation."[4]

This was how Hugh Moore described his release from Florence: "We were embarked on the railroad train without breakfast, and at 2 o'clock, p.m. arrived at Charleston. When we left the cars we went to the wharf and got on board a boat which put off towards the south... In a few minutes we saw through the fog a large steamship coming towards us... As the stars and stripes glimmered through the fog, a shout of joy and triumph came up from the boat we were in...

[1] Ralph O. Bates, *Billy and Dick From Andersonville to the White House* (Santa Cruz, Cal.: Sentinel Pub. Co., 1910), pp. 45-91.

[2] Stephen Payne diary, in private hands.

[3] *Mass. Monument*, p. 35.

[4] *Bangor* (Maine) *Jeffersonian*, December 6, 1864.

**Ex-prisoners on Board a Side-wheeler Transport** - They were usually given another bath, tobacco, whiskey, and small portions of food. Some died from gorging themselves on food. Surpisingly, some were given pork and cornbread. The transports usually went to Annapolis or New York City. A couple sank off of Cape Hatteras.

"The vessel, the steamship, *U.S.*, a large three-decked steamship, came alongside and the plank was thrown out and we were taken aboard. The first thing that the Dr. ordered was that we should take off our clothes and throw them into the harbor, and put on a new suit of blue, that was furnished us, and wash our hands and faces with soap (this was the first soap that I had used for six months). We then had our supper, which was one large cracker, a small piece of broiled, pickled pork, and a pint of weak coffee. The Dr. explained that there was plenty on board the vessel for us... but that was all we could safely have at first. He said the pickled pork was to cleanse the stomach... some of the poor fellows laughed, some cried, and some shouted for joy...The next morning the breakfast was more sumptuous and something more was added each meal, as we grew more accustomed to a square meal.

"On the evening of the third day, we came in sight of Annapolis, Maryland, where we were to land... As we approached nearer to the wharf, we could hear the notes of *the Red, White and Blue*, that came over the water from the band that awaited us on the wharf, along with the U.S.A. officers...

"After the vessel landed and the plank was thrown out, the dead, of whom there were about twenty, were carried on shore, and after them the sick were also helped ashore.

"Then came the rest of us... The Col. in command ordered the citizens not to approach us, as our strength might be too severely taxed, and we were soon marched to a number of large bathing houses, in which we... washed and were made clean; we then put on another new suit of clothes, and threw the others away. We then went to the barracks prepared for us, which were large, airy, and pleasant, where we rested until strength came again to us. We were granted sixty days leave of absence, with three months pay, and told that we might go to our homes or stay at Annapolis until we were ready for duty. The Colonel also informed us that he would send a detail of one man with any of us who felt unable to go alone."[5]

Clifton related, "When we got on to our boat they had new clothes for us. The first thing we did was to throw our old rags off in the river and take a bath and put on our new clothes. Then they began to give us something to eat, it was a cup of coffee, a few crackers and about a spoonful of rice. Of course that didn't anything like satisfy our appetites, but they told us they would give us more after while. That was all we must have at once but that they had plenty and would give it to us just as fast as we could stand it but they must be the judges. The boys that came with the boat was awfully good to us and seemed to have great sympathy for us. They had a good doctor on the boat but in spite of all that could be done, several died before they got off the boat. They were so weak, [that] the voyage killed them. Well, we landed at Annapolis, Maryland. Those that were not able to travel, went to the hospital. Those able to travel, went to Camp Denison, Ohio."[6]

**Passing the Line for Exchange** - Prisoners removed their rags and put on new blue uniforms. This depicts prisoners arriving by train at Wilmington, NC. (Abbott)

From Annapolis, Lyon was taken to Baltimore and put in Jarvis Hospital for 3 weeks. Lyon had lost weight from a normal weight of between 150 to 180 pounds down to 100 pounds. Another prisoner said he went from his normal weight of 175 pounds down to 80. Another prisoner with a normal weight of 154 said he lost down to 96 pounds. Another lost from 197 down to 91; another from 175 down to 94. Fosdick, who had weighed 115 pounds before his ordeal, eventually weighed 66 for a loss of 49 pounds. Blessing lost 10 pounds during his first month of captivity.

Near the 10th of February, a group of prisoners, including Fosdick, was placed on a train and, after a 2-day trip,

---

[5] Hugh Moore, pp. 459, 460.

[6] Clifton, p. 14.

arrived at the Confederate fortifications on the Cape Fear River. They were carried across the river on a ferry boat to Wilmington on the opposite shore. There, they were loaded into a train again for a one-day trip to Goldsboro, N. C. After a march through a swamp, they were placed in a clearing guarded by North Carolina troops. These troops were very kind, saying they had been pressed into the Confederate service; some expressed Union sympathies. After having been there about 10 days, they were aroused in the middle of the night and put on board a train for Wilmington; a detachment of Union cavalry had been as close as 25 miles from Goldsboro. There at Wilmington about half were loaded on trains and taken back to the same camp at Goldsboro from which they had come. During the last days of February, they were asked to sign parole papers by the Confederate officers. After this formality, some were again loaded on a train bound for Wilmington. Others waited for several days and were then loaded on flat cars pulled by an engine with two white meal sacks attached to the engine as flags of truce. They were taken through the lines about 12 miles north of Wilmington. They were given blankets and small portions of food with some medicinal stimulants. Fosdick was placed on the *General Lyon*, a huge steam and sail vessel. After about three days, they reached Annapolis at night and remained on board until dawn. They were given a new uniform and had their hair cut. Two men bathed and dried each man. They received twenty-five cents per day commutation pay for each day in prison.[7]

Major Randlete, the provost marshal of Wilmington, said, "One day, 40 of the men which came into our lines were absolutely as naked as they were born." At Wilmington was located the Geer Hospital, probably named for Chaplain J. J. Geer of the 183rd Ohio Volunteers. It seems to have been a receiving hospital for ex-prisoners, especially those suffering from orthopedic problems of the legs related to confinement at southern prisons. Sometimes the debilitated ex-prisoners would stay there a few days until they could gain strength by eating an adequate and nutritious diet. When strong enough, the patient could then bear the stress of a needed amputation. Abbott described the patients at this hospital, "... there were two hundred and eighty-seven cases of the character represented by our illustrations."

On April 9th, there were 2,500 poor fellows still left at Andersonville, who basically remained there because they were too feeble to undertake the march homeward.

Vawter's last month or so of captivity was very interesting. "One day, early in March, an order was read at the gate, that declared that a general exchange of prisoners had been agreed upon, and that they would begin at once, and empty the prisons in Virginia and Carolina first, and would probably reach Andersonville in two weeks, or ten days. This news threw the camp into a wild excitement, though I must confess that many of us did not believe it...

"But in a few days they gave us copies of papers that contained accounts of the release of prisoners from Richmond and Salisbury, Then we began to believe and to grow feverish with excitement.

"In due time rebel officers came in and began to enroll names, putting down rank and regiment. The first call was to take out all the sick; but they gave us the wink, and told us that if any one had any greenbacks, or gold, they would enroll him as sick, and take him out on the first train...

"The whole prison was crowded around the gate; and as the names were called by a loud-voiced rebel, some countenance would light up with joy as he answered, 'Here!'

"Two trainloads... were taken to Vicksburg, Mississippi, for exchange. Then came word that Wilson's Cavalry had raided through Mississippi and Alabama, and destroyed the railroad over which they were shipping the prisoners, so the exchange was stopped.

"About eight thousand came from Blackshear - and about four thousand remained when Wilson's raid stopped the exchange. For the next two weeks they kept hearing of the rumors of Wilson's raid...

"About four o'clock one day, toward the last of March, two long trains stopped at the station. A guard was detailed in a hurry. The counting-sergeants came in and ordered us to get ready to go out at once... 'Every son of a bitch has to be out a-foah mawnin'!'

"The men thinking that Wilson was near, some decided to lag back and catch the last train. They hurried us all they could. The first train was loaded, and pulled out about sunset. They loaded into the darkness. They would count off eighty men, and crowd them up to a car door, and keep saying - 'Hurry up, dah! hurry up, dah!'...

"In Vawter's train were five flat-cars, containing about three hundred prisoners. He was on one of these. They were well to the rear of the train, with perhaps two or three box-cars and a caboose behind. The guard did not seem to fancy these flats, so most of them climbed onto the box-cars ahead of us. Soon after we started, someone discovered that there were but three guards on the five flats, and conceived the bold project of cutting the train and giving

[7] Fosdick, pp. 113-130.

them the grand bounce. The plan was, to uncouple the rear boxes, and as soon as they were sufficiently to the rear - a mile or so - to then uncouple the flats; and as soon as they stopped, to jump off and take to the woods. We knew that those three guards could not stop us, even if they tried.

"Going down a grade, the pin was drawn; and we soon saw the space widen, and the rear cars grew dim in the distance. The train ran about four miles before the guard made the engineer understand that he had lost a part of his train. He then ran on to the first station, and left Vawter's group, while he went back for the rear…

"About daylight we ran into Macon, and stopped, but they did not take us off the cars. From our train we could see up into the business part of town, and noticed a number of large, white flags floating over the principal houses. We asked a negro what they were for, and he said -'Specks de Yanks is comin'!'

"The engine was turned around and hitched to the other end of our train, and by eight o'clock we were steaming away down the same road we came up the night before.

"About two or three o'clock p.m. we passed Andersonville, and from the cars we took our last look at that pen of woe. They took us to Albany - to Thomasville, over the same route that we came in December... They took us eastward from Thomasville to a junction... There we took another road, and ran southward till we struck the Jacksonville & Tallahassee railroad, thence eastward again till we reached Lake City, Florida.

"In sight of the railroad, about four miles east of Lake City, on an island - or more properly, a peninsula - in a vast cypress swamp, we were corralled for the last time. Our prison was a palmetto-covered knoll, of about two acres area, surrounded on all sides by swamp and water, except a narrow low neck across which a corduroy road connected us with the main land.

"Here we had plenty of fuel. Pine and cypress logs lay in rich abundance all about us. When we were there, during April, the weather was warm and dry...

"I had gone without a shirt all winter, using my blouse instead. It had now become so rotten and ragged that it was not worth picking the lice off for all the protection it afforded, so I threw it away. My wardrobe then consisted of pants, ending in a neat fringe about the knee, and a leathern gun-sling, which did duty as a suspender...

"While we were in this prison our rations consisted of a pint of meal per day. We were there one month, and drew nothing but meal during our stay… One day one of the guard shot an alligator, about eight feet long, which he gave to the prisoners. Some of the boys tried steaks off of its tail. That was the only meat eaten in that prison.

"It was the last of April. Thirty-three hundred prisoners were encamped on that little island. The quartermaster brought in our ration, and we noticed more sacks than usual. The old quartermaster gave a knowing wink, and said he was going to fatten us...

"The rations measured out three pints of meal per man… [The next morning] a train of cars came down. We were loaded on and went eastward a few miles - as far as the rails were laid, as the iron had been taken off this road, to mend others, nearly all the way from Jacksonville to Lake City.

"When we got to the end of the railroad we were ordered off the cars, and marched out on the old road bed ahead of the engine. The colonel who had command of our guard then made us a speech.

"He told us that they were tired of guarding us. They knew our time was up, and that we were anxious to get home. They were going to the front to fight, and so had decided to turn us loose. He advised us to go home, and stay there; and to tell our friends at the North that we 'could never whip the rebels in the world!' He told us to follow the railroad-bed and it would take us to Jacksonville - which was in possession of the Yanks.

"The whole speech was a lie. He was included in Johnston's surrender to Sherman and was then under orders to go to Tallahassee to turn over his arms to the United States authorities. This we learned after we got out.

"After this speech the guard opened ranks, and we marched out. 'Good-bye, Johnnies!' 'Good-bye, Yanks!' were the parting salutations."[8]

They were within 8 or 10 miles of Jacksonville. Some rushed towards freedom rapidly, and, because of weakness and overexertion, had to lie down. Some went a mile and gave out, some two, some six. They were strung out along the railroad cut. Most had to sleep that night in the forest beside the cut. They hid, just in case. They were trudging before sun-up; at about noon they came to a creek where some bathed. By mid-afternoon they saw a mounted Yank ahead, about three miles from Jacksonville. They were welcomed by their comrades who set up hospital tents and gave them a ration of whiskey. By dark, they had wheat bread and four barrels of boiled meat known as "mess pork," coffee by the barrel and a gill of whiskey. A train of wagons and ambulances with surgeons and nurses, went out on the rail bed to look for stragglers. It took them three days to search the cut and return to Jacksonville. Vawter's

[8] The synopsis was taken from Vawter, pages 167-185.

group stayed in Jacksonville for about three weeks, then went to Fernandina, where they were put on an ocean steamer called the *Cassandra.* Vawter went by way of Fortress Monroe, Annapolis, then to Camp Chase, Ohio, and then home.[9]

**Off for 'God's Country** - Prisoners being led away from Andersonville to be exchanged. (McElroy)

This was how Private Asbury Stephen spent his last days in Dixie, according to his brief diary. He said he was told by Wirz, on March 24th, that all would be leaving Andersonville soon. Stephen said that, on April 2nd, Wirz left the post and went to find transportation. Wirz returned the next day and reported all were to leave on the 4th. Stephen was placed on a train that morning with "grub" and arrived at Albany at 3 p.m. His group continued on to Blue Springs and spent the night there. They got up and marched 19 miles, stopped in some woods where they received supper, and spent the night. They got up the next morning early and rode on a train, crossing one bridge, then made camp for the night. On the 7th, they got three hardtack biscuits and arrived at Thomasville at 2 o'clock. They stayed there on the 8th and then received orders to go back to Andersonville where they returned on the 12th. On the 17th, the Masons from Albany brought some "C. & G." At Andersonville, Stephen's group was again ordered back on the train to Thomasville, but they "flanked the place." They were placed on another train for Jacksonville and stopped at a place called Live Oak on the 23rd. They continued on to Lake City on the 24th and signed paroles for a couple of days. They arrived at Jacksonville on the 28th and, for recreation, Stephen went fishing, where he had bad luck. He was detailed to a hospital, lived in a tent, and spent most of his time fishing in order to relax. Stephen went on to Maryland, arriving there on May 29th; he was mustered out on June 27th in Ohio.[10]

"Communication with Richmond being cut off, General Imboden held a conference at Macon with General Gideon J. Pillow, the newly-appointed Commissary of Prisoners and, therefore, his superior officer, and with General Cobb, commander of the Georgia troops, from whom he hoped to obtain sufficient force to guard the prisoners under his charge. General Imboden add[ed], concerning the situation during those last weeks: 'The difficulty of supplying the prisoners with even a scanty ration of corn was increasing daily... We decided that the best thing that could be done was to make arrangements to send off all the prisoners we had to the nearest Federal post, and having paroled them not to bear arms until regularly exchanged, to deliver them unconditionally, simply taking a receipt on descriptive rolls of those turned over.'

"General Sherman having destroyed all railroad communication with Savannah and at the west, the only available outlet was at St. Augustine, Florida. General Imboden continued, 'It was resolved to open communication with the Federal commander at that place. With this view, about the middle of March, Captain Rutherford, an intelligent and energetic officer, was sent to St. Augustine. A few days later after his departure, he telegraphed, 'Send on the prisoners.' He had, as subsequently reported, arranged with the Federal authorities to receive them. Three days' cooked rations were prepared, and at once all were ordered to be sent forward who could bear the journey. All but 12 or 15 men reported themselves able to go, and did go. The number sent was 6,000. To my amazement, the Federal commandant at St. Augustine refused to receive or [give] receipt for the prisoners until he could hear from General Grant at Petersburg, with whom he could communicate only by sea, along the coast. Knowing that 2 or 3 weeks must elapse before hearing from Grant, and it being impossible to subsist our men and prisoners, I could pursue only one course. I ordered them returned to Andersonville...

"The old routine was resumed at Andersonville, but it was not destined to continue long. Before any communication was resumed from St. Augustine, I learned that General Wilson, with a large body of cavalry, was approaching Georgia from the west. It was evident that his first objective point was Andersonville. Finding that we were powerless to prevent Wilson reaching Andersonville, where he would release the prisoners and capture our officers and troops, it was decided without hesitation to send the prisoners again to Jacksonville and to turn them loose to make their way to their friends in St. Augustine. In a few days the post at Andersonville was broken up, and in a short time the surrender of Johnston, embracing all that section of the country, occurred. The Confederate prisons ceased to exist.'"[11]

The following was how Major N. Cutler of the Second Maine Cavalry described the releases in this vicinity: "On

[9] *Ibid.*
[10] Asbery Stephen diary, pp. 34-37.
[11] Ashe, pp. 13-15.

the 28th of April, 1865, having been a prisoner of war in the hands of the rebels, I was released at Lake City, Florida, together with 1,819 men of U.S. troops, who had also been prisoners. Upon application to the so-called Confederate authorities I obtained transportation from Lake City to Baldwin, Florida, a distance of thirty miles, for myself and men. I then marched the men nine miles to the rebel lines, and, passing through them, marched eleven miles to the lines of the U.S. army, at Jacksonville, Florida. There were in addition to the above, 12 officers and about 1,500 enlisted men released at Lake City on the same day, and, as I am informed, under the same circumstances. On my arrival at Jacksonville I reported the whole number of officers and men released by the rebels to Brevet Brigadier-General Tilghman, commanding post at Jacksonville, Florida. None of the officers or men released were turned over to any U.S. officer. At different times from four weeks to three days before they were released these officers and men had signed to a descriptive list of prisoners of war, which was afterward headed a parole; but nearly all, if not all, had for three weeks after they had signed such a list been held under guard and had been sent to the interior of the so called Confederacy on the approach of the Union forces, to which the rebel authorities had promised they should be turned over."[12]

Doctor William Balser, a contract surgeon with the rank of assistant surgeon, was stationed at Hilton Head, South Carolina. He treated the prisoners at Jacksonville, Florida, who had been released from Andersonville from the 1st to the 26th of May. There arrived at Jacksonville, near the first of May, about 3,300 prisoners. Balser described them this way: "If they did have anything on it was only rags. They were covered with filth and lice. They had sores all over them. A great number of the prisoners had their arms and legs swelled up three or four times their natural size and actually black with extravasated blood. They had ulcers three or four inches in diameter on their arms and calves of their legs. Some of them, from the effects of scurvy, had necrosis of the jaws, so that I was obliged to pull out pieces of bone nearly an inch long. Some of them had lost the eye from ulceration of the anterior portion of the cornea. A good many were idiotic and demented from softness of the brain. There were 3,300 at Jacksonville altogether, and I do not believe there were 200 who did not require treatment. From the 1st of May to the 26th of May, there had died between 80 and 90. I know from the records that between 40 and 50 died at the hospital at Hilton Head."[13]

Beginning as early as 1862, the Federal government found it necessary to establish camps where returnees from Southern prisons could be housed until they had convalesced, been given their back pay, and sent on their way. The main receiving camp in the East was established on the tiny grounds of St. John's College in Annapolis, Maryland. "On the back campus there had been erected eight wooden barracks, each ninety by twenty feet in size and each to hold 150 men. There were also such cook-houses as were necessary, and, eventually, there were added bath-houses and a chapel. The Quartermaster's Corps maintained at all times a vast store of supplies; 2,000 suits, 2,000 overcoats, as well as shoes and blankets and whatever else the men might want. Lazelle reported that, as soon as the men had landed and been brought to the college, they were compelled to wash thoroughly and to throw their old clothes and shoes into the creek, after which they were outfitted."[14] This particular facility soon proved very inadequate.

"On May 1, 1863, the Federal Government signed a lease with Charles S. Welch and Ann Rebecca Welch, his wife, for the use of their 250-acre farm outside of Annapolis, at a rent of $125 per month. A camp for paroled Union prisoners, it was called Camp Parole. According to records found in the United States Archives, forty of the eighty-three authorized buildings were occupied by December of that year. In evidence of the hasty building of these last century 'Government tempos' is the report of an inspection made of the camp after complaints of soldiers who suffered from the cold. The clapboard walls were 'impracticable' to batten but certain siding boards, warped apart, might be mended; also, six inch boards should be used around the buildings where they were raised above the ground, to cut off winds that whistled through the floors.

"By December 15, Surgeon Pittinos of the camp claimed that the 168 bed hospital was totally inadequate for the 6,750 men then in Camp Parole barracks, and suggested adding two more wards and a wash house."

Here the prisoners received a suit of clothing, a bath, a shave, and a new pair of shoes. The emaciated prisoners were well-fed until they felt well enough to either return to their regiments after a 30-day furlough to visit their loved ones or if their terms of service had expired, be mustered out and returned home.

"By June 21, 1865, Capt. John Power, in charge of the Camp, was writing that he expected 'the business of the camp would be closed in 2 or 3 weeks.' He respectfully suggested that Quartermaster stores including horses, wagons, carts, ambulances, harness, lumber, policing tools, barracks, (all military surplus) be sold at public auction. By July 18, 1865, Camp Parole was nearly vacated. The question then arose as to what to do with the 44 barracks, each

[12] *O.R.*, VII, p. 555.

[13] Chipman, p. 139.

[14] Tench Francis Tilghman, Maryland Historical Magazine,Vol. XLV, "The College Green Barracks; St. John's During The Civil War," June, 1950, p. 85.

104′ x 25′ and 10′ high along with the other buildings 'all in good condition.' These, too, were finally sold at auction.

"Long after the camp was turned back to farming, this stop on the Annapolis and Elkridge Railroad was known as Parole Camp Station.

This was how the prisoners reacted when the doors of Andersonville prison were actually opened: "The following day, when I got up I could see the soldiers drawing the artillery into the forest and swamp. Men seemed to be going in all directions, alone or in small squads, with knapsack and gun, and we knew that the war was ended.

"Before noon our gates were thrown open, and we could go where we chose. Our first thought was to go to the rebel camp for something to eat; found plenty of meal and flour. The next day we thought we must start for the Union army, and were sure they were at Macon. We went up the railroad, and in two days made about ten miles to Oglethorpe. We found a guard on the railroad bridge, who would not permit us to go further, as they had only heard that President Lincoln was dead. In a few days a detachment of General Wilson's men came and took us to Macon, where we were put in the Blind Asylum Hospital. Here we remained until after July 4, when my brother found me, and together we started for 'God's land.' On my journey north I wore a rebel uniform, which I still keep."[15]

John M. Tate was released via the South Gate on April 17th and, when he looked back over his shoulder, there was no one left in the prison. He was turned loose at Baldwin Junction, Florida, and, after a walk of about 20 miles, he arrived at Jacksonville on the 29th.[16] The author, Lessel Long, was among those released from Andersonville and taken south to Albany; he was then to be taken on to Florida. They stayed in Albany for two or three days when orders came for them to return to Andersonville. "After we got in the stockade an officer got in one of the perches and said that Colonel Gibbs would make us a speech late in the evening, when it was cool. Said he, 'The Colonel will speak from this stand, and when the bugle sounds he requests that you will come here and hear what he has to say.'... At the sound of the bugle a large body collected near the gate where they could hear the Colonel. He began by saying, 'Prisoners, I hold in my hands an order from General Gideon J. Pillow, which was received at this camp this day, and it is for the removal of you to your lines. It will go into effect between this and the 18th of this month. You will be taken to Vicksburg for exchange. I want you to take as good care of yourselves as you can under the circumstances. Prisoners, I call on you for witnesses that during your long confinement, when you were being removed from one prison to another, have I ever said you were going home? It has often pained me to see you so badly deceived. I did not at that time, nor do I now, think it was right to so cruelly deceive you. It has often pained me more than I can express to you, to witness the horrors of this prison. Many months ago I resolved that I would never knowingly deceive one of you. Many of you will remember when you asked me about exchange I would say that it was not for me to say when an exchange would take place. If I had had the power I would have caused an exchange many months ago, or I would have made your condition different from what it has been. But I now speak from authority and can say that there will be no extending the time beyond the 18th, and it may be sooner."... There was much speculation as to whether it was genuine or not...At last, on the evening of April 17th, an order came to get ready to move... Soon we passed outside of the gates, and away to the railroad and here we go for Macon." "... I saw Captain Wirz coming along giving orders to the officers. He said, 'We will go back to Andersonville, but will stop only to draw rations,' ... At the rear of our train was attached one passenger coach which was filled with rebel officers and among them was Captain Wirz. Negroes informed the prisoners that General Wilson was approaching... When we came in sight of the stockade we fairly strained our eyes to see if we could see any of our boys inside. As we came near and could see better we saw no one inside the stockade, nor were there any guards in the perches... Arrived at the station we saw no rebels there, but learned from our men who had been left to take care of the sick, who were unable to be moved, that there was a call for men to go for rations. While they were getting rations one of our boys who had remained to help the sick came to our car and related the following: 'Early in the morning word was sent to the officer of the prison to destroy all the artillery and ammunition together with the muskets, and for the guards to disperse in every direction and not more than two of them go together, and keep in the woods as much as possible.' He said, 'There is no doubt but that some of Wilson's men are near here now and the rebels do not want to be caught guarding us. They have destroyed all the artillery in the forts, cut down the wheels of gun carriages, thrown their muskets in that deep well at Wirz' headquarters...'

"At last Colonel Gibbs came along the train and said we would go to Albany and march across the country to Thomasville, where we would take the cars for Tallahassee or Lake City, Florida."[17] After the cessation of hostilities,

[15] *Mass. Monument*, p. 36.

[16] John M. Tate, *Half Hour With an Andersonville Prisoner*, Delivered at the Reunion of Post 9, G.A.R., at Gettysburg, Pa., Jan. 8th, 1879 (Published by author, 1879), pp. 10, 11.

[17] Long, pp. 140-146.

General Wilson continued the mopping up operations and pacification of the area. As he had for most of his march through Georgia, he fed his troops from the gleanings from the land under his domain. Colonel George Welling, of the Fourth Kentucky Cavalry, a part of General Wilson's command, captured the Confederate commissary, which was located at Albany about 35 miles by railroad from Andersonville. There, Captain John Davis, Confederate commissary, turned over to him the stores and provisions consisting of 31,000 pounds of bacon, 700 bags of salt, large supplies of corn, and other foodstuffs. In the country nearby, there were large enough quantities of corn and bacon to easily supply General Wilson's army.

A large grain mill at Albany, built by the Confederate government, had "two run of stones." This mill was capable of grinding from 400 to 500 bushels of corn in a 24-hour period. It had a very good "bolting cloth" in it and ground a very good quality flour which was used by the Federal troops who came to the vicinity. The Confederate government had set up a large baking facility there with four ovens in which they baked hard bread or hardtack crackers. The Southern troops surrendered over twenty wagons with thirty or forty mules though many more mules had been lent out when capture was imminent. There were two other grain mills in the vicinity. One of them, four miles away, also had "two run of stones." Transportation was no problem, because many small farmers and every large plantation along the line of march from Macon to Albany had ox teams. At Vienna, about 40 miles from Andersonville, there had been considerable stores captured, but the citizens had raided them when they heard of the approach of the Yankee army and most of the stores vanished.[18]

In January, Captain Dick Winder was made chief quartermaster of all prisons east of the Mississippi River and was assigned to Headquarters at Columbia, South Carolina. Soon after Columbia was evacuated, when there was a general exchange of prisoners, he was ordered to the new headquarters at Salisbury, North Carolina. Because of his loyal service and because of his increased responsibilities, Captain Dick Winder received a promotion to major. On March 25th, Major Winder was assigned to Richmond with Commissary-General of Prisoners Daniel Ruggles after Ruggles had asked Dick Winder to be his chief quartermaster because of his experience. He was awaiting orders to Texas, when he left Richmond with Ruggles on the night of the evacuation; he went to Danville. From there, Major Winder was ordered to Augusta, Georgia, where he was paroled May 2, 1865, by General Fry.[19]

The closing of Florence was very similar to Andersonville as witnessed by Doctor Mann: "The tone of the prison authorities began to change, particularly to those of us who were enjoying the outside parole. The guard began to fraternize with us, showing a disposition to be neighborly. One of them made the burial squad a present of a very fine ham, such a ham as they at the South only know how to cure, and a bushel of sweet potatoes. They began to lounge into our little log hut and chat with us during the evening, and play cribbage, chess, and checkers. We were invited into their camp. The last two or three weeks of our stay at Florence we could go and come pretty much as we pleased after our day's duties were done. At last we were told that they could hold us no longer, and that we would be placed on board the cars as fast as they could be obtained and run into the Union lines at Wilmington. Adjutant Cheatham requested that all the paroled men remain to help those coming off the last trainload, which would consist of the sick and totally disabled... The last load left the fourth day after. We worked till near midnight in loading the box-cars with their half-living, half-dead human freight, the remnants and dregs of the Florence prison. Seven died on the way to the train, and more than twenty while en route between Florence and Wilmington. We placed aboard the train nearly a hundred cases of smallpox, and two hundred cases in the last stages of scurvy... Soon after daylight of March 1, 1865, I saw the first free Union soldier."[20]

George C. Gibbs, who lived in Quincy, Florida, was appointed Captain of Infantry in the State of Florida, on May 20, 1861, and was ordered to duty at Fort Marion, Florida. He was promoted to Major and assigned to the four companies, A, B, C, and D, which made up "Gibbs' Prison Guard Battalion, North Carolina Troops." On January 10th, '62, Major Gibbs reported to General Winder who sent him to Salisbury where he was "Inspector and Mustering Officer" in April '62. The battalion was raised to a regiment about May by the addition of six companies of recruits and designated the 42nd Regiment North Carolina Infantry (State Troops). In a letter to General Sam Cooper, Adjutant and Inspector General Gibbs said, on May 9th, that he had been on duty at Salisbury for almost four months with three companies. The other seven companies were in the Camp of Instruction near Salisbury. Gibbs asked that three other companies be assigned there and that he be allowed to take his regiment "into service." Gibbs was still in Salisbury in the middle of June but, on August 14th, he was ordered to proceed to Drury's Bluff and to report to Brigadier General James Green Martin for assignment to a brigade of General Daniel H. Hill.

---

18 Chipman, pp. 189, 190.

19 Military Records obtained from the National Archives.

20 *Ibid.*

Colonel Gibbs was in Garysburg, N.C., during the month of January of 1863. He signed requisition slips for forage at Kinston and Wilmington in October and in Wilmington in November and December. He was admitted to the C.S.A. General Hospital, No. 4, Wilmington, N.C., on October 18, 1863, with a complaint of a fever, "Feb. Int. Quotidiana." He returned to duty on the 23rd, but was readmitted on the 25th. Two days later, he was granted a 30-day leave of absence upon Surgeon's Certificate. He wrote, from Wilmington, to Secretary of War Seddon, submitting his resignation on December 15th to take effect on Jan. 7th. He resigned on account of the objection of North Carolina Troops to serve under officers from other states. On December 30th, Gibbs asked General Cooper for orders to report to General Gardner, commanding in Middle Florida for assignment to duty because his health condition required a southern climate. He was assigned to the command of the Federal prisoners in Macon to which place he was to go without delay. He would have the exclusive charge of the prisoners and prison discipline and was to make requisition upon the commandant of the post for the necessary guard. He was still in Wilmington on January 11, 1864, but left that day for Quincy, Florida.

Captain Gibbs wrote, to General R. H. Chilton, in Richmond on May 14th, from Charleston, informing him that the Special Orders issued on April 26th had only reached him in Tallahassee on the 10th of May and that he was leaving immediately for Columbia.

Gibbs was at Camp Macon on July 5th, 1864, in command of Federal prisoners. The temporary rank of Colonel was conferred upon Captain Gibbs on July 6th. Henry M. Clarksow, Surgeon in Charge at Camp Oglethorpe, Macon, on August 13th, stated, "I do hereby find that Colonel Gibbs suffers from Chronic Diarrhea of three month's standing and should be granted a thirty days' leave of absence." Gibbs, in Macon, asked for the leave of absence on August 15th, from General Winder, Commanding Military Prisons in Georgia and Alabama, whose headquarters was at Andersonville.

On October 27th, a Medical Examining Board at Andersonville comprised of Doctors H. H. Clayton, Surgeon; E. D. Edward, Surgeon, and G. G. Roy, assistant Surgeon, declared Gibbs was "... unfit for duty in consequence of an ulceration of the face, with strong phagaedenic tendency and therefore recommend a thirty day leave of absence. In February of 1865, he was still commanding the post at Camp Sumter and listed the 2nd Regiment Georgia Reserves as having its "band" with them in January and February.

On March 29, 1865, Gibbs said he reported to General John D. Imboden, Commander of All Military Prisons West of the Savannah River. Gibbs stated "... He was here recently and gave this much-abused post a thorough inspection. The result was entirely satisfactory. I had no chance to 'fix' for inspection for I did not expect him and his inspection was made within two hours after his arrival." General Imboden said, 'I have with pleasure in my report given expression to my high appreciation of your services and qualifications and hope your sphere of usefulness will be enlarged by a larger command than a mere post.' Imboden expects to rejoin his brigade and recommend me to succeed him in command of all military prisons west of the Savannah river. Now without vanity I say that if this post and prison had been inspected before I took command of it, no such report could have been made. Two years of field service has so impaired my health, I cannot attempt that again, and this prison duty I have learned thoroughly."

On March 29th, Gibbs said all Federal officers at Andersonville were sent to Vicksburg for exchange. Gibbs was still at Andersonville on April 12th, serving as Colonel Commanding. "Directly, I have never had anything to do with the prisons. I rode through the stockade almost every day (less about seventy days sick leave out of seven months command), and though the prisoners then had ample opportunity there to complain of ill-treatment, no complaint was ever made to me. Though I was powerless to redress grievances, yet I could and would have represented their cases to higher authority. In paroling for exchange (by order) at Baldwin, Florida, 3,400 prisoners, the whole line as I passed it gave expression to the kindest feeling toward myself. In everything which officially I have done in this connection I have acted by order."[21]

"Gibbs returned on May 3rd, after having paroled for exchange all the prisoners at Baldwin, Florida. Also, last night, in the absence of all guard, a raid of soldiers, their wives and the citizens was made upon the military stores and all the small amount here taken off. Provisions, unused clothing and bedding were taken."

Gibbs was listed on the Register of Prisoners, Provost Marshal General, Washington, under the following heading: "List of Rebels who have reported under General Orders 104." He was paroled in Tallahassee, Florida, under the Amnesty of May 29th. The oath was administered by Lt. Sharp in Washington on June 16th. Under remarks it said, "Stopping at Willard's temporarily; Witness in the case of Capt. Werz"(sic).[22]

[21] Mann, p. 622.

[22] Military Records obtained from the National Archives.

The Confederates could not allow a prisoner to go into a prison with lots of money. It would be too much of a temptation if offered as a bribe to a guard. Routinely, all prisoners were searched and stripped of all money and items of enough value to possibly become a bribe. These were kept and were to be returned to that prisoner upon his release. Between 35,000 and 40,000 dollars in U.S. currency was collected that belonged to those prisoners shipped to Andersonville and Macon. It was entrusted to the keeping of Captain Clarence Morfit, assistant quartermaster, who was quartermaster of prisons with offices in Richmond. He retained the money of each prisoner in a separate parcel. Provost-Marshal Major I. H. Carrington wrote to Secretary Seddon and asked what should be done with the money. Seddon suggested that the money be turned over to the Treasury of the Confederate States and that it be forwarded to the quartermaster of the prisons where the prisoners were kept so they might have use of the funds for their purchase of necessities.[23]

Though there were many instances when prisoners were not credited with the full amount taken from them, there was an attempt to return funds to them from a general pool of funds collected from all the prisoners at all prisons. "I estimate it to reach an aggregate of $750 coin, $44,000 U.S. Treasury notes, $3,000 bank bills, and Confederate notes."[24] "It will also include about $6,000 in U.S. Treasury notes, which had been forwarded by Salisbury and Andersonville in March last with a list of the owners."[25]

Captain Morfit, wrote from Charlotte on April 25th to Brigadier-General Ruggles, the Commissary-General of Prisoners then in Charlotte, of the final disposition of the prisoners' monies. "The property belonging to prisoners was sent by railroad from Richmond to Danville, and was left there upon the evacuation of that place as I did not know where it was stored... and I brought it in an ambulance as far as Ca Ira, Cumberland county, Virginia. At this place there was a probability of being intercepted by the enemy, and Major I. H. Carrington deemed it best to divide the risk and took charge of $670.50 in gold and $5,400 in greenbacks. I brought the remainder to Danville, and as that place was reported to be surrounded by the enemy, Major Carrington took charge of about $2,500 in U.S. currency and bank notes. I have left in my possession about $674 in bank notes, $362 in greenbacks, and $400 in U.S postal currency, and $13,000 in C.S. old issue... I have learned since leaving Danville that the chest of valuables, containing also the books and papers relating to prisoners' funds, was in a house with Major Bentley's stores and that he turned everything over to the civil authorities."[26]

On April 9th, of 1866, the Commissary-General of Prisoners, Major-General Hitchcock, wrote to Secretary Stanton and asked for permission to settle the accounts of the Federal ex-prisoners who had filed claims to regain funds lost to search and seizures by the Confederate officers at various prisons of the South. There were 361 applicants who claimed to have lost about $35,000, but the Federals only had on hand about $28,000 for distribution. There was, also, about $8,000 belonging to Confederates that was unclaimed and which he wished to add to the above to make up the deficiency. [27]

Several times the Confederate authorities gathered prisoners into trains, carried them to the Federal lines, or tried to send them through the lines. In March and April, they were often rebuffed and returned to Andersonville or to some other holding pen. Finally, in disgust, the authorities took the prisoners to the Federal picket lines; there, they told the prisoners they were free and told them to make their way as best they could. As the condition of the Federal prisoners improved with the closing of the prison doors, conversely, the conditions of some of the Confederate personnel took a turn for the worse. Several would soon see themselves confined behind closed doors; one would pay the supreme penalty for his involvement in the treatment of Federal prisoners at Andersonville.

---

[23] *O.R.*, VII, p. 461.
[24] *Ibid.*, p. 772.
[25] *Ibid.*, p. 771.
[26] *O.R.*, VIII, p. 512.
[27] *Ibid.*, p. 895.

## *Chapter Thirteen*

# The Trials and Tribulations

*"Be of good cheer, I have been told on yesterday by Gen'l Bacher that it is well understood among high officials, that they are not trying me or you, but have to try me apparently to get hold of the big men, such as Cooper, Seddon, Jeff Davis. If you can give me any information as to the fact that the authorities in Richmond knew or even authorized the state of affairs at Andersonville as to rations, food, shelters, let me know. I think it will save me, at any rate you."*

*Reply: "I know of nothing except the reports from the prisons, the reports of inspecting officers and newspaper statements."*

Wirz' note to and reply from Dick Winder written from prison.
(Author's collection)

About the 1st or 2nd of May, Major General J. H. Wilson, in Macon, sent his aide-de-camp, Captain Henry E. Noyes, Second U.S. Cavalry, to Eufaula, Alabama, the nearest command, to tell General Grierson the news of the repudiation of the Sherman-Johnston armistice. The train carrying Captain Noyes stopped at Andersonville to take on wood and water. While stopped there and while off the train, Captain Noyes noticed a number of debilitated prisoners. They were being processed by Captain Wirz to be sent to Macon. General Wilson had ordered all sick prisoners were to be sent to Macon. At Andersonville, Noyes noticed two or three Confederate officers mingling with the Federal prisoners, trying to get them to sign their paroles. There were, at that time, over 250 of the most feeble prisoners still remaining at Andersonville. Most were not able to walk except when being supported under each arm. As Captain Noyes was boarding the train, he heard Wirz bellow the following (or something to this effect), "Hurry up and sign these paroles, or you'll die here anyhow."[1]

When Noyes got back to Macon, he told General Wilson what he had witnessed at Andersonville. General Wilson, at once, by verbal order, sent Captain Noyes and a Lieutenant Rendelbrook back to Andersonville to arrest Captain Wirz. Noyes and Rendelbrook left on or near the 6th of May. Since there were no public accommodations in Andersonville, they went on to Americus, about ten miles past the post. They returned the next morning by hitching a ride on a freight train. Noyes attempted to gather any records or papers he thought important or pertinent for any future trial. He did not gather the hospital records because Doctor G. G. Roy had said they were not yet complete. Doctor Roy requested that Captain Noyes send him several clerks and he would see that the records were completed. Captain Noyes agreed to that request.

Prior to that time, General Wilson had already ordered a party to go to the prison to "... investigate matters connected with the Andersonville Prison, and the atrocities alleged to have been perpetrated there."[2] This party of Federal troops must have had orders to search buildings and offices because Noyes said the following letter was brought to General Wilson by this party and it had been "... found among the papers of Captain Wirz' office":[3]

[1] Chipman, p. 46.
[2] *Ibid.*, p. 48.
[3] *Ibid.*, p. 45.

*Andersonville, Georgia, May 7, 1865*
*Maj. Gen. J. H. Wilson, U.S. Army*
*Commanding, Macon, Ga.:*

*General: it is with great reluctance that I address you these lines, being fully aware how little time is left you to attend to such matters as I now have the honor to lay before you, and if I could see any other way to accomplish my object I would not intrude upon you. I am a native of Switzerland, and was before the war a citizen of Louisiana, and by profession a physician. Like hundreds and thousands of others, I was carried away by the maelstrom of excitement and joined the Southern Army. I was very severely wounded at the battle of Seven Pines, near Richmond, Virginia, and have nearly lost the use of my right arm. Unfit for field duty, I was ordered to report to Brevet Major General John H. Winder, in charge of the Federal prisoners of war, who ordered me to take charge of a prison in Tuscaloosa, Ala. My health failing me, I applied for a furlough and went to Europe, from whence I returned in February, 1864. I was then ordered to report to the commandant of the military prison at Andersonville, Georgia, who assigned me to the command of the interior of the prison. The duties I had to perform were arduous and unpleasant, and I am satisfied that no man can or will justly blame me for things that happened here and which were beyond my power to control. I do not think that I ought to be held responsible for the shortness of rations, for the overcrowded state of the prison (which was in itself a prolific source of the fearful mortality), for the inadequate supplies of clothing, want of shelters, &c. Still I now bear the odium, and men who were prisoners here seem disposed to wreak their vengeance upon me for what they have suffered, who was only the medium, or, I may better say, the tool in the hands of my superiors. This is my condition. I am a man with a family; I lost all my property when the Federal army besieged Vicksburg. I have no money at present to go any place, and even if I had, I know of no place where I could go. My life is in danger, and I most respectfully ask of you help and relief. If you will be so generous as to give me some sort of a safe-conduct, or, what I should greatly prefer, a guard to protect myself and family against violence, I shall be thankful to you, and you may rest assured that your protection will not be given to one who is unworthy of it. My intention is to return with my family to Europe as soon as I can make the arrangements. In the meantime I have the honor, general, to remain,*

*Very respectfully, your obedient servant,*
*Hy. Wirz,*
*Captain, C.S.Army*[4]

General Wilson read Wirz' letter and, on May 19th, endorsed on it, "Attention called to the letter of Captain Wirz and accompanying statement of escaped prisoners." This letter was forwarded to George H. Thomas, Major-General at the Headquarters, Department of the Cumberland, in Nashville, who endorsed on it, on May 26th, "… The writer of this will be sent under guard, in charge of Captain Noyes, Second U.S. Cavalry, this day to Washington for final disposition."[5] Wilson "… ordered his arrest for the purpose, and with the special intention that he should not have the benefit of amnesty or armistice between Sherman and Johnston."[6]

Captain Noyes located Wirz at his house and went there to arrest him. Wirz was there with his wife, Elizabeth, and their two young daughters. It was a very difficult task to take a man away from his wife and family. One of the daughters and his wife were crying and very upset. Noyes tried to soothe them by telling them that, if after taking the Captain to Macon, General Wilson decided Wirz had performed his duty the best he could and only had followed the orders of his superiors, he would probably be allowed to return to his family. Noyes made no promises or guarantees of freedom and said this only to calm Wirz and his family. Captain Noyes told Wilson the family expressed "… great fear that he was going to be hanged or made away with."[7] Noyes testified that he, at the time, had no doubt but that the general would retain him as a prisoner.

The actual words of the arrest supposedly were these: "'I have been directed, Major,' said Captain Noyes, 'by General Wilson to take you to his headquarters.'

"'Very well, sir, I have no objection; but before we go, had you not better have something to eat? We have but little in the house, but, little or much, you and your men are welcome to it.'

"The captain thanked him and they sat down with the Wirz family to bread and bacon."[8] He apologized for having no coffee or tea saying "… coffee and tea are luxuries of the past."[9]

---

[4] *O.R.*, VIII, pp. 537, 538.
[5] *Ibid.*, p. 538.
[6] Chipman, p. 48.
[7] *Ibid.*, p. 49.
[8] Page, p. 187.
[9] Mildred Lewis Rutherford, "Facts and Figures vs. Myths and Misrepresentations," A Reprint of the *U.D.C. Bulletin* of 1921 (Athens, Ga: 1921), p. 5.

After dining, Wirz was taken to Macon and put in prison there by order of General Wilson under headquarters guard. The general immediately wrote to the Secretary of War, suggesting that Wirz might be brought to trial. General Wilson had sent an officer back over to Andersonville for the hospital records from Doctor Roy as well as all the records and some flags that had been captured in campaigns through Alabama and Georgia; these items were taken on the trip to Washington. Wilson said, "I put a man in charge of the place in order to protect it."[10] About the 20th of May, Noyes was ordered to take Wirz to Washington, along with all the records from Andersonville, for final disposition.

The group was tormented and heckled from the very start. Ex-prisoners recognized their ex-keeper and crowds gathered at all points; they attempted to overpower them and to kill Wirz. Noyes stated he did not think Wirz would have made it to their destination if he had not been accompanied by an officer of the United States army.

Noyes put Wirz in the prison at Chattanooga. Wirz was wearing a regulation Confederate uniform with hat when he was taken to the prison at Chattanooga. When Noyes went to pick Wirz up in order to continue on their way, he said, "I hardly knew him; all his clothes were stripped off him, he had only a part of his hat, no coat, a very dirty shirt, a portion of a pair of pants pretty badly torn, and shoes."[11]

They had a particularly bad time at Nashville. While trying to get him on the boat there, a crowd tried to eliminate the necessity for a trial. At Louisville, Noyes ordered him disguised to prevent further attacks. While in Louisville, Wirz mentioned he had friends there. With the help of these friends and Noyes, they "... succeeded in getting a complete suit of black and a beaver hat."[12] They had him shaved; with the full beard missing and the bland clothing, they were not bothered for the remainder of their journey even though they were seen by many soldiers, especially while in Cincinnati.

Upon reaching Washington, Wirz was first taken to the "central guard-house" by Captain Noyes. On May 31st, he was taken to the Old Capitol Prison by order of the Secretary of War. The Old Capitol Prison was located at the corner of First and A Streets. It was built in 1800, originally designed as a tavern or boardinghouse, but, owing to bad management, it had been a failure and was closed shortly before the War of 1812. In August, 1814, when the British troops under General Ross entered Washington, they burned the Capitol and other public buildings. The government bought this old tavern or boardinghouse, in which Congress held its sessions and conducted public business until the Capitol could be rebuilt.

The interior of the building was completely renovated and reconstructed, and there both Houses of Congress had sat for a number of years. There two Presidents were inaugurated, and some of our most distinguished statesmen began their careers. It was in this building the Honorable John C. Calhoun died.

When it was abandoned by Congress upon the completion of the new Capitol, it was called the Old Capitol. Later, it was used as a boardinghouse, a school, etc., until, in 1861, it was taken by the authorities in Washington to be used as a prison.[13]

Wirz was probably admitted, much as other prisoners had been, by entering the prison on First Street. They were probably halted by the sentry patrolling the pavement in front of the prison door, who called out with a loud voice, "Corporal of the guard; Post No. 1." This brought out the corporal with his musket at his shoulder, and he escorted them inside through a broad hallway to a room where prisoners were first taken to be questioned and searched. Then he walked on to his room, on the third floor, which had the designation "No. 9-Wirz, H., Captain C.S.A." A guard was assigned to sit in Wirz' room day and night to prevent any attempt by Wirz to take his own life.

After Wirz' capture, Judge-Advocate General Joseph Holt advised Secretary of War Edwin Stanton that he should order Norton Parker Chipman to prepare for Wirz' trial. By the middle of August, all the evidence had been collected, mostly by Colonel E. D. Townsend, Assistant Adjutant-General. The necessary witnesses were gathered, and the charges were drawn up and served upon Wirz.

A special Military Commission met first on Monday afternoon, August 21, 1865, in the Court of Claims room in the Old Capitol Building pursuant to the instructions in Special Order No. 449.

At one-thirty, Captain Wirz was brought into the room, guarded on each side by a Federal soldier. The prisoner was asked to rise, at which time Colonel N. P. Chipman, Judge-Advocate, asked, "Captain Wirz, you are to be tried by this Military Commission. Have you any personal objection to any of its members?"[14] Judge James Hughes, one of

[10] Chipman, p. 187.
[11] *Ibid.*, p. 47.
[12] *Wirz Trial*, p. 20.
[13] James J. Williamson, *Prison Life in the Old Capitol* (West Orange, N. J.: 1911), p. 20.
[14] *Demon of Andersonville*, p. 29.

the counsels for Wirz' defense, stated that, if his client was to be tried by a Military Commission, Wirz was satisfied with this one; however, he added that, at a later time in the trial, the defense would object "... to the mode of constituting the Court."

**Quarters of Captain Wirz Within the Old Captol Prison in Washington** - Dick Winder's quarters were directly across the hall. The doors were kept open at times and a guard posted in the hall between the rooms. Wirz and Dick Winder corresponded by writing notes and putting them within the spout of the common coffeepot. (Frank Leslie's Illustrated Newspaper, November 25, 1865)

Wirz was defended by Louis (Frederick) Schade, "... a fellow-countryman of Wirz," as well as by Judge James Hughes, General J. W. Denver, and Charles F. Peck, members of the Washington law firm of Hughes, Denver and Peck.

The members of the Military Commission were then sworn in. Colonel Chipman read the charges and specifications against Wirz.

Wirz was arraigned on two charges. The first charge stated that Wirz was responsible for "Maliciously, wilfully, and traitorously, and in aid of the then-existing armed rebellion against the United States of America, on or before the 1st day of March, A.D. 1864, and on divers other days between that day and the 10th day of April, 1865, combining, confederating, and conspiring, together with Robert E. Lee, James A Seddon, John H. Winder, Lucius C. Northrop, Richard B. Winder, Joseph [Isaiah H.] White, W. S. Winder, R. R. Stevenson, and others unknown, to injure the health and destroy the lives of soldiers in the military service of the United States, then held and being prisoners of war within the lines of the so-called Confederate States and in the military prisons thereof, to the end that the armies of the United States might be weakened and impaired; in violation of the laws and customs of war."[15] The only specifications in this charge simply enumerated the ways Wirz injured the prisoners, (i.e., "... by confining in unhealthy and unwholesome quarters, by exposing to the inclemency of winter and to the dews and burning sun of summer, by compelling the use of impure water and by furnishing insufficient and unwholesome food,... [by taking] and [by] caus[ing] to be taken from them their clothing, blankets, camp equipage... by fastening large balls of iron to their feet... by maliciously confining them within an instrument of torture called 'the stocks,'... [by using] and [by] caus[ing] to be used for the pretended purposes of vaccination, impure and poisonous vaccine matter... etc.).[16]

The second charge had thirteen specifications, allegedly for murders, "... in violation of the laws and customs of war." For the sake of brevity, these specifications will be condensed:

Specification 1. - Wirz did shoot on or about the eighth of July, 1864, a prisoner, "... whose name is unknown," who died the 9th day of July.

Specification 2. - Wirz "... did jump upon, stamp, kick, bruise, and otherwise injure, with the heels of his boots," a prisoner "... whose name is unknown," who died on the 20th day of September, 1864.

Specification 3. - Wirz did shoot, on or about the 13th day of June, 1864, a prisoner, "... whose name is unknown," who died instantly.

Specification 4. - Wirz did shoot on or about the 30th day of May, 1864, a prisoner, "... whose name is unknown," who died that day.

Specification 5. - Wirz did, on or about the 20th day of August, 1864, "... confine and bind, with an instrument of torture called 'the stocks,' a prisoner;" as a consequence, the soldier died on the 30th day of August.

Specification 6. - Wirz did, on or about the 1st day of February, 1864, "... confine and bind within an instrument of torture called 'the stocks,' a prisoner, whose name is unknown," who died soon thereafter on the 6th day of February."

Specification 7. - Wirz did, on or about the 20th day of July, 1864, "... fasten and chain together several persons... binding the necks and feets of said prisoners closely together." As a consequence of this treatment, one of the prisoners, "... whose name is unknown" died on the 25th day of July, 1864.

Specification 8. - Wirz did, on or about the 15th day of May, 1864, order a rebel soldier, "... whose name is unknown," then on duty as a sentinel or guard to kill a prisoner, "... whose name is unknown."

Specification 9. - Wirz did, on or about the 1st day of July, 1864, order an unknown sentinel to kill a pris-

[15] *Wirz Trial*, p. 3.
[16] *Ibid.*, pp. 3-5.

oner, "... whose name is unknown."

Specification 10. - Wirz did, on or about the 20th of August, 1864, order an unknown sentinel to fire on a prisoner, "... whose name is unknown," who soon thereafter died.

Specification 11. - Wirz did, on or about the 1st day of July, 1864, "... cause, incite, and urge certain ferocious and blood-thirsty animals, called bloodhounds, to pursue, attack, wound, and tear in pieces a soldier whose name is unknown." The prisoner died on the 6th day of July.

Specification 12. - Wirz did, on or about the 27th day of July, 1864, order an unknown sentinel to shoot a prisoner, "... whose name is unknown." The prisoner died soon thereafter.

Specification 13. - Wirz did, on or about the 3rd day of August, 1864, make an assault upon a prisoner, "... whose name is unknown," and beat him with a pistol, causing his death the next day.[17]

**Woodcut of the Trial of Captain Wirz** - Wirz was sick and spent most of the trial on a sofa. (Culver)

After the arraignment, Wirz entered the plea of "Not Guilty." Judge Hughes filed several pleas. "First. Denying the jurisdiction of the Court to try the prisoner, it having no authority to do so either by statute or well-established usage. Second. That this case is not brought before it by competent authority. Third. That the prisoner is a naturalized citizen, and was never in the land or naval service of the United States, now being at peace, and civil war ceased, there is no authority to punish him. The prisoner protests he ought not, therefore, to be tried, but discharged from custody. He also claims that just before the time of his arrest at Andersonville, Captain Noyes, on duty near that place, applied to him for information, which he cheerfully communicated to him, and he accompanied Captain Noyes to General Wilson's quarters, the former promising him safe conduct, and giving him assurance that he should not be arrested. The prisoner relied on the good faith of Captain Noyes, but notwithstanding the above repeated assurances, the prisoner was seized, held in confinement, and brought to Washington. The prisoner further protests that he ought not to be held any longer, for the reason as set forth at length, that he came within the terms of the capitulation between General Johnston and General Sherman. The defendant also asks the Court to quash the several charges and specifications, because they are each and every one uncertain and indefinite as to the time and the offence; and the allegations are so indefinite and vague that he ought not to be tried upon them; and further, that they do not charge him with any offences punishable under the laws of war."[18] Then the court adjourned for twenty-four hours.

"Secretary of War Stanton personally read the charges on the opening day but became furious when he found Chipman's conspiracy charges couched in extravagant language similar to that which had embarrassed him in the Lincoln murder trial, charging Davis, Lee, and other high-ranking Confederates as accomplices. Stanton had the court adjourned, and the next morning Wallace announced that President Johnson had 'dissolved' the commission so that a new indictment could be drawn up."[19]

---

[17] *Ibid.*, pp. 5-8.

[18] *Demon of Andersonville*, p. 34.

[19] Robert E. and Katharine M. Morseberger, "After Andersonville: The First War Crimes Trial," *Civil War Times Illustrated*, July 1974, p.33.

On the next day, Tuesday, August 22nd, the Secretary of War, by order of the President of the United States, dissolved the court. The court was reconvened on Wednesday, the 23rd at eleven o'clock, by the following order:

*War Department, Adjutant General's Office*
*Washington, August 23, 1865*

***Special Orders No. 453***

*A special military commission is hereby appointed to meet in this city at 11 o'clock a.m., on the 23rd day of August, 1865, or as soon thereafter as practicable, for the trial of Henry Wirz, and such other prisoners as may be brought before it.*

*Detail For the Commission*

*Major General L. Wallace, United States Volunteers.*
*Brevet Major General G. Mott, United States Volunteers.*
*Brevet Major General J. W. Geary, United States Volunteers.*
*Brevet Major General L. Thomas, Adjutant General, U. S. Army.*
*Brigadier General Francis Fessenden, United States Volunteers.*
*Brigadier General E. S. Bragg, United States Volunteers.*
*Brevet Brigadier General John F. Ballier, Colonel, 98th Pennsylvania Volunteers*
*Brevet Colonel T. Allcock, Lieutenant Colonel, 4th New York Artillery*
*Lieutenant Colonel J. H. Stibbs, 12th Iowa Volunteers*
*Colonel N. P. Chipman, additional Aide-De-Camp, Judge Advocate of the Commission, with such assistants as he may select, with the approval of the Judge Advocate General.*

*The commission will sit without regard to hours.*

*By order of the President of the United States:*
*E. D. Townsend,*
*Assistant Adjutant General"*[20]

Brevet Brigadier General John Howard Stibbs, Twelfth Iowa Infantry Volunteers, a member of the commission, described the commission this way: "It was made up as follows: At the head of the table sat Major General Lewis Wallace, the President of the Court. He was at that time a man of mature years, a lawyer by profession, and of recognized ability. On his right at the table sat Major General Gershom Mott, who subsequently became Governor of New Jersey. He was a man then of forty-five or fifty years, a lawyer, and a man of excellent judgment and discretion. Opposite him sat Major General Lorenzo Thomas, the Adjutant General of the United States Army. He was then fully sixty-five years of age, had been for many years connected with the regular service, and was an acknowledged authority on military law and the rules and usages of war. On General Mott's right sat Major General John W. Geary, who after his discharge from the military service was made Governor of the great State of Pennsylvania - a man aged fifty or more, and possessed of more than ordinary ability. Opposite him sat Brigadier General Francis Fessenden of Maine, son of old Senator Fessenden, a man aged about thirty-five, a lawyer, and one who in every sense might have been called an educated gentleman. On General Geary's right sat Brevet Brigadier General John F. Ballier of Philadelphia, Pennsylvania, an educated German, aged fifty or more, who had commanded the Ninety-eighth Pennsylvania Infantry. On his right sat Brevet Colonel T. Allcock of New York, a man of forty or more, and a distinguished artillery officer, and finally on the opposite side of the table, was placed the boy member - your humble servant. Possibly it might have been truthfully said of me that I was too young and inexperienced to fill so important a position, since I was then only in my twenty-sixth year; but I had seen four years of actual warfare, had successfully commanded a regiment of Iowa men, and I thought then, as I think now, that I was a competent juror. The Judge Advocate of the Commission was Colonel N. P. Chipman, who early in the war served as Major of the Second Iowa Infantry. He was severely wounded at Fort Donnelson in February, 1862. When sufficiently recovered to return to duty he was promoted and became Chief of Staff for General Samuel R. Curtis, and later was placed on duty in Washington. He was a lawyer by profession, a man of superior education and refinement, and withal one of the most genial, kindhearted, companionable men I have ever had the good fortune to meet."[21]

The charges against Wirz were different on Wednesday than they had been on Monday. The major difference

[20] *Wirz Trial*, p. 2.
[21] Stibbs, pp. 25, 26.

was in the first charge. It was amended by the deletion of several names from the list of persons who had been previously charged with having conspired with Wirz to destroy the lives of Federal soldiers. The co-conspirators deleted were Jefferson Davis, James A. Seddon, Howell Cobb, and Robert E. Lee.

The defense counsels vigorously contested the charges. Wirz had been arraigned on the former charges and his life placed in jeopardy; he was now entitled to acquittal or at least to trial on the former charges. Their demand for Wirz' freedom, based on the prohibition against double jeopardy, was denied after a full hearing. "When Wirz protested that Captain Henry E. Noyes, who arrested him, broke his promise that Wirz should have safe conduct back to his home, Chipman countered that the agreement for surrender by rebel soldiers did not extend amnesty for '... offences and crimes in violation of the laws of war' and that any violation of safe- conduct was irrelevant and had no bearing upon the court; that upon learning of the crimes at Andersonville, General Wilson had no power to absolve the prisoner and was justified in revoking the safe-conduct. Only a special pardon by the President could '... give exemption from trial for actions in violation of the laws and customs of civilized warfare.'

**Photo of Wirz' Attorney, Louis Frederick Schade**

"In 1865 military commissions operated under *Instructions for the Government of Armies of the United States in the Field*, prepared by Francis Lieber, a German emigre` and veteran of Waterloo, who was professor of law and political science at Columbia University. In May 1863 Lincoln approved these as General Orders No. 100. Lieber wrote that warfare does not justify atrocities, that 'Men who take up arms against one another in public war do not cease on this account to be moral beings, responsible to one another and to God.' In 1865, the precedent was yet to be established, and a major issue in the trial was the jurisdiction of the court."[22]

In protest, Judge Hughes put on his hat, gathered his law books, and walked out. Then Peck and Denver disassociated themselves from the defense. "Wirz shouted that without counsel he was being delivered to the hangman."

On the next day, Thursday, August 24th, Louis Schade, Esq., himself an alien, told the Court that he could not abandon the helpless Wirz, especially since he sincerely thought him innocent. Schade asked for an eight-day postponement to allow him to prepare his case. This was denied. Otis S. Baker, Esq., who just happened to be in the courtroom that day, volunteered his services as assistant counsel for the defense.[23]

"Baker responded that Chipman had no right to assume Wirz guilty and that in any case he should be tried by a proper civilian tribunal. A military court could not hold subordinate officers as criminals for every killing committed under their command unless it was prepared to indict hundreds of thousands from both armies. Lewis Wallace overruled all of these objections and ordered the trial to proceed. Repeatedly Baker argued that his client would have certain rights in a civil court, only to have Chipman and Wallace reply that it was a military tribunal.

[22] Morseberger, p. 33.
[23] *Ibid.*

A few days later, on Sunday, August 27th, Major Wirz wrote to the *New York News* describing his situation, defending his conduct during the war, and soliciting funds for his defense:

*Old Capitol Prison*
*Washington City, D.C.*
*August 27th, 1865*

*To the Editor of the New York News:*

*Although a perfect stranger to you, I take, in my unfortunate and helpless condition, the liberty to address you this letter, knowing that, as a friend to the downtrodden South, you cannot but have some sympathy for a man who, as he believes, is innocently about to be sacrificed - a sympathy which I hope will prompt you to interest yourself in his behalf. I am a native of Switzerland, and, have been for years before the war a resident of Louisiana, could not do otherwise than take up arms to defend the State and country of my adoption when it was invaded. I joined the Confederate army in 1861, and served faithfully the cause I considered to be a rightful one. In 1862, the United States troops destroyed my home, and my wife and three children had to seek shelter among friends. I lost all I possessed, but a few negroes who still remained faithful. In 1864, I was ordered to report to the officer of the military prison at Andersonville, Georgia. By this officer I was put in command of the prison, and remained in that position from April 1864 until 1865. When the South ceased the struggle, I was still in Andersonville with my family, believing myself fully protected by the terms of the agreement between Generals Sherman and Johnston, and never dreaming that I, a poor captain and subaltern officer, would be made to answer with my life for what is now alleged to have been done at Andersonville. I was, in violation of a safe-conduct which was given me by a staff officer of General Wilson, arrested in Macon, Georgia, was kept there in confinement for two weeks, and then sent on to Washington, and am now, by order of the President of the United States, brought before a court to be tried under the most atrocious charges. I have no friends here. I am helpless; and unless I can get help, will have to lose the last thing which I possess in this world - my good name and my life. My conscience is clear. I have never dealt cruelly with a prisoner under my charge. If they suffered for want of shelter, food, clothing and necessaries, I could not help it, having no control over these things - things which the Confederate Government could give only in very limited quantity, even to our own men, as everybody knows who will be just and impartial. My legal advisers (Messrs. Schade and Baker), seeing my helplessness, have undertaken to conduct my defence. They are both doing it from generosity and compassion, knowing full well that I have not the means to remunerate them for their trouble. But I cannot expect them to furnish the means which it absolutely requires in the conducting of a case of such importance. Copies of depositions have to be made, messengers have to be sent here and there to get up testimony; and how can this be done without money? I have none to give; and, no doubt, my case will be lost - my life sacrificed - for want of the money to defray the expenses of such a trial. But my counsel believe, from the evidence already in their possession, that if the necessary means can be obtained, my acquittal must be the result. On this condition, I take the liberty to appeal to you to assist me, and let me not be the victim of injustice. Your influence is such that it will not require very great efforts to collect the necessary means for a vigorous carrying on of the defence. I am myself without clothes, without any means to alleviate the hardships of a close confinement. My health is bad, and the prison fare is not calculated to benefit a sick, or at least a suffering man. Still, these things I have borne without murmuring, and hope, with the help of God, to bear yet for a while longer.*

*Hoping that this petition will receive a favorable reception on your part, and assuring you again that nothing but the direst necessity could induce me to address you, I remain, sir, with the greatest respect, your obedient servant,*

*H. Wirz*
*Late Capt. and A.A.G., C.S.A."*[24]

"Early in the trial Wirz became sick, and a lounge was brought into the room on which he was permitted to recline; and during many days of the trial he lay on the lounge with his handkerchief over his face, apparently oblivious to all that was taking place. Finally a witness was placed on the stand who told of his escape from the stockade in company with a comrade whose name he did not know, of their pursuit by the blood hounds, and of their recapture and return to the Confederate camp. He said that when brought to Wirz' tent and their escape and recapture was reported, Wirz became furious, and rushing from his tent he began cursing and damning them for having attempted to escape. The comrade, who was nearly dead from exposure and suffering, had staked his last effort on this attempt

[24] Stibbs, pp. 32-34.

to regain his freedom, and the recapture had discouraged him completely and caused him to feel that death itself was preferable to a return to the stockade. Like a caged animal he turned on Wirz and gave him curse for curse, challenged him to do his worst, and told him he would rather die than return to the hell hole from which he had escaped. This so enraged Wirz that he sprang at the man, knocked him down with his revolver, and then kicked and trampled him with his boot heels until he was dead. When the witness began this story Wirz became interested. First he removed the handkerchief from his face; then propped himself on one elbow; and as the story progressed he gradually rose up until he stood erect. His fists were clenched, his eyes were fairly bursting from their sockets, and his face presented a horrible appearance. As the witness finished his story Wirz fairly screamed at him: 'You say I killed that man.' 'Yes sir', replied the witness. 'You trampled him to death in my presence'. At this Wirz threw up his hands and exclaimed, 'Oh my Gott', and fell back in a faint on the lounge."[25] "This was one of a number of stories that told of Wirz' personal acts of cruelty. In addition, he was directly chargeable with the unwarranted punishments which he caused to be inflicted on men who attempted to escape or in other ways violated the rules of discipline which he had established. These punishments consisted of stopping of rations, establishment of a dead-line, use of the stocks, the chain-gang, use of hounds, bucking and gagging, tying up by the thumbs, flogging on the bare back, and chaining to posts, from all of which causes deaths were shown to have resulted."[26]

"Wirz was five feet ten inches in height, of a thin, spare figure, which made him seem taller than he really was. His complexion was dark; hair, beard, and mustache, black, mixed with gray. During the trial he was dressed in a black cloth coat and pantaloons, with white shirt, collar turned down, a la Byron, over a thick, heavy black silk handkerchief. His head gear consisted of a well-worn, greasy-looking old silk hat, and this, with his seedy looking, threadbare clothes, gave him a shabby genteel appearance."[27]

Wirz wrote to Colonel Chipman, asking for Father Whelan and Father Hamilton to be assigned to spiritually comfort him: "You will, I hope, excuse my liberty to address you these lines; but, not knowing to whom to appeal, I refer the matter to you. I am now a prisoner since the 7th of May, 1865. I have been deprived of all the chances to receive the consolations of religion even necessary to anybody, and truly more so to a man charged with crimes so heinous, so terrible that the mere thought of them makes me shudder. Although I know myself full well that I am wrongfully accused, that an all-seeing, all-knowing God knows my innocence, still I need some encouragement from others not to sink under the heavy burden which is placed upon me. Under these circumstances, I respectfully ask that permission be granted to Rev. Fathers Whelan and Hamilton to visit me and administer such spiritual comforts as my unfortunate position requires. They are both men of integrity, and will not profit by the occasion to see or do anything but what their duties as ministers of the gospel will permit. Hoping that this, by humble request, may be favorably received and the permission be granted, I remain, Colonel, most respectfully, "Your obedient servant, H. Wirz."[28]

"For weeks after the trial began the Judge Advocate presented only such testimony as went to show the general conditions existing at the prison and which tended to establish the charge of conspiracy, and he held back until near the close of the trial the evidence on which he depended to establish the fact that Wirz had by his own acts been guilty of willful murder. As a result Wirz evidently concluded that no such evidence had been found, and on repeated occasions he addressed the Court through his counsel, saying that he was ready to admit the truth of all evidence that had been presented, but that he was not personally responsible for the conditions shown to have existed in the prison; that he had simply acted in conformity to the orders of his superior officers, and should not be held responsible for them; and he therefore asked for an acquittal and discharge. These requests, one after another, were denied by the Court."[29]

With the fall of Richmond, the graphic report of Colonel Chandler was discovered. "This original report was introduced before our Court, and Colonel Chandler was brought there to testify concerning it. He was an officer who had been educated at West Point, a polished gentleman in manner and speech; and his testimony, given in a frank, straightforward way, made a deep impression on the Court. He swore that he wrote the report and that the statements embodied in it were true. He told of his very minute inspection of the stockade, of his measurements and computations, showing the amount of space allowed each inmate, and of the horrors he encountered on every hand. The picture he drew of the place served to confirm the stories of the men who had been held there as prisoners. He

[25] *Ibid.*, pp. 28, 29.
[26] *Ibid.*, p. 29.
[27] *Demon of Andersonville*, p. 118.
[28] Ashe, p. 34.
[29] Stibbs, p. 28.

told of calling on Winder and remonstrating with him regarding the care of the prison, and Winder's infamous language in connection therewith. He said that, when he had mailed his report to the Secretary of War, he confidently expected that General Winder would be removed from the command of the prisoners, and that he felt disgusted and outraged when he learned that, instead of being removed, Winder had been promoted to be Commissary General and Commander of all Military Prisons and prisoners throughout the Confederate States.

When Colonel Chandler was at Andersonville, he was under orders to inspect all the prisons in the South and West. Considerable time elapsed before he got back to Richmond. He then made an investigation and found that his report, relating to Winder, had been received and considered by Seddon, the Secretary of War. He threatened to resign unless his report was taken up and acted upon; but, at about that time, Seddon was succeeded by Mr. Breckenridge as Secretary of War; soon thereafter General Winder died. Then followed the closing days of the war and collapse of the Rebellion."[30]

On the back of the report were endorsements indicating that the horrid conditions at Andersonville were possibly known by people as high in the government as Secretary of War Seddon.

On the back of Chandler's report was endorsed the following,

> *Adjutant and Inspector General's Office*
> *August 18, 1864*
>
> *Respectfully submitted to the Secretary of War*
>
> *The condition of the prison at Andersonville is a reproach to us as a nation... Col. Chandler's recommendations are concurred in.*
>
> *By Order of General Cooper*
> *(Signed) R. H. Chilton, A. A. & I. G.*

This was followed by a second endorsement. "This report discloses a condition of things imperatively demanding prompt and decisive measures of relief... No effectual remedy for all these evils seems available so long as the numbers are in such large excess over that for which the prison was designed; but some things can be done at once to ameliorate the condition..."[31]

"These reports show a condition of things at Andersonville which calls very loudly for the interposition of the Department in order that a change may be made." This additional endorsement was signed by J. A. Campbell, Assistant Secretary of War.

And, finally, there was endorsed: "Noted -File. J. A. S." The initials are those of James A. Seddon, Secretary of War.[32]

These endorsements were used to support the contention of the prosecution of a conspiracy at the highest levels of the Confederate Government. No evidence was ever produced to show the existence of such a conspiracy.

"Men of high social standing from Georgia were subpoenaed by Wirz' counsel and went to Washington, ready and eager to testify to his character and humane conduct towards the Union prisoners, but were not allowed to do so.

"The Confederate Commissioner of Exchange, General Ould, and the Federal Commissioner, General Mulford, were prepared to give evidence of the earnest desire of the Southern authorities for exchange of prisoners, but were not called upon.

"On the trial the reports of Drs. White and Stevenson were suppressed, and garbled extracts from those of Dr. Jones and others were used. While all the evidence against the prisoner was received, nothing tending to exculpate him was admitted. The prisoner's counsel was not permitted to have access to records which were open to the counsel for the prosecution.

"As part of the defense it was intended to show the brutal treatment of prisoners in Northern prisons, and that systematic cruelty was practiced for the purpose of forcing them to take the oath of allegiance. The names of witnesses by whom it was intended to prove these things were handed to Mr. Baker, assistant counsel to Judge Advocate Chipman. None of these witnesses appeared; the subpoenas for them were never issued, having been suppressed by the Judge Advocate on the ground that '... it was not proper that such testimony should see the light.'

"Chipman afterwards admitted that he refused to have subpoenas issued for some of the '... rebel functionaries whose testimony was considered important to the defense.' Among the men whose testimony was thus rejected was

[30] *Ibid.*, pp. 22, 23.
[31] *O.R.*, VII, pp. 550-551.
[32] Stibbs, p. 22.

General Lee, whose simple word would have gone far to prove to the world the truth."[33]

"Witnesses were often vague about dates by as much as several months. Naturally, they would be uncertain as to exact day, as they had no accurate way of keeping a calendar. But sometimes Chipman changed the specifications to fit the testimony. When the defense proved that Wirz was absent from Andersonville from August 4 to 20, one charge of murder had its date changed to August 25. Only one witness gave the name, rank, and regiment of a man Wirz supposedly murdered, in the middle of September. None of the thirteen specifications charged murder at that time, so the court revised a charge from June 13 to a September date."[34]

Doctor Joseph Jones, the Andersonville medical investigator, described his experiences related to the Wirz trial. On September 22nd, Doctor Jones was ordered to come to Washington as a witness in the trial and to bring with him "... all papers, reports, records, etc., of every kind in his possession, pertaining to the Andersonville Prison." Colonel Chipman, said he had heard of Jones's research from "southern sources." Doctor Jones thought a colleague who had visited him at his home after the war had furnished Chipman with the knowledge of the document.[35] Jones immediately appealed the summons of the Wirz tribunal to General James B. Steedman, Provost Marshal of the Department of Georgia, whose office had issued it, insisting that he had "... none of the original records of Andersonville" in his possession. He did admit to having copies of some of the prison hospital records which had been incorporated in an unfinished report but questioned whether the order applied to "... matter which had never been formally and officially presented to the Medical Department of the Confederate States." Steedman rejected Jones' appeal, informing him that the summons was irrevocable and pertained to everything in his possession connected in any way with Andersonville. This material, including his unfinished report, was to be immediately surrendered to the judge advocate. Jones was dismayed since he had no recourse but to comply with Steedman's instructions. "To a paroled prisoner of war," he remarked, "there was neither option nor appeal in the matter."

"With a heavy heart Jones left for Washington at the end of September. 'I cannot express to you,' he wrote his wife, 'the pain which I feel in being compelled to use my labors which were pressed solely for the advancement of the course of Humanity & my profession in the prosecution of criminal cases'."[36]

"Jones arrived in Washington on October 2... One of Jones first acts in Washington was the drafting of a lengthy appeal to Chipman in a last-ditch attempt to prevent the use of his Andersonville report against Wirz. He began by pointing out that he had gone to Andersonville '... to determine the causes of the great mortality amongst the Federal prisoners' and included a copy of his orders from Moore to prove the trip's official nature. As for the Federal prisoners, Jones argued that they had been moved to southwestern Georgia not only for reasons of security 'but also to secure a more abundant and easy supply of food.'"[37]

"The same principle," Jones asserted, "which led me to endeavor to deal humanely and justly by those prisoners, and to make a truthful representation of their condition to the Medical Department of the Confederate States army, now actuates me in recording my belief that as far as my knowledge extends there was no deliberate or wilful design on the part of the Chief Executive, Jefferson Davis, and the highest authorities of the Confederate Government to injure the health and destroy the lives of these Federal prisoners."[38]

Jones went to the Old Capitol Building on October 3rd and gave Chipman the manuscript. Jones was sworn, on October 7th, as a witness and briefly testified. He was not allowed to report mitigating circumstances but only to identify the report as his. The 600-page report had been reduced to a mere 20 pages. Jones was upset because "... any passage favorable to the Confederacy and even those in which he had attempted to explain the reasons for the abominable conditions at Andersonville had been expunged."[39]

Jones believed Chipman "... deliberately endeavored to arouse the hatred of the entire North" against him and the other medical officers of the Confederacy.[40]

One witness for the prosecution was especially damaging to Wirz. His name was Felix de la Baume, who said he had been born in France, on the French side of the Rhine. "He was the one who testified to most of the killing. His omnipresence at Andersonville was supernatural.

"He was a good address, he had a pleasant voice and he was intelligent. He swayed the crowd by his oratory.

[33] Ashe, pp. 27, 28.
[34] Morseberger, p. 37.
[35] Breeden, pp. 169, 170.
[36] *Ibid.*, p. 170.
[37] *Ibid.*, p. 171.
[38] *Ibid.*
[39] *Ibid.*, p. 172.
[40] *Ibid.*

He glibly rehearsed the manifold atrocities of Henry Wirz. He held the crowd spellbound. He made the statement that he was related to Marquis de Lafayette, Washington's friend, the hero of Brandywine was his grand uncle. So great was the impression he made that after the trial he was given a position in the Department of the Interior at Washington.

**Felix La Baume** - He had a print made, of the hospital at Andersonville, that was entered as evidence. (Authhor's Collection)

"Eleven days after Wirz was hanged some German soldiers recognized in Lafayette's grand nephew a deserter from the Seventh New York Volunteers and his name was not de la Baume at all but Felix de la Baume Oesser, born in Saxony, on the German side of the Rhine. After his discovery he disappeared and was known no more."[41]

Felix de la Baume had published a print measuring about 29 by 22 inches titled, *Let Us Forgive But Not Forget*. This print was "Dedicated to my Fellow Survivors and to all sons of Veterans in Memory of 14,000 Martyrs Who Perished." It also stated, "Address all orders to Felix LaBaume, Chicago, Ill."

This print was shown to Doctor Bates during his testimony and these were some of the comments by him about the print: "The great point in which it is not facsimile is that too few men are represented. If there were forty delineated where there is one it would be more correct. These men walking on their hands and knees and on crutches, some carrying their tin cups in their mouths, represent men who could not go there otherwise. They were afflicted with scurvy as a general thing. The man represented here I recognize as a man named Ison, who was a subject of dementia; he only crept along on his haunches and feet...That man with the bucket in his mouth, I frequently saw crawling up for his rations. I see one man here representing 'Dr. Bates examining the character and quantity of the beef,' together with the Confederate surgeon and Ed. Young, boss of that cook-house. I also see one figure representing 'Dr. Bates giving beef-bones to the cripples."[42]

The following was taken from a diary kept by Major Wirz while the trial was ongoing:

Old Capitol Prison, Oct. 1, 1865

Everything is quiet around me. No sound but the measured steps of the sentinel in the corridor can be heard. The man who is sitting in my room is nodding in his chair. Poor, short-sighted mortals that we all are! This man is here to watch me, to prevent any attempt I might make to take my own life. My life - what is it worth to anyone except myself and my poor family, that they should be so anxious? I think I understand it very well, they are afraid I might cheat them and the public at large from having their revenge, and giving, at the same time, the masses the benefit of seeing a man hung. If that is all, they are welcome. I have no desire to live; perhaps there was never a more willing victim dragged to the scaffold than I am. Why should I desire to live? A beggar, crippled, and with my health and spirit broken - why, oh why, should I desire to live? For the sake of my family? My family will do as well without me as with me. Instead of providing for and taking care of them, I would be a burden to them. And still knowing all that, why do I not put an end to my life? Because, in the first instance, what I suffer now is the will of God. God - how much is not in this word - what tower of strength, of consolation! Yea, Heavenly Father, if it was not Thy will I would not be a prisoner. I would not be looked at, spoken of as a monster such as the world has never seen and never will see. If that what I suffer now was not put on me by you for some wise purpose, I would be as free as the bird in the air. Thou and I - we two alone - know that I am innocent of those terrible charges. Thou and I, we both know that I never took the life of a fellow man - that I never caused a man to suffer and die in consequence of ill-treatment inflicted by me; and still I am tried for murder. Men have sworn that they saw me do it; they have called on Thee to witness that they would tell the truth, the whole truth, and nothing but the truth, and still they told a lie - a lie black as

[41] Rutherford, pp. 14, 15.
[42] Chipman, pp. 131, 132.

hell itself. Why did you not send a thunderbolt from the high heavens - why, oh God, why? Because it is Thy holy will, and in humility I kiss the rod with which Thou seest proper to chastise me.

The second reason why I did not destroy a life which is a burden to me, is because I owed it to myself, my family, my relations, even the world at large, to prove that there never existed a man so utterly devoid of all humanity, such a fiend incarnate, as it has been attempted to prove me to be. I see very well that I have no earthly show - that I am a doomed man; but thanks be to God that I am enabled to say with holy Stephanus, Lord, lay not this sin to my charge. They judge from what they hear and I must abide by it.

It makes me feel very sorry, and at the same time I could almost smile when I see men like Col. Persons and Captain Wright give their testimony; how careful they first weigh every word! how afraid they are to say something which might, perhaps, implicate themselves! I pity them. A day will come when they will be sorry that they took not a more manly stand than they did. Perhaps one of the hardest things I have to bear is when I hear such men speak now and recollect what they have said and now they acted a year ago. Then they did not say that they did not wish to associate with me. Oh! no; then they visited my house and invited me to theirs. But enough. I despise and always have despised a coward.

My wife has tried again to see me to-day, but could not because Gen. Baker, who, by order of the Secretary of War, has to be present at the interview, is still sick. I think it is pretty hard; because a man is sick, I have been deprived now for two weeks of almost the only joy, to see my poor wife. It looks to me that, among the hundreds of officials at Washington, one could be entrusted with the fearful responsibility to let a sick prisoner see his wife, talk with her for thirty minutes about their dear children, their domestic affairs. But why should I grumble or have any bitterness in my heart. I think I ought to be proud that a Government like the Government of the United States considers me of such importance to take such extraordinary measures.

For five weeks have I asked in vain to have the permission to see a minister of the gospel - to get such consolation as I thought I needed. Part of the time I was at death's door; and finally, on yesterday, I was allowed to see the Rev. Father Boyle; but during the whole time, except during confession, the officer was present. I think it is high time to blot out the eagle in the American escutcheon, and substitute a buzzard. I have heard, when I was a boy, that the eagle was the king of birds; if he is, how is it that the stoops so low to tear with his talons an humble Captain, and is afraid to strike men such as I could name. Poor eagle, I pity thee; thy acts are more like those of a buzzard.

October 2, 1865. - Again a day has passed. I am tired and worn out; whichever way I turn my eyes everything looks gloomy and dark. Can it be possible that, knowing what I do know, I shall fall a victim? But why do I doubt? What right have I to grumble, as if it was a thing unheard of in history that men suffered the death of a felon as innocent of the crimes alleged as I am; and if I dare to make a comparison between our Savior and myself, did not He also suffer death? True, he died as an atonement for a sinful world; true, He died willingly, He had a holy mission to fulfill; but I? Why should I die? I can only say, because it is God's will. Oh, God! our Heavenly Father, give me the grace, give me the power to bear the cross which they seest fit to lay on me. Have I not often sinned against Thee, and neglected the holy commandments? If I suffer now innocently, can't I, dare I say, I never offended Thee? Therefore, be calm, my poor heart. Give thyself into His hands and say Abba! Father!

October 3, 1865 - What a mockery is this trial. I feel at times as if I ought to speak out aloud and tell them why do you wrong yourself and me too? Why not end the game at once? Take me and hang me, and be done with it. A few days I asked to arrange my defense: it was refused on the ground that I had ample time. Ample time indeed! May the day be far distant for Gen. Wallace when he may plead with grim death for a day, and receive the answer, No! I just received a note from my wife, saying she has tried in every way to see me, but impossible. She says she is going to her mother in Kentucky, and hopes to be able to do more for me there than in remaining here. Poor, deluded woman, what do you expect to accomplish, what can you do for me but pray? Oh, what a consolation is it to a person in a situation like mine, that there is in the wide, wide world at least one being that will pray for me. Yes, pray; but pray for thyself; the road thou hast to travel is a hard one; when thou findest out that when you pressed my hand two weeks ago, when thy lips touched mine, it was in all probability the last time, then dost thou need all the comfort prayer can give. May God bless you, and take care of you and the dear, dear children. I must end. Everything swims before my eyes. God, oh, God have mercy upon me.

October 4, 1865 - What a mockery this trial is. They say that they are anxious that I should have justice done to me, and then when a witness is put on the stand to give testimony they try everything to break him down; if they cannot do it they try to assail his private character. When they had their own witnesses up, they not alone were allowed to state everything I said, everything I done, but even what they heard others say that I had said so and so, done such and such things, and now, when I wish to prove by my witnesses what I also said and done, it is said it is inadmissible. I just as well might be up on the stand myself, as if I had said those things now and not a year ago, when I had no idea that I should be held to account hereafter. But so the world goes, and all I can say is, Oh, God, give me strength to bear with patience and humility what Thou seest fit to put on me. Be Thou my judge.

October 5, 1865 - When I left the court-room to-day, I heard a lady remark: 'I wish I could shoot out his eyes,' meaning me. Foolish woman! The time will come when my earthy eyes are shut up; are you in such a hurry. But is it very natural that people do think and pass such remarks. For weeks and weeks they have heard men testify to cruelties done by me, and now a very slim chance have I to contradict these statements. It seems to me as if Gen. Wallace had a personal spite against me or my counsel, or he would not act the way he does. If he has one against me, I pity him that he has not more magnanimity of soul than to crush me in such a[n] unheard of arbitrary way; if he has a spite against my counsel, it is a cowardly act to do as he does, for in the end I am the sufferer, and not my counsel.

October 6, 1865 - Another day passed. I wish the trial was over. I wonder what unheard of resolutions the Court will pass again to-morrow. I did not feel it so keenly to day as I felt it other days, and I have to thank God for it in permitting me to partake of the Holy Communion this morning. I feel less contempt for those who are sitting in judgment over me. If it is God's will to open their eyes and hearts, He alone has the power to do it. I am certain that none of the Court, nor the Judge-Advocate considers and believes me guilty. They all know that the whole think is a farce. Cruelties have been committed at Andersonville: some one has to suffer for it; they have me; therefore, I am the one, *voila tout.* Talk about the Roman Catholic institution of Inquisition. What is the difference? There they forced an innocent man to confess crimes he never committed; here they bring witnesses against him who swear downright lies, and when he tries to defend himself, he is curtailed as much as possible in his privilege to do so. If anything, I prefer the first; there least it was plain that the object was to punish a man; here the object is the same, only a thin vail down over it, so thin, as airy, that all who wish to see can see though it."[43]

One of the points of contention during the trial was that Wirz was not physically able to assault the prisoners as the prosecution described. On October 24th, "At the request of counsel for the accused, Dr. C. M. Ford and Dr. John C. Bates made, in the presence of the court, an examination of the physical condition of the prisoner.

"By consent of the judge advocate,

"Dr. C. M. Ford was called as a witness for the defense, and, being duly sworn, was examined as follows:

"By Counsel:

Q. State what is your position.

A. I am acting assistant surgeon in the army of the United States, in charge of the hospital at the Old Capitol.

Q. Have you during some time past, been in the habit of seeing the prisoner?

A. Yes, sir; since June, I believe, ever since his imprisonment, he has been under my care when sick.

Q. Have you during that time examined his right arm, and have you examined it to-day?

A. Yes, sir.

Q. What do you find to be the present condition of his arm?

A. It is swollen and inflamed, ulcerated in three places; ... it has the appearance of having been broken. In addition to that, I believe that portions of both bones of the arm are dead.

Q. State your professional opinion as to the strength of his arm in its present condition? Would he be capable with that arm of pushing or knocking down a person, or using any heavy or even a light instrument in doing so?

A. I don't know that I can answer that question entirely. I don't know how much strength he has in the

[43] "Andersonville, Diary of Henry Wirz," *New York Tribune*, Nov 14, 1865, p. 1.

arm; but I should think him incapable of knocking a man, or lifting a very heavy instrument of any kind, without doing great injury to the arm.

Q. Have you examined also the prisoner's left shoulder?

A. Yes, sir.

Q. State what you found to be its condition.

A. There is a very large scar on the left shoulder, and a portion - about half, I should suppose - the outer half of the muscle of the shoulder. The deltoid muscle is entirely gone - I suppose from the wound; it has been carried away, only the front part of the muscle or the shoulder remaining.

Q. How does that influence the strength of the arm?

A. It prevents in a great measure the action of the deltoid muscle, the use of which is to elevate the arm. It would prevent the perfect elevation of the arm. It has no influence at all on the flexion of the arm at the elbow, or striking out with the fore-arm from the elbow; it does not have any material effect as to that.

Q. How do you find the fingers of the prisoner's right hand?

A. I believe that two fingers, the little finger and the next, are slightly contracted; not permanently so, I believe. I am not positive, but I think I could straighten them. The contraction is due to the injury of the nerve leading down to the fingers.

Q. Have you examined the legs of the prisoner?

A. I have.

Q. What do you find to be their condition?

A. I find both of them covered with dark brown scars, as if they had been ulcerated at one time.

Q. Do you find traces of his having had the scurvy?

A. Yes, sir.

Q. State your professional opinion as to the body strength of the prisoner, so far as regards his ability to do my injury to any one?

A. He is now in a very prostrated condition; and I should not think him now capable of doing much violence to any one in the present condition of his system.

Q. Taking into consideration the general condition of his arms, legs, and bodily frame, do you think him capable of exerting himself to any extent in doing injury to anybody, pushing a man down, or anything of that kind?

A. I believe that he might push a person down, but I do not think he would be apt to exert himself to do any act of violence, because in doing that he would be very apt to do injury to himself.

"By the Judge Advocate:

Q. In what you have said, you speak of the prisoner's present condition?

A. Yes, sir.

Q. The opinion which you give has no reference to the condition in which he was a year ago?

A. No, sir.

Q. From the symptoms presented, can you reason back and tell us what was his condition in 1864?

A. I should not think the right arm was any better in 1864 than it is now. The scurvy, if he was suffering from it then, might make the wound worse. Scurvy or similar disease will often cause fractures to open again after being united.

Q. Can you say with certainty what was the prisoner's condition a year ago?

A. I cannot; but the external appearances would indicate that there had been a very extensive injury to the bones and the tissues.

"By the court:

Q. Can you say whether the wound has ever healed, and this is the second breaking out of it?

A. No, sir: I do not know: I first met the prisoner in June, when he came to the prison. The wound was then in very nearly the same condition as now.

"The prisoner:

In 1863, my health failing, I asked a furlough to go to Europe, and received it after an examination by the chief surgeon at the hospital at Richmond. I went to Europe and had my wound operated upon at Paris. The doctor there thought that all the dead bone had come out. After spending several months in Switzerland, I returned to England, and from there to the Confederate States. On shipboard, three or four months afterwards, the wound broke open again, and has been in its present condition since February, 1864.

"By consent of the judge advocate, Dr. John C. Bates, being recalled, was examined as a witness for the defence.

"By Counsel:

Q. You have heard the opinion just given by Dr. Ford; give us your general opinion about the state of the prisoner's health.

A. I have the advantage of Dr. Ford in having seen the prisoner at Andersonville; but while there I never examined him professionally. I noticed on several occasions that he had difficulty in using his right arm. I never inquired what was the matter. As I stated some time since, he was feeble in September, 1864, and did not look like a man enjoying the best of health. The impression of some of the medical gentlemen at Andersonville (you can take it for what it is worth) was that there was in his system a constitutional syphilitic taint. For that reason, I asked him to let me examine his shanks. This is, it seems to me, an intermingling of the scorbutic and syphilitic taint. When this first manifested itself I do not know. I agree with Dr. Ford in all that he has said; there is nothing from which I would dissent. I concur in his opinion in reference to the left shoulder, the destruction of a portion of the deltoid muscle, and also in his opinion in reference to the right arm, the inability to use it with any considerable degree of force in fighting or striking. He could not use the right arm very extensively, without injury to the bones, which are partially destroyed.

"By the Judge Advocate:

Q. May not a man disabled in the arm so that he cannot strike out straight, without danger of injury to himself, be still able to use a pistol with great effect by exercising the wrist?

A. In the case of injury or partial destruction of the main muscle of the shoulder, he might use the arm from the elbow; but the upper portion of the arm would remain partially inactive.

"By Counsel:

Q. Would it cause the prisoner any pain if he should use a pistol or any instrument, by striking from the elbow with his right arm?

A. I should think so; considering the condition of the bones and the ulceration, it might be a serious injury to them"[44]

After 63 days of testimony, the trial was brought to a close on October 24th. But even before the verdict was in, Schade wrote to the President, pleading for mercy for his client:

*Washington, D. C., October 26, 1865*

*His Excellency Andrew Johnson,*
*President of the United States:*

*Sir: One of the principal prerogatives of your high position is that of mercy and pardon. It becomes still more important in dubious cases, where it is not quite clear whether justice has been done or not. Such one, I regret very much to say, is my duty not only as counsel for the defendant, but as friend of humanity, to lay before Your Excellency today.*

*Captain Wirz, my client, has been tried, and, as I apprehend, condemned to die. In your hand it rests whether this sentence shall be carried out or not. It is true that if you are solely guided by the evidence which will be or has been laid before you, little or no hope is to be entertained; but there is something else which cannot fail to command Your Excellency's regards, and that is the following:*

*1. That this commission, before which the prisoner has been tried, has in many instances excluded testimony in favor of the prisoner, and, on the other hand, admitted testimony against the prisoner, both in violation of all rules of law and equity. That the whole country knows. Every lawyer in this city and elsewhere has regarded this and the treatment the counsel suffered at the hands of the president of the commission and the judge-advocate with indignation and as an insult to the profession. My former colleagues, Messrs. Hughes, Denver, and Peck, left for that reason, and then I would have followed their example had not the prisoner had my word of honor not to for-*

[44] *Wirz Trial*, pp. 803-805.

*sake him.*

*2. The testimony for the prosecution is loose, indefinite, and in the most part contradictory. Before any other court but that military commission it would have been an easy matter to uncover and bring to light a tissue of perjuries [such] as the world has seldom seen. Time will show that this assertion of mine is no empty one.*

*Captain Wirz was almost a prisoner himself at Andersonville. If permitted we could have proven by our witnesses that at different times he requested to be discharged, or to be sent to the Trans-Mississippi Department away from Andersonville. He took the responsibility of enlarging the stockade against the orders of his superiors, as appears from Colonel Persons' testimony, a witness for the prosecution; and 'worked indefatigably' for the benefit of the prisoners. Colonel Persons, commandant of the post, in harmony with Wirz, approved what the latter had done. Both sent remonstrances to Richmond, and the consequence of these remonstrances was that General Winder was sent to Andersonville to stop them. It was Captain Wirz who complained of the bad bread (see his letter published in the testimony); who asked for shoes or leather from the rebel authorities for paroled Union prisoners; who paroled about fifty young Union drummer boys in order that they might escape the horrors of the stockade; who remonstrated against having so many prisoners sent there; who gave writing material to our boys to prepare a petition for exchange to Washington, and permitted six of our men to go North for that purpose in order to see the President and the Secretary of War; and when all hopes for exchange were gone he told Judge Hall, one of the witnesses for the prosecution, that he (Wirz) would wish all the prisoners paroled and set at large, instead of letting them die in the stockade. All that and many other facts prove that Captain Wirz did certainly not conspire to kill the prisoners.*

*Thirteen cases of acts of personal cruelty and murder alleged by the prosecution to have been committed by Captain Wirz are located in the month of August, 1864. About sixty witnesses (thirty-four for the defense and over twenty for the prosecution) have positively sworn that Captain Wirz was not at Andersonville and Lieutenant Davis in command of the prison during that time. Not a single one has contradicted that statement. That proves sufficiently how much stress is to be laid upon such testimony. Some ten to twelve on both sides swear that he was sick in the latter half of July and the most part of September; that he was fetched in an ambulance from his residence to his office, and was unable to ride on horseback, &c. And almost all the alleged cruelties and murders are said to have been committed in July, August, and September, 1864.*

*Among the 35,000 prisoners were many bounty-jumpers and bad characters. Some six of them were hung by their own comrades. If I have the Government's patronage, and perhaps the prospect of an office or two (as actually has been the case with some of the witnesses for the prosecution in the Wirz trial), and can also give a promise of safe conduct and perhaps a reward, I do not doubt in the least that among those 500 raiders at Andersonville (as they are styled in the testimony) I shall within four weeks find enough testimony to try, condemn, and hang every member of the Wirz military commission on any charge whatever, provided it is done before such a military commission.*

*Your Excellency knows me. It is unnecessary to state that nothing but a feeling of humanity urges me to ask you for clemency. No remuneration, but labor and vituperation have been the reward of the counsel in this case. God knows that I would not ask you to do anything which was not right. And therefore let the miserable, crippled, half-dying man, at the worst a tool in the hands of superiors, a subaltern officer who had to obey orders, live out the few remaining days of his life, and do not let our hands be tainted with the blood of this miserable and unfortunate being. I know you will believe me if I, with all my heart, declare that he does not deserve that fate. Spare the cripple! Be merciful!*

*Yours in haste and with all the old attachment and respect,*
*Louis Schade*[45]

On August 31st, Dick Winder arrived at the Old Capitol Prison and became the across-the-hall neighbor of Wirz. It was during this time of Wirz' confinement that the two communicated with one another by hiding notes within the spout of the coffee pot. The following was a note Wirz sent to Winder: "Be of good cheer, I have been told on yesterday by Gen'l Bacher that it is well understood among high officials, that they are not trying me or you, but have to try me apparently to get hold of the big men, such as Cooper, Seddon, Jeff Davis. If you can give me any information as to the fact that the authorities in Richmond knew or even authorized the state of affairs at Andersonville as to rations, food, shelters, let me know. I think it will save me, at any rate you." The "General Bacher" mentioned in the note was undoubtedly Brigadier-General La Fayette C. Baker, "the well-known detective" and provost marshal. Dick Winder sent Wirz the following reply: "I know of nothing except the reports from the prisons, the reports of in-

[45] *O.R.*, VIII, pp. 773, 774.

specting officers and newspaper statements."[46]

Some historians have intimated Wirz tried to commit suicide by having his wife sneak poison to him in his cell. Brigadier-General La Fayette C. Baker wrote a rambling autobiography and historical narrative in 1904. In the last chapter, titled "Attempted Suicide of Wirz" Baker told about this alleged attempt: "I had taken no part in Wirz' trial, most of the evidence having been procured by military officers then on duty in the South. During the last days of the trial, Mrs. Wirz appeared in Washington, and desired an interview with her husband. The Secretary of War had directed the officer in command of the prison to exercise the utmost caution in respect to the prisoner. It was feared that he would commit suicide. Orders were issued not to allow any interview to be had with him under any pretense whatever. He was to be kept entirely secluded from the other prisoners, and only visited by the clergy and his counsel. Mrs. Wirz applied to me for permission to see him. She claimed that she desired only to administer to his comfort, as far as possible, and had no objection to the interview taking place in the presence of an officer of the Government. Wirz sent me a request to visit him, and accordingly I repaired to his apartment in the 'Old Capitol.' During the conversation, he expressed earnest desire to see his wife, when I reminded him that the orders of the Secretary prohibited such interviews. His anxiety was so great, that I stated the prisoner's request to Mr. Stanton, who consented to a meeting in my presence, with no communications in their own language between them. He then gave me the following order:

**General Baker Foils Wirz' Attempt at Suicide**

*War Department, Adjutant-General's Office*
*Washington, November 9, 1865*

*Major-General Augur*
*Commanding Department of Washington: -*

*General - Henry Wirz has sent a request to General L. C. Baker to visit him. The Secretary of War desires that the authority be given General Baker.*

*I am, very respectfully, your obedient servant,*
*E. D. Townsend,*
*Assistant Acting Adjutant-General*

"With this document I procured a permit, and requested Mrs. Wirz to be at the prison at four o'clock that day. The interview took place, and I shall never forget the first meeting between Wirz and his wife. She exhibited the most stoical indifference, and simply said, 'How are you, Wirz?' Instead of embracing him, as would naturally have been expected under the circumstances, she sat down in a chair in front of him, and looked at the doomed man a moment, and then gave utterance to the most vindictive words against the Government, in which he joined. Instead of talking of their family affairs, the unfortunate position in which Wirz was placed, and the probability of his execution, she took occasion to denounce Colonel Chipman, Judge-Advocate of the commission before whom Wirz was being tried, and the witnesses as perjurers, and in the most threatening manner defied the Government to carry the findings of the commission into execution. This interview finally closed in their making an appointment for another.

"The conduct of Wirz and his wife was to my mind very suspicious. I did not conceive that such indifference was natural under the circumstances, and determined to watch their next interview very closely. It came in due time, and was very similar to the first one. Mrs. Wirz sat in front of her husband, and I took a position where I could casually observe the movements of each. Mrs. Wirz took from her hand a glove, inside of which I noticed she had a small package; what it was I could not tell. The interview was short, as both were conscious that I was observing every movement. At the third interview the same thing was repeated. As we all rose to go to the door leading to the hall, Wirz walking first, Mrs. Wirz next, and myself at the rear, she for the first time approached him, when they em-

[46] Original note in author's collection.

braced and put their lips up to kiss each other. I watched the motion, and perceived that she was conveying something from her mouth to his. I sprang forward in an instant, caught him by the throat, and threw him on the floor. He raised a pill from his throat, brought it within his teeth, crushed it and spit out. I picked it up and found it to be a small round piece of strychnine enclosed in a piece of oiled silk. Upon this discovery I informed Mrs. Wirz that she could have no more interviews with her husband. She was compelled, therefore, to leave him to his fate. My next step was to inform the Assistant Secretary of War and Judge Holt of the singular occurrence. I also showed to the former the strychnine pill. On the day of the prisoner's execution, I related the poison scene to a reporter of a New York paper. It was given to the public by him. The copperhead press immediately opened their artillery of abuse, making me the target of bitterest attack. The whole statement was pronounced a fabrication, while it was verified entirely by Louis Skade [sic], the counsel of Wirz, and by Mrs. Wirz. It is a fact, which should make the loyal men of the land reflect deeply, that these reckless detractors of the administration of Mr. Lincoln, and all who aided him in checking the insane revolt, who defended the vilest actors in the drama of rebellion, are to-day the friends of Mr. Johnson and his 'policy.' No reflective patriotic mind can exclude the doubt whether the infamous keeper of the Andersonville prison pen would have been executed at all had the merited fate been delayed a few months longer, until the change in the tone of the Presidential feeling toward rebels, whom he had so warmly condemned and warned that their treason must be made 'odious' for all coming time. It is more sad and stinging to know this, for those of us who necessarily were familiar with the character and deeds of the brutal servants of Davis and his counselors and commanders."[47]

On November 13, 1865 the *New York Tribune* said, "Louis Schade, esq., published a card denying the truth of the statement that Mrs. Wirz introduced strychnine into her husband's mouth while kissing him. Mr. Schade shows that at the time of the alleged interview Mrs. Wirz was in Kentucky, and says: 'Whether the statement comes from Gen. Baker or from any one else, it is an infamous lie from beginning to end.'"

On November 6th, the following verdicts were returned against Wirz with some modifications of the specifications:

"To the First Charge, 'guilty' and the co-conspirators were amended by adding the names of Jefferson Davis, James A. Seddon, and Howell Cobb.

To the Second Charge: 'Guilty.'

To the First Specification of the Second Charge: 'Guilty,' adding the words 'or about' immediately before the phrase 'the 9th day of July.'

To the Second Specification of the Second Charge: 'Guilty.'

To the Third Specification of the Second Charge: 'Guilty,' after striking out 'June,' and inserting, instead,'September.'

To the Fourth Specification of the Second Charge: 'Guilty.'

To the Fifth Specification of the Second Charge: 'Guilty,' after striking out the phrase 'on the 13th day,' and inserting instead the phrase, 'on or about the 25th day.'

To the Sixth Specification of the Second Charge: 'Guilty,' after striking out the word '1st' and inserting '15th' and also striking out the phrase 'on the 6th day,' and inserting instead the phrase,'on or about the 16th day.'

To the Seventh Specification of the Second Charge: 'Guilty,' after striking out the word '20th' and inserting the word '1st,' and also after inserting 'on or about' immediately before the phrase of 45th day.'

To the Eighth Specification of the Second Charge: 'Guilty.'

To the Ninth Specification of the Second Charge: 'Guilty.'

To the Tenth Specification of the Second Charge: 'Not Guilty.'

To the Eleventh Specification of the Second Charge: 'Guilty,' after striking out the word '1st,' and inserting instead the word '6th,' after striking out also the phrase 'incite and urge,' and the phrase 'encouragement and instigation,' and by adding the words 'or about' after the word 'on' where it last occurs in the specification; and also after striking out the word 'bloodhounds' where it afterward occurs, and inserting 'dogs,' and also striking out the words 'given by him.'

To the Twelfth Specification of the Second Charge: 'Guilty.'

To the Thirteenth Specification of the Second Charge: 'Not guilty.'

---

[47] La Fayette C. Baker, *Spies, Traitors and Conspirators of the Late Civil War* (Philadelphia: 1894, John E. Potter & Co.), pp. 392-397.

"And the court do therefore sentence him, the said Henry Wirz, to be hanged till he be dead, at such time and place as the President of the United States may direct, two-thirds of the members of the Court concurring therein."[48]

The proceedings, findings, and sentence" of the Wirz case were submitted to the President of the United States, who issued the following orders:

> *Executive Mansion*
> *Nov. 3, 1865*
>
> *The proceedings, findings, and sentence of the Court, in the within case, are approved, and it is ordered that the sentence be carried into execution by the officer commanding the Department of Washington, on Friday, the 10th day of November, 1865, between the hours of 6 o'clock A.M., and 12 o'clock noon.*
>
> *Andrew Johnson, President*

"Major-General C. C. Augur, commanding the Department of Washington, is commanded to cause the foregoing sentence in the case of Henry Wirz, to be duly executed in accordance with the President's order.

"The military commission of which Major General Lewis Wallace, U.S. Volunteers, is president is hereby dissolved."[49]

On the same day the verdicts were returned, Wirz wrote to the President of the United States:

Old Capitol Prison
November 6, 1865
To the President of the United States,

> Mr. President: With a trembling hand, with a heart filled with the most conflicting emotions, and with a spirit hopeful one moment and despairing the next, I have taken the liberty of addressing you. When I consider your exalted position; when I think for a moment that in your hands rests the weal or woe of millions - yea, the peace of the world - well may I pause to call to my aid courage enough to lay before you my humble petition. I have heard you spoken of as a man willing and ready at all times and under all circumstances to do justice, and that no man, however humble he may be, need fear to approach you; and, therefore, have come to the conclusion that you will allow me the same privilege as extended to hundreds and thousands of others. It is not my desire to enter into an argument as to the merits of my case. In your hands, if I am rightfully informed, are all the records and evidences bearing upon this point, and it would be presumption on my part to say one word about it. There is only one thing that I ask, and it is expressed in a few words: Pass your sentence.
>
> "For six weary months I have been a prisoner; for six months my name has been in the mouth of every one; by thousands I am considered a monster of cruelty, a wretch that ought not to pollute the earth any longer. Truly, when I pass in my mind over the testimony given, I sometimes almost doubt my own existence. I doubt that I am the Captain Wirz spoken of. I doubt that such a man ever lived, such as he is said to be; and I am inclined to call on the mountains to fall upon and bury me and my shame. But oh, sir, while I wring my hands in mute and hopeless despair, there speaks a small but unmistakable voice within me that says: 'Console thyself, thou knowest thy innocence. Fear not; if men hold thee guilty, God does not, and a new life will pervade your being.' Such has been the state of my mind for weeks and months, and no punishment that human ingenuity can inflict could increase my distress.
>
> "The pangs of death are short, and therefore I humbly pray that you will pass your sentence without delay. Give me death or liberty. The one I do not fear; the other I crave. If you believe me guilty of the terrible charges that have been heaped upon me, deliver me to the executioner. If not guilty, in your estimation, restore me to liberty and life. A life such as I am now living is no life. I breathe, sleep, eat, but it is only the mechanical functions I perform, and nothing more. Whatever you decide I shall accept. If condemned to death, I shall suffer without a murmur. If restored to liberty, I will thank and bless you for it.
>
> "I would not convey the idea to your mind, Mr. President, that I court death. Life is sweet; however lowly or humble man's station may be, he clings to life. His soul is filled with awe when he contemplates the future, the unknown land where the judgement is before which he will have to give an account of his

[48] *O.R.*, VIII, pp. 789-792.
[49] *Ibid.*

words, thoughts, and deeds. Well may I remember, too, that I have erred like all other human beings. But of those things for which I may perhaps suffer a violent death, I am not guilty; and God judge me. I have said all that I wished to say. Excuse my boldness in addressing you, but I could not help it. I cannot bear this suspense much longer. May God bless you, and be with you; your task is a great and fearful one. In life or death I shall pray for you, and for the prosperity of the country in which I have passed some of my happiest as well as darkest days.

Respectfully,
H. Wirz [50]

John Howard Stibbs, a member of the Military Commission which tried Wirz, gave a few insights into the verdict returned against Wirz. "When our verdict was rendered and the record made complete it was submitted for review to General Joseph Holt, Judge Advocate General, a man noted for his high character, patriotism, and ability as a lawyer and a judge."[51]

"We took it for granted that if our verdict was approved by the President the government would accept our finding as an indictment of the persons named, and that they would be brought to trial. I am pleased to say, however, that the Court found no evidence showing that General Lee was cognizant of, or was in any measure a part to, this conspiracy, and his name was not included in the verdict."[52]

**Father B. F. Wiget**

"The average level-headed citizen while considering the verdicts rendered in an ordinary criminal case is generally ready to say: 'The jury are the best judges of the evidence, they heard it all as it was given, had an opportunity to judge of its value and estimate the credibility of the witnesses, and their judgment should be accepted as correct and final.' It seems to me that the American people, and especially the future historian, should be equally fair in dealing with the Wirz Commission. Indeed, I do not see how it would be possible for an intelligent, unprejudiced, fair-minded reviewer to conclude that such a Court could or would have rendered a verdict that was not in full accord with the evidence presented. I assure you that no attempt was made to dictate or influence our verdict; and furthermore, there was no power on earth that could have swerved us from the discharge of our sworn duty as we saw it. Our verdict was unanimous. There were no dissenting opinions. And for myself I can say that there has been no time during the forty-five years that have intervened since this trial was held when I have felt that I owed an apology to anyone, not even to the Almighty, for having voted to hang Henry Wirz by the neck until he was dead."[53]

The *New York Times* of November 11, 1865, described, in detail, the last few hours of Wirz on this earth in a "Special Dispatch" dated Nov. 10th:

"Yesterday afternoon, Louis Schade, Wirz' junior counsel, communicated to him the result of his last appeal to the President. Wirz said he had no hope. He was ready to die. He had sought and received religious consolation, and it mattered little whether he died now or was spared to die a natural death, for die soon he must. An attaché of the Swiss Consulate also called to ascertain the residence of his relatives, that they might be officially apprised of his death. Wirz said he had been greatly wronged by the refusal of the Swiss Consul to receive money to enable him to conduct his defence.

"Wirz ate his supper as usual, and retiring, slept soundly the best part of the night. This morning he arose early and partook of a moderate breakfast. Soon after, R. B. Winder, who was associated with Wirz in the command at Andersonville, was allowed to visit him, and the two had a long conversation, devoted to a review of their career at the stockade, a review of the evidence, and mutual assertions that they were equally guilty, or rather, equally innocent,

[50] Rutherford, pp. 39, 40.
[51] Stibbs, p. 27.
[52] *Ibid.*, p. 24.
[53] *Ibid.*, pp. 26, 27.

and that if Wirz deserved hanging, so did Winder. Winder then bade Wirz an emotional farewell at half-past eight o'clock. Mr. Schade was admitted for a farewell interview, during which the prisoner reiterated his thanks for his counsel's efforts, and expressed himself as to his innocence, much as he had done before. It is due to Mr. Schade to say that he has been indefatigable in seeking to prolong the life of his client. He left the prison at the close of the interview, and went to the President's, where at ten thirty-five he made his last appeal. Wirz was hung at ten thirty-two.

"After Mr. Schade left Wirz, his spiritual advisers, Father Boyle and Wiget entered and remained with him until he was led forth to the scaffold.

"The arrangements for the execution which had been under the management of Maj. Russell, Provost-Marshal of the District, and Captain Walbridge, commandant of the prison, were completed at an early hour this morning. The scaffold was erected in the southern portion of the prison yard. Wirz is the eighth criminal who has been executed upon it. ... (The scaffold had been in use for 15 years for the execution of seven prisoners before the hanging of Wirz.)

**Father F. E. Boyle** - Pastor of St. Peter's Roman Catholic Church, Washington, DC.

"The capacity of the yard for holding spectators having been closely estimated, directions were given by Major Russell for the issue of two hundred tickets of admission. He had applications for ten hundred. The hour for the execution not being generally known, people began to assemble as early as 7 o'clock; but no one was admitted to the yard until nearly 10. The crowd who couldn't get in at all soon became very large, and was chiefly composed of soldiers, many of whom well remembered Andersonville. The facilities for observation for this outside crowd were few - chiefly confined to the tops of a row of shade trees in the capitol grounds, a few house-tops, and the dome of the capitol, a quarter of a mile distant. The house-tops were peopled at an early hour, and favorable places for seeing commanded a premium.

**Wirz Being Prepared for His Execution** - He is being helped into his black robe and hood. Reverends Wiget and Boyle are to his right (Frank Leslie's Illustrated Newspaper, November 25, 1865)

"At 10 o'clock, all being ready Major Russell and Captain Walbridge and the guard entered Wirz' room to bring him to the scaffold. Wirz greeted the officers in a quiet and easy manner. He had been engaged for the previous hour with the confessors, and now complied with the request to prepare for the final scene. Without any exhibition of nervousness, he even indulged in pleasantry as to his appearance in the black shroud, and said also that he 'Hoped to have a white gown soon.' The officers proceeded to pinion his arms behind his back, but found the handcuffs would not slip on to his right arm, it being much swollen. His limbs were therefore all left free until he reached the scaffold. As they were leaving the room, Wirz turned to the mantel, and with as much nonchalance as if he had been in a bar-room, took up a bottle of whisky, and pouring out a liberal draught, drank it down with apparent relish. Then taking a chew of tobacco, he took his place in the procession, which was led by the Provost-Marshal, then the two Priests, then Wirz, the guards next, and Captain Walbridge in the rear, in which order they mounted the scaffold, the prisoner exhibiting much steadiness in his movements. Stepping upon the trap, he seated himself upon a stool, the noose, so soon to be his fatal snare, dangling over his head. Maj. Russell then proceeded to read the order, reciting the finding of the court, and the approval of the sentence by the President...

**The Warrant Read to Wirz** - Wirz sat on a small, wooden stool for about 20 minutes and listened as the charges were read against him.

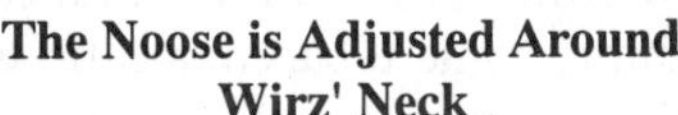

**The Noose is Adjusted Around Wirz' Neck**

**Wirz' Dead Body is Lowered to the Ground**

"The reading was finished at 10:20, and Wirz was directed to stand up. Major Russell asked him if he had anything to say publicly, to which he replied, 'No.' Father Boyle then recited the service of the Catholic Church for the dying, to which Wirz responded in a low tone.

"During these few moments shouts could be heard from the soldiers in the tree-tops of 'Hang him,' 'Andersonville,' 'Remember Andersonville,' and others not calculated to increase his calm demeanor, but he paid no attention to them, and preserved his cheerful expression of countenance throughout.

"At thirty minutes past ten, his hands and legs having been pinioned by straps, the noose was adjusted by L. J. Richardson, Military Detective, and the doomed man shook hands with the priests and officers. At exactly thirty-two minutes past ten, Sylvester Ballou, another detective, at the signal of the Provost-Marshal, put his foot upon the fatal spring, the trap fell with a heavy noise, and the Andersonville jailor was dangling in the air. There were a few spasmodic convulsions of the chest, a slight movement of the extremities, and all was over. When it was known in the street that Wirz was hung, the soldiers sent up a loud ringing cheer, just such as I have heard scores of times on the battle-field after a successful charge. The sufferings at Andersonville were too great to cause the soldiers to do otherwise than rejoice at such a death of such a man.

"After hanging fourteen minutes the body was examined by Post-Surgeon Ford, and life pronounced to be extinct. It was then taken down, placed upon a stretcher, and carried to the hospital, where the surgeon took charge of it.

"No sooner had the scaffold and the rope done its work, and become historically famous, than relic seekers began their work. Splinters from the scaffold were cut off like kindling wood, and a dozen feet of rope disappeared almost instantly. The interposition of the guard only saved the whole thing from being carried off in this manner.

"The surgeons held a post-mortem, and an examination of the neck showed the vertebrae to be dislocated. His right arm, which has been the chief cause of his physical misery, was in very bad condition, in consequence of an old wound having broken out afresh. His body also showed severe scrofulitic eruptions.

"Agreeably to a request from Wirz, Father Boyle received the body to-day, and delivered it to an undertaker, who will inter it, to await the arrival of Mrs. Wirz, who is expected soon. Wirz left few or no earthly effects. The only things in his room after the execution were a few articles of clothing, some tobacco, a little whisky, a Testament, a copy of Cummings on the Apocalypse, and a cat, which was Wirz' pet companion. This is all there is left of him."

The following is an extract from a letter to Mrs. Jefferson Davis, from Major R. B. Winder, written on January 9, 1867:

"The door of the room which I occupied while in confinement in Old Capitol Prison, Washington, was immediately opposite Captain Wirz' door, and both were occasionally open. About two days before Captain Wirz' execution I saw three or four men pass into his room, and, upon their coming out, Captain Wirz assured me that they had given him assurances that his life would be spared and his liberty given him if he (Wirz) could give any testimony that would reflect on Mr. Davis or implicate him, directly or indirectly, with the condition and treatment of prisoners of war, as charged by the authorities of the United States; that he indignantly spurned these propositions, and assured them that, never having been acquainted with Mr. Davis, either personally, officially or socially, it was utterly impossible that he should know anything against him, and that the offer of his life, dear as the boon might be, could not purchase him to treason and treachery to the South."[54]

Schade told of the last 24 hours of Wirz on this earth. "On the night before the execution of the prisoner a telegram was sent to the Northern press from this city, stating that Wirz had made important disclosures to Gen. L. C. Baker, the well-known detective, implicating Jefferson Davis, and that the confession would probably be given to the public. On the same evening some parties came to the confessor of Wirz, Rev. Father Boyle, and also to me, one of them informing me that a high cabinet officer wished to assure Wirz that, if he would implicate Jefferson Davis with the atrocities committed at Andersonville, his sentence would be commuted. He (the messenger, or whoever he was) requested me to inform Wirz of this. In the presence of Father Boyle, I told Wirz next morning what had happened. The Captain simply and quietly replied: 'Mr. Schade, you know that I have always told you that I do not know anything about Jefferson Davis. He had no connection with me as to what was done at Andersonville. If I knew anything of him I would not become a traitor against him, or anybody else, even to save my life.' He likewise denied that he had ever made any statement whatever to General Baker. Thus ended the attempt to suborn Captain Wirz against Jefferson Davis. That alone shows what a man he was. How many of his defamers would have done the same? With

[54] Ashe, p. 45.

his wounded arm in a sling, the poor paroled prisoner mounted, two hours later, the scaffold."[55]

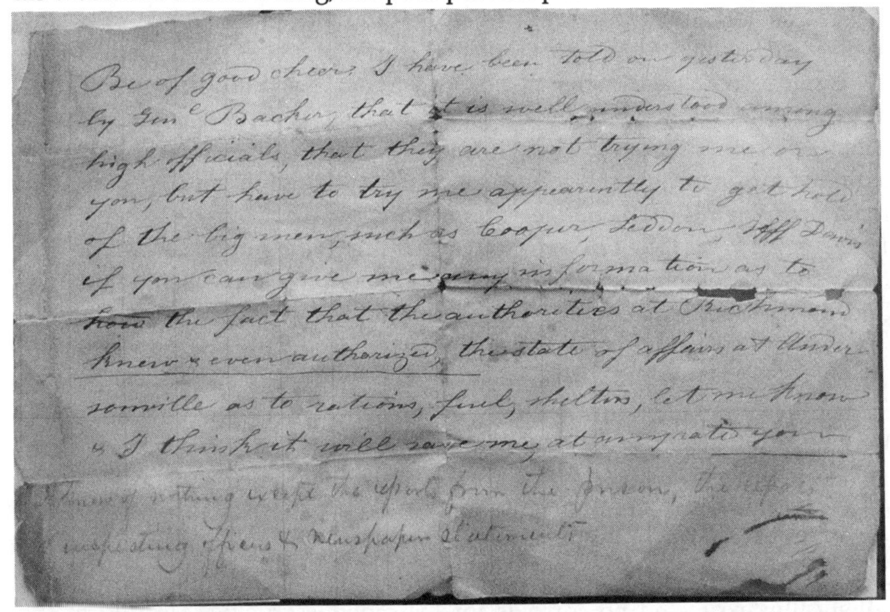

Be of good cheer I have been told on yesterday
by Genl Bacher that it is well understood among
high officials, that they are not trying me or
you, but have to try me apparently to get hold
of the big men, such as Cooper, Seddon, Jeff Davis
if you can give me any information as to
how the fact that the authorities at Richmond
knew & even authorized, the state of affairs at Andersonville as to rations, fuel, shelters, let me know
& I think it will save me, at any rate you

I know of nothing except the reports from the prison, the reports
inspecting officers & newspaper statements

"... To get hold of the big men, such as Cooper, Seddon, Jeff Davis if you can give me any information as to how the fact that the authorities at Richmond knew & even authorized, the state of affairs at Andersonville as to rations, fuel, shelters, let me know & I think it will save me, at any rate you." The reply, "I know of nothing except the reports from the prison, the reports of inspecting officers & newspapers statements." (Author's Collection)

In reply to a letter in inquiry from the Hon. Jefferson Davis, Rev. Father Boyle wrote of this incident: "On the evening before the day of the execution of Major Wirz a man visited me, on the part of a cabinet officer, to inform me that Major Wirz would be pardoned if he would implicate Jefferson Davis in the cruelties at Andersonville. No names were given by this emissary, and upon my refusing to take any action in the matter, he went to Mr. Louis Schade, counsel for Major Wirz, with the same purpose and with a like result.

"When I visited Major Wirz the next morning he told me that the same proposal had been made to him and had been rejected with scorn. The Major was very indignant, and said that while he was innocent of the charges for which he was about to suffer death, he would not purchase his liberty by perjury and a crime such as was made the condition of his freedom.

"I attended the major to the scaffold, and he died in the peace of God and praying for his enemies. I know that he was indeed innocent of all the cruel charges on which his life was sworn away, and I was edified by the Christian spirit in which he submitted to his persecutor. Yours very truly, F. E. Boyle."[56]

"Wirz spent the greater part of the night before his execution in writing, but slept for a few hours before daylight and awoke cheerful and refreshed. He was calm and self-possessed and had left nothing undone. His own books, as well as those borrowed, were all neatly done up and left for delivery to the proper parties. His diary was completed up to the last day.

"He felt keenly the abuse that was heaped upon him. As he bade farewell to his old associate, Captain R. H. [sic] Winder, he said:

"'Promise me, if you live, to do all in your power to wipe out this awful stain upon my character. Make my name and character stand as bright before the world as it did when you first knew me. Promise me you will do something to assist my wife.'

"Winder turned his face away to hide his tears, as he replied: 'Captain, I will.'

"One of the daily newspapers, after relating this parting with Winder, said: 'Wirz passed on down the stairs, out between the files of men facing outward, up to the scaffold, showing something in his face and step which in a better man might have passed for heroism.'

"How contemptible! His courage and fortitude shone out in spite of the infamous position in which his enemies sought to place him, but even the eyes blinded by prejudice and the callous hearts around him could not fail to note, though they could not appreciate, the lofty spirit of the man.

"From the little room in the third story, designated 'No. 9 - Wirz, H., Captain C.S.A.,' he was marched to the scaffold, erected in one corner of the prison yard. Here he took a seat on a small stool, immediately under the gaping noose swaying over him. A soldier stood at shoulder arms on either corner of the platform, and four companies, one each from the 195th and 214th Pennsylvania, and two from the 9th Regiment of Hancock's Corps, formed a hollow square around the scaffold. Fathers Boyle and Wiget never left his side until the last moment. Indeed, when the

[55] *Ibid.*, pp. 38, 39.
[56] Williamson, pp. 139-141.

noose was adjusted his face wore a smile and he was still talking to Father Boyle.

"For eighteen minutes he was compelled to sit and listen to the reading of the findings and sentence - the enumeration of the crimes with which he was charged, while on the housetops and in the branches of the trees in the Capitol grounds men and boys crowed, all eager to witness the ghastly spectacle; and their inhuman shouts, and brutal jests about the 'dead-line,' pendant above him, could be heard by Wirz, who sat apparently calm and unmoved, save when amid the groans and outcries, a voice called out 'Hang the scoundrel.' As this reached his ears he turned quickly, with a defiant look in the direction from which the sound proceeded, then, giving a cool glance on the surroundings, he resumed his self-command, giving his undivided attention to his spiritual advisers.

"At the close of the reading Major Russell asked Wirz if he wished to say anything to the public before the execution. He replied: 'I have nothing to say, only that I am innocent, and will die like a man, my hopes being in the future. I go before my God, the Almighty God, and he will judge between me and you.' At twenty minutes to eleven o'clock Sylvester Ballon kicked away the prop and Henry Wirz passed from life to the dark valley of the shadow of death."[57]

"On the 6th of November, he was informed by General Augur, that he was sentenced to be hanged, and would suffer the penalty of his crimes on the 10th. Wirz received the news of his doom with perfect unconcern, merely remarking, 'Well, I suppose it must be done.' He then went to the door of his cell and called out to General Briscoe, who was confined on the opposite side of his cell, 'General, I am to be hung on Friday.' As General Augur was leaving him he said, 'After I am dead I will come back and haunt all of you.'

"Having been born in the Roman Catholic faith, a priest was sent to him, to prepare him for his end. He received the ministrations of the priest apathetically; expressed no sorrows for his hideous cruelties, scoffed at the United States Government, and on the night before his execution, he remarked to Colonel Baker, that the 'American Eagle was a damned turkey buzzard.' He slept soundly during his last night on earth, but was aroused at three o'clock by his spiritual comforters to engage in prayer, and prepare for the end. He listened to the prayers, insisted he was innocent, and would not forgive any one.

"On the morning of the 10th of November, the preparations were all complete, one hundred civilian spectators were present, and a battalion of soldiers. The latter were arranged in a hollow square about the gallows. This instrument of justice was made of heavy timber, and presented a somewhat weather-worn appearance. Its extreme height was twenty-two feet; the platform was twelve feet from the ground, and twelve feet square; in the centre of this platform, and elevated one foot above it, was the fatal drop; a chair stood upon it, and from the stout beam overhead dangled a noose of fine manilla rope.

"At fifteen minutes past ten o'clock, the prisoner emerged from his cell, walking between father Boyle and Wiget. He had a loose robe of black cambric thrown over his person, carried his right arm in a sling, had no manacles of any kind upon his person, and walked with a light, careless step, toward the gallows. He ran briskly up the steps, and walked at once toward the chair, and seated himself directly under the fatal noose. The roofs of the surrounding houses were packed with people, who looked in upon the punishment of the monster.

"Major Russell took his station directly in front of him, and read in a clear, loud tone, the charges, specifications, findings, and sentence. During this long reading, Wirz listened, shaking his head and smiling occasionally. No shade of sorrow or remorse flitted across his countenance. The reading ended, he was asked if he had anything to say; he replied with a broad grin 'No, I have nothing to say to the public.'

"The priests whispered their parting admonitions; the black cap was drawn over the face of the condemned; he was told to stand up; the rope was fastened around his neck, and his legs and arms secured with cords. At twenty minutes to eleven o'clock, Major Russell made a signal, and on the instant the trap fell, and the demon of Andersonville was swinging between heaven and earth. The clatter of the falling trap was answered by a loud yell from the crowd congregated outside of the prison walls. A few convulsive jerks, and life was extinct. At eleven o'clock the corpse was taken down, examined by the physicians, and officially declared dead. It was then placed in a coffin, and given to Father Boyle. And thus ended the career of a faithful servant of the Devil and Jeff. Davis."[58]

---

[57] *Ibid.*, pp. 141-143.

[58] *Demon of Andersonville*, pp. 118, 119.

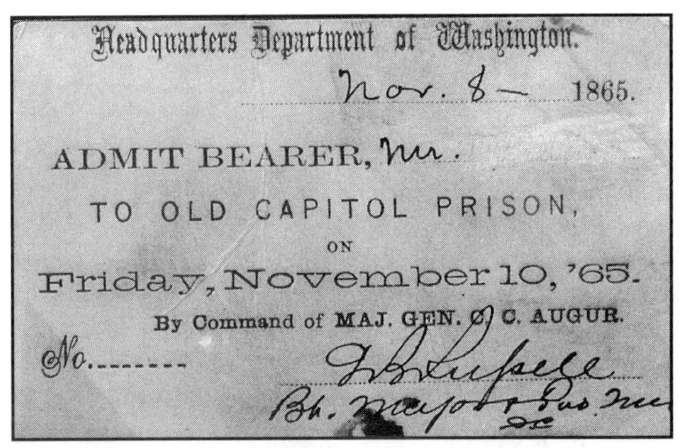

Headquarters Department of Washington.

Nov. 8 — 1865.

ADMIT BEARER, Mr.

TO OLD CAPITOL PRISON,

ON

Friday, November 10, '65.

By Command of MAJ. GEN. C. C. AUGUR.

No.--------

There were issued 250 passes by the government to allow the bearer to enter the Old Capitol Prison to witness this execution. They were printed on yellow cards and the one in the author's collection was issued two days before the execution:

> *Headquarters Department of Washington*
> *Nov. 8 1865.*
> Admit Bearer, *Mr.*____________
> *TO OLD CAPITOL PRISON*
> *FRIDAY, NOVEMBER 10, 1865*
> *By Command of Major General C. C. Augur*
> *No* _____ *Signed G. P. Russell*
> *Bvt. Major, Prov. Mar.*

The person who had been issued this pass had scratched his name off so as to make it illegible.[59]

Besides these 250 spectators, the hanging was witnessed by members of the press from papers around the world. Around the prison yard at the arsenal grounds, where the four Lincoln conspirators had been hanged four months earlier, were dozens of people who had climbed high into elm trees that they might catch some glimpse of the proceedings. As Wirz made his way up the scaffold, the four companies of Federal troops chanted "Wirz, remember Andersonville." Major Russell, almost apologetically, said he was sorry as he adjusted the noose around Wirz' neck, but added that he was only following orders. Wirz said, "I know what orders are, Major. And I am being hanged for obeying them." Because of poor technique or intention, the fall did not break Wirz' neck. In those days, when hangings were more-or-less common, most people knew, by computing the weight of the prisoner, how much slack was needed to break the neck. Several stories are extant about how prisoners asked for more slack so as to ensure that the neck would break. Nevertheless, in Wirz' case, his neck did not break and he had to slowly strangle to death over a period of several seconds when the trap door sprung at 10:32 a.m.

After Wirz' execution, in his cell were found a *French Missal, Spiritual Conferences*, two volumes of Bulwer's *Caxtons, The Jews of Verona*, and several books on religion and metaphysics. These were the books Schade's grandson, Frederick Louis McCoy said were found.[60] The *New York Tribune* dated November 13, 1865, said, "All the heritage left by Wirz consisted of four books - a Bible, a Testament, an A'Kempis, and Tschoke's Meditations on Life. In the well-worn Bible, formerly in use in some hospital, he wrote just before going to execution:

"My Dear Wife: This Bible I send to you. You see the marks where I left off reading. God bless you. Keep this Bible to remember me. H. Wirz. Nov. 10, 1865.

The Testament bears the inscription, 'To Cora from her father, H. Wirz. (Cora was his only daughter.) The inscription in the Tschoke is, 'To my dear children, Susan and Cornelia.' These were his step-children."

Also found was this letter thanking his counsel, Louis Schade:

> *Old Capitol Prison*
> *Washington, D.C., Nov. 10, 1865*
>
> *Mr. Louis Schade*
>
> *Dear Sir: It is no doubt the last time that I address myself to you. What I have said to you often as often I repeat. Accept my thanks, my sincere, heartfelt thanks, for all you have done for me. May God reward you, I cannot. I still have something more to ask of you, and I am confident you will not refuse to receive my dying request. Please help my poor family - my dear wife and children. War, cruelest, has swept everything from me, and today my wife and children are beggars. My life is demanded as an atonement. I am willing to give it, and hope that after a while, I will be judged differently from what I am now. If any one ought to come to the relief of my family, it is the people of the South, for whose sake I have sacrificed all. I know you will excuse me for troubling you again. Farewell, dear sir.*
>
> *May God bless you.*
> *Yours thankfully,*
> *H. Wirz"*[61]

---

[59] Author's collection.
[60] Edwin W. Beitzell, Editor, "Chronicles of St. Mary's," Monthly Bulletin of the St. Mary's County Historical Society, August 1961, p. 194.
[61] *Ibid.*

Wirz bid farewell to his family with this letter:

*Old Capitol Prison*
*Washington, D.C., Nov. 10, 1865*

*My dearest Wife and Children:*

*When these lines reach you the hand who wrote them will be stiff and cold. In a few hours from now I shall be dead. Oh, if I could express myself as I wish, if I could tell you what I have suffered when I thought about you and the children! I must leave you without the means to live, to the miseries of a cold cruel world. Lise, do not grieve, do not despair. We will meet again in a better world. Console yourself, think as I do - that I die innocent. Who knows better than you that all these tales of cruelties and murders are infamous lies, and why should I not say it? A great many do call me hard-hearted, because I tell them that I am not guilty, that I have nothing to confess. Oh, think for a moment how the thought that must suffer and die innocent must sustain me in that last terrible hour; that when I shall stand before my Maker I can say, 'Lord, of these things you know I am not guilty. I have sinned often and rebelled against Thee, oh, let my unmerited death be an atonement.' Lise, I die reconciled. I die, I hope, as a Christian. This is His holy will that I should die, and therefore let us say with Christ, 'Thy will, O Lord, be done.'*

*I hardly know what to say. Oh, let me beg you, do not give way to despair. Think that I am gone to my Father, to your Father, to the Father of all, and that there I hope to meet you. Live for the dear children. Oh, do take good care of Cora. Kiss her for me. Kiss Susan and Cornelia, and tell them to live so that we may meet again in the heaven above the skies; tell them that my last thoughts, my last prayer shall be for them.*

*You ask me about Cora's schooling. My dear wife, you must do now as you think best. In regard to your going to Europe, I would advise you to wait until you hear from them. I have written to my father; if he should be dead, my brother, I hope is still alive. I send you his address. You had better get a certificate of our marriage; also of Cora's birth, and have it approved before a magistrate. If you should go to Europe you would need it. I shall hand this letter to Mr. Schade, who will send it to you with some other papers and books; this is all I can leave you; but now I can leave you something more, something better; my blessing.*

*God bless you all and protect you. God give you what you stand in need of, and grant that you all so live that when you die you can say, 'Lord, Thou callest me, here I am.' And now, farewell wife, children, all, I will and must close, farewell, farewell; God be with us.*

*Your unfortunate husband and father,*
*H. Wirz"*[62]

The day after the execution, the commanding general of the Department of Washington sent the following letter to the Adjutant General of the Army:

*Official:*
*E. D. Townsend*
*Assistant Adjutant General*
*Headquarters Department of Washington*

*Sir. I have the honor to report that the sentence and orders of the President in the case of Henry Wirz, as promulgated in General Court-martial Orders No. 607, dated War Department, Adjutant General's Office, Washington, November 6, 1865, have been duly executed (between the hours of 10 and 11 a.m.) yesterday, November 10, and his body has been interred by the side of Atzerodt, in the arsenal grounds.*
*I am, general, very respectfully, your obedient servant,*

*C. C. Augur*
*Major Gen. Vols., Commanding Department*
*The Adjutant General of the Army"*[63]

It will be remembered that, after Wirz' marriage at Cadiz, Kentucky, he inherited two small step-children, Susie and Cornelia Wolfe. Wirz and his wife had their own daughter on February 25, 1855, whom they named Cora. She was but ten years old when her father was executed. "She well remembers the agonizing grief of her mother during that awful November of 1865, and how she begged for the body of her husband and was refused it by the authorities.

[62] "Andersonville, A letter to His Wife," *New York Tribune*, p. 1.
[63] *Wirz Trial*, p. 815.

They bluntly informed the weeping woman that she could not have the remains; that they had concluded to bury the body by the side of Mrs. Surratt and Herold, the 'Lincoln conspirators,' in the prison-yard. This was done."[64]

"Mr. Louis Schade made application, in behalf of Wirz' family, for his remains; and Mrs. John F. Tucker, of the sixth ward, undertook on behalf of the family, to arrange for his interment. The necessary order was given on Wednesday last, and the remains were delivered to Mr. Augustus Burgdor, undertaker, and by him placed in a handsome Mahogany coffin and carried to the vault at Mount Olivet Cemetery, where they remained until yesterday, and in the meantime, Mr. Schade, considering it a matter of duty addressed the President the following letter:

*Washington, D.C.*
*February 26,1869*
*To His Excellency Andrew Johnson*
*President of the United States*

*Sir:*

*When you gave the order to have the remains of Captain Wirz delivered to me it was your intention that I should get the whole body and not a part of it. The coffin, however, which was delivered to me at the Arsenal contains only the frame, the head, right hand and the spine being missing. If they had been retained for the benefit and in the interest of Science, I would certainly have no objection to it, nor would the relations of Captain Wirz in whose benefit I act. But the skull and some other parts of his body had been exhibited at the Old Capitol Prison by a discharged soldier for money. For that reason, and no other I respectfully ask you to give an order that the missing parts of the remains of Captain Wirz, said to be at the Surgeon General's Office, may be delivered to me for interment along with the other parts on Sunday afternoon at 3 o'clock.*

*I am, your obedient servant,*
*Louis Schade*

"No answer was received to this up to yesterday and at 2 o'clock in the afternoon a number of persons assembled at St. Peter's Church and took carriages to Mount Olivet Cemetery, where they arrived just before 3 o'clock. There were on the ground about 50 persons, including the Reverend Father Boyle, Mr. Schade, Mr. Therkeld? and a number of them having been - at the door of the receiving vault - Mr. Schade in behalf of the daughters of the deceased placed on the coffin a handsome wreath. Reverend Father Boyle read the services of the Church and the remains were carried to the grave in the Southeast portion of the grounds, where the services were concluded. Reverend Father Boyle remarked that he had fulfilled a long-promised request in conducting the service.

"I have no record that the missing parts of Wirz' body were returned by the Government, but they may have been. Louis Schade"[65]

The grave was marked by "... a small marble block inscribed with the name 'Wirz' on the upper face."

In the fall of 1864, Captain Winder was assigned as Chief Quartermaster of Prisons in Georgia, a charge which included the prison at Andersonville and the officers' prison at Macon, with headquarters at Andersonville. In January, 1865, he was promoted to major, sent to Columbia and made Chief Quartermaster of prisons east of the Mississippi River. "Soon after this the general exchange of prisoners took place. Columbia was evacuated and I was ordered to Salisbury, N. C. I had been there but a short time when I was relieved of duty with the prison department and ordered to report in Richmond, and was there awaiting orders to Texas. At this time, however, General Daniel Ruggles was assigned to duty as Commissary-General of Prisoners, and at his earnest solicitation I was temporarily assigned to duty with him as his chief quartermaster, in order to furnish him with such information as he might need in regard to my department. General Ruggles and myself left Richmond the night of the evacuation. As soon as we got to Danville he ordered me to Augusta, Ga., at which place I was paroled, and thus ended my connection with the prison department."[66]

While commanding a wagon train moving supplies and prisoners from the threatening path of Sherman's Army, Winder and his train were captured at Augusta, Georgia. One of Dick Winder's last duties for the Confederacy was his assignment in charge of returning all properties that had been removed from Federal prisoners in the Confederate prisons east of the Mississippi.

Dick Winder was paroled on the 2nd of May, 1865, at Augusta, by General Fry under the convention between General William T. Sherman, of the U.S. forces, and General Joseph E. Johnston, of the Confederate forces. He re-

---

64

65 Rutherford, pp. 58, 59.

66 *O.R.*, VIII, pp. 734, 735.

turned to Accomac county and reported to John Sample, the captain commanding the Federal troops there. Though he was assured that he was covered under the Sherman-Johnston Convention, he was apprehensive. With the newspapers full of accounts of post-war arrests and knowing that preparations were being made for the trial of his friend, Wirz, two months after the war, Dick Winder feared arrest by the authorities. This was a letter sent by Winder to his friend, George T. Garrison, who was his lawyer.

*Richmond, May 5, 1865*

*Mr. George T. Garrison, Accomac County, Va.:*

*Dear Sir:*

*Having an idea of leaving the United States, and unwilling to leave myself connected with any transaction which could by any possibility be tortured into any reflection upon myself, I give you the following facts: Some time during the summer of 1864, General Stoneman and his command, while on excursion through the State of Georgia, were captured and the privates were sent as prisoners of war to Andersonville, Ga. Owing to the fact that they had been pillaging and stealing everything that they could lay their hands on from the citizens of Georgia, General J. H. Winder ordered all species of property found in their possession to be taken from them and deposited in my hands as post quartermaster. This order was executed by the commandant of prison. I was then instructed to return all property identified to original and rightful owners and to hold the balance subject to orders. I have thus returned all identified property, and in obedience to orders have the balance on hand. Knowing the bitter feelings of the Federals to any one connected with the prison department, I have not considered it advisable at present to call the attention of any Federal officer to these facts or to turn over said property to them for their action in the matter, but at the same time am unwilling to hold them without a proper explanation to be used in my defense hereafter in case any charges are brought against me. Some of the property evidently belongs to citizens of Georgia, while other of it was evidently the property of the prisoners themselves. No list of prisoners' names from whom these things were taken was ever furnished me, and consequently I can give no information as to the individual ownership. I place these facts and property in your hands, subject to your discretion, and in order that, as a friend of mine, you can protect me from any complaints which may be brought against me in the matter. Any of the officers stationed at Andersonville at the time of this transaction will confirm my statement, as will also my clerks. All other property in my hands belonging to prisoners of war has been turned over to them through the proper channel, the moneys through the hands of Captain Thomas R. Stewart, Company G, First Maryland Regiment, to Colonel Ould, agent of exchange, and other property through the commandant of prison at Andersonville. Hoping that it will not be asking too much of a favor to protect me as far as in your power in this matter,*

*I am, your very true friend,*
*R. B. Winder*

*P.S. -- Enclosed find W. H. Hatch's receipt for Federal funds and Wirz' receipt for other articles, viz, thirty-nine watches and parts of same, four teaspoons, one tablespoon, two forks, one lot of trash too worthless to enumerate....*

*R. B. W. "*[67]

Dick Winder stated that, on August 30th, he had: "... the receipt of the assistant agent of exchange, Captain Hatch, for all moneys in my hands belonging to prisoners of war; Captain Wirz' receipt for their watches which were in my possession (General Winder after his arrival at Andersonville ordered all prisoners' watches returned, and, if my memory serves me rightly, no sum of money under $100 was taken from them). I have also Lieutenant Davis' receipt for all prisoners' clothing, &c., sent to Andersonville and issued by Lieutenant Davis during Captain Wirz' extreme illness there. The boxes sent to prisoners I never had anything to do with. They were always turned over to commandants of prisons."[68]

These personal properties and receipts of the prisoners were given by Winder to Garrison. "By a strange consistency of events, even while the trial of one of the principals in this transaction was occurring at Washington in 1865, a police detective captured from a man, a friend of R. B. Winder, on board of a James River steam-boat, the two identical sacks with the watches therein."[69]

On September 11th, the provost marshal of Norfolk wrote to the Provost-Marshal-General of the Department of

[67] *O.R.*, VII, pp. 534, 534.
[68] *O.R.*, VIII, p. 735.
[69] Spencer, p. 74.

Virginia and said: "I have the honor to herewith forward a true copy of statement of R. B. Winder, assistant quartermaster (late Confederate States), in regard to watches, &c., belonging to Federal prisoners which were confined in Andersonville prison, Ga.; also copies of receipts from W. H. Hatch, agent of exchange, and H. Wirz, captain, commanding prison. On the 10th of the present month my assistant and chief detective found in the possession of George T. Garrison (citizen) a box containing thirty-four old watches, which he (Mr. Garrison) states that he received from Mr. Winder. The original receipt states that there were thirty-nine watches, but only thirty-four can be found. Mr. Garrison lives on the Eastern Shore, and claims to be counsel for the defense of Mr. Winder, who is now confined in the Old Capitol Prison at Washington, D.C. I would respectfully ask what disposition I shall make of Mr. Garrison, watches, &c., and original statement and receipts."

The response was: "I would respectfully suggest that the watches and property recovered be turned over to Bvt. Brig. Gen. John E. Mulford, Assistant Agent of Exchange for the United States, who now has charge of money and property belonging to Federal prisoners of war. The only criminality that appears to attach to Garrison in this transaction is the fact that on receiving the property from Winder he did not promptly notify and turn it over to the U.S. military authorities."[70]

Captain Samuel Gilmore, of the 39th Illinois volunteers, who was on duty at Norfolk, Virginia, was a witness for the prosecution and testified: "I am on duty at Norfolk, Virginia. I did, while on duty, make a seizure of property in the hands of one Garrison.

"Q . What were the circumstances?

"A. On the 10th of September of this year I sent men to search the passengers on the Richmond boats. The object of the search was to find some watches that had been stolen. The men came back with a box of watches that had been taken from one Garrison. They were watches that were taken from the Stoneman raiders at Andersonville; Garrison came on with the men. That was his representation. It is George T. Garrison, of Accomac county, Virginia. He stated at that time that he was acting as counsel for Richard B. Winder. There were thirty-four watches; also some other trinkets, silver spoons and forks, and some watch chains and lockets. There were some photographs or pictures. There were some two or three ambrotypes; I do not remember the exact number. I recognize the article now handed me as one of the things that I saw at the time in the box.

"The Judge Advocate: This is a watch chain with a medal attached to it, which is about the only evidence seeming to connect the plunder with our federal prisoners. The watches were marked in no way, and I cannot introduce them in evidence, but this medal bears the inscription, 'Darius Morris, company A, 169th New York volunteers, Rensselaer county, New York;' on the reverse is, 'Abraham Lincoln, President of the United States, war of 1861.'

"Q. Is the paper now handed to you one that you received at that time?

"A. It is one of the papers that I received from Garrison.

"The paper, of which the following is a copy, was offered in evidence, and is as follows:

"Received from R. B. Winder, A. Q. M., this 1st day of July, 1864, the following lot of property belonging to federal prisoners, to wit:

Silver watch, No 12,252; R. W. Kelley.
Do............ 11,697; N. R. Leaver.
Brass watch..... 37; J. Champany.
Silver watch.... 13,037; N. J. Smith.
Do.............26,326; J. G. Blocke.
Do.............23,956; J. D. Wolfe.
Do............ 8,771; D. Bilman.
Do............ 546; F. Foster.
Do............ 161; Jacob Metzger.
Do.............14,554; H. Mansfield.
Brass watch and pencil; Nottingham.

H. Wirz.
Captain Commanding Prison
Camp Sumter Andersonville, Ga.

[70] *O.R.*, VIII, pp. 744, 745.

"I have compared the numbers on the watches with the numbers on the list. I did not find the one corresponding with the other.

"The Judge Advocate. I submit this document to show that the property here referred to passed into the hands of the prisoner, since which time it has not been heard of, and the property found in the hands of R. B. Winder, last September, is not the property herein enumerated.

"Cross-examin[ation] by Counsel:

"Q. Do I understand you to say that you searched the passengers on the Richmond boats in September last?

"A. We searched the passengers who came down from Richmond and City Point on the 10th of last month for a lot of property. I had received a telegram from the provost marshal at City Point that there had been a heavy robbery committed there on the night of the 9th, and he wished me to search the passengers on the Richmond boat for this property, which consisted of watches and jewelry.

"By the Judge Advocate: Garrison came down from Richmond on one of the boats. I did not arrest Winder; he was arrested, I think, before that. I think he lives in the neighborhood of Mr. Garrison; I am not certain.

"By the Court: I was serving in the capacity of provost marshal..."[71]

Dick Winder lived on the Eastern Shore, undisturbed, until the 9th of July. On that day, he went before the provost-marshal and took the oath as required to receive a parole as a loyal citizen of the United States. He received his certificate of parole marked "No. 3," which was duly certified and delivered to him. He continued to live unmolested and unquestioned as a paroled prisoner of war.

During the summer of 1865, many of the officers who were assigned to duties within the Confederate prison system were fearful of arrest. Some of Dick Winder's family and in-laws tried to make an attempt to warn him that his arrest was imminent. Dick Winder's sister, Mary Catherine, had married Major Charles Howard of Baltimore. His mother's father was Francis Scott Key. Charles's brother, McHenry Howard wrote *Recollections of a Maryland Confederate Soldier and Staff Officer*. McHenry Howard writes, "In the early Summer my father and mother looked about for some retired place where they could spend a few months in quiet with their reunited family and they fixed on Cobb's Island, ten miles out in the Atlantic off the coast of the Eastern Shore of Virginia. Shortly after our return to Baltimore, in October I think, one morning a lady, closely veiled, drove to our house on Cathedral Street and after a few minutes private conversation with my father and mother drove as mysteriously away. She had stopped on her way from Washington to New York to say that she had received private information in Washington that both Captain William Sidney Winder, a son and aide de camp of Brigadier-General John H. Winder, commandant of Confederate prisons, and Captain Richard B. Winder, a cousin and who had been quartermaster at the Andersonville prison, were to be arrested, as Captain Wirtz, commanding at Andersonville, had been. She was on her way to warn the former in New York, and as the wife of my brother Charles Howard was a sister of Captain Richard Winder, she thought we would find a way to notify him on the Eastern Shore of Virginia. I undertook to do this. I had lost a piece of baggage - an old fashioned carpet bag - in our return from Cobb's Island and I thought I could make a fair pretext for my trip in pretending to be looking it up. So I took the next Norfolk steamboat, both on it and on the wharf at Norfolk proclaiming my object, as also on the boat to which I changed to cross the Chesapeake to Cherrystone on the Eastern Shore. But on this boat I found Dr. Alex. Thom who told me I was too late, as Captain Winder had been arrested the evening before. I necessarily continued on to the Eastern Shore and I spent a day at the house of Captain Winder's sister, Mrs. Kerr, in Eastville, where he had been, and to this day I have a vivid recollection of the great variety and excellence of the figs in the large garden."[72]

On the 26th of August, Dick Winder was arrested by two officers of the Federal army, put in manacles and confined in the Accomac County jail. Winder wrote, on August 30th, from the Accomac County jail to Major N. Church, the Acting Assistant Adjutant-General of the Chipman Commission, asking to be paroled or to remain in custody on the Eastern Shore with enough freedom to allow him to continue to attend to his personal endeavors.

"Sir; I know not what charges have been preferred against me, causing my arrest, but, as I was paroled under Generals Sherman's and Johnston's terms of agreement, came home, took the required oath of allegiance to the United States, and am confident that no conduct of mine since has rendered me liable to any charges, I must conclude that my connection with the prison at Andersonville, Ga., is the reason of my arrest. When I came to Virginia

[71] *Wirz Trial*, pp.642-644.

[72] McHenry Howard, *Recollections of a Maryland Confederate Soldier and Staff Officer* (Baltimore: Williams & Wilkins Company, 1914; reprint ed., Dayton, Ohio: Morningside Bookshop, 1975), p. 396 n.

and found so much prejudice against the officers who had been stationed at Andersonville, Ga., I determined to quit the country, but domestic troubles of the severest nature caused me at once to hurry home and see after two little helpless and penniless children. After arriving here I determined to make my home in this country, and have been making arrangements with a friend of mine to go into business with me in Baltimore. I merely mention these facts to let you know that it is my fixed purpose to make my home in this country and become, of course, a law-abiding and loyal citizen. If there are charges against me of maltreatment of prisoners, I scorn the imputation and am desirous of meeting them and will meet them fearlessly and with a clear conscience. But, owing to extreme domestic troubles which require my whole attention at this time, I most respectfully ask that either an investigation of the matter be given me at once or that I be paroled, giving my word of honor (or, if you prefer it, security) for my appearance at any time I may be called for, or that I be allowed to remain in custody on the Eastern Shore with sufficient privileges to enable me to attend to my business..."

He then told of the prison and his duties there, ending with: "It is extremely humiliating to be held in prison in manacles, but much more so to be held up to our countrymen as a demon, accused of charges of which you are not guilty."

With this letter he enclosed a group of letters attesting to his character and "... standing as a man," signed by "... nearly every citizen of the town near which I have for the last ten years, before the war, resided, and also all my near neighbors."[73]

This letter was referred to Colonel Chipman who put this endorsement on it on October 25th: "The findings in the Wirz trial inculpate R. B. Winder. I think he ought to be tried for complicity, though there is no evidence of his being a cruel or brutal man."[74]

On the 31st, Winder was taken from the jail and carried to the Old Capitol Prison in Washington. He was not told of any charges or allegations at that time nor was he told during the time of his imprisonment in the Old Capitol Prison as of the 13th of November. Thus, for several months while he was in prison, his business was being neglected and his wife and small children were without a husband and father.

In relation to Winder, Judge-Advocate-General Holt reported to Secretary Stanton on November 3rd; "While the evidence at the trial of Wirz was deemed by the court to implicate him in the conspiracy against the lives of all Federal prisoners in rebel hands, no such specific overt acts of violation of the laws of war are as yet fixed upon him as to make it expedient to prefer formal charges and bring him to trial."[75]

On November 16th, Holt recommended that Winder be released and allowed to resume his former status as prisoner of war on parole. On November 23rd, the ex-Confederate General J. E. Johnston wrote to Lieutenant-General Grant and asked him to intercede on Dick Winder's behalf. Grant, on December 21st, wrote: "In my opinion the paroles given to the surrendered armies lately in rebellion against the Government should be held inviolate, unless in cases where all rules of civilized warfare have been violated, and in such case of such charges an immediate trial should be had. I would respectfully recommend, therefore, that Captain Winder either have an immediate trial or that he be released on bonds for his appearance when called on for trial."[76]

On November 22nd, Dick Winder received a message from the Secretary of War that stated that his petition had been rejected and "... that they had the matter under consideration." Dick Winder said that he had good reason to believe that this application had been brought up before the Cabinet and that it would be brought up before them on the 24th. Winder said his counsel, William Linn Brown, "... who is one of the counselors of the Supreme Court of the United States" thought that they would act favorably. "I have good reasons for knowing that there has been an order to convene a military commission to try me and I also know that the order has been suspended."[77]

On November 29th, the President directed that Dick Winder should be conveyed to Richmond under suitable guard and delivered to Major General A. H. Terry, commanding the Department of Virginia. By December 2nd at 3 p.m. he had been sent to Richmond and the necessary papers containing the charges would follow by mail as soon as they were received from the Judge-Advocate-General.

On December 12th, J. Holt, the Judge-Advocate-General, wrote to Maj. Gen. Terry, saying, "I am instructed by the honorable Secretary of War to request you not to proceed with the trial until you shall be furnished with such testimony in the case as is in the possession of the Government, as well as with the specific charges, in case it shall be

---

[73] *O.R.*, VII, pp. 730-735.
[74] *O.R.*, VIII, p. 736.
[75] *Ibid.*, p. 783.
[76] *O.R.*, VII, 814, 815.
[77] *Ibid.*, p. 817.

determined to prepare the same at this Bureau."[78]

When the Confederate forces evacuated Richmond in April, Grant ordered the 20th New York State Militia, with the 24th Massachusetts Volunteers, to jointly assume the martial control of Richmond under the command of Brigadier General M. R. Patrick, Provost Marshal General. Captain J. M. Schoonmaker was ordered to take general charge of both Libby Prison and Castle Thunder.

In early 1866, Captain J. M. Schoonmaker was relieved, at his own request, of the command of these military prisons by Lieutenant Edward Hunter. One of the prisoners under Schoonmaker's charge in Libby was Dick Winder. He stated, "... one of the most valued of my treasured mementoes of the war is a letter received from that prisoner three days before I was relieved by Lieutenant Hunter. Its references for a personal nature are very dear to me, while the sentiments so elegantly and eloquently voiced are such as well warrant its introduction here:

*Richmond, Va., January 26, 1866*

*Captain J. M. Schoonmaker*
*Twentieth New York*

*Captain:*

*As you are about to retire from military life to the much more pleasant duties of a peaceful occupation, allow me to tender you my warm well wishes for your future, and to sincerely thank you for the kindness and consideration which has characterized the treatment I have received while a prisoner in your hands. In the present state of our country's troubles, when excitement and virulent prejudice are rampant, it is gratifying and consoling to know that there are many men - officers in our late contending armies - who have thrown aside their vindictiveness and are willing to do justice to all. To these same true and tried men, as in the hour of conflict, our country will again have to turn. We can then hope for peace - actual peace - good will and a national brotherhood.*

*R. B. Winder*"[79]

By March 10th, 1866, Winder had not been brought to trial because "Mr. Ambrose Spencer, who professes to be well informed in regard to the criminal conduct alleged against Winder, has given distinct assurances from time to time that he would furnish such details in regard to this man's offenses, with names of witnesses, &c., as would enable the Government to put him on trial, but as yet he has not done so."[80]

Dick Winder was released from his cell in Libby prison by the following order:

*Hd. Qrs. Dept. of Virginia*
*Richmond, Virginia April 11, 1866*
*Special Orders*
*Extract # 84*
*II Pursuant to instruction from the Secretary of War, Adjutant General's Office, Washington April 10th, 1866. R. B. Winder is hereby released from confinement at Libby Prison, Richmond, Virginia.*

*By Command of Bvt. Maj. Gen. Turner*
*Official William L. Hulbert,*
*Assistant Adjutant General*
*J. Kensington*
*1st. Lt. 11th U. S. Infantry*
*Com'd'g Mil. Prisons*[81]

When Richmond was evacuated on Sunday, the 2nd of April, Captain W. Sidney Winder was almost certainly on board the presidential train as it left late that night on the 140-mile trip to Danville. The presidential party arrived at mid-afternoon the next day and Danville became the temporary capital of the Confederacy until April 11th. At that time, the President again left by train for Greensboro and other points south. Since the railroad tracks leading south from Greensboro had been severed by the raiders of General Stoneman, Captain M. H. Clark, Chief Clerk of the Executive Office made up a train of wagons, carriages and ambulances. On April 15th, the President left Greensboro accompanied by an escort of Tennessee cavalry commanded by Brigadier General George G. Dibrell and a com-

[78] *O.R.*, VIII, p. 834.
[79] J. M. Schoonmaker, "Annals of the War, "Philadelphia Weekly Times, July 24, 1880.
[80] *O.R.*, VIII, pp. 887, 888.
[81] Document in author's collection.

pany of Kentucky cavalry under Captain Given Campbell to act as scouts, guides, and couriers. Secretaries Breckenridge and Mallory and Postmaster General Reagan rode on horseback with the President, while Secretary Benjamin, Attorney General Davis, Secretary of the Treasury Trenholm and some of the older army officers, including General Cooper, rode in the wagons. Carried by this group of wagons were $35,000 in gold coins, the official papers of the Confederacy, and the necessary provisions and baggage for the trip.

At Abbeville, South Carolina, on May 2nd, President Davis, Secretary of State Benjamin, Postmaster General Reagan (who was also Acting Secretary of the Treasury), and former Secretary of the Navy Mallory, accompanied by the President's Staff and a small escort, separated from the rest of the wagons, leaving behind what was called the baggage train. It was in this remaining baggage train that Captain W. Sidney Winder rode. In fact, troops and individuals left and rejoined this wagon train almost continually as it wound through South Carolina and Georgia.

Captain M. H. Clark, Chief Clerk of the Executive Office and Quartermaster Watson Van Benthuysen, assisted by a small number of highly-trusted officers and men, immediately followed the President with his baggage, the remaining papers of the President and Cabinet, and the two boxes of money amounting, originally, to $35,000 when they had been placed in the Presidents's ambulance at Greensboro. At Washington, Georgia, President Davis performed his last official act as President by appointing Captain M. H. Clark Acting Treasurer. On May 6th, near Sandersville, Georgia, after several men and units had separated from the baggage train, Captain Clark and his guard with the now $25,000 were on their way to Tallahassee or Madison, Florida. There they were to unite and buy a boat to go to the Bahamas, Cuba or Texas.

"If, by interference of the Federals, Davis were prevented from uniting his small escort with the baggage train, the understanding was that Captain Clark, who was in charge of the train, would take the money, official papers, and baggage to Cuba or to Mexico."

"Captain Clark had with him a group of the most trusted young men of the Confederacy, members of prominent families, some of whom were related by marriage or friendship to the Confederate President. They were Captain Watson Van Benthuysen, Captain Alfred C. Van Benthuysen, and Captain Jefferson Davis Van Benthuysen. Also in the group were five 'Eastern Shoremen' of Maryland - Captain Fred Emory, William Sidney Winder, John White Scott, William Elveno Dickinson, and Tench Francis Tilghman - two scouts from Captain Given Campbell's company, and five negro servants, including Watson, the President's cook."

At first, the train consisted of one four-mule wagon and two ambulances, but one of the ambulances was soon abandoned. The train was carefully guarded during the night by the men, who served in relays of two. Captain Clark and his guards were making good progress toward Florida the first week or so of May. The baggage train passed over the Ocmulgee River on May 11th. "Winder was very ill for several days and had to be carried in the ambulance." Tilghman said they ate blackberries on their way and that their destination was most likely Cuba and "thence God only knows." On May 15th, they entered Florida, ignorant of the fact that Davis had been captured and was on his way to prison. They were fearful because Florida was occupied and, if they were not paroled in ten days were to be outlawed. On May 22nd, after learning that the President had been captured, "Captain Clark announced to the Van Benthuysen brothers and several of the Marylanders who were in his tent, that the capture of President Davis placed upon him, as Chief Clerk of the President's office, personal responsibility for the safekeeping of the Davis papers and baggage, and as Acting Treasurer of the Confederate Government with 'verbal orders from the Secretary of the Treasury Reagan,' the care of the balance of some $25,000 remaining in the Confederate Treasury. He proposed to hide the papers and baggage in Florida until he could return for them. He would pay to members of the guarding party a fair salvage from the money in recognition of the risk and trouble borne by them." He would place the remaining funds in England to await orders or funds for the defense of the President and Cabinet members who might be tried by the United States government.

This announcement produced a heated discussion between Clark and Watson Van Benthuysen. The latter declared that the money had been turned over to him as a quartermaster fund, that he had exclusive control of it, that the Confederate Government had ceased to exist, and that all quartermasters and financial agents would appropriate such funds as remained in their care. Van Benthuysen told Clark that he had consulted his two brothers and the five Marylanders and, with their approval, he would lay aside one quarter of the entire fund for the benefit of Mrs. Davis and her children, and that he would divide the balance equally among those who had guarded the funds, papers, and baggage. This decision was reached on May 23rd. The money was divided according to the following schedule:

| | |
|---|---|
| Captain Watson Van Benthuysen<br>400 gold sovereigns at $4.85 | $1,940 |
| Captain Alfred C. Van Benthuysen<br>400 gold sovereigns at $4.85 | $1,940 |
| Captain Jefferson Davis Van Benthuysen<br>400 gold sovereigns at $4.85 | $1,940 |
| Captain Fred Emory<br>400 gold sovereigns at $4.85 | $1,940 |
| W. E. Dickinson<br>400 gold sovereigns at $4.85 | $1,940 |
| W. S. Winder<br>400 gold sovereigns at $4.85 | $1,940 |
| T. F. Tilghman<br>400 gold sovereigns at $4.85 | $1,940 |
| John W. Scott<br>400 gold sovereigns at $4.85 | $1,940 |
| Captain M. H. Clark<br>400 gold sovereigns at $4.85 | $1,940 |
| To each of the above, $55 for traveling expenses | $ 495 |
| One month's pay to Captain Clark | $ 125 |
| To Howard and Staffin, (Davis's cook and guard) each $250 | $ 500 |
| To five negro servants $20 each | $ 100 |
| Miscellaneous | $ 250 |
| Total | $18,930 |

It was the understanding of Clark, Dickinson, Scott, Tilghman, and Winder that Watson Van Benthuysen retained the balance of 1,400 gold sovereigns at $4.85 ($6,790) for Mrs. Davis and her children. They buried the papers in one trunk and two chests "... at midnight in a cow stable." They then split up with all their worldly possessions with them and rode away to seek paroles. Tench Tilghman and Sidney Winder stopped overnight at "Kanapaha," the plantation of Thomas Evans Haile, eight miles southwest of Gainesville. "El" Dickinson and John Scott were accommodated a quarter mile away at the home of Haile's brother-in-law, James Chesnut. The four Confederate officers stopped at Gainesville and swam in the nine-mile-long Sante Fe Lake northeast of Gainesville. They arrived at Jacksonville on May 26th.

"Today we have been subjected to a trial such as I had hoped never to have been called on to endure," wrote Tilghman. "We were halted by negro pickets and taken to a tent where our names were registered by a negro sergeant. We were then stripped of our revolvers and escorted into town. The remarks of the negro soldiers were unendurable. I feel disgraced and degraded."

Each man kept his $2,000 in the bottom of his pantaloons, which he then stuffed into his boots; the money was not disturbed. They registered at the Taylor House and sold their horses for $50 each. The Marylanders were not allowed in Jacksonville to take the oath of allegiance to the United States but were given a pass to Hilton Head. They waited for a steamer until June 7th and reached Hilton Head, Federal headquarters for the district, on June 8th. They took the oath on the 10th and were "... informed that we were free to go anywhere we chose in the United States." Late that afternoon, they boarded the *S. S. Haze* and started home.[82]

Sid Winder arrived in New York, "... sold the gold for slightly over $3,000 in United States currency, and arrived in Baltimore on 22 June... Shortly after his arrival, he learned that his arrest had been ordered, and he hurriedly departed for Canada... He did not return to Baltimore until after March, 1866... he returned to the practice of law."[83] Sidney spent the twenty-five years immediately following the Civil War trying to disprove the legitimacy of an order supposedly issued by his father, General Winder. This document became infamous as "Order No. 13." This order, allegedly discovered among papers at the prison, was printed in the Northern press time and time again; it was used to inflame anti-Southern sentiment by "proving" General Winder's murderous nature.

Sidney sought the aid of many of General Winder's friends and fellow officers to help clear his father's name. He submitted several of his letters from friends to Samuel B. Davis so that he might include them in his booklet, *Escape of a Confederate Officer From Prison.*

---

[82] Alfred J. Hanna, *Flight into Oblivion* (Richmond, 1938: Johnson Publishing Co.), pp. 38, 39, 88, 108-111, 114-116, 121-124.
[83] Blakey, pp. 203, 204.

"The order, as it appeared in the *Congressional Record* on April 22, 1890, was supposedly as follows:

*Order No. 13*
*Headquarters Military Prison*
*Andersonville, July 27th, 1864*

*The officers on duty and in charge of the Florida Artillery, at the time, will, upon receiving notice that the enemy has approached within seven miles of post, open upon the stockade with grape shot without reference to the situation beyond these lines of defense.*
*John H. Winder,*
*Brig.-Gen. Com."*[84]

Northrop entered, in his diary on August 10th, "Steward Brown, who is an Englishman and not a soldier, on parole, expresses the belief that it was fortunate for prisoners that Stoneman's expedition failed, for it was the intention of Gen. Winder to use the Florida battery on the prison had any considerable Union force approached Andersonville within seven miles, and had so ordered in the regular way in writing, on July 27th."[85] Since this was a diary written within the pen and, therefore, before the post-war controversy, it might lend credence to Order No. 13's existence.

Despite denial about the validity of the order, it and several other versions persisted and were resurrected at every opportunity. "The *Baltimore Herald* of September 23rd, 1887, contained the following dispatch:

Chicago, Ill., September 22nd

The Federal Ex-Prisoners' Association is in session in this city. General Pavey in his address read the following circular issued at Andersonville.

Headquarters
Confederate States Military Prison
Andersonville, Ga., July 27th, 1864

The officers on duty and in charge of the Battery of Florida Artillery, at the time, will, upon receiving notice that the enemy have appeared within seven miles of the post, open fire upon the stockade with grape shot without reference to the situation beyond these lines of defense.

It is better that the last Federal be exterminated than be permitted to burn and pillage the property of loyal citizens, as they will do if allowed to make their escape from prison.

By order of John H. Winder,
Brig.-Gen.
W. S. Winder,
Adjt.-Gen."[86]

These orders differed very materially. One was an "order" and one was a "circular." The circular gave the reason for its being issued in a second paragraph. One had the heading "Headquarters Confederate States Military Prison." One was signed by General Winder, the other by his son, his adjutant-general.

Sid Winder said, "When Gen. Winder went to Andersonville, in June, 1864, he continued the use of the order book and letter book, at Headquarters, as used by Col. Persons, who had been in command. The last General Order issued, by Col. Persons, was No. 44, dated June 14th, 1864. The first General Order issued, by Gen. Winder, was No 45, dated June 17th, 1864 (this was the order assuming command of the post). The last Special Order issued by Col. Persons was No. 103, dated June 16th, 1864. The first Special Order issued by Gen. Winder was 104, dated June 18th, 1864.

"It is clearly-proven by the above statement that there was no such order as No. 13 issued by General Winder. As for myself (W. S. Winder), I am prepared to state, under oath, that I never saw, signed or heard of any such order said to have been issued by me as Adjutant General.

"Captain C. E. Dyke, who commanded the Florida Artillery, in a letter to me (W. S. Winder) dated Tallahassee, Fal., February 7th, 1876, says "...I have not the remotest recollection of ever having received such an order; it was inconsistent with General Winder's character..."

---

[84] Davis, pp. 36, 37.
[85] Northrop, pp. 103, 104.
[86] Davis, p. 37.

The following letter is from E. W. Gamble, Esq., a well-known citizen of Tallahassee, Florida, who was a lieutenant in the Battery of Florida Artillery during the time it was stationed at Andersonville.

Tallahassee, Fla., May 19th, 1890
W. S. Winder
No. 2117 St. Paul Street
Baltimore, Md.:

Sir - Yours of the 4th came while I was away from home, calling my attention to the following order purporting to have been given to the Florida Light Artillery then at Andersonville, Ga.
(Mr. Gamble here quotes Order No. 13).

I have to say so far as I know this is a malicious slander, as no such order was ever given to the Battery, and I feel sure my Captain, Charles E. Dyke, would have made me acquainted of it, as the officers of the company took each a day to be on duty at the guns and it would have been necessary for each of us to have known of such an order.

Yours truly,
E. W. Gamble.

Col. F. B. Pavy, a citizen of Florida, a gentleman well-known and highly esteemed, was first sergeant of the Battery of Florida Artillery while it was stationed at Andersonville, and wrote the following letter:

Savannah, Ga., May 12, 1890
W. S. Winder, Esq.,
Baltimore, Md.:

My Dear Sir - I am in receipt of your esteemed favor of the 4th inst.; my absence caused delay in replying, which I greatly regret.
I am astonished to learn that your good father was charged with the issuance of the order which you quoted. My relations with Captain Dyke and the battery he commanded was, perhaps more close than was ever enjoyed by a soldier occupying my position; while only a sergeant, I acted and performed more the duties of an adjutant, and was, therefore, in a position to learn even of matters that was confidential. I say to you positively, that I never saw such an order, nor did I ever hear of it.
Yours respectfully,
F. B. Pavy

Mr. Jackson Marshall, who was a clerk in Gen. Winder's office, writes as follows:

No. 530 Carey St.
Baltimore, Md.
November 5th, 1887

Capt. W. S. Winder:

My Dear Sir - I have received the papers containing the notice of an address delivered by a General Pavey, before the Federal Ex-Prisoners Association at Chicago, at which he read the following order or circular issued at Andersonville:

(Mr. Marshall here quotes the order as given above).

When your father, Gen. John H. Winder, assumed command at Andersonville, June, 1864, I was a clerk at Headquarters and Gen. Winder retained me in that position, giving me charge of all the books in the office. I remained with him till his death, February, 1865.

I have no recollection of having seen or heard of any such order, and no such order was ever entered on the order book by me. It is only another of the many lies that have been circulated in connection with the treatment of the prisoners of war. I was almost constantly with Gen. Winder, and knew him to be incapable of anything like inhumanity or inconsistent with true nobleness of character. I resided at Madison, Ga., during the war and at Oxford, Ga., for 15 years before, the home of Secretary Lamar to whom I can refer.

Yours truly,
Jackson Marshall.

Dr. R. R. Stevenson writes as follows:

"As Chief Surgeon of the Andersonville Prison Hospital, I can truthfully say that no such order as that referred to ever emanated from Gen. John H. Winder or his subordinates. I never saw or heard of such an order until after the war, and then it was through a partisan press.

In no instance can I find either in the orders issued by Col. Persons or by Gen. Winder, among those in my possession, the heading 'Military Prison,' or 'Confederate States Military Prison.' I have examined their general orders down to No 58 inclusive, and their special orders to No. 114 inclusive. The last general order in my possession issued at Andersonville is No. 58, dated June 30, 1864. The last special order is No 114, date July 1, 1864; but the following letter, dated July 28, 1864, the day after the date of the alleged order No. 13, speaks of special order No. 143, which was issued either on the 27th or 28th of July, 1864."

Camp Sumpter
Andersonville, July 28, 1864
Captains -
By special order number one hundred and forty-three (143) you will proceed as directed to select a site for a new prison in the neighborhood therein designated. After selecting the site you will secure by rent the land, water privileges, timber and such houses adjacent as may be thought advisable. You will use a sound discretion, conferring with reliable men in the vicinity as to the health of the location, etc., etc. Notify me by telegram as soon as you have made the selection.

Very respectfully,
John H. Winder.
Brig-Gen.
Captains D. W. Vowles and W. S. Winder

"When the order read by General Pavy in Chicago was published, I wrote to the Secretary of War asking to be informed if any such order was on file among the Confederate records in his department. He replied as follows:

War Department
Washington City, Oct. 12, 1887

Sir –

I am in receipt of your letter of the 1st instant requesting a copy of an order said to have been issued by Gen. John H. Winder and dated 'Headquarters Confederate States Military Prison, Andersonville, Ga., July 27, 1864,' directing the officers in charge of the Florida Artillery, upon receipt of information that the enemy had appeared within seven (7) miles of the post, to open fire upon the stockade with grape-shot.

In reply, I beg to inform you that a careful search has been made, but no record of this order is found on file among the Confederate records.

Very respectfully,
W. C. Endicott,
Secretary of War"[87]

All of these letters published in Davis' booklet support the contention the order was, indeed, a forgery. It is interesting that the letter above, purporting to be a letter ordering Sid Winder to establish the prison, written and signed by his father, lists the address as "Camp Sumpter" with a misspelling of "Sumter."

"Sidney's health deteriorated during the 1870's as did his grandmother's, his mother's, and his sister's, but all were alive (except Gertrude, who died in 1872 at age ninety) when Winder's body was returned to Baltimore in 1878. Caroline died the next year and was interred beside her husband, and Sidney and Carrie withdrew into a world of their own. Neither ever married, and they shared a comfortable house at 2117 St. Paul Street until Carrie died on 3 April 1903. She left all of her possessions to her 'dear brother,' whom she appointed her sole executor.

"Old and alone, almost blind, and in ill health, Sidney saw few people after Carrie's death... He drew up his

---

[87] *Ibid.*, pp. 38-42.

will, bequeathing the house and its contents plus $39,500 to his nephew and nieces, and then killed himself on 25 February 1905... According to John Winder Hughes, a grandnephew, Sidney cut his throat with a straight razor."[88]

Another of the personnel at Andersonville who was arrested after the war was Private James W. Duncan, who had served in the Commissary Department as "commissary sergeant." During the Wirz trial, on Thursday, September 21st, a witness for the prosecution, after relating the story of Duncan's having kicked the prisoner who had stooped down to pick up a crust of bread, was asked, "... if Duncan was now in Court, when he responded in the affirmative, and pointed him out; Duncan, after standing up to show himself, was requested to take a seat, and the Court informed Duncan that he must remain here."[89]

Judge-Advocate-General Holt, after the Wirz trial, recommended that J. W. Duncan should be tried for at least this one case of murder, numerous cases of robbery, and cruelty perpetrated by him at Andersonville, where he was commissary-sergeant.[90]

In November, the President directed that Duncan should be delivered to Major-General Steedman, commanding the Department of Georgia, and that he should stand trial in Savannah. By December 2nd, he had been sent there, and the papers containing the charges were sent by mail as soon as they had been forwarded by the Judge-Advocate-General.

James W. Duncan was brought before a military commission convened at Savannah on March 26th, 1866, pursuant to orders from headquarters of the Department of Georgia at Augusta. Bvt. Lieut. Col. H. A. Darling presided. Duncan was tried on three charges, the third having five Specifications. To all the charges and specification, James W. Duncan pleaded "not guilty."

"Charge I: Murder, in violation of the laws of war. Of the Charge, not guilty, but 'guilty of manslaughter, in violation of the laws of war.'
Specification: When an unnamed prisoner belonging to an unknown Tennessee regiment picked up a crust of bread which fell from the food wagon, Duncan did knock him down and kick him several times, inflicting mortal injuries. He died about three days later, on June 13th.
Of the Specification, guilty.

"Charge II: Robbery, in violation of the laws of war.
Of the Charge, 'not guilty.'
Specification: In October, Duncan did confine James Armstrong of an unknown Ohio regiment in the 'spread-eagle stocks' and rob him of $8 in U.S. Treasury notes, and a likeness of his mother or sister, of the value of $1.
Of the Specification, not guilty.

Charge III: Violations of the laws of war.
Of the Charge, 'guilty.'
Specification 1: Duncan near the 15th of June did knock down and cruelly kick an unnamed prisoner and after he got up, did knock him down again though the prisoner was idiotic or half-witted.
Of the specification, 'guilty.'
Specification 2.: Identical as Charge II's specification.
Of the Specification, 'not guilty.'
Specification 3.: While having charge of the rations from the commissary to the time when they were issued and while having charge of the cook-house, did wrongfully deprive the prisoners of vast amounts of rations by subsisting himself and his private mess upon them. He also engaged in speculating, selling, giving away and feeding to his hogs some of the items meant for the prisoners such as, bacon, beef, bread, meal, rice peas, sirup and whiskey. He also was accused of boiling down and straining about twenty barrels of grease from the bacon for his own use.
Of the Specification, 'not guilty.'
Specification 4.: Duncan did assault, strike, and knock down weak prisoners and put many in stocks.
Of the Specification, 'guilty.'
Specification 5.: Duncan did take into his possession the boxes and packages which were forwarded to

---

[88] Blakey, p. 207 and endnote 18.
[89] *Demon of Andersonville*, pp. 84, 85.
[90] *O.R.*, VIII, p. 783.

the prison from prisoners' families and did take the contents including clothing, cigars, coffee, sugar, cheese, etc.

Of the Specification, 'guilty'.

"Duncan was sentenced to be confined at hard labor for the period of fifteen years at Fort Pulaski, Georgia. "It appears from the records of Fort Pulaski that Duncan escaped July 11, 1867."[91]

After the war, Doctor White returned to the Medical College of Virginia and took the position of Demonstrator of Anatomy from 1865 to 1876.[92] He was the first Secretary of the Richmond Academy of Medicine in 1866. "When after the war the Federals hanged Col. Wertz [sic], the commanding officer, Dr. White got away to Canada to save his neck and had in 1869 but recently located again in Richmond, where he made a fine teacher."[93] After he returned and from 1868 until 1882, he taught at his alma mater. In 1868 through 1870, he was the Superintendent of the Medical College Hospital. He married, in 1871, Mrs. Caroline W. Brooks, nee Kern, daughter of Daniel Kern, Esq. of Waterloo, New York.

"In 1890, White fitting up several rooms of his own home at 115 E. Franklin St., advertized trained nurses, massage, baths, electricity and douches, stating that he would receive selected female patients for treatment."[94]

In 1893-1894, he was Professor of Diseases of Women.

Doctor Isaiah H. White died on July 15, 1907.[95]

After being named as a co-conspirator in the First Charge against Wirz and fearing arrest, Doctor Stevenson fled to Upper Stewiache, Nova Scotia. He arrived there in 1865 and remained there until about 1873. In an 1874 newspaper was an announcement to the public that he was practicing on Hollis Street in Halifax. In 1874, he returned to the South to prepare to publish *The Southern Side; or Andersonville Prison.* He remained in Virginia and practiced medicine for some years until his wife died. His wife was remembered by Upper Stewiache folks as "... regal, aristocratic, and very, very proud." After her death, Doctor Stevenson returned to Nova Scotia and married again. He married a Miss Lydia Jane Morton on March 24, 1887. He settled at Little River (now Elderbank), Halifax County, Nova Scotia, and practiced there until his death, June 18, 1891.[96]

George C. Gibbs, on May 12, 1865, wrote a letter to General E. M. McCook, Commanding Tallahassee, Florida, giving a brief synopsis of his duties at the pen. He said, "From the fact, doubtless, that General Wilson has confounded the officer (myself) commanding the post at Andersonville and the officer (Captain Wirz) commanding the prison at that post, my parole was delivered at Albany. I write this at your suggestion, and I have to-day reported to you in person, as per my verbal parole given you in Albany, Ga. ... So far as General Wilson's or your power to arrest me is concerned I freely admit it. So far as his or your right is concerned I totally deny it. I am a colonel, or was, in the army of the Confederate States. General Johnston's surrender necessitated mine, and I respectfully claim as a right, not a favor, the customary parole." General McCook, endorsed on it, "... I will retain Colonel Gibbs as prisoner and send him to Macon unless the general commanding orders otherwise, although I think this is the wrong man, and Captain Wirz (that you have already) the guilty party. If you desire him paroled and released, please notify me at an early day, as he lives below here, and it will be a long way to send him as prisoner unless he is retained."[97]

Another prison official arrested by Secretary Stanton was Samuel Boyer Davis. He was the one-time substitute commandant of the interior of the prison while Wirz was away sick in the summer of 1864. Davis told about his being transported around the country during the trial to prevent his being called as a defense witness by Wirz. "I do remember that during his trial I was confined in the prison at Albany; that I was run off to Fort Warren in order to keep me from being taken, at Wirz' request, to Washington to prove that on the specified dates upon which he was charged with murder, which charge was sworn to by three witnesses. I was in charge of the Andersonville prison, and Wirz in Augusta, Ga."[98]

A very enlightening biography of Davis was included in the *Confederate Military History* edited by Jed Hotchkiss. "Samuel Boyer Davis, of Alexandria, Va., whose service in the cause of the Confederate States was one of the most romantic in the history of the war, was born at Wilmington, Del., December 5, 1843. Early in life his home was made

[91] *Ibid.*, pp. 926-928.
[92] *Virginia Medical Monthly*, 1890-1891, Volume 17, p. 496.
[93] S. W. Dickinson, "Some Professional Recollections," *Virginia Medical Semi-Monthly*, Volume XXI, No. 23, p. 575.
[94] *Virginia Medical Monthly*, p. 496.
[95] Medical College of Virginia Archives.
[96] The sketch was taken from personal correspondence in the possession of the author.
[97] *O.R.*, VII, pp. 552, 553.
[98] Davis, p. 33.

at Baltimore and, with other young Marylanders, his sympathies were earnestly with the South at the opening of the war in 1861. In his nineteenth year, July, 1862, he enlisted in the Confederate service, as a member of Latimer's battery of artillery, in time to participate in the important engagements of Cedar Run, Second Manassas and Sharpsburg. Subsequently his intelligence and efficiency caused his promotion to the position of orderly with Colonel Hoke, then in command of Trimble's brigade, and he afterward served as aide-de-camp upon the staff of General Trimble, who was promoted major-general and put in command of a division of the Second army corps. While serving in this capacity, in the support of Pickett, during the third day's fight at Gettysburg, he was shot through the lung and taken prisoner by the advance of the Federal forces. Though assured by a surgeon that he would die, he was carried to a field hospital and soon was under care at the Chester hospital, Pennsylvania. His determination to live was no sooner clearly in prospect of realization that he formed a plan to escape before being transferred to a prison. He found a sympathizing comrade in Captain Slay, of the Sixteenth Mississippi, and bribed a guard to permit them to escape on the night of August 16, 1863. After some hairbreadth escapes from detection, they reached Dover, Del., greatly fatigued, the next night, and there received aid in their effort to reach the Potomac. Crossing Maryland, they received help from friends and finally took a boat over the Potomac and reached the Confederate lines. After arriving at Richmond, both were prostrated by the forced march they had made from the Pennylvania hospital and were for a long time sick with typhoid fever. Late in October, Lieutenant Davis reported for duty and was assigned to Gen. John H. Winder as acting assistant inspector general, with duty at Richmond. In the following May he was ordered to Goldsboro, N. C., and thence in June to Andersonville, Ga., where he arrived about the same time as did General Winder. The condition of affairs there, 24,000 prisoners confined in an area of 28 acres, guarded by 1,200 militia, led to his being sent with dispatches to Adjutant-General Cooper, urging the establishment of another prison and that no more prisoners should be forwarded there. On July 21 he was ordered to take charge of the prison at Macon, Ga. On account of a brief parole he granted a prisoner he was relieved and returned to Andersonville, where he relieved Captain Wirz, who was seriously ill, about August 14th. On Christmas day, 1864, he was in Richmond and accepted an opportunity to be the bearer of important dispatches through the United States to Canada. These dispatches, conisting of a manifesto from President Davis that John Beall, of Virginia, had been ordered to make the attempt to capture Johnson's Island, and a copy of Beall's commission in the Confederate States navy, he carried safely through Washington and thence to Toronto, without exciting suspicion; but on his return, at Sandusky, Ohio, he fell in with a party of returned Federal prisoners from Andersonville, who instantly recognized him, and he was put in jail at Newark, Ohio. There he was able to remove the dispatches for the Confederate government, which had been executed on white silk and sewed in the lining of his coat, and burn them in the stove. Accused of being a spy, he was taken to the 'McLean Barracks,' at Cincinnati, and confined there in a small room, wearing a ball and chain, and furnished with a block of wood for a pillow, which he was not to raise his head from until called in the morning, on pain of being shot by the sentinel. He was tried on the 17th and 18th of January and, though he made, according to the Cincinnati papers of that date, a most eloquent and forcible argument that he was a bearer of dispatches but not a spy, the case was prejudged and public sentiment clamored for his death. To his accusers he said: 'I know I have only done my duty. I have done it as best I could. God knows what I intended and He knows I do not deserve death; but if I die I go without asking pity, as a soldier should die.' About February 1st a gentleman called upon him and promised to advise his friends of his situation, but he soon learned that he had been condemned to death by hanging February 17th, 1865. He was taken to Johnson's Island and soon was advised that his friends were working for him and had secured some influential help; but beyond the mysterious assurance of a strange visitor that he would not be executed, he heard no word as to his fate. On the morning of the 17th he was aware that his gallows had been completed; he had perceived the arrangements for his execution, had given up all hope, and was in fact already dead to the world, though unmoved and undaunted, when, as the band was playing the dead march, the commanding officer announced that the sentence had been commuted to imprisonment for life. He started at once for Fort Delaware prison, passing a trainload of people on an excursion to witness his execution. At Fort Delaware he was put in irons and treated with inhuman brutality by General Schoepf, the officer in charge. Subsequently transferred to Albany, N. Y., he was for six weeks confined in a cell and finally, through the intercesssion of friends, was permitted to remain in the prison hospital. Meanwhile the Confederacy had ceased to be, but his imprisonment continued. In November, 1865, he wrote to Mr. Bradley, the president of the Andersonville Prison Survivors association, and asked his assistance. This was promptly promised by that gentleman, who wrote in reply: 'You were the first to introduce anything like sanitary regulations in the prison at Andersonville; at Savannah, where you were in command, the prisoners were treated like men, so far as you were concerned... You never used any violence and never punished anyone for trying to escape.' Finally, on December 7th he was released, though Secretary Stanton declared that it was by mistake and that he ought to have been hanged. After the war he learned that the kind heart of Abraham Lincoln had been interested in his behalf and that it was to him that he owed his escape from an ignominious death on an unjust charge. Returning to Virginia, he lived upon a farm until 1868, regaining his former strength and vigor, and then took charge, as captain, on a steamer on the Potomac river. During the last administration of President Cleveland he served as assistant postmaster at Alexandria. He is an honorary member of R. E. Lee camp, No. 2, Confederate Veterans. Four of his children are living; two daughters, married, and two sons, one of whom is a leading member of the Alexandria bar and the other holding a position in the United States Fishery commission. His experiences during the war which have led to his designation as the 'Andre' of the Confederacy have been well described by him in a brochure published in 1892, after the story had been partly told before the Loyal Legion by a member of his court martial."[99]

With the cessation of hostilities, there was initiated an immediate roundup of many other members in the higher echelon of the Confederate government. President Jefferson Davis was taken to the casemates of Fortress Monroe. Vice-President Alexander H. Stevens of Georgia and Postmaster-General Reagan were placed in Fort Warren. On May 22nd, Secretary of War Stanton ordered former Confederate Secretary of War James A. Seddon and Assistant Secretary of War John A. Campbell arrested and placed in Libby prison. Nearly all the men who had been in supervisory positions in the military prisons of the South were arrested and detained for varying lengths of time.

Dick Turner was arrested immediately after the war and kept in Libby prison until late in May of 1866. No charges were ever filed against him and, since none seemed to be forthcoming from Washington, Major-General Terry asked for permission to release him. Finally, Terry, on June 16, 1866, ordered Dick Turner be released on parole.

Judge-Advocate-General Holt, after the Wirz trial, recommended that Captain Vowles, who had been at Millen, and Lieutenants Wilson, Cheatham, and Mosely, of the Florence prison, should be the subject of further investigation and possibly prosecuted. Judge-Advocate-General Holt recommended that Lieutenant-Colonel Iverson, of the Forty-seventh Georgia volunteers, and Captain Barrett should be arrested and tried for their actions at Florence. "The testimony fixes upon them not only a series of the most cruel and inhuman acts of neglect, abuse, assault, robbery, &c., but a considerable number of well-established homicides. In these Barrett was the principal agent, but Iverson, as his commanding officer, was clearly no less criminal."[100] Iverson lived in Columbus.

**Major Richard B. Winder's Pistol** - Pocket Model Colt - 36 Caliber - Down the brass backstrap is engraved, "Major R. R. Winder, C.S.A." {Author's Collection)

Boggs, in the back of his book, told about what became of the officers who had charge of the Confederate prisons. He mentioned, "... Major Thomas P. Turner, commandant of the famous Libby at Richmond, Va., resides at Memphis, Tenn.; his Adjutant, (little dandy Ross), was burned up in a hotel in Richmond a few years after the war. The red-headed barbarian of Florence, S. C., Lieut. Barrett, lives at Augusta, Georgia. At the close of the war he fled to Europe; but has since returned, despised by his own countrymen as a brute, coward, and assassin, afraid to live, and afraid to die..."[101]

After his release from Libby prison, Dick Winder returned to his family in Accomac county but, as a result of the war, he was almost destitute.

"It was said of him by the late Governor Henry A. Wise, who had known him from boyhood, that 'Dick Winder had lost and suffered more than any man he knew, and with less complaint.'"[102] He soon settled the affairs at his farm and decided to study dentistry. He was very good with his hands as a young man and had carved trinkets and various objects and had given them to his friends. He graduated from the Baltimore College of Dental Surgery in 1869, at the age of forty-one, after working under the guidance of Doctor F. J. S. Gorgas and Doctor T. S. Waters of

[99] Jed Hotchkiss,ed., *Confederate Military History* , Volume III; (Atlanta, Ga.: Confederate Publishing Company, 1899), pp. 831-833.
[100] *O.R.*, VIII, p. 783.
[101] Boggs, p. 91.
[102] The Odontographic Journal, p. 143. Obtained from A.D.A.

Baltimore. He set up a practice at 716 Park Avenue in that city and rapidly built a large and prosperous practice. "During all the years of his life he retained a warm spot in his heart for the Eastern Shore of Virginia, his birthplace, and it is said of him that he would not accept pay for professional service, when an Eastern Shore Virginian was his patient."[103]

**Maryland College of Dentistry** - Founded by Richard B. Winder, D.D.S., in 1873. (Author's Collection)

Dick Winder, hoping to upgrade his professional competency, "... took a course of lectures" and graduated with an M.D. degree from the College of Physicians and Surgeons at Baltimore in 1873. Doctor Winder, in company with others, organized the Maryland Dental College in the year 1873, gathering a fine faculty of the foremost talent then in America. An innovation of this school was that each graduate was interviewed and given an oral examination by a board of regents. This board, composed of fifty or more dentists from throughout the United States, was appointed for a term of three years. Each year, the president of this board would appoint a committee of three of the dentists to supervise this examination. Doctor Winder was elected Dean of the Faculty and Professor of Physiology and Hygiene. This small school flourished but could not compete with the Baltimore College of Dental Surgery. In 1879, the Maryland Dental College was assimilated into the Baltimore College of Dental Surgery. A new faculty chair was created and Doctor Winder was made Professor of Dental Surgery and Operative Dentistry. In 1882, Doctor Winder was elected the Dean of this enlarged Baltimore College of Dental Surgery. He succeeded Doctor Gorgas as dean, a position he held until his death. The school year began on November 1st and commencement was usually held near March 4th.

One of the greatest contributions made to dentistry by Doctor Winder was his organization of the National Association of Dental Faculties. "To Dr. Winder was largely due the credit of having dentistry assigned to the list of professions by the Census Bureau," along with medicine and law.[104]

He was responsible for the rejuvenation of the then-lethargic and unpopular Maryland State Dental Association. He tried to heal the rift between the dentistry of the North and the South and, through his influence, the Southern Dental Association and the American Dental Association joined, forming the National Dental Association in 1879. It was the forerunner of the present American Dental Association, formed in 1922.

**Small, 8-inch wooden jewlry box** carved by Richard B. Winder and given to his third wife in Petersburg, Virginia, possibly as a first anniversary gift. (Photo in Author's Collection)

"He was a Democrat, Mason, Knight of Pythias and member of the Episcopal Church."[105]

After the death of his first wife, Elizabeth Custis, he married her sister, Miss Sarah Custis, who bore him two children. Young R. Bayly Winder, Jr., of Baltimore became a dentist and followed in his father's footsteps. His daughter, Mary Custis Winder, married Henry Augustus Miller of Wilmington, Delaware. After the death of Professor Winder's second wife, he married Miss Kate H. Dorsey of Maryland at New Market, Frederick county, Maryland, on the 15th of April. The ceremony was performed by the Reverend James D. McCabe, according to a wedding announcement in *The Daily Express* of Petersburg on Monday, April 19, 1869.

Doctor Winder carved a small, wooden chest of drawers for his third wife to use as a jewelry box, possibly as a present to her on their first wedding anniversary. On the bottom of this chest he wrote: "128 Madison Street, Petersburg, Virginia; Kate D. Winder, Dr. Richard B. Winder, in 1870."

[103] Charles R. E. Koch, D.D.S., Editor, *History of Dental Surgery*, Vol. III, Burton Lee Thorpe, M.D., D.D.S., *Biographies of Pioneer American Dentists and Their Successors* (Chicago, 1909), p. 462.
[104] *The Dental Cosmos*, p. 758.
[105] Koch, p. 463.

In an Eastern Shore of Virginia newspaper (probably the *Eastern Shore Herald*), on April 22nd, 1892, appeared the following announcement:

> "Dr. Richard B. Winder, a native of this town, but for twenty-five years a practicing dentist of Baltimore, where he has distinguished himself in his chosen profession, and is dean of the dental college, spent this week in Eastville with his sister, Mrs. Geo. Kerr. Dr. Winder was warmly welcomed by the friends of his earlier years. It has been over twenty years since he has been on the Eastern Shore. Mrs. Winder accompanied him."

Doctor Richard B. Winder died of Bright's disease (i.e., glomerulonephritis) on July 18, 1894, at age sixty-seven, and was buried at London Park Cemetery, Baltimore. Another obituary said he died of "heart-disease."

It was said "… he was a man of courtly manners, handsome of features and possessed of high courage, true in his friendship and honest in all his dealings with his fellow men."[106]

In Memoriam.

Bro. Prof. R. B. WINDER M.D. D.D.S.

*Dean of the Baltimore College of Dental Surgery.*

Born, July 17th, 1828;

Died, July 18th, 1894.

And hast thy spirit soared beyond the blue,
Thy staunch brave heart for ever ceased to beat?
Alas! 'Tis so, but Heaven's Divinest hue
Shines with all glory on thy life complete.
Yet why lament an earthly winding sheet?
It is the last frail garment of the dead;
And now thou walkest with no earthly feet
In that glad realm where holiest angels tread!
O Brother mine, my heart is sore to day—
With loving grip I fain would clasp thy hand;
But lo! Thou listeth with no worldly clay—
Thrice thrilling thought, to know and understand
The Signs and Passwords of the far away
A sure admittance to the Promised Land!

CHAS. F. FORSHAW LL.D. D.D.S
*in the "Freemasons Chronicle"*

Winder House,
Bradford, Eng.
*July 30th, 1894.*

**Memorial Card** - Commemorating the Death of Doctor Winder. He died one day after his 66th birthday.
(Doctor' Winder's Grandson)

[106] *Ibid.*, p. 464.

Louis Schade (shä-dá), lawyer and journalist, was born in Berlin, Germany, Apr. 4, 1829, son of Friedrich and Wilhelmina (von Sydow) Shade. As a law student at the University of Berlin, he became implicated with other students in the revolution of 1848-51, and as a penalty for erecting barricades in the streets of Berlin against the government troops was condemned to death. He succeeded in making his escape, however, and came to the United States in 1851. After spending a few months with friends at Weehawken, N. J., he went to Washington, D.C., where through his ability to speak four foreign languages and translate with ease five others, he obtained a position as assistant librarian at the Smithsonian Institution. He held that post until 1854, when he transferred to the U. S. census bureau, and in 1855 he was made a translator and statistician in the department of state. There he came to the notice of Senator Stephen A. Douglas (q.v.), of Illinois, who in 1856 induced him to go to Chicago as editor of the "National Demokrat," a German language newspaper owned by the senator, and also as editor of the "National Union," printed in English. As a result of this association he became a staunch supporter of Douglas and a champion of the cause of the South in the inter-sectional controversy then approaching its climax. He had gained a reputation as a public speaker and at the suggestion of the Democratic national committee stumped the German-American districts in Illinois and Iowa for the Democrats in the political campaigns of the period. He was admitted to the bar in Burlington, Iowa., in 1858. He was especially active in the Lincoln-Douglas campaign of 1860 and at its conclusion returned to Washington, D. C., and engaged in the practice of law, acquiring an extensive clientele. He achieved national prominence in 1865 as the attorney for Captain Henry Wirz, superintendent of the Confederate military prison at Andersonville, Ga., during the civil war, who was arrested, tried before a military commission, convicted and executed (Nov. 10, 1865), on the charge of having murdered Union soldiers who were prisoners of war. The trial now appears to have arisen out of a desire to secure criminal charges against Jefferson Davis, who, with Wirz and several others, was named in a conspiracy to murder Union soldiers. No evidence of such a conspiracy was forthcoming and although the charges against Davis were dropped, Wirz was convicted. Two years after the execution, Mr. Schade published an open letter to the American people in which he revealed that on the night preceding Wirz' execution, messengers from some "high cabinet officer' offered to secure a commutation of Wirz' sentence if he would implicate Jefferson Davis in the Andersonville "atrocities." In the same letter he pointed to proven cases of perjury on the part of the prosecution and of intimidation of defense witnesses. The truthfulness of Schade's letter has never been denied. He secured the removal of Wirz' body from the arsenal grounds, in which it had been interred, to a Washington cemetery, and during the remainder of his life, faithful to a promise to Wirz, he did his utmost to clear his name and memory. In 1870, with the assistance of W. W. Corcoran (q.v.), he established the Washington *Sentinel*, a weekly newspaper, which he conducted successfully for thirty years, until over taken by ill health. Deeply interested in all public questions, he frequently appeared before committees of congress in behalf of measures calculated to safeguard personal liberty and he was active in espousing the development of the national capital. As solicitor of the Prussian legation in Washington, he induced President Grant to place an embargo on the shipment of arms to France in the Franco-Prussian war in 1871. When it appeared that speculators were about to purchase the house in which Lincoln died, Mr. Schade purchased it himself in 1879 and occupied it as his own residence until 1893, when he sold it to the District of Columbia Memorial Association as a memorial to the martyred president. He was a lifelong student, a man of unusual culture and scholarshiip, absolutely fearless, of an extremely generous and sympathetic nature, and exhibited the highest devotion to his adopted country. Mr. Schade was married in Stettin, Germany, Sept. 18, 1867, to Anna, daughter of Heinrich Krieger. They had five children: Anita, Frederick A. L., Ella, wife of Joseph S. McCoy, Hermann and Clara Antonie, who married Max F. Mueller. Mr. Schade died in Washington, D. C., Feb. 25, 1903.[107]

[107] *The National Cyclopaedia of American Biography* , Volume XXI, (New York; James T. White & Company, 1931).

# Conclusion

The Confederate States established, in a brief three months, a prison in rural, southwest Georgia equivalent to a very large city. The requirements of the large concentration of prisoners were overwhelming. It was remarkable that the authorities could supply water, food, shelter, and sewage in such a short time and to such a remote site. No wonder so many died.

The total number of the dead at Andersonville prison, as the doors were finally swung open wide, are as follows:

| | |
|---|---|
| Alabama | 15 |
| Connecticut | 315 |
| D.C. | 14 |
| Illinois | 850 |
| Indiana | 594 |
| Iowa | 174 |
| Kansas | 5 |
| Kentucky | 436 |
| Louisiana | 1 |
| Maine | 233 |
| Maryland | 194 |
| Massachusetts | 768 |
| Michigan | 639 |
| Minnesota | 79 |
| Missouri | 97 |
| New Hampshire | 24 |
| New Jersey | 170 |
| New York | 2572 |
| North Carolina | 17 |
| Ohio | 1030 |
| Pennsylvania | 1811 |
| Rhode Island | 74 |
| Tennessee | 738 |
| Vermont | 212 |
| Virginia | 288 |
| Wisconsin | 244 |
| U.S. Army | 399 |
| U.S. Navy | 99 |
| Civilians | 165 |
| Unknown | 504 |
| Hanged | 6 |
| Total | 12,912 [1] |

The deaths at Andersonville compare interestingly with the carnage that took place on the battlefields. "More Union soldiers perished at Andersonville than were killed on the six most bloody battlefields of the war. The total deaths at Andersonville are reported as 13,714. The numbers of Union men killed in the six battles referred to are as follows:

| | |
|---|---|
| Gettysburg | 3070 |
| Spotsylvania | 2725 |
| The Wilderness | 2246 |
| Shiloh | 1754 |
| Stone's River | 1730 |
| Chickamauga | 1656 |
| Total | 13181"[2] |

[1] Long (back index), p. ii.
[2] Melvin, pp. 145, 146.

Only 15 or 16 of the witnesses at Wirz' trial, most of whose views were skewed towards the prosecution, said that he was directly responsible for homicides at the prison. Of the two hundred or so prisoners who wrote about their stays there, about the same number concurred. Did all 30 of these persons perjure themselves?

Perhaps the most interesting item brought forth in this book is the note Wirz sent to Dick Winder in the Old Capitol Prison which stated that Colonel Baker had, indeed, offered Wirz his life if he would implicate President Jefferson Davis in a conspiracy to take the lives of prisoners at Andersonville.

Did General Winder truly do the best he could to care for his charges? How high a priority was the feeding of the prisoners? How large a part did regional hatreds play in the lack of care?

The responsibility for the deaths at Andersonville must be shared equally by both sides. Secretary of War, Edwin Stanton, and a few other Northern politicians wanted someone to pay and pay dearly for the atrocities at Andersonville. Only reluctantly did the North release Southern "war criminals."

Old animosities only now are beginning to be soothed by the passage of time. The civil rights that were trampled one hundred and forty years ago are still thought by some to be trampled today. Perhaps in a hundred more years...

# Index